D0593373

COUNSELING AND PSYCHOLOGY

Counseling and Psychology

VOCATIONAL PSYCHOLOGY AND ITS RELATION TO EDUCATIONAL AND PERSONAL COUNSELING

by MILTON L. BLUM, Ph.D

Associate Professor of Psychology and Subchairman of the Department of Psychology, School of Business and Civic Administration of the City College of New York

and BENJAMIN BALINSKY, Ph.D.

Assistant Professor of Psychology, School of Business and Civic Administration of the City College of New York

PRENTICE-HALL, INC.

Englewood Cliffs, N. J.

Fifth printing . . September, 1959

PRINTED IN THE UNITED STATES OF AMERICA

18147

To

TWO WIVES *and*

FOUR CHILDREN

for their insistence on non-authoritarian counseling

PREFACE

THE PRIMARY OBJECTIVE of *Counseling and Psychology* is to present the authors' views on the contributions of psychology to the body of knowledge known as vocational counseling. The profession of vocational counseling is growing fast. More schools and communities are coming to recognize the fact that it is no longer a luxury to be indulged in if and when the budget allows. Vocational counseling has reached the stage in which it is accepted as the necessity it really is, to help people be most productive in adult years through the attainment of adequate adjustment. Parents are generally aware that their children need vocational guidance and are willing to admit that specialists are in the best position to offer this service. As a result, schools on all levels of education as well as community organizations are engaged in programs of guidance.

The field of counseling attracts people with varied backgrounds; teachers, social workers, and just plain counselors are among a few of the professionals, in addition to psychologists, working in this field. Although each contributes his share, psychologists seem to be primarily involved in perfecting interviewing techniques and constructing measuring instruments to increase the validity of vocational guidance. They are realistically in the vanguard. However, many psychologists have, in their writings, been too willing to confine their contributions to tests. This book attempts to cover in a broader fashion the psychologists' contribution to the field.

Such contributions are likely to be subtle and to gain acceptance only over a period of time. For example, the term "guidance" now seems to be in disrepute because of its active connotation, and the term "vocational counseling" is much more acceptable. It is entirely possible that the transition from guidance to counseling has been not purely a matter of semantics but rather evidence of the importance that psychologists have had in the progressive development of the field.

The information presented in this book is not limited to any one point of view. As psychologists we favor integration, not because we are eclectic "middle-of-the-roaders," but because we recognize the value of different approaches and contributions. However, we firmly believe that a clinical point of view must be recognized as the core of vocational psychology. Although the authors are not wedded to any one system, they recognize that Gestalt psychology and psychoanalysis have offered much to the advancement of vocational psychology. We are neither "pro" nor "anti" non-directivists but see quite a bit of value for vocational psychology in the non-directive development.

It has been our desire to write a book of moderate size, capable of being read by non-psychologists who are interested in and perform counseling duties. The literature surveyed has been vast and yet we cannot claim to know it all. Accordingly, we have undoubtedly committed errors of omission. Furthermore, since we have not adhered to any one system, we will be accused on many fronts. Our main purpose was to write a book which would integrate the points of view of others and our own biases into a workable system of counseling.

The chapter organization as well as the specific material covered in each chapter is logical to us; but other equally logical (if not more logical) chapter organizations are possible. For example, the chapter on interests is number thirteen, though interest tests are discussed much earlier. Interest tests are widely used in counseling and so are described as part of testing. Interests are also determined through the interview and so must be considered in the interview chapters. However, interest is a basic concept in counseling, and so a separate chapter considers its theoretical implications as well as its implications for successful counseling. We have chosen to have this chapter precede the one on occupational information, but we are aware that it might have preceded the testing chapters or even the chapters on the interview. This problem of placing also occurred with the chapter on statistics. Depending upon the statistical background of the reader, it may be read after or before the chapters on testing.

The major difficulty is that vocational counseling is a dynamic and integrated process. Division into chapters artificially breaks this process into unreal parts; but for purposes of study, chapters are to be recommended because they can be grouped into various kinds of units. Those who decide to use this book as a text will surely desire to assign chapters in the order most suitable to their organization of the subject matter. We believe that the book has been written so that this change in assignment order could readily be accomplished.

To cover the field, 19 chapters have been written. Chapter 1 is introductory. It traces the influences of psychology in the field of counseling. It expounds the interrelationships among the various types of counseling: vocational, educational and personal. The relationship between counseling and therapy is also discussed.

Chapter 2 attacks the pseudo-scientific systems by referring to studies investigating their claims of validity. A positive note is a description of those qualified to give guidance.

In Chapter 3, a survey of the variety of guidance centers is made. This includes school and community agencies, both public and private. To give the reader a picture of the complete counseling process in operation, the Vocational Advisory Service is described.

Chapters 4 and 5 deal with the interview, the most important technique in counseling. In Chapter 4 the framework for discussing interviewing is set. The major emphasis is that counseling is seldom only vocational. It most usually is vocational with educational and/or personal nuances. Three interviewing techniques are discussed and evaluated: the authoritarian, the non-directive, and the non-authoritarian. We prefer the non-authoritarian but are aware of the need for further research. Chapter 5 is devoted to discussion of general principles for conducting the interview. To a limited extent, these two chapters have as their objective the teaching of the interviewing technique, insofar as the written word is capable of doing it.

Although psychologists have done most of the work in the construction, administration, and evaluation of psychological tests, it is incorrect to consider guidance as synonymous with testing. Nevertheless, anyone giving vocational guidance must have some fundamental knowledge of the variety of tests. Chapters 6 through 9 present material about tests.

Chapter 6 is concerned primarily with the discussion of principles and problems of psychological testing. Chapter 7 discusses the varieties of tests: intelligence, aptitude, achievement, interest, and personality. Each variety is evaluated in accordance with the principles discussed in Chapter 6, and special consideration is given to validity, reliability, and the characteristics of norms.

Chapters 8 and 9 describe and critically evaluate the specific tests most widely used in vocational counseling.

Chapter 10 treats the clinical approach in vocational counseling. This approach is organismic and dynamic; the individual is considered a unified whole. Tests that are primarily clinical in nature, and the clinical use of tests that are not, are treated as essential parts of the clinical approach.

Chapter 11 demonstrates that successful counseling cannot take place until tests and interviews have been integrated; and it discusses ways and means of interpreting test results to the client through the interview. As the person seeking guidance becomes older, the likelihood is that the problem is less strictly one of vocational guidance, and more one of vocational and personal guidance. Awareness of this is a necessity, and in Chapter 11 this view is expounded.

For the guidance worker, a knowledge of statistics, at least on the verbal level, is necessary. Chapter 12 describes those statistical terms widely used in counseling on a nonmathematical level. Some of the terms discussed are measures of central tendency, measures of variation, the coefficient of correlation, and factor analysis.

Chapter 13 deals with the very important matter of interests. Although knowledge of a client's interests is obtained through both the interview and psychological tests, the theoretical basis of interests as well as their development must be understood. The relationship between interests and abilities and the degree of permanence of interests are problems of vital concern in counseling; evidence is offered in this chapter toward their solution.

It is impossible to do vocational counseling without knowledge of occupational information. Chapter 14 outlines and describes the necessary occupational information as well as its sources and uses.

Chapter 15 attempts to demonstrate the relation of occupational information to vocational psychology. Vocational psychology integrates information about jobs with information about the individual. When this is done, the matching of men and jobs becomes more precise. It takes into account such important aspects as job satisfaction. There is also discussion of the job psychograph and the occupational ability pattern, as well as job classification systems which include psychological characteristics.

Next to the client, the most important person in counseling is the counselor. Chapter 16 attempts to describe the background and training qualifications necessary for the counselor, whether he be employed in the school system, in a public or private agency, or as an individual. The necessity for improving the standards and requirements of the counselor is recognized and articulated. The subject matter included in the training of counselors is detailed.

Evaluation is the topic in Chapter 17. For the progressive development of counseling, evaluation is a necessity. The various methods of evaluating counseling are reviewed and themselves critically evaluated. The results of evaluative studies are summarized.

Chapter 18 presents the need for counseling in industry. The social bases for counseling as well as a review of a few of the companies already counseling their workers are presented.

Chapter 19 deals with vocational selection. In this chapter the attempt is made to describe in summary fashion six aids used in employment screening from the points of view of both the employer and the applicant seeking a job.

ACKNOWLEDGMENTS

THE AUTHORS are indebted to many sources and individuals, so many that it is even difficult to know where to begin in expressing our debt of gratitude. Our students have enabled us to develop our ideas; their patience and valuable criticisms are deeply appreciated. The persons we have counseled have benefited us not only in preventing our seclusion in "ivory towers" but also by enriching our knowledge.

Our professional colleagues have been most kind. To Professor Donald G. Paterson we owe everlasting thanks. He was a source of inspiration while we were learning; he has been a friend and scholar in his encouragement. His very studious reading of the manuscript has resulted in invaluable suggestions. We are indeed fortunate that he was willing to take an interest in this work. For valuable suggestions we are also indebted to Mrs. Gertrude Aull, Dr. Alexander Mintz, Dr. Carroll Shartle, Dr. Max Smith, Dr. Joseph Tiffin, Dr. Brian Tomlinson, and Mr. Allen Williams.

To the Vocational Advisory Service of New York City, we owe much of our early experience and practical training. We thank this organization for its investment in our careers. We are indebted to Dr. Helen Smith, its director, and to Mrs. Bea Pruski, who gave us a very sound foundation and contributed a great deal to our present ideas.

Miss Ellen Silbowitz, Miss Lenore Antine, Miss Ann Giordani, Miss Irma Richter, and Miss Winifred Kennard have been very helpful to us.

To the many authors and publishers who have graciously made possible quotations from their works we are indebted

Last we thank the two wives and four children who encouraged and humored us and who willingly underwent the sacrifices entailed in writing this book.

MILTON L. BLUM

BENJAMIN BALINSKY

CONTENTS

COUNSELING AND PSYCHOLOGY

1

INTRODUCTION

THIS COUNTRY's most precious resource is its citizens. The intention of the authors is to help in developing this resource. People have problems; counseling is intended as an aid in the solution of these problems. Since problems arise at any time in life, counseling must be recognized as a continuing process.

The major objective is to have individuals who are adequately adjusted, efficient, and well balanced. They will then be able to contribute their maximum share to society. A society consisting of such people will be most productive and well balanced. In such a world, want would be lacking and peace would reign. Counseling, in other words, is intimately related to the adjustment of people, vocational as well as personal.

Counseling is appropriate for persons of all ages. To avoid many future problems, one should be especially concerned with the counseling of youth, the future citizens. Such counseling can best be done when it is intimately integrated with the educational system. Counseling is not an added thrill or luxury; it epitomizes education. When used as suggested, it can make its most definite contribution, enabling people ultimately to benefit from their education to the utmost.

The perplexing problems of today and tomorrow can be more readily solved if the individuals who are called upon to deal with them do not have problems of their own which often prevent their maximum functioning. Counseling is the solution to an individual's problems.

Point of view

In this book we are concerned primarily with the vocational aspects of counseling. However, we recognize that vocational counseling is only part of a more comprehensive concept. The term counseling is all-inclusive and is accordingly the most proper term to use. The term vocational counseling is used when the vocational aspects of counseling are being emphasized, but it is not intended that vocational counseling be exclusive of the other aspects of counseling, which are simultaneously contributing factors to the individual's problems.

Vocational guidance is the process of assisting the individual to choose an occupation, prepare for, enter upon, and progress in it. This is the definition offered in each issue of *Occupations,* the Journal of the National Vocational Guidance Association.

Super (8) defines vocational counseling as "the process of helping the individual to ascertain, accept, understand and apply the relevant facts about himself to the pertinent facts about the occupational world, which are ascertained through incidental and planned exploratory activities."[1] These two definitions are offered as basic and most germane to our subject matter. It is to be noted that the definitions of vocational guidance and vocational counseling are rather similar. This raises the question of the use of the words guidance and counseling. At the present time, the word counseling is in favor and is fashionable. The word guidance has historical significance but is somewhat outmoded. Possibly the reason for this is that formerly guidance practices were more directive and advisory, whereas at the present time, the practices and techniques require a less active role and the word counseling implies this characteristic better than the word guidance. To conform with the trend, we have accepted the word counseling and, in fact, included it in the title. However, for

[1] Reprinted by permission from *Appraising Vocational Fitness,* by Donald E. Super, Harper & Brothers, New York, 1949.

purposes of writing style we shall use the terms counseling and guidance as synonymous. Whenever the word guidance is used, we are not concerned with the directive, advice-giving aspect implied in the term, but rather assign to it the more passive, client-centered connotation.

At times the word vocational precedes the term counseling or guidance. The question arises as to which to use and what are the precise relations between counseling and vocational counseling. The latter is a delimiting term which indicates correctly a point of emphasis but also may introduce an error. The term vocational counseling can be correctly used to indicate the locus of the problem and enable the counselor to focus on the area the client most often can understand and accept. However, no matter how simple and direct the vocational problem, there is usually a more complex situation involving not only the educational aspects but also the personal problems of the client. This tripartite—vocational, educational, and personal—is the essence of counseling. Although any one area may be emphasized it is unlikely that a solution for an individual can occur when the others are neglected. In other words vocational counseling can indicate an emphasis on the vocational aspects of a client's problem but cannot completely solve his problem without duly considering the total situation.

There is one further aspect of terminology that needs clarification. Ordinarily the term vocational psychology includes both vocational guidance and vocational selection. In vocational guidance, the frame of reference is one individual and potentially many jobs. The objective is to match the individual with the job or jobs he can do best. In vocational selection, the orientation is quite different; here there is one job and potentially many individuals. The objective is to match the job with the individual or individuals who can be most reasonably expected to perform the job best. The use of the word "best" needs a further qualification since the present stage of development in measurement makes it absolutely untrue that an individual can perform only one job. Conversely, it is absolutely untrue that any one job can be performed by just one individual. The likelihood is that we will not achieve for a very long time the degree of perfection in measurement and prognosis that will enable us to claim that there is one job for one individual.

In practice, vocational guidance and vocational selection are regarded as two separate entities of vocational psychology. Ordinarily guidance assumes importance in the schools and public or private agencies, whereas selection assumes importance in the personnel departments of business organizations. Actually, interviewing, administering psychological tests, and giving information about occupations apply equally to both vocational guidance and vocational selection and can be integrated in the subject matter known as vocational psychology. The frame of reference in this book emphasizes vocational guidance, although all or most of the techniques apply equally well to both aspects of the subject matter.

The influence of psychology

Psychology studies the behavior of man with the aid of scientific methodology. It uses the experimental method—that is, observation under controlled conditions—to gather data. It uses other methods as well, such as the case history method and observation of development as it takes place. Psychology accepts introspection—or a subject's report that describes mental processes—as a source of data. It is interested in obtaining facts which can be readily verified and duplicated (1). Vocational psychology draws upon the facts, generalizations, and principles of psychology. It uses the methods prescribed in psychology. Vocational psychology is the application and extension of psychological facts and principles to the problems concerning the matching of men and jobs. It is the only system that applies scientific procedures in such matching. Its rigid discipline demands that conclusions be based upon data rather than wishing and a priori reasoning. Because of this, psychologists and psychology are in the driver's seat in the field of vocational counseling or guidance. In his 1950 presidential address to the membership of the National Vocational Guidance Association, Robert Hoppock (3) stated, "Today it is the psychologist who dominates the scene, commands our attention, does our research and takes the lead in establishing our professional standards." He goes on to say, "It does not require fantastic reaches of imagination to anticipate what may happen to vocational counselors and to other personnel workers if our negligence or our delay forces or encourages the psychologist to define our field and to write our standards for us." Hoppock submits that guidance is more than psychology. He refers to the fact that psychologists who undertake to do vocational guidance often do not have an adequate knowledge of vocational information and so must refer clients to other sources for such information.

It is to be recognized that schoolteachers and personnel workers and others administer guidance. They are not primarily psychologists. But it must be insisted, from our point of view, that training in that aspect of psychology related to the matching of jobs and men is essential. The psychological basis of counseling is so important in effective counseling it cannot be overlooked.

Viteles (10), in reviewing the application of psychology to vocational guidance, has cogently named three stages. The first stage was the wide-spread dissemination of all kinds of psychological tests. The second stage, according to Viteles, might be considered the application of the clinical method to the study of the individual seeking advice. The clinical method is the synthesis of all available data concerning the individual to arrive at a comprehensive understanding of his potentialities and liabilities. The third stage of the contributions by psychologists is essentially one of intensive research designed to evaluate and improve psychological procedures in vocational guidance. In other words, the psychologists have contributed not only in psychological testing, but also in the devising of the clinical method as well as the intensive research in the evaluation of the procedures of vocational guidance. It is obvious, therefore, that psychology is the core of vocational guidance.

Psychology has contributed to vocational guidance in the area of tests, interviewing techniques, and occupational information. In these areas, psychologists have not only contributed methodology but also technique and evaluation.

Psychology as a science readily admits no secrets. The methods and techniques devised and used by psychologists are available to all who will seek them out in the various publications. In fact, this availability has been another contribution by psychologists to the field of vocational guidance. Such a system aids in preventing those who would be mystical from having their spurious claims gain widespread adherents. Psychology is an aid in uncloaking those who do not have a scientific system because it insists that there are really no secrets in science. All one needs is knowledge and experience, which are available to all who will study.

The psychologist very willingly describes the steps involved in counseling. He insists that the conclusions be derived from the data gathered and further he insists that the data be gathered in as objective a manner as possible. The means of gathering data must also be described so that the conclusions drawn cannot be attributed solely to the person who gathered the data but rather to the instruments used. It is therefore necessary to develop sound instruments for gathering data. This requirement applies to techniques of interviewing, psychological tests, and transferable knowledge about occupations, as well as all the other aspects of vocational guidance to be discussed.

An example of a description by psychologists of the steps involved in counseling is afforded by a reference to the procedure outlined by Williamson (11). It also refers to the concept—clinical—which psychologists believe to be very important.

He has very aptly described six steps involved in clinical counseling.

> These steps are analysis, synthesis, diagnosis, prognosis, counseling (treatment), and follow-up. *Analysis* refers to the collection from a variety of sources of data which provide for an adequate understanding of the student. *Synthesis* refers to the summarizing and organizing of the data from analysis in such a manner as to reveal the student's assets, liabilities, adjustments, and maladjustments. A case history or cumulative record form may be used to summarize the mass of data about the student's life, and test scores are summarized on a profile or psychograph. *Diagnosis* refers to the end result of diagnosing; it is the clinician's conclusions concerning the characteristics and causes of the problems exhibited by the student. *Prognosis* refers to the clinician's statement, or prediction, of the future development of the student's problem; whether he will readjust or what will be

the probable outcome of a choice of a particular course of study. Prognosis is a statement of the implications of the diagnosis. *Counseling* refers to the steps taken by the student and by the counselor to bring about adjustment and readjustment. The final step in clinical work, *follow-up*, includes what the clinician does to assist the student with new problems, with recurrences of the original problems, and what is done to determine the effectiveness of counseling.

In actual clinical practice these steps do not necessarily follow in sequence; moreover, the counselor proceeds at a different pace for each problem exhibited by the student. He may be counseling a student's emotional problem at the same time that he is diagnosing a vocational problem. In other cases a vocational problem may "clear up" through the counseling of an associated emotional problem. Obviously the clinician uses a flexible procedure rather than adhering rigidly to a sequence of procedures. Every student must be dealt with in that way which produces the optimum results. The clinician has so immersed himself through experience in the techniques of his art that he uses them as resources to be utilized in terms of the way the case "breaks."[2]

The relation between types of guidance and counseling

Briefly, there are three major types of counseling: vocational, educational, and personal. In reality, it is best to consider these three types of counseling as aspects of the same thing. Even though vocational counseling has the major frame of reference in this book, it is impossible to administer vocational guidance without recognizing the implications necessary in educational guidance. It is very often impossible, as the previous quote by Williamson states, to administer vocational counseling without first clearing up the problems of a personal variety. Counseling must be recognized as a continuing process. At one phase in the individual's development, educational guidance is in the forefront; at another it may be vocational guidance, and continually interwoven is the necessity of recognizing the third or personal type of counseling. Let us chronologically follow a variety of typical individual problems and see how impossible it is to separate vocational counseling from the others.

---

[2] From *How to Counsel Students* by E. G. Williamson. Copyright, 1939. Courtesy of McGraw-Hill Book Co.

The major aspect of counseling until the individual reaches 14 years of age is educational. During the first eight years of one's educational life, the basis is obtained for either his higher education or his eventual life's work. Those who are entrusted with the responsibility of teaching this group have much more than teaching to do.

In this group evidences of the well-adjusted pupil who eventually becomes the well-adjusted adult appear (9). The well-adjusted pupil is the socialized pupil and early aspects of socialization are the product of home and school treatment marked by tolerance, respect, and affection. It is in the school that the child and, in many instances, the youth acquire both the feeling of personal acceptance which lays the groundwork for being well disposed toward other individuals and the expanding social outlook which insures adjustment in the larger environment outside of the school. The adequate school makes provision for social growth, which is fundamental to the maintenance of mental health. In this age group it is important not only to teach the child but to also observe his behavior while he is learning. Those children with anti-social or destructive activities may be objecting to the learning process in the only way they know. Children who withdraw or who have regressive tendencies may be manifesting overtly feelings of insecurity, anxiety, or frustration. These are very often the earliest signs that all is not going well with the child. It is for this reason that it is no longer fashionable to treat such children as merely behavior problems. It is more appropriate to try to understand why they are behaving that way. It should not be inferred that any form of unacceptable behavior must be directly attributable to the school system, but on the other hand, the school system can well relieve itself of any possible guilt by determining to what extent the educational system is responsible.

At this point the problem is for the school to attempt to understand the child in relation to his I.Q., his reading ability, his arithmetic ability, his personality adjustment, and his social relations. It is valuable to obtain at least two or three measures of the child's I.Q. within this age period. Ordinarily one would not expect the I.Q. to change, but if such variation occurs it should be investigated. It is important to compare the child's rate of learning with his I.Q. Children will learn to read more or less rapidly, and if the child's difficulties in reading are not recognized at the earliest possible moment they may become a veritable thorn in the side of the child's educational life forever.

In other words, accompanying the education of a child is the need for integrating educational and personal counseling so that vocational adjustment is a logical outgrowth. One should not be too concerned with any specialization or even preparation for specific occupations during this age. At best only superficial exploration of the occupational world should be encouraged and this only when the child approaches the end of elementary school. For the large number in this group the major guidance activity might be regarded as testing to determine the intelligence level and to measure the basic skills of reading, arithmetic, and language. As the child becomes older, tests of personality should be included. This testing should be done, not to obtain records, but rather to be able to determine how well the child is doing in relation to his abilities. Provision should also be made to match the test results with the behavior of the child. In the classroom it is desirable to spot those with problems and begin counseling at the earliest age that the problem can be detected. The varieties of problems may be many, but if they are nipped in the bud, the individual has been salvaged for a useful and happy adult life.

During the next four years the problems more closely approach those that might be regarded as vocational. It is in this group that we find many in the high schools. Those who have been subjected to severe economic pressure or those with limited intelligence have dropped by the wayside. In the former group, many are not limited intellectually and may eventually be successful. The latter group can become useful citizens doing the many tasks required of those with limited ability. It is during this age that the educational process becomes differentiated. There are academic, general, commercial, and vocational high schools. The students who do well in academic subjects prepare for college. Others will not go beyond high school and will require preparation for commercial or trade jobs. Counseling can improve the haphazard selection which often takes place when the choice is left to the child or his parents.

At this age, the interests of a person are basically mature and so in evaluating an individual the dimension of interest should be added to the dimensions of intelligence, aptitude, ability, and personality.

This group is likely to split into what is known as the work group and the college group. And so, it is exceedingly important that a complete appraisal take place of all individuals in the senior year at high school. It is, of course, assumed that previous appraisals have been made, but at the time when a person is ready to be graduated from high school it is most appropriate to investigate each intensively in relation to the dimensions of intelligence, aptitude, ability, personality adjustment, and interest. With reference to intelligence, it is known that there are many who have sufficient intelligence for successful completion of high school but may not have sufficient intelligence for successful completion of college. For these people, insisting upon a college education might lead to maladjustment. With reference to aptitude, abilities, and interest, when these match in the individual one can think of the person as potentially able to attend a college of engineering, business, liberal arts, or any of the other further degrees of specialization.

In the case of those who because of economic or other reasons do not go on to college, it is of the greatest importance that they be given the opportunity to have vocational guidance. At this age the individual can easily go in the wrong direction vocationally. Emphasis should be placed upon adequate vocational orientation and occupational information. The world of work in which a person will ultimately be found ought not to be left to haphazard or chance circumstances.

To summarize, the problems of guidance or counseling in the age group from 14 to 18 is to separate correctly those who are likely to be successful in college from those who are not. For those who are likely to be successful in college, it is important to try to select that type of college which would lead to the greatest success and greatest rewards.

For those who are not likely to be successful in college it is important to open to the individual the vast amount of information in relation to the varieties of occupations or jobs in which such a person may find himself.

The years between 18 and 22 might best be called "the emerging adult." By this time, most individuals have begun to solve their adolescent problems and to resemble the adult. However, in terms of responsibility they are not quite adults. Persons in this age group often have to cope with personality problems to a large extent related to psychosexual matters. Such problems are recognized in counseling.

This group forms two sub-groups: the out-of-school group and the college group. For the college group, educational guidance problems continue. The bright youngster in high school may now find real intellectual challenge on the college level; this sometimes erroneously leads him to the conclusion that he is not as bright as he used to be. Very often, these people have been functioning successfully on the academic level because of their high level of mental ability. This is no longer enough for many and they must for the first time learn how to study.

The out-of-school group presents equally as serious, if not in many respects more serious, problems which deserve counseling. For one, many of the people in this group have met with only limited success in school and as a result they face the future and the occupational world with considerable insecurity. When these people do not have correct evaluations of their intelligence, aptitudes, abilities, personality adjustment, and interests, they very often will be found floating in and out of jobs with little satisfaction.

Whether they enter white-collar jobs or the trades, they most usually are found in the beginning jobs, and this adds to their problems. Since the early job histories of these people are likely, in many cases, to determine their future occupation, considerable attention should be given to these jobs. For example, a person might get a job as a shipping clerk and although he may not remain such, he is not likely to progress too far beyond it; or when job changes occur he will often remain in the same industry. At this point, the pattern of manufacturing, wholesale business, or retail trade is also likely to emerge as a result of the first, second, or third job. It is therefore important that further guidance be made available to these people who are out-of-school, especially to help them see new vocational directions that might be possible for them.

In this age group, personal problems emerge. These personal problems are often related to choice of occupation or college, and if the person does not have the counseling to help him work through them, they will tend to continue and become more intense as he grows older.

The type of problem that a person in the young adult group has presents considerable challenge to the counselor. In this group is the person who has had one or more jobs with varying degrees of success. Added to the previous problems of earlier age groups are the new ones. Characteristic of the people in this group is the fact that they do have job experiences. Some may have only one year of it, but others may have five to eight years or more. Very often experience has been accumulated in a number of jobs. As many as four or even eight jobs is not unusual for this group of job-experienced adults. They are not necessarily drifters, nor people who earned low incomes. They may show determination in seeking employment. They are not invariably lacking in ability nor always essentially disturbed emotionally. They present in a most striking form the typical vocational guidance problem, that is, fitting a job to the individual's abilities and experiences. For these individuals, a testing program is likely to be very unsatisfying in its results. Actually, the ability and aptitude tests are not particularly geared to these people and, in any event, in the light of the job experiences that they have had, the record stands out more clearly.

Nevertheless, the problem is present, and is expressed by the person in his question, "What kind of job shall I seek so that I can really get some place?"

Another major type of vocational problem of the "young adult" is the one where the individual is experiencing little success and much difficulty on the job. For some, it may be advisable to encourage either retraining or additional training. Many of the G.I.'s under the G.I. Bill of Rights benefited materially as a result of the opportunity for additional training. Very often, these people are presently capable of benefiting from training but previously did not have the motivation necessary for success.

Then too there are people who do not evaluate their abilities correctly and as a result of limited ability are more or less doomed to the menial "run of the mill" job. For these people, very little can be done except possibly to encourage them to enter the occupational area that is likely to lead to security as well as moderate satisfaction.

In the middle-aged adult group, there are still people who need the benefit of counseling. For most of these people, the problem is intensified as a result of economic, or more appropriately, socio-economic pressures. Among these people are those who have already acquired considerable financial responsibilities; an example would be the married group with children. These people very often realize they are not in the right job, but as a result of the experience they have acquired they are now earning more than they would if they had to start all over. They are unable to start all over because of responsibilities, and as a result, the guidance these people can receive is extremely limited. For these, it is possible to encourage a more rounded life by following hobbies that would lead to greater satisfaction than possibly the job alone can afford.

Among this group we find the misplaced owner of a retail store, the misplaced professional man, and many others. In part, it is necessary to recognize the personality problems accompanying the lack of vocational adjustment and to counsel along personal lines. In this group there are very few who are courageous enough or are free enough to start over. Rather it is necessary to try to build a more firm foundation with what they have been doing for so many years of their adult life.

One of the major problems that must be faced in counseling this group is the fact that often, consciously or unconsciously, they are aware of their limitations and decide that since they have not handled the problem correctly, they will make every effort to see that the same thing does not happen to their children. It is at this point that the problem becomes serious, since they are very likely to play a major role in now spoiling a second person's life. It is desirable to help these people gain insight to the point where it is possible to demonstrate that the decisions they are making concerning their children may not be the most appropriate.

Very often, these people reach the counselor indirectly. They are likely to refer the child for counseling, not even aware that they can benefit as much as their children.

Within recent years, a new area in guidance has begun to emerge. As this country gets older, it faces for the first time a considerable population sixty or more years of age.

Depending upon the success that these people have achieved prior to that age, they may have more or less difficulties. Of course, with the pressure of industry and the relatively recent emphasis on pension plans, from the point of view of a younger person the problem is solved by merely retiring these people. Actually, the older person very often cannot face retirement with such calm. At the time at which retirement is offered or insisted upon, the individual hurriedly runs through his life in retrospect and sees that he has not accomplished all that he has set out to do.

It is for this reason that one finds such people, when faced with retirement, planning a burst of activity which, of course, will not materialize, since the previous period did not produce such activity.

For some of these people, the economic pressure is great because there may not be a nest egg or retirement plan or an annuity. These people cannot afford to retire, and the question as to the type of job such a person can obtain is a difficult one. Actually, the solution is not readily available. It is entirely likely that many of these people can successfully perform more sedentary jobs; or they may find part-time work, or be able to put former hobbies on an income basis.

The solutions reached in counseling the older person probably lie in having him engage in that work which he is still capable of performing with success.

Community houses for the aged are beginning to appear, and it is very likely that within the reasonable future they will be as numerous as nursery schools. Actually, this presents another and likely solution for such people.

At the community house, they will be able to mix socially with people of similar age and the program of arts and crafts can be made very meaningful in relation to the person becoming or continuing to be creative and productive. It is ridiculous to assume that the aged are senile; some may be, but the normal aged person, although he may be less strong and slower physically, retains his mental abilities without any appreciable loss. Such a person is likely to obtain gratifications through social relations with people of his age group, and also through the family.

The relation between counseling and therapy

Since counseling aids an individual to solve his problems it is necessary to ask whether counseling is similar to therapy. If therapy is to be considered a process fostering an individual's growth, so that he can now handle problems that he formerly could not, then counseling might be considered as synonymous with therapy. Rogers (6) states: "While there may be some reason for this distinction, it is also plain that the most intensive and successful counseling is indistinguishable from intensive and successful counseling psychotherapy. Consequently, both terms will be employed as they are in common use by workers in the field."[3] Rogers will be referred to especially in relation to interviewing technique. At this time it might be mentioned that he has evolved the type of interviewing technique known as nondirective. The inroads that this technique has made not only in the field of counseling and therapy but also in the field of vocational guidance have been great.

The view expounded is that counseling is therapy. In many instances it is exceedingly difficult to separate the counseling aspect from the therapeutic aspect. It is precisely because of this belief that we recommend that psychological training be given prior to the administration of vocational guidance. It must be remembered that when an individual has a problem, be it vocational or any other type, it is important that he be helped to solve it. The best way to help him

[3] From *Counseling and Psychotherapy* by Carl R. Rogers, copyright 1942 by Carl R. Rogers. Reprinted by permission of and arrangement with Houghton Mifflin Company, the authorized publishers.

is to enable him to see the problem and the varieties of solutions, and then to allow him to experience that growth which is necessary for the correct and successful solution of the problem. Therefore, guidance when correctly handled is similar to or identical with therapy.

Guidance or counseling can, therefore, not only be considered as having therapeutic value, but actually be therapy. The typical vocational guidance agency dares only to whisper the word therapy at the present time. This is nonsense. If the agency has adequately trained individuals in counseling, then it must boldly recognize that it does the very important job of therapy which may in this instance be primarily related to vocational problems, but as pointed out, is also related to emotional as well as educational problems. Shellow (7) considers vocational planning as a process of growth. The goal of vocational guidance, according to Shellow, should not be to give a specific answer to a groping client. As she states,

> Our goal is rather to train the individual in self-evaluation and in realistically relating himself to the economic world. Vocational guidance is a learning process. The client learns to approach his problems through the understanding of himself. It is a process of integration and drawing together of the several aspects of the personality into a related pattern directed to a goal in line with this pattern.[4]

Shellow courageously states that vocational guidance has always had a therapeutic value. "When a person comes bewildered and confused and through the use of tests and counseling is directed toward an occupation which seems to remove the confusion and give him a feeling of security, is this not therapy?"[5] asks Shellow. According to her, the question is no longer "Should we do therapy?" but "How far should we go?" In an increasing number of cases, vocational guidance is the only acceptable straw at which a disturbed client can grasp. As Shellow astutely points out,

> Many will accept the services of a stigma-free agency for vocational guidance who would never get to a social agency or a mental hygiene

[4] "The Increasing Use of Clinical Psychology in Vocational Guidance," by Sadie M. Shellow. *Occupations, the Vocational Guidance Journal,* published by National Vocational Guidance Association, Incorporated, 28:304(1950).

[5] *Loc. cit.*

> clinic. Sometimes it is necessary for the counselor to lend a receptive ear to the problem uppermost in the client's mind until he finds release and recognizes that his basic need is not for vocational guidance but for emotional adjustment. The vocational guidance agency serves as a bridge to bring the disturbed client into contact with agencies whose function is intensive therapy.[6]

We are in complete agreement with Shellow's point of view. It is not recommended that vocational guidance agencies handle involved and seriously maladjusted personality problems. However, it is recognized that a person with a vocational problem is likely to be confused not only in the realm of the occupational world but also within himself and therefore both kinds of problems must be appreciated and clearly attacked. In this context, counseling must be accepted as synonymous with therapy.

History of vocational guidance

Brewer (2), in an exacting historical survey of the movement known as vocational guidance, reaches the conclusion that Frank Parsons deserves the designation of founder of organized vocational guidance. From this survey, Brewer reaches the following conclusions concerning the importance of the contributions of Frank Parsons:

1. Vocational guidance grew out of voluntary educational, civic and social work; it did not originate in any of the fields of business, industry, psychology, placement, personnel work, scientific management, division of labor, public education, vocational education, government, employer associations, labor unions, or religious or parental effort.
2. Parsons paved the way for undertaking the work in schools, both by the methods he used and by the direct statement that schools and colleges should undertake the work.
3. He began the training of counselors, planning group meetings for that purpose.
4. He used all the scientific tools available to him; there is evidence that he would have used various kinds of standardized tests if these had then been available. He used rating sheets, interview techniques, and specific assignments. His book has hints of the tryout plan, versatility, and follow-up.

---

[6] *Loc. cit.*

5. He refrained from the use of phrenology and other false methods, in spite of their popularity during his entire lifetime.
6. He analyzed the problem of vocational guidance far enough to furnish what later writers called "six steps in the vocational progress of an individual."
    1. laying a broad foundation of useful experiences
    2. studying occupational opportunities
    3. choosing an occupation
    4. preparing for the occupation
    5. entering upon work
    6. securing promotions and making readjustments
7. He organized the work of the Vocation Bureau of Boston for the collection of information, group study of such information, study of the individual, counseling, etc., in a way which laid the groundwork for successful operation of such effort in schools, colleges, and other agencies.
8. He recognized the importance of his work and secured appropriate publicity for it. He secured financial support for the bureau and the endorsement and supervision of educators, employers, and other public men and women.
9. He enlisted friends and associates in such a manner as to lead to the continuance and expansion of the movement. For their help he prepared much written material, including the manuscript for *Choosing a Vocation.*[7]

Parsons recognized that in the wise choice of a vocation there are three broad factors: (1) a clear understanding of yourself, your aptitudes, abilities, interests, ambitions, resources, limitations and their causes; (2) a knowledge of the requirements and conditions of success, advantages and disadvantages, compensations, opportunities and prospects in different lines of work; (3) true reasoning on the relations of these two groups of facts. These three factors were stated in his book, *Choosing a Vocation* (5), published in 1909. It must be remembered that in that period psychology, especially as it is known today, was almost nonexistent. In fact, psychological testing, knowledge of personality, and the area of mental hygiene were not available. It is a tribute to the insight of Parsons that at that stage he was able to recognize the importance of matching the individual with job information.

[7] Reprinted by permission from *History of Vocational Guidance,* by J. M. Brewer, Harper & Brothers, New York, 1942.

Parsons served as the first director of the first bureau dedicated to vocational guidance. In May of the year the Boston Bureau was founded, he issued his first, and as it turned out to be, his only report. This report is valuable not only because in it for the first time the term vocational guidance was used, but also because Parsons advocated that this work become a part of the public school system in every community. From the time of this report until his death, Parsons was most occupied with the gathering of material for his book, *Choosing a Vocation.* This book was published posthumously and to a large extent must have been written by Ralph Albertson, a coworker of Parsons in the Boston Bureau.

Hoppock (3) correctly characterizes the early workers in the field of vocational guidance as social workers interested in the problems of child labor and in the transition of youth from school to work. Their efforts were rewarded when they helped to force the school administrators to recognize that these problems were not only important but related to their work.

In the 1920's and 30's guidance had been so well received in the schools that it was actually dominated by the school administrators. The third phase occurs, according to Hoppock, in the late 1930's when the focus was on the problems of unemployment, of placement, of technological change, of occupational trends and occupational mobility.

Of considerable influence in the growth of vocational guidance were certain governmental agencies organized as a result of the economic depression of the 1930's. Each of these agencies was primarily concerned with improving the conditions that resulted from widespread unemployment and each in its own way fostered vocational guidance activity. The Works Progress Administration published many volumes of occupational information (4). The two agencies devoted to unemployed youth, The National Youth Administration and The Civilian Conservation Corps, made use of vocational guidance not merely to help place young people in the most appropriate work but also to counsel them in the general sense of the term.

In the development of any profession, membership organizations play an important role. In guidance there have been at least four important bodies contributing heavily to advancement in the field.

The National Vocational Guidance Association has played the most important role. This organization can trace its origin to the period of approximately the time that Parsons was doing his work and has shown a steady and continued growth. It has various divisions and also various local branches. Its committees constantly study the entire field of guidance and issue reports that affect both progress and standards. Its official publication is *Occupations,* the most widely known magazine devoted to vocational guidance.

The American Vocational Association, through its professional activities, has also promoted vocational guidance and its work was very important in relation to the passing of the George-Barden Act of 1946, under which federal aid became available to the states for the purposes of vocational guidance. The National Education Association has also been interested in vocational guidance. The fourth organization is the American Psychological Association. It has a division which is interested in guidance work and has been instrumental in raising the professional standards of counseling. The status of clinical psychologists as well as consulting psychologists is being defined, clarified, and raised as a result of the efforts of this professional organization.

The outstanding publication of a professional nature in the field of vocational guidance is the magazine known as *Occupations,* a vocational guidance journal. It had its origin in a four-page pamphlet issued in April 1915 by Dr. W. C. Ryan, the first secretary of the National Vocational Guidance Association. About 20 issues of this bulletin appeared between April 1915 and March 1918. At that time it was expanded to an eight-page pamphlet. The first issue of the National Vocational Guidance Association bulletin, a 12-page document, appeared in 1921. It had a foreword, a report of the meeting of the Association at Atlantic City, plans for the year, and abstracts of four papers delivered. In December 1922 this publication was taken over by the Bureau of Vocational Guidance of the Graduate School of Education at Harvard University. This is the bureau that succeeded the older Vocational Bureau established by Parsons. It was moved to Harvard in 1917 with R. W. Kelly as director. In 1919 Brewer succeeded Kelly; in 1923 F. J. Allen became the editor; and in 1924 the magazine was named the *Vocational Guidance Magazine.* In 1933 the National Occupational Conference became the joint publisher of this periodical with the National Vocational Guidance Association, and the title became *Occupations.* At the expiration of the National Occupational Conference, the Association again became the sole publisher. In 1944, the magazine finally became known as *Occupations, the Vocational Guidance Journal,* with Harry Dexter Kitson as the editor. It publishes articles on all aspects of vocational guidance.

Another agency important in the development of vocational guidance was the National Occupational Conference, which was organized in 1933. This agency was supported by funds from the Carnegie Foundation. In the six years of its existence, more than half a million dollars was spent by the Conference. It had a great influence not only because it made possible the publication of books which were very valuable to the development of guidance but also because it was able to give much financial and scholarly support to the magazine *Occupations.* It allowed for a considerable expansion of this publication. The third major contribution of the National Occupational Conference was its promotion of vocational guidance in the school system by its organized tours and conferences. It was able to influence the administrators of education of the importance of vocational guidance. The Conference before winding up its affairs assisted greatly in the work of the United States Office of Education. This office became the federal nucleus in a system of assisting state education departments.

In World War I and in World War II the importance of vocational guidance as a contributor to the efficiency of the nation's economy as well as to the winning of the war was recognized. In fact, during World War II the necessity of vocational guidance was demonstrated. If one were to consider the armed forces as a huge industrial organization in the process of unprecedented expansion, and one in which it was necessary to place people, many of whom did not have training, it can be seen how important vocational guidance actually is. Since so many millions of people had to be placed in jobs that were in accord with their abilities, previous experiences, and so on; and since in many cases this meant not making use of their civilian experience, it can be readily recognized that the need for testing, interviewing, job analyses, and the extension of occupational information was not only useful in the direct services of the armed forces but necessary. This was also true for industry. They had quite suddenly to hire and train many workers to meet the war effort.

With the end of the war, guidance again assumed great importance in the shifting of people back to their civilian occupations and in designating civilian occupations for those who went directly into the armed forces from schools. The decade beginning with 1950 is characterized by a changing employment market, emphasis on more specialized and still higher forms of learning, and rewards for the person trained in specialties. All of this requires the still further recognition of vocational counseling.

Preview of the book

Chapter 2 is titled "Pseudo-Scientific Guidance." It attempts to describe such pseudo-scientific systems as physiognomy, phrenology, astrology, and palmistry, and to show the confused cause and effect relationships upon which these quackeries are based.

Systems of guidance not based upon psychology can do untold harm to the many people who have problems. There are many who foolishly seek the advice of charlatans. The charlatans either tell people what they want to hear or allow them to make their own specific interpretations of glittering generalities. To indicate clearly what vocational guidance is not, this chapter describes the fakery existing in our times.

Chapter 3 describes the types of counseling centers. In order for the student to obtain a panoramic view of vocational guidance, a survey of a variety of agencies in both the school and the community is presented. A complete description of the procedure of counseling at the Vocational Advisory Service is also presented to provide a picture of the steps involved in counseling, as well as to describe what happens to a client from the time he presents himself to a guidance agency until the case is designated as closed.

Chapters 4 and 5 are devoted to the interview, the most important aspect of counseling. Chapter 4 describes and evaluates three major categories of interviewing techniques. Based upon an evaluation of authoritarian interviewing and non-directive interviewing, it promotes the type of interviewing described as non-authoritarian. Chapter 5 is intended as a training manual in which general principles for conducting an interview as well as the areas to be covered in the interview are specifically described.

Chapters 6 and 7 describe the general and theoretical bases for psychological testing. Chapter 6 is concerned primarily with the description of those principles and problems of psychological tests that are basic and fundamental to the understanding of the theoretical structure on which all psychological tests should be constructed. Chapter 7 describes in general the major areas of psychological testing—intelligence tests, aptitude tests, achievement tests, interest tests, and personality tests.

Chapters 8 and 9 are a continuation of the presentation of psychological tests except that rather than a general description, a review of the specific tests most widely used in counseling is presented. This review includes not only a description of these tests but also a critical evaluation of the tests for guidance purposes. It happens that many of the widely used tests are not as good as their popular usage would imply. Pointing this out indicates the need to evaluate tests critically prior to their use in vocational batteries.

In Chapter 10 is a discussion of the clinical approach in its two aspects. The first is the idea of the individual as a unified whole to whom an organismic, dynamic approach must be made. This idea is the antithesis of the rather sterile concept of the analysis of an individual into small units based upon insignificant single test scores. The second is those psychological tests that are essentially clinical in nature but can have meaningful usage in vocational counseling. Special reference is made to the Wechsler-Bellevue Intelligence Test and the Rorschach Inkblot Test for personality diagnosis. As a matter of fact, many tests not originally clinical in nature do allow for successful application of the clinical approach. Counseling will be more effective when the concept "clinical approach" has shed its mystical aura and is more widely used. The authors have attempted to reduce this concept to the everyday meaning that can be understood and applied by professional workers in guidance.

Chapter 11 is "Integrating Tests and Interviews." Too often books adequately describe interviewing techniques as well as psychological tests without integrating the two as is necessary in the counseling of any individual. The client can benefit from the interviews and the psychological tests only when the psychological tests are made meaningful to him. This, of course, must be done during the interview. Probably the most important skill of the counselor is his ability to integrate psychological tests in the interview. This chapter attempts to enable the counselor to achieve this all-important integration.

Chapter 12 consists of subject matter which is often the bane of the counselor's existence. As counseling becomes more objective it needs objective study. This means at least familiarity with statistical concepts. This chapter describes the statistical terms most widely used in counseling on a verbal non-mathematical level. It may not be necessary for a counselor to know how to make certain statistical computations, but it is necessary for him to understand the concepts. For the reader who has not had a course or courses in statistics, this chapter might offer more benefit if it is read before the chapters on psychological tests.

Chapter 13 deals with the vital area of interests. Although knowledge of a client's interests is attained through both the interview and psychological tests, the theoretical basis of interests as well as their development must be understood by the person who is to be a successful counselor. The relationship between interests and abilities as well as the degree of permanence of interests are some of the problems that must be dealt with in order to evaluate correctly the importance of a client's interests.

Chapters 14 and 15 are concerned with the sources and uses of occupational information as well as the contributions of psychologists to this area. For counseling to be successful, the world of occupational information must be made known to the client. A counselor, regardless of his skill in interviewing or test administration, will not be able to offer the client what he needs unless he has a large store of knowledge of occupations. While the area of occupational information has not been objectively developed to the extent that other areas in vocational guidance have, it is making rapid progress.

Chapter 16, entitled "The Counselor," attempts to describe the background of training qualifications necessary for the person who does the work of counseling whether he be employed in the school system, in a public or private agency, or as an individual doing counseling work. The necessity for improving the standards and requirements of the counselor is recognized and articulated. The subject matter to be studied is also included. The day is fast passing when anyone will be able merely to assume the title of counselor.

For the development of counseling, evaluation is a necessity. The various methods of evaluating counseling as a total process are reviewed and in turn critically evaluated so that the adequate techniques can be differentiated from the less adequate ones. Evaluation is the topic in Chapter 17.

Although this book is oriented along vocational guidance lines, it has been stated that all the techniques have application in vocational selection, the other aspect of vocational psychology. Not only within the profession but also within industry the need for counseling workers is becoming recognized.

The social bases for counseling in industry as well as a review of a few of the companies already counseling their workers is presented in Chapter 18, "Employee Counseling."

Chapter 19 is on vocational selection. This chapter attempts in summary fashion to describe the tools used in employment screening, not only from the point of view of the employer, but also from the point of view of the applicant seeking a job.

This brief thumb-nail description of the chapters to follow has been included so that the reader may, at the outset, have an understanding of the subject matter covered and the points of view expressed.

Bibliography

1. Blum, M. L., *Industrial Psychology and Its Social Foundations.* New York: Harper, 1949.

2. Brewer, J. M., *History of Vocational Guidance.* New York: Harper, 1942.
3. Hoppock, R., "Presidential Address, 1950," *Occupations,* 28:497–499 (1950).
4. Jager, H. A., "Vocational Guidance in the United States," *International Labor Review,* 57:1–15 (1948).
5. Parsons, F., *Choosing a Vocation.* Boston: Houghton Mifflin, 1909.
6. Rogers, C. R., *Counseling and Psychotherapy.* Boston: Houghton Mifflin, 1942.
7. Shellow, S. M., "The Increasing Use of Clinical Psychology in Vocational Guidance," *Occupations,* 28:302–305 (1950).
8. Super, Donald E., *Appraising Vocational Fitness.* New York: Harper, 1949.
9. Thorpe, L. P., "Guiding Child and Adolescent Development in the Modern School," *Educational Bulletin #16,* California Test Bureau, California (1946).
10. Viteles, M. S., "Psychological Practice and Research in Vocational Guidance," *Journal of Consulting Psychology,* 5:258–264 (1941).
11. Williamson, E. G., *How To Counsel Students.* New York: McGraw-Hill, 1939.

2

PSEUDO-SCIENTIFIC GUIDANCE

When a person has a problem, of course he would like to solve it correctly. However, too often he cannot do so. He may not be able to think clearly. He may not have the ability to obtain the correct solution. He may not have sufficient information or even know where to obtain it. In many cases the solution may not be easily obtained and can occur only as a result of a chain of correct responses rather than a single one. Eventually he becomes so involved and harassed that he does not know what to do. At this point he may realize that he needs help but may not want to reveal his need to a qualified person or agency; or he may not know how to determine who is qualified. Rather than reveal his problem he may even prefer to be surreptitious.

Such a person is easy prey for quacks and charlatans. They often advertise widely and glowingly in newspapers, pulp magazines, and telephone directories. They have convenient "offices" in restaurants, fairs, resorts, or centrally located office buildings in the cities. Such charlatans speak in superlatives about their mysterious powers and abilities. No problem is too difficult for them to solve. They exercise no caution or hesitancy. They call themselves by various names and grant themselves odd and worthless degrees. Such a person's problem cannot be solved or even lessened by these charlatans, yet he often seeks their advice and too often is left more damaged than unharmed.

His problem may be far from simple. Most of the problems concerning him do not resemble the simple problems of arithmetic, in which there is only one correct answer attained briefly and with assurance. For example, John does not know whether to continue his last year of high school, enlist in the Navy, or take the job that his uncle has offered him as a plumber's helper. Here is what seems to be a simple problem in vocational guidance, but it is no simple problem for John. John is not the only person involved since his parents as well as other adults enter the picture, and very often they confuse more than help. John's parents advise him to stay in school, the recruiting officer advises enlistment, and the uncle definitely knows that his job offer is best.

At this point one of the following characters may enter: the physiognomist, the phrenologist, the palmist, the astrologist, the graphologist and the just plain faker. Many of these alleged experts are nothing more than confidence men who ply their trade on gullible and harassed people. If John were to seek the services of such a person, he most assuredly would not obtain the best answer to his problem. Nevertheless, since John and his parents do not know how to solve the problem by themselves, they will be glad to seek the recommendation of someone who claims omniscience. It will be the task of this chapter to shed some light on this sort of person.

The quacks in vocational psychology are many. Roback (16) estimates that there are approximately 15,000 psychological quacks at the present time. He estimates that they spend $12,000,000 per year for advertising. Since it is not known what part this $12,000,000 is of the total take, one cannot say definitely how much money people waste on such services. It must be enormous. For example, if advertising expenditures average 10 per cent of income then the total sum spent by people who go to quacks for advice is more than one hundred million dollars a year.

By now the reader is probably saying, "There ought to be a law against this." Be assured that the legal aspects are complicated. Very few cases are prosecuted. These quacks thrive because few states have laws to prevent their existence. A rare instance of indictment is reported by Brotemarkle (2):

> Last Spring it fell to my lot to be summoned as a witness of fact and also to be qualified as an expert in what I deem to be the first

> case involving the direct problem of psychological service. During the January 1939 term the Grand Jury presented to the District Court of the United States for the District of Columbia an indictment against an individual, charging that that individual "stated and represented herself to be an international authority and lecturer on nutrition and psychology and a mental healer," and that the individual "unlawfully, knowingly, designedly and with intent to defraud, feloniously did pretend and represent . . ."
>
> The facts developing out of this indictment led to the conviction and sentencing of this most charming individual . . . one readily recognized to be among the cleverest of the entire group. She has appealed the case and therefore I think it best for me to delay any detailed discussion of the same. Nor need I present to you any of her advertising which on the whole is duplicated by hundreds of others. It might seem amusing to you, were it not pathetic. To read from her "Master University Course in Personality Building and Character Development for the Individual" would be even more amusing, yet even more pathetic.[1]

Even if the laws were perfect in this instance, it must be remembered that it is not only the quack who is involved. There are always the people who seek out these charlatans and are willing to pay for their "service." The person who visits the quack is usually confused and gullible. It is no wonder that advantage is taken of him. Most of these people do not know the difference between what psychology is and what charlatans claim it to be. They know nothing of the experimental method through which facts about behavior are established. They are naive and often confused in determining cause and effect relationships. A statement about behavior not derived from conclusions based upon experimentation may often result in confusion between cause and effect. For example, the statement that red heads have tempers can lead to a confusion between cause and effect. Knowledge resulting from experimentation reveals that hair coloring is not the cause of tempers. Therefore, red hair does not cause temper.

It must be recognized that a person's anxiety to solve his perplexing problem makes him willing to receive a ready-made "solution" and so encourages and invites the pseudo-solutions of the charla-

[1] Reprinted from the *Journal of Applied Psychology*, 24:17(1940), by permission of the American Psychological Association, publishers.

tan. Brotemarkle in an address as chairman of the clinical section of the American Association for Applied Psychology aptly remarked:

> The specific challenge of quackery to Consulting Psychological Service is probably greater than to any other specific service today save the diversified fields of religious cult practice in which may be found the origins of the quack and to which he even now seems prepared to take final flight. The dissemination of knowledge fundamental to most other professions rendering service to human kind is sufficient to have driven the charlatan to seek other activities especially for cover and defense. Psychological practice is today his greatest opportunity. No field has ever offered the quack richer opportunities. The potency of the human mind has ever been a fertile field for his endeavors; now enriched by the amassed experience and culture of the past the charlatan readily employs this so-called "omnipotence" of the human mind as the basis of his predatory activity.[2]

Munn (11) defines psychology as the science of experience and behavior. Ruch (17) conveys the meaning of psychology by referring to such objectives as the description, prediction, and control of behavior. Psychology as a science collects facts about behavior systematically, organizes them into coherent bodies of information, and finds their relationships and their explanations. Vocational psychology is a branch of psychology related to the aspect of experience and behavior that involves people and occupations. Its task is to collect facts involving the relation between occupations and people, systematically organize them into a body of knowledge, and ultimately contribute to vocational planning. The pseudo-systems do not do this. Regardless of their grandiose claims, they never allow such claims to be subjected to the rigors of the experimental method. Whenever these pseudo-systems and their mumbo-jumbo are checked, the invariable result is to remove the mystical nonsense from their gibberish and to show them to have the confusion between cause and effect that they started out with.

An experiment is simply an observation under controlled conditions. In the case of John, it is not possible to cut him into three parts and have each part follow one of the three vocational plans men-

---

[2] Reprinted from *ibid.*, page 12, by permission of the American Psychological Association, publishers.

tioned. However, it is possible to collect facts and organize them as is done in vocational psychology, and with his cooperation, arrive at the best possible vocational step. Facts must be gathered and organized about such elements as age, family background, educational history, intelligence, aptitudes, abilities, and interests. Prediction must be based solely upon these data. Furthermore, it is possible to observe John and many others like him and to make a generalization. Although vocational psychology does not lend itself to the "ideal" type of experimentation afforded the physical sciences, in which all factors are eliminated, neutralized, or held constant except the single experimental factor, it nevertheless allows with suitable modifications findings based upon data collected. Such a modification allows for the advisability of using the clinical method in vocational psychology. The confusion between cause and effect is generally prevented.

As each of the "systems" is discussed, it is hoped that the major differences between vocational psychology and the pseudo-science of the "lunatic fringe" will become clear.

Physiognomy

Physiognomy is the supposed art of discovering traits of character, personality, and so on from the outward appearance, especially the face. All physiognomists take advantage of the fact that too often people are uncritical and will accept the incorrect conclusion of reasoning by analogy, which often leads to confusion between cause and effect. Many people either like or dislike a face and accordingly judge behavioral accompaniments which do not have anything to do with the face.

According to physiognomists, the face can be divided into many minute areas, each related to mental traits and ultimately to vocational success. Physiognomists claim that by studying people's faces they have been able—with never a failure—to guide these people correctly in choosing their vocations. There is ordinarily no evidence offered to support these assertions; there are no experimental controls. And without such scientific support, the cause and effect relationship that physiognomists claim exists cannot be accepted.

Phrenology

Phrenology is the system which claims that the brain is divided into small parts, each section controlling an independent faculty or power; any overdevelopment of a faculty causes a bump on the head. Therefore, an analysis of the bumps tells all. In a very remote way, phrenol-

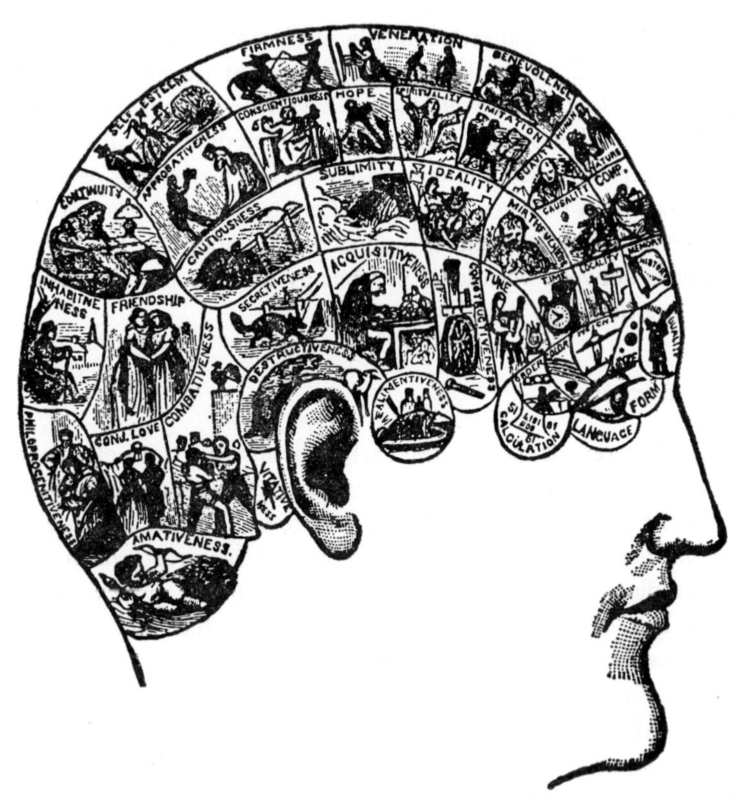

From Floyd L. Ruch, Psychology and Life, *3rd ed., published by Scott, Forsman and Co.*

ogy might be considered as being related to the mind-body problem or, as stated in a more modern way, the problem of localization of cerebral function. Gall, who is considered historically important in phrenology, developed his system primarily by observing friends and acquaintances. He assumed that when a friend had a bump and also a certain trait that these two went together, not only for the friend but for everyone else.

The specific brain location alleged by phrenologists to be related to amativeness has been determined by experiment to maintain equilibrium. Destructiveness, according to phrenologists, is located in the area that physiologists know determines auditory sensations.

Phrenology has been disproved by experimentation, but it is necessary to mention the obvious fallacy of reasoning by analogy and drawing conclusions on limited samples. Also fallacious is the peculiar notion that the soft tissue of the cerebrum can make dents in the bone tissue of the cranium.

Most phrenologists are found at amusement parks and state fairs. The figure on page 32 is their trademark.

Examining phrenology with the criteria of experimental methodology, one readily sees that there is no basis for any serious consideration.

Astrology

Astrologers claim to be able to tell all about your past, present, and future by ascertaining the position of heavenly bodies particularly in relation to your date of birth. The continued appearance of columns on astrology in some of our most accepted and respected newspapers indicates man's willingness to accept this nonsense. The confusion between cause and effect is obvious. The particular date a person is born is not related to the position of heavenly bodies; anyone with a knowledge of biology knows this to be true.

Parr (15) reports an interesting study on the effectiveness of horoscope readings. Sixteen astrologers advertising in pulp magazines were requested to send him horoscopes. In all, sixty personality traits were assigned to him. Only five were in any way objectionable, illustrating the principle used by most of these charlatans of favoring "molasses over vinegar." Tabulation of the days which the horoscopes referred to indicated that all but three of the three hundred sixty-five were designated as either lucky or unlucky days and each of the days in the year were termed lucky by most of the astrologers and unlucky by the others. In six cases supplemental horoscopes were sent (of course for an additional fee). In each of these six cases, three questions were asked: (1) "In what line of work have I the best chance to

TABLE 1

ANSWERS TO QUESTIONS ON OCCUPATIONS BY SIX INDEPENDENT ASTROLOGERS*

Astrologers	*Question 1* *In what line of work have I the best chance to succeed?*	*Question 2* *How long will I be in my present position?*	*Question 3* *When will I receive a raise in pay?*
A	It would not be to your advantage to make a decided change in your line of work.	Present work offers you a chance for advancement.	No immediate prospect.
B	You will get into a different type of work within the next year.	You will make a change in the fall of this year.	A change in position will take you to a larger place.
C	I see no change in your present position.	Present position will last another year and you will get a promotion from same company. I see no change in view.	Before end of present year.
D	You should do well in scientific work.	No immediate change.	You will get one this summer.
E	Your traits point toward a business career.	You will change when conditions improve.	Because of depression a raise will be postponed.
F	In whatever you attempt to do.	It would not pay you to change. Sit tight.	More pay right away.

* *Occupations, the Vocational Guidance Journal,* published by National Vocational Guidance Association, Incorporated, 16:238 (1938).

succeed?" (2) "How long will I be in my present position?" (3) "When will I receive a raise in pay?"[3] The person asking these questions of the six astrologers was a commissioned officer in the U.S. Army. Table 1 indicates the answers he received to each of these questions.

[3] *Occupations, the Vocational Guidance Journal,* published by National Vocational Guidance Association, Incorporated, 16:238(1938).

Palmistry

According to a palmist the creases, lines, folds, and tufts of the hand are related to vocational as well as other forms of advice. A book (not on our suggested reading list) by W. B. Benham, entitled *How to Choose Vocations from the Hands,* describes the work of the palmists. An abstract from a typical palmist is quoted as follows:

> The hand of a good judge is very long to give him patience and has a dominant first finger for rule, and he always has a remarkable line of head. . . . The peculiarity of the hands of a physician is a certain elasticity of palm, soft yet very firm, wide with long fingers, a turned thumb, high Luna and Mercury mounts; the line of head ought to be sloping, and the third finger dominant.[4]

Again it is not advisable to select vocations on such a basis; no experimental evidence is offered, and the relationship between cause and effect is not at all clear.

Graphology

Both quacks and scientists are found as exponents of graphology. The quacks indulge in generality and unsubstantiated claims. The scientists are more cautious. When one views handwriting as an expression of the individual and therefore a revealer of personality, then we are in the realm of possibility. Murphy (12) states that much of the theory offered by contemporary graphology makes sense and is very reasonable. But he is concerned about the problem of validation which he thinks needs more clear-cut definition and solution.

There are a number of psychologists who are seriously investigating through experimental and clinical techniques many possible hypotheses and theories. Until such time as the evidence is conclusive, it will be necessary to maintain an open mind.

As an example of a favorable statement by a psychologist the following private communication by Gertrude Aull is offered:

---

[4] From Katherine St. Hill, *The Book of the Hand.* New York: Putnam, 1928, pages 259–260, as quoted in *Readings in Industrial Psychology.* New York: D. Appleton and Co., 1931, pages 87–88.

Graphology, as applied by Central European psychologists, is based in its present form predominantly upon the works of Ludwig Klages, otherwise known as the originator of a holistic, personalistic system of personality theory. His basic postulate is the absolute uniqueness of individual personality, seen as a unitary, meaningful psycho-physical process. In this sense, all of an individual's behavioral moves and gestures are assumed to have psychic correlates, and to be actually expressive and highly characteristic of his needs, impulses and attitudes, in short of his total personality.

Handwriting is conceived as a trail of expressive moves, which affords a picture of the writer's typical manner of structuring and organizing space. The characteristics of handwriting differ from person to person regardless of the uniformity of instruction and the medium or instruments used. Furthermore, in a normal adult, volitional effort to change the handwriting results in only superficial changes in script.

Modern personality diagnostics has made frequent use of expressive efforts of subjects (for example, figure and other controlled and free drawings, paintings, and acting), giving attention to both the form and the spatial orientation revealed. The use of handwriting in diagnostics has the advantage over these techniques of dealing with products which are easily accessible and which may be obtained naturally without the artificiality of a staged laboratory test situation. All that is needed for a handwriting diagnosis is a large enough sample (at least several lines), unhurriedly and informally written and, as with all projective tests, information as to the subject's sex and age.

Diagnostic interpretation of handwriting is concerned neither with content or calligraphic beauty of the script, but with its form as such. The significance of form in handwriting may be considered under three different aspects:

1. Handwriting as a trace of an individual's hand and arm movements, unique and characteristic for him, and so of his typical and recurring gestures.
2. Handwriting as a task to be performed.
3. Handwriting as the creation of an individual pattern, which develops not consciously planned yet under the watchful eye of the writer.

Observation and contemplation of form along these lines leads to further inquiry:

1. What are the muscular operations involved in the given writing movements (such as contraction and release)? What ac-

tions or experiences is a gesture remindful of and what does it convey? What needs and impulses prompted it? What is the writer trying to do? Writing moves all may be translated into behavioral axioms illustrative of typical efforts, attitudes, emotions (for example, hiding, dealing a blow, protecting, asserting).

2. While performing his task the writer is moving along through space towards a certain goal and towards a meeting with the environment. How does he get there? Slow or fast, graceful or clumsy, plodding along with regulated steps or striding boldly. Surely, his image of the goal (as close, distant, promising or indifferent) and his perception of the road (as free and open, endangered by obstacles, wide or narrow) will help to determine his pace.
3. What are the structure, quality, style of the writing pattern? What is the effect intended upon the observer? How does the writer deal with the available space and how successful and original is his departure from the conventional school pattern?

Meaningful interpretations along these lines must, as in all projective tests, proceed by the Gestalt principle. Criticism of graphology is frequently based upon the faulty assumption of an absolute point-to-point relationship between any definite "signs" or symptoms of scripts in general and psychological correlates or traits. Handwritings must be diagnosed "from above," that is: individual aspects gain their significance and meaning from the general level of form in the total pattern, which serves as a specific frame of reference. They are not interpreted absolutely, but in view of a configurational interdependence and relationship between all aspects presented in the handwriting. A given characteristic then can extend along an ambivalent scale, and so may be found to be of positive or negative value, according to the total pattern in which it occurs. The trait of domineeringness, for example, may be qualified either by assertiveness and self-reference or, in another case, by the capacity to understand and to adapt to others. Thus any major aspect of the script, such as smallness, may have a large scale of possible meanings, ranging from modesty and tolerant devotion down to compulsiveness and self-torture. Its specific meaning in a given sample will depend upon the context of which smallness is but one aspect.

Diagnosis proceeds by major and minor dimensions, which have been empirically found to correlate with certain dimensions or aspects of personality, such as vertical and horizontal dimensions (related to the writer's orientation towards the self and to reality), rightward and leftward (future, contact, goal vs. past, self); more specifically, aspects of extension (large, small, narrow, wide), velocity, impact, degree of fluctuation (regulated or rhythmical) forms of binding, ductual dispersion and their psychological counterparts.

The final product should be a highly specific yet complex picture of the personality, his way of doing things, his style of life, his means and manner of externalization and self-realization.

Objections to graphology as a diagnostic device have been raised mainly on two grounds: it cannot be expressed in quantitative terms, and it may not be readily taught to every student of psychology. These same objections, however, hold true for all of the other conventional projective tests. The fumbling beginner relies upon quantification, while the experienced clinician frowns upon pragmatic acceptance of absolute rules and formulas and prefers to exploit the qualitative data. Adequate handling of psycho-diagnostics requires more than adequate instruction. It requires keen perception, knowledge of personality dynamics both normal and abnormal, and in addition a thorough familiarity with the psychology, for example isomorphistic meanings, of expression. Graphology, as any other projective test, cannot be validated by correlating "factors" with those of other tests. Much rather it must validate itself (and has done so) by success in daily exposure to practical clinical experience.

As for the vocational significance of graphology: whatever was said of personality diagnosis can be applied for purposes of vocational guidance. That means that there is no point-to-point relationship between symptoms of the script and specific absolute vocational aptitudes or prospects. Vocational guidance which conceives of vocational choice not as a mere means of making a living, but as a socialized outlet and field of satisfaction for personal needs and tendencies, as a way of realizing personal goals and attitudes, can profit considerably from as complex and specific a personality picture as graphology affords. It may not yield an infallible prediction of success and failure, but vocational guidance which is aware of occupation as a human phenomenon requiring specific physical and psychological attitudes, will find the same physical and psychological attitudes behaviorally expressed in handwriting.

However, there is a kind of graphologist who does not deserve serious consideration: the kind who claims, without offering evidence, that ambition is related to lines that slope upward, force to heavy lines, and perseverance to long bars on the letter *t*. There again crude analogy is self-evident. It is most likely universally true that those graphologists who advertise or write columns in the newspapers and are able to give you a diagnosis for ten cents are not scientific.

To illustrate this point, one of the authors made an investment and received a list of the following traits, which are a reflection of his personality according to quack graphology. Since the traits that go with the advice as to whom he should and should not marry is likely to apply to most of the readers, he passes along this advice for nothing, which is exactly what it is worth.

Qualities that add to your charm:

An intensively ACTIVE MIND makes you interesting company.
Everything you do is with ARTISTIC insight and CULTURED taste.
Your excellent ENTHUSIASM aids in making others enthusiastic.
Others are unable to resist that certain MAGNETIC quality you possess.
With such PERSEVERANCE and COURAGE you never really give up.
SELF-ASSURANCE keeps you—and often others—from doubting your success.
VITALITY and a DYNAMIC FORCEFULNESS are yours.

Qualities that may detract from your charm:

IMPATIENCE or RESTLESSNESS can make some of your friends uneasy.
STUBBORNNESS is never an asset to charm.

"Tips"

Seldom let others realize your strong desire to dominate.
Your emotions are dynamic. Be careful not to use them to disadvantage.
You will be happiest in marriage with the type of person checked:
An agreeable partner who enjoys being told what to do—by you.
A responsive person who forgives and forgets easily.
With your temperament you should NOT marry the type of person checked here:
A really obstinate person who won't do as you say.

Another graphologist checked the following traits for the same author. This analysis cost 25 cents. Again with the same devotion the checked traits are presented with the view that it might apply to a lot of others.

Affectionate	Imaginative
Active	Moody
Aggressive	Love of beauty
Broadminded	Responsive
Congenial	Sense of humor
Concentration	Executive ability
Demonstrative	Artistic nature
Idealistic	Good mixer

Open-hearted

Super (21) conducted an investigation of a woman who claimed to be a graphologist and wrote articles for many leading newspapers. Each of 24 students in a psychology class checked a question asking for vocational help on the coupon in the newspaper and wrote three sentences in accordance with the directions: "Dear Miss D——, Please tell me what I am best fitted for. I will greatly appreciate your help. Thank you in advance." These were mailed at different intervals with the necessary 10 cents per enclosure.

All students were given an American Council of Education Intelligence Test, the Bernreuter Personality Inventory, and the Strong Interest Test. The findings of these psychological examinations reveal that the assignment of the suggested occupation range as proposed by the graphologist, when compared with the occupation range suggested by the Intelligence Test, is no better than might have been achieved by guess-work.

In only one case did the graphologist suggest that a student enter the type of occupation in which the Strong Interest Test indicated he was most likely to find satisfaction. The graphologist recommended that thirteen of the twenty-four enter the field of physical science or a skilled occupation. The test revealed only one student scoring highest in those fields. The occupations recommended by the graphologist were quite different from those that would have been recommended on the basis of the interest inventory; certain unsuitable occupations being recommended with more than chance frequency by the graphologist were affected by a constant error in favor of certain types of occupations for men, namely engineering, skilled trades, and sales work.

In addition, the graphologist had a check list of 29 personality traits. Six of these seemed comparable to those measured on the Bernreuter. Three students were not told they lacked self-confidence, and twenty-one were so told. Oddly enough, the average score of the twenty-one indicated more self-confidence than the average score of the other three. The graphologist's diagnosis of personality traits was similar to chance in all cases except two, and for these two traits, it was considerably worse than chance.

An interesting analysis of graphology is offered by Crider (3). He furnished handwriting specimens to two handwriting specialists and requested analysis. Although the analyses seemed astonishingly correct, more careful study revealed that they were cloaked in such generalities that it was hardly possible for them to be wrong. At this point Crider administered 13 standardized psychological tests to 18 subjects, and also wrote out in detail a description of the traits the tests purported to measure. These traits were then carefully explained to both graphologists, and they were requested to rank the specific handwritings in the order in which they revealed the various traits. The results are presented in Table 2.

TABLE 2

CORRELATIONS REPORTED IN THE CRIDER EXPERIMENT*

Graphologist I and tests	.146
Graphologist II and tests	.268
Graphologist I and II	.175
Graphologist I and I	.818

* From the *Journal of Applied Psychology*, 25:323–325 (1941), by permission of the American Psychological Association, publishers.

Crider concludes that the correlations indicate that graphologists do not agree with what the psychological tests purported to measure and the two graphologists do not agree with each other. One graphologist agrees with himself indicating that whatever he ranks, he ranks consistently.

It is necessary to report that graphology is used in industry. For example, Long and Tiffin (9) sent a questionnaire to 12 companies which had been suggested as possible advocates of graphological analysis. The replies from nine led to the conclusion, according to Long and Tiffin, that graphology—and not the reputable kind—may be enjoying a more cordial reception in business and industry than most of us realize. The following quotes are typical:

> The vice-president of a furnace manufacturing company wrote as follows:
>
> "This filled-in application form is submitted to a graphologist—more for character analysis than for any other purpose—and our experience over the past four years indicates that the percentage of misses on the part of the graphologist are (sic) less than 10%."
>
> The director of a retail sales organization wrote as follows:
>
> "For instance, in a group of about fifty applicants answering a blind ad, I easily selected the most intelligent and forceful personality by the handwriting alone. Subsequent interview of this large group proved that the person thus selected was head and shoulders above the others.
>
> "The axones of the brain cells extend down the spinal cord and the arm into the hand. Hence, it is literally with a part of the brain that we write. It is entirely logical, therefore, that handwriting should reflect the quality of mind."
>
> The president of a construction company wrote as follows:
>
> "Graphology when in the hands of such an experienced and ethical person as ——— takes its place with any of the sciences.
>
> "We feel we have saved money in being guided by graphology when employing help. In the case of temporary employees who have to handle large sums of money, a handwriting check-up is as good as a surety company check-up, where time is limited."[5]

An attempt to evaluate the offerings of these charlatans according to the rigorous standards of science always leads to the same conclusion—they have no value. Humiston (8) demonstrates this point very clearly. He had his future read by 25 practitioners. In 13 instances, he visited them personally, and in 12 he consulted them by mail. Included were five astrologers, five clairvoyants, five palmists, three numerologists, one vibration reader, one analyst of human chemistry.

[5] Reprinted from the *Journal of Applied Psychology*, 25:470–471 (1941), by permission of the American Psychological Association, publishers.

The writer sought vocational information based upon the following 28 major headings:

- agriculture
- arts
- building trades
- business
- clerical
- communication
- domestic and personal service
- education
- engineering
- fishing
- food and home economics
- forestry
- government and public service
- health
- labor
- languages
- law
- library
- manufacturing and industrial executives
- manufacturing industries and trades
- metal and mechanical trades
- mining and quarrying
- publishing and printing
- religious work
- science
- social work
- transportation
- writing

Twenty-one of the major fields were suggested by a variety of the advisors, and the reasons are as varied as the suggested vocations. For preparation for a vocation, college, night school, and special training schools were advised, although four practitioners definitely advised against college. One astrologer advised working in a drugstore as the best preparation for becoming a chemist. With reference to personality diagnosis, eleven described Humiston as strong-willed, stubborn, determined, and persistent, while eight others thought that he was changeable, vacillating, and procrastinating and had a lack of perseverance. Nine of 18 made the sage remark that home life and family would contribute most to happiness. From the data gathered, Humiston concludes that fortune tellers whether of the same type or of a different type do not agree among themselves. The advice given is general, vague, and contradictory.

Specific advice rarely occurs, and when it does, it is not accompanied by sound, adequate, or practical explanations. He found the fortune tellers to be uninformed on the psychological, educational, and economic aspects of vocational guidance, with no knowledge of job opportunities or occupational information. Humiston also discovered that the amount and kind of advice is frequently contingent upon the fee paid.

Forer (6) makes a very good point when he emphasizes the possibility of committing the error of "universal validity." He uses this term to refer to personality evaluations couched in such generalities that they apply to everyone. Such descriptions are likely to be verified on the basis of "personal validation" and are useless. Forer states:

> The crystal-gazer is likely to be aware of some of these points and other pseudo-diagnosticians, though they may be unaware of the fallacies inherent in their procedures, make effective use of "universal

Reprinted by permission of the artist

"YOU LIVE WITH A GREAT MANY MEN; YOU ARE NOT VERY WEALTHY; YOU KEEP REGULAR HOURS. . . ."

> validity" and "personal validation" in deceiving their clients. Allport states that "one way in which character analysts secure a reputation for success is through the employment of ambiguous terms that may apply to any mortal person." A naive person who receives superficial

> diagnostic information, especially when the social situation is prestige-laden, tends to accept such information. He is impressed by the obvious truths and may be oblivious to the discrepancies. But he does more than this.[6]

Thirty-nine students in a class taught by Forer were given Diagnostic Interest Blanks and one week later each student was given a typed sheet with his personality sketch. Unknown to the students, each one was given the identical sketch as follows:

> 1. You have a great need for other people to like and admire you.
> 2. You have a tendency to be critical of yourself.
> 3. You have a great deal of unused capacity which you have not turned to your advantage.
> 4. While you have some personality weaknesses, you are generally able to compensate for them.
> 5. Your sexual adjustment has presented problems for you.
> 6. Disciplined and self-controlled outside, you tend to be worrisome and insecure inside.
> 7. At times you have serious doubts as to whether you have made the right decision or done the right thing.
> 8. You prefer a certain amount of change and variety and become dissatisfied when hemmed in by restrictions and limitations.
> 9. You pride yourself as an independent thinker and do not accept others' statements without satisfactory proof.
> 10. You have found it unwise to be too frank in revealing yourself to others.
> 11. At times you are extroverted, affable, sociable, while at other times you are introverted, wary, reserved.
> 12. Some of your aspirations tend to be pretty unrealistic.
> 13. Security is one of your major goals in life.[7]

These statements came largely from a newsstand astrology book. To describe the results of the experiment, Forer's remarks are most relevant.

> After the papers had been returned to the writer students were asked to raise their hands if they felt the test had done a good job.

---

[6] Reprinted from the *Journal of Abnormal and Social Psychology,* 44:119 (1949), by permission of the American Psychological Association, publishers.

[7] *Ibid.,* page 120.

> Virtually all hands went up and the students noticed this. Then the first sketch item was read and students were asked to indicate by hands whether they had found anything similar on their sketches. As all hands rose, the class burst into laughter. It was pointed out to them that the experiment had been performed as an object lesson to demonstrate the tendency to be overly impressed by vague statements and to endow the diagnostician with an unwarrantedly high degree of insight. Similarities between the demonstration and the activities of charlatans were pointed out.[8]

Forer's study seems most useful insofar as he was able to duplicate or surpass the results of the pseudo-diagnostician without even the use of a diagnostic instrument or a supposed system based upon the confusion between cause and effect.

Donald Paterson has used a form called "character reading at sight of Mr. X." It is a further illustration of the use of a vague statement having "universal validity." In correspondence with the authors, he states, "I have used this on innumerable occasions for reading character at sight on members of rotary clubs, etc. and have had the person being read and two of his friends check on the accuracy of each statement made. They always certify that my readings have been from 90 to 95 per cent accurate." The character reading used is illustrated in the accompanying figure.

Before accepting the claims of a system or diagnostic instrument it is necessary for it to stand the test of experimentation. The relationship between the method of analysis and the results derived must be verified experimentally. The procedure must be sufficiently objective so that others can repeat it to obtain the same results and conclusions. Athough it is not necessary that a cause and effect relationship be immediately obvious it should be possible to examine the claims based upon the data presented in order to verify the validity of the conclusions.

The material previously presented indicates that most of the systems described are mystical and subjective and do not stand objective evaluation. It is generally true that these systems are not supported when relatively careful experiments are conducted to check the claims.

[8] *Loc. cit.*

CHARACTER READING AT SIGHT OF MR. X

According to the System of Mr. P. T. Barnum.

Abilities: Above average in intelligence or mental alertness. Also above average in accuracy—rather painstaking at times. Deserves a reputation for neatness—dislikes turning out sloppy work. Has initiative; that is, ability to make suggestions and to get new ideas, open-mindedness.

Emotions: You have a tendency to worry at times but not to excess. You do get depressed at times but you couldn't be called moody because you are generally cheerful and rather optimistic. You have a good disposition although earlier in life you have had a struggle with yourself to control your impulses and temper.

Interests: You are strongly socially inclined, you like to meet people, especially to mix with those you know well. You appreciate art, painting and music, but you will never be a success as an artist or as a creator or composer of music. You like sports and athletic events but devote more of your attention to reading about them in the sporting page than in actual participation.

Ambitions: You are ambitious, and deserve credit for wanting to be well thought of by your family, business associates and friends. These ambitions come out most strongly in your tendency to indulge in day-dreams, in building air-castles, but this does not mean that you fail to get into the game of life actively.

Vocational: You ought to continue to be successful so long as you stay in a social vocation. I mean if you keep at work bringing you in contact with people. Just what work you pick out isn't as important as the fact that it must be work bringing you in touch with people. On the negative side you would never have made a success at strictly theoretical work or in pure research work such as in physics or neurology.

Donald G. Paterson,
Professor of Psychology.

Who is qualified to give guidance

It is necessary at this point to mention that many who claim to be psychologists are not. It is important to know the qualifications of an accredited psychologist. Usually an accepted member of a profession belongs to the national professional body. For psychologists, this group is known as the American Psychological Association. It has two classes of membership, fellow and associate. The fellow has higher status. Educational requirements, professional experience, and scientific contributions determine election to the Association. It is rare that a person who deserves recognition as a psychologist does not belong to the American Psychological Association. In addition to professional recognition through membership in the A.P.A., psychologists may be granted Diplomate status as a result of the organization in 1947 of the American Board of Examiners in Professional Psychology. Until 1950, the Board granted diplomas (in clinical psychology, industrial psychology, and counseling and guidance) on the basis of training, professional experience, personal integrity, and special competence in the specific professional field. With the expiration of the "grandfather clause," or examination waiver, passing of examinations was added to the requirements.

This is not to claim that the only one entitled to give vocational guidance is a psychologist. For example, there is a national professional body known as the National Vocational Guidance Association with two types of membership. This professional group has definite standards of admission for professional members although it does admit others as members who are interested in vocational guidance. It is likely that the percentage of competent people in these associations is far greater than that in the group outside them who claim to be guidance experts.

David (4) analyzed the status of psychologists who advertise in telephone directories and discovered that the proportion among them who are members of the American Psychological Association is small. Table 3 is presented to show the distribution in 20 of the larger cities in the United States.

The safest procedure for any individual seeking vocational guidance is to contact the local college or state university. In most instances, a member of the Psychology Department will be able to make a referral to either an accredited agency or a professionally qualified individual.

In most large cities there is likely to be a Welfare Council. The In-

TABLE 3

PSYCHOLOGISTS WHO ADVERTISE IN TELEPHONE DIRECTORIES*

Cities in Order of Size, 1940 Census	*Rank by Population*	*Rank by No. of Advertisements*	*Total No. of Advertisements*	*No. of Separate Individuals Listed*	*Advertisers Listed in A.P.A. Yearbook*	*Advertisers Listing Academic Degrees*	*Advertisers Listing A.P.A. Membership*
New York City	1	1	105	71	17	3	—
Chicago	2	3	40	25	6	8†	—
Philadelphia	3	5	10	7	2	—	—
Detroit	4	8½	6	3	1	—	—
Los Angeles	5	2	71	55	8	11	3
Cleveland	6	15	3	3	1	—	—
Baltimore	7	8½	6	5	0	1	—
St. Louis	8	10½	5	3	0	—	—
Boston	9	7	7	6	0	—	—
Pittsburgh	10	16	1	0	0	—	—
Washington	11	18½	0	0	0	—	—
San Francisco	12	4	18	13	1	1	1
Milwaukee	13	13	4	2	0	—	—
Buffalo	14	18½	0	0	0	—	—
New Orleans	15	18½	0	0	0	—	—
Minneapolis	16	13	4	2	0	—	—
Cincinnati	17	6	8	5	2	1	—
Newark	18	13	4	2	0	—	—
Kansas City	19	10½	5	3	0	—	—
Indianapolis	20	18½	0	0	0	—	—

* Reprinted from *The American Psychologist*, 3:206 (1948), by permission of the American Psychological Association, publishers.

† Through Illinois Association for Applied Psychology.

formation Bureau of such an agency is also in a position to make referrals on a sound professional level.

This chapter has attempted to eliminate at once any pseudo-scientific system as a part of vocational guidance. The chapters to follow will discuss the scientific aspects of vocational guidance.

Summary

People with problems are easy prey for charlatans. For many reasons they inadvertently seek the services of sponsors of pseudo-scientific systems and support them to the extent of one hundred million dollars annually.

The charlatans do not draw conclusions based upon sound scientific experimentation; and they willingly confuse cause and effect to the extreme disadvantage of naive and harassed people with problems. Specific investigations of physiognomy, phrenology, astrology, and palmistry show decisively that these systems are based upon mystical or confused ideas of the relationship of cause and effect, rather than upon sound experimental evidence. Graphology was conceded the chance of being a revealer of personality and possibly useful in guiding vocational choice, but emphasis was placed upon the large amount of nonsense existing in this field.

The experiments of Humiston and Forer were especially desirable in pointing up the explanation of why such nonsense is often given credence.

Care must be exercised in selecting a professionally acceptable expert and one should at least be wary of anyone not belonging to the appropriate national professional body. A good and sage source for referrals is either the local college or the welfare council.

Bibliography

1. *Are You in the Right Vocation?* New York: Merton Institute, Inc.
2. Brotemarkle, R. A., "The Challenge to Consulting Psychology; The Psychological Consultant and The Psychological Charlatan," *Journal of Applied Psychology,* 24:1, 10–19 (1940).
3. Crider, B., "The Reliability and Validity of Two Graphologists," *Journal of Applied Psychology,* 25:3, 323–325 (1941).

4. David, Henry P., "Advertising in Telephone Directories," *The American Psychologist,* 3:6, 206 (1948).
5. David, Henry P., "An Analysis of Psychologists in the Classified Telephone Directory," *The American Psychologist,* 3:4, 133–134 (1948).
6. Forer, Bertram R., "The Fallacy of Personal Validation: A Classroom Demonstration of Gullibility," *Journal of Abnormal and Social Psychology,* 44:118–123 (1949).
7. Harris, Daniel, "Gold-brick Salesmen of Vocational Guidance: A List, with Comments," *Popular Psychology Guide,* 3:5, 12–15 (1941).
8. Humiston, T. F., "Fortune Tellers as Vocational Guidance," *Occupations,* 21:3, 229–232 (1942).
9. Long, W. F., and J. Tiffin, "A Note on the Use of Graphology by Industry," *Journal of Applied Psychology,* 25:4, 469–471 (1941).
10. *Merton News Letter,* Mertonian Society, New York, December, 1941.
11. Munn, Norman L., *Psychology: The Fundamentals of Human Adjustment.* Boston: Houghton Mifflin, 1946.
12. Murphy, Gardner, *Personality.* New York: Harper, 1947.
13. "N.O.C. Clearing House: News of the National Occupational Conference," *Occupations,* 12:3, 52 (1942).
14. *New York World Telegram, The,* April 4, 1941.
15. Parr, Frank W., "How's Your Horoscope?" *Occupations,* 16:3, 236–239 (1938).
16. Roback, *Psychology of Common Sense, Psychology of Character.* New York: Harcourt, Brace, 1928.
17. Ruch, Floyd L., *Psychology and Life.* Chicago: Scott, Foresman, 1941.
18. St. Hill, Katherine, *The Book of the Hand.* New York: Putnam, 1928.
19. Stafford, Muriel, *Your Charm Rated According to Your Handwriting,* 1941.
20. Steiner, Lee R., *Where Do People Take Their Troubles?* Boston: Houghton Mifflin, 1945.
21. Super, D. E., "A Comparison of the Diagnoses of a Graphologist with the Results of Psychological Tests," *Journal of Consulting Psychology,* 5:127–133 (1941).
22. Valentine, Willard L., *Experimental Foundations of General Psychology.* New York: Rinehart, 1946.

3

TYPES OF COUNSELING CENTERS

ALTHOUGH COUNSELING should be regarded as a continuing process, most of our institutions are not geared to administer it in this manner. As a result, we find a wide variety of agencies specializing in different types of counseling problems. Sometimes these guidance centers are organized along the arbitrary lines of age divisions; at other times they are geared to serve a particular community; and at still other times, they are subdivided according to nationality, religion, or other special categories.

The previous chapter emphasized the need for recognizing the professional status of the person administering vocational counseling; we should like to emphasize here that ordinarily the single individual, regardless of his personal qualifications and background, is not likely to be as capable of administering guidance as efficiently and validly as a guidance center or agency. Although it is true that a number of inadequately trained individuals cannot become effective merely as a result of the magic of being affiliated with a guidance center, it must also be remembered that such individuals are infrequently hired by an agency. In other words, the place to seek guidance is a guidance center. In such an establishment one is likely to find professionally qualified people who contribute to each other, with the result that the guidance administered is probably on a higher professional level.

Of course, there are some organizations administering guidance that can be severely criticized because of ridiculous and preposterous unprofessional conduct. Some of these agencies are inadequate because they are more concerned with making money than in giving guidance; while others are groups unaffiliated with professional associations because they do not meet standards or because they use questionable scientific methods and instruments. The individual using an agency service must check its qualifications and reputation. A valuable aid in this matter is the National Vocational Guidance Association Directory of Vocational Counseling Services (8). This directory lists 82 agencies in the United States and Canada which have voluntarily applied for approval by the Ethical Practices Committee of the Association. This list is not complete and additions will be made to it from time to time, but it is valuable since it is the first listing based upon uniform and objective evaluation. Additional listings of approved agencies appear from time to time in *Occupations.*

Purely for the purpose of logical treatment, counseling centers can be considered as one of two types: those affiliated with a school or educational institution, and those attached to a community. The first type usually caters to the students attending the school, whereas the second type is more likely to have a clientele more diversified in such respects as age and economic status.

Both types of guidance centers may be either public or private. In the public center, either no fee or a very nominal fee is charged for the service rendered to the individual. Among the private agencies, it is more usual to expect a fee to be charged. Because of the large number of people involved in the administration of a single guidance case and because of various other overhead charges, the cost of guidance for an individual is usually between $25 and $50. Counselors, registrars, psychologists, administrators, and clerks are only a few examples of the type of personnel needed before a single case may be considered closed. Regardless of whether the individual pays for the service directly, or the service is paid for by a government agency, or a philanthropic bequest lessens the direct cost, guidance costs money. While it is impossible to evaluate a guidance center solely on the basis of cost, it is well to remember that the cost per case is considerable, and somebody must pay for the service rendered. From the point of view of the value of guidance, the $25 to $50 item is negligible, especially when the counseling leads to a better adjusted and potentially more productive individual.

School guidance centers

Junior high schools. Although the need for guidance may arise before the seventh year of school, it is generally agreed that the school system must seriously face the problems of vocational guidance by this time. According to Smith and Roos (19), a junior high school guidance program serves four purposes:

1. To assist the child to *orient* himself to a broader life situation;
2. To guide pupils toward planned *exploration* as a means of discovering "individual differences" and of studying whatever area seems worthy of exploration;
3. To assist the child in *appraising* his own abilities and interests;
4. To *acquaint* him with what lies ahead.

Ordinarily the "home room" teacher is the one charged with the responsibility of carrying out these purposes. To the extent that "home room" teachers are familiar with the scope and purposes of vocational guidance, such guidance is likely to be helpful. It can be immediately seen that "home room" teachers must therefore be trained in the subject matter of vocational counseling.

Although it would be more advisable to have qualified and specially trained counselors handle the problems of educational and vocational guidance on the junior high school level, it would be Utopian to expect it at this time. Regardless of economic conditions it appears that educational budgets are always limited. School administrators are continually harassed by such conditions and are forced to make choices that impede the development of guidance in the schools. Too many local and state officeholders regard anything besides a classroom teacher as a luxury. A counselor, therefore, is regarded by them as possibly desirable but as something to be considered in future plans. The annual educational reports reveal this. Such reports make good reading and satisfy those who want small budgets *now* as well as those who want increased facilities but will compromise with the hope of future attainment. An example of compromise exists in the 83 New York City Junior High Schools. According to a report issued by the Division of Educational and Vocational Guidance (1), individual counseling programs were conducted by 17 licensed counselors and by more than four hundred specially selected teachers assigned part-time. Actually this means that the time alloted to counseling these students is equivalent to one full-time person per school. The average number of students per school is 1187. The reader may draw his own conclusion on the adequacy of this program. When it is readily admitted that even this amount of time is far greater than exists in most other communities, one can see the severe problems caused by lack of trained personnel, which in turn is caused by insufficient allotments in the budgets.

A major problem in the counseling of junior high school students involves the transfer of students from such schools to academic or vocational high schools. To meet this need with the available staff, group guidance and assemblies play important roles. Speakers from the school system as well as the business world address student groups. Films on vocational information and guidance are also moderately useful.

As part of the junior high school guidance program in New York City, in-service courses are offered for teachers. Two such course titles are: "The Organization of Guidance Programs in Junior High Schools" and "Employment Opportunities for Beginning Workers."

Since few junior high school students are likely to terminate their formal education at this point, the major task is to direct them to the most appropriate high school or course within the high school that is most likely to lead to a successful future occupation. In other words, while the task is primarily educational guidance it must nevertheless be remembered that educational and vocational guidance are really two parts of the same integrated whole.

Senior high schools. As the student becomes older and reaches the senior high school stage, it is obvious that the problems of vocational guidance become more severe. A study of the present practice in certain selected schools is reported in a pamphlet published by the U.S. Office of Education's Vocational Division (14). A rather comprehensive 12-page questionnaire was sent to approximately 1300 schools previously reporting that one or more persons devoted at least half their time to counseling. Data were obtained from approximately 870 high schools in 44 states. It is very likely that these schools are not typical of high schools in the United States but rather, as a group, excel in guidance facilities. A review of the highlights of the report is in order. It shows the existing sad state of affairs and points to the compelling need for the development of guidance programs in our secondary schools.

Leonard and Tucker (14) summarize their analysis of these data in five major divisions: Records received from elementary schools; Use of cumulative records; Use of tests; Counseling; and Problems. The major conclusions for each of these divisions will be presented.

With reference to the type of records received by the high schools the evidence indicates that they do not have very much to begin with. The major findings are:

1. Practically all of the high schools received from the elementary school some kind of record for each entering pupil. This transfer was reported by 95 percent to 98 percent of the different types of high schools.
2. From one-half to nearly all of the high schools regularly receive from the elementary schools such information as personal data, teachers' marks, intelligence test scores, attendance records, medical and dental data, achievement test scores, and parents' occupations. When these items are supplied, the information is in complete form in about three-quarters of the cases and as an abstract in about one-quarter of the cases.
3. Such items as social, personality, and interest ratings, extracurricular activities, home and family conditions, special aptitudes, nongainful activities, counselor's interviews, parents' education, and employment record are regularly received from the elementary schools by fewer than one-quarter of the high schools, and occasionally received by about another one-quarter of the high schools. These items are rather difficult to record but would supply valuable information to the high schools. The use of a folder type of record would facilitate the transfer of this kind of information.
4. Test results for entering pupils are received by about three-quarters of the high schools. About three-quarters of these test scores are received regularly and one-quarter occasionally. Practically all of these test results cover achievement and intelligence tests.

5. The test results reported cover tests given in all grades from one through nine but the largest number were given in the sixth and eighth grades.[1]

Although the high schools do a slightly better job of record-keeping than elementary schools, there is considerable room for improvement if these records are to be put to maximum use. The records to be most effective should be cumulative. Leonard and Tucker report the following eight items with reference to the practices of high schools in keeping cumulative records.

1. More than three quarters of the schools record regularly personal data, teachers' marks, attendance records, and intelligence test scores. More than one-half record regularly, in addition to the above, parents' occupations, medical data, extracurricular activities, achievement test scores, dental data, and counselors' interviews.
2. From one-quarter to one-half of the schools record regularly those items so helpful in understanding the whole personality of the pupil such as social, personality, and interest ratings, home and family conditions, out-of-school and nongainful activities, employment records, special aptitudes, teachers' observations, and parents' education.
3. From 1 percent to 27 percent of the schools record occasionally the various types of information on the cumulative records.
4. The instruments most commonly used for recording the individual inventory are the cumulative record card, several separate forms, and the cumulative record folder. About one-half of the schools use each of these three methods, about 30 percent of the schools reporting that they use more than one method.
5. Fifty-five percent of the schools report keeping the individual inventory record, either original or duplicate, in the secretary's or registrar's office and 44 percent report keeping the records in the counselor's office. No other place was reported by as many as 25 percent of the schools.
6. Access to the complete individual inventory is available to the principal in three-quarters of the schools, to the counselor in two-thirds of the schools, and to the teacher and home-room teacher in about one-half of the schools.

---

[1] A. Leonard and A. C. Tucker, *The Individual Inventory in Guidance Programs in Secondary Schools, a Study of Present Practices in Selected Schools* (Vocational Division Bulletin #215), Federal Security Agency, U.S. Office of Education, 1941, page 8.

7. The use of cumulative record forms for occupational, educational, and general reference after the pupil has left school is reported by about one-half of the schools. Only 13 percent of the schools reported using these records for a follow-up.
8. Only 14 percent of the schools report sending in cumulative records, or any part or summary of them, to any employment office or agency. Another 35 percent sometimes supply records to employment agencies.[2]

Psychological tests are used in varying degrees by the high schools. Intelligence tests are most commonly administered and then achievement, aptitude, and personality and interests tests follow in that order. To give some idea of the slight extent of psychological test usage by these 780 schools, Table 4 lists the number of schools reporting types of tests used.

TABLE 4

USE OF APTITUDE TESTS BY 780 REPORTING HIGH SCHOOLS*

Type of Test	*No. of Schools Reporting*
Mechanical	171
Clerical	105
Art	45
Music	45
Form Board	43
Algebra	35
Manipulative Dexterity	31
Latin	21
Geometry	19
Spatial Relation	19
Modern Language	16
Scientific	11
Stenographic	10
Nursing	3
Teaching	3

* A. Leonard and A. C. Tucker, *The Individual Inventory in Guidance Programs in Secondary Schools, a Study of Present Practices in Selected Schools* (Vocational Division Bulletin #215), Federal Security Agency, U.S. Office of Education, 1941, page 20.

The major findings of this investigation in this area are:

1. Intelligence tests are used in 87 percent of the schools. About one-fifth of the schools give 3 or more intelligence tests.
2. Achievement tests are used in 70 percent of the schools with more

[2] *Ibid.*, page 15.

than one-half of the schools giving 2 or more tests. About one-fifth of the schools give 5 or more achievement tests. Forty-two percent of the reported achievement tests are in the field of English and 18 percent cover mathematics.

3. About one-third of the schools give aptitude tests. One-fourth of all the aptitude tests given by these schools are for the purpose of measuring mechanical aptitude. Clerical aptitude tests are also commonly used.
4. About one-third of these schools use measures of personality and interest. The types most commonly used are vocational interest blanks, personality rating scales, and adjustment questionnaires.
5. These schools consider the most important purposes for which test results are used to be: Discovery of individual abilities and disabilities for guidance purposes, and the classification and gradation of pupils.
6. Intelligence tests are generally scored under the direction of the counselor, teacher, or test specialist such as a psychologist. Most achievement tests are scored by or under the direction of the teacher. The counselor handles the scoring of most aptitude tests and measures of personality and interests.
7. About 1 percent of the tests are scored by machine.
8. In fewer than one-quarter of the schools do the persons having professional training in tests and measurements such as counselor, psychologist, or director of guidance, participate in the determination of the tests to be given. The decision regarding tests to be used is made largely by administrative officials.[3]

In this study the term counseling was used in the more narrow sense of interviewing, and as can be seen from the findings the interview is rarely conducted by a person designated and trained as a counselor.

1. The replies to the questionnaire confirm the belief that any division of counseling into such categories as academic, personal, and vocational is arbitrary and that in most cases the pupil is helped on all types of problems by the same person.
2. Academic counseling is done regularly by the counselor in two-thirds of the schools, by the principal and home-room teacher in about one-third of the schools, and by the teacher, vice principal, and dean or adviser of girls in about one-quarter of the schools.

---

[3] *Ibid.*, page 25.

In more than one-third of the schools the principal, home-room teacher, and teacher perform this function occasionally.

3. Personal counseling is done regularly by the counselor in three-fifths of the schools, by the principal, home-room teacher, and dean or adviser of girls in one-third of the schools, and by the vice principal and dean or adviser of boys in about one-quarter of the schools. Personal counseling is done occasionally by the principal and teacher in almost one-half of the schools and by the home-room teacher in more than one-third of the schools.
4. Vocational counseling is done regularly by the counselor in two-thirds of the schools. No other person counsels regularly on vocational problems in as many as one-quarter of the schools. In more than one-half of the schools the principal, home-room teacher, and teacher perform this function at least occasionally.
5. There is generally good cooperation between the counselor and other school agencies. In practically all schools the counselor may refer pupils to the classroom teacher, attendance officer, and public health nurse. In over one-half of the schools pupils may be referred to the vocational department and psychologist. Fifty other persons or agencies are mentioned as cooperating with the counselor.
6. Cooperation with nonschool activities is reasonably good. In about two-thirds of the schools the counselor may refer pupils to social case work agency, probation officer, and relief agency. In more than one-half of the schools pupils may be referred to attendance officer and mental hygiene clinic. Fifty-nine other agencies are mentioned as cooperating with the counselor. There is an average of four agencies per reporting school.
7. Disregarding junior high schools, regular contact with local employers is maintained by about two-thirds of the schools with reference to employment and by about 40 percent of the schools with reference to training opportunities and follow-up of former pupils.[4]

The Leonard and Tucker study was also noteworthy for its attempt to determine what the respondents considered their most difficult problems. The three general problems which appeared to concern them most were:

1. Many recognize the superficiality of their present counseling programs and want to individualize and lengthen the contacts between counselor and pupil. They are aware of the lack of facilities for

[4] *Ibid.*, page 32.

following up on the information obtained and decisions made by the pupil while in school.

2. A need is felt for coordinating not only the curricula of the elementary schools with their own curricular opportunities but also the guidance procedures of the lower schools with the procedures in the high schools so the pupil may consistently and continually secure guidance through his school life and attack better his early vocational ventures.
3. Many indicate in their responses an appreciation of and an exasperation at the limitations of the present high-school curriculum which is predominantly concerned with college preparation and ignores the needs of the great majority of young people who cannot or do not wish to go to college.[5]

For better understanding of the specific nature of these general problems they list nine items: Lack of time (44 per cent); lack of trained personnel (40 per cent); inadequate philosophy of guidance (12 per cent); lack of cooperation with home and family (12 per cent); lack of cooperation by teachers (12 per cent); curricular inadequacies (10 per cent); lack of testing facilities (8 per cent); inadequate records (7 per cent); lack of occupational information (6 per cent).

This listing can be very valuable in evaluating any guidance system. It is also useful as a check list when one is contemplating the initiation of a counseling program. If care is taken to avoid the dangers that result from not meeting these requirements, it is likely that an effective counseling program exists.

The Leonard and Tucker report shows the need for improving the high school counseling programs. This early chapter merely attempts to survey the situation. It is obvious that improvements are necessary. It is not enough to be thrilled by the fact that some schools have teachers who devote part of their time to counseling. It is necessary to strive for a foundation that is sound to begin with and then build.

There is no doubt that many educators recognize the value of guidance. That is not enough, however. The present development indicates that guidance is in its infancy. Much growth is necessary. The growth in guidance should proceed with the development of

[5] *Ibid.*, page 34.

methods, techniques, and the instruments of the scientist. As the following chapters will indicate, these tools are available.

The colleges. Most students entering college do so without the benefits of counseling. Their choice of college is too often left to the decisions of their families, who are not able to decide on the basis of professional counseling. At this point one may wonder whether this situation results in maladjustment often enough to be disturbing. The idea is, though, that conditions could be much better; that in a society where vocational problems can be solved with the aid of scientific instruments and methodology, there should be more well-adjusted and productive people.

Characteristic of counseling in colleges is the high degree of individuality of the various college programs. Each has been developed to suit particular needs; consequently none is really typical.

The American Council on Education has listed 23 functions as the constituents of a complete personnel program. They are:

1. Interpreting institutional objectives and opportunities to prospective students and their parents and to workers in secondary education.
2. Selecting and admitting students, in cooperation with secondary schools.
3. Orienting the student to his educational environment.
4. Providing a diagnostic service to help the student discover his abilities, aptitudes and objectives.
5. Assisting the student throughout his college residence to determine upon his courses of instruction in light of his past achievements, vocational and personal interests, and diagnostic findings.
6. Enlisting the active cooperation of the family of the student in the interest of his educational accomplishment.
7. Assisting the student to reach his maximum effectiveness through clarification of his purposes, improvement of study methods, speech habits, personal appearance, manners, etc., and through progression in religious, emotional, social development, and other non-academic personal and group relationships.
8. Assisting the student to clarify his occupational aims and his educational plans in relation to them.
9. Determining the physical and mental health status of the student, providing appropriate remedial health measures, supervising the health of students, and controlling environmental health factors.

10. Providing and supervising an adequate housing program for students.
11. Providing and supervising an adequate food service for students.
12. Supervising, evaluating, and developing the extra-curricular activities of students.
13. Supervising, evaluating, and developing the social life and interests of students.
14. Supervising, evaluating, and developing the religious life and interests of students.
15. Assembling and making available information to be used in improvement of instruction and in making the curriculum more flexible.
16. Coordinating the financial aid and part-time employment of students, and assisting the student who needs it to obtain such help.
17. Keeping a cumulative record of information about the student and making it available to the proper persons.
18. Administering student discipline to the end that the individual will be strengthened, and the welfare of the group preserved.
19. Maintaining student group morale by evaluating, understanding, and developing student mores.
20. Assisting the student to find appropriate employment when he leaves the institution.
21. Articulating college and vocational experience.
22. Keeping the student continuously and adequately informed of the educational opportunities and services available to him.
23. Carrying on studies designed to evaluate and improve these functions and services.[6]

As Lloyd-Jones points out (13), there are infinite variations in college personnel programs. These programs differ not only in their concern for the previously mentioned 23 functions but also in their proportions. Characteristic of each college program is its particular organization and its ideas of who is to carry out the functions of the organization. According to Lloyd-Jones, the University of Minnesota distinguishes very clearly the areas of competence and incompetence of the instructional staff as regards counseling. At Sarah Lawrence College the counselors devoted their primary efforts to encouraging and developing instructors as counselors to their students. Iowa State

[6] Reprinted from the *Journal of Consulting Psychology*, 4:201–202(1940), by permission of the American Psychological Association, publishers.

College is in the middle of these two positions since certain faculty members who are interested and able are designated for this work.

The University of Minnesota. Minnesota has been for many years one of the outstanding leaders in the field of college counseling. As a result of its work not only have the students benefited but the profession has gained. Many worthwhile books have been published by its very capable and active faculty. A few of the more well-known volumes are: *How to Counsel Students* (22), *Testing and Counseling in the High School Guidance Program* (6), *Student Guidance Technique* (17), *Student Personnel Work* (21), and *Trends in Student Personnel Work* (23).

According to Williamson (21), the Minnesota counseling system was profoundly influenced by its originator, D. G. Paterson, following the early leadership of Dean Johnston in 1914. To aid understanding of the so-called Minnesota point of view, seven significant characteristics are described.

The first of these is the emphasis on testing. However, the group has always been concerned with more than testing; as early as 1925, Paterson described 15 varied activities.

The second characteristic is the bringing of measurement and testing into the field of educational and vocational guidance as a means of helping individual students.

The third characteristic is the refinement of human judgments through the use of objective devices. The fourth characteristic is the insistence that counseling is a mutual process between counselor and counselee. The counselor participates by contributing significant items of information and suggestions which are reviewed and evaluated by the counselee.

The fifth characteristic of the Minnesota group is the attempt to evaluate counseling through experimental verification. The sixth is the continuous emphasis on research.

The seventh characteristic is the concept of a balanced service; such a service exists at Minnesota and includes a clinic or counseling bureau, specialized services in such diversified fields as speech disabilities and financial counseling, and an extensive program of counseling in the colleges of the university.

According to Williamson (21), "the student learns and relearns his adjustments in this total environment and the college once more assumes its earlier societal role of facilitating the learning or development of personality." This statement clearly summarizes the point of view of the Minnesota program as it has been carried on for many years.

Many colleges emphasize the personality adjustment problems of their students. For example, McKinney (15) concludes that the type of problems presented by students at the University of Missouri may be classified as primarily emotional, motivational, social, familial, academic, sexual, schedule, disciplinary, financial, and health. Students, according to McKinney, are troubled by multiple rather than single problems.

The Counseling Center at the University of Chicago deals with the emotionalized attitudes of the client toward his problems and himself rather than with the problems per se. During the year starting in May 1946, 1059 clients came to the Center. About 60 per cent of the clients were students and the remainder were from the neighboring community. This center is the focal point of the non-directive technique to be described in Chapter 4. This center is interesting because it serves not only the college but also the community. It is an attempt to bridge the gap between the two types of centers described in this chapter; those serving educational institutions and those serving the community.

It should be noted that counseling on the college level is broad and includes vocational and emotional problems. As one approaches adulthood it becomes difficult to separate these two types of problems; the separation is really artificial, and the individual cannot be fully helped unless both aspects are solved.

Community centers

The State or United States Employment Service can make a considerable contribution to the field of guidance whenever its budget allows it to live. Too often budget cuts have been large and unpredictable, preventing not only necessary planning and growth but even reasonable work. The contributions of such an employment service to guidance and present problems are clearly depicted by Stocking (20). He points out that there are six coordinated functions which are the minimum requisites of a sound employment service:

1. An effective placement service to facilitate the employment and reemployment of returning servicemen and women, displaced former war workers, youth entering the labor market, disabled veterans and other handicapped workers, in short all persons seeking jobs.
2. An employment counseling program to assist workers to determine their present or potential occupational abilities and interests in the light of realistic information about job requirements and employment opportunities.
3. A special service to veterans including employment counseling and preferential service by the local offices, as well as priority of referral to any job for which the veterans are qualified.
4. A personnel management service to assist employers and labor organizations in the use of personnel tools and techniques which have been developed by the employment service for effective selection, assignment and transfer of workers.
5. Labor market analyses and information to aid workers in choosing among various employment careers; for employers in locating plants or in scheduling production to utilize most effectively available labor resources; and for training authorities, community groups, and other agencies whose programs are concerned with manpower.
6. Participation, in cooperation with community organizations, and government agencies, in programs for increasing economic activity and maintaining high levels of stabilized employment.[7]

The Detroit program. Two major conclusions of a survey of certain problems of Detroit's youth were that there was a lack of coordination of youth services and that there were markedly inadequate facilities for counseling out-of-school youth (12). To correct this situation, a Council for Youth Service was formed in 1930 with 25 agencies represented. About six years later this group together with the National Youth Administration formed its Junior Consultation Service (appropriating the title of the New York Agency) for counseling

[7] *Occupations, the Vocational Guidance Journal,* published by National Vocational Guidance Association, Incorporated, 25:500–501(1947).

youth. The need for a still larger coordinated counseling program resulted in the establishment of the Detroit Counseling Service. This agency provided a full counseling service to the Youth of Detroit between the ages of 16 and 25. This program was curtailed by the federalization of the state employment services in 1942 and the discontinuance of the N.Y.A. in 1943; but the public schools have continued to operate on the same pattern but with a smaller budget, staff, and service. The problems of the clients seeking service have been classified as follows:

1. Those who have made no plan, or only a vague or partial plan, who need help in discovering the occupation which they would like to enter, and who need information about how best to prepare for it.
2. Those who have made a plan unsuited to their abilities. For example, the boy who wishes to be a tool and die man because he has heard of the advantages, yet who has received his poorest marks in related subjects and who, on tests, reveals little aptitude in this field.
3. Those who have no realization of what their chosen occupations involve, like the girl who wants to be a health education teacher because she likes basketball and other sports.
4. Those who because of economic necessity have had an unwise decision forced upon them, like the boy who for three years was a helper on a delivery truck and who on the *American Council Achievement Tests in Mathematics, English,* and *Science* obtained scores in the 99th and 100th percentiles, and would like to prepare himself for engineering.
5. Those who are in conflict with their families over a choice of plans, like the girl who wants to become a nurse, but whose parents insist upon her becoming a stenographer because of probable immediate employment.
6. Those who have lost interest in school, but who through assistance in making an occupational plan begin to realize the importance of further training and would like to make plans to get it. The problem here is increased of course, if a long period of time has elapsed since leaving school.
7. Those who are drifters and need to be encouraged to find immediate employment which will stimulate them in establishing better habits, like the boy who hitch-hiked and wandered about the country for a year, sleeping in parking lots and all night

movies, and who now would really like to settle down, but does not know where to begin.

8. Those who have special personal problems and who need help in making adjustments before success in any occupation may be possible, like the girl who because of an unhappy home situation and many conflicts, adopts a defensive attitude and feels that all of the adult world is her enemy.
9. Those who have made good plans, but who desire confirmation of their choice.
10. Those who have severe handicaps, mental, physical, or emotional.[8]

This service has emphasized testing, and although no one battery has been used the testing has measured such things as achievement, intelligence, interest, dexterity, and personality.

The interesting feature of the Detroit program is that although many parts of the community have contributed to the out-of-school counseling program it has been carried on primarily by the public school authorities. Other school systems in various cities might well copy the Detroit plan and thereby give impetus to the counseling of out-of-school youth.

Vocational Advisory Service

One of the very valuable vocational guidance agencies is the Vocational Advisory Service in New York City, which has been in existence for many years. Previously known as the Vocational Service for Juniors, it has been a pioneer in demonstrating how private and public agencies can cooperate. Two examples are its work with the New York State Employment Service, through the division known as the Consultation Service, and its cooperation with the National Youth Administration.

The Consultation Service of the Vocational Advisory Service has two main divisions, consisting of counselors and psychologists. The counselors conduct the interviews with the clients, and the psychologists have as their main task the testing of clients and preparation of psychological reports for the counselors. Psychologists also interview

[8] *Journal of Educational and Psychological Measurement,* 7:130–131(1947).

clients, in order to write more meaningful reports. In addition, this agency has an Information Department which assembles, classifies, and evaluates occupational and educational materials and information for the counselors. In many respects this agency is a model deserving very careful study by anyone contemplating setting up a vocational guidance center or evaluating other existing agencies (5).

Because the Vocational Advisory Service is relatively old and has benefited by maturity and experience, the authors believe it is worth describing in detail. However, there is another and more important reason for including a description of the Consultation Service of the V.A.S. It is to give a description of a total organization in process. Too often students studying a subject learn each of the separate topics without understanding how each fits into an integrated unit. Such a criticism of the education process applies to vocational psychology. Test knowledge, interest measurement, occupational information, statistics, and other elements of vocational psychology can all be taught without the student ever seeing how these tools and techniques really fit together. So that the reader may be given a general picture before these subjects are discussed, the experiences of a client as well as the work of the many professionals on the staff of the Vocational Advisory Service will be described.

The clients. Many people between the ages of 16 and 25 reach the offices of the Consultation Service which is sponsored by the V.A.S. and the N.Y. State Employment Service. The fact that a guidance and employment agency cooperate is to be noted and commended. It illustrates a sincere attempt to unify the problems of guidance and selection. Some of these clients are referred by employment interviewers who recognize the disparity between a likely job placement and the job the applicant seeks. There are other reasons for such referrals; among the more common ones are inability to hold a job, vocational confusion, and a need for training. Other major sources of referral are the social agencies and hospitals. Recently a few of the mental hygiene clinics handling seriously disturbed personalities have recognized the value of administering guidance to the patient after some progress has been made in his treatment. While such clients need the most skillful care this agency is geared to work with

CONSULTATION SERVICE
93 Madison Avenue, New York 16, N. Y.
Murray Hill 3-5425

Explanation of the Service

The purpose of the Consultation Service is to assist young people in choosing a vocation and developing and carrying out a program to reach their vocational objective, or if they have already made tentative vocational plans, to help them with the evaluation of these plans.

This service is free and is available to young people who do not know what field of work to enter, or who are contemplating a change of work. There is no age limit for veterans or persons with physical handicaps. The Consultation Service is jointly sponsored by the Vocational Advisory Service and the New York State Employment Service.

The Consultation Service helps by:-

1. Discussing with the applicant his vocational plans in the light of his school record, job experience, aptitudes, interests and ambitions.

2. Giving aptitude tests.

3. Planning with the applicant a program of training, or work experience for the purpose of entering a vocational field.

4. Informing applicants about occupations and occupational opportunities.

5. Obtaining vocational training, educational and recreational opportunities which fit into the vocational program.

If applicants are not employed and are interested in securing employment, but have not registered with the New York State Employment Service, it is to their advantage to go to the appropriate office and register immediately. Visits to the Consultation Service do not take the place of the scheduled visits to the employment office.

In order that the Counselors at the Consultation Service may become well acquainted with applicants and their needs, they are asked to return several times for interviews.

JCS-3 (6-47)

By permission of the V.A.S.

FORM USED TO EXPLAIN THE SERVICE OF THE V.A.S.

them. The third major source of referrals is the "word of mouth" recommendations. Elders, friends, or "others" have heard of the agency or consulted it, and so send people in. When the prospective client

CONSULTATION SERVICE
95 Madison Avenue, New York 16, N.Y.

REGISTRATION

Name________________ Date________________

Present Address________________ Tel. No.________________
(Number and street)

________________ Date of Birth________________
(Town or boro) (Zone No.) (State)

Former Address________________ Soc. Sec. No.________________

Height______ Weight______ Health______ Married? Yes______ No______

If married, wife's full maiden name before marriage________________

Referred by________________
(Person) (Organization)

First Name	Age	Health	Occupation	Now Employed
Father				
Mother				

Mother's Full Name Before Marriage________________

Names of Bros. & Sisters	Age	School Grade or Term Completed	Living at Home	Married	Occupation	Now Employed

Name of School	Address	Last Term Completed	Date	Day-Eve.	Gen'l	Com'l	Art	Other
Grade Sch.								
High Sch.								
College								
Other								

Are you attending any classes now?______ Where?________________
What subjects?________________

List all types of work you have done including after school, vacations, part time.

Employer	How Long	Kind of Work	Pay	Did you like or dislike it?	Why?

How long have you been looking for work?________________
What kind of job are you looking for now?________________

What would you like to be doing 10 years from now?________________

What special problems would you like to discuss with us?________________

JCS- (9-47)

By permission of the V.A.S.

REGISTRATION BLANK USED BY THE V.A.S.

reaches the offices, however he came, he is greeted by a receptionist, made to feel at ease, and given a mimeographed sheet explaining the service. The figure on page 70 is a sample of the form used.

CONSULTATION SERVICE

Name...Age....................Sex....................Date..............................

1. What do you do that you like best outside of work or school hours?

   Outdoors / Indoors

   a)..............................a)..............................

   b)..............................b)..............................

   c)..............................c)..............................

2. What is your special hobby?

3. What things outside your job would you now like to learn to do either in connection with work or with recreation?

4. What school or college subjects did you
   a. like best?

   b. find most difficult?

5. Which of the following subjects, if you had them, did you like better?
   a) English or Mathematics..............................
   b) Science or History..............................

6. What have you studied outside your regular school course that you liked?

7. What course of training or special subjects would you like to take if you could?

8. Have members of your family or friends suggested any particular career to you?..................
   What?..
   How do you feel about their suggestion?

9. What have you often thought that you would like to do for a living?

   a) Why?

   b) How long have you been interested in it?

10. What occupations or fields of work would you like more information about?

11. What kind of work are you trying to get now?

12. If you have worked, in what jobs did you feel you were most satisfactory to the employer?

13. Do you read newspapers?
    Which ones?

    What parts?

14. What magazines do you read often?

15. What three books outside of school books that you have read do you especially like?

16. What radio programs do you like particularly?

17. What club meetings or athletic groups do you attend frequently?

18. What do you like best to do there?

19. What further kind of recreation would you like if you could arrange it?

(*Use other side*)

By permission of the V.A.S.

INTEREST BLANK USED BY THE V.A.S. FOR CLIENTS WHOSE HISTORIES ARE CHIEFLY THEIR SCHOOL RECORDS (*front*)

The intake counselor. The applicant is then introduced to the intake counselor, a very important person. She is an experienced coun-

A. Check the activities in the list below which especially attract you and tell why you like them.

1. Working outdoors
2. Writing prose or poetry
3. Solving puzzles
4. Being "on the go" always
5. Using tools
6. Meeting lots of people
7. Tinkering and repairing things
8. Making speeches
9. Doing research work
10. Facing dangerous situations
11. Working at many things
12. Working at one thing steadily
13. Raising garden products
14. Doing new things all the time
15. Doing work for which you have to put on old clothes and get your hands dirty.

B. Check 2 of the following things which you would like to do best about either a radio or a garment.

(Place a check after radio........or after garment.......to indicate choice.)

Make it
Plan (or design it)
Sell it
Repair it
Improve it practically
Use it
Draw a picture of it
Write an article about it
Teach others about it
Handle the buying of it
Improve its beauty
Prepare the advertising of it

C. Glance through this list of occupations. What occupations do you think you would like best to follow?
(Check Five)

Actor
Accountant
Advertising
Air Conditioning
Aircraft Mechanic
Apprentice (in a trade)
Architect
Artist (com'l)
Artist (painter)
Athletic Director
Author
Auto Mechanic
Aviation Mechanic
Aviator
Bacteriologist
Baker
Bank-teller
Beauty Specialist
Bookkeeper
Bricklayer
Builder (contractor)
Buyer (dept. store)
Cabinet Maker
Carpenter
Cashier
Caterer
Chauffeur
Chemical Engineer
Chemist
Civil Engineer
Civil Service
Cleaner and Dyer
Clerk (dept. store)
Clerk (hotel)
Clerk (office)
Clerk (sales)
Clerk (shipping or stock)
Construction Worker
Cook
Counseler (camp)
Dancer (professional)
Demonstrator
Dental Mechanic
Dental Assistant
Dentist
Designer (clothes)
Designer (textiles)
Designer (jewelry)
Designer (machines)
Detective
Dietician
Doctor
Draftsman
Draftsman
Dressmaker
Editor
Electrician
Electrical Engineer
Elevator Operator
Engineer, Building
Enginere, Chemical
Engineer, Civil
Engineer, Electrical
Engineer, Industrial
Engineer, Mechanical
Engineer, Mining
Engraver
Farmer
Fashion Illustrator
Fireman
Fireman (city)
Florist
Forester
Furrier
Gem Appraiser
Grocer
Hostess
Housekeeper
Illustrator (magazine)
Insurance Agent
Insurance Claims Adjuster
Interior Decorator
Industrial Engineer
Inventor
Jeweler
Journalist
Judge
Laboratory Technician
Lawyer
Librarian
Machine Operator
Machinist
Mail Carrier
Mason
Mechanical Engineer
Mechanic
Milliner
Mining
Minister
Movie Operator
Musician
Naturalist
Nurse
Nursery School Teacher
Optometrist
Painter (house)
Painter (sign)
Personnel Worker
Pharmacist
Photographer
Playground Director
Plasterer
Plumber
Poultry Farmer
Policeman
Priest
Private Secretary
Printer
Prison Warden
Probation Officer
Psychologist
Publisher
Rabbi
Radio or Wireless Operator
Railroad Worker
Refrigeration Service
Research (scientific)
Restaurant Manager
Retailer
Roofer
Salesman (inside)
Salesman (outside)
Seaman
Serviceman (electrical equipment)
Serviceman (office machines)
Serviceman (radio)
Sheet Metal Worker
Sign Painter
Singer (professional)
Social Worker
Statistician
Steamfitter
Stenographer
Surgeon
Surveyor
Tailor
Taxi Driver
Tea Room Proprietor
Teacher
Telephone Operator
Textiles
Tool Maker
Traffic Manager
Transportation Manager
Tree Surgeon
Typist
Undertaker
Upholsterer
Veterinary
Waiter
Waitress
Watchmaker
Welder
Window Dresser
X-Ray Technician

VOCATIONAL ADVISORY SERVICE — 95 MADISON AVENUE — NEW YORK 16, N. Y.

By permission of the V.A.S.

INTEREST BLANK USED BY THE V.A.S. FOR CLIENTS WHOSE HISTORIES ARE CHIEFLY THEIR SCHOOL RECORDS (*reverse*)

selor who conducts a brief interview with the prospective client. She must decide whether this is a case for a vocational counselor or whether a referral should be made to a social agency, or employment service. She must also decide whether the person is merely in need of educational or occupational information, or on the other hand, will benefit from guidance.

If another agency has made the referral, as is often the case, the intake interview can be brief, since ordinarily the agencies refer only those who can benefit from guidance.

When the interview indicates the need for counseling the applicant is registered. This consists of having the person complete the registration blank as shown in the figure on page 71.

This form requests important and relevant information from the client. In Chapter 5, on the interview, reasons for including such items will be discussed. Briefly, it can be stated that these items are necessary background information if a valid job of guidance is to be done.

In addition the applicant is given an appropriate interest blank which is not labeled as such. There are two kinds, one for clients whose histories are chiefly their school records, the other for clients with some work experience; the former is illustrated on pages 72 and 73. No attempt is made to score the blank numerically. The blank serves to bolster the intake counselor's judgment as to the interests and activities of the client and supplements the brief 15- to 30-minute interview she conducts.

The applicant is then told that he will receive an appointment by mail. The time lapse depends upon the waiting lists. In cases of extreme emergency, the case assignment is hurried.

The intake counselor then contacts the schools to complete the educational record and obtain a picture of the client's academic ability and performance. The form sent to the high schools is illustrated on page 75. The client's name is also cleared with the Social Service Exchange for any additional information. This would be available if the family was known to other agencies.

When all this material has been assembled, the intake counselor takes inventory and assigns the case to a counselor. This is done according to her estimation of which counselor would be best for the client. Counselors in this organization have previously had different

CONSULTATION SERVICE
95 Madison Avenue
New York 16, N.Y.

Date____________

To the Recorder of________________________High School:

The applicant listed below has been referred to us for vocational guidance. In connection with plans for future work and training we find the school record of great value. Will you please fill in the record below and return as soon as possible? This information will be considered confidential. It will be most helpful to us to have the complete school record. We shall appreciate your help.

______________________Registrar

Name________________________Address________________________

Birth Date____________________Father__________Mother__________

School________________Annex____________Address____________

Course________________School Previously Attended________________

Please verify: Date of entering________ Terms completed__________

Date of discharge________ Was student graduated?________

SUBJECT	GRADE RECEIVED								
	1ST TERM	2ND TERM	3RD TERM	4TH TERM	5TH TERM	6TH TERM	7TH TERM	8TH TERM	REGENTS
PLEASE LIST GRADES ACCORDING TO TERM IN WHICH SUBJECT WAS TAKEN, AND INCLUDE FAILURES.									

Please give information about student's abilities and traits, and his extra-curricular activities. (Use reverse side if necessary.)

Signature________________________Position________________

JCS-15 (9-47)

By permission of the V.A.S.

FORM SENT TO SCHOOLS BY THE V.A.S. TO COMPLETE THE CLIENT'S EDUCATIONAL RECORD

backgrounds and work experiences. The former engineer, the former school teacher, the former salesperson—each is assigned cases in relation to former experiences whenever possible. Even the sex of the counselor obtains the consideration it deserves. For example, the boy who reveals through the intake interview that he is having a difficult father relationship but gets along well with his mother is usually assigned to a female rather than a male counselor.

Although the actual work of investigation and assignment is done within one week, there may be a delay in the client's first appointment. The staff of the V.A.S. is determined by its budget, and so practical considerations enter. While it would be ideal to have more immediate appointments, the organization can handle only the case load that is reasonable for its 14 counselors.

The first interview. The first interview with the counselor assigned to the case usually lasts about one hour but may run from 45 to 75 minutes. When the counselor believes that more time is needed, a second "first" interview is scheduled.

The purpose of the first interview is to get the facts, get acquainted, and encourage the client to think about his own problem. The counselor has reviewed the registration blank and other forms before this interview and now adds the flesh and blood to the skeleton of cold facts these forms reveal.

No specific method of interviewing is used, except that the counselor does not give final answers. Even when the client pushes and asks, "What shall I do?" the counselor says, "I don't know. I would have to know you better." This answer applies even when the counselor thinks he or she knows the answer. The counselor's concern is to establish the facts about the client, and their interrelationships, so that he can properly understand the client's problem.

For example, it is one thing to know how many brothers and sisters the client has, but it is much more important for the counselor to fit this into the total picture of socio-economic status of the family, educational level and aspiration of the parents, and so forth. Then the family situation, as well as the reality of the problem, becomes more clearly established.

Toward the end of the interview or at an appropriate time during it, the counselor suggests that the client take some psychological tests and explains their purpose. The appointment is made for a definite time within one week after the "purpose" of testing has been explained. The counselor makes two main points: first, that tests will not make up the clients' minds and thereby relieve them of their responsibilities to make their own decisions; and second, that the tests may show strengths and weaknesses but do not result in failure in the sense that school tests do.

When the first interview is completed, the counselor then dictates his notes and also completes a check list of suggested psychological tests to be administered by the psychologists.

As can be seen from the form illustrated on page 78, the counselor is asked to justify the reasons for requesting specific tests and also to place the tests into two categories, one being more important than the other. Giving the counselor such responsibility demands that he know the tests the psychologist uses. This is important since it allows counselor and psychologist to work together more smoothly.

In some organizations, counselors do not appreciate the value of tests. They probably do not know the tests and have not learned their value.

Psychological tests. The psychological department of the Vocational Advisory Service receives the counselor's test recommendations together with the client's folder. Prior to testing, the psychologist reviews the case and is at liberty to add or delete any test or tests. All psychologists are trained to administer either the individual or group tests, so that each staff member may rotate and have an opportunity to do all types of testing as well as research. This is valuable since it adds variety to the work as well as allowing for easier administrative control.

A testing room is always likely to present sudden problems, and so the psychologists must be observant as well as flexible. Sometimes slow people cannot finish all the tests scheduled and this requires last-minute changes in proposed batteries. At other times unexpected emotional behavior must be appropriately handled.

Almost all clients are tested; occasionally even a graduate university student. An important feature of testing is the mature observation of test performance and related behavior that psychologists can make while a client is taking tests. Often the client reacts quite differ-

CONSULTATION SERVICE

COUNSELOR'S CHECK SHEET

Client__________ Counselor__________ Date__________

Tests	Tests Desired*	Reason for Requesting Tests**
Vocabulary		
Verbal Reasoning		
Minn. Clerical		
Simple Posting		
Complex Classification		
Filing		
Arithmetic		
Fractions		
Spelling		
Finger Dexterity		
Tweezer Dexterity		
Placing and Turning		
Two-Dimensional Simple		
Two-Dimensional Complex		
Three-Dimensional		
Wechsler-Bellevue		
Personnel		

*Check the tests desired and double check those tests considered essential in the event time does not permit the administration of all tests which have been checked.

**Record the reason for requesting each test checked unless the reason is obvious from the material in the folder. Please always note the reason for requesting the Verbal Reasoning, the Kohs, the Complex Classification.

JCS 22 (2-18-46)

By permission of the V.A.S.

THE V.A.S. COUNSELOR'S CHECK LIST OF PSYCHOLOGICAL TESTS DESIRED

ently in testing than in an interview situation, and so different facets of personality are revealed through his answers and manner of performance. All clients tested are given the Wechsler-Bellevue, and this test is used as a clinical instrument rather than merely an attempt to obtain the I.Q. In addition, verbal, spatial, and clerical tests are usually given to all clients, and then other tests are added to fit the specific needs of the client and his problem.

The department tests six or seven clients each morning. One psychologist is in charge of the testing room and an additional two or three do the individual testing in private rooms. The client is smoothly brought in and out in such a fashion as to maintain rapport and create minimum confusion.

During the afternoon the psychologists score the tests, draw up a profile (see the figure on page 80), and write supplementary reports which are essentially clinical analyses of the Wechsler together with any observation made during the client's test performance. The psychologist's report is returned to the counselor together with the case folder and then the counselor arranges for the case conference.

Case conference. The case conference is one of the most important steps in guidance. Although it is a behind-the-scenes affair and the client does not necessarily know of its existence, a second interview is seldom held without it. The main purpose of the case conference is to serve as a safeguard against any subjective and snap judgments by a counselor.

There are often three or four professional people at the case conference. Included are the counselor, a senior counselor who serves as a consultant, the professional person who has made the referral, and a psychologist. Always included in the conference are the counselor and the senior counselor. The referrant is invited only when he is a professional person connected with a referring agency. Relatives or non-professional people are never invited to the conference. Without training they usually do not have sufficient insight to handle the case objectively. The psychologist either may request that he attend the conference or may be called in. Whenever special problems arise and it is believed that the psychologist has useful information, he attends.

The discussion at the case conference includes a presentation of the case by the counselor, and all present attempt to understand the client. No final plans are made, since the V.A.S. recognizes that a plan that is not the client's will not help him. The conference results in suggestions to the counselor as to what directions or possibilities might be sound for the client to consider. The counselor is prepared to point out possible actions but must allow the client to make his own

PSYCHOLOGICAL PROFILE

CLIENT__________ COUNSELOR__________

Male___ Female___ Age___ Grade Completed______ Date______

Test No.	Test Name	Poor	Below Av.	Average	Above Av.	Except	Score	Errors	School Grade
	Standard Score Scale	2.0 2.5 3.0	3.5 4.0	4.5 5.0 5.5	6.0	6.5 7.0 7.5 8.0			
	Percentile Rank Scale	0 1 2 5	10 20 30	40 50 60	70 80 90	95 98 99 100			
1	Wechsler Bellevue, Total								
2	Verbal								
3	Performance								
4									
5	Vocabulary, O'Rourke								
6	Wonderlic Personnel								
7									
8	Reading, rate								
9	Reading, comprehension								
10	Arithmetic								
11	Spelling								
12	Minn. Clerical: Numbers								
13	Minn. Clerical: Names								
14	Simple Posting								
15	Complex Classification								
16									
17	Minn. Spatial Relations								
18	O'Connor Wiggly Block								
19	Revised Kohs								
20									
21									
22									
23									
24									
	σ Score Scale	-3.0 -2.5 -2.0	-1.5 -1.0	-.5 0 .5	1.0	1.5 2.0 2.5 3.0			

Entered by______ Checked by______

THE V.A.S. PSYCHOLOGICAL PROFILE *By permission of the V.A.S.*

plans. If the plan is totally inadequate, the counselor is prepared to point out this to the client and help him to develop a more appropriate one.

Second interview. The second interview takes place soon after the conference. It usually begins with such a question as, "What have you thought about your problem since you last were here?" Most often the client shows some growth and is prepared to discuss his problem more fully. The client is usually also interested in discussing the test results, and the counselor does this not in terms of specific test scores but rather in terms of the vocational implications of the results. If the client is ready to make a decision then he and the counselor work out the necessary practical steps. If not, then another interview is scheduled. The counselor is expected to follow through with the client not only to see that the client "gets started" but also so that the counselor is provided with information on results.

To evaluate the service of the V.A.S. as well as to keep records of its work, the counselor completes one additional form, the case analysis form, which summarizes the case in terms of the type of problem, the recommendation made, and the type of service completed. This form is presented on pages 82 and 83.

Information Service. There is one additional department of the V.A.S., the Information Service. It has two functions, the first of which is to furnish information directly to the client when he seeks educational or occupational information and is not really in need of guidance. This task falls primarily on the intake counselor.

Its second function is to serve the counselors. It helps staff committees arrange for regularly scheduled lectures by experts from firms, educational institutions, and other organizations. These guest lecturers are briefed in advance as to the needs of the counselors and so the discussions are usually very helpful. Such matters as hiring practices and policies, union situation, organization set-up are discussed. Following the talk a field trip is arranged and the counselors by visiting the plant learn even more of the things that a client is likely to want to know. The following is a list of some of the fields recently reviewed in this program: hotels; building and construction; a railroad; federal civil service; the traffic division of a manufacturing

CONSULTATION SERVICE

CASE ANALYSIS FORM

IDENTIFYING DATA

Office________Date 1st Interview______

Client________________________M____F____

Counselor______________________________

Relief: Yes____No____

Worked Before: Yes____No____

Age: Under 16___16 to 18___18 to 21___
21 to 25___Over 25___

Referred by:
- NYSES office______________
- School______________
- Social Agency or Church__________
- Friend or Relative__________
- Self______________
- Other______________

EDUCATION

Level Completed:

Less than 8th Gr.___8th Gr. Grad.____
Some H. S.________H. S. Grad.______
Some College_______Col. Grad.______

Course Taken in School or College:
General____________Technical________

Com'l.____________Art & Music______
Indus. (Tr.)__________Other__________

Additional Training: (Predominate)

Com'l____________Art or Music_____
Tech. or Trade______None__________

Other______________________________

TYPE OF PROBLEM
(as seen by Counselor)

RECOMMENDATIONS MADE

(Check "P" column for primary and "S" for secondary problems and recommendations)

Type of Problem	P	S
A) Needs advice on securing or preparing for immediate work		
B) Needs advice on planning further training or work for the following reasons:		
1. Has no plan		
2. Needs help in choosing between plans		
3. Needs confirmation of plan		
4. Needs change in plan because preparation, abilities or interests not suited to present plan		
5. Needs change in plan because of change in circumstances		
6. Unadjusted in present employment		
7. Unadjusted in present training program		
8. Other (specify)		
C) Needs financial aid for training		
D) Vocational problem complicated by personality factors		
E) Other (specify)		

Recommendations Made	P	S
A) Take new or additional training or revive plans for training		
B) Make or improve contacts leading toward employment		
C) Make long term vocational plan		
D) Confirm client's own vocational plan		
E) Change or modify inappropriate vocational plans		
F) Refer to agency for specialized service (health, relief, psychiatric, or other)		
G) Undertake recreational or avocational activities		
H) Undertake measures for improving personal fitness		
I) Secure financial aid for training		
J) No satisfactory recommendations made		
K) Other (specify)		
L) In process at end of month		

JCS-21 (Rev. 12/5/46)

By permission of the V.A.S.

V.A.S. CASE ANALYSIS FORM

company; editor of a weekly magazine; a lithographing company; a chemical firm; a radio station; an air line; and the public relations field.

Complete notes of each of the talks and field trips are made and

OUTCOME

1. SERVICE COMPLETED (Check "P" column for primary and "S" column for secondary results)	P	S
A) Specific information given		
B) Contact with employment office improved or established		
C) Secured employment		
D) Plan for further training:		
a) Undertaken		
b) Decided upon		
E) Decision to continue present plan		
F) Unwise plan for work or training altered		
G) Referred to specialized agency		
H) Avocational or recreational plan undertaken		
I) Helped to achieve more personal fitness for work		
J) Financial aid obtained for training		
K) Morale improved		
L) Client failed to adopt plan		
M) No satisfactory recommendations made		
N) No certain information on outcome		
O) Other (specify)		

2. SERVICE NOT COMPLETED	
A) Plans interrupted by new developments:	
a) Moved away	
b) Secured employment	
c) Other (specify)	
B) Did not keep appointment (reason unknown)	
3. IN PROCESS	

By permission of the V.A.S.

V.A.S. CASE ANALYSIS FORM

filed for reference use whenever necessary. In addition a weekly newsletter is prepared for the counselors; it covers pertinent information on new items in the field of occupational and educational information.

Other community agencies

Vocational guidance agencies on a community level may be found in such places as boys' clubs, Y.M.C.A.'s, religious organizations, philanthropic organizations, community houses, and even prisons.

Cole (4) reports an interesting study in which an attempt has been made to evaluate a guidance program in a boys' club in Worcester. Two groups of 100 members each were selected on the basis of age, I.Q., school marks, physical development, parental education, and social and economic status. Cole reports that in 1931, these two groups were rather similar. One group received vocational guidance and the other did not. In 1936, these two groups were followed up, and the results are presented in Table 5.

TABLE 5

COMPARISON OF FOLLOW-UP OF TWO GROUPS AFTER FIVE-YEAR PERIOD*

	Counseled	*Non-counseled*
Per cent of group in school	45%	22%
Average grade attained in school	11.88	10.86
Average weekly earning	$21.85	$19.15
Never shifted jobs	59%	32%

* Adapted from Robert C. Cole, "Evaluating a Boys' Club Guidance Program," *Occupations, the Vocational Guidance Journal*, published by National Vocational Guidance Association, Incorporated, 17:705–709 (1939).

The results of Cole's study indicate clearly the advisability of boys' clubs in community centers seriously considering attempts to guide youth vocationally as well as in the more obvious social ways.

The Vocational Service Center of the Young Men's Christian Association provides counseling and placement facilities for its clients. It serves to complement rather than supplant the counseling services of the local branches. During the period beginning January 1944 and ending August 1946, a total of 22,658 new applicants received one or more of the services offered by this agency. It has four divisions: Counseling and Testing; Placement; Credit Aid; and Veteran's Advisement.

A Jewish service organization known as B'nai B'rith has a vocational service program offered on a national level. Its present work consists primarily of occupational research, the publication of occupational literature, and sponsorship of group activities in guidance. It is also experimenting with employment of traveling counselors, who conduct part-time individual counseling programs in the small communities of Michigan, Pennsylvania, New Jersey and Texas. The B'nai B'rith, in a fashion similar to the United States Government Printing Office, publishes many worth-while occupational information items on a purely service basis. It also maintains a counselors' information service. Through this service mimeographed releases of value to vocational counselors are issued approximately every two weeks. The vocational service program has taken the lead in promoting group vocational guidance. While they do not believe that group guidance should take the place of individual guidance, they consider the two kinds as complementary in a vocational guidance program. The values of group activities as distinct from individual counseling are reported by Baer (2) as follows:

1. They provide *some* orientation to many individuals who are not reached through individual counseling. In many cases such orientation may be sufficient to enable an individual to make his plans without further help from a counselor.
2. They may focus attention on individuals particularly in need of individual counseling.
3. They tend to stimulate demand for individual counseling.
4. They help establish *rapport* for subsequent individual counseling.
5. They provide an economical means of imparting information of common interest and value.
6. They provide an economical means of obtaining certain information about individuals (such as through group testing).
7. They provide a more effective means of obtaining certain information about individuals (character and personality traits as revealed in a natural group setting).
8. They facilitate use of such effective educational techniques as dramatizations, quiz contests, occupational tours, motion pictures, talks by experts in different occupations, etc.
9. They facilitate use of natural group activities for tryout experiences and other guidance purposes.
10. They make possible the pooling of experiences of many for the benefit of each member of the group.

11. They make it possible for the group to influence the thinking of the individual.
12. They provide opportunities for improvement of character and personality traits, especially facility in human relationships.
13. They offer one of the best opportunities for self-diagnosis.[9]

Another example of the use of vocational guidance is reported by Martin (16). He describes a rather interesting program of vocational guidance in a prison system. While the person is in the prison, a complete work history is collected from his first job to the one held at the time of the current offense, in order to learn the man's principal as well as secondary occupation as determined by previous experience. Then a battery of psychological tests is administered; these include mechanical, manual, intelligence, and interest tests. During further interviews a vocational plan is developed, which includes consideration of the prisoner's educational status, vocational experience, aptitude pattern as well as occupational preferences and temperament pattern. This results in a vocational training program which may include assignment to certain types of prison jobs, vocational courses, or related educational courses. It is entirely possible that such a system can go a long way in the correction of those who have erred.

The Veterans Administration has played a large role on the community level in the administration of counseling veterans both by providing its own service and by paying acceptable agencies for the services rendered veterans. Many schools and colleges as well as community agencies have co-sponsored veterans' advisement units. The quantity and quality of counseling was very definitely influenced by the program of the V.A., in which it was recognized that counseling was an important aspect of deciding educational and occupational objectives.

Summary

Although it is impossible to describe each vocational guidance agency in the United States, an attempt has been made to present in-

[9] *Occupations, the Vocational Guidance Journal,* published by National Vocational Guidance Association, Incorporated, 24:277(1946).

formation on the wide variety of vocational guidance centers available on either the school or the community level. The program of guidance in the junior high schools shows the need for integrating educational and vocational guidance. A survey of practices among the high schools indicates the need for improving the counseling programs. The type of guidance program in the colleges varies considerably with different universities emphasizing different aspects of the total program.

Community programs were described as they occur in the City of Detroit and at the Vocational Advisory Service in New York. A complete description of the procedure of counseling at the V.A.S. was presented, not only because this agency can be regarded as effective and progressive but also because it was thought desirable to give the reader a picture of the total process of guidance in operation. It included references to clients, the intake counselor, the interview, psychological tests, the case conference, and the information service.

In addition a few other community services were briefly mentioned.

Bibliography

1. *Annual Report, 1947–1948,* Division of Educational and Vocational Guidance, Board of Education, City of New York (1948).
2. Baer, M. F., "The B'nai B'rith Vocational Service Program," *Occupations,* 24:277–280 (1946).
3. Bennett, H., "Ypsilanti Community Counseling Service," *Occupations,* 18:429–432 (1940).
4. Cole, R. C., "Evaluating a Boys' Club Guidance Program," *Occupations,* 17:705–709 (1939).
5. Culbert, J. F., and H. R. Smith, *Counseling Young Workers.* New York: Vocational Service for Juniors, 1939.
6. Darley, J. G., *Testing and Counseling in the High School Program.* Chicago: Science Research Associates, 1947.
7. ——— and D. G. Marquis, "Veterans' Guidance Centers: A Survey of Their Problems and Activities," *Journal of Clinical Psychology,* 2:109–116 (1946).
8. Directory of Counseling Services, *Occupations,* 27:570–596 (1949).

9. Grummon, D. L., and T. Gordon, "The Counseling Center at the University of Chicago," *The American Psychologist,* 3:166–171 (1948).
10. Hanna, J. V., "The Counseling and Guidance Program of the YMCA of the City of New York," *Counseling,* 4:6 (1946).
11. Kirkpatrick, F. H., "Vocational Guidance in an American College," *The Human Factor,* 11:409–415 (1937).
12. Layton, W. K., "Community Relationships in Out-of-School Counseling," *Journal of Educational and Psychological Measurement,* 7:127–132 (1947).
13. Leonard, A., and A. C. Tucker, *The Individual Inventory in Guidance Programs in Secondary Schools, a Study of Present Practices in Selected Schools* (Vocational Division Bulletin #215), Federal Security Agency, U.S. Office of Education, 1941.
14. Lloyd-Jones, E., "Variations in College Personnel Programs," *Journal of Consulting Psychology,* 4:201-205 (1940).
15. McKinney, F., "Four Years of a College Adjustment Clinic," *Journal of Counsulting Psychology,* 9:203–217 (1945).
16. Martin, G., "Vocational Guidance in a Prison System," *The American Psychologist,* 1:542–543 (1946).
17. Paterson, D. G., G. G. Schneidler, and E. G. Williamson, *Student Guidance Techniques.* New York: McGraw-Hill, 1938.
18. Ryan, J., "Children's Aid Society Gives Vocational Guidance," *Occupations,* 30:597–600 (1942).
19. Smith, M., and M. M. Roos, *A Guide to Guidance.* New York: Prentice-Hall, 1941.
20. Stocking, C., "Contributions of the U.S.E.S. to Guidance and Personnel Problems," *Occupations,* 25:500–503 (1947).
21. Williamson, E. G., "Counseling and the Minnesota Point of View," *Journal of Educational and Psychological Measurement,* 7:141–155 (1947).
22. ———, *How to Counsel Students.* New York: McGraw-Hill, 1939.
23. ——— (ed.), *Trends in Student Personnel* Work. Minneapolis: University of Minnesota Press, 1949.
24. Williamson, E. G., and J. G. Darley, *Student Personnel Work.* New York: McGraw-Hill, 1937.

4

THE COUNSELING INTERVIEW—GENERAL

THE INTERVIEW allows the client and counselor to exchange ideas and attitudes through conversation. Its purpose is to lead to a solution of the client's problems or at least to some change in attitude or behavior.

Different methods of interviewing have been used in vocational counseling. The category considered least valid may be called authoritarian. Another method is a technique of interviewing developed originally for use in personal counseling and more recently applied to vocational counseling; it is known as non-directive. The third category and the one we consider most usable in vocational counseling is called non-authoritarian.

Before dicussing each of these types of interviewing it is advisable to cut across the methods and consider the interview from one of two frames of reference. One is client-centered and the other is counselor-centered. The participation in conversation on the part of the client or counselor varies depending upon whether the interview is client- or counselor-centered.

Client-centered interviews revolve about the client. The client is encouraged to lead in the conversation and to express his attitudes, feelings and thoughts. The counselor is more passive and does not interrupt the client's free flow of ideas, thoughts, expressions and feelings. The counselor helps the client to talk freely by his manner of tactfully indicating he understands and by not attempting to fill lulls in the conversation with his talk. He aids the client to crystallize his ideas and attitudes toward more positive and successful behavior. Fundamentally, he establishes rapport, the feeling of mutual confidence between the two parties in the interview, by his understanding attitude and manner.

The client-centered interview primarily makes use of open-end questions. These are loosely structured and allow for considerable verbalism by the client. In answering such relatively unstructured questions, the client projects his own personality. The counselor is more concerned with summarizing the emotional content of what the client has said than in asking specific questions and expecting direct answers.

In replying the client is allowed and encouraged in subtle ways to speak at length. The form of the question and the manner in which it is posed permits the client to feel that the interviewer is interested in him as a person, respects his opinion, and is not merely probing for facts which may seem of dubious value to the client. Facts as such are not sought. The goal is to weave the facts into an integrated whole. Any probing that is done is in the context of what has been said or implied and is to help clarify the feelings and thoughts expressed. Mere disconnected facts, unweighted for value to the client, are not really important. They are like the legal yes or no to complexly motivated behavior and may even be confusing. The following is a brief description of a client-centered interview:

Jack felt that he was making very little progress in his job and came to a vocational counseling agency for help.

Counselor: What did you want to discuss with us?

Client: I've been on my job now for five years and feel that I'm in a rut. When I got the job, I was 18 years old. I was told that there would be great opportunities to advance, but there haven't been. I was just out of high school at the time and even went to evening college to prepare myself for advancement. I'd like to change my job or maybe go to school or something.

Counselor: You feel that you are in a rut and want to get out of it but don't know exactly what to do.

Client: I was thinking of engineering school, but then I'm 23 years old and would have to start from scratch.

Counselor: You think you're too old to start engineering school.

Client: Not only that, but maybe I'm rusty with school subjects and I don't think I could go in the evening. I'd rather go in the day and finish up quickly, but I have to discuss that with my parents. Maybe if I showed my parents I'm not dumb, they would back me in day college. Could I take some tests?

Counselor: You feel that tests would help convince you and your parents that you could get through college and your parents would be willing to finance you.

Client: Yes.

Counselor: Tests can be arranged. (An appointment was made for them.)

Client: Thanks. Now what shall I do about my job in the meantime, and suppose I can't convince my parents?

Counselor: We can start discussing these matters now.

The interview continues in similar fashion. The client is allowed to take the lead, to crystallize his attitudes and feelings, see his problems clearly and begin to discuss action to solve the problems.

Counselor-centered interviews revolve about the counselor. He may try to establish rapport by being friendly and helpful. The counselor is very active and often expresses his own attitudes and feelings freely. He evaluates the client's expressions. He leads the interview, often makes premature suggestions and is inclined to be free with advice. In the counselor-centered interview, the interviewer usually asks a series of standardized questions and each may be answered briefly. The following is a brief description of a report on an interview that was extremely counselor-centered. This kind of interview is rarely reported verbatim.

> Nora was all mixed up. She didn't know her own mind. She wanted to leave high school, but then she wanted to be a nurse. I pointed out that these two moves were incompatible. To be a nurse, she would have to finish high school. She wanted to leave high school because her mother was an invalid and she wanted to be a nurse for the same reason. I asked her about her school marks and she said they were good. But they really weren't. I advised her to drop school and get into some factory work. I thought she would be happier at this.

This illustration is rather extreme to point up the centering about the counselor. From the description, the counselor does not allow much development of feeling and attitude expression on the part of the client. As an expert, he takes the lead, evaluates and gives advice. In this illustration the evaluation and advice may have been given prematurely. The client may not have weighed the alternatives for herself. She may have been told without understanding why.

Personal and vocational counseling interrelated

One cannot do vocational counseling without considering such personal aspects as home situation, health condition, and personality factors. The client in discussing his vocational plan will, if allowed by the counselor, talk of his finances, his aspirations, his failures and successes, his health, even his fears and personal involvements. The vocational counselor cannot refuse to listen to such discussions or consider these matters as irrelevant to the vocational problem presented.

A good deal of the difficulty lies in the incomplete training of counselors in interviewing techniques, as well as in the lack of standards and definition as to what is a professionally trained vocational counselor. The kind of personal problems to be dealt with by a vocational counselor also lack definition. The Veterans Administration tried to solve the problem by training a selected staff in personal counseling (5). The Personal Counselor would "screen and refer to the Mental Hygiene Unit cases that might need psychiatric diagnosis and treatment, to counsel with veterans presenting personal problems, and to consult with Vocational Advisers and Training Officers in their dealings with the adjustment problems of veterans." The counseling on personal problems was given the major emphasis in the training program since few of the counselors had any training in psychotherapy.

The Veterans Administration found it necessary to train some of their staff for personal counseling. In some vocational guidance agencies this separation of function takes place over a period of years, with those more adept at dealing with the personal problems involved in vocational counseling taking over the function. The uncomplicated vocational problems remain in the hands of those who do not have the skills to go beyond such problems. A vocational counselor should also be able to counsel with personal matters that impinge on the vocational adjustment. He should be able to discuss the need for psychiatric treatment and know how to make a referral.

It is unfortunate that certain vocational counselors are mainly concerned with the occupational aspects of counseling and do not have the skills needed to recognize and handle the individual with personal problems. On the other hand, those counselors who stress adjustment and do not have occupational information cannot do a complete job in the vocational interview. Evelyn Murray, an employment counseling specialist, correctly states: "Vocational counselors need to use wide, deep knowledge of *people* and *jobs*." In a letter to the Editor of *Occupations* she writes (14):

> All authorities agree that in giving vocational guidance we must know people and we must know occupations. But, unhappily, among those persons who claim to give vocational guidance those who pay equal attention to jobs and to people are in the glorious minority.
>
> Having recently served as Chairman to the Ethical Practices Committee of the New York City Branch of NVGA, I examined the reports covering surveys of local guidance agencies which had applied for certification by the National Association. Most of these agencies dwelt on the pains they take in examining clients. A few mentioned their occupational libraries. Some pointed out their proximity to a placement agency. To questions asked them about knowledge of occupations, the answers were usually in the affirmative, but few details were given. Many, particularly the private practitioners, spoke only of their "clinical work," "deep therapy," and of their "psychology" connections.
>
> Reading these reports, one gained the impression that many practitioners feel that training in psychology alone qualifies them to practice vocational guidance. They seem to attach little importance to knowledge of jobs, industry, and labor market trends. Their chief aim is to "adjust the individual." This aim is, of course, legitimate and often has to come before, or in the process of, vocational guidance, but it is not, in itself, Vocational Guidance. A psychologist may be trained in counseling techniques but without vocational content his interview sometimes resembles a beautifully wrapped—but empty—box.
>
> Let us look at the other side of the picture. There are those who think only of "opportunities." Some are my co-workers in public employment offices. They use the results of occupational and labor market research as though these constituted the chief substance of vocational guidance. They pour out their occupational knowledge to the counselee as though it were the whole story for him or her. If there is a scarcity of jobs for draftsmen, they hasten to inform each person who asks about such work of this condition. It doesn't matter that the coun-

selee may have had the best possible training or experience in this field. The counselor must tell him all he knows of the job. And, worse, the counselor often gives out full job information before examining the individual; he asks too few preliminary questions. A boy may have great potentiality for art work, but if this field is crowded he must be told about it at once—even though he may already realize this fact but believes his talent to be unusual enough to form a reasonable insurance of success. The counselor who over-emphasizes the labor market in his counseling will seldom delve deeply enough to find out if his client should be encouraged even though jobs in his line are relatively few.

Often, too, those counselors with a labor-market bias give out the facts they have amassed even where they are not needed. They talk as if the statistical mean applied specifically to the person then being interviewed. Placement personnel who do vocational guidance often do not know enough about individual appraisal—the analysis of the total individual. The research worker also gives us trouble. A researcher in medicine seldom attempts to treat a patient. But in the field of vocational guidance, some researchers (psychologists and economists) will advise any individual who will listen to them.

Vocational guidance is a difficult profession. Even though it may draw on many other disciplines, it still remains a separate and distinct profession. The trained vocational counselor draws on the findings of the psychologist and the expert in individual and group adjustment. He also utilizes the work of the economist and statistician in the course of his own unique task of assisting the individual to choose a satisfactory field of work or to adjust to his job.

Vocational counselors need to use wide, deep knowledge of people and jobs. Neither the imparting of information nor the process of helping the individual to know or accept himself is the whole job to be done. Let us not continue to have our work discredited because we still permit those who take some supplementary part in it to operate as though they were masters of the entire process.[1]

Personal counseling involves attitude change and reorientation of social and emotional values. Where the changes and reorientation do not involve adjustment in vocations, then only personal counseling is required. Where they do, a combination of personal and vocational counseling is demanded for fullest adjustment of the individual.

Personal counseling is the special contribution of psychologists to

[1] *Occupations, the Vocational Guidance Journal,* published by National Vocational Guidance Association, Incorporated, 27:404–405(1949).

the field of vocational counseling. Personal counseling has its theoretical and methodological roots in the teachings of Freud and those who followed him to some degree but dissented on some issues; as well as in the progress of psychological knowledge in personality dynamics. Some of its practical roots are to be found in the expansion of the services of vocational guidance. Many different kinds of problems come to vocational counselors.

A person may come to a vocational guidance organization because he feels that a change in job might relieve him of marital problems. He obviously has a personal problem although he is primarily aware of the vocational problem. Most probably he has both. The individual who believes that a different kind of job might help rid him of persistent headaches also may have personal problems.

The case of Alfred illustrates how personal problems are often concealed under the guise of a vocational problem. It is presented to demonstrate how one kind of problem cannot be solved without the other. Alfred, who was 40, had worked for 20 years as a stock clerk in a large corporation. After three years of academic high school he left at the age of 17 to seek work because his father had died and his mother was ill. He had a younger sister who subsequently married. He never married.

Before he found work with the large corporation, he had a series of nondescript jobs. He started with the corporation as a messenger boy. Many times he wanted to change jobs, but his mother was too sick. Many times he thought of going to evening school to improve himself but if he did his mother would be left alone at night. He used to "hop rides" on the maintenance truck and would have loved to change over to that kind of work. His mother thought that was not clean work and so he did not. Now at the age of 40, he came for vocational counseling. He wanted to know if he could take tests; he came to see what job would be suitable for him. His mother was still living but quite old and "about to die."

Merely finding out about his abilities and interests and interviewing strictly along vocational lines would not have been sufficient. This man, through several interviews, came to understand the true nature of his problem. He said he had assumed great burdens, his mother was too possessive, he was weak and should have been stronger. He really hated his mother at times, but would not dare show it or even let himself think about it. So, he did her bidding because he felt any show of independence would reveal to himself his hatred of his mother. And this he could not bear. Alfred had originally stated that his problem was vocational and it turned out to be personal. The interview had allowed him to see how his work objective and adjustment at his job were affected by his personal problems. He expressed his attitudes toward his mother and was able to see himself in a new light. The vocational problem was no longer a problem. Alfred said that he did not dislike his job, and after exploring the difficulties attendant with a change of occupation, stated that he thought it best to remain at his present job. However, he felt that he had neglected his social life and now wanted one. This he decided to do by joining organizations. In a later interview he remarked that he had left his mother home to go out to a social affair and found himself feeling more "like a man." This case illustrates that a client will often have a problem that is more complex than originally stated. Clarification of the problem is necessary before it can be fully understood and a solution reached.

Ray and Virginia Bixler (4) report on a comparison made between the initial and later statements of the problem in a group of 50 college students who came for counseling. Eleven, or 22 per cent, decided after the interview that their problems were entirely different from those given in the initial statement. They had come seeking vocational guidance and felt at the conclusion that their problems were emotional. Twenty-two students or 44 per cent made changes similar to the above eleven, retaining their desire for vocational guidance, but including emotional problems. The Bixlers note that in 1943 the University of Minnesota changed the name of its bureau from the University Testing Bureau to the Student Counseling Bureau, apparently to include service for those who needed personal counseling as well as vocational counseling.

Bailey, Gilbert, and Berg (3) state that of 1617 clients who came to the Student Personnel Counseling Bureau at the University of

Illinois, 74.5 per cent were considered to have educational-vocational problems. The remaining 25.5 per cent had emotional problems, with some of them having vocational problems as well. Hahn and Kendall (10) report on a review of cases at Syracuse University from which they gather that educational-vocational problems outnumber problems with an emotional complication by about three to one. Nelson (15) has supplied more detailed data on the frequency of types of counseling problems. He refers to a group of 200 disabled male veterans who had come for guidance. Two thirds of the men were in the age group 20–29 and all of them varied from 18 to 51 years of age. The problems were defined by the counselor after interviewing had proceeded sufficiently to make the problems clear. The following five groups of problems emerged:

1. Counselee came with one specific vocational objective in mind. Furthermore, he had formulated an educational plan. The counseling process generally involved merely approving a clear-cut plan.
2. The counselee had one definite goal but was not decided on the type and amount of training.
3. The counselee had interests in two or more specific vocations.
4. The counselee had an interest in one or more general kinds of work, such as agriculture, mechanics, clerical; or in one or more specific objectives plus one or more general fields.
5. a. The counselee had no specific or general vocational interests—"The tests would tell him what to be."
   b. The counselee had formulated definite vocational and educational plans but they were inconsistent with the individual's characteristics.
   c. The counselee displayed symptoms (physical and/or psychological) which indicated he needed therapy beyond vocational counseling.[2]

The distribution of the types of problems according to Nelson is presented in Table 6.

This list of problems conforms in general with the types of problems found in a larger sampling of non-veteran, non-disabled individuals preponderantly between the age groups of 16–25, and re-

[2] *Journal of Clinical Psychology,* 3:255(1946).

TABLE 6

TYPES OF COUNSELING PROBLEMS ACCORDING TO NELSON (15)*

Type	Frequency	Percentage
1. One specific vocational objective	39	19.5
2. One objective but undecided about training	46	23.0
3. Two or more specific vocations	31	15.5
4. One or more general kinds of work or one or more specific objectives plus one or more general fields	32	16.0
5. No specific or general objective or goals inconsistent with individual's characteristics or needed therapy beyond vocational counseling	52	26.0
TOTAL	200	100.0

* *Journal of Clinical Psychology*, 3:255(1947).

ported by Culbert and Smith (9). They list the following types of problems as seen by the counselors:

1. Needs information on entering or training for specific vocation.
2. Needs advice on securing or preparing for immediate work.
3. Needs advice on planning further training or work for the following reasons:
   a. Has no plans.
   b. Needs help in choosing between plans.
   c. Needs confirmation of plan.
   d. Needs change in plan because preparation, abilities or interests not suited to present plan.
   e. Change in plan necessary because of change in circumstances.
   f. Unadjustment in present employment.
   g. Unadjustment in present training program.
   h. Other.
4. Needs financial aid for training. (This problem would not occur in disabled veterans because of government grants for training.)
5. Vocational problem complicated by personality factors.
6. Other.[3]

The evidence clearly indicates that there is an interrelation between personal and vocational counseling. Depending upon the type

[3] J. F. Culbert and H. R. Smith, *Counseling Young Workers*. New York: Vocational Service for Juniors, 1939, page 188.

of agency or the age of the population, the incidence of multiple problems varies.

Methods of interviewing

Despite the fact that interviewing is an old technique in vocational counseling, study of its methods and evaluation is recent. The impetus to the study of the vocational interview was given largely by Carl Rogers (17) in 1942, when he published his book *Counseling and Psychotherapy*. The vocational counselor, generally untrained in the science of psychology and limited in his knowledge of and experience in clinical psychology, was probably aware of the general conduct of the interview but did not consciously formulate the merits or limitations of any specific interviewing technique for different kinds of problems. Jaqua (11) remarked, in the introduction to the manual *The Training of Vocational Counselors:*

> Perhaps it should be added that running through all the deliberations and recommendations of the Advisory Committee was the hope that something might be done to elevate the profession of Counseling, to lift it from the plane of random advising, which anyone can do who is "fond of people," into the realm of an exacting professional task requiring expert training and mature judgment.[4]

This training program includes instruction in personality adjustments and techniques of vocational interviewing as well as the more standard fields of occupational information, training opportunities, labor problems, and tests and measurement. It demonstrates the need of vocational counselors for more thorough training. However, the present writers believe that even more emphasis should be placed on interviewing techniques, especially as they apply to different kinds of problems. It has been reported previously that at least 25 per cent of those who come for vocational counseling have personal problems.

The kinds of vocational interviewing in use can be distinguished as authoritarian, non-directive, and non-authoritarian. The authoritarian is counselor-centered; the non-directive is client-centered; the

---

[4] E. J. Jaqua, *The Training of Vocational Counselors.* Washington, D.C.: Bureau of Training, War Manpower Commission, 1944, page 3.

non-authoritarian is mainly client-centered, but may occasionally shift when necessary.

The authoritarian type of interview submerges the client and his problems and elevates the interviewer to the level of authority. He is the expert. The non-directive type of interview swings the pendulum to the other extreme. Here the client "runs the show" and the interviewing method is rigidly prescribed.

In between is the type of interview we prefer to call non-authoritarian. It rejects the authoritarian role and yet allows for freedom in the choice of interviewing techniques which may be judged by the counselor as suitable to the client and his problems.

Authoritarian interviewing. The authoritarian interview evolved without scientific formulation and appraisal. It is simplest to conduct since it has no generally accepted rules. It allows anyone to conduct an interview as long as he "knows" what is best. Those who conduct such interviews have the necessary skills by their own evaluation. It dates from the era when having a fondness for people was the major prerequisite for a counselor. The interview usually consists of obtaining work and educational history from a client and giving information about jobs or training in return. Psychological tests are very frequently given by a psychologist who reports the results to the counselor. The results are then used by the counselor to give advice about jobs. The advice frequently does not allow for discussion, and the client, in altogether too many instances, does not have the opportunity to bring in other needs fully enough. Authoritarian interviewing is completely directed by the counselor.

The case of Edward illustrates how it can easily fail. Edward was 18 years old and the oldest of three children. He had completed three years of an academic high school course during the day and at the time of counseling was attending school in the evening to obtain his diploma. He had worked on any job he could find to help his parents financially. His father was sick and could work only a few days a week. He was wondering about his vocational future and so came to a vocational counselor.

The vocational counselor gave him a battery of tests including aptitude, personality, and interest measures. Edward had thought he might like selling and had wanted to discuss this matter among others. He was told by the counselor, however, that he did not have the personality for selling. He was advised to go into other kinds of work and was given information about the job requirements, as well as other items. Some of these jobs were on a professional level, requiring college, but the college question with its ramifications was not discussed. Edward had no opportunity to really express himself and analyze all the possibilities from his own point of view.

Edward did not follow any of the advice or take advantage of any of the information. He was seen sometime later by one of the authors and after a series of non-authoritarian interviews decided to try his hand at selling. Follow-up demonstrated that he was selling effectively enough to have remained on a job for a year and to have earned a substantial salary.

Lipsett and Smith (13) report a follow-up of 200 disabled veteran clients six months after completion of advisement. They found that of the 200 clients, 148 had their own vocational objectives confirmed by advisement and 52 had their objectives significantly changed by advisement.

Of the 148 whose vocational objectives were confirmed, 68 per cent were continuing in their objectives, whereas of the 52 whose vocational objectives were significantly changed, only 37 per cent were continuing in their changed objectives. Lipsett and Smith state that "The relatively large number of veterans who changed objectives for no reason which is apparent in the records (listed as 'change of interests') suggests that if there is any means of reducing this number, it might be through a more searching interview."

Although the method of interviewing is not described, it appears to have been similar to the authoritarian type of interview. Further attention to the interviewing method should have been given in the handling of these cases. Then "more searching interviews" would not have been necessary and the real motivation for changing objectives would have been known. As long as the client has an objective that is practical and the counselor recognizes it, authoritarian interviewing will not be too harmful. It is when a client's objective needs change or when the authoritarian interviewer believes this to be true that the shallowness of authoritarian interviewing is revealed. Under these circumstances it can be harmful to the client.

Corsini (7) conducted vocational counseling with male prisoners using

> . . . free interviewing following an examination of the criminal-social record, the testing of various psychological areas, and the final integration of all elements in a summary to the subject.[5]

A negligible percentage of the men followed the advice. In interviewing the men as to why, after gaining their cooperation, they said:

> . . . they weren't convinced of the value of the advice, or it was spring, or it was summer, fall or winter, or the programs were too strenuous, or sacrifices would have to be made, etc.[6]

As a result of the lack of success in this method of interviewing, Corsini then introduced a non-directive type of interviewing and he described the results as "far better." However, according to Rogers (7) the method used was not truly non-directive. In a discussion of Corsini's paper, Rogers writes:

> It would seem accurate to call Mr. Corsini's new approach "less directive" rather than "non-directive." The counselor still selects and administers tests and gives the results willy-nilly to the client. It is only then that he becomes non-directive. In other words Mr. Corsini, like many other clinical workers, has discovered that his results are better if he is less directive, but he has hesitated to go the full way and actually place his professional reliance upon the client as the vital force in counseling.[7]

What Corsini did was to become more aware of the emotionalized attitudes, and by responding to them, create better rapport and eventually help the individual gain more insight. This responding to the client's emotions and feelings is a key to successful interviewing. Unfortunately, the authoritarian type of interviewer never really recognizes this. One of the reasons for the delay in understanding the principle has been the assumption that people who come for vocational counseling are not under emotional stress and that they are quite cap-

[5] *Journal of Clinical Psychology*, 3:96(1947).
[6] *Ibid.*, page 97.
[7] *Ibid.*, page 100.

able of moving forward on their own when their vocational direction is clarified.

Non-directive interviewing. The non-directive interview is essentially a client-centered interview. The technique was formulated by Carl Rogers as an outgrowth of his experiences in personal counseling. It is based on the theory that the individual has the capacity and drive to grow and develop so that he can meet the conditions found in reality. Therefore the counselor is most passive. The individual is fully accepted for what he is; he is free to express any attitude. The counselee-counselor relationship permits any client-expression except, of course, destruction of objects or violence toward the counselor.

The non-directive interview is not as deep as the psychoanalytic type. It permits the client to express present attitudes. It allows for the reflection and clarification of the client's feelings. There is no attempt to explain why the client has the present attitudes, no probing into the past, no suggestions, no persuasion, no attempts at re-education or changing environment. Rogers is closest to Rank, an unorthodox analyst, who emphasized the client-centered relationship and renounced the past for the present. However, Rank used interpretation in his counseling and did not abandon completely all counselor direction.

Rogers (18) describes six conditions which will aid the expression of the growth forces within the individual:

1. If the counselor operates on the principle that the individual is basically responsible for himself, and is willing for the individual to keep that responsibility.
2. If the counselor operates on the principle that the client has a strong desire to become mature, socially adjusted, independent and productive, and relies on this force, not on his own powers, for therapeutic change.
3. If the counselor creates a warm and permissive atmosphere in which the individual is free to bring out any attitudes and feelings which he may have, no matter how unconventional, absurd, or contradictory, these attitudes may be. The client is as free to withhold expression as he is to give expression to his feelings.
4. If the limits which are set are simple limits set on behavior, and

not limits set on attitudes. (This applies mostly in children. The child may not be permitted to break a window, or leave the room, but he is free to feel like breaking a window, and the feeling is fully accepted. The adult client may not be permitted more than an hour for the interview, but there is full acceptance of his desire to claim more time.)

5. If the therapist uses only those procedures and techniques in the interview which convey his deep understanding of the emotionalized attitudes expressed and his acceptance of them. This understanding is perhaps best conveyed by a sensitive reflection and clarification of the client's attitudes. The counselor's acceptance involves neither approval nor disapproval.
6. If the counselor refrains from any expression or action which is contrary to the preceding principles. This means refraining from questioning, probing, blame, interpretation, advice, suggestion, persuasion or reassurance.[8]

To illustrate the non-directive interview, a brief excerpt of one of Rogers' records is presented (19). This is excerpted from the third interview with an attractive young lady, Mary Jane Tilden (fictitious name), 20 years old. Mary was referred for counseling by her mother because she slept all the time, was afraid of people's opinions about her and often feared insanity. The interview is annotated to describe the specific conditions in the non-directive technique. The case was phonographically recorded.

S. 57[9] That's right. (*agreement*) (*Long pause*) Well, in the first place, if I were to take a job right now, I don't think that it would be fair to the employer, I mean, I really don't think it would be—when I'm in a rut like this. (*Problem—negative attitude toward self*) The point is, am I just raising that as a defense mechanism for not getting out? Or am I really thinking that it just wouldn't be fair. That's an important question to me. (*Insight—ambivalent toward self*).

C. 58[9] You feel that it wouldn't be fair, and at the same time there arises in your mind a question, are you just putting that up to keep from undertaking what would be a hard thing to do. (*Clarification of feeling*).

---

[8] Reprinted from *The American Psychologist*, 1:416(1946), by permission of the American Psychological Association, publishers.

[9] S. 57 signifies subject's 57th statement; C. 58, the counselor's 58th statement. S. 58 and C. 59, subject's and counselor's 58th and 59th statements, respectively, and so on.

S. 58 That's right. (*agreement*) (*Pause, laughs*) You shake your head. Is that all? (*asking for information*).

C. 59 You feel perhaps I should know the answers then. (*Clarification of feeling*).

S. 59 That's right. (*agreement*) Is it fair to an employer to go out and take a job that you feel, well, it may help you but it may not do very much for him? (*pause*) Is it justifiable? (*asking for information*).

C. 60 You feel you might really be cheating the employer by doing that? (*clarification of feeling*).

S. 60 That's right. I've said that before. I know we've covered that once before. Uhuh. (*agreement*) (*long pause, laughs*) Well, what's the answer? Am I supposed to get the answers? (*Asking for information–negative attitude toward counselor*).

C. 61 You are wondering that, too, aren't you, whether maybe the answer is in you? (*clarification of feeling*)

S. 61 In other words, I'd have to make a radical change before I–I'm supposed to change in attitude, and change in everything. (*Insight*)[10]

Clarification of feeling helped Mary achieve some insight. She goes on to speak about how work would affect her. She feels it would force her to do something, but that it would also bring up many other problems. She also speaks again of the problem of finding the answers in books. She feels that most of the ideas in the books are not much related to her individual situation; that if she does find an idea she likes, she does not know what to do with it.

This was a rather difficult counseling case. Rogers was doubtful about the outcome after eleven interviews. The young lady had a resurgence of some of her old feelings after a year had elapsed since counseling. Rogers stated (19), "It will be seen that the evaluation of the final outcome in this case remains somewhat in doubt. There can be no question that the eleven counseling hours were followed by a period of improved adjustment. Whether the recent regression is temporary remains to be seen."[11]

Both Covner (8) and Combs (6) have used the non-directive tech-

[10] From *Casebook of Non-Directive Counseling* by William U. Snyder, copyright 1947. Reprinted by permission of and arrangement with Houghton Mifflin Company, the authorized publishers.

[11] *Ibid.*

nique in vocational counseling and report that it can successfully reach clients who have combinations of emotional and vocational problems.

The method of non-directive interviewing is rather rigidly prescribed. The lack of flexibility permitted an interviewer is a shortcoming of this method, especially in relation to certain types of problems. A case described by Robinson (16) illustrates a shortcoming and at the same time demonstrates the need for flexibility of method. He cites the example of a client, who "after discussing various problem areas decides he wants to work on remedying a study skill difficulty."[12] In this instance the non-directive technique has made the client aware of his difficulty but does not permit direction toward remedying it. As Robinson states, "For instance, in such a situation a counselor response of, 'You feel that you need help in improving your reading rate' leads the conference toward a consideration of *why* he wants to improve his reading and not toward its actual improvement."[13] The problem is now understood but the client still has his reading difficulty.

Non-authoritarian interviewing. The term non-authoritarian is used to encompass those techniques which are neither authoritarian nor rigidly non-directive. The non-authoritarian interviewer may be regarded as an authority by the client but does not act as an authoritarian. He is attentive to the feelings and attitudes of the client and may use a variety of techniques during the interviews.

Those who use non-authoritarian techniques are at times client-centered, but they are not rigidly bound to only this frame of reference. There is an attempt to adapt such techniques as seem effective at the time. Many techniques should be known by the counselor so that he is fully prepared to help with any problem whether it is a simple vocational, or a more complex personal problem. Thus non-authoritarian interviewing will make use of the techniques of suggestion, persuasion, and advice; reassurance; interpretation; giving information; and manipulation of the environment. These techniques will be described.

---

[12] *Journal of Clinical Psychology,* 2:368(1946).
[13] *Loc. cit.*

Suggestion, persuasion, and advice. These three techniques are grouped because they are similar. In all three the individual is being influenced more or less indirectly by the interviewer. Suggestion implies less forcefulness than persuasion. Persuasion may start as suggestion, with the suggestions taking on the flavor of persuasion as they are reiterated and more definitely expressed. A suggestion may be, "Perhaps this is a good idea." The statement may be made in such a way as to be an instance of persuasion, such as, "You'd rather do that, you know." Advice is inherent in both suggestion and persuasion. In both, the counselor is more or less subtly trying to get the client to see a point or act in a certain way.

These techniques have been widely used, but often abused. Suggestion, persuasion, and advice tend to be ineffectual if given without understanding the needs of the individual and before good rapport has been established. They must be in accord with actions already contemplated or attitudes felt, even if vaguely. Thorne (22) in writing about suggestion, persuasion, and advice, states that "clinical experience indicated the superiority of a quiet, tactful, indirect approach which does not stimulate interpersonal tensions."[14] He gives examples of acceptable and unacceptable approaches, which fit the experience of the authors of this text. They apply to most situations in which there is an attempt made to influence the client either through suggestion, persuasion or advice.

Acceptable

"Another way of looking at it might be ______________."
"What would you think of ______________."
"You feel that is the only solution of the problem."
"Perhaps you would like to know the latest psychological (medical) theories on this point."
"I wonder what the smartest way of doing it might be."
"How would you like to ______________?"

Unacceptable

"I think that you should ______________."
"The only thing for you to do is ______________."
"I'm going to tell you what to do."

[14] *Journal of Clinical Psychology,* 4:74 (1948).

"There's only one right way to do it."
"I want you to do this ____________."
"There is a better way to do ____________."
"There is only one smart way to do this."
"If you don't do this, you'll be sorry."[15]

Reassurance. Reassurance is another technique that, if used properly, can serve many clients. An individual client may be very much in doubt and concerned about whether or not he can make good in a certain kind of work. The basis for his attitudes may be known, but he may still feel the need for reassurance. Reassurance must not be theoretical or hypothetical. There must be some real concrete evidence. Andrews (2) regards reassurance as perhaps the simplest of counseling and therapeutic techniques, but one that has often been misused. She states that reassurance "is most effective when it involves a factual presentation rather than expressions of opinion or mere consoling terms."[16] As an example Andrews presents the case of F. R.:

> F. R. is a 21 year old college senior whose academic career has been marked by extreme variations in grades and achievement. Although scoring an I. Q. of 145, his high school record was extremely spotty with grades ranging from failures in languages to almost perfect in mathematics. He barely passed the work of the first college year and failed 4 out of 5 subjects the first semester of the second college year. Without benefit of outside counseling, his marks jumped to honor levels during the 3rd and 4th years and he went on to become a promising graduate student.
>
> Up until the 3rd college year, F. R. had never really tasted success. Never really happy because of poor physical development and an unprepossessing appearance, he had gone along without ever developing adequate motivation and frequently so tied up in his own conflicts as to be unable to devote proper attention to school work.
>
> The turning point in his academic career came when a sociology instructor became interested in him and indicated his belief that F. R. was a potentially brilliant student. F. R. was so stimulated by this surprising evaluation that he extended himself to do excellent work and secured an A grade for the first time in his college career.[17]

[15] *Loc. cit.*
[16] *Journal of Clinical Psychology*, 1:55(1945).
[17] *Ibid.*, page 60.

This young man was burdened with feelings of inadequacy. Reassurance seemed to help motivate him. However, it must be remembered that mere reassurance given by just anyone or without any real factual basis will probably not be helpful.

Interpretation. Interpretation is a powerful tool provided it is used very skillfully and with perfect timing. It is widely used in counseling and therapy, but too often without proper training and skill on the part of the counselor. It is the method of integrating present attitudes and past experiences. The memories of the past experiences are largely unconscious, but they influence present attitudes and behavior. They must be brought to consciousness in order that the problems may be fully understood.

A client, Nancy, was confused about whether to accept an offered position and give up school or continue with school and take a chance on finding a position after graduation some six months later. She thought she could handle the available position well, and that it was in accord with her abilities and interests. But she stated she had doubts that the position really was all she thought it would be.

It developed during the interview that the available position was held by a close friend of hers who was resigning to get married. The friend had recommended Nancy. Nancy thought this act on the part of her friend was most generous. But she was hesitant about taking the position, even after a successful interview with the employer. Although basically well adjusted, Nancy unconsciously felt competition with her friend and was afraid she would not do as well and so suffer injury to her ego. There was some unconscious rivalry between them. Through interpretation Nancy understood her feelings of rivalry toward her friend and they were related to her attitude toward the available position. After this, Nancy was able to make up her mind without hesitation. She decided to undertake the work and complete the remaining six months of schooling in the evening.

It must not be assumed that immediately after interpretation, the way is clear for quick decision and success. Many new resistances can develop. This was not so in the case of Nancy because her problem was simple and she was well adjusted. Many more complex problems require skillful interpretations as growth and progress are made.

Information. In the non-authoritarian interview, the interviewer seeks information from the client and in turn is prepared to give two kinds of information. To obtain information, the counselor begins by allowing the client to discuss himself in relation to the way in which he sees his problem. Most useful information will be expressed in this way, and it is not necessary to ask the client directly for specific information. After the matters under discussion are well along and good relationship has been established between the client and counselor, specific questions may be asked when they are necessary to further the understanding of the nature of the problem.

The two kinds of information most often given during these interviews can be called vocational and psychological. Giving occupational information as well as educational information is a significant part of counseling. Very often clients need information about job requirements and opportunities, steps to take in job-seeking, or schools to attend. Information is most useful after the individual being interviewed has weighed his needs, expressed his attitudes toward various goals, and is ready to take some action. The information supplied will then be discussed in relation to how to satisfy the needs, and some decision will be made. A caution must be exercised in seeing that supplying educational or occupational information does not occur before the client is able to utilize and integrate it. Otherwise there is little chance that the client will be able to accept it, and his decision may not be stable.

Psychological information refers to explanations of motivation, attitude formation, setting values, and other similar matters. After a client has some understanding of the nature of his problems, he sometimes wants to know how to help himself. At this point, non-authoritarian counselors give information to their clients on such matters.

An illustration of the use of psychological information is offered by the case of John F. He was a high school senior and determined to enter college to study engineering. His school counselor tried unsuccessfully to counsel him away from this goal. John had a difficult time with mathematics, having failed it twice and barely passing the subject all other times. His grades in science were mediocre.

His father was a skilled mechanic who brought John up to be "one of those engineers." To John's father, the engineer was the "big man" and embodied all the virtues he would have wanted for himself.

John had been taught to set a high value on the position of engineer. In the process of growing, he developed an attitude toward engineers that was enmeshed with his being accepted or rejected by his father; reaching the goal meant acceptance, failing to reach it meant rejection.

It was difficult for John to come to grips with his real problem. However, after several interviews, he achieved insight. But he was anxious about whether his father would accept this decision. He wanted more information about how the process of setting values on jobs worked, both to make it clearer to himself as well as to be better able to explain it to his father. At this point, the necessary psychological information was given with examples from John's own experiences as gathered from previous interviews.

Manipulation of the environment. This is a technique that is often found to be necessary in counseling, personal as well as vocational. By manipulation of the environment is meant helping the individual to effect a change in his environment that will allow him to develop more freely and in accord with his abilities and interests. There are instances when a client, ready in all other ways, for college or a special course, needs funds. Loans or scholarships are in order and part of good counseling. Because of financial difficulties, there have been instances of anxiety attacks resulting in a strong impulse to change an otherwise satisfactory position. Sometimes it is necessary to interview parents, wives, or husbands to improve the environment of a client. If John had not been able to work through his relationship with his father, an interview with the father would have been in order.

The type of interviewing we have preferred to call non-authoritarian is characterized by flexibility of method. It recognizes that different problems can more readily be solved by different interviewing techniques.

Non-authoritarian interviewing resembles rather closely the type of interviewing referred to by Thorne (23) as "directive psychotherapy." He too calls for flexibility. Thorne reports: "Directive psychotherapy requires that the therapist will be trained and able to make use of every known method in his field as indication may arise."[18] He believes that clarification of the client's feelings does not

[18] Reprinted from *The American Psychologist,* 3:165(1948), by permission of the American Psychological Association, publishers.

complete the interviewing process. Thorne (21) writes, "After having recognized and clarified feelings and conflicts, it is usually necessary to go beyond the stage of understanding and to elaborate a constructive plan for future action."[19] This implies that the individual may not be able to work out a constructive plan for himself.

Williamson (24) describes the function of the counselors at the University of Minnesota "as somewhat similar but not identical to that of the classroom teacher who participates in the learning process, not by dominating either teaching or learning but rather by contributing significant items of information and suggestions which are then reviewed and evaluated by the student-counselee and accepted or rejected by that same counselee."[20]

Some indirect evidence on the desirability of flexible interviewing technique is offered by psychoanalysis. Alexander and French (1) write:

> In addition to the original decision as to the particular sort of strategy to be employed in the treatment of any case, we recommend the conscious use of various techniques in a flexible manner, shifting tactics to fit the particular needs of the moment. Among these modifications of the standard techniques are: using not only the method of free association but interviews of a more direct character, manipulating the frequency of the interview, giving directives to the patient concerning his daily life, employing interruptions of long or short duration in preparation for ending the treatment, regulating the transference relationship to meet the specific needs of the case, and making use of real-life experiences as an integral part of the therapy.[21]

Evaluating interview methods

The authors have shown a distinct preference for the non-authoritarian type of interview. It must be admitted that exponents of other interviewing methods are equally enthusiastic. The time must come

---

[19] *Journal of Clinical Psychology*, 2:182(1946).

[20] *Educational and Psychological Measurement*, 7:149 (American College Personnel Association Supplement, 1947).

[21] Franz Alexander and Thomas Morton French, *Psychoanalytic Therapy*. Copyright 1946 by The Ronald Press Company.

when self-evaluation and personal preference can no longer be the means of determining the most effective method of conducting an interview. The interview must be subjected to rigorous scientific tests and this demands the use of the experimental method. Many difficulties are present in the attempt to evaluate the efficiency of an individual technique. Strang (20) lists six conditions that must be considered before thorough evaluation is possible:

1. Comparable groups, one serving as a control. Otherwise we do not know whether the therapy is more effective than a good school or hospital environment alone would have been. But equating groups with respect to variables that may influence the results of treatment is a difficult task. For example, groups should be equated with respect to (a) their initial capacity for adjustment, (b) the kind, intensity, and pervasiveness of the maladjustment, (c) the appropriateness of the therapy for the individual, (d) the therapeutic values of the environment, including work experience, to which they return after treatment.
2. Standard means of describing research populations and their potentialities for clinical improvement.
3. Scientific basis for ascertaining the significance of the individual's responses to standardized and to real-life situations.
4. Standard means of determining the degree of clinical improvement.
5. Sufficient number of cases to warrant generalizations.
6. Follow-up for a sufficiently long time to ascertain delayed effects of treatment.[22]

A step in the right direction has been taken in an excellent study by Keet (12). It is the first attempt to evaluate by experiment the effects of two interviewing techniques, the expressive and the interpretive. The expressive technique resembles rather closely the non-directive and the interpretive resembles the technique we refer to as non-authoritarian. In this technique the method shifts and the interviewer may be passive when free expression is desirable and more active when interpretation is deemed necessary. The expressive technique limits itself to one method.

Keet had 30 normal subjects in the experiment. They were given a word association test to discover areas of emotional disturbance. Then

[22] *Journal of Clinical Psychology*, 3:182–183 (1947).

an ingenious learning situation was established which included neutral words as well as the word associated with the disturbance, the traumatic word. The subjects were to recall the words and it was expected that they would not recall the traumatic word. Five subjects actually did and so were not included in the remainder of the experiment. The next step was to use one of the two interviewing techniques to help the subject recall the traumatic word. For this purpose the subjects were divided into two groups, one of 13 and the other of 12. Keet used the expressive technique with the 13 and the interpretive with the other 12 subjects.

The final step was to check the effect of the techniques. For this purpose, a second learning situation was established which included neutral words and the word given as a reaction to the traumatic. The reaction word would have disturbing associations for the subject which were similar to those for the traumatic word. If the subject recalled the word in this part of the experiment, it would mean that the word no longer had disturbing associations. The interpretive technique succeeded in 11 out of 12 cases, while the expressive did not succeed in any of the 13. This is a very significant finding. This study indicates that variation in technique allowing for interpretation and expression is superior to the single technique of expression.

To be certain that the techniques used were expressive or interpretive, Keet had three qualified judges assess 10 interviews. The agreement of the judges as to which interviews were expressive and which interpretive was excellent. Keet also checked for the differences in age, education, and sex between the two groups and found that these factors could not account for the differences between the effects of the interviewing. Keet reports that the disturbance created in the subjects resembled a compulsion neurosis which, of course, was temporary. It was this condition that yielded to the combination of expressive and interpretive interviewing but not to the expressive alone. This experiment should be repeated using different subjects and a different interviewer. Other methods of experimental attack should be formulated to determine the relative effects of different techniques on different problems.

It is likely that the richest findings in the evaluation of the interview method can come from the use of experimentation.

Summary

The interview is a conversational process through which the client and counselor exchange ideas and attitudes. Its purpose is to lead ultimately to a solution of the client's problems. It must be understood that many people with vocational problems also have personal problems. Personal and vocational counseling are interrelated.

The interview may be understood in one of two frames of reference: the client-centered and the counselor-centered. We have categorized the interviewing methods into three types: the authoritarian, the non-directive, and the non-authoritarian. The authoritarian is always counselor-centered. The non-directive is always client-centered. In it the counselor is passive and tries to establish a permissive and warm atmosphere that will allow the client freedom of expression. The counselor reflects and clarifies the client's feelings.

The non-authoritarian interview is generally client-centered but not always passive. In it the counselor is flexible and will shift to directive when necessary. He will use various techniques such as suggestion, persuasion, advice, reassurance, interpretation, information, and manipulation of the environment.

We prefer the non-authoritarian but are aware of the need for further research. The experimental method needs to be applied to interviewing techniques. Keet, whose study is the first well-organized experiment with interviewing techniques, found for his group of subjects that a flexible combination of free expression and interpretive techniques was superior to the non-directive used alone. Other experiments are necessary with different groups and under different conditions.

Bibliography

1. Alexander, F., and T. M. French, *Psychoanalytic Therapy—Principles and Applications.* New York: Ronald Press, 1946.
2. Andrews, J. S., "Directive Psychotherapy: I. Reassurance," *Journal of Clinical Psychology,* 1:52–66 (1945).
3. Bailey, H. W., W. M. Gilbert, and I. A. Berg, "Counseling and the Use of Tests in the Student Personnel Bureau at the University of Illinois," *Educational and Psychological Measurement,* 6:37–60 (1946).

4. Bixler, R. H., and V. H. Bixler, "Clinical Counseling in Vocational Guidance," *Journal of Clinical Psychology,* 1:186–192 (1945).
5. Blocksma, D. D., and E. H. Porter, "A Short-Term Training Program in Client-centered Counseling," *Journal of Consulting Psychology,* 11:55–60 (1947).
6. Combs, A. W., "Nondirective Techniques and Vocational Counseling," *Occupations,* 25:261–267 (1947).
7. Corsini, R. J., "Non-directive Vocational Counseling of Prison Inmates," *Journal of Clinical Psychology,* 3:96–100 (1947).
8. Covner, B. J., "Nondirective Interviewing Techniques in Vocational Counseling," *Journal of Consulting Psychology,* 11:70–73 (1947).
9. Culbert, J. F., and H. R. Smith, *Counseling Young Workers.* New York: Vocational Service for Juniors, 1939.
10. Hahn, M. E., and W. E. Kendall, "Some Comments in Defense of Non-directive Counseling," *Journal of Consulting Psychology,* 11:74–81 (1947).
11. Jaqua, E. J., *The Training of Vocational Counselors.* Washington, D.C.: Bureau of Training, War Manpower Commission, 1944.
12. Keet, C. D., "Two Verbal Techniques in a Miniature Counseling Situation," *Psychological Monographs: General and Applied,* 62:1–55 (1948).
13. Lipsett, L., and L. F. Smith, "The Rochester Veteran's Guidance Center Takes Stock," *The American Psychologist,* 3:12–15 (1948).
14. Murray, E., Editorial Comments, *Occupations,* 27:404–405 (1949).
15. Nelson, A. G., "Types of Vocational Counseling Problems: A Study of 200 Disabled Male Veterans," *Journal of Clinical Psychology,* 3:252–256 (1947).
16. Robinson, F. P., "Are Non-directive Techniques Sometimes Too Directive?" *Journal of Clinical Psychology,* 2:368–371 (1946).
17. Rogers, C. R., *Counseling and Psychotherapy.* Boston: Houghton Mifflin, 1942.
18. ———, "Significant Aspects of Client-centered Therapy," *The American Psychologist,* 1:415–422 (1946).
19. Snyder, W. U., *Casebook of Nondirective Counseling.* Boston: Houghton Mifflin, 1947.
20. Strang, R., "Criteria of Progress in Counseling and Psychotherapy," *Journal of Clinical Psychology,* 3:180–183 (1947).
21. Thorne, F. C., "Directive Psychotherapy: VII. Imparting Psycho-

logical Information," *Journal of Clinical Psychology,* 2:179–190 (1946).

22. ——— "Directive Psychotherapy: XIV. Suggestion, Persuasion and Advice," *Journal of Clinical Psychology,* 4:70–82 (1948).
23. ——— "Principles of Directive Counseling and Psychotherapy," *The American Psychologist,* 3:160–165 (1948).
24. Williamson, E. G., "Counseling and the Minnesota Point of View," *Educational and Psychological Measurement,* 7:141–155 (American College Personnel Association Supplement, 1947).

5

THE COUNSELING INTERVIEW —SPECIFIC

ALTHOUGH THERE will be variations in individual cases, there are characteristic general principles which may serve as a conceptual schema for the interview as well as offer some rules for its conduct. These principles are extracted from the recommendations of Roethlisberger and Dickson (2) as well as from Rogers (3), Bingham and Moore (1), and our own experiences. They are listed below and will be followed by descriptive elaborations of each of the principles.

General principles

1. Establish and maintain rapport.
2. Let the client talk freely.
3. Do not criticize.
4. Do not argue with the client.
5. Serve as an understanding listener, not as an authoritarian.
6. Have the client understand his emotional needs.
7. Treat what is being said in its context.
8. Be aware of different values or feeling-tones on the subjects expressed.
9. Be aware of what the client omits or tries to say but cannot.
10. Talk or ask questions only at appropriate times:

a. When the client seems to want to say something but finds it hard to do so.

b. When fear and anxiety are interfering with the interview relationship.

c. To direct the interview toward an omitted or incompletely discussed topic.

d. To clarify, interpret or explain a matter only implicitly assumed.

e. To give approval.

1. *Establish and maintain rapport.* Rapport is basically essential to the success of any interview. It is the feeling of mutual confidence and trust without which the client will not truly and freely express his attitudes and thinking and, in consequence, will gain nothing by continuing the interviews. Rapport, once established, must also be maintained. Its maintenance is dependent upon what the interviewer does during the subsequent interviews. The interviewer must not only be accepting and understanding but give continuous evidence by what he says and does of being able to help the client. Following the rest of the principles will aid in maintaining rapport. The interviewer must be careful not to foster too dependent a relationship but rather to allow the individual to make decisions for himself. If rapport is properly established and maintained, the client will see himself more clearly through this relationship and be able to plan towards greater development.

2. *Let the client talk freely.* If the client is allowed to talk freely, he will eventually come to the crux of whatever he is concerned about, be it a simple vocational problem, a more complex one, or a personal problem. The client will express himself more freely if he feels confidence in the interviewer. Taking the lead from the client or interrupting him may tend to limit expression and break down any rapport already established. The interviewer must listen patiently and with interest and understanding. He may ask questions in context to facilitate the client's talking. He may ask for further discussion of a topic if he believes that it is important.

3. *Do not criticize.* Psychologists are in general agreement as to the inadvisability of criticizing or moralizing during an interview. Care-

less use of this technique seems to promote guilt feelings. Clients are aware either consciously or unconsciously of their errors and misjudgments. They probably have had enough criticism from members of their families and their friends. If a person states that he believes he has received abuse in all the jobs he had and thinks they were "lousy jobs," he is not to be told that that is the wrong thing to say. Instead, the client should be encouraged to express these feelings, by being asked to speak more about these situations if he does not continue spontaneously. It will be found that sometime after he has made the negative remarks, he will begin to express himself more positively. He may say such things as, "It really wasn't as bad as all that. I liked some of the people."

4. *Do not argue with the client.* Arguing can destroy rapport. It indicates non-acceptance of the individual. It demonstrates lack of understanding on the part of the interviewer of the interviewee's problems. It will cut off free expression by the client. The interviewer should be objective and, even though irritated or annoyed, must be able to control himself. The interviewer should not argue with the client because of a clash in sentiment. Roethlisberger and Dickson (2) state,

> The only way in which the interviewer can guard against having his own sentiments acted upon is not by denying their existence but by admitting and understanding them. Anyone who has had experience in interviewing realizes that often he learns more about himself than about the person being interviewed. Frequently he finds himself becoming irritated and annoyed at what a person is saying. It is not sufficient to brush these moods lightly aside; he must ask himself what sentiments of his own are involved. Otherwise, in a quite unexpected fashion, he may find himself doing and saying things which may evoke the very attitude on the part of the speaker that he is trying to avoid. The interview might then become a battle of opposing sentiments.[1]

Such a battle would, of course, disrupt the counseling process.

5. *Serve as an understanding listener, not an authoritarian.* An understanding listening attitude helps establish and keep rapport. The counselor who acts in an authoritative manner is most frequently not

---

[1] Reprinted by permission of the publishers from Fritz Jules Roethlisberger and William John Dickson, *Management and the Worker,* Cambridge, Mass.; Harvard University Press, 1939.

accepted. Although there is some element of authority in the interviewing relationship, this does not mean that the counselor must be authoritarian. The client must feel accepted and have a sense of self-worth created. The counselor must be aware of any display of authoritarian manner either direct or subtle, so as to guard against it. He should not say, "This is best for you!" "You must mend your ways!" "Other people usually don't think that way," and the like.

6. *Have the client understand his emotional needs.* To have real value for the client, the interview must offer him the opportunity to recognize and clarify his needs. Interviews should not be abstract philosophical discussions unrelated to the needs of the client. Many a client has been dissatisfied with vocational counseling because he really did not have a chance to weigh and clarify his needs. It is necessary to know about the psychological principles of needs in order to function adequately as a counselor.

Needs vary in strength at different times. In the infant the visceral, activity, and sensory needs predominate. Thus the baby wants to be free of hunger and thirst, to be kept comfortably warm, sleep an optimum amount of time, eliminate regularly, and play. Needs, however, become socially structured and personalized as the child grows older and lives in a more complex environment. The visceral, activity, and sensory needs are quite readily satisfied but other needs begin to predominate.

In the adolescent and the adult the socially structured and personalized needs predominate. These needs vary with the social group. In our society the need for achievement and prestige is great. The individual needs to feel accepted as a member of the group. However, these needs are more difficult to satisfy because they may conflict with the needs of others. When a need goes unsatisfied, it sets up strivings and tensions that seek satisfaction. Work is one of the means of providing the satisfaction, either directly or indirectly.

Personal needs vary with the individual's experiences. To illustrate this the case of Anthony F. is cited. Anthony F. was 35 with a college degree in business administration. He had taken a business course at the insistence of his father, whom he described as always pushing him. His father was a government worker in a position of authority and wanted his son to earn a large salary. The father felt that his own work put him in a financial position inferior to that of many of his friends who were in business. The client never went into business, and in fact, never stayed long at a job. He had felt unhappy in every position he had ever held. He had tried his hand at an accounting position but had soon left it because he "could not get the numbers straight." His father had been disdainful of the client's ability with figures while he was in school, often telling him how slow and stupid he was. These unfortunate experiences with figures brought about a distaste for them.

Anthony F. said he felt uneasy, that he was unsure of his status with other people. He would try very hard to please and exhaust himself in meticulousness. When in the Army he took on special burdens. He did not know why precisely, but later felt he did so to reduce his restlessness and to give himself something important to do. Anthony F. needed to feel more important and secure. He needed to build up a greater sense of self-worth. When the client understood his needs, he was able to evaluate his abilities, education, and interests with better judgment. Before this he felt confused, often acted confused. He could now regard himself as more able than he had felt previously and planned a vocational program that was most satisfactory to him and possible of fulfillment. He decided to study law. This field suited his abilities, interests, and personal needs, and turned out successfully.

7. *Treat what is being said in its context.* This principle requires that the interviewer be alert to the latent and truer meaning of what is being said. The manifest or surface meaning is often not correct. The principle also requires that the interviewer let the client speak more, or subtly direct him so that he will ultimately arrive at the latent meaning by recalling those experiences which will throw light upon it.

Roethlisberger and Dickson (2) give an excellent illustration:

> At an afternoon tea in New England, attended by members of both sexes, a woman made a remark to the effect that the English public school system tended to make men brutal. All in the group took sides, some agreeing and some disagreeing with the generalization. A heated and lengthy discussion followed in which the merits and demerits of

the English public school system were thoroughly reviewed. In other words, the statement was taken at its face value and discussed at that level. No one, seemingly, paid attention to the fact that the woman who made the statement had married an Englishman who had received an English public school education and that she was in the process of obtaining a divorce from him. Had it occurred to the others, as it did to one person in the room, that the woman had expressed more clearly her sentiments towards her husband than she had expressed anything equally clear about the English public school system, and that the form in which she expressed her sentiments had reacted on the national and international sentiments of her audience, which they, in turn, had more clearly expressed than anything equally clear about the English public school system, such an idea would have been secretly entertained and not publicly expressed, for that is the nature of polite social intercourse.

But in an interview things are otherwise. Had this statement been made in an interview, the interviewer would not have been misled by the manifest content of the statement. He would have been on the alert for a personal reference, and, once he had learned about the woman's husband, he would have guided the conversation on this topic rather than on the English public school system. Furthermore, he would have been on his guard not to allow any sentiments which he as a social being might entertain toward the English to be acted upon by the form of this statement.[2]

Every statement made in an interview should fit. Why a person likes or dislikes things, why he is more or less interested in different matters can have meaning only in the context of the individual's experiences. The interviewer must pursue the lead until it is clear.

8. *Be aware of different values or feeling-tones on the subjects expressed.* The experiences that an individual has in life result in different degrees of satisfaction or dissatisfaction. These feelings are connected or attached to the objects, people, or events that were part of the experiences, and the kind of feeling attached will color the individual's behavior toward these objects, people, or events. He may prefer certain things, avoid others. He may be scornful, guarded, contemptuous toward some, and be delighted and gay and feel secure toward others. He will value things in different ways and with greater or less degree.

[2] *Ibid.*

If an individual has learned to attach a negative feeling-tone to commercial enterprise, or a mechanical trade, or working in a noisy place, there will generally be a strong tendency to avoid the situations so valued. He will be driven in some other direction, even if he has the abilities and opportunities for work in the area for which he has a negative feeling-tone. Counseling experiences indicate that significance must be attached to feeling-tone. Why does a certain person want so much to go into selling and to avoid anything reminding him of desk work? It is necessary that the counselor recognize why he feels that way and what needs he is to satisfy by his vocational direction.

Needs and feeling-tones are dynamically interrelated. Every individual has the need to feel secure and to have a sense of importance. Those aspects of his experience to which have become attached feeling-tones or values that are negative, ego-destructive, or deflating will be circumvented or avoided. The individual reacts to them as not satisfying his need for security, whether or not he is conscious of the reasons why.

9. *Be aware of what the client omits or tries to say but cannot.* These are crucial matters. They may be the difference between successful and unsuccessful counseling. What is left unsaid is usually more important than what is said. The client's true feelings and attitudes are often contained in what is omitted. If they are left unexpressed the client's decision will not be based on all the data, and will therefore be unstable. Sometimes he will decide on a plan or course of action, only to disregard it later because the unexpressed thoughts and feelings conflict with it.

That which a person wants to talk about but finds difficult to express is also significant. These are usually emotionalized matters, otherwise he would have been able to express them without difficulty. The mere fact that the client finds it hard to discuss a subject often demonstrates its strength and importance. The counselor must not only be aware of this but be able to act in such a way that he can help the person say what he finds difficult to talk about. If, at the moment, the client is too resistant to discussing the subject, it can be brought up at a later time in the same interview or in a later interview where the subject is hinted at again. Often when the client has involved himself more with the counselor and found him understanding and dependable, the client will be more willing to discuss the emotional material.

Roethlisberger and Dickson (2) have written very clearly on this subject.

> Things about which a person does not care to talk are often likely to be connected with unpleasant or painful experiences. There has already been occasion to mention examples of such omissions: the worker who did not want to say *x is black* because that assertion was associated in his mind with the possibility of losing his job, and hence with unpleasant feelings of insecurity; the woman who in a discussion about English public schools failed to mention her husband, with whom unpleasant memories were associated. Such omissions are likely to indicate areas of emotional significance, which, should the opportunity arise, should be explained. These explorations cannot be rushed. The interviewer has to wait for an appropriate time to break into such critical zones. Many times the procedure has to be indirect. Instead of trying to lead the interviewee directly into such critical areas, the interviewer tries to remove the 'resistance,' that is, the fears or doubts which he believes are preventing the interviewee from expressing himself freely. In the case of the previously mentioned worker who is afraid of losing his job, the interviewer does everything to assure the worker that what is said in the interview has no connection with the security of his position. In this way he hopes the interview will be directed into more fruitful channels.
>
> However, most omissions that occur in an interview involve not only things about which the speaker does not wish to talk but also things which lie so implicitly in his thinking that they have not become conscious discriminations. A person may not want to talk about a particular topic and yet he may not be quite clear as to why he refrains. In the case of most omissions, therefore, the interviewer is on the alert for both contexts.
>
> Take, for example, the case of an interviewee who changes the subject of conversation and begins to speculate (aloud, of course) on whether or not a psychologist can handle his personal affairs, and whether or not a psychologist follows the advice he so freely gives to others. In such an instance the uncomplimentary things which the speaker thinks and feels about the interviewer, but which he does not choose to mention directly, are probably clear even to the speaker. But

it is doubtful if the speaker could have stated explicitly the source of his antagonism toward the interviewer.

For the interviewer, therefore, it is important to note what the speaker regards in his own mind as obvious and of such universal application that it has never occurred to him to doubt or question it. By listening carefully to him as he discusses a variety of topics, the interviewer can frequently detect things which underlie what is said but are themselves not expressed. These implicit assumptions are of the greatest importance in assessing a person's ultimate values and significances, for, although they cannot be expressed explicitly by the person, nevertheless for that very reason they enter into the determination of his everyday judgments and thoughts.[3]

10. *Talk or ask questions only at appropriate times:* a. *When the client seems to want to say something but finds it hard to do so.* Under this condition it is advisable to ask questions. It is better to wait several seconds or even minutes before asking a question, to give the person the opportunity to say spontaneously what he wants to say. If he seems to want to speak but needs help, then questions such as, "Would you tell more about it?" or simply, "Why?" are appropriate to ask. Sometimes, when the person is speaking more in terms of generalizations and then blocks upon trying to relate the generalization to a concrete example from his own experiences, it is good technique to encourage him by saying, "Go ahead," or, "Tell about the examples."

b. *When fear and anxiety are interfering with the interview relationship.* It is occasionally found that a client is fearful or anxious about the confidential aspects of the interview. He wants to be sure that all that he is going to say will not be held against him or harm him. In these instances it is necessary to structure the interview relationship to allay this fear or anxiety. Explanations of the nature of the relationship and reassurance in words as well as manner will reduce the anxiety.

Most frequently the reassurances and explanations given at the beginning are sufficient. But there are clients to whom it is necessary to give reassurance frequently during the course of an interview and perhaps over several interviews. As a particularly anxious client speaks more about his real difficulties, he may want to break off the

[3] *Ibid.*

relationship. Or, as happens occasionally, a client who is somewhat depressed as a result of anxiety and has low regard for himself may feel that he is not meeting what he believes to be the interviewer's standards for him and will break off his contacts. He may need explanations of this tendency on his part and reassurance and approval for gains in insight and behavior.

c. *To direct the interview toward an omitted or incompletely discussed topic.* There will be topics that need fuller discussion in order for the client to see more clearly the origins as well as the interrelationships of his present feelings and behavior. The skilled interviewer can discern which topics to develop further or which to go into anew. Where there are resistances against speaking about something, this is usually omitted or just touched upon. This resistance serves as a clue to which the interviewer should return when better rapport has been established. In some instances a client will speak too well of someone or some experience, saying, "Oh, he was good, all right," or, "That really was a healthy experience." He really may not mean it to be so favorable and may make the statements with inappropriate feelings. This also indicates an area into which it will be necessary to probe.

After the client has more understanding, he can more easily return to omitted topics if they are important to speak about at this time. An individual may have come to really know what his problem is, and so be able to discuss aspects of it which he could not see, as has been discussed previously. Thus when the client Anthony F. saw his problem as not being purely vocational, he discussed his personal experiences, especially those related to his father, much more freely. Once he did this, he could return to the vocational problem of discussing his planning for the future much more realistically and rationally.

d. *To clarify, interpret, or explain a matter only implicity assumed.* A matter implicitly assumed is what the interviewer thinks is lurking behind the client's statements, but not explicitly said by him. Much skill is required to detect something of this kind and to know when and how to bring the matter up consciously. The non-directive interviewer would try to have the client speak explicitly by reflecting and clarifying what he said. The non-authoritarian interviewer might employ interpretation or explanation and possibly clarification of feelings. This would depend upon what the interviewer judges to be the strength of rapport, the verbal fluency of the client, and the client's ego strength. The fact that the client does not state the matter explicitly indicates that he is not ready to do so as yet. If the interpretation is made too soon, it will be rejected and rapport may be harmed. Clarification of the stated feeling is safer but may not lead to the implicit assumption if the individual is not verbal and has a weak ego, that is, needs much help and support to think about himself and to make plans that are more possible of fulfillment.

An illustration from our experience demonstrates this. Eleanor said she wanted to change her job. She was 25 and had six years of clerical experience. She said the work fatigued her, and although her boss thought she was a good worker, she feared that eventually she would show herself to be a poor worker. She spoke little about her relationships with other people on the job. But in speaking about the job she would like to have, she stated that she would prefer to work in a small place, alone. She worked better alone. She said that she was happier alone. At this point she blocked, changed the subject, and became tense. It was obvious that there was an implicit assumption for changing the job that was not stated but that was related to social matters. This could not be interpreted at the moment, but after about a minute of silence she spoke about what a fool she was. She was given reassurance and began to talk again of a job away from people. This was reflected. She said nothing but seemed to want to be helped by being asked a question. The counselor then asked indirectly, "Perhaps you had trouble with people and want to be alone now?" She reacted with a flash that that was it and poured a torrent of words about the abuse she had received from some co-workers. This, of course, opened the way to further counseling.

e. *To give approval.* Approval has been found to be valuable in interviewing. Roethlisberger and Dickson recommend its use when the client tries to express himself freely and frankly. Approval helps the individual feel more important. But it must not be given indiscriminately for any sentiment expressed. What the client has regarded as important and what seems important in terms of the total context can be given approval. For instance, if an individual client speaks about how much better he regards certain abilities which he had previously underestimated, this might be met with the statement, "That's fine," or "That's good." Or if he sees himself in a clearer light in respect to meeting issues formerly difficult for him, his insight should be given approval.

Subject matter covered during interview

Certain subject matter should be covered during the course of interviewing. These subjects concern: (1) the problem or reason for coming for counseling, (2) previous work history, (3) educational history, (4) hobbies, avocational and recreational activities, (5) interests, (6) family situation and background, (7) social activities, (8) physical condition, and (9) self-evaluation of appearance, abilities, and personality.

These areas are not to be covered in a systematic, point-by-point manner. Each of the areas, in fact, will be more or less covered depending upon how important it is for the client and his problem. The client will usually show the way and take the lead if the proper atmosphere exists and the counselor is familiar with the interviewing principles previously described. If it is necessary to ask questions about any subject, it is best to start off with a general question such as, "What about your family?", "What do you think about your past jobs?", or "What do you think about your schooling?"

The problem, or reason for seeking counseling, is basic. It can set the tone for the interview. As was discussed earlier in the chapter, the problem presented to the counselor may not be the most important one. People come for counseling for varied reasons; some are referred and come reluctantly, others are referred but do not really know why, and still others come to avoid deeper problems. A good opening to structure the problem situation is, "What did you want to discuss with us?" This throws the responsibility on to the client and sets the stage for his clarifying the reasons why he came.

Previous work history focuses on the past to elucidate future work plans. When the individual discusses his past jobs, he sees them more clearly in perspective, discovers the good and bad about them, determines what he wanted from them and perhaps did not receive. He can talk about his aspirations and goals, about his limitations in realizing them, and about what he needs to do to achieve them. In discussing work history, the client also has the opportunity to discuss his personnel relations, both toward supervision and toward his colleagues. He can discuss the features of the work he liked, was best at, and found congenial. These can be in terms of the work itself and the work conditions, both physical and social.

Educational history includes not only how far the client progressed and what courses he took, but also whether he liked or disliked them. The client can be brought to discuss why he liked some and not others, whether he thinks he took the proper courses, and whether he feels the need for more training and education. He will discuss any extracurricular activities and his attitudes toward them. Another important matter is the relationship with teachers and fellow students.

Hobbies and avocational and recreational activities are an important source of information on interests. They may reflect the kinds of vocations suited for the person. When the client is young and has not yet had any work experiences, they serve as a means through which leads about vocational interests can be obtained. For the person with some work experience, they can add more knowledge about his real interests. The counselor will usually find that the hobbies and avocational and recreational activities form patterns related not only to interests, but even to attitudes toward self and others. In discussing this subject matter, the client can reveal the reasons for his preference for certain activities and talk about how he regards himself as a person.

Interests are ascertained from the various experiences the client has had. In discussing interests the focus is on the possible future vocations. The client is to weigh his experiences in discussing his interests. He is to judge how they relate to his abilities and what the possibilities are for achieving them. In so doing, the client weighs the reality picture against his assessment of himself. Interests may be varied, and they may form a hierarchy. Sometimes the interests are undeveloped in his real occupations, as happens frequently with younger clients. Suggestions based upon knowledge of the person's experiences and attitudes are then in order. If there is conflict between interest and ability, personal counseling is necessary to help the client understand why the conflict exists and to be able to resolve it. It is necessary not only to have the person know his interests clearly but to discuss how they came about and how they can be fulfilled.

The family situation and background cannot be neglected in counseling, vocational or otherwise. Interests are most frequently derived from the family influence. The socio-economic level of the parents, their education, their ambitions, play a very significant role in their children's development. Often this is for the good but sometimes it brings about conflict. In the latter instance, the family interrelationships must be discussed more fully in order to help the client arrive at a stable vocational goal. Finances occasionally come up in discussing the family situation, and this can be a vital factor in vocational adjustment.

Social activities are separated from hobbies and avocational and recreational activities in our listing of subjects to be covered because social activities have different values and standards. They are usually in different settings, although sometimes they are combined with the others. Social activities relate to parties and mixed affairs. A person may manage very well in sports, for example, yet not feel comfortable in a party setting. From discussion of social activities comes information helpful to the client about his relations with people, and this has implications for different kinds of vocations.

Physical condition is concerned not only with actual handicap but also with how the client regards his health, strength, and stamina. It is important not only for the physically handicapped. The individual without any overt handicap may have attitudes toward his health that affect his thinking about vocations. One client may feel he can work all day and study each night to gain his end; another feels that he is not strong enough. A client may use a minor illness as the reason for not continuing as a mechanic and preferring clerical work. This can lead to many complications unless it is discussed and cleared up.

The final category of subject matter serves as a summary for all the preceding points. Self-evaluation of appearance, abilities, and personality indicates how the person regards himself and his possibilities. This self-evaluation should be going on during the interview. The client should ask himself how his capabilities measure up to the vocational possibilities for him. The counselor must be constantly aware of this requirement throughout the interview in order to help the person evaluate himself properly. The self-evaluative features also set the direction for later interviews, showing what aspects need fuller discussion.

In order to highlight the kind of coverage recommended for each of the subject matters, we are listing a series of questions. These questions are not to be asked in order nor are they all necessarily to be asked in an individual instance and in the same manner. They are intended to demonstrate the emphases to make in interviewing on the various subjects.

1. *The problem or reason for coming for counseling*
   What would you like to discuss with us?
   Who referred you? (If had been referred by an agency or school)
   Why do you think you were referred?
   What made you come to this place? (If came on his own)
2. *Previous work history*
   What did you do?
   How did you like the jobs?
   Which did you like best?
   What made you like that one best?
   Which did you like least?
   What made you like it least?
   What did you expect to get out of the work?
   How did you get along with the people?
3. *Educational history*
   What schools did you go to?
   How did you like school?
   What subjects did you like?
   What made you like the subjects?
   What subjects did you dislike?
   What made you dislike them?
   Why did you choose the course?
   What extracurricular activities did you participate in?
   What did you think about the activities?
   What did you think about your fellow-students?

What did you think about your teachers?
What made you leave school? (If left before graduation)

4. *Hobbies and avocational and recreational activities*
   What hobbies do you have?
   What do you think of them?
   How do you think you can use your hobbies vocationally?
   What recreational activities do you have?
   What do you think of them?
   How good are you in them?
5. *Interests*
   What vocational interests do you have?
   What do you think of them?
   How did you get interested in them?
   What do you think about your chances to achieve them?
6. *Family situation and background*
   Are you living with your parents?
   How are things at home?
   What does your mother (father, wife, husband) think about your vocational plans?
7. *Social activities*
   What social activities do you participate in?
   Which do you prefer?
   What makes you prefer them?
   Which don't you like?
   What makes you dislike them?
   How do you feel about your social life?
   Have you ever thought about the relationship between your social activities and work plans?
8. *Physical condition*
   What about your health?
   Do you think you are limited in any way by your physical condition?
9. *Self-evaluation of appearance, abilities, and personality*
   (These questions are put in the third person because information about them is obtained indirectly during the course of the interviews.)
   What impression does he think he makes on others?
   How does he regard himself?
   Does he seem to be confident?
   Does he overrate or underrate himself?
   What does he think of his abilities?
   What does he think of his chances for vocational success?

In covering these areas, the interview should include not only the present but also the past. As many of the client's previous experiences are discussed as will make the present meaningful to the client and help him plan his future intelligently. The counselor should be able to make some estimate of the needs of the individual even during the first interview in order to use the appropriate interviewing techniques. If the counselor is alert to the personality as a dynamic system, he will be able to interview more effectively.

Length of interview

The common practice is to schedule appointments in advance. The time agreed upon is one that will be convenient to both parties, although the client must be able to fit the working hours of the counselor. In authoritarian vocational counseling, there is no specific length of time set on the interview. The first interview is usually the longest and may be as long as one hour. Most information is obtained from the client during the first interview. Succeeding interviews, if any, in authoritarian vocational counseling, are shorter.

In non-authoritarian interviewing, there may or may not be a set length of time, depending upon the counselor and the agency. The tendency, however, is toward a set amount of time; this is usually one hour. The same time may be spent on succeeding interviews. Where no definite length of time has been set, the interview may last as long as one and one half hours as in the Western Electric counseling, and succeeding interviews may take that long if necessary. However, it is not wise to spend too much time in one interview. Fatigue may set in, and it has been found that giving the client the opportunity to let things "sink in" leads to good results. The subsequent interviews can start fresh with new angles and new examples from the client's experiences.

In non-directive interviewing, a specific time length is given the interview. Whether first or last, one hour is allotted. This is the client's hour but he cannot exceed it. The rationale for the specific time comes from psychoanalysis and is to the effect that the client knows the limit and must take the responsibility for making the most of the hour.

Number of interviews

In authoritarian vocational counseling there is usually a single interview when the test results are explained and advice about the vocational objective is given. There is extremely little follow-up. Where the non-authoritarian technique is employed in vocational counseling, the first interview will usually discuss problems in terms of the information given by the client. An appointment for tests may be made at this time. Whether or not tests are given, a second appointment is arranged. Sometimes a case conference between counselor and supervisor precedes the second interview so that they will more fully understand the client and his problems and can decide on how to proceed in the next interview. No set vocational plan results from the conference, but rather a clearer understanding of the possible vocational directions to take.

The second interview then revolves about consideration of vocational plans, taking into account all the subject-matter. As a result of the second interview, the client may take his first step toward implementing the vocational plan decided upon, if one was. Whether or not a plan is decided upon, subsequent interviews are possible. They can be spaced weeks and months apart, depending upon the particular needs of the individual.

Non-directive counseling, like non-authoritarian, allows for several interviews. There will not be the planning of action and more deliberate spacing of interviews. However, the number of interviews can be as many as are needed for the individual to make his own decisions.

Summary

General principles for conducting the interview were described. They follow what we believe to be the best features in non-authoritarian and non-directive interviewing. The usefulness of the practices depends upon the skill of the counselor.

Certain information should be obtained during a vocational interview: work and educational history, hobbies, interests, family situation, social activities, physical condition, and self-evaluation of appearance, abilities, and personality.

The length of each interview and the number of interviews for a client vary.

Bibliography

1. Bingham, W. V., and B. V. Moore, *How to Interview.* New York: Harper, 1941.
2. Roethlisberger, F. J., and W. J. Dickson, *Management and The Worker.* Cambridge, Mass.: Harvard University Press, 1946, esp. Chapter 13.
3. Rogers, C. R., *Counseling and Psychotherapy.* Boston: Houghton Mifflin, 1942.

6

PRINCIPLES OF VOCATIONAL TESTING

PSYCHOLOGICAL TESTS are standardized instruments designed to measure samples of the characteristics of people in a scientific manner. Each test has standardized instructions for administration and scoring. These insure the same presentation for every examinee and eliminate subjectivity in scoring. The environmental conditions for testing are free from as many distracting influences as possible. Every examinee is put at ease but is motivated to do his best. Under these conditions the measurement can be a truer sampling of whatever characteristic is being measured. Unfavorable conditions may lower the score; if any have existed, this possibility must be taken into account.

Administering tests demands not only knowledge of instructions but a considerable amount of prior information. This holds true even for the simplest test.

There are many tests. It has become an encyclopedic task to be familiar with all of them. Buros has recognized this and assumed the responsibility of compiling reviews of tests. His first edition in 1935 comprised 44 pages. His most recent edition in 1949, *The Third Mental Measurements Yearbook*, consists of 1047 pages (8). This indicates the phenomenal growth of testing. The availability of so many tests makes difficult the decision of selecting the few to be used in any individual case.

There are many different kinds of tests. They can be categorized as intelligence, aptitude, achievement, interest, and personality tests. Each category of tests takes different soundings of the individual and within each category specific tests ascertain these soundings more or less accurately. However, unlike physical soundings, those taken of people are affected by the attitude of the person. There is then an impact between the test and the individual that causes resultant forces varying in direction and quanta which demand more than mere reading of the scores on the tests. The scores on tests are only surface reflections within certain limits. In order to interpret a score properly, one needs knowledge of the basic principles underlying human measurement. These principles are important in two ways. They are guideposts to what lies behind and within the specific tests; and they are guideposts to the present state and background of the individual being tested.

Psychological principles and background information

Individual differences. Basic to all measurement is the desire to determine the degree to which individuals differ from one another. This knowledge indicates the person's absolute position as well as his relation to others. Very often the variability of large samples of test measures conforms to the curve of normal distribution. The accompanying figure, adapted from Bingham (4), graphically illustrates the curve.

The number of individuals is represented by the height of the curve cut by the ordinates or vertical lines. Thus at M, the symbol for mean or average, is found the greatest number of people. As the scores vary from the mean toward either extreme, the height of the curve recedes and there are fewer and fewer individuals who make such scores. The distances from either side of the mean are set off by standard deviation (σ) units, each unit measuring an equal distance on the base line. The standard deviation scores are convertible into percentile scores. Both standard scores and percentile scores locate one's position in relation to others. These statistical matters will be discussed in greater detail in Chapter 12.

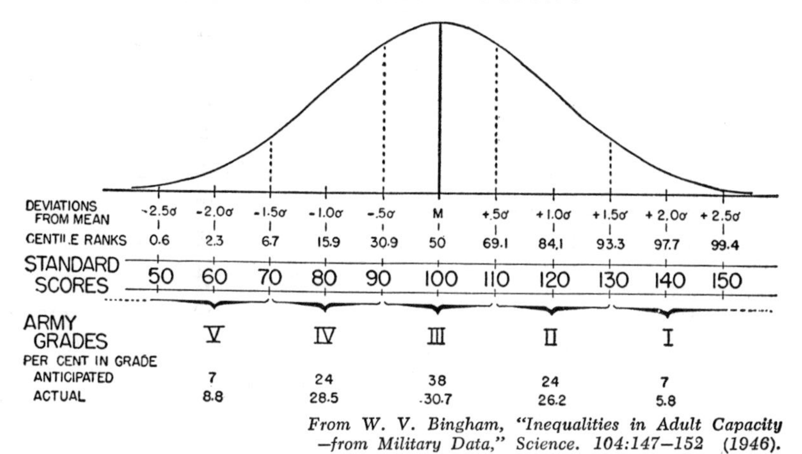

From W. V. Bingham, "Inequalities in Adult Capacity —from Military Data," Science. 104:147–152 (1946).

NORMAL DISTRIBUTION CURVE

For all measurement, whether it be of intelligence, as illustrated in the accompanying figure, of aptitudes, personality traits, or interest patterns, the scores made by a representative sampling of the population often conform to the normal distribution curve. If all people measured the same there would be no need to test. All that would be necessary would be a measure of one or several persons; the score obtained would fit all. This is not the case. People do vary so that testing is necessary to establish one's position in relation to others.

Variation within the individual. Not only do people vary in the continuum represented by the normal distribution curve, but the abilities and characteristics of an individual vary in amount. Thus one individual may have more ability in verbal expression than in the ability to put parts of an object together. A person may show a better social adjustment than home adjustment, or greater interests in one area than in others.

This intrapersonal variation is basic to vocational counseling. The goal of vocational counseling is to help the person know his abilities, interests, and personality traits so that he can relate them to different kinds of work. Much more is known about the relationship between abilities and different fields of work than about personality traits and occupations. Interest tests have been developed in such a way as to be directly useful for comparison with known occupational groups so that the relationship between interest patterns and fields of work is also quite well established. Thus on the Kuder Preference Record, mechanical engineers have their highest interests in the mechanical and scientific areas. Male high school teachers of social studies have their highest interests in literary and social service areas.

In the case of personality traits, the variation is much more complex. That is because personality theory and measurement is still far behind theory and measurement of abilities and interests. It cannot be said with certainty what are the traits of personality suitable for success in different jobs. It can be stated, however, that the traits of personality vary within any one individual so that he may feel very self-confident but have low dominance in relation to others. On the other hand, a person may have lower feelings of confidence and have high dominance. The examiner must be aware of this variation and try to find the dynamic interrelationship among the traits and then relate them to vocational success.

With regard to intellectual abilities, generally the person with superior intelligence has good abilities and the person with inferior intelligence, few well-developed abilities. Unger and Burr (33), in studying the minimum mental age levels of accomplishment of employed girls of low-grade intelligence, found that the higher the mental age level the greater the number of jobs as well as more difficult ones they could manage.

Just as a superior person may have well-developed abilities in several areas but have outstanding abilities in one or two, the individual of low-grade intelligence may have one comparatively well-developed ability with which he can gain a foothold in a job, providing he has the interest and is well enough adjusted.

An individual may be superior in spatial ability, an ability requisite for success in such work as engineering, but have above average ability or even below average ability in the use of language. On the other hand, there are many instances of individuals who have average spatial ability with superior verbal ability. The person of low-grade intelligence more frequently shows higher ability in spatial and manual activities than in verbal.

For any one individual, variation of any one test score can be studied as the distance from the average of his tested abilities, all test scores having been converted into comparable units (standard or percentile scores). This variation of test scores from the average of all the test scores, in comparable units, has been found in normal as well as abnormal groups, and the amount of variation differs on different kinds of tests. Schafer and Rapaport (27) found that their normal group tended to have a greater "mean scatter" (a term having a meaning similar to variation from the average) on the performance part of the Wechsler-Bellevue Intelligence Scale than on the verbal part. Bingham (3) has stated, "The widest variations are apt to be in his (the individual's) various motor abilities which, indeed, bear but little relationship to each other. His different sensory and perceptual powers also do not tend to cluster as closely about his average as do his more complex and ordinarily much more important intellectual abilities. But here also, in certain respects he is deficient, and in others superior, as compared with his average."[1]

TABLE 7

VARIATIONS IN VERBAL AND PERFORMANCE ABILITIES FOR DIFFERENT LEVELS OF INTELLIGENCE IN TWO AGE GROUPS AS MEASURED ON THE WECHSLER-BELLEVUE

	Chronological Age 10–16			*Chronological Age 20–49*		
I.Q. Category	*% Performance Higher*	*% Verbal Higher*	*% No Difference*	*% Performance Higher*	*% Verbal Higher*	*% No Difference*
79 and below	67.5	25.0	7.5	74.3	23.0	2.7
91–110	52.3	43.9	3.8	46.7	48.9	4.4
120 and over	12.2	82.9	4.9	21.0	77.4	1.6

Adapted from D. Wechsler, *Measurement of Adult Intelligence.* Baltimore: Williams and Wilkins, 1944, page 126.

Table 7 indicates that for the two age groups there is an increasing tendency for those with higher intelligence to do better with verbal than with performance material. The performance tests in the Wechsler-Bellevue Intelligence scale are mainly spatial with some manipulative ability required.

Environmental influences on test results. Capacity is the maximum potential ability of an individual. It depends for its fullest develop-

[1] Reprinted by permission from *Aptitudes and Aptitude Testing,* by W. V. Bingham, Harper & Brothers, New York, 1937.

ment upon a stimulating and healthy internal and external environment building upon the original hereditary endowment. If the external environment is poor in quality, capacity will not be developed to its highest potential. If an internal environment of high motivation and emotional balance does not exist, capacity will not be allowed to express itself in its true stature.

Moreover, differences in kind of opportunities make for unequal development of capacities. An environment that puts greater stress on the use of language leads to greater development of the capacity for language. Economic status also influences the development of capacities. Apropos of this is the story told by Leonard Lyons in his column, "The Lyons Den" (20), "When a hinge fell off a piece of furniture in her room, Beatrice Lillie sent for a carpenter to restore it. 'Couldn't you do a simple thing like that yourself?' one of her friends asked. 'Have you no mechanical ability at all?' Miss Lillie shrugged, 'Mechanical ability usually is something possessed by people who can't afford to hire somebody else to do it.' "[2] This does not necessarily mean that Miss Lillie or any other person on a higher socio-economic level originally did not have good mechanical capacity. They probably did not care to develop it.

Ability is an individual's present level of functioning as measured by a test. The ability measured is the result of the interaction of heredity and environment. If capacity is to develop, it must have environmental stimulation. Tests measure ability, not capacity.

Abilities as measured by tests may fluctuate, depending upon factors within the individual, factors concerned with the test administration, and environmental factors. Studies by Ribble (25) and Goldfarb (15) have shown the effects of a cold institutional environment on personality development. Not only did the children lack self-confidence but their development was retarded. They were not up to their true level in motor ability and alertness. Clinical studies of adolescents and adults with such backgrounds continue to show a lower level of ability than their capacity would warrant. The external environment has affected their personality as well as their intellectual development.

---

[2] Reprinted by permission of the author.

When children are adopted into superior foster homes, their intelligence quotient increases (12). If they are adopted into better homes when younger, the intelligence quotient will rise even more than if adopted at a later age (24).

However, the rise in ability is limited by heredity. One cannot go beyond his inherited potential. It may well be that there was a selective factor operating in the placement of the adopted children studied. For example, adoption agencies knowing favorable facts about the true parents are likely to be influenced and place such children in favorable homes. This "selective placement" was pointed out in studies by Burks (7) and Leahy (18) as a caution in otherwise allowing for the interpretation that the rise in the I.Q. is solely a function of the environment.

The degree of motivation in an individual when taking a test, as well as the manner in which the test is administered, can make for differences in the final result. Seashore (28) conducted a study on the Minnesota Rate of Manipulation, Placing Test, to determine if there was any improvement in test performance when bonuses as well as penalties were given. In the manual for the test, statements are made to the effect that the basic rate of manipulation is primarily native and can be only slightly improved. If this were so then bonuses should be able to increase the score only slightly. However, for the seven subjects tested by Seashore for nine days over a period of three weeks with three trials each day, when bonuses and penalties were given, the differences between initial time and final time in seconds ranged from 3.08 to 13.72. The largest gain in percentile was from the 64th to the 99th percentile. This improvement cannot be interpreted as slight. The individuals were highly motivated by the special test conditions so their scores rose. To paraphrase Seashore, this indicates that capacity is probably not measured but that the present status or ability can be measured easily.

Another important matter related to environment is the effect of special experience on test results. An individual with experience in a particular line of work may do better on a test measuring functions similar to the work because he had that special environmental opportunity. Blum and Candee (5) experimented with the use of three tests, the O'Connor Finger Dexterity Test, and the Minnesota Rate of Manipulation Placing and Turning Tests, as aids in the selection of department store wrappers and packers. They had a group of permanent employees and a larger group of applicants, of whom those with the poorest test scores were eliminated. The authors summarized their findings thus:

> In this study the satisfactory permanent employees excel less experienced workers in production, in supervisor's rating and in test scores, the indications being that this is due primarily to experience on the job. That experience rather than selection is the chief factor is indicated by the fact that there are no significant differences on the tests between the satisfactory and less satisfactory permanently employed groups and between the two seasonal employed groups but only between the more and less experienced workers, regardless of the supervisor's ratings.[3]

That experience is an important matter to consider in test results also came out clearly in a study on the use of a work sample by Steel, Balinsky, and Lang (29). Here a work sample involving the hooking together of an electric bell circuit was administered as part of a group of vocational tests to 86 individuals who had come for vocational guidance over a period of two months. The counselees had been classified according to degree of experience in mechanical type activities. The authors found "a consistent trend for those with more experience to complete the work sample in less time."

The differences in test results between people of more or less experience may mean that the experience in itself has brought about differences in test results or that the more successful workers as evidenced by years of employment or experience had better ability to begin with.

Paterson *et al.* (23) have considered this problem in their research on mechanical ability testing. Their attempts to isolate environmental influences that produced the striking differences in mechanical ability yielded negative results. In comparing males and females, they found that the sexes did equally well on most of the tests. They attributed the better performance of boys on the Minnesota Assembly

---

[3] Reprinted from *Journal of Applied Psychology*, 25:76–85 (1941), by permission of the American Psychological Association, publishers.

Test to practice and stated that "When such practice effects fail to influence test performance, the differences between the sexes tend to disappear."

The key to much future knowledge on testing depends upon the solution of the heredity and environment problem. At present the last word is not known. Although different authorities will sometimes interpret similar problems in accordance with either hereditary or environmental predispositions, the evidence available seems to support the view that the importance of neither heredity nor environment can be overlooked.

Identification of abilities and traits. Tests measure different abilities and traits. What abilities or traits are being measured is important in the analysis of tests and their relationship to different kinds of work. A test may measure more than one ability or trait; and the various tests overlap a good deal. There are many tests with similar names but with combinations of different kinds of items. It becomes necessary to identify the abilities and traits common to the tests. In this way the multiplicity of tests can be grouped into fewer categories, thus making for greater clarity in interpretation. For example, instead of using the term mechanical ability, under which can be grouped several abilities measured differently by various tests of mechanical ability, the abilities can be described in terms of a few basic factors common to all.

Psychologists have been searching for the factors common to tests for many years. They have always felt the need to sharpen their knowledge of what the test measures. Clinical observation and analysis of test performance is the main method used. This method requires an experienced psychologist, thoroughly familiar with psychological concepts and terminology. Clinical observation and analysis can be checked by statistical methods and refined accordingly, but can never be replaced by them. Even factor analysis, the statistical technique employed to find common elements among tests, does not name the abilities. The description of the abilities is left to the psychologist. He describes the abilities and traits through his clinical experiences. Thurstone (32), one of the leaders in factor analysis, writes that factor analysis is a scientific method useful for testing psychological hypotheses offered by the clinician.

Interest and personality tests have been subjected to clinical and factorial analyses, but so far with less success than have those of intellectual abilities. Interest patterns and personality have many descriptive terms and they are complexly interrelated. It would be valuable to be able to discover the major traits by means of which the complexities could be simplified.

The simplest classification of interests is in terms of interest in ideas, in people and in practical matters (26). Thurstone (31) did a factorial analysis of eighteen of the occupational categories of Strong's Vocational Interest Blank and found that four terms could describe the 18. They were science, language, business, and people. Strong (30) later conducted several more factor analyses on his test and found that four or five factors could account for all the scales developed. Vernon (34) conducted a factor analysis study of occupational interests among university people or people of equivalent intellectual level. He started with 58 varied occupations and identified four bipolar factors as descriptive of them: gregarious vs. isolated, social welfare vs. administrative, scientific vs. display, and verbal vs. active. These interest types overlap. They point the way for understanding interest patterns more clearly. In counseling, one is not concerned with finding the degree of interest in a specific job; there are too many. But if we can determine fundamental interest patterns, they could be applied constructively to narrow the field to a few kinds of jobs in a certain area.

Cattell (10) and Eysenck (11) made factorial studies of personality in an attempt to reduce to basic terms the numerous trait names used in personality description. The factors described, however, are still quite large in number and subject to varieties of interpretations, according to what personality theory is held by the psychologist. Flanagan (13) factor-analyzed Bernreuter's Personality Inventory and found that two traits, confidence and sociability, accounted for Bernreuter's original four descriptive terms of neurotic tendency, self-sufficiency, introversion-extroversion, and dominance-submission. Flanagan's two terms, however, did not replace the original four but were added to them. It seems that for personality measurement, the four original terms were so intrenched in usage that they could not be discarded for just two. Because personality is so complex, it requires probably more terms than do interests and abilities for adequate description.

It must be admitted that tests of ability include non-intellectual factors. When a test of ability is administered to a person, it does not measure only intelligence, aptitude, or achievement. It measures at the same time such motivational and personality factors as perseveration, flexibility and carefulness. In regard to tests of intelligence, Wechsler (36) has cogently written that "general intelligence cannot be equated with intellectual ability, but must be regarded as a manifestation of the personality as a whole." Tests of intelligence contain elements that are essentially factors of personality. The intellectual factors measured by a test of ability may account for a relatively small part of the test score. Jastak (17) found that intelligence accounted for only 20 per cent to 25 per cent of the variance of any one test. The rest was accounted for by the non-intellectual factors.

In an analysis of the tests in the Army Air Forces Psychological Program, Guilford (16) discovered such factors as carefulness and pilot interest. He described carefulness and pilot interest as seeming "to be temperamental or motivational variables rather than abilities." The non-intellectual factors have a very important impact upon the test score. In practice, these factors should be recognized so that appropriate analysis of the test results are made.

Clinical observations describe the motivational and personality aspects of ability test performance. Without these qualitative observations the test score becomes rather pointless in many instances. For example, on a manipulative test, a careful performer may take a longer time than a careless performer. The quality of work is often important vocationally and must be included in the interpretation of the test score. Similarly, a person may be more relaxed and less tense on verbal tests than on performance tests. This is also significant.

The non-intellectual factors and observations are not to be noted as mere interferences with intellectual or ability functioning. They should be regarded as part of the total behavior, which is the result of the interplay of intellectual, motivational and personality forces. All of the facts obtained by means of tests, the intellectual as well as the non-intellectual, are to be considered in the counseling process.

Ability and age. The organization of mental abilities changes with age. The same test may measure different functions over the expanse of years. In children less than 15 years old, various abilities, such as verbal, numerical, and spatial have higher intercorrelations than they do in later adolescence and adulthood. This means that an I.Q is more general in children and can be used to predict quality of performance in several areas of school work and other activities. As Garrett (14) states: "It seems likely that the 'g' factor (general intelligence, more specifically abstract intelligence) which appears strongly at the elementary school level is, in large part, verbal or linguistic in nature. If the school child can read well, he can very probably do the rest of his school work well."[4]

However, at the high school and college levels, the general factor is fractionated. Garrett states: "It would seem to be theoretically more defensible, therefore, and practically more useful, to measure verbal, numerical, perceptual or spatial ability, and perhaps other factors at these ages, than to give the subject a single over-all score."[5] Practically speaking, vocational guidance must await the period of fractionation which comes at about age fifteen. Before that time only the broadest predictions can be made on the basis of the test results. One can say the child would be suitable by ability for any number of occupational areas. However, later he may test much better in some areas than in others and the field of occupations can be narrowed. Also the lack of experience must be considered in children. Generally under age 15 educational guidance is more appropriate than is vocational.

An example is the results of Balinsky's study (1) of the mental factors of age groups 9, 12, 15, 25–29, 35–44, and 50–59. Using the Wechsler-Bellevue Intelligence Scale on selected samplings of each age group, he found that the mental organization changes over the years; that the same tests measure different functions at different age levels; and that there is "a definite decrease in the average of the subtest intercorrelations through the age group 25–29, followed by a decided increase for the older ages."

[4] Reprinted from *The American Psychologist,* 1:376 (1946), by permission of the American Psychological Association, publishers.

[5] *Ibid.*, page 377.

Table 8

AVERAGE OF THE INTERCORRELATIONS AMONG SUBTESTS OF WECHSLER-BELLEVUE INTELLIGENCE SCALE CHANGES WITH AGE

	Chronological Age					
	9 yrs.	*12 yrs.*	*15 yrs.*	*25–29 yrs.*	*35–44 yrs.*	*50–59 yrs.*
Average of the Intercorrelations	.37	.34	.23	.18	.31	.43
Standard Deviation	.106	.128	.111	.110	.100	.126

From B. Balinsky, "An Analysis of the Mental Factors of Various Age Groups from Nine to Sixty," *Genetic Psychology Monographs,* 23:219 (1941).

This suggests increasing fractionation or differentiation in abilities from 9 to 29 with probable greater specialization. Beyond 35 years of age, a reorganization of abilities takes place which may be due to complete maturation and to a greater flexibility in the use of the various abilities in performance.

Study of the subtests of the Wechsler-Bellevue Scale shows different meanings at different ages. For instance, the Digit Span Test, a test of rote memory, is included in the "g" cluster for children 9 years of age, and it also has a significant loading in the verbal factor. At age 12, it is part of the verbal cluster. At age 15, it is indefinite, and at age 25–29, it clearly measures the memory factor. In the age group 35–44, it is included in the memory cluster but loses its identity as a measure of memory in the age group 50–59. Any generalized statement about what functions or factors a test is measuring must clearly be modified by the age group to which reference is made.

Data indicate that most abilities continue to mature up to the early twenties. Wechsler (35) reported, "The age at which the maximum is attained varies from ability to ability but seldom occurs beyond 30 and in most cases somewhere in the early 20's."[6] Intelligence reaches its peak at 20–24. Miles (21) measured various motor functions among samplings from 8 to 80 and found increases until 18 years of age. The functions included hand movements such as reaching and grasping, speed of simple reaction of hand and foot to an auditory stimulus and

[6] D. Wechsler, *The Measurement of Adult Intelligence.* Baltimore: Williams and Wilkins, 1944.

accuracy of pursuit reaction by hand. The declines after the peak was reached were not large.

Studies on timed intelligence tests show speed to be affected by age. Lorge (19) found that on the Army Alpha Test, the Otis Self-Administering Test, and other timed tests, that the older adults (40 or over) scored significantly lower than the younger group (aged 20–25) although both age groups were equated with respect to the C.A.V.D. Test, an intelligence test with no time limit. Brown (6) obtained essentially similar results on speed and non-speed tests when given to samplings from three age groups of below 30 years, between 31–50 years and above 50 years. There is variation from individual to individual in rate of maturation as well as decline. The slowing up

"Satisfied?"

Reprinted by permission of Cosmopolitan Magazine.

with age may be the result of conservation. The older person may also compensate for decrease in speed by improved techniques developed over a period of years. This is demonstrable by comparing experienced older men at work with younger less experienced. The older men pace themselves and have learned to organize their movements so that they maintain a good rate of speed. However, if both younger and older people were to learn an entirely new task, the younger would probably outstrip the older.

Differences in test administration

Tests are administered in different ways. These differences in administration in themselves make for varied results. It is therefore necessary to consider the manner of administration in interpreting the results. Tests in general can be categorized as: (1) group or individual, (2) performance, paper and pencil, or oral, (3) time limit or work limit.

Group or individual. A group test is given to a number of examinees at the same time by a single examiner, or several if the group is very large. An individual test is administered to a single examinee by a single examiner.

An advantage of group tests is saving in time and money. This is important in mass testing when large numbers of people have to be examined in a brief time. It was necessary during the war. If all service men had been examined individually the emergency would have been over before the tests were completed. Group tests are rather valid for most people. However, where they are not, an individual test must be given.

Individual testing allows for correction of any conditions that may interfere with the individual's best performance. In group examination, some individuals may not be well-motivated, and the examiner may not know about it. An examinee may be nervous, and the group examiner can do little about it. In the individual test, the examiner will try to put the person at ease. He will establish a friendly, warm atmosphere conducive to a good relationship in which the examinee will work at his best. The group examiner may frequently be an inexperienced psychologist or sometimes a clerk. The individual examiner must always be a more experienced psychologist.

In individual testing, the experienced psychologist sees the person as a whole. He is clinical in his approach. He will not only try to induce the best test conditions possible but will also observe how the person reacts on different parts of the tests. As has been pointed out previously, this behavior may be more important than the test results themselves. Burtt (9) illustrates this as follows: He was examining a man who had supposedly recovered from shell shock. The man was being tested as a preliminary to employment on a fatiguing job requiring considerable patience and involving rather complex machinery. The man reacted normally at the beginning, but during the first test "blew up," protested violently against the tests, and manifested other psychopathic symptoms. It would have been dangerous for him to undertake the work in question and accordingly he was given an unskilled, out-of-doors job. In a group test, it is difficult to know just what he would have done, but it is certain that his test results would not have been as illuminating as his remarks, which might even have gone undetected. In individual testing, the examinee often expresses his feelings and attitudes about the tests and himself, because he feels it a more personal situation.

A group testing program is usually not as flexible. Since the psychologist does not know how the people in the group are doing, he cannot adjust the tests to make them more suitable for the particular individual. An individual who is a slow reader will not be discovered in group testing unless he previously knew this and reported it. The individual examiner will discover it and give other kinds of tests not involving reading to obtain a fuller picture.

Since group testing is so prevalent, the group examiners should be trained to acquire skill in motivating the examinees as well as in developing rapport with them. If this training were given group examination would be improved considerably.

Performance, paper and pencil, or oral. Performance tests are those which consist of simple or complex apparatus. They may be simple blocks like those that children use to make designs, or complicated pieces that resemble machine equipment. Instructions are given orally (or by pantomime if necessary) about what to do, and practice is sometimes given. Performance tests are often referred to as nonverbal because the examinee does not have to know how to read, write, or speak English. The designation non-verbal allows for the inclusion of picture tests where the examinee is to identify the part missing. There is actually no performance in terms of moving parts about.

Paper and pencil tests are generally understood to mean the large body of verbal group tests where the person is given a test blank and instructions. He reads the items and writes or underlines the correct answers. The answers are usually simply recorded like a number or a letter, or in machine-scored tests, a darkened line. Sometimes more writing is required. There are paper and pencil tests that are non-verbal; such as tracing mazes or numbering disarranged pictures to show their correct order. Many mechanical aptitude tests are given in paper and pencil form.

In oral tests, questions are stated orally and responses to them are oral. The individually administered tests of intelligence are oral. So are some proficiency tests of skill. Where performance material is given the instructions are oral, but the responses are such actions as manipulating the apparatus or showing where the part may be missing.

Paper and pencil tests are obviously most adaptable to group administration, whether verbal or non-verbal. However, if the non-verbal material is apparatus, then group testing is limited to two or three at a time. This is so because of the expense of providing many pieces of equipment. Orally administered tests are usually administered to single individuals. Both oral tests as well as performance tests lend themselves more to clinical observations. Paper and pencil tests do not permit this but have the asset of economy.

Time limit or work limit. Time limit tests are those on which there is a set time in which to do the task. It may be as short as 30 seconds and as long as 30 minutes. The test is stopped, no matter how much the examinee has completed, when the time limit has been reached. The score is usually the number of items done correctly in the time limit.

Work limit tests are those which have a set amount of work to be done. The whole task is to be completed and the time taken to do it is recorded. The score is usually the time taken and often a measure of accuracy.

Group tests have time limits, obviously to control the time uniformly for all. The time limits are more or less generous. In some instances they are made long enough for almost everyone to finish without feeling hurried. When this is the case, they are more in the nature of power tests which measure the upper level of difficulty that the individual can accomplish. An example of this type of test is the Miller Analogies. This has a 50-minute time limit but it is primarily a power test. Speed is of negligible importance. With few exceptions, those who take the test answer all the items in the time limit and if more time is given the score is not raised significantly. A group of 54 clinical psychologist trainees was given an additional 40 minutes. They raised their average score only 1.2 points. The correlation between 50- and 90-minute scores was .99 (22).

The time limit and work limit are equivalent in this instance. The individual has finished all he could and extra time will not raise his score significantly. Baxter (2) found a correlation of .85 between time limit and work limit scores on the Otis test.

However, there are some group tests that few people can finish. In fact, the time limit is so set to prevent all but relatively few from finishing the task. The factor of speed is more important on these tests and although it may not affect the score of the younger client significantly it will be more likely to do so on older people.

Apparatus or performance tests usually have work limits. The examinee is, for example, to finish putting pins into holes, or different-sized or shaped pieces into correct places. If a time limit is put on such tests, it is usually so generous that those who do not finish obtain a very low score anyway.

Attributes of psychological tests

The general principles apply to all tests with certain modifications dependent mainly upon the validity, reliability, and norms in the standardization of the particular tests. In order to interpret test results on all kinds of tests, it is necessary to consider the three aspects: validity, reliability, and norms.

Validity is the most important characteristic of a psychological test.

A test is valid if it measures what it purports to measure. Validity is determined by finding the degree of correlation between the test and a criterion. A test of intelligence should measure intelligence. A test of aptitude should measure the kind of aptitude it claims to measure. The same holds for personality and interest tests. However, one cannot expect a perfect relationship between test and criterion at this stage of test development. Tests are not yet perfect predictors. On the other hand the criteria used to measure the validity of tests are also frequently incomplete or too subjective.

A test is valid when it correlates significantly with the trait or complex of traits it is designed to measure. If the test can improve our ability to prognosticate the trait or traits it is demonstrating validity. Some tests improve upon this ability more than others and are therefore more valid. The criteria employed to test the validity of a test are sometimes themselves in need of improvement. The criteria which involve subjective estimates, like foremen's judgments of workers' ability or teachers' of students', may not be themselves very valid. They will therefore tend to lower the correlation between test and the criterion.

Different criteria may be employed to determine the validity of a test. A scholastic aptitude test like that of the American Council on Education could be validated against college grades in the freshman year or the average of college grades over four years. Different degrees of validity may then eventuate. A clerical aptitude test can be validated against the performance of various groups such as routine clerks, bookkeepers or stenographers. Again the validity of the test will vary with the adopted criterion. For tests of interests and personality the variety of criteria possible is even greater.

Bingham (3) has stated the problem of validity very well. In writing of aptitude tests he reports:

> The main explanation, however, of the fact that most of the apparently good tests of aptitude have relatively low coefficients of validity is not that the test is unreliable, or the criterion used as a measure of success against which the test is validated. The trouble is more often to be found in the narrowness, inadequacy or impurity of this criterion. We need to validate a medical aptitude test, for instance, before using

> it as a means of estimating the likelihood that a student will be able to master his medical courses. Scholarship grades obtained in medical school furnish a possible criterion of success. But here are three students of equal ability. One has to earn his expenses; the others do not. Another crams industriously before each examination while the third prefers instead to put in extra time in the clinics. Are the marks these students receive—no matter how reliable the examinations—perfect measures of their relative ability to do the work of the medical curriculum? Obviously not. Are the annual earnings of two lawyers—even though these earnings are reliably ascertained—adequate measures of their relative legal ability when one chooses to accept only the most profitable clients, while the other prefers to devote half his time to the problems of neighbors in trouble who can afford to pay only modest fees?[7]

The counselor and psychologist must always bear in mind the criteria employed in validating a test. The test score will then have more value and its meaning will be more validly interpreted.

Another important attribute of tests is reliability, which is consistency of test measurement. If a test had to be readministered or a duplicate form of the test given, the results should be similar to those of the first administration unless there were actual changes in the person or test administration. Of course there may well be such changes but they do not affect the reliability of the test.

If a person's blood pressure were taken by the sphygmomanometer, the usual instrument used to measure blood pressure, and there was a significant change between two such measures, the implication would not necessarily be that the blood pressure apparatus was unreliable. The person might have actually had a rise in blood pressure. This, of course, would be checked by other clinical means. It is necessary to ascertain whether a difference in test performance is to be attributed to unreliability of the test or to a change in the behavior being tested. A person may be a slow reader and receive a low score on a verbal test with a time limit. He may then receive aid to develop his reading rate. The next time he takes the test, the score will be higher. This again does not reflect upon the reliability of the test.

---

[7] Reprinted by permission from *Aptitudes and Aptitude Testing*, by W. V. Bingham, Harper & Brothers, New York, 1937.

The reliability is obtained by testing a group of people. This procedure minimizes any undue individual variability resulting from change in behavior. However, one must know certain characteristics of the group. If it is homogeneous, the reliability will necessarily be lower than that for a more heterogeneous sampling. This is due to the narrowness in range of scores of homogeneous populations. A test should have a high reliability, because the size of the reliability coefficient necessarily must affect the size of the validity coefficient. In other words, a test in order to be valid must have reliability. The converse is not true. A test can be reliable and yet not be valid.

Norms are standards of reference, derived from a sampling of the population, against which an individual score is to be compared. These norms vary from test to test, and frequently a single test may have several sets of norms. If a person is to be compared on a test of clerical aptitude with norms derived from experienced clerical workers, his rating will be lower than when he is compared to the norms derived from the general population. If a person takes a vocabulary test and his score is compared with a college norm, he will rate lower than if his score were to be compared with a population of industrial workers. Any score must be interpreted in terms of the norms against which it has been compared. The counselor and psychologist must constantly bear in mind the characteristics of the sampling from which the norms are derived.

Knowledge of the validity, reliability, and norms of tests facilitates more precise evaluation of the tests and more complete interpretation of their results. Tests vary in their validity and reliability, and in the characteristics of their norms. It is not possible to select tests appropriately or to interpret them with insight without full knowledge of the attributes of the specific tests.

Summary

Psychological tests are standardized instruments designed to measure samples of the characteristics of people in a scientific manner. There are many tests and it is often difficult to determine which tests to use in a particular situation. Evaluative information is an aid to specific test usage.

Psychological testing is a complex matter. In order to test properly and obtain results which are most meaningful, it is necessary to have knowledge of psychological principles and certain background information, ways of administering tests, attributes of tests, and varieties of tests.

All testing is based upon the principle of individual differences. Not only do people differ from one another; differences in ability occur within the same individual. The environment influences test performance in many ways.

It is necessary to know about the differences in test administration because these differences make for varying interpretations. The differences in test administration were described under the categories of group or individual; performance, paper and pencil, or oral; and time limit or work limit.

The three attributes of psychological tests are validity, reliability and norms. Validity is the measure of how well the test measures what it purports to. Reliability indicates the consistency of measurement. The norms are the standards against which individual scores are compared.

Bibliography

1. Balinsky, B., "An Analysis of the Mental Factors of Various Age Groups From Nine to Sixty," *Genetic Psychology Monographs,* 23: 191–234 (1941).
2. Baxter, B., "An Experimental Analysis of the Contributions of Speed and Level in an Intelligence Test," *Journal of Educational Psychology,* 32:285–296 (1941).
3. Bingham, W. V., *Aptitudes and Aptitude Testing.* New York: Harper, 1937.
4. ———, "Inequalities in Adult Capacity—from Military Data," *Science,* 104:147–152 (1949).
5. Blum, M. L., and B. Candee, "The Selection of Department Store Packers and Wrappers with the Aid of Certain Psychological Tests, I," *Journal of Applied Psychology,* 25:76–85 (1941).
6. Brown, R. R., "Effect of Age on the Speed-Power Relationship with Reference to Tests of Intelligence," *Journal of Educational Psychology,* 29:413–418 (1938).

7. Burks, B. S., "The Relative Influence of Nature and Nurture upon Mental Development: A Comparative Study of Foster Parent–Foster Child Resemblance and True Parent–True Child Resemblance," *Yearbook of the National Society for the Study of Education,* 27 (I), 219–316 (1928).
8. Buros, O. K., Editor, *The Third Mental Measurements Yearbook.* New Brunswick, N.J.: Rutgers University Press, 1949.
9. Burtt, H. E., *Principles of Employment Psychology.* New York: Harper, 1942.
10. Cattell, R. B., *Description and Measurement of Personality.* Yonkers: World Book, 1946.
11. Eysenck, H. J., *Dimensions of Personality.* London: Kegan Paul, Trench, Trubner, 1947.
12. Flanagan, J. C., *Factor Analysis in the Study of Personality.* Stanford: Stanford University Press, 1935.
13. Freeman, F. N., *et al.,* "The Influence of Environment on Intelligence, School Achievement and Conduct of Foster Children," *27th Yearbook of the National Society for the Study of Education,* 27: Part I, 103–217 (1928).
14. Garrett, H. E., "A Developmental Theory of Intelligence," *The American Psychologist,* 1:373–377 (1946).
15. Goldfarb, W., "Effects of Early Institutional Care on Adolescent Personality," *Journal of Experimental Education,* 12:106–129 (1943).
16. Guilford, J. P., "The Discovery of Aptitude and Achievement Variables," *Science,* 106:279–282 (1947).
17. Jastak, J., "A Plan for the Objective Measurement of Character," *Journal of Clinical Psychology,* 4:170–178 (1948).
18. Leahy, A. M., "Nature-nurture and Intelligence," *Genetic Psychology Monographs,* 17:236–308 (1935).
19. Lorge, I., "The Influence of the Test upon the Nature of Mental Decline as a Function of Age," *Journal of Educational Psychology,* 22:100–110 (1936).
20. Lyons, L., "The Lyons Den," New York *Post,* August 1, 1949.
21. Miles, W. R., "Measures of Certain Human Abilities throughout the Life Span," *Proceedings of the National Academy of Sciences,* 17:627–633 (1931).
22. *Miller Analogies Test Manual.* New York: The Psychological Corporation, 1947.

23. Paterson, D. G., *et al.*, *Minnesota Mechanical Ability Tests.* Minneapolis: University of Minnesota Press, 1930.

24. Reymert, M. L., and R. T. Hinton, "The Effect of Change to a Relatively Superior Environment upon the IQ's of One Hundred Children," *39th Yearbook of the National Society for the Study of Education,* 39: Part II, 255–268 (1940).

25. Ribble, M., *The Rights of Infants.* New York: Columbia University Press, 1943.

26. Rodger, A., "How People Compensate or Adjust Themselves for Lack of Ability," *Human Factor,* 11:385–393 (1937).

27. Schafer, R. and D. Rapaport, "The Scatter in Diagnostic Intelligence Testing," *Character and Personality,* 12:275–284 (1944).

28. Seashore, H. G., "The Improvement of Performance on the Minnesota Rate of Manipulation Test When Bonuses Are Given," *Journal of Applied Psychology,* 31:254–259 (1947).

29. Steel, M., B. Balinsky and H. Lang, "A Study on the Use of a Work Sample," *Journal of Applied Psychology,* 29:14–21 (1945).

30. Strong, E. K., *Vocational Interests of Men and Women.* Stanford: Stanford University Press, 1948.

31. Thurstone, L. L., "A Multiple Factor Study of Vocational Interest," *Personnel Journal,* 10:198–205 (1931).

32. Thurstone, L. L., "Psychological Implications of Factor Analysis," *The American Psychologist,* 3:402–408 (1948).

33. Unger, E. W. and E. T. Burr, *Minimum Mental Age Levels of Accomplishment.* Albany: The University of the State of New York, 1931.

34. Vernon, P. E., "Classifying High-grade Occupational Interests," *Journal of Abnormal and Social Psychology,* 44:85–96 (1949).

35. Wechsler, D., *The Measurement of Adult Intelligence.* Baltimore: Williams and Wilkins, 1944.

36. ———, "Cognitive, Conative, and Non-intellective Intelligence," *The American Psychologist,* 5:78–83 (1950).

7

TYPES OF VOCATIONAL TESTS

In vocational counseling the kinds of tests employed are intelligence, aptitude, achievement, interest, and personality. Each variety of test has its particular function or functions. All the tests are subject to the general principles, are administered in one of several ways, and have particular validity, reliability, and norms, as discussed in the previous chapter.

Intelligence tests

Individual intelligence tests. Historically, intelligence tests were coupled with the criterion of academic success. Because of this they are frequently referred to as scholastic aptitude tests. However, the first tests to be applied in practice as measures of intelligence were not the kind used today. They were mainly measures of physical and physiological processes derived from the experimental laboratory. Cattell, in 1890, recommended such tests as strength of grip, measurement of the smallest difference in weight that an individual could discriminate, the speed of reaction to sound, and the accuracy with which one could produce an interval of ten seconds. These tests were tried out on students and the results compared with estimates of intelligence by teachers and with school grades. Needless to say, the test results showed very little relationship to teachers' estimates and to grades.

It was in relation to an education problem that intelligence testing made a significant step forward. In France, at the turn of the century, schoolteachers and administrators recognized the problem of unequal progress by pupils. There was particular concern for the children doing poorly. This problem was studied by a committee appointed by the ministry of education. Binet and Simon, two members of the committee, were instrumental in devising tests that proved to have a high degree of validity for predicting school success. These tests measured more complex mental processes like judgment, reasoning, comprehension, and memory.

The discovery of this kind of testing with high validity for school success was significant and established the basis for all subsequent intelligence tests. Goddard, director at the time of an institution for mental defectives at Vineland, New Jersey, translated and adapted the Binet-Simon tests for use in the United States. Terman began to work on an English version, and by 1916, he had produced the Stanford-Binet Intelligence Test. This test became the prototype for the many tests of intelligence developed later. The Terman revision itself became the standard for intelligence testing in schools and elsewhere until 1937, when Terman and Merrill revised it. The new revision is now extensively used and is considered the best test of intelligence for children from age 2 to about 14. The Wechsler-Bellevue Intelligence Scale, completed in 1939, is considered the best measure of adolescent and adult intelligence. In 1949, Wechsler (24) standardized a new test designed for the measurement of children's intelligence.

The Binet tests and the Wechsler-Bellevue Scale are individually administered tests and enjoy the advantages of such tests. The Binet is an age scale; that is, for each age, there are several tests, usually six, that have been determined passable by the average person of that particular age. The Wechsler-Bellevue is a point scale; that is, an individual accumulates a certain number of points as he passes items in each of the subtests that make up the scale. There is no dependence on age levels.

The validity of the latest revision of the Stanford-Binet is based upon increasingly higher test results with age. In other words, the assumption of validity is that an older person (up to a certain age) knows more and should pass more tests. The weakness of the Stanford-Binet is that its standardization does not include older populations, so that norms at these ages are weak. The Wechsler-Bellevue corrected this deficiency by providing norms for adolescents and older adults.

Studies like the one by Anderson *et al.* (2) demonstrate the ability of the Stanford-Binet Test to measure achievement in school or academic success. It is mainly a verbal test and was originally standardized to measure school success. However, the Wechsler-Bellevue Scale contains five non-verbal subtests, as well as five which are verbal. Anderson *et al.* found the verbal tests of the Wechsler-Bellevue Scale to have a higher correlation with grade-point averages among college freshmen than even the combined Wechsler-Bellevue verbal and non-verbal tests. The non-verbal or performance group of tests correlates only +.19 with grade-point average; so low as to "cast considerable doubt on the validity of the performance scale at the college level."

Apparently the non-verbal subtests are not measuring academic ability. The Wechsler-Bellevue, however, has been generally accepted as more suitable for testing adult intelligence. For this test, the criterion must be broadened to include not only academic ability but also worldly ability. A study by Balinsky, Israel, and Wechsler (5) throws some light on this matter. It concerned the diagnosis of mental deficiency. In a mental hygiene clinic, the problem of commitment to a state institution for mental defectives often arises. The intelligence test results are only one factor, and the social and psychiatric histories are often more important. The psychiatrist makes the final decision on commitment after a full consideration of the psychological tests, the social history, and his own clinical evidence. In the study, the Stanford-Binet and the Wechsler-Bellevue I.Q.'s were available for one group of patients prior to the final diagnosis. The Bellevue Full Scale (both verbal and non-verbal) I.Q. gave the highest correlation with the recommendation for or against commitment to an institution for mental deficiency. The Bellevue Performance I.Q. was next. Both the Bellevue Verbal I.Q. and the Binet I.Q. were low.

TABLE 9

CORRELATION BETWEEN STANFORD-BINET I.Q.'s, WECHSLER-BELLEVUE I.Q.'s, AND RECOMMENDATION FOR COMMITMENT TO INSTITUTION FOR MENTAL DEFECTIVES

I.Q.	*Recommendation for Commitment or Not*	*Correlation*
Stanford-Binet	Recommendation for Commitment or Not	.274 ± .100
Bellevue Full Scale	Recommendation for Commitment or Not	.785 ± .054
Bellevue Verbal	Recommendation for Commitment or Not	.330 ± .097
Bellevue Performance	Recommendation for Commitment or Not	.693 ± .066

From B. Balinsky, H. Israel, and D. Wechsler, "The Relative Effectiveness of the Stanford-Binet and the Bellevue Intelligence Scale in Diagnosing Mental Deficiency," *American Journal of Orthopsychiatry*, 9:798–801 (1939), p. 800.

Apparently the performance type of test measures something other than academic success. In the case of mental defectives or those below average in intelligence, it is probably related to their worldly ability to make a vocational and social adjustment. The verbal type of test is not as adequate a measure. Notice, however, that the Full Scale has the highest correlation. The more rounded ability, including verbal and non-verbal, has highest relationship to life success.

The reliability of the revised Stanford-Binet, obtained from average differences between the duplicate forms L and M, ranges from .98 for subjects below 70 I.Q. to approximately .90 for subjects above 130 I.Q. For subjects near 100 I.Q., the reliability is .925 (22). The reliability of the Wechsler-Bellevue Scale, four tests by four tests, is .90±.014. The minimum reliability coefficient should be about .90 to be useful in practice. Both tests satisfy this criterion, but this does not mean that they have perfect reliability.

Both the revised Stanford-Binet and the Wechsler-Bellevue have carefully chosen samplings. Each age group is representative of the general population of that age. Attempts were made to include the same percentages found in the school population in the sampling of each group. In the older age groups for the Wechsler test, the samplings were made to correspond as far as possible with the occupational categories of the U.S. Census. This careful selection of samplings is extremely important, because the norms are derived from them. In intelligence testing, care must be taken to obtain heterogeneous and representative sampling of the population for various ages.

The problem of sampling is by no means solved just by obtaining percentages similar to actual educational distributions or to occupational groupings. Much depends also upon what schools are selected and what specific kinds of work are included in the larger occupational groupings. Terman and Merrill selected schools of average social status in each community they used. This method was necessary to obtain a school sampling that was not highly selected or that possibly had a better than average social environment. They had their greatest difficulties in selection with their 15- to 18-year-olds. Terman and Merrill report (22): "Dozens of studies have shown that the regular academic high school is highly selected, how highly depending on the nature of the community and on various other factors."[1] Different states have differences in compulsory school age. In some communities, the quality of schooling is better or poorer than in others.

In the use of the census data, the same difficulties may arise. For example, the category, "manufacturing and mechanical" is the largest occupational grouping, representing well over 30 per cent of the total working force. There are numerous specific kinds of jobs within that large category. The sampling must be done randomly within each category so as to assure obtaining a spread of occupations that approximates the true average.

Group intelligence tests. The same considerations that apply to the Stanford-Binet and Wechsler-Bellevue tests, both individual tests, apply to group tests of intelligence. The first group test, the Army Alpha, was devised under the pressure for examining recruits in World War I. It consists of items much like the Stanford-Binet. Since there were many recruits unable to read English, for whom a verbal test would not be valid, a non-language group test of intelligence (the Army Beta) was devised. It included such tests as pictures, images, and cube counting. The two became prototypes for many to follow.

If a recruit made a low score on the Alpha and Beta Scales, he was tested individually. For the English-speaking group, the Stanford Revision was used most frequently; for the foreign-born and illiterate,

[1] From *Measuring Intelligence* by Lewis M. Terman and Merrill, Maud A. Copyright 1937 by Lewis M. Terman and Maud A. Merrill. Reprinted by permission of and arrangement with Houghton Mifflin Company, the authorized publishers.

an individual performance test was devised. Individual tests of intelligence, verbal or performance, give a truer picture of the examinee. Where there is doubt about intelligence level because of background or motivation, the individual test is to be given.

The following illustration demonstrates what happens when a group test is taken for granted. Joe S. was 17 when he came for counseling to help him determine if he could do some kind of mechanical work. He had been tested in school with a verbal group test, and found to test low enough to be called mentally defective. Accordingly, he was placed in an ungraded class where he learned very little. Consideration had not been given to the fact that he was rather shy and needed reassurance during the test. In addition, his parents spoke a foreign language at home and as a result he was not fluent in English. Upon being re-examined with the Wechsler-Bellevue test he tested as low average and even rated higher on the performance part. Although his general fund of information and vocabulary were comparatively low, he rated well on the abstract verbal ability subtest. On the latter test he rated a standard score of nine, which is rarely accomplished by true mental defectives (25). Without doubt, Joe is not mentally defective.

Soon after World War I, many group tests were devised. Not all are equally well standardized; hence it becomes extremely important to select the test which is most appropriate to the age group being considered and which has the greatest validity and reliability. In the case of Joe S., a non-verbal group test would have been more valid than the verbal because of his language background.

As has been stated previously there is not one kind of intelligence; rather there are different kinds. These can be expressed as abilities rather than intelligences. This holds true for both individual and group tests of intelligence. The S.R.A. Primary Mental Abilities test developed by L. L. and T. G. Thurstone demonstrates the ability or factorial composition of tests most clearly. This test measures such intellectual abilities as verbal-meaning, space, reasoning, number, and word-fluency.

The *Examiner's Manual* (23) gives the following descriptions of these abilities. (The manual referred to here was published in 1947. A revised manual was issued in 1949.)

VERBAL-MEANING is the ability to understand ideas expressed in words. It is needed in activities where one gets information by reading or listening. High ability in V is especially useful in such school courses as English, foreign languages, shorthand, history, and science. V is needed for success in such careers as secretary, teacher, editor, scientist, librarian, and executive.

Fifty problems similar to the one below are presented to measure V:

ANCIENT. A. Dry B. Long C. Happy D. Old

The word meaning the *same* as the first word is to be marked.

SPACE is the ability to think about objects in two or three dimensions. Blueprint reading, for example, requires this ability. The designer, electrician, machinist, pilot, engineer, and carpenter are typical workers who need ability to visualize objects in space. S is helpful in geometry, mechanical drawing, art, manual training, radar, physics, and geography classes.

Twenty problems similar to the one below are given in the test for S:

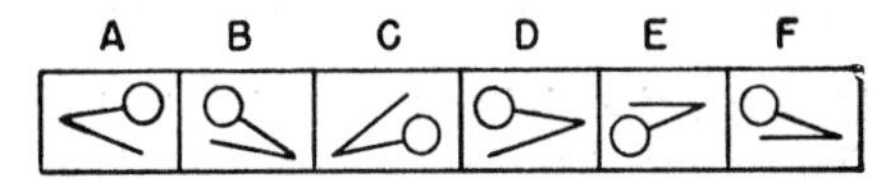

Every figure which is *like* the first figure is to be marked.

REASONING is the ability to solve logical problems—to foresee and plan. It is the ability that helps to make inventors, doctors, teachers, executives, statesmen, scientists, and supervisors outstanding. The higher a student goes in school, the more R he needs for success. Understanding science and mathematics takes a lot of R. Recent research has shown that R is really two separate abilities: *inductive* reasoning, the ability to reason from a specific case to a general rule; and *deductive* reasoning, the ability to reason from stated premises to a logical conclusion. The present test is a composite measure of both abilities. Thirty problems of the type below are presented in the R test:

a b x c d x e f x g h x [h] [i] [j] [k] [x] [y]

The box containing the next letter in the series is to be marked.

NUMBER is the ability to work with figures—to handle simple

quantitative problems rapidly and accurately. Accountants, cashiers, comptometer operators, bookkeepers, bank tellers, salesclerks, and inventory clerks should be high in N. NUMBER ability is useful for school success in business arithmetic, accounting, bookkeeping, and statistics.

Seventy problems similar to the one below are included in the N test:

17
84
29
—— [R] [W] Whether the answer given is right
140 or wrong is to be indicated.

WORD-FLUENCY is the ability to write and talk easily. People to whom words come rapidly and fluently are high in W. Careers requiring W include actor, stewardess, reporter, comedian, salesman, writer, and publicity man. Being high in W helps in drama classes, public speaking, radio acting, debate, speech, and journalism.

The test for W requires writing words beginning with the letter "s."[2]

In addition to these five abilities, this form of the Primary Mental Abilities also included reference to memory, motor, and perceptual speed. Brief descriptions of these three abilities follow:

Memory, the ability to recall paired associations. If a person is shown several pictures of people with the name of each written under it, his memory ability can then be measured by showing him the pictures alone after a given time has elapsed and asking him to recall the name that goes with each picture. It seems probable that memory is important for success in many types of school work. Future research may prove that what is ordinarily called memory actually comprises several abilities.

Motor, the ability to coordinate eye and hand movements. This ability, which is important in learning to read, has been included in the PMA (Primary Mental Abilities) battery for ages 5 and 6. It has not been included here, because by the age of 11, nearly all children have achieved a good enough motor coordination so that it does not affect materially their intellectual accomplishments. A high degree of motor coordination is important, however, for certain types of athletics and for many occupations requiring the assembly of small parts.

Perceptual-speed, the ability to locate details quickly. This ability

---

[2] *Examiner's Manual, Preliminary Edition, for the SRA Primary Mental Abilities* (the 1947 edition). By permission of the authors, L. L. and T. G. Thurstone, and the publisher, Science Research Associates.

> is probably important in school courses and occupations in which speed of recognizing likenesses and differences is required. It is known to be important for example, in several types of clerical jobs.[3]

Analysis reveals that the various intelligence tests measure abilities similar to those described above. However, they are not pure measures of these factors. A single test may measure more than one intellectual factor and, as previously stated, non-intellectual factors as well. For predictive purposes in vocational psychology, they can be compared with the Thurstone abilities. The factors are not independent of each other. There is a relationship between them. Thurstone called it curious that some insist that the factors be uncorrelated. The fact is that they are uncorrelated only when statistically forced.

That abilities are not independent of each other is in line with the thesis that the individual functions as a whole. The individual is not merely a mass of separate abilities but rather a well-coordinated organism of many abilities, some more highly developed than others, but all interrelated.

In discussing group intelligence tests it is almost mandatory to discuss the Miller Analogies Test (17). This test primarily interests college undergraduates seeking admission to those graduate schools requiring it as a condition for entrance. It was developed to measure scholastic aptitude at the graduate school level. Form G has been in use since 1940 and consists of 100 analogies. The test is really a power or work limit test although it has a time limit of 50 minutes.

It has been standardized with extreme care and its reliability is over +.90. Its validity varies from group to group but is correlated with grades in graduate courses to the extent of approximately +.50. Percentile norms are available for 13 graduate and professional school groups such as engineering, psychology, social work and education.

The most outstanding characteristic of the test is its requirement of rapid ability to shift on the part of the examinee both as to subject matter and the missing part of the four-part analogy. To do well on this test one must "see relationships" in the verbal, mathematical, and informational areas.

---

[3] *Ibid.*

Sample items similar to those on the test are as follows:

(a. spelling, b. physics, c. calculus, d. engineering): RHETORIC:: ARITHMETIC: ALGEBRA
COMMONPLACE: USUAL:: (a. variety, b. scarcity, c. possibility, d. expense): RARITY
DECIMAL: BINARY:: 10: (a. π, b. π^2, c. 2, d. 12)
MECHANISM: (a. principle, b. equipment, c. procedure, d. element):: STRUCTURE: PROCESS
LEAVE: PERMISSION:: WIT: (a. remark, b. wag, c. joke, d. inanity)
TABLE: (a. chair, b. defer, c. educate, d. rostrum):: TILL: CULTIVATE

Answers are: (A) (B) (C) (C) (B) (B)[4]

The publishers plan to have a new form available every two years beginning with Form H, released in 1950. It is distributed by The Psychological Corporation and is rigidly controlled as to usage and administration.

Vocational significance of intelligence tests.—Intelligence tests are useful to determine expected level of academic success as well as optimal range within occupations. Scores below or above this range are considered indicators of poor chance for success, other things being equal. For instance, an I.Q. of 110 is usually considered minimal for success in college. Scores below this are more likely to result in failure than success. A skilled craftsman needs a higher level of intelligence than a semi-skilled or unskilled worker.

The figure shown on pp. 172–173, derived from the Army General Classification scores made by recruits in different civilian occupations, is a sample of the general use of intelligence tests. The figure refers to 125 different occupations. The dark bar with the occupation in it shows the middle 50 per cent of scores in that occupation and the thin extension lines on either side, the 10th and 90th percentiles. In the case of tailors, for instance, 50 per cent of the individuals in the sampling make scores between about 83 and 112 on the A.G.C.T. Ten per cent of them make scores below 68; and 10 per cent make scores above 120.

Notice the extent of overlap. Fifty per cent of tailors score between 83 and 112. Fifty per cent of draftsmen score between 108 and 128.

[4] Reprinted by permission of The Psychological Corporation.

Fifty per cent of surveyors fall between 97 and 120. Fifty per cent of laborers rate between 76 and 108. On the basis of intelligence test score alone, vocational predictions must be made with caution. Education, interest, and personality must certainly be taken into account. Also it may well be that the laborers with high scores are occupationally maladjusted as far as "intelligence" is concerned.

Another consideration is the kinds of intelligence or ability traits. Some jobs require higher verbal ability, others higher spatial, and so on. Not enough is known about each particular kind of job to determine explicitly by means of intelligence tests the probable degree of success. At best it can be said that the probability of success in a certain line of work is greater or less depending upon the optimal range for the specific occupation.

Aptitude tests

Aptitude tests are related to intelligence tests. They measure intellectual components such as verbal, spatial, and perceptual abilities. However, they measure other abilities like motor (known also as manual or manipulative) which are not intellectual measures except for children under 11. They are also more subject to the influence of the environment than an intelligence test because they take for granted equality of experiences among people which do not exist. Aptitude tests can be further differentiated from intelligence tests in that they are more specific, measuring only certain aspects of functioning and within a limited range. The usual aptitude test norms also are derived from more specific and homogeneous populations and therefore interpretations must be limited. For example, clerical tests have norms based on various samplings of clerical workers or commercial students or other special groups. The reason for this limited range is that aptitude tests were developed as aids for the selection of possibly successful workers in different kinds of work. In vocational guidance they are employed to determine the abilities of the individual so as to predict success in particular areas of work.

There is confusion about the term aptitude itself. Some believe that aptitudes are special capacities. Aptitudes are only in part inborn or native. The basic neurological and anatomical structures

AGCT SCORES FOR

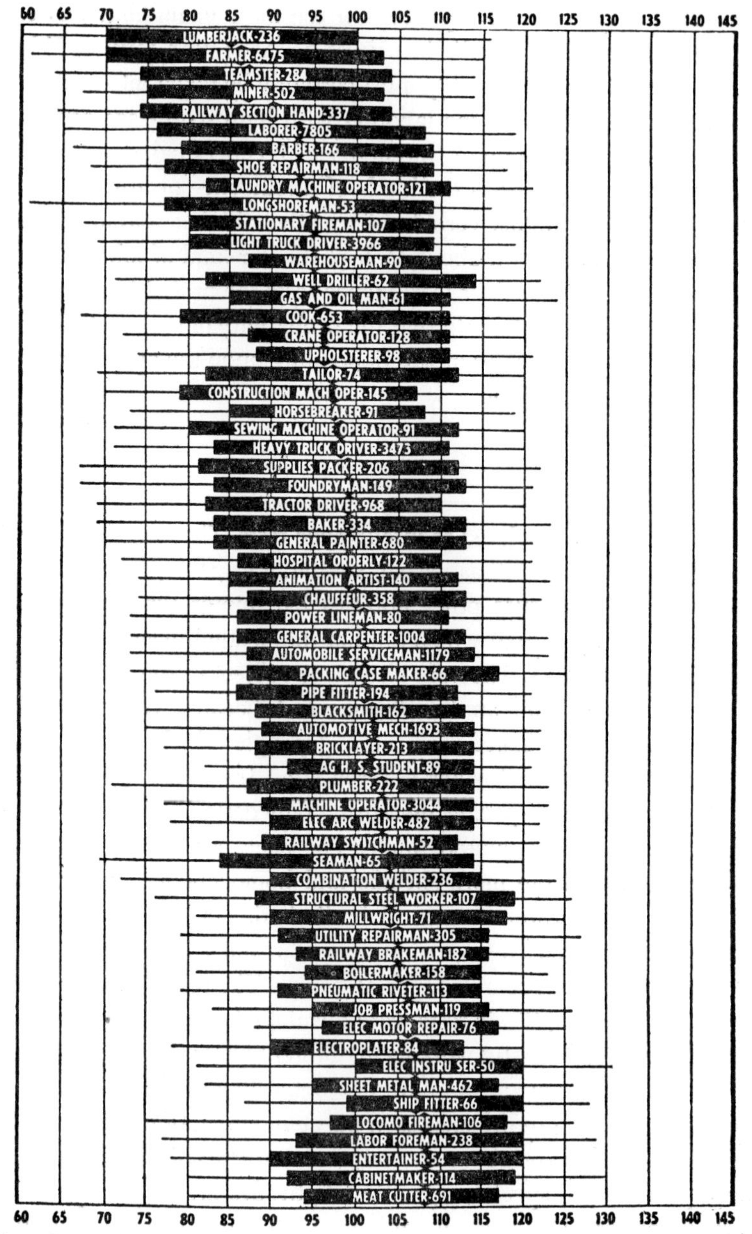

From Examiner's Manual for The Army General Classification Test, First Civilian Edition.

CIVILIAN OCCUPATIONS

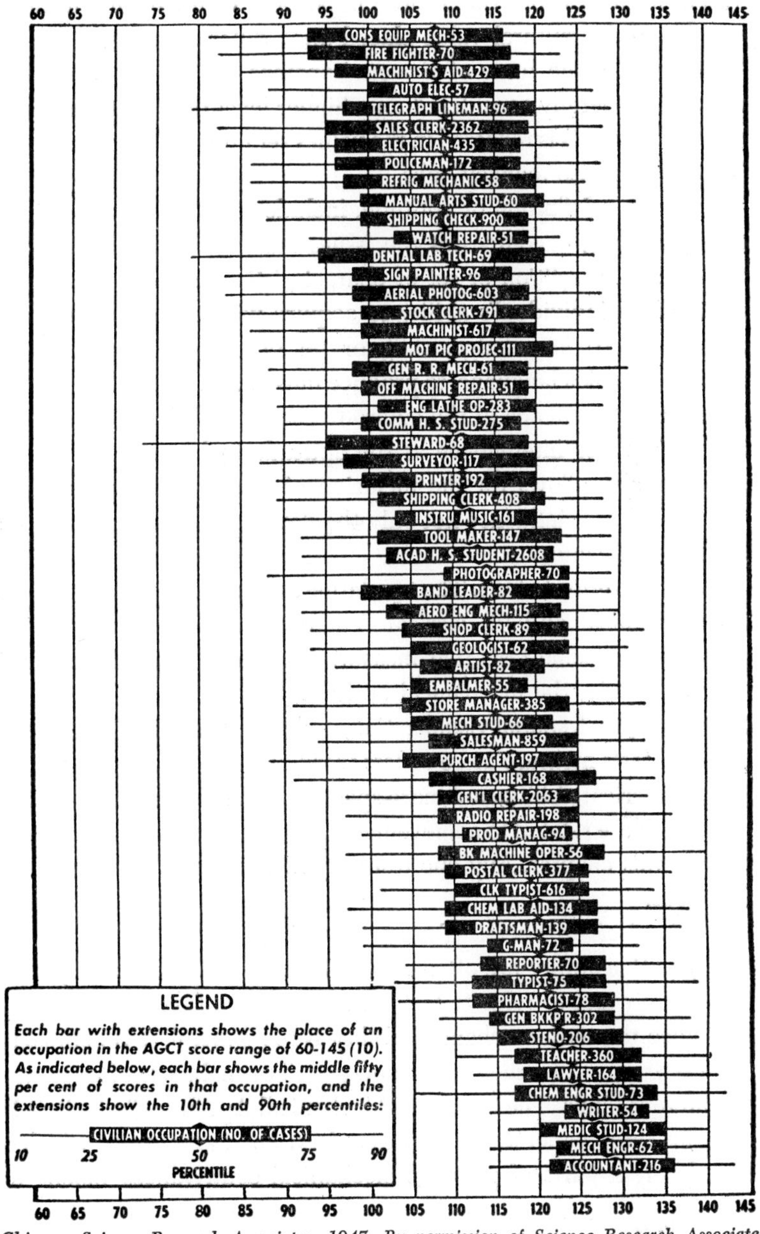

Chicago: Science Research Associates, 1947. By permission of Science Research Associates

play a role, but the environmental role is important too, and in individual instances sometimes more important. One has only to be reminded of the cultural value placed upon different kinds of abilities to appreciate the force of the environment. In our culture, verbal ability is generally considered on a higher level than spatial and mechanical and this is reflected in the values set upon white-collar versus "dirty" or "grease-monkey" jobs.

Bingham's definition of aptitude, included in Warren's *Dictionary of Psychology*, encompasses the issues succinctly. He defines aptitude as: "A condition or set of characteristics regarded as symptomatic of an individual's ability to acquire with training some (usually specified) knowledge, skill, or set of responses, such as the ability to speak a language, to produce music. . . ." This definition allows for the influence of the environment through learning or training. It includes intelligence as the aptitude to learn academic material. It also allows for the inclusion of interests and personality, which we know influence not only the development of attitudes, but their present status.

Kinds of aptitude tests. The two largest groups of aptitude tests are (1) mechanical and (2) clerical. There are tremendous variations among the specific tests that measure mechanical and clerical aptitude. Basically, the mechanical aptitude tests measure to some degree perceptual, spatial visualization, and motor abilities. The clerical aptitude tests measure more or less word fluency, verbal comprehension, numerical ability, and more specialized tasks like filing and typing, which are related to achievement. Achievement will be discussed later in this chapter. Any one test may measure one or more of the functions.

Mechanical aptitude. Tests measuring spatial relations and manipulative ability are often referred to as mechanical ability tests. It is more exact to refer to tests in terms of the function measured, and since the term mechanical ability is too general, it is confusing. Such tests may be either paper and pencil or make use of apparatus of different kinds. The Stenquist Mechanical Aptitude Tests, Part II, contains three paper and pencil exercises: one to recognize which of two different parts of pictured mechanical contrivances belong together; the second to answer such questions on mechanical knowledge as "Oil is kept from dripping on the floor by —"; and the third, to answer questions on principles of mechanics, such as, "Look at pulleys 1 and 3. Which carries the heavier load?" The MacQuarrie Test for Mechanical Ability, another paper and pencil test, has seven different subtests. This test and others frequently used will be described and illustrated in Chapter 8. Other mechanical ability tests have different content and are differently administered.

Wittenborn (26) conducted a factor analysis of mechanical ability using the data employed in the preliminary Minnesota experiment. Twenty-six different tests had been administered to a sampling of 217 boys in the seventh and eighth grades of a Minneapolis junior high school. Their courses of study included shop work.

> Boys were chosen rather than men, because it was felt that in boys, individual differences would be determined less by differences in the amount of mechanical training and more by stable abilities which accrue from general sources. Boys from the middle class were selected rather than a more heterogeneous sample. The reason for this selection was that in all probability the boys in the upper classes have had a restricted opportunity to acquire mechanical abilities, and the boys from the low, under-privileged class have had restrictions in their development also. Selection of boys who were enrolled in shop courses was determined by the need for a suitable criterion, which could not only be reliably determined, but which would also suitably represent the varied operations which are considered to comprise mechanical ability.[5]

The following group of 26 tests was administered. The tests had been grouped originally into seven parts in accordance with the kind of functions they appeared to be measuring. The factor analysis was done later by Wittenborn (26). Both group and individual tests of the paper and pencil and of the performance variety were administered.

I. Standard group intelligence tests:
   1. Army Alpha, Form 6 (group paper)

[5] J. R. Wittenborn, "Mechanical Ability, its Nature and Measurement. I. An Analysis of the Variables Employed in the Preliminary Minnesota Experiment." *Educational and Psychological Measurement,* 5:244 (1945).

2. Otis Self-Administering Tests of Mental Ability, Higher Examination: Form A (group paper)

II. Simple motor tests
1. Tapping Test A (group paper)
2. Tapping Test B (group paper)
3. Tapping Test C (individual apparatus)
4. Steadiness of Motor Control (individual apparatus)
5. Accuracy of Movement or Tracing Paper (group paper)
6. Accuracy of Movement or Tracing Board (individual apparatus)
7. Aiming (individual paper)
8. Speed of movement (group paper)

III. Balancing tests
1. Body Balancing (individual apparatus)
2. Stick Balancing (individual apparatus)

IV. Complex eye-hand coordination tests
1. Link's Machine Operator's (individual apparatus)
2. Card Sorting (individual apparatus)
3. Card Assembly (individual apparatus)
4. Packing Blocks (individual apparatus)

V. Assembly tests involving manipulation and responses to spatial relations
1. Stenquist Assembly (group apparatus)
2. Paper Form Board (group paper)
3. Link's Spatial Relations (individual apparatus)
4. Cube Construction (group apparatus)

VI. Tests of mechanical knowledge
1. Stenquist Picture Tests I and II (group paper)

VII. Miscellaneous tests
1. Slow Movement or Motor Inhibition (individual paper)
2. Digit-Symbol Substitution (group paper)
3. Letter Cancellation (group paper)
4. Number Cancellation (group paper)
5. Rhythm or Perception of Time (group apparatus)[6]

Six factors were found to account for the variance in the 26 tests: (1) spatial visualization, (2) stereotyped movement, (3) scholastic ability, (4) manual dexterity, (5) perceptual speed, and (6) steadiness.

Three points should be noted in the array of factors. (1) Some tests

[6] *Ibid.*, pages 243–244.

measure more than one factor. For example, Link's Spatial Relations measures spatial and dexterity factors, and the Paper Form Board measures spatial and scholastic factors. (2) The factor analysis reveals that spatial visualization differs from perceptual speed. (3) The factor of perceptual speed found in the letter and number cancellation tests, which are similar to those used in clerical tests, is also a factor in mechanical ability.

TABLE 10

FACTORS FOUND AMONG 26 TESTS IN A STUDY OF MECHANICAL ABILITY*

Factors	*Tests*
1. Spatial visualization	Link's Spatial Relations, Paper Form Board, Stenquist Assembly, Stenquist Pictures I and II.
2. Stereotyped movement	Link's Machine Operator, Speed of Movement, Tapping A, Tapping B, Tapping C.
3. Scholastic ability	Army Alpha, Otis, Stenquist Picture II, Paper Formboard.
4. Manual Dexterity	Card Assembly, Time; Card Sorting, Time; Digit Symbol; Link's Machine Operator; Link's Spatial Relations; Packing Blocks.
5. Perceptual speed	Letter cancellation, Number cancellation.
6. Steadiness	Aiming; Body Balancing; Steadiness, No. contacts; Tracing Board, No. errors; Tracing Paper, No. errors.

* Adapted from J. R. Wittenborn, "Mechanical Ability, its Nature and Measurement. I. An Analysis of the Variables Employed in the Preliminary Minnesota Experiment." *Educational and Psychological Measurement,* 5:241–260 (1945).

Harrell (15) found perceptual and spatial factors high in mechanical ability tests. Guilford (14) recognized the difference between spatial visualization and perceptual speed. He calls one factor spatial relations, defining it as a "perceptual awareness of the arrangements of objects with respect to right-left, up-down and out-in dimensions."[7] This is similar to the direct recognition of different sizes and shapes and can be called perceptual speed for the sake of uniformity and simplicity. He describes the visualization factor as

> requiring one to imagine transformations, movements, or other changes. A typical test represents a picture of a square paper being folded one or more times, in successive steps, and a hole of a given

[7] J. P. Guilford, "The Discovery of Aptitude and Achievement Variables," *Science,* 106:280 (1947).

shape being cut out. The examinee selects one of five other pictures, each showing plausible creases and holes, as the paper might appear after being unfolded.[8]

Factor analysis allows for the breakdown of the tests into components which can be psychologically identified. Perceptual speed and space visualization have been identified by this means; this identification has important vocational implications. The tests of perceptual speed are not as difficult as those of space visualization; they are more concrete and not as highly correlated with scholastic ability. Tests of perceptual speed are therefore related to less difficult mechanical jobs than space visualization tests. The latter are related to engineering and highly skilled jobs. The dexterity or motor factor is known to be significant too, but less so for the more complex jobs. This factor, however, probably has several components, not all identified as yet.

Examination of the standardization data reported by Bennett and Cruikshank (6), in *A Summary of Manual and Mechanical Ability Tests,* reveals significant facts about the reliability and validity of such tests. By the descriptions and evaluations of the tests as given in the summary, as well as our own knowledge of and experience with the tests, it was possible to classify them as mainly spatial or mainly motor or manual. Table 11 shows the validities and reliabilities of the tests so categorized.

The validity coefficients are lower than the reliability coefficients. Yet validity is more important than reliability, and is more difficult to obtain. This is so because reliability can be measured by means of the test alone, either through repetition of the test, or through a duplicate form of the test, or by splitting the test in half and correlating one half against the other (usually odd-numbered items against even-numbered items, where there are a large enough number of items arranged in order of difficulty). But validity has to be measured against standards outside of the test itself, like shop work grades, production records, or foreman's ratings. The outside criteria are never perfect in themselves and present extraneous as well as uncontrolled factors that tend to lower the validity coefficient.

The validity of motor tests is generally lower than that of spatial

[8] *Loc. cit.*

tests, probably because motor tests generally measure a narrow aspect of total functioning. Motor tests must be used with greater caution than spatial tests.

TABLE 11

VALIDITY AND RELIABILITY COEFFICIENTS OF SPATIAL AND MOTOR TESTS

	Spatial Tests	*Motor Tests*
Validity coefficient	Range from .48 to .91 with four tests indefinite	Range from .11 to .53 with three tests indefinite
Reliability coefficient	Range from .60 to .90 with two tests indefinite	Range from .77 to .90 with one test indefinite

Data derived from G. Bennett and R. B. Cruikshank, *A Summary of Manual and Mechanical Ability Tests*. New Yoık: The Psychological Corporation, 1942.

Blum and Candee (10) used two motor tests, an intelligence test and a clerical test, in a study on the selection of department store wrappers and packers. On the surface, one would expect the motor tests to be highly involved in successful wrapping and packing. However, the authors found that

> clerical speed and accuracy seem to have a much higher relationship to production in the long run. Apparently, initial adjustment to the job is influenced in packers to some extent by speed of relatively gross movements, but long term superiority on the job depends more on clerical ability with both wrappers and packers.

Apparently, a clerical test is more valid for selecting wrappers and packers than motor tests which ordinarily might be assumed to have higher relations to such jobs.

To interpret test results, norms or standards of reference must be available too. The size of the population as well as its special characteristics must be known before one can evaluate the norms. Large populations are ordinarily better than small ones in considering the value of norms. The appropriateness of the population in relation to the person tested must also be considered. Is the examinee being compared with norms derived from a group of assembly workers or skilled mechanics? Such factors as age, sex, socio-economic status, educational level, occupational level are some of the more commonly considered variables in the interpretation of test results.

The Revised Minnesota Paper Form Board (to be described and

illustrated in Chapter 8) has several sets of norms: for engineering students, liberal arts freshmen, high school seniors, business college students, adults applying for positions, vocational school boys, boys age 9–15, and printer's apprentices. In interpreting a score of a client, it must be decided which of the norms would be most applicable.

The interpreter of test results in vocational guidance must know the validity and reliability of the tests used as well as the characteristics of the norms, so that they will be of the greatest advantage to the individual client. This means that there must be even greater caution because the focus is on the individual. If a test is generally valid, the question of validity for the individual must be asked. This can be determined only by a full clinical study of how the individual fits into the norm group and in what respects he deviates.

Clerical aptitude. Clerical aptitude is not just one aptitude. It consists of several abilities. Although there are common elements from clerical job to clerical job, there are differences in level as well as differences in skills required, such as bookkeeping and typing.

Bingham (9), in describing the abilities required in clerical work, states:

> Aptitudes for clerical occupations then are evidenced in part at least by four different kinds of abilities. The first and simplest of these is strictly perceptual: ability to observe words and numbers, to see instantly and correctly what is on the paper. The second is intellectual: ability to grasp the meaning of words and other symbols and to make correct decisions regarding the questions raised. . . . The third group of clerical abilities consists of various mental skills peculiarly susceptible to improvement through special training. The most elementary of these skills include the ability to add and multiply, to spell correctly, to punctuate, and to use a wide variety of English words and expressions correctly; while the most advanced may require a technical knowledge of some learned profession. The fourth kind of ability is motor. With agile fingers and hands, the various papers, cards, pencil, typewriter, comptometer, and other office tools are adroitly manipulated.[9]

Not only do the various clerical tests have different kinds of items; they have not been equally well standardized. Anderson (3), in a re-

[9] W. V. Bingham, "Classifying and Testing for Clerical Jobs," *Personnel Journal*, 14:170 (1935).

view of six clerical tests published between 1929 and 1942, and 14 tests published before 1929, found the validity coefficients, reliability coefficients, and norms to be quite varied. Table 12 summarizes his findings.

TABLE 12

VALIDITY COEFFICIENTS, RELIABILITY COEFFICIENTS, AND NUMBER OF SUBJECTS USED TO OBTAIN NORMS FOR CLERICAL TESTS DEVISED BEFORE 1929 AND BETWEEN 1929 AND 1942

	Before 1929		*Between 1929 and 1942*	
	No. of Tests	*Coefficient of Correlation*	*No. of Tests*	*Coefficient of Correlation*
Validities Reported	11	Range 0.19 to 0.82; "average" 0.53	3	Range 0.28 to 0.72; "average" 0.48
	3	Not given	3	Not given
Reliabilities Reported	1	0.26 and 0.49	1	0.85 and 0.90
	1	0.82	1	0.85 and 0.96
	12	Not given	1	0.85
			1	0.89
			2	Not given
	No. of Tests	*No. of Cases*	*No. of Tests*	*No. of Cases*
Number of Subjects Used	9	50 to 200	5	139 to 1500
	5	Not given	1	Not given

From R. N. Anderson, "Review of Clerical Tests," *Occupations, the Vocational Guidance Journal*, published by National Vocational Guidance Association, Incorporated, 21:659 (1943).

There has been some improvement since 1929 in reliability and in size of sampling used, but none in validity. And this is crucial. The validities reported for tests since 1942 in Bennett and Cruikshank (7), a very serviceable manual for clerical tests, show great variability. Undoubtedly, much of the difficulty in validation of clerical tests is due to the wide coverage extended for each test. A single clerical test purports to measure different kinds and levels of clerical work, from routine duties to accounting. Unlike intelligence tests, the aptitude tests do not measure broad functions. This fact, and the fact that validity is measured against ratings by supervisors or grades, makes for lower validities. This is not to excuse the low validities but to point up the need to examine them more carefully with due regard to all factors. The tests do serve the purpose of improving upon the ability to predict clerical success, but will be even more useful if interpreted together with knowledge about the individual and with other tests.

The same situation holds for the characteristics of norms that was true for mechanical aptitude tests. They vary in size and kind of sampling and must be interpreted with due regard to those attributes. There is an additional feature about clerical aptitude tests which we will discuss under achievement tests. This is the fact that many clerical test items like spelling, grammar, and typing are very similar to those of achievement tests.

Other aptitudes. There are other aptitude tests developed more specifically for various occupations. They may measure potential ability for engineering, selling, law, music, or art. Usually, they consist of several kinds of subtests. For example, tests for engineering include such subtests as mathematics, physical science comprehension, verbal comprehension, and mechanical comprehension. Selling aptitude tests measure such functions as social consciousness, arithmetical ability, memory, ability to follow directions, and personality. The tests may be used as supplementary to the interview with some mild degree of success. However, they require much more research before they can be used to select personnel. Different jobs have different requirements and the tests would have to be tested for validity for the various kinds of jobs.

Some law schools and medical schools use tests as part of their entrance requirements. The aptitude tests for law and medicine measure aspects of intelligence like ability for accurate recall, ability to reason by analogy and analytically, ability for logical reasoning, and ability to acquire scientific vocabulary (for medical schools). These tests have validity when considered along wtih college grades, references and interviews.

Tests of aptitude for music and art generally measure appreciation rather than actual ability. The assumption is that there is a relationship between the two. However, the validities of the tests as predictors of success are questionable. There is considerable controversy about the relative importance of heredity and environment as contributing factors to success in music and art. For example, although pitch discrimination is considered basic to musical talent, some believe it is largely inherited and others that it is greatly influenced by experience and training. Neu (18) critically evaluated the research on absolute pitch, or the ability to correctly name a particular tone without reference to another tone. This is considered the highest level of pitch discrimination. He believes that even absolute pitch can be acquired. But Bachem (4) disputes this, claiming that one can learn high pitch discrimination but not absolute pitch. The latter, he claims, is inherited; he cites its occurrence in families, the close association with musical talent, its appearance at an early age, and the fact that no adult person has ever acquired it. The question needs further research, especially in terms of what it means for success in music.

For art, Meier (16) believes that nature and nurture play interacting roles. He writes:

> . . . let it be understood that there is no heredity involved as heredity is sometimes conceived, namely as inheritance of acquired characteristics from parents. What is involved is simply stock inheritance, or in other words, merely that the present individual comes from a line of ancestors who found the acquisition of skills in artistic pursuits relatively easy. The present individual, coming from the same stock, likewise finds the acquisition of these skills easy.[10]

It would seem that both heredity and environment play important interacting roles in music and art aptitude. A person cannot become a concert pianist as easily, if at all, if he discovers his ability late in life, because of the other intricacies involved in virtuoso playing. Of course, talents display themselves in different forms and for the talented person who could not become a concert pianist late in life

[10] N. C. Meier, *Examiner's Manual, The Meier Tests. I. Art Judgment.* Iowa City: Bureau of Educational Research and Science, State University of Iowa, 1942, page 20. Reproduced with the permission of the author and the publishers.

there is the garment worker who became an artist at an advanced age.

The music and art tests can generally be classified as having high reliabilities but doubtful validities. Taylor (21) in her study on the prognosis of musical talent concludes that, "It is evident that, as a whole, the music test batteries do not evidence sufficient predictive power to be used by themselves for guidance purposes, yet neither do they have so little value as to warrant discarding them entirely." Carroll (11) in a study of two art tests found that they did not correlate much with the judgment of university art instructors on the creative ability of art majors in college.

Achievement tests

Achievement tests measure acquired skill or knowledge in a trade or school subject. Although they measure the present status, they may afford implications about future potentialities. In this sense they are also measures of aptitude. Trade tests are not as widely used in vocational guidance as are the other kinds, since people who have reached a high level of skill in a trade generally do not come for vocational counseling. Trade tests are used more widely in selection.

Educational achievement tests are used in vocational guidance. These estimate the level of knowledge attained in subject matter. The most widely used of subject-matter tests are those of English and mathematics. There are achievement tests in algebra, arithmetic, calculus, geometry, agriculture, business education, education, engineering, science, social studies, and foreign languages. They all have implications for school success. Together with tests of intelligence, aptitudes, interest, and personality, they help round out the picture of the individual's potentialities.

These tests differ in their suitability for different groups. Some are for elementary grades, some for high school, and some for colleges. Obviously, the norms must differ for the different groups. The validities vary too. When careful study is made of the suitability of the tests, they can serve useful functions. For example, they are helpful in determining discrepancies between intelligence and how much has been learned. The level reached on an achievement test may be in line with the intelligence level. However, it may be lower, due to special environmental circumstances. In such instances the intelligence test will prognosticate the probable level of achievement. The achievement test will demonstrate the need for training in the subject.

As an illustration, the case of John J. is offered. He had had to leave school early to work in unskilled jobs because of family circumstances. He was now interested in learning a trade like machine shop work. His intelligence was above average on a non-verbal test. Arithmetic achievement was very low and he did not know decimals. For success in machine shop work it is necessary to read a micrometer which uses decimals. The achievement test demonstrated that John did not have the requisite knowledge, but the intelligence test showed that he could acquire it. Training was indicated and turned out to be successful.

Although aptitude tests are not supposed to have items that are dependent upon formalized training, clerical and mechanical tests sometimes do. Clerical tests may have items of spelling, grammar, arithmetic, and business knowledge. In this respect, they resemble achievement tests. However, there is justification for including achievement items in a clerical test in that they indicate degree of readiness for clerical work. Since high school graduation is usually a prerequisite for clerical work, the achievement type of item is appropriate. Items of achievement can be similar to aptitude items in this instance since they project how well one will learn a clerical job, on the basis of how well the particular items that go into successful clerical work have been learned previously. However, caution must be used in interpreting the test results when the educational opportunities were much different from the average or the circumstances were peculiar to the individual.

Typing and stenography tests are achievement tests. These are usually given in the form of a work sample; that is, a sample of typing or stenography is obtained under standardized conditions. These tests are given mainly in employment situations for hiring purposes. They may be given in vocational guidance if the interest exists and the individual has had the opportunity to learn the skills.

Some mechanical ability paper and pencil tests have subtests of mechanical information or knowledge. This type of exercise is also closely akin to achievement tests since it requires experience with machinery, tools, and objects. The justification for the inclusion of such items in an aptitude test is that the individual who has mechanical aptitude would have come in contact with such items through his experience. The people who do not presumably would have avoided them. This may or may not be true in individual instances and such items or exercises would have to be interpreted with respect to more knowledge about the individual.

Interest tests

The measurement of interests is generally considered to be as important as the measurement of abilities in vocational guidance. It is needed to account for part of the variance in job success that ability does not measure. Without interest, ability may be wasted. Interest tests are valuable to measure and predict the strength of motivation that may be expected in relation to fields or types of work. A knowledge of the interest patterns obtained from the tests becomes a convenient frame of reference during an interview. An individual may not be fully aware of his interests and their relative strength and, in some instances, he may be unfamiliar with the variety of occupations that fit his vocational preferences. The interest test can be a means through which the individual is helped to clarify his interests in terms of occupations.

Interest tests measure attitude toward various occupations, school, and social and recreational activities. They are generally standardized by administering the test items to samplings of people in different occupations. In this way different interest patterns are identifiable for different fields of work. The Kuder Preference Record, which will be described in Chapter 9, measures nine fields of interest: (1) mechanical, (2) computational, (3) scientific, (4) persuasive, (5) artistic, (6) literary, (7) musical, (8) social service, and (9) clerical. The Strong Vocational Interest Blank measures degree of interest in 15 different vocations for women and 39 for men. Some of these are: artist, psychologist, architect, physician, accountant, and lawyer.

Super (20) in his review of Strong's book on *Vocational Interests of Men and Women* states:

> That patterns of vocational interests begin to be clear cut in adolescence and remain fairly stable throughout life, indicates that the test (Strong's Vocational Interest Blank) can be used in vocational guidance at the high school level, and that vocational interests are not acquired as the result of vocational experiences. The interests of high school boys can and do resemble those of experienced engineers, printers, accountants, even though they have never had direct and intimate contact with their work, and these resemblances are relatively stable.[11]

The assumption of stable patterning of interests is basic to interest measurement and must hold in order for the tests to have any value as predictors of interest.

Individuals may have one or more interest patterns in varying degrees. The higher the rating or percentile in the specific interest, the stronger the interest is presumed to be. Thus in the Kuder Preference Record, a percentile rating of 75 or better is considered a significantly high interest. In the Strong Vocational Interest Blank, ratings of A and B+ are considered presumptive of interest. However, lower percentile or letter ratings are not to be disregarded. Low ratings may point to areas that should be eliminated from consideration. Judgments made by the interpreter should not be based upon single ratings, but various ratings should support each other in the final analysis.

Darley (12) has proposed that the analysis of a person's scores on the Strong Interest Blank be made on the basis of three patterns. The primary pattern includes a preponderance of scores of A or B+ on specific occupational keys. The secondary pattern includes scores of B+ and B and the tertiary pattern shows a preponderance of B and B–. An analysis of 1000 men students at the University of Minnesota revealed the distribution of patterns shown in Table 13.

---

[11] Reprinted from *Psychological Bulletin*, 42:361 (1945), by permission of the American Psychological Association, publishers.

TABLE 13

FREQUENCY OF OCCURRENCE OF PRIMARY, SECONDARY, AND TERTIARY INTEREST PATTERNS IN 1000 CASES*

	Number	*Percentage*
1. A primary pattern only	62	6.2
2. A secondary pattern only	54	5.4
3. A tertiary pattern only	160	16.0
4. No primary, secondary, or tertiary pattern	28	2.8
5. Primary and secondary patterns together	86	8.6
6. Primary and tertiary patterns together	111	11.1
7. Secondary and tertiary patterns together	283	28.3
8. Primary, secondary, and tertiary patterns	216	21.6
	1000	100.0

* J. G. Darley, *Clinical Aspects and Interpretation of the Strong Vocational Interest Blank.* New York: The Psychological Corporation, 1941.

It can be seen from the table that some people present no primary pattern at all. In fact roughly half the population is to be found in this category.

It is dangerous to recommend a job or even a broad field of work on the basis of a high rating in one area alone. One should not just array the ratings in ascending order and say scientific is the first choice, literary the second, and so forth. Rather one should pattern the various ratings. The interest tests will not tell specifically and with finality what job is the one and only. Other tests must be used too, and all the test results integrated in the interview.

There are individuals who either deliberately or unconsciously respond to interest items in different ways and for different reasons. Miss Shirley F. responded to an interest questionnaire so as to come out highest in social service interest. In the interview she denied this interest as a career. It would have had to be on a lower level too because she was low average in intelligence. She is interested in social service activities because of her particular personal experiences but really disliked the actual activities involved in such work, when these were described. She felt she needed social service help herself but really could not give it to others.

Michael D., aged 20, rated highest in persuasiveness and moderately high in mechanics and science on an interest test. When interviewed, he stated that he would not really like to persuade people unless it was for something he believed in wholeheartedly. He just could not be persuasive in other situations. However, he felt that he could be convincing with technical and scientific things, and that he would feel inclined toward selling and pushing them. For any one individual the test results must be interpreted in terms of what meanings he attaches to them. And he will attach those meanings which are related to his background of experiences, and his emotional adjustment.

The reliabilities of interest tests are high. The measures are generally stable upon repetition after the lapse of several months and in some cases, years. This speaks well for their consistency of measurement.

The validity of the tests is really measured by their use in practice. If the interest patterns obtained seem to the counselor to be consistent with the picture he gets of the individual from such other sources as other tests, work history, and interview, the test is considered valid. The manner of the standardization of interest tests also offers intrinsic support for its validity. Only those items in a field of work or occupation are included which check with individuals already established in these fields and occupations.

Although the more commonly used interest tests have accepted validity, scores from any two interest tests made by the same person will not necessarily show the same strength in the various interest areas. Wittenborn, Triggs, and Feder (27) compared the measurement of interest by the Kuder Preference Record and the Strong Vocational Interest Blank and found some consistencies and some inconsistencies. The items that make up each test are different and so are the norms. One cannot then expect complete agreement between two tests of interest.

It is necessary to study the norms carefully. Scores will differ in accordance with the norms used as a standard of comparison. Sex differences are significant on interest tests. The culture determines pretty much the development of male and female interest patterns. For instance, clerical work is considered more feminine, whereas mechanical work is considered more masculine. There are substantial differences between the sexes in their relative interest in the two kinds of work. The female average is higher for clerical interest and the male average, for mechanical interest. This means that a female must make a higher score than a male to obtain the same percentile rating in clerical interest, but a male needs a higher score in mechanical. Thus a score of 71 by a male in the clerical area of the Kuder Preference Record rates a 90th percentile, while a female requires a score of 84 to receive the same percentile score.

Personality tests

Personality tests are used in vocational guidance to help complete the picture of the individual. Tests of ability and interest do not measure such personality traits as confidence, dominance, and sociability, which account for a significant part of vocational adjustment. Paper and pencil personality tests of the questionnaire variety are used predominantly in guidance, mainly because they are easily scored and can be given to groups.

Most of the personality questionnaires can be traced to the original Psychoneurotic Inventory, which was developed as a result of problems arising during World War I. The necessity for mass screening encouraged the development of group personality tests. The questions in the Inventory were to be answered *yes* or *no* by the subject or an observer. They were developed from psychiatric examinations of neurotics. Some of the questions in the Inventory are, "Are you frightened in the middle of the night?" "Do you make friendships easily?" "Do you ever feel an awful pressure in or about the head?" "Are you troubled with the idea that people are watching you on the street?" Almost all subsequent paper and pencil personality tests use similar questions with some variations. Typical personality tests will be described in detail in Chapter 9.

Personality tests differ in terms of the several categories they purport to measure. For instance, the Bell Adjustment Inventory (Student Form) measures four areas of adjustment: home, health, social, and emotional. The Bernreuter Personality Inventory purports to measure six traits: neurotic tendency, self-sufficiency, introversion, social dominance, self-consciousness, and sociability.

The Mental Health Analysis test by Tiegs, Thorpe, and Clarke breaks down the scoring into assets and liabilities of personality. The Guilford-Martin Personnel Inventory measures cooperativeness as opposed to fault-finding, objectivity as opposed to personal reference, and agreeableness as opposed to belligerence. Other tests like the Humm-Wadsworth Temperament Scale and the Minnesota Multiphasic Personality Inventory allow for more complete analyses by using clinical patterns. The former employs Rosanoff's grouping of traits: normal, hysteroid, or anti-social; cycloid (manic phase), cycloid (depressed phase); schizoid (autistic phase), schizoid (paranoid phase); and epileptoid. The latter has nine scales within it called the hypochondriasis scale, the depression scale, the hysteria scale, the psychopathic deviate scale, the interest scale (masculinity or femininity of interest patterns), the paranoia scale, the psychasthenia scale, the schizophrenia scale, and the hypomania scale.

Group paper and pencil personality tests originally were intended for screening purposes. That is, the intent was to detect quickly the few seriously maladjusted persons in a population. Later the use of trait descriptions was developed. Still later, attempts to diagnose personality patterns emerged. A major shortcoming of the questionnaires that measure multiple traits is their inability to integrate the results into a meaningful, dynamic, and living personality. The trait descriptions result in relatively stagnant and somewhat unreal personality patterns. The group tests do not indicate how one trait affects another. They do not reveal the deep undercurrents of the individual and the way in which they affect behavior.

For example, there is the instance of Edward F., who was advised by some guidance person not to go in for selling because in a personality questionnaire he scored low in the trait extroversion and high in introversion. The young man was interested in selling and otherwise had the abilities for it. He found another counselor and after completing tests and interviews, took a sales job, and was successful in it. The original guidance person overlooked the fact that different personality patterns may be suitable for different selling jobs. He had arrived at a conclusion on the basis of a single trait. In some selling situations, introversion is not necessarily a deterrent. The particular kind of work that Edward does is selling quality standard items, which does not require the extensive socialization of the extrovert. He is thought to be friendly and steady in his relationships although not a glowing back-slapper.

Personality questionnaires are also greatly affected by honesty with oneself. Dishonesty is not always deliberate; it is often the result of unconscious motivation. Individuals interpret the qualifying words such as *frequently* or *occasionally* in different ways. A person may say he *frequently* feels like crying, but his interpretation of *frequently* may mean less in number than one who answers that he does not feel like crying *frequently*. Also he may feel that way at appropriate times, and he may overcome the feeling quickly. This is normal behavior. In fact, the normal person may, because of his greater feelings of inner security, feel free to answer many items indicating problems than a poorly adjusted person. The tremendous overlap in scores between normal and abnormal persons on personality questionnaires bears this out. A known mentally ill person may make a better score than a normal person with ordinary adjustment problems.

In guidance the personality questionnaire can be used to help screen a person for psychiatric attention or to get some clues about the type of job for which he might be more suited. However, the personality questionnaire has to be checked carefully against other personality data obtained from the interview and the vocational and social history. Where the counselor is skilled, this will be done and done well. Where the counselor is not skilled, too much reliance may be placed on the test and the ensuing results may be harmful to the person.

Some of the personality questionnaires have been used for diagnostic purposes, especially the Minnesota Multiphasic, which measures clinical symptoms. This test is usually administered individually and has been shown by Altus (1) and others to have some relationship with the more dynamic projective Rorschach personality test. The Rorschach test, consisting of ten inkblots, is considered a good projective test of personality structure and is only beginning to be used in vocational guidance. We shall discuss this test further in Chapter 10. Of the personality questionnaires, the Minnesota Multiphasic seems to have higher validity than the others for diagnostic purposes.

Ellis (13) reviewed the validity of personality questionnaires. Essentially the review is in terms of the diagnostic competence of the various questionnaires. Do they "adequately differentiate neurotics from non-neurotics, introverts from extroverts, dominant from submissive persons, and so on"? He concludes that, on the whole, they do not. Their validities are dubious. Some of the tests are better than others, but none have high validity, except for the Minnesota Multiphasic, which is administered individually.

Super (19) reviewed the research on the Bernreuter Personality Inventory. This test has been the most widely used of the paper and pencil personality tests. He writes,

> The Bernreuter scores tend to distinguish neurotics and various types of psychotics from normal individuals, although not perfectly; abnormals in the mass are not differentiated, because of the cancelling out of extreme tendencies. Unfavorable scores are indicative of maladjustment, but "favorable" scores do not necessarily indicate good adjustment. . . .[12]

About occupational differences he notes that they have been disappointing.

> There is considerable overlapping, suggesting that there is sufficient variety among the jobs in a given occupation to allow scope for all kinds of personalities in any occupation. In spite of this fact, the tendencies are rather definite; those in work involving contact with individuals tend to be more dominant than others, whereas those working with records and objects tend to be less so. Differences in other traits have not been found to be reliable, and in no case are they great enough for individual guidance; other factors are of more importance.[13]

As we pointed out in the case of Edward F., even in work involving contacts with individuals, there are varieties of contacts differing in degree of challenge and intimacy. The degree of dominance needed

---

[12] Reprinted from *Psychological Bulletin*, 39:115 (1942), by permission of the American Psychological Association, publishers.

[13] *Loc. cit.*

would vary considerably and in any event would have to be related to other traits of personality, such as how the dominance trait is used.

The reliability of personality questionnaires is high. Retest results after a period of time are still quite similar to the original test results. The relationship is higher between two test administrations the closer they are in time. Benton and Stone (10) found that the consistency of response to personality test items (in this case, the Personal Inquiry Form of Landis and Zubin, whose items were derived from the Bernreuter Personality Inventory and other questionnaires) progressively decreased in accordance with the length of the time interval between test and retest until the four-day interval was reached. Thereafter the responses were consistent. Other studies have shown similar results. The tests are in general reliable, but the validity is doubtful.

Summary

The varieties of tests were categorized as intelligence, aptitude, achievement, interest, and personality. Each category was evaluated in accordance with certain psychological principles. In each instance special consideration was given to the attributes of validity, reliability and norms. Validity was considered the most important of the three attributes since ultimately the interpretation of test results is for the individual, who is, after all, the focus in vocational counseling.

Bibliography

1. Altus, W. D., "Some Correlates of the Group Rorschach and the Schizophrenia Scale of the Group MMPI Among Two Groups of Normal College Students," *Journal of Consulting Psychology,* 12:375–378 (1948).
2. Anderson, E. E., *et al.*, "Wilson College Studies in Psychology: I. A Comparison of the Wechsler-Bellevue, Revised Stanford-Binet, and American Council on Education Tests at the College Level," *Journal of Psychology,* 14:317–326 (1942).
3. Anderson, R. N., "Review of Clerical Tests," *Occupations,* 21:654–661 (1943).

4. Bachem, A., "Note on Neu's Review of the Literature on Absolute Pitch," *Psychological Bulletin,* 45:161–162 (1948).
5. Balinsky, B., H. Israel, and D. Wechsler, "The Relative Effectiveness of the Stanford-Binet and the Bellevue Intelligence Tests in Diagnosing Mental Deficiency," *American Journal of Orthopsychiatry,* 9:798–801 (1939).
6. Bennett, G. K., and R. M. Cruikshank, *A Summary of Manual and Mechanical Ability Tests.* New York: The Psychological Corporation, 1942.
7. ———, *A Summary of Clerical Tests.* New York: The Psychological Corporation, 1949.
8. Benton, A. L., and I. R. Stone, "Consistency of Response to Personality Inventory Items as a Function of Length of Interval Between Test and Retest," *Journal of Social Psychology,* 8:143–146 (1937).
9. Bingham, W. V., "Classifying and Testing for Clerical Jobs," *Personnel Journal,* 14:163–172 (1935).
10. Blum, M. L., and B. Candee, "The Selection of Department Store Packers and Wrappers with the Aid of Certain Psychological Tests: Study II," *Journal of Applied Psychology,* 25:291–299 (1941).
11. Carroll, H. A., "What do the Meier-Seashore and the McAdory Art Tests Measure?" *Journal of Educational Research,* 26:661–665 (1933).
12. Darley, J. G., *Clinical Aspects and Interpretation of the Strong Vocational Interest Blank.* New York: The Psychological Corporation, 1941.
13. Ellis, A., "The Validity of Personality Questionnaires," *Psychological Bulletin,* 43:385–440 (1946).
14. Guilford, J. P., "The Discovery of Aptitude and Achievement Variables," *Science,* 106:279–282 (1947).
15. Harrell, W., "A Factor Analysis of Mechanical Ability Tests," *Psychometrika,* 5:17–33 (1940).
16. Meier, N. C., *Examiner's Manual. The Meier Art Tests, I. Art Judgment.* Iowa City: Bureau of Educational Research and Science, State University of Iowa, 1942.
17. *Miller Analogies Test Manual.* New York: The Psychological Corporation, 1947.
18. Neu, D. M., "A Critical Review of the Literature on 'absolute pitch,'" *Psychological Bulletin,* 44:249–266 (1947).

19. Super, D. E., "The Bernreuter Personality Inventory: A Review of Research," *Psychological Bulletin*, 39:94–125 (1942).

20. ———, "Strong's Vocational Interests of Men and Women," *Psychological Bulletin*, 42:359–370 (1945).

21. Taylor, E. M., "A Study in the Prognosis of Musical Talent," *Journal of Experimental Education*, 10:1–28 (1941).

22. Terman, L. M. and M. A. Merrill, *Measuring Intelligence.* Boston: Houghton Mifflin, 1937.

23. Thurstone, L. L., and T. G. Thurstone, *Examiner's Manual, Preliminary Edition, for the SRA Primary Mental Abilities.* Chicago: Science Research Associates, 1947.

24. Wechsler, D., *Manual for Wechsler Intelligence Scale for Children.* New York: The Psychological Corporation, 1949.

25. ———, H. Israel, and B. Balinsky, "A Study of the Subtests of the Bellevue Intelligence Scale in Borderline and Mental Defective Cases," *American Journal of Mental Deficiency*, 45:555–558 (1941).

26. Wittenborn, J. R., "Mechanical Ability, its Nature and Measurement. I. An Analysis of the Variables Employed in the Preliminary Minnesota Experiment," *Educational and Psychological Measurement*, 5:241–260 (1945).

27. ———, F. O. Triggs, and D. D. Feder, "A Comparison of Interest Measurement by the Kuder Preference Record and the Strong Vocational Interest Blanks for Men and Women," *Educational and Psychological Measurement,* 3:239–257 (1943).

8

THE GUIDANCE USE OF INTELLIGENCE, APTITUDE, AND ACHIEVEMENT TESTS

The previous two chapters attempted to familiarize the reader with the principles and background information underlying psychological tests, their validity, reliability, and norms. It also indicated that there are many, many tests. All of this is important, but two more kinds of information are necessary before complete knowledge about psychological tests can be presumed. First there should be more precise familiarity with specific tests and their contents. Second and more important, the knowledge must be available to help one decide what specific tests to administer to a client.

This chapter will describe those intelligence, aptitude, and achievement tests most frequently used in vocational counseling. It will also indicate the extent and variety of their uses. This discussion will acquaint the reader not only with general but also with specific test information, so that he will not be in a dilemma if he has either to decide what battery of tests to administer or to evaluate a battery already in existence.

In selecting the tests to be described in this chapter and Chapter 9, such clinical instruments as the Rorschach Inkblot Test and the Wechsler-Bellevue Intelligence Scale have been deliberately omitted. Both of these tests require much more clinical experience and training not only in administration but also in interpretation.

These two tests as well as a few of the more commonly used projective tests will be discussed in Chapter 10.

The decision as to which tests to describe and still limit the material to reasonable proportions was not easy. The relationship between the validity of a test and its usage is surprisingly enough not always too high. If only high validity was the criterion then some tests included in this chapter would not have been described. However, the intent is primarily to describe the tests that are most frequently used in counseling and that have *reasonable validity*. The tests described are critically evaluated so that the shortcomings are revealed as well as the good points. This procedure should make it clear that wide usage of a test is not necessarily the best criterion for selecting it.

To bolster the judgment of the authors four surveys were used. In 1935 Pallister (56) undertook an investigation to determine which of 53 well-known tests were best known by reputable American psychologists, and how efficient they thought the 53 tests were. She sent questionnaires to 74 qualified psychologists, of whom 38 replied.

The tests known to 50 per cent or more of the 38 psychologists were regarded as best known. Seven tests were in this category: the Bernreuter Personality Inventory (71.1 per cent); the Strong Vocational Interest Blank (71.1 per cent); the Otis Self-Administering Test (68.4 per cent); the MacQuarrie Test for Mechanical Ability (60.5 per cent); the Minnesota Vocational Test for Clerical Workers, now known as the Minnesota Clerical Test (52.6 per cent); the O'Connor Finger and Tweezer Dexterity Tests (50.0 per cent); and the Stenquist Mechanical Aptitude Test (Picture Test) (50.0 per cent). These consist of one personality test, one interest test, one intelligence test, and four tests usually included among aptitude tests.

A test was considered efficient if 75 per cent or more of those who marked it classified it as such. Twenty-three tests were so classified: Aids to the Vocational Interview (100 per cent); the Pressey Senior Classification Test (100 per cent); the Pressey Senior Verifying Test (100 per cent); Test VI Mental Alertness (100 per cent); the Otis Self-Administering Test of Mental Ability (96.2 per cent); the Minnesota Vocational Test for Clerical Workers (95 per cent); the Minnesota Assembly Test (93.8 per cent); the Minnesota Spatial Relations Test (93.3 per cent); the Minnesota Paper Form Board Test (93.3 per cent); the Otis Group Intelligence Scale, Advanced (92.3 per cent); Rating Scales (90.9 per cent); the Minnesota Card Sorting Test (90 per cent); the Minnesota Rate of Manipulation Test (90 per cent); the Revised Minnesota Paper Form Board Test (90 per cent); the O'Connor Finger and Tweezer Dexterity Tests (89.5 per cent); the Strong Vocational Interest Blank (88.9 per cent); the Minnesota Packing Blocks Test (88.9 per cent); the O'Rourke Mechanical Aptitude Test, Junior Grade (87.5 per cent); the Willoughby Emotional Maturity Scale (85.7 per cent); the O'Rourke Clerical Aptitude Test, Clerical Problems (81.8 per cent); the Minnesota Interest Analysis (80 per cent); the Bell Adjustment Inventory (78.6 per cent); and the Thurstone Attitude Scales (75 per cent).

Darley and Marquis (24) surveyed veterans' advisement units in 1945 concerning the kind of programs they had. The survey included information on kinds of tests used and considered most valuable. The following tests were among those most frequently mentioned by the 51 clinics surveyed: the Kuder Preference Record (94 per cent); the Otis Series (73 per cent); the Wechsler-Bellevue (69 per cent); the American Council on Education (67 per cent); the Strong Vocational Interest Blank (67 per cent); the Minnesota Vocational Test for Clerical Workers (61 per cent); the Cooperative Test Service Series (59 per cent); the Minnesota Multiphasic Inventory (55 per cent); the Bennett Mechanical Comprehension Test (53 per cent); the O'Connor Finger-Tweezer Dexterity Tests (43 per cent); the Revised Minnesota Paper Form Board Test (43 per cent); the Purdue Pegboard (39 per cent); the U. S. Armed Forces Institute Tests (38 per cent); the Ohio State Psychological (37 per cent); the Minnesota Spatial Relations Test (37 per cent); the Bell Adjustment Inventory (35 per cent); the Bernreuter Personality Inventory (29 per cent); the Minnesota Rate of Manipulation Tests (29 per cent); the Detroit Mechanical Aptitude Test (27 per cent); the Iowa Placement and Achievement Tests (27 per cent); the Stanford Achievement Test (27 per cent); and the Meier-Seashore Art Judgment Test (22 per cent).

Of the 22 tests most frequently mentioned by Darley and Marquis four are intelligence tests, four educational achievement, two interest, three personality, and nine aptitude.

In 1946 Baker and Peatman (6) surveyed by means of a questionnaire the various psychological tests used in Veterans Advisement Units. They received replies from 188 units and found that the tests most frequently used, adjudged so by the criterion of at least once for every five or six veterans, were (1) the Kuder Preference Record (85 per cent); (2) the Bennett Mechanical Comprehension Test (64 per cent); (3) the American Council on Education Test (A.C.E.) (54 per cent); and (4) the Minnesota Clerical Test (39 per cent). As for the number of advisement units using the tests, frequency not being considered, the Kuder Preference Record had some use in 99 per cent of the units replying; the Minnesota Clerical in 92 per cent; the Bennet Mechanical Comprehension and the Revised Minnesota Paper Form Board in 90 per cent; the American Council on Education in 87 per cent; the Wechsler-Bellevue in 85 per cent; the Purdue Pegboard in 79 per cent; the Minnesota Multiphasic Personality Inventory in 77 per cent; the Ohio State Psychological Examination and the Minnesota Rate of Manipulation Test in 75 per cent; and the Strong Vocational Interest Blank and the Minnesota Spatial Relations in 70 per cent.

Of the 12 tests most used by the advisement units, irrespective of how frequently, two are group intelligence tests, one an individually administered intelligence test, six aptitude tests, one personality and two interest tests. An analysis of the units reporting indicates that 96.5 per cent frequently used at least one test of general intelligence. Ninety-three per cent frequently used an interest inventory; 83 per cent used either manual or mechanical tests. Personality tests were used frequently by 50 per cent of the centers, clerical by 43 per cent, achievement tests by 32 per cent. The two smallest categories included certain special tests like music and art aptitude tests and projective tests. Both of these were used frequently by only 6 per cent of the centers reporting. In addition to the 52 tests appearing on the Baker and Peatman questionnaire, unit directors were requested to list other tests used. Altogether 175 tests were reported. Among the more commonly listed tests were the O'Connor Finger and Tweezer

Dexterity Tests. They were reported as being used by 83 of the advisement units, although 18 said they used them rarely.

Failor and Mahler (27) surveyed the tests selected by counselors in a vocational counseling agency. They reported the selections by one counselor for 20 consecutive cases and by eight counselors in 20 cases each. Among the tests the counselor employed are the following (listed in order of frequency): Strong Interest, English Achievement, American Council on Education (entrance test results of the University), Iowa Mathematics, Kuder Preference Record, Wechsler-Bellevue, Minnesota Paper Form Board, Personal Audit, Physics Achievement, Minnesota Multiphasic, Engineering and Physical Science Aptitude, Minnesota Spatial Relations, Ohio State Psychological, and Reading Achievement. In addition several other tests were used in from one to three cases.

The eight counselors selected the following tests in order of frequency: Kuder Preference Record, Bennett Mechanical Comprehension, Minnesota Paper Form Board, Otis Test (Higher), American Council on Education, Occupational Interest Inventory, O'Connor Finger Dexterity, Wechsler-Bellevue, Strong Vocational Interest, Army General Classification Test, Cardall Arithmetic Achievement, O'Connor Tweezer Dexterity, Minnesota Clerical, Woody-McCall Arithmetic, Detroit Retail Aptitude, Personal Audit and Purdue Pegboard. Several other tests were selected but with less frequency.

The Failor and Mahler survey is limited to one vocational agency whereas the Darley and Marquis, and Baker and Peatman surveys are much larger in scope. However, it is a contemporary survey of test usage.

The four surveys show rather high agreement among the tests widely used. Of course, there are variations but they are likely to have arisen because of differences in time the surveys were taken, differences in sampling, differences among the counselors surveyed, and differences in the wording of the questionnaires. With the surveys and the experience of the authors as a basis for selection, 22 tests were chosen for description and discussion in this chapter and Chapter 9. They include three widely used intelligence tests, twelve tests of aptitude selected for range of testing as well as frequency, three tests of personality and two tests each to illustrate achievement testing and the measurement of interests. The remainder of the chapter will present and discuss three intelligence tests, 12 aptitude tests, and two achievement tests.

Intelligence tests

American Council on Education Psychological Examination. The American Council on Education has constructed a "Psychological Examination for College Freshmen," and a similar test for high school students. The A.C.E. Psychological Examination for College Freshmen is a time-limit group test of intelligence yielding three scores, linguistic (L), quantitative (Q), and a total score. It has gone through several revisions over a number of years and new editions are planned in the future. It is considered an excellent test of academic ability.

The L-score is more closely related to successful work in liberal arts colleges. The meaning of the Q-score is not as clear, perhaps because it measures several abilities and their relationships have not been established in terms of success in different courses. Guilford (32) has described the Q-score as "conglomerate factorially."[1] He writes, "Besides measuring numerical facility, this part also probably measures three kinds of reasoning as well as other factors to a small degree."

Anderson *et al.* (2) administered the A.C.E. as well as other tests to 112 women of the freshman class in a small college and found that the L-scores yielded correlations with grade-point averages as high as those of the total A.C.E. score. The correlations were of the order .50. The Q-scores yielded lower correlations (.39 and .36) with grade-point average. However, Berdie (13) found a correlation of only .21 between the total A.C.E. score and honor point ratio in a group of 154 engineering students. Traxler (78) reported correlations of .41 and .26, respectively, between the Q-score and Minnesota Paper Formboard and between the Q-score and the Bennett Mechanical Comprehension Test. The Q-score is not as good a measure of technical ability

[1] Reprinted by permission of Oscar K. Buros, Editor, *The Third Mental Measurements Yearbook* (New Brunswick: Rutgers University Press; 1949). Page 298.

as the L-score is of verbal ability. The test predicts college success well, but its interpretation must be bolstered by "other evidences of ability such as grades in high school and in content examinations that are uniformly given to all students" (75).

No reliability data on the current test are available. However, the reliability figures on earlier editions of the test are adequate, and it is assumed that the present test has similar reliability.

The norms are very extensive as a result of rather wide usage. They are obtained from many colleges throughout the country. Percentile norms are available for males and females for L-scores, Q-scores, and total scores for four-year colleges, junior colleges, and teachers' colleges.

The A.C.E. consists of six tests grouped as follows:

- Quantitative tests (Q-score)
  - Arithmetic–10 minutes
  - Number Series–8 minutes
  - Figure Analogies–5 minutes
- Linguistic tests (L-score)
  - Same-Opposite–5 minutes
  - Completion–5 minutes
  - Verbal Analogies–5 minutes

Each test is preceded by practice problems to accustom the examinee to the task expected. The time limits on the practice problems are not rigid, since it is important that the examinee understand the task. The six tests have separate time limits. Once the time limit for a test is past the subject may not go back to the task. The entire test, including time for practice problems, takes about one hour.

The six figures accompanying this discussion are the practice problems of each of the six tests. They are representative of the entire test for the 1946 edition. It is not considered ethical to present test items as illustrations. Obviously, presenting test items would tend to invalidate at least in part the tests so abused. However, it is desirable to illustrate the kind of items used in tests; and so practice problems will be presented as illustrative material, since they are not exactly the parts of the test that directly contribute to the final score.

Arithmetic

PRACTICE PROBLEMS

In this test you will be given some problems in arithmetic. After each problem there are five answers, but only one of them is the correct answer. You are to solve each problem and blacken the space on the answer sheet which corresponds to the answer you think is correct. The following problem is an example.

1. How many pencils can you buy for 50 cents at the rate of 2 for 5 cents?
(a) 10 (b) 20 (c) 25 (d) 100 (e) 125

Find on the answer sheet the space labeled "ARITHMETIC, Practice Problems, Page 3." The correct answer to the problem is 20, which is answer (b).
In the row numbered 1, space (b) has been blackened.

In the *second* row, blacken the space which corresponds to the answer to the second practice problem.

2. If James had 4 times as much money as George, he would have $16. How much money has George?
(a) $4 (b) $8 (c) $12 (d) $16 (e) $64

You should have blackened space (a), which corresponds to $4, the correct answer.

Blacken the spaces corresponding to the answers to the following problems:

3. In 5 days Harry has saved a dollar. What has his average daily saving been?
(a) 20¢ (b) 22½¢ (c) 25¢ (d) 30¢ (e) 40¢

4. John sold 4 magazines at 5 cents each. He kept ½ the money and with the other ½ he bought papers at 2 cents each. How many did he buy?
(a) 3 (b) 4 (c) 5 (d) 6 (e) 10

When the signal is given (not yet), turn the page and work more problems of the same kind. Work rapidly and accurately. Your rating will be the total number of correct answers. You may not be able to finish in the time allowed.

Stop here. Wait for the signal.

1946 Edition

A.C.E. PRACTICE PROBLEMS

Ohio State University Psychological Test. The Ohio State University Psychological Test is a group test of general intelligence or academic ability. It is known as a power test since it has no time limits.

Number Series

PRACTICE PROBLEMS

The numbers in each series proceed according to some rule. For each series you are to find the *next number*.

In the first series below, each number is 2 larger than the preceding number. The *next number* in the series would be 14. Of the five answers at the right, answer (e) is, therefore, correct. In the section of the answer sheet labeled "NUMBER SERIES, Practice Problems, Page 11," space (e) in the first row has been blackened.

Series						*Next Number*				
2	4	6	8	10	12	10 (a)	11 (b)	12 (c)	13 (d)	14 (e)

Find the rule in the series below, and blacken one of the answer spaces in the second row on the answer sheet.

2.	20	19	18	17	16	15	10 (a)	12 (b)	14 (c)	15 (d)	16 (e)

Each number in this series is 1 less than the preceding number You should have blackened space (c), which corresponds to 14, the next number in the series.

Find the rule in the series below and blacken the space on the answer sheet which corresponds to the next number.

3.	10	8	11	9	12	10	9 (a)	10 (b)	11 (c)	12 (d)	13 (e)

The series above goes by alternate steps of subtracting 2 and adding 3. You should have blackened space (e) which corresponds to 13, the next number.

In each series below, find the rule and blacken the space on the answer sheet which corresponds to the next number. There is a different rule for each series. Go right ahead. Do not wait for any signal.

4.	8	11	14	17	20	23	10 (a)	13 (b)	23 (c)	25 (d)	26 (e)
5.	27	27	23	23	19	19	15 (a)	16 (b)	17 (c)	18 (d)	19 (e)
6.	16	17	19	20	22	23	18 (a)	20 (b)	22 (c)	24 (d)	25 (e)

When the starting signal is given (not yet), turn the page and work more problems of the same kind. Work rapidly because your rating will be the total number of correct answers. You may not be able to finish in the time allowed.

Stop here. Wait for the signal.

1946 Edition

A.C.E. PRACTICE PROBLEMS *(continued)*

It consists of three subtests, all verbal: (1) Same-opposites, (2) analogies, and (3) reading comprehension. The test has a high correlation with college success; correlations of the order of .60 have been re-

Figure Analogies

PRACTICE PROBLEMS

Look at the figures A, B, and C in Sample 1 below. Figure A is a large circle. Figure B is a small circle. By what rule is Figure A changed to make Figure B? The rule is "making it smaller." Now look at Figure C. It is a large square. What will it be if you change it by the same rule? It will be a small square of the same color as the large square. Figure 2 is a small white square. In the section of the answer sheet labeled "FIGURE ANALOGIES, Practice Problems, Page 7," the space numbered 2 in the first row has been blackened to indicate the correct answer.

A B C 1 2 3 4 5

1

In Sample 2 below, the rule is: "Turn Figure A upside down to make Figure B." Now look at Figure C and think how it would look when turned upside down. It would look like Figure 4. The space numbered 4 has already been blackened on the answer sheet.

A B C 1 2 3 4 5

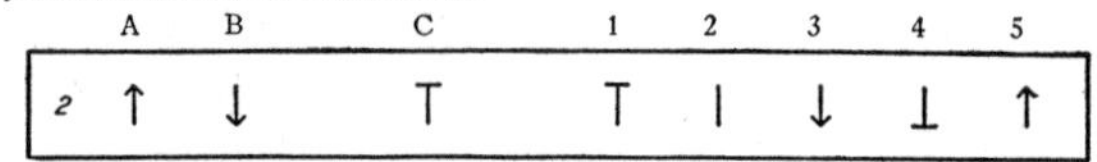

In Sample 3 below, the rule has two parts: "Make Figure B of the opposite color and larger than Figure A." Apply the rule to Figure C and blacken the space which corresponds to the correct answer.

A B C 1 2 3 4 5

3

You should have blackened the space numbered 1, which corresponds to the large white square.

Notice that the rule changes from one example to another. You are to do four things to each exercise on this page and the next.

a. Decide what rule is used to change Figure A to Figure B.
b. Apply this rule to Figure C.
c. Select the resulting figure from the five figures at the right.
d. Blacken the space on the answer sheet which is numbered the same as the figure you have selected.

Proceed to the four exercises below, marking your answers on the answer sheet. Go ahead.

A B C 1 2 3 4 5

4

5

6

7

Stop here.. Wait for the signal.

1946 Edition

A.C.E. PRACTICE PROBLEMS *(continued)*

ported between the test and knowledge of college subject matter (53). The correlations are somewhat lower for natural science and mathematics courses than they are for social studies and English. This is to

Same-Opposite

PRACTICE PROBLEMS

The word at the left in the following line is "many.

1. many	(1) ill	(2) few	(3) down	(4) sour

One of the four words at the right means either the *same* as or the *opposite* of "many." The word "few," which is numbered 2, is the opposite of "many." In the section of the answer sheet labeled "SAME-OPPOSITE, Practice Problems, Page 9," space number 2 in the first row has been blackened.

The word at the left in the second example is "ancient." Select one of the four words at the right that means the *same* as or the *opposite* of "ancient." In the second row on the answer sheet, blacken the space which corresponds to the answer you have selected.

2. ancient	(1) dry	(2) long	(3) happy	(4) old

You should have blackened the space numbered 4, because 4 corresponds to "old," which means the same as "ancient."

In each of the following lines select the word that means the *same* as or the *opposite* of the word at the left. On the answer sheet, blacken the space which corresponds to the answer you have selected.

3. deep	(1) blue	(2) shallow	(3) tense	(4) watery
4. awkward	(1) clumsy	(2) loyal	(3) passive	(4) young
5. hot	(1) dry	(2) cooked	(3) red	(4) cold

When the starting signal is given (not yet), turn the page and work more problems of the same kind. Work rapidly because your rating will be the total number of correct answers. You may not be able to finish in the time allowed.

Stop here. Wait for the signal.

1946 Edition

A.C.E. PRACTICE PROBLEMS *(continued)*

be expected since the test emphasizes verbal material. The reliability estimate is .93 (32).

The test is one of the most carefully developed of the group tests.

Completion

PRACTICE PROBLEMS

Look at the following definition. You are to think of the word that fits the definition.

1. A contest of speed. B F M P R

The word is *race*. The letter *R* is the first letter in the word *race*. In the section of the answer sheet labeled "COMPLETION, Practice Problems, Page 5," the space indicated by *R* in the first row has been blackened.

Blacken the space corresponding to the first letter of the word which fits the following definition.

2. A place or building for athletic exercises. C D G H T

The word is *gymnasium*. You should have marked the space indicated by *G* because it is the first letter in the word *gymnasium*.

Do the following examples in the same way:

3. The thin cutting part of an instrument, as of a knife or sword. A B D H W **4.** The wife of a king. F N P Q V **5.** A small or portable bed, as of canvas stretched on a frame. C G N P T

When the starting signal is given (not yet), turn the page and work more problems of the same kind. Work rapidly because your rating will be the total number of correct answers. You may not be able to finish in the time allowed.

Stop here. Wait for the signal.

1946 Edition

A.C.E. PRACTICE PROBLEMS *(continued)*

Since the first form appeared in 1919, it has undergone many revisions; and new revisions are planned for the future. The items that comprise this test have been very thoroughly planned, the non-dis-

Verbal Analogies

PRACTICE PROBLEMS

Read the following words:

1. foot-shoe hand- (1) thumb (2) head (3) glove (4) finger

The first two words, *foot-shoe*, are related. The next word is *hand*. It can be combined with one of the remaining words in the row so as to make a similar pair, *hand-glove*. In the section of the answer sheet labeled "VERBAL ANALOGIES, Practice Problems, Page 13," space number 3 in the first row has been blackened.

Read the following words:

2. father-son mother- (1) aunt (2) sister (3) child (4) daughter

The first pair is *father-son*. The next word is *mother*. It can be combined with the word *daughter* to make the similar pair, *mother-daughter*. In the second row on the answer sheet, blacken space number 4, which corresponds to the word *daughter*.

In each row of words, the first two words form a pair. The third word can be combined with another word to form a similar pair. Select the word which completes the second pair. On the answer sheet, blacken the space which corresponds to the word you select.

3. sky-blue grass- (1) green (2) sod (3) path (4) blue
4. ice-solid water- (1) hard (2) fire (3) iron (4) liquid

In the third row on the answer sheet, you should have blackened space number 1, which corresponds to *green*. In the fourth row, you should have blackened space number 4, which corresponds to *liquid*.

Select the answers to the following problems and blacken the corresponding spaces on the answer sheet. Go right ahead. Do not wait for any signal.

5. ear-music nose- (1) face (2) perfume (3) breath (4) tone
6. cloth-dye house- (1) shade (2) paint (3) brush (4) door
7. green-grass yellow- (1) silver (2) color (3) golden (4) gold
8. cattle-hay man- (1) eat (2) bread (3) water (4) life

When the starting signal is given (not yet), turn the page and work more problems of the same kind. Work rapidly because your rating will be the total number of correct answers. You may not be able to finish in the time allowed.

Stop here. Wait for the signal.

1946 Edition

A.C.E. PRACTICE PROBLEMS *(continued)*

criminating items having been in the main eliminated. One of the major refinements of the test is its shift from time-limit to work-limit. This was done to achieve greater differentiation among superior people and accordingly increased the validity of the test. More difficult items were added during this process.

The test consists of 150 items distributed among the three tests: 30 for the same-opposites, 60 for the analogies, and 60 for the reading

TEST 1 Do not write on Test Booklet Page 1

Directions and Samples for Test 1:—

Look at the first sample below. At the right, find one word of the five in the same row which will finish the sentence and make the best sense; then notice its number and then note how the corresponding answer space (little square) is marked with an X. When you do the real test questions, on the opposite page at the right, you would now punch a hole through the right answer space of the answer pad or (if you have been told to use the special pencil) would black in the answer space here-marked X. The samples, A, B, C, show you how to do it. Thus in Sample A, "Good" is the opposite of "bad" so, if this were a real test question, you would now punch (or mark with the special pencil) answer space No. 3. **Do not punch or mark the test booklet. Punch or write only on the Answer Pad. Be sure to answer every question.**

SAMPLES:							1 2 3 4 5
	A. Good is the OPPOSITE OF	1excellent	2cheerful	3bad	4wrong	5true	A ☐ ☐ ☒ ☐ ☐
	B. Little is the SAME AS	1coarse	2small	3prodigious	4immense	5feeble	B ☐ ☒ ☐ ☐ ☐
	C. Return is the OPPOSITE OF	1advance	2surround	3revolve	4go	5send	C ☐ ☐ ☐ ☒ ☐

After you have read the above directions, and noted carefully the three samples, go now to the opposite page, at the right, and do all the questions 1 - 30 in exactly the same way.

TEST 2 Page 2

Directions and Samples for Test 2:—

Find among the five numbered choices a word which fits the third word in the same way that the second word fits the first word. Then punch a hole in the appropriate answer square on the answer pad. The samples, A, B, C, show you how to do it. If you are using the special pencil (and not the stylus), carefully black-in the correct answer space. Write only on the answer pad, but be sure to **get it very black**. It has to be black to score correctly by electricity. Do not make any stray marks on the answer pad. **Be sure to answer every question.**

SAMPLES:									1 2 3 4 5
	A. boy	boys	man	1girls	2men	3man's	4men's	5gentlemen	A ☐ ☒ ☐ ☐ ☐
	B. push	pushed	run	1running	2runs	3runner	4ran	5runned	B ☐ ☐ ☐ ☒ ☐
	C. friend	friend's	John	1Johns'	2Johnes	3John's	4Jones	5Jons	C ☐ ☐ ☒ ☐ ☐

After you have read the above directions, and noted carefully the three samples, go now to the opposite page, at the right, and do questions 31 - 60 in exactly the same way. Then turn the page and do questions 61 - 90. There are two pages in this test. Do both pages.

Reprinted by permission of the publishers

DIRECTIONS AND SAMPLES FROM THE OHIO STATE UNIVERSITY PSYCHOLOGICAL TEST

comprehension. The test ordinarily requires about two hours, but a third hour should be made available for those who may need the extra time (52). Norms for each test as well as for the total score are provided for each year of high school and for college freshmen. The norms are in terms of percentiles and expected grades. The sampling is based upon an adequate size population (32) but is not as national in representation as is that of the A.C.E.

Illustrated here are practice problems for tests 1 and 2 of the Ohio

TEST **3** Do not write on the test booklet. Page **4**

Directions for Test 3:—

Read each paragraph and then answer each of the questions asked on the opposite page, by punching a hole in the center of the answer square of the answer pad corresponding to the answer which is most nearly correct. If you are using the special pencil, carefully black-in the correct answer space. **Be sure to answer every question. Each question has only one right answer.**

Read Paragraph 1 first; then answer questions 91-98 at the right. Then read paragraph 2, and so on.

Paragraph 1 **The following paragraph refers to questions 91-98 on the opposite page.**

Smoke is unburned carbon in a finely divided state. The amount of carbon carried away by the smoke is usually small, not exceeding 1 percent of the total carbon in the coal. Its presence, however, often indicates improper handling of the boiler, which may result in a much larger waste of fuel. Smoke is produced in a boiler when the incandescent particles of carbon are cooled before coming into contact with sufficient oxygen to unite with them. It is necessary that the carbon be in an incandescent condition before it will unite with the oxygen. Any condition of the furnace which results in carbon being cooled below the point of incandescence before sufficient oxygen has been furnished to unite with it will result in smoke. Smoke once formed is very difficult to ignite and the boiler furnace must be handled so as not to produce smoke. Fuels rich in hydrocarbons are most apt to produce smoke. When the hydrocarbon gas liberated from the coal is kept above the temperature of ignition and sufficient oxygen for its combustion is added, it burns with a red, yellow, or white flame. The slower the combustion the larger the flame. When the flame is chilled because the cold heating surfaces near it take away heat by radiation, combustion may be incomplete, and part of the gas and smoke pass off unburned. If the boiler is raised high enough above the grate so as to give room for the volatile matter to burn and not strike the boiler surface at once, both the amount of smoke given off and of coal used will be reduced.

TEST **3** **Be sure that the number on the answer pad agrees with this page number.** **Do not write on Test Booklet** Page **4**

Write or mark only on the answer pad.

According to Paragraph 1, Form 23, Test 3, (Page 4)

Questions on Par. 1:—

What condition other than temperature is necessary for hydrocarbon gas to burn with a yellow flame?
1sufficient oxygen 2reduced oxygen 3keep temperatures low 4keep flame yellow 5keep smaller flame **91**

What phrase of two words, used in the paragraph, has the same meaning as "extremely fine"?
1finely divided 2unusually small 3incandescent particles 4volatile matter 5incomplete combustion **92**

In what substance are fuels, that are most apt to produce smoke, most rich?
1oxygen 2hydrocarbons 3carbon 4gas 5smoke **93**

What, besides additional smoke, is a result of placing the boiler too close to the grate?
1gas is formed 2explosions 3imperfectly burned hydrocarbons 4reduction in coal needed 5waste of fuel **94**

What two characteristics would one be able to note in a very hot fire?
1red flame, little smoke 2no smoke, small flame 3small flame, white flame 4colored flame, no smoke 5white flame, much smoke. **95**

What is a general solution to the problem of a smoking furnace?
1raise the boiler 2less stoking 3provide more oxygen 4burn volatile matter 5increase the heat **96**

What one word, used in the paragraph, best characterizes the condition of the flame when combustion is incomplete?
1lignite 2chilled 3incandescence 4unburned 5white **97**

What one word best describes the condition of the carbon particles as they unite with the oxygen?
1smoky 2combustion 3cooled 4incandescent 5cool **98**

Reprinted by permission of the publishers

A PROBLEM FROM THE OHIO STATE UNIVERSITY PSYCHOLOGICAL TEST

State University Psychological Test, and the first problem of test 3. (This test has no practice problems. The illustrations are from Form 23, the 1947–48 edition of the test. Since this form will be replaced, this illustration can be condoned.)

Otis Self-Administering Tests of Mental Ability. The Otis tests are time-limit group tests. They are modeled after a group test developed in 1918 for use in business. There is an Intermediate Examination for grades four to nine and a Higher Examination for high school students and college freshmen. Each examination has four alternative forms, A, B, C, and D. The Otis tests have wide usage as predictors of school and college success as well as part of a battery of tests in vocational guidance and selection.

Kuder (40) reports that the tests have a high relationship with the A.C.E. and that the Otis tests bear as high or even a higher correlation with college grades. Hay (34) reports a study to predict success in machine bookkeeping in which the Otis Self-Administering test has a correlation of .56 with production and when used together with the Minnesota Clerical test gives a multiple correlation of $+.65 \pm .06$. This is considered high as a predictor of vocational success.

The Otis tests are simple and economical to administer and score. The Higher Examination takes 30 minutes and can also be given in 20 minutes. This is of importance for mass testing. The 20-minute test, however, is not considered as accurate a measure as the 30-minute test. The test has 75 test items ranged in order of difficulty. It is mainly verbal, but consists also of some numerical items and a few spatial questions. It has no subtests, so only a gross score is obtainable. This is a weakness of the test.

The score can be expressed in terms of I.Q., I.B. (Index of Brightness), and percentiles. The I.Q. is obtained by using Binet mental age equivalents. However, the I.Q.'s do not correspond precisely to the Stanford-Binet I.Q.'s because of the differences in tests and the greater inaccuracy of group tests. The I.B. is derived from the Otis directly without using the corresponding Binet mental ages. Thus, if an 18-year-old student receives a score of 53 on the Higher Examination, his I.B. is 53+100—42 (the norm for his age)=111. There is a discrepancy between the two scores, I.Q. and I.B. For instance, if we used the Binet mental age, a score of 53 is equivalent to a Binet mental age of 16 years, 10 months. The I.Q. would be the quotient of 16 years, 10 months divided by 16 years (the norm usually taken in figuring I.Q.'s of people over 16). The I.Q. is then 105. This discrepancy can be corrected by using a lower age as a norm for adults (7). Terman and Merrill (74) report corrections starting at age 13 with 15 becoming the norm for adults 16 years of age and over. These corrections should be applied when the test is given to older subjects. Thus the score of 53 would yield the I.Q. 112 (16 years, 10 months divided by 15 years). Both the A.C.E. and Ohio State avoid the use of mental age and I.Q. for adults over 16. More appropriately these tests use percentiles.

The reliability of the Otis Higher Examination is of the order .92 (55). Norms are based on large populations of students. Where they are used in business, norms are developed on the workers or applicants.

The figure on page 214 is a copy of the instructions for the Otis Self-Administering Tests of Mental Ability, Higher Examination.

Aptitude tests

Bennett Mechanical Comprehension Test. This test was designed to measure a high level of mechanical ability. It is a paper and pencil test to be administered to groups but, as is the case with all group tests, can be given individually. It has three forms, AA, BB and W-1. Form AA, for high school boys and for adults of similar educational attainment, has the widest usage. The more difficult Form BB, which is more discriminating among the highest technical levels, is for engineering school students and candidates as well as applicants for mechanical work. Form W-1 is specially designed for women; it has more feminine mechanical items, like those found in a kitchen.

Form AA, the most widely used of the tests, consists of 60 items arranged in order of difficulty and pictorially represented. The test has no time limit but usually does not take more than about thirty minutes. It measures understanding of mechanical principles in everyday situations, not rote knowledge. The problems minimize "the effect of training and formal knowledge" (10). The test shows fair relationships with tests of intelligence (11). Traxler (78) found the Mechanical Comprehension Test to have a correlation of .37 with the A.C.E. for 230 cadets, 18–22 years old, in the U.S. Merchant Marine

This is a test to see how well you can think. It contains questions of different kinds. Here is a sample question already answered correctly. Notice how the question is answered:

Which one of the five words below tells what an apple is?
1 flower, 2 tree, 3 vegetable, 4 fruit, 5 animal.......(4)

The right answer, of course, is "fruit"; so the word "fruit" is underlined. And the word "fruit" is No. 4; so a figure 4 is placed in the parentheses at the end of the dotted line. This is the way you are to answer the questions.

Try this sample question yourself. Do not write the answer; just draw a line under it and then put its number in the parentheses:

Which one of the five words below means the opposite of North?
1 pole, 2 equator, 3 south, 4 east, 5 west..........( )

The answer, of course, is "south"; so you should have drawn a line under the word "south" and put a figure 3 in the parentheses. Try this one:

A foot is to a man and a paw is to a cat the same as a hoof is to a – what?
1 dog, 2 horse, 3 shoe, 4 blacksmith, 5 saddle......( )

The answer, of course, is "horse"; so you should have drawn a line under the word "horse" and put a figure 2 in the parentheses. Try this one:

At four cents each, how many cents will 6 pencils cost?..........( )

The answer, of course, is 24, and there is nothing to underline; so just put the 24 in the parentheses. If the answer to any question is a number or a letter, put the number or letter in the parentheses without underlining anything. Make all letters like printed capitals.

The test contains 75 questions. You are not expected to be able to answer all of them, but do the best you can. You will be allowed half an hour after the examiner tells you to begin. Try to get as many right as possible. Be careful not to go so fast that you make mistakes. Do not spend too much time on any one question. No questions about the test will be answered by the examiner after the test begins. Lay your pencil down.

Do not turn this page until you are told to begin.

PRINTED IN U.S.A.
Published by World Book Company, Yonkers-on-Hudson, New York, and 2126 Prairie Avenue, Chicago. OSATMA:HE:B-50

From Otis Self-Administering Test of Mental Ability: Higher Examination. *Copyright by World Book Company. Reproduced by special permission.*

DIRECTIONS FOR
OTIS HIGHER EXAMINATION

Cadet Corps. However, Sartain (60) found a correlation of .18 between the Mechanical Comprehension and the Otis for 46 employees in the inspection department of an aircraft factory. Some of the employees were new and many were experienced. Apparently the differences in sampling make for variations in the relationships with tests of intelligence. The relationship may be due to the characteristic of comprehension of physical principles. Jacobsen (37) has found the Mechanical Comprehension Test to have predictive significance, especially in combination with other tests, for success as a Mechanic Learner. He believes that this significance is due to the abstract concepts found in the test. Tests that measure abstract thought are, of course, found in intelligence tests, and this fact may account for the relationship.

The factor of abstract thinking is probably related to the factor of spatial visualization. Wechsler (80) reported the Block Design Test, a test involving spatial visualization, as having a high correlation with intelligence. Bennett and Cruikshank (10) report fairly high correlations with the Minnesota Paper Form Board, a measure of visualization, and Humphreys (36) believes the test should have high validity because of this factor.

The test is apparently valid for work requiring a higher type of mechanical ability. Jacobsen (37) found that it had validity in predicting successful Mechanic Learners and Shuman (65) reported it valid for such skilled factory jobs as machining precision parts, testing aircraft engines, and inspection.

One question usually raised in criticism of the test concerns the physical principles. Some believe that formal training in physics would bring about a higher score. However, Bennett's Manual (11) for the test refers to two studies that show no significant difference in scores between those who have had courses in physics and those who have not. The difference is only four points, on the average, in favor of those who have had a physics course.

Although the test has reasonable validity, like any other test it should not be used as the sole criterion in predicting success. Other tests, grades in school, and experience must be taken into account.

The reliability is quite high, .84 for a relatively homogeneous group of 500 ninth grade boys. It would probably be higher for a more heterogeneous group. The norms are varied for the particular use to which the score is to be put. There are educational norms for 9th, 10th, 11th, and 12th grades, for technical high school, introductory engineering courses, and engineering school. There are also industrial and other norms for various kinds of occupations and special courses. Also provided in the manual is a set of women's norms. Illustrated here are the directions and practice problems for Form AA of the test.

Revised Minnesota Paper Form Board. This is a revision by Likert and Quasha of the Minnesota Paper Form Board Test by Paterson, Elliott, Anderson, Toops, and Heidbreder. The revision has more problems and a longer time limit. It correlates .75 with the original. In the original, 56 geometric figures and a group of parts are given; the examinee is to draw lines in each figure to show how the parts fit into it. In the revision the correct solution is given among five multiple-choice possibilities and the examinee is to identify it. This method increases the ease and objectivity of scoring, eliminating the possibility of errors in judging the adequacy of the lines drawn by the examinee. The revision has 64 geometric figures and practice problems. The time limit is 20 minutes. The test is usually given to groups. There are two hand-scoring forms, AA and BB, as well as two machine-scoring forms, MA and MB.

Both the original and the revision measure ability to perceive spatial relations (spatial visualization), which is a fairly complex intellectual factor. The ability is related to the more complex mechanical occupations, such as engineering. Tests of spatial ability are found in tests of intelligence and, indeed, the geometrical figures used in the Minnesota Paper Form Board are derived from the Army Beta, a non-verbal test of intelligence. However, tests of intelligence include varieties of subtests, while the Minnesota Paper Form Board consists of only one kind of item. It may therefore be taken to measure spatial ability more nearly exclusively, and its validity for this ability may be determined by comparing its results with occupational success. In itself it is not a complex measure of mechanical success but may be employed as a partial measure of mechanical and engineering aptitude (68). School grades and other tests are used to bolster the prediction of success.

TEST OF
MECHANICAL COMPREHENSION
FORM AA
George K. Bennett, Ph.D.

DIRECTIONS

Fill in the blanks on your ANSWER SHEET. Write your last name first, the date, your age in years and months, and your school. Now draw a circle around the highest grade that you have finished in school.

Now line up your answer sheet with the test booklet so that the "Page 1" arrow on the booklet meets the "Page 1" arrow on the answer sheet. Then look at Sample X on this page. It shows pictures of two rooms and asks, "Which room has more of an echo?" Room "A" has more of an echo because it has no rug or curtains, so a circle is drawn around "A" **on the answer sheet.** Now look at Sample Y, and answer it yourself. Draw a circle around the right answer **on the answer sheet.**

PAGE 1 →

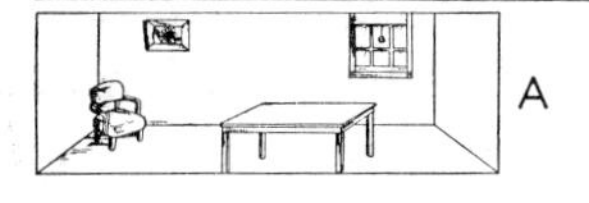

A

X

Which room has more of an echo?

B

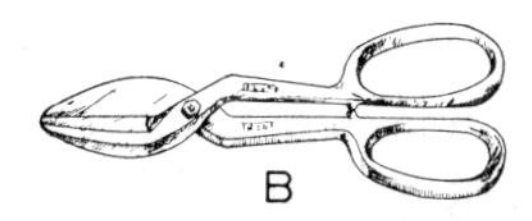

A

Y

Which would be the better shears for cutting metal?

B

On the following pages there are more pictures and questions. Read each question carefully, look at the picture, and draw a circle around the best answer on the answer sheet. Be sure that you use the right column on the answer sheet for each page. The arrow on the page should meet the arrow on the answer sheet.

DO NOT MARK THIS BOOKLET — PUT YOUR ANSWERS ON THE ANSWER SHEET.

The Psychological Corporation

DIRECTIONS AND SAMPLES FOR THE BENNETT MECHANICAL COMPREHENSION TEST, FORM AA

Berdie (13) obtained a correlation of .22 between the Revised Minnesota Paper Form Board and honor point ratio of 154 engineering students. This was significantly different from 0.00 correlation at the one per cent level of probability. Brush (18) found the test to be a promising predictor of mechanical ability as related to engineering aptitude among engineering students. He reports, however, that "the actual predictive power of most single tests of mechanical ability is not great." Other studies summarized in the Manual (44) report the use of the test as an aid in the prediction of success in such occupations and subjects as drafting, blueprint reading, technical drawing, and machine design.

The test shows moderate relationships with other tests of spatial visualization like the Crawford Tridimensional and the Wechsler-Bellevue Block Design test as reported in the Manual. Manual dexterity is not an important part of this test.

The reliability of the test is adequate. The Manual reports correlations of .85 for one form and .92 when the two forms (AA and BB) are both given. The norms are varied, for educational and industrial groups, and there are separate norms for men and women. The score is the number right minus one fifth the number wrong which is a correction for guessing. The directions and practice problems of Series BB of the test are illustrated in the accompanying figure.

Minnesota Spatial Relations Test. This is a performance test given individually. The test is adapted from Link's Spatial Relations test and has four large form boards, each containing 58 cutouts of different shapes and sizes. Most shapes have three sizes: small, medium and large. Form boards A and B use the same cutouts and form boards C and D another set of blocks. The test can be administered in a number of ways: using all four boards with board A as practice, or boards A and B alone, or C and D alone. The first method seems to be most widely used. Boards A and B alone are employed at the Consultation Service of the Vocational Advisory Service as well as in other places. Blum (16) reports that the method of using boards A and B alone saves time and requires only slightly modified directions to administer. He writes that percentile norms are available on a large group between ages 16 and 24.

The test measures simple spatial ability. It is not abstract like the Minnesota Paper Form Board test and does not involve combining and integrating. Brush (18) reports that it has rather low correlations with success in engineering courses. This is to be expected, since the

DIRECTIONS AND PRACTICE PROBLEMS

READ THE FOLLOWING DIRECTIONS VERY CAREFULLY WHILE THE EXAMINER READS THEM ALOUD

Look at the problems on the right side of this page. You will notice that there are eight of them, numbered from 1 to 8. Notice that the problems go DOWN the page.

First look at Problem 1. There are two parts in the upper left-hand corner. Now look at the five figures labelled A, B, C, D, E. You are to decide which figure shows how these parts can fit together. Let us first look at Figure A. You will notice that Figure A does **not** look like the parts in the upper left-hand would look when fitted together. Neither do Figures B, C, or D. Figure E **does** look like the parts in the upper left-hand corner would look when fitted together, so E is PRINTED in the square above [1] at the top of the page.

Now look at Problem 2. Decide which figure is the correct answer. As you will notice, Figure A is the correct answer, so A is printed in the square above [2] at the top of the page.

The answer to Problem 3 is B, so B is printed in the square above [3] at the top of the page.

In Problem 4, D is the correct answer, so D is printed in the square above [4] at the top of the page.

Now do Problems 5, 6, 7, and 8.

PRINT the letter of the correct answer in the square above the number of the example at the top of the page.

DO THESE PROBLEMS NOW.

If your answers are not the same as those which the examiner reads to you, RAISE YOUR HAND.

DO NOT OPEN THE BOOKLET UNTIL YOU ARE TOLD TO DO SO.

Some of the problems on the inside of this booklet are more difficult than those which you have already done, but the idea is exactly the same. In each problem you are to decide which figure shows the parts correctly fitted together. **Sometimes the parts have to be turned around, and sometimes they have to be turned over in order to make them fit.** In the square above [1] write the correct answer to Problem 1; in the square above [2] write the correct answer to Problem 2, and so on with the rest of the test. Start with Problem 1, and go DOWN the page. After you have finished one column, go right on with the next. **Be careful not to go so fast that you make mistakes. Do not spend too much time on any one problem.**

PRINT WITH CAPITAL LETTERS ONLY.

MAKE THEM SO THAT ANYONE CAN READ THEM.

DO NOT OPEN THE BOOKLET BEFORE YOU ARE TOLD TO DO SO.

YOU WILL HAVE EXACTLY 20 MINUTES TO DO THE WHOLE TEST.

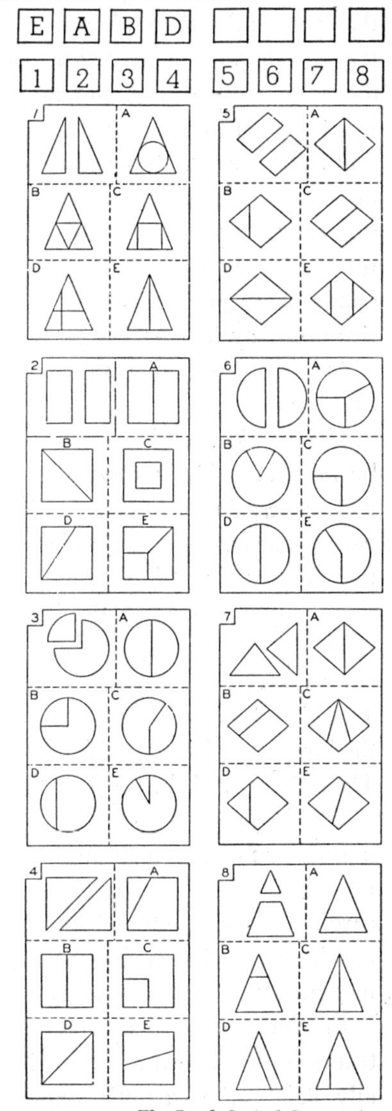

The Psychological Corporation

REVISED MINNESOTA PAPER FORM BOARD

test measures simple spatial ability. Speed is an important element; the score is the time taken to complete it. Manual dexterity is relatively unimportant according to Super (69). Practice can increase the score considerably. Greene (31) repeated boards A, B, C, and D five times on five college students at intervals of approximately two days. The average student placed about .207 pieces per second on the first trial and .364 pieces per second on the fifth trial. And the limit of improvement was not reached at the fifth trial. The last two trials correlated higher than the first and fifth, indicating that ratings may change with practice. Subjects improve their time scores with practice on many if not most performance tests. Accordingly, psychologists should discourage subjects from performing the tests before actual administration.

The test does not have as wide use in industry as it has in guidance because it is individually administered. It is more suitable for predicting success in the less technical mechanical occupations such as garage mechanics' work and ornamental ironwork. Super (69) writes that for people of low average intelligence, a high average spatial score may indicate promise in the skilled trades.

The test takes about eight minutes per board. The test should be given with the examinee standing and using only the dominant hand. Time is taken for each board; the score is simply the total time on the boards used, except, of course, where board A is used for practice. The reliability of the test is within acceptable limits, .84 corrected for attenuation in one instance and .91 in another. There are different norms for men, women, and high school boys. Many of the sets of norms are derived from local samplings, so it is necessary to check carefully the characteristics of the sampling and, if necessary, to make another set of norms more representative of the particular group being studied. Given here is an illustration of this test.

In selecting a test, the practical question of whether to use a paper test or a form board test must be decided. Practical expediency usually dictates the use of the paper test. However, as Levine (42) points out, this choice is not always correct. Most paper and pencil tests designed to measure aptitudes correlate positively in varying degrees with tests of general intelligence, whereas apparatus tests are not correlated with general intelligence. This fact means that paper and pencil tests are less effective when used in considering the relatively low I.Q. person for jobs that require only a modest level of intelligence but require a high degree of the special ability.

MacQuarrie Test for Mechanical Ability. The MacQuarrie is described because it is a popular group paper and pencil test of the omnibus kind. Baker and Peatman (6) report it as being used in 66

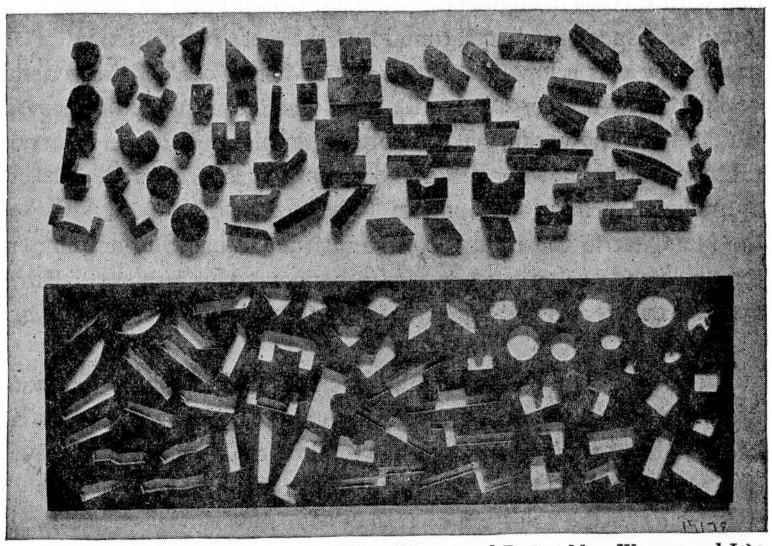

From Paterson and Darley, Men, Women, and Jobs. *Minneapolis: University of Minnesota Press, 1936*

MINNESOTA SPATIAL RELATIONS TEST

per cent of the Veterans Administration Advisement Units. It is one of the older tests, having been published in 1925. It consists of seven subtests, each introduced by a brief practice session. Each subtest has a time limit so that the entire test consumes about 30 minutes. The seven subtests are tracing—drawing a curved line through small openings in a series of vertical lines; tapping—placing three dots in circles as rapidly as possible; dotting—putting one dot in each of a series of small circles irregularly spaced; copying—reproducing figures of simple design in a dotted space; location—finding the letters in a large square and placing them in corresponding positions on dots in smaller squares; block counting—visualizing and recording how many blocks are touched by certain given blocks; and pursuit—following lines in a maze-like pattern by eye.

Although the Manual of Directions (45) for the test claims that it is useful for a wide variety of jobs "from the highly skilled trade of the tool and diemaker to the relatively unskilled but highly specialized machine operator," research does not quite bear out this assertion. Brush (18) found the MacQuarrie test to have a rather low correlation with success in engineering courses. Ghiselli (29), in a study of a group of inspector-packers, found that the test's correlation with job proficiency was a low .19; and that only 46 per cent of the general population made scores lower than the median of inspector-packers. He did learn, however, that the dotting, tapping, blocks, and pursuit subtests were somewhat better indicators of success than was the test as a whole. Sartain (60) reports a higher correlation, +.65, between the MacQuarrie and ratings by two instructors based upon job performance and performance in a refresher course for inspectors. However, Sartain reports fair and rather high correlations for all the tests used.

The total score masks the subtest scores, which are generally more useful than the total score. Brush (18) found four of the subtests to be better indicators of success than the total score. McDaniel and Reynolds (46) report that the tapping and dotting tests contribute high weightings to the selection of trainees for mechanical occupations. Blum (15) adapted the tracing test as a measure of selecting sewing machine operators and found it better than the total score. Barrett (9) found the tracing, dotting, and pursuit tests to be of some value for differentiating inferior from superior college students in typing. He discovered, similarly, that the pursuit test was useful in differentiating students in a shorthand course.

The tracing, tapping, and dotting tests measure manual dexterity; copying, location, and block counting measure spatial visualization; and pursuit measures speed of perception. The variety of functions in the total test make it desirable to use the separate tests or combinations of them rather than the total score. The Manual of Directions has norms for the total score for ages from 10 to average adult and for the several subtests by sex. The grouping of the sexes in the combined score is questionable, since there are some sex differences (39). The reliability of the test is as high as .90 but considerable variability is also reported (10).

If the total score on the MacQuarrie test is used, it should be interpreted with other test information and data from the client's history. The subtests have more meaning and some degree of validity for different kinds of occupations. However, the reliability of each subtest is generally lower than that of the entire test; the subtests as well, then, must be bolstered with other data.

The figures on pages 224 and 225 illustrate the practice exercises of three of the subtests.

O'Connor Finger Dexterity and Tweezer Dexterity Tests. The Finger and Tweezer Dexterity Tests are discussed simultaneously. Opposite sides of the same apparatus are usually used for the two tests. They have been frequently employed together in test batteries. The tests were devised in 1920 by Johnson O'Connor (54) as measures of manual dexterity for small assembly work. They are individually administered performance tests.

The Finger Dexterity Test consists of a plate sometimes made of metal, sometimes of wood and metal. One end has a shallow recess to hold small brass pins; this is always to be placed at the side of the dominant hand. The rest of the plate consists of 100 holes, large enough for three pins to fit, 10 rows across and 10 columns down. The examinee is seated when he works on both Finger and Tweezer Tests (preferably at a table of 30 inches in height with appropriate chair). For the Finger Dexterity Test he is to pick up three pins at a time and place them into each hole three at a time, starting from the upper left hole if right-handed and the upper right hole if left-handed and work across each row, going back to the next row until the whole board is completed.

The Tweezer Dexterity Test is usually the opposite side of the plate. The tray is similarly situated in accordance with dominant hand and is filled with the same small brass pins. There are 100 holes, 10 across and 10 down. However, these holes are smaller, holding

PRACTICE LOCATION

INSTRUCTIONS: Read these instructions to yourself as the examiner reads them aloud.

This is the practice page for the LOCATION test. Notice the letters in the large square, and the five dots in each of the small squares below. For each dot in a small square, there is a letter in the same place in the large square. When the examiner says GO, but not before, put right on each dot the letter that stands in its place in the large square. For instance, the upper dot in the small square to the left is in the position of the letter K in the large square, so you will put a letter K on that dot.

F	E	D	C	B	A
G	H	J	K	L	M
T	S	R	P	O	N
U	V	W	X	Y	Z
A	B	C	D	E	F
M	L	K	J	H	G

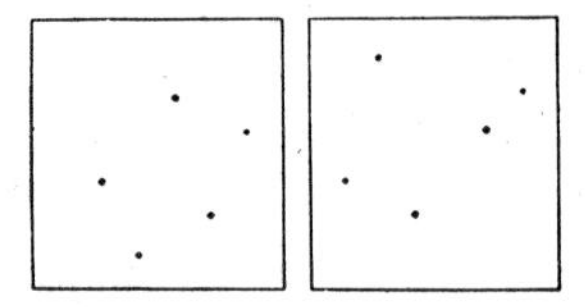

PRACTICE BLOCKS

INSTRUCTIONS: Read these instructions to yourself as the examiner reads them aloud.

This is the practice page for the BLOCKS test. Here is a pile of blocks, all the same size and shape. On five of the blocks, you will see X's. When the examiner says GO, but not before, you are to find out how many blocks touch each block that has an X on it, and then place that number to the right of the X. For example, the lowest block which has an X on it touches four other blocks. Please locate them now and place a 4 to the right of the X. Put it there now, and you may have twenty seconds in which to place the correct numbers to the right of the other X's.

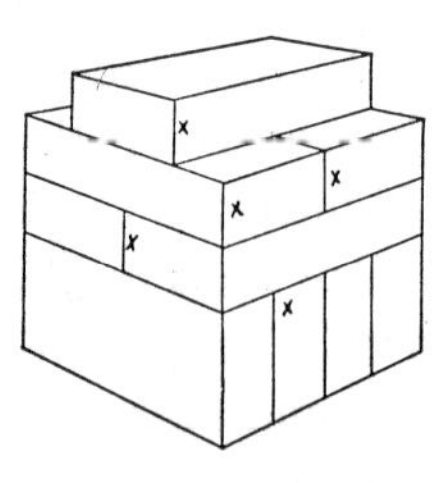

Reproduced by permission of the California Test Bureau, Los Angeles, California

SAMPLE SUBTESTS FROM THE MACQUARRIE MECHANICAL ABILITY TEST

only one pin at a time. The examinee is to pick up one pin at a time with a tweezer of specific gauge and place it in a hole. He places the pins in the same order as in the Finger Dexterity Test.

Candee and Blum (20) found that both the Finger Dexterity and the Tweezer Dexterity ability were desirable for superior work in a watch factory. They also found the amount of improvement on the last half of the Finger Dexterity test to be important in selecting superior workers. O'Connor had suggested scoring the improvement by adding a constant fraction, one tenth of the second half. Candee and Blum do not support this method of scoring; they use total time as the score, considering any improvement between first and second

PRACTICE PURSUIT

INSTRUCTIONS: Read these instructions to yourself as the examiner reads them aloud.

This is the practice page for the PURSUIT test. Notice the numbers in the little squares at the left, where the curving lines begin. When the examiner says GO, but not before, follow each line by eye from the square where it begins at the left to the square where it ends at the right. Remember the number at the beginning of the line, and put it in one of the small squares at the end. Do not be concerned if two lines end in the same place, but just use both squares for your answers. Do not use your pencils to follow the lines if you can help it. You will work much faster if you depend entirely upon your eyes.

Reproduced by permission of the California Test Bureau, Los Angeles, California

SAMPLE SUBTEST FROM THE MACQUARRIE MECHANICAL ABILITY TEST

halves as an additional indication of success. They also found the quality of performance as rated by the examiner on the Finger Dexterity Test to be useful as a predictor of success in watch assembling.

A later study by Blum (14) also obtained distinctive correlations between time scores on the tests and certain criteria of proficiency. The subjects were females in a watch factory. He found the performance quality ratings to be of value when measured against the criterion of foremen's ratings. The discovery of a relationship between quality of test performance and quality of actual work adds another use to performance testing. Performance tests allow for observation of method, neatness, steadiness, and so on. Study of the quality of work on a performance test deserves further research in connection with later on-the-job performance.

The Finger and Tweezer Dexterity Tests are not highly correlated with each other, nor are they highly correlated with other manual tests measuring different psychomotor patterns. Consequently, the tests cannot be used as general measures of manipulative ability but must be studied in relation to more specific types of work like that in a watch factory. Harris (33) used the tests as part of a battery in predicting achievement in dental school. In the preliminary study the criterion was the average grade received by the student in the first-year courses in Dental Anatomy and Dental Technology, which involve more manipulation and more understanding of spatial relationships than do the other first year courses. In general the students did markedly above average on the Finger and Tweezer Dexterity Tests. The correlations were low but statistically significant. In the main study the criteria were all courses during the first year and the average of all courses during the four years. The group of students were above average on the tests, but the correlations were very low. The Otis Intelligence test and the pre-dental scholarship test showed substantial relationships with the criteria. Apparently the dexterity tests have some value for courses where fine work is significant but become relatively unimportant in the overall picture. However, it must be noted that even in the main study the students had above average dexterity; this finding can be regarded as significant.

Jacobsen (37) found the Finger and Tweezer Dexterity Tests to have little relationship to Mechanic Learner courses, a fact possibly due to the more abstract nature of the courses. The tests have no correlation with measures of intelligence. Blum and Candee (17) employed the Finger Dexterity Test together with other tests in a study on the selection of department store wrappers and packers. The test was not found to be selective. Another finding was that the females made better scores than the males.

In general, the tests have some usefulness in jobs requiring rapid movements of hands, wrists, and fingers on small objects. However, the degree of validity has to be determined in each instance; the tests cannot be taken at face value without specific research.

The reliability of the Finger Dexterity test is about .90. There are no reliability data for the Tweezer Dexterity test. The norms on the tests vary. O'Connor reports adult norms which are not considered as

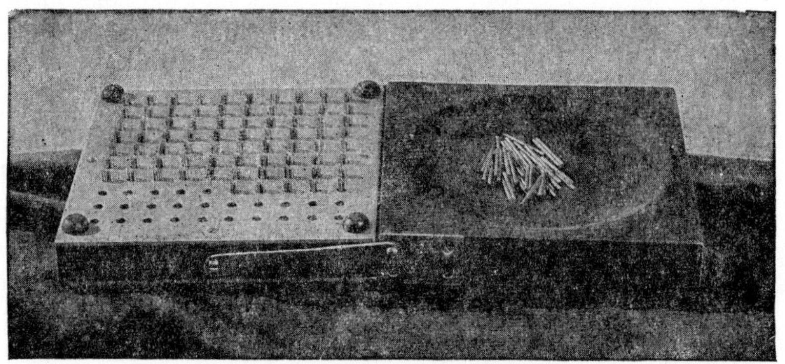

O'CONNOR FINGER DEXTERITY TEST

O'CONNOR TWEEZER DEXTERITY TEST

representative as those of the Minnesota Employment Stabilization Research Institute. The latter are based on employed adults. Also available are norms derived from scores which are based on total time, without the O'Connor correction mentioned previously. In using any set of norms it is necessary to know the characteristics of the group from which they were derived. Further development of norms is required for the tests in respect to other tasks involving fine dexterity. The accompanying figures illustrate the two tests.

Minnesota Rate of Manipulation Test. This test, in its most usual form, consists of two tasks, placing and turning. The tasks are administered to an individual or a small group. Both employ the same apparatus, a rectangular-shaped board with 60 round holes into which 60 discs are fitted. The discs are colored differently on either flat surface. In the Placing Test, they are put back into the holes in the board as quickly as possible in a standardized manner. In the Turning Test all the discs are in place in the board; each one is removed with one hand, turned over with the other, and returned to the hole from which it was removed.

The usual procedure is to have, for each task, one practice trial, then four actual trials. After each test trial the examinee is motivated to perform faster. The scores are the sum of the four test trials for each of the tests. The 1946 Examiner's Manual of the Minnesota Rate of Manipulation Test (26) includes three new tasks: displacing test, one-hand turning and placing test, and two-hand turning and placing test. The Manual cites Jurgensen's study of the validity of the two original tasks and the last two of the additional tasks. The coefficients of correlation between test performance and supervisors' ratings of men hired as converting machine operators in a paper mill range from .33 for the Placing Test to .57 for the turning and placing done with both hands simultaneously. The intercorrelations among the older and new tasks range from .46 to .55 (38). Further study of the applicability of the newer tests to different kinds of work is needed to discover whether they are useful.

The Placing and Turning Tests are essentially measures of gross manipulative ability. They bring into play the muscles of the hands and arms and not so much the fingers as do the Finger and Tweezer Dexterity Tests. Ghiselli (29) found the Turning Test to have a validity coefficient of .40 with supervisory ratings of job proficiency of inspector-packers. The Placing Test yielded a lower correlation. One test alone gives only slight indication of success; however, when used with other tests having a fair degree of validity with the criterion, it is found useful. Blum and Candee (17) in their study of wrappers and packers found a low but reliable correlation between the Placing Test and the production of inexperienced packers. The packers were faster on the test than the wrappers. The wrappers do more complex work than the packers and gross dexterity is therefore less important. However, the Placing Test had little value with experienced packers, indicating that gross dexterity becomes less important even among packers after a period of time on the job. The analysis of the operations of machine bookkeepers would lead one to believe that manipulative dexterity was important. However, Hay (34) found that the results of these tests had insignificant relationships with success in this work. He reports that "the mental abilities required are so overwhelmingly important that the dexterities can be ignored." Manipulative ability is not significant in the more complex tasks.

Jacobsen (37) found the Placing and Turning Tests to be of no significance in predicting mechanic learner achievement when the criterion was ratings by the instructors. Unfortunately neither Hay nor Jacobsen gives the average scores made by his group. Although a test may have low correlation with a criterion, the averages made by different groups may vary considerably and be differentiating. A certain minimum of dexterity may be necessary for different occupations; more than this minimum may not be very important for the more complex tasks. Teegarden (73) determined the percentile scores on various spatial and manipulative tests, including the Placing and Turning, for different occupational groups. She found that the median of helpers in skilled trades surpassed 67 and 55 per cent of an unselected group on the Placing and Turning Tests. However, the helpers were surpassed on these tests by wrappers and packers. Both the Placing and Turning Tests were found to strikingly differentiate food wrappers and packers and butter wrappers and packers from the general population (30). The median of woman assemblers, inspectors, and testers surpassed the largest percentages of unselected applicants on the Placing and Turning Tests. (These were 76 and 72 per cent, respectively.) The various percentages were not tested for significance but indicate that the scores required vary for occupations of different levels. The minimum score necessary for each occupation would have to be separately determined.

For guidance purposes the test scores must be considered together with other test results and in the light of the interests and the existing occupational opportunities. Very low scores and very high scores would be important in deciding whether the client should choose an occupation requiring manipulative ability. The counselor would have to know in what kinds of work a certain minimum of the ability is necessary.

These tests have little relation to finger and tweezer dexterities. This is in agreement with the U.S.E.S. study (66), in which two separate factors, finger and manual, are reported. The Placing and Turning are almost pure tests of manual dexterity. Super (69) reports no significant relationship between manual dexterity and spatial visuali-

From Paterson and Darley, Men, Women, and Jobs. *Minneapolis: University of Minnesota Press, 1936*

MINNESOTA RATE OF MANIPULATION TEST

zation. Seashore (64) found the tests unrelated to scholastic aptitude. Interestingly enough he also found that college students not in physical education or engineering were superior to the general norm on the tests. This finding is in line with Harris' findings on dental students. Although college students may never need much manual or finger dexterity to get ahead in their occupations, they do have, on the average, at least a minimum of it.

Coefficients of reliability of approximately .90 (corrected) are reported for the Minnesota Rate of Manipulation Test when the first trial is used as practice and the next four are totaled to obtain the score (10). Norms are given in the Manual of Directions, but the populations from which they were derived are not described. However, Teegarden (72) has norms for a group of 860 applicants, 16–25, for various jobs in an employment agency. Tuckman (79) supplies norms for a large group ranging in age from 18–58, who had come for counseling. Cook and Barre (22) have norms for 2475 applicants for factory work in a large manufacturing plant. These are higher than the norms in the original standardization, possibly reflecting the group's greater interest and experience in manipulative work. Norms based upon such diverse groups must bear close scrutiny, and be interpreted with care. It is often necessary, moreover, to develop a set of norms more appropriate to the group being counseled. Cook and Barre also report "sufficiently significant difference between the scores of men and women on the Placing Test to warrant a separate table of percentiles." The Turning Test does not warrant separate norms. The accompanying figure illustrates the Rate of Manipulation Test.

Purdue Pegboard. The Purdue Pegboard Test has been available since the early 1940's. It is a performance test that can be individually administered but can be given more readily to groups than the other performance tests because it has time limits rather than work limits. The test consists of a rectangular board with four small cups at the top and two rows of holes going down the center. The extreme right and left cups contain 25 metal pins each; the cup to the right of the center has 20 metal collars and the cup to the left has 40 washers. The examinee is seated at a table approximately 30 inches high with the board placed so that the cups are furthest away from him. The first test is to pick up one pin at a time from the right-hand cup with the right hand and insert it into the right-hand row. Three or four placements are used for practice; the pins are then removed. The examinee is then allowed the time limit of 30 seconds to insert as many pins as he or she can. The score is the number of pins placed. The second test is with the left hand and the same procedure is followed except that the left cup and left-hand row are employed.

The third test is for both hands. The examinee picks up two pins, one with the left hand from the left cup and one with the right hand from the right cup, and inserts them simultaneously into the two rows of holes. Thirty seconds is the time limit; the score is the number of pairs of pins placed. A fourth score is obtained by totaling the scores on the first three tests.

The fourth test, the assembly test, yields the fifth score. The examinee is required to pick up a pin with the right hand and while placing it in the first hole of the right row, pick up a washer with the left hand. The washer is placed over the pin and while this is being done, the right hand picks up a collar and places it over the washer. Then the left hand picks up another washer and places it over the collar. This action completes the first assembly. The next assembly is started immediately with the left hand; this procedure continues until the time limit of one minute is reached. Practice is allowed for this sequence too. The score is the number of complete assemblies and fractional parts made.

The purpose of the test, as described in the Preliminary Manual (59), is to measure manipulative ability to aid in the selection for such work as "assembly, packing, operation of certain machines, and other routine manual jobs of an exacting nature." It measures two types of dexterity: gross movements of hands, fingers, and arms, and "tip of finger" dexterity for small assembly work.

The test requires many more studies of validity. In the Preliminary Manual validity is claimed for work requiring dexterity. The data were obtained in a large ordnance plant and could not be released because of governmental restrictions at the time. The revised manual (1948) provides validation data on very small samplings of workers in light machine operation, textile quilling, and simple assembly on small parts. The correlations found, although of the usual order for single tests against a criterion, are probably unreliable because of the small samplings. Only Surgent's (70) study on radio tube mounters shows a reliable correlation for validity. There are as yet no data reported on the intercorrelation of the various parts of the total test.

Each of the four tests can be given once, twice, or three times. The reliability is highest for three trials, reaching about .83 for placing of pins and .89 for assembly. It would seem that lengthening of the tests to three trials would be more valid for guidance purposes, since a more reliable measure results.

Norms are available for men and women on a college and an industrial level. Also available are norms developed from a sampling of veterans by Long and Hill (43). There is a need for norms on more varied manipulative jobs. Since many use the test and apparently think well of it as a testing instrument, more adequate norms as well as validation studies will very likely be forthcoming. The test is illustrated in the accompanying figure.

PURDUE PEGBOARD

Minnesota Clerical Test. This test, formerly called the Minnesota Vocational Test for Clerical Workers, is widely known and has had extensive use since its publication in 1933. It is a simple test to administer and score. The test can be given to large groups at one time and scored by clerks. It consists of two parts, Number Comparison and Name Comparison. The former has 200 pairs of numbers varying in length from three to 12 digits; the latter has 200 pairs of names varying in length from seven to 16 letters. The examinee is to compare each pair and put a check mark in the line between the members of each pair that are the same. If the pairs of numbers or names are not the same, the line is left blank. The Number test has a time limit of eight minutes and the Name test, seven minutes. The entire test takes 15 minutes plus several minutes for directions.

The test was designed to measure "certain aspects of clerical work" (5). Andrew and Paterson (4) found the test to have some validity with grades in accounting; some value distinguishing the rapid and average typist from the slow; and some value in differentiating the employed clerical workers from workers in general, and employed clerical workers from unemployed workers. They also reported that the test does not distinguish among the various clerical workers to a statistically significant degree, although those on the higher level tend to make higher scores than do routine clerical workers and stock and shipping clerks. Hay (34) found the Minnesota Numbers to correlate .51 with production of machine bookkeepers, and the Minnesota Names to correlate .47 with the same criterion. Together with the Otis test, a multiple correlation of .65 was obtained. The three tests have been used as a battery in the selection of new bookkeepers with good results (35). Blum and Candee (17) reported the test to have a relationship to production of wrappers and packers over the long run. They reported that "Initial adjustment of packers to the job is influenced to some extent by gross manipulative ability, but long term superiority on the job depends more on clerical ability with both wrappers and packers."

Andrew and Paterson (4) report that age does not much affect the test results. However, there is evidence that after 40 there is a decrement, although slight, in speed of number and name checking (57). This finding agrees with other data on the relation between age and scores on tests that measure the speed factor. A striking sex difference in the general population was also found. Only 20 to 25 per cent of males reach or exceed the median of females. The difference is as pronounced in the elementary grades as in high school or among adults (61). However, when both sexes are at a given level or kind of clerical work, the sex differences tend to disappear. Andrew and Paterson also found negligible relationships between years of clerical experience and test performance, slight relationships with years of schooling, and slight relationships with intelligence for employed clerical workers. However, if the sampling is more heterogeneous, the correlation between the clerical test and academic ability is greater (57).

Andrew (3) found in a factorial study of the test that for homogeneous groups, scores in the number and name checking tests were relatively independent of academic ability. For a heterogeneous group, the number test was independent of academic ability, and the name checking test had a higher relationship than the number checking with intelligence tests. She also found that scores on both tests were relatively independent of spatial and dexterity abilities. Number checking includes a measure of numerical ability (probably routine computations) and name checking of verbal ability. The correlation between the two parts is .66. Although this correlation indicates considerable overlap, there is still a large difference between them.

The greatest usefulness of the test is as a predictor of success in routine clerical jobs. When other tests, like the Thurstone Examination in clerical work and the O'Rourke Clerical, are correlated with advancement (estimated as job level reached after five or more years of work), they show greater relationship than the Minnesota Clerical (25). The Thurstone and O'Rourke are more complex tests measuring intellectual functions in clerical settings. The simpler Minnesota measures primarily speed and accuracy of perception. An intelligence test should supplement the Minnesota Clerical for greater usefulness in selection of those who are to be considered for advancement.

Bennett and Cruikshank (12) report the median coefficient of reliability in thirteen groups to be .85. All reliabilities are from alternate forms or test-retest situations. The test is usually scored as Rights minus Wrongs (R—W). The authors of the test were concerned primarily with speed but recognized accuracy as a factor not to be eliminated. According to the Manual for the test, it is usually performed "at a high level of accuracy." The R—W scoring formula penalizes those who go so fast as to sacrifice accuracy. For employment situations where many applicants are to be tested at a minimum cost, Copeland (23) recommended the score as the "number of items attempted." The correlation between the R–W score and number attempted score for the number checking is .96, indicating interchangeability for practical purposes. However, the name checking correlation is .89, which implies that caution should be exercised in substituting the "number of items attempted" score for the R—W score. Candee and Blum (20) advocate obtaining a speed score and an accuracy score separately. This scoring system has been used for many years at the Vocational Advisory Service. It has lent itself to descriptions of habits of work which the counselors there have found useful when related to other test observational and vocational history data. In counseling inexperienced people, a highly accurate performance of a relatively slow person, together with other information, has allowed the counselors to draw inferences about possible success in routine clerical work. An employer may prefer an accurate even though relatively slow clerk for some jobs or a very fast worker for other jobs where accuracy is not important at all. Filing accounts receivable might be an example of the former whereas addressing envelopes in a mass mailing would illustrate the latter.

Norms are available for the separate scoring system both at the Vocational Advisory Service and at the College of the City of New York. The Manual includes norms for the R—W scoring. These norms (separate for males and females) are for various educational grades, geographical regions, and classifications of employed and unemployed clerical workers. The norms for the various clerical workers are generally derived from small samplings. Where they are mixtures of two kinds of occupations, like accountants and bookkeepers, the groups are not differentiable. In using the norms in counseling, the grade norms and the more general norms for employed clerical workers and gainfully occupied adults might better be used first and then comparison made with the specific occupations. Again as with all testing, the normative results for a single test cannot be used alone but rather along with other test results and interview data.

The instructions and samples of the test are illustrated here.

Meier Art Tests: I. Art Judgment. This is the revision of the original 1929 Meier-Seashore Art Judgment Test. Before the publication of the revision in 1940, extensive research had been carried out concerning the nature and functioning of artistic talent. This test is the first of three to be published, the other two being Creative Imagination and Aesthetic Perception. Meier (48) writes that the three tests

MINNESOTA CLERICAL TEST

(formerly the Minnesota Vocational Test for Clerical Workers)

by Dorothy M. Andrew, Donald G. Paterson, and Howard P. Longstaff

Name__________ Date__________

TEST 1—Number Comparison	TEST 2—Name Comparison
Number Right________	Number Right________
Number Wrong________	Number Wrong________
Score = R—W________	Score = R—W________
Percentile Rating________	Percentile Rating________

Instructions

On the inside pages there are two tests. One of the tests consists of pairs of names and the other of pairs of numbers. If the two names or the two numbers of a pair are *exactly the same* make a check mark (√) on the line between them; if they are *different*, make no mark on that line. When the examiner says "Stop!" draw a line under the last pair at which you have looked.

Samples done correctly of pairs of *Numbers*

79542 ___ 79524

5794367 √ 5794367

Samples done correctly of pairs of *Names*

John C. Linder ___ John C. Lender

Investors Syndicate √ Investors Syndicate

Now try the samples below.

66273894 ___ 66273984

527384578 ___ 527384578

New York World ___ New York World

Cargill Grain Co. ___ Cargil Grain Co.

This is a test for Speed and Accuracy. Work as fast as you can without making mistakes.

Do not turn this page until you are told to begin.

Printed in U. S. A. 47-109T

The Psychological Corporation

INSTRUCTIONS AND SAMPLE PROBLEMS FOR THE MINNESOTA CLERICAL TEST

"will complement and supplement each other." He believes that their use together with tests of personality and intelligence will considerably advance the prognosis of art ability.

The test has 100 artistic reproductions included after analysis of the items. Each plate has two reproductions, in black and white, of works of established merit. Each has some principle singled out so that the subject has two versions almost identical except for an impairment of a principle. One is therefore better than the other. The examinee is to select the better one. According to Ziegfeld (81), "94 of the plates are of paintings (or of related graphic media); 3 are of vases and urns, 3 are of design which appear to be derived from or suitable to pottery."[2]

Meier considers aesthetic judgment "one of the most important, if not the most important, single factor in artistic competence."[3] It is the ability to discern the relationships of form organized in accordance with universal principles found in all good art. The 100 plates finally selected to measure judgment were favorably reviewed by 25 art experts and received a 60 to 90 per cent preference by 1081 subjects, varying in age from 11 years to "middle age," with various degrees of schooling. The plates were also analyzed for prognostic significance.

Meier (48) states that aesthetic judgment is not positively correlated with general intelligence nor with information about art. "A twelve-year-old child without training may make as high a score as an adult with the benefit of the best training."[4] Barrett (8) found no difference in intelligence between her control group of 40 non-art majors and an experimental group of 40 art majors on the Q, L, or Total scores of the A.C.E. Psychological Examination. Carroll (21) reports on the effect of art training. He administered the Meier-Seashore Art Judgment Test (the original) to 152 college students, art majors, and non-art majors, before and after a one-year period of art instruction. Both groups improved their scores, with the non-art students gaining a negligible amount and the art students improving more but not with statistical significance. Aesthetic judgment according to

---

[2] Reprinted by permission of Oscar K. Buros, Editor, *The Third Mental Measurements Yearbook* (New Brunswick: Rutgers University Press; 1949). Page 258.

[3] N. C. Meier, *Examiner's Manual, The Meier Art Tests: I. Art Judgment,* page 4. Reproduced with the permission of the author and the publishers.

[4] *Ibid.,* page 15.

Meier is not merely the result of inheritance; it is the result of the interaction of nature and nurture. He writes,

> . . . the process is a developmental one; but it should not be lost sight of that, if he has at the beginning, the craftsman attitude and manner of work, he will have almost by nature a certain regard for order in arrangement. This order in arrangement represents the functioning of aesthetic judgment.[5]

Carroll found a correlation of .40 between the Art Judgment Test and ratings of creative art ability by university art instructors. Morrow (49) found a correlation slightly higher. Aesthetic judgment is related to ability at about the same level that most aptitude tests are related to various criteria. Barrett (8) showed that the Meier test differentiated the art majors from the non-art with some overlap. She also used three other tests which differentiated the groups, the Strong Vocational Interest Blank scored for artists, the Study of Values, and the revised Minnesota Paper Form Board. Those tests when combined with the Art Judgment test gave results that differentiated between the art and non-art majors with 85 per cent accuracy. The use of other tests together with the Art test allows for safer and more accurate prediction. Although intelligence is not closely related to Art Judgment, one of the Carnegie Studies cited by Meier notes the average I.Q. of very successful artists to be 119. This indicates that while very superior intelligence is not essential it is certainly helpful for success.

Ziegfeld (81), writing in *The Third Mental Measurements Yearbook,* states that since most of the plates of the test are in the graphic arts medium, it is limited to this medium. He writes that it is not necessarily a measure of aesthetic judgment in other areas like architecture and sculpture. He also notes that the differences between the plates are based upon design factors; "that is, the balance has been destroyed, emphasis altered, proportions changed, and the rhythm of continuity broken."[6] There are other factors in aesthetic judgment such as color, subject matter, and expression. However, he believes

---

[5] *Ibid.*, page 22.

[6] Reprinted by permission of Oscar K. Buros, Editor, *The Third Mental Measurements Yearbook* (New Brunswick: Rutgers University Press; 1949). Page 258.

that what it measures it measures well; and that "it is the most satisfactory of all the art tests that have been constructed."[7]

The reliability of the test as given in the Examiners' Manual ranges from .70 to .84 on samplings from junior high schools, senior high schools, college undergraduates, the Pratt Institute, and the Rhode Island School of Design. These reliabilities are not very high, especially for individual prediction. However, in combination with other tests and measures of art ability, the Art Judgment can be useful. The scoring is very simple. The number of correct responses plus an extra point for every item marked with an asterisk gives the score. The extra point for the asterisked items makes for better discrimination between the lower and higher scores. The test is given to groups, with no time limit. Most people finish the task in about 45 minutes.

Norms are available for Junior High School Grades 7, 8, and 9, Senior High School Grades 10, 11, 12, and College-Adult Art Schools. Those examinees who fall into the highest quartile range (76th–100th percentiles) are likely to be successful in art, other factors being favorable. The intermediate groups need further study, especially in the light of the varieties and levels of art careers possible. For those obtaining scores in the lowest quartile, careful check with other test results as well as other factors should be considered. The accompanying figure illustrates two sets of the plates.

Seashore Measures of Musical Talents. These tests have a long history. They were originally published in 1919 and revised in 1939. The 1939 measures consist of two series of records, each series having three double records. Series A, an easier form than Series B, is used for screening purposes. Series B is employed for individual and more precise testing. Both series measure six musical capacities: pitch, loudness, time, timbre, rhythm, and tonal memory. The tests are based on the principle of discriminating smaller and smaller differences between pairs of each of the six measures. The tests take about one hour. They can be repeated several times and the results averaged to achieve greater reliability. Evidently little learning takes place. Parts of the records, non-consecutive excerpts at the begin-

[7] *Loc. cit.*

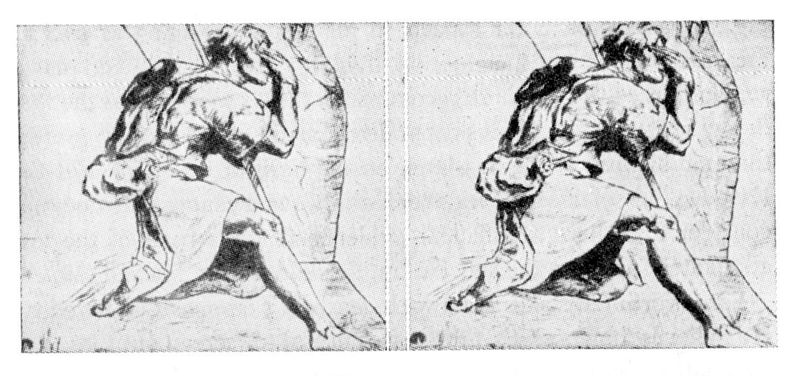

Reproduced with the permission of the author and the publishers

SAMPLE PLATES FROM MEIER ART JUDGMENT TEST

ning and end, are given for demonstration purposes without having any practice effect, according to Super (69).

Seashore (63) believes "musicality" to consist of a number of specific traits and not as a single omnibus trait. He considers the six measures basic, but not as constituting the whole of musical talent. He writes (62), "They do not measure the musical mind as a whole, but they do measure specific and fundamental traits of musical hearing." Measures of motor aspects in playing and singing as well as measures of memory, imagination, thinking, feeling, and so on play a role in musicality. Seashore recommends the six measures as the first in any series of tests of musical ability. Larson (41), however, prefers the omnibus use of the Seashore, on the basis of experiences at the Eastman School of Music for over a quarter of a century. He does not consider that there is sufficient evidence that the parts of the test adequately measure the specific traits. Neither does Mursell (50).

Farnsworth (28) takes issue with Seashore's emphasis on heredity. He believes, however, that the test is useful to "screen out those unfortunates who will not achieve success in music without enormous effort." The complexity of musicality is recognized by Seashore. As noted above, he writes of other factors being important. He also admits the need for favorable environmental conditions. As Super (69) states, "Talents may be a sine qua non, but they cannot be sufficient in and of themselves."[8]

Taylor (71) conducted a rather comprehensive study in the prognosis of musical talent. During a five-year testing program at the College of Music of Cincinnati (from 1930–1935), she employed several tests including the Seashore. A follow-up in 1939, after three to seven years had elapsed since the 185 students tested had left school, provided the criterion data. She had marks of students in certain college subjects in music, judgments by competent persons of the students' professional success as musicians, and other data. She did not find the Seashore tests to be good predictors of success in music courses in the college. The Detroit Intelligence Test was found to have substantial predictive value for success in musical dictation (.59) and in sight singing (.43). Sight singing shows the highest relationship with professional success; dictation has the next highest. These two subjects involve "ear training." Harmony and history, the other two subjects studied, show less correlation with professional success. Apparently, the music students were a rather homogeneous group with a certain minimum of musicality, but the variation in intelligence made for differences. However, they probably varied also in the several musi-

[8] Reprinted by permission from *Appraising Vocational Fitness,* by Donald E. Super, Harper & Brothers, New York, 1949.

cal abilities; this variation would make for differences in success in different fields of music.

In regard to musical success, Taylor reports that musical talent is a prerequisite, but that "the individual who possesses that musicality will reach a limit above which he cannot rise unless his musical ability is accompanied by no small degree of intelligence."[9] Stanton (67) also demonstrated that intelligence is necessary to really master the more difficult music. Taylor believes in Seashore's specific theory of the nature of musical talent; she notes that the various elements do not occur in equal amounts and that "one element usually tends to dominate another, thus leading different persons into the various fields of musical endeavor. . . ."[10]

The Seashore tests, then, can be used, but guardedly. If the individual has had some practice, an audition by a competent professional person would probably be wise as a supplement to the tests. For younger people without much training, the tests have some possibilities. Seashore recommends the use of the test beginning with the fifth grade or at about ten years. If abilities exist, there is still time for training. However, not everyone can be trained to be a great classical musician. There are different fields of music requiring different levels of ability as well as different personality traits. The differences become more obvious with maturation and training.

The reliabilities of the various measures vary. They are somewhat higher for tonal memory, pitch, and intensity, and they are within the range of acceptability. The tests of consonance, timbre, and rhythm cannot be considered reliable.

Decile norms are provided for both Series A and Series B. For Series A, there are norms for pupils in fifth, sixth, seventh, and eighth grades as well as for adults. Series B has only adult norms. No in-between norms are given because of the small increase in test performance from eighth grade to adult. However, the norms are not highly discriminating. A single point can make for a marked change in rating.

---

[9] E. M. Taylor, "A Study in the Prognosis of Musical Talent," *Journal of Experimental Education*, 10:27 (1941).
[10] *Ibid.*, page 19.

Achievement tests

Cooperative General Achievement Tests (Revised Series)—A Test of General Proficiency in the Field of Mathematics. The Cooperative General Achievement Tests, Revised Series, actually consist of three tests: Test 1, A Test of General Proficiency in the Field of the Social Studies; Test 2, A Test of General Proficiency in the Field of Natural Sciences; and Test 3, A Test of General Proficiency in the Field of Mathematics. These tests were devised to measure general proficiency in the three fields, not mastery of specific courses as were the Survey Tests. Each test may be used separately.

The Mathematics Test consists of two parts, "terms and concepts," and "comprehension and interpretation." The former has a time limit of 15 minutes, and the latter, 25 minutes. If the second part is completed before the time limit, the examinee may go back and work on either part. Indiscriminate guessing is penalized by the scoring method, which provides penalties for wrong responses.

The test items are constructed in the form of multiple-choice questions. There are no practice problems. There are three equivalent forms; S, T, and X. The "terms and concepts" part consists of 45 questions in the areas of business arithmetic, algebra, geometry, and trigonometry. Typical examples from Form S are the following:

Money paid for the use of money is called

1. rebate
2. interest
3. premium
4. collateral
5. commission

The longest side of a right triangle is called the

1. hypotenuse
2. leg
3. perimeter
4. median
5. base[11]

[11] Published by permission of the copyright holder, Cooperative Test Division, Educational Testing Service, 20 Nassau Street, Princeton, New Jersey.

The correct number is to be written in the parenthesis provided in the test blank.

The "comprehension and interpretation" part consists of 36 questions involving knowledge of the same fields of mathematics as the first part. However, here a complete problem is stated, some with charts and graphs, and then various questions are posed about the problem. The problems are all quite practical. Examples follow:

Flaked Corn Pie Crust

4 cups flaked corn
¼ cup sugar
¼ cup melted butter
½ teaspoon cinnamon

Put the flaked corn through a food chopper, using the fine cutter. This will make 1 cup of fine crumbs. Mix with sugar, butter, and cinnamon. Butter a circular pie tin 9 inches in diameter and line the bottom and sides with the crumbs. Bake in a 400-degree oven about 10 minutes.

1. How much crumbs will 1 cup of flaked corn make
   1–1 1 cup
   1–2 ½ cup
   1–3 ¼ cup
   1–4 4 cups
   1–5 ⅛ cup . . . . ( )

3. If you had two 9-inch tins to place in the oven together, they would need to bake for
   3–1 about 5 minutes
   3–2 about 10 minutes
   3–3 about 15 minutes
   3–4 about 20 minutes
   3–5 more than 20 minutes . . . . ( )[12]

There are four questions in all about the first problem. Other problems have as many as six or seven questions.

It is obvious that the test is for high school and college students. McQuitty (47) writes of the usefulness of the test for those whose academic background is "widely divergent or where a long period of

[12] *Ibid.*

time has elapsed since the examinee studied the field involved." He warns that the results should not be taken to indicate course mastery and, in addition, that the test is after all only a sampling of a broad field. It may perhaps be used for college placement of freshmen; but this possibility has not been completely verified.

The manner of construction of the test has a certain degree of validity. The test is the result of cooperation between subject-matter specialists and test technicians. Adkins (1) considers this sort of cooperation ideal for achievement test construction. The subject-matter specialist selects items, knowledge of which correlates with school success; the test technician makes up the form of the examination, paying attention to how well it discriminates and to how accurately it predicts.

The test should not be used alone in guidance. Other tests, especially of intelligence and interest, must accompany it. It could be employed for those clients interested in occupations like accountancy, actuarial work, and engineering who have been out of school for some time. Their school grades may still be available, but they may be unsure of how good they are in mathematics. Also, as is the case of many veterans, mathematics grades may not have been too good previously, but with heightened interest in work requiring mathematics, they might have learned more on their own. The test will discover this fact.

The reliability of the test is given in terms of the standard error of measurement, a measure of the degree of accuracy of the score. For the standard errors given for selected scores, reliability seems adequate. All raw scores are transmuted into scaled scores that make for comparability among the different achievement tests. Norms are available for ninth, tenth, eleventh, and twelfth grades.

Cooperative English Test. This test has two levels, the lower level for grades 7–12 and the higher level for grades 13–16. Only the higher level will be described. There are three forms, R, S, and T, and they can be used interchangeably. The Single Booklet Edition contains three different tests, Reading Comprehension, Mechanics of Expression, and Effectiveness of Expression. Each of the three tests takes 40 minutes, for a total of two hours.

The Reading Comprehension Test consists of two subtests, vocabulary and reading. The former has a time limit of 15 minutes and the latter 25 minutes.

If the work on a later test is finished before the time limit, the examinee is not allowed to go back to the preceding tests. As in the Mathematics tests, "wild" guessing should be avoided for all parts of the English test, since the scoring includes penalties for wrong answers. The Mechanics of Expression test includes subtests of grammatical usage (15-minute time limit), punctuation and capitalization (15-minute time limit), and spelling (10-minute time limit). The Effectiveness of Expression Test has three subtests: sentence structure and style (15 minutes), active vocabulary (10 minutes), and organization (15 minutes).

The vocabulary subtest (with 60 five-choice items) is according to the Manual (77) a test of recognition and uses words of increasing difficulty, with increasingly close discrimination required among choices. Examples of this subtest are given below:

inquisitive
1. cruel
2. curious
3. peculiar
4. unselfish
5. uninterested

insignia
1. naval officers
2. emblems
3. records
4. equipment
5. witnesses[13]

The number of the correct choice is to be placed in the parenthesis provided in the test booklet.

The reading subtest has 90 five-choice items. According to the Manual, the reading involves determining meanings of words from the context, organizing the meanings, understanding the writer's meaning, and making conclusions from the content.

An example follows:

> "It was all Mrs. O'Malley. She *would* do it," urged Mr. O'Malley, first looking around to ascertain that his partner had left the room.
>
> "That is no excuse," replied the Constable. "You were present on the occasion of the destruction of those trinkets, and indeed are the

[13] Published by permission of the copyright holder, Cooperative Test Division, Educational Testing Service, 20 Nassau Street, Princeton, New Jersey.

more guilty of the two in the eye of the law, for the law supposes that your wife acts under your direction."

"If the law supposes that," said Mr. O'Malley, squeezing his hat and looking around again, "the law is an ass, an idiot. If that's the eye of the law, the law is a bachelor; and the worst I wish the law is that his eye may be opened by experience."

MECHANICS OF EXPRESSION
PART I: GRAMMATICAL USAGE
(15 minutes)

Directions: Read each sentence and decide whether there is an error in usage in any of the **underlined** parts of the sentence. If so, note the number printed under the **wrong** word or phrase, and put this number in the parentheses at the right. If there is **no** usage error in the sentence, put a zero (0) in the parentheses.

No sentence has more than one error, and some sentences do not have any errors. The sentences are to be judged on the basis of suitable usage for general written English.

Samples:

8. He says that he ain't coming home with us today. . . . . .8(**2**)
says = 1, ain't = 2, home = 3, us = 4

In this sentence, ain't is wrong. The number printed below this word, 2, is therefore written in the parentheses.

9. She isn't ready to go home . . . . .9(***0***)
isn't = 1, ready = 2, home = 3

In this sentence, there is no error in any of the underlined words. A zero is therefore written in the parentheses.

DIRECTIONS AND SAMPLES FROM COOPERATIVE ENGLISH TEST

2. We may infer that Mr. O'Malley
   - 2–1 has destroyed some property
   - 2–2 told his wife to destroy some property
   - 2–3 is trying to protect his wife from the law
   - 2–4 usually does what his wife tells him to do
   - 2–5 is happily married
4. Mr. O'Malley apparently thinks that his wife
   - 4–1 is not responsible for her acts

4–2 is innocent of any wrongdoing
4–3 is self-willed
4–4 is amusing
4–5 has been insulted by the Constable[14]

Six multiple-choice items are given for this paragraph. Other paragraphs have as many as eight multiple-choice items. This subtest measures speed and level of comprehension and the test directions

PART II

PUNCTUATION AND CAPITALIZATION

(15 minutes)

Directions: In the passages below, at each place where there is a number below the line of text, decide what punctuation, if any, is needed there. At the right of that line, in the group numbered to correspond to the place in the text, locate the punctuation you consider correct for that place. ("N" means "no punctuation.") Write the **number** of the correct choice in the parentheses at the right, as in the sample.

Sample:

8–1 N
8–2 ,
8–3 ; .... 8(*1*)

We came home yesterday
8 9

9–1 N
9–2 .
9–3 ? .... 9(2)

In the sample, at the place in the sentence marked 8, no punctuation is required. "N," meaning "no punctuation," is choice 1, so you would write 1 in the parentheses, as shown above. At the place marked 9, a period is needed. The period is choice 2, so you would write 2 in the parentheses.

Published by permission of the copyright holder, Cooperative Test Division, Educational Testing Service, 20 Nassau Street, Princeton, New Jersey.

DIRECTIONS AND SAMPLES FROM COOPERATIVE ENGLISH TEST

state that "enough material has been included so that even the most rapid readers probably will not finish in the time allowed."

The grammatical usage subtest of the Mechanics of Expression contains 60 items. The directions and samples are shown on page 248.

[14] Published by permission of the copyright holder, Cooperative Test Division, Educational Testing Service, 20 Nassau Street, Princeton, New Jersey.

The punctuation and capitalization subtest consists of 45 multiple-choice type items. The directions and a sample illustrate this subtest.

The spelling subtest has 60 items; we have illustrated the directions and samples on this page.

Sentence structure and style of the Effectiveness of Expression part consists of sets of sentences differing in structure and style. The examinee is to choose the better version and to answer questions about the sets. The items are in multiple-choice form. An illustration is given on page 251.

PART III: SPELLING

(10 minutes)

Directions: In each of the items below, a word is spelled in two ways. Choose the correct spelling of the word, and put its **number** in the parentheses at the right, as in the samples. In a few items, both spellings given may be wrong. If neither spelling is correct, the space for that item should be left blank.

Samples:

0–1 speling
0–2 spelling .... 0(2)
00–1 right
00–2 rihgt ....00(*1*)

Published by permission of the copyright holder, Cooperative Test Division, Educational Testing Service, 20 Nassau Street, Princeton, New Jersey.

Some of the questions are given below:

A. Section A is better expressed in
A–1 Column 1
A–2 Column 2 ....A( )

a. The inferior version of Section A is poor because
a–1 it lacks emphasis
a–2 two separate sentences are punctuated as if they were a single sentence
a–3 it is not a complete sentence
a–4 the vocabulary is inappropriate ....a( )

c. In the inferior version of Section C
c–1 an incomplete sentence is punctuated as if it were a complete sentence
c–2 there is a dangling participle
c–3 a modifier is wrongly placed
c–4 the vocabulary is less dignified than in the other version c( )

D. Section D is better expressed in
D–1 Column 1
D–2 Column 2 ....D( )[15]

---

[15] Published by permission of the copyright holder, Cooperative Test Division, Educational Testing Service, 20 Nassau Street, Princeton, New Jersey.

EFFECTIVENESS OF EXPRESSION
PART I: SENTENCE STRUCTURE AND STYLE

(15 minutes)

Directions: Different versions of each passage of prose are given in the two columns below. In this part of the test, you will be asked to choose the better version of each section, and to answer certain questions about the sections. First, read quickly through Column 1 of the passage to get the meaning of the whole passage. Then read the directions below.

	Column 1		Column 2
A–1	A boy has many hard problems to deal with; for example, there is the difficult task of getting the whole world into your head.	**A–2**	An example of the many hard problems a boy must deal with, the difficult task of getting the whole world into your head.
B–1	You have to make a picture of it, and that is easy, but it must correspond with the world outside, but that keeps changing.	**B–2**	You have to make a picture of it; that's easy, but the picture has to correspond somewhat with the world outside, which keeps changing.
C–1	You succeed in picturing the sun going around the earth; then you suddenly learn something more, and are forced to picture the earth whirling around the sun. This means a complete readjustment.	**C–2**	Having the sun going around the earth, something more is suddenly learned and the earth must be pictured whirling around the sun, necessitating a complete readjustment.
D–1	At one time I thought the earth was flat, I had to put China and the Far East to the west of me, this was not an easy task for a boy.	**D–2**	I remember how, when I thought the earth was flat, I had to put China and the Far East to the west of me—no easy task for a boy.
E–1	I did accomplish that, but shortly after, I studied a book which made the earth round like an orange. China's location again was made uncertain to me.	**E–2**	Then, when I had accomplished that, I studied a book which made the earth round like an orange. Where was one to put China then?

Compare the two different versions of each lettered section as given in Columns 1 and 2 above, and answer each of the following questions by putting the number of the correct choice in the parentheses at the right.

Active vocabulary is tested by the second subtest of the Effectiveness of Expression; a recognition type vocabulary. A sentence is used to describe what is wanted and the examinee is given multiple-choice items with first letter and total number of letters as clues. There are 25 multiple-choice items. Directions and a sample are given below:

PART II—ACTIVE VOCABULARY

(10 minutes)

Directions: Each sentence below describes a certain word. The number in parentheses shows how many letters there are in the word. You are to think of the exact word which best fits the sentence and find its **first letter** among the choices given below the sentence. Put the **number** of this initial letter in the parentheses at the right.

Do not spend too much time on any one item; if you cannot think of the right word, go on to the next item.

Sample:

0. The thin cutting part of an instrument, as of a knife or sword, is called its –(5)–.
0–1 A
0–2 B
0–3 C
0–4 D
0–5 E . . . . 0(2)

The 5-letter word referred to in the sample sentence is "BLADE." The first letter of the word, **B,** is choice **2.** The number **2** has therefore been written in the parentheses.

Published by permission of the copyright holder, Cooperative Test Division, Educational Testing Service, 20 Nassau Street, Princeton, New Jersey.

DIRECTIONS AND A SAMPLE FROM COOPERATIVE ENGLISH TEST

The final subtest is designed to measure ability to organize materials. According to the manual for the tests (76) the factors involved in the ability to organize are:

ability to discriminate between relevant and irrelevant material
ability to recognize the relative breadth of scope of various topics
ability to classify material under appropriate headings
ability to arrange material in an effective order
ability to handle transitional material effectively.[16]

[16] Published by permission of the copyright holder, Cooperative Test Division, Educational Testing Service, 20 Nassau Street, Princeton, New Jersey.

Two kinds of items are used. In the first, various thoughts are presented randomly and the examinee is to arrange them in the best order in a sentence or paragraph; or topic sentences of whole paragraphs of a theme are given for the examinee to arrange in the order that would give the best organization for the theme. In the second kind of item, the examinee is to organize topics presented randomly and to answer questions designed to test how well the topics were classified and organized. The directions and an illustration of part of the subtest are shown in the figure on page 254.

The Cooperative English test is very thorough. Its subject-matter is derived from experts in English; and it is constructed in accordance with the basic principles of psychological measurement. The validity of the test is primarily dependent upon how well it measures the skills actually involved in reading, in mechanics, and in effectiveness of expression. According to the manuals very complete analyses were made of these processes and the subject-matter developed accordingly. This method can be used more readily with achievement tests than with aptitude or intelligence tests, where the subject-matter is not as definitive.

Noyes (51), an associate professor of English, considers the Reading Comprehension Test as better than the others. Concerning the Mechanics of Expression Test he states, "College freshman English sections are full of students who have done reasonably well on such exercises as these but who are still lamentably prone to solecisms almost as bad." He also writes that the Effectiveness of Expression Test measures critical rather than creative ability. A truer indication of effectiveness of expression, he believes, would be discovered "by giving the student a blank page and a pencil and setting him to write."

Pooley (58), another English professor, considers the test "one of the best available in the field of English skills." He considers its main defect to be that shared by all other objective tests, namely that:

> It does not test ability in English, if ability is defined as the power to use English effectively in speech and writing. It does test the power to correct errors, to proofread, to organize or reorganize material composed by others. It does not test the power to compose English and

PART III—ORGANIZATION

(15 minutes)

Directions: Read each of the following groups of sentences, and decide what would be the **best order** in which to put the sentences, to form a well-organized paragraph. Write the letters of the sentences **in this best order** on a piece of scratch paper. Then answer the questions below each group by putting in the parentheses at the right the **number** of the best answer, according to the order you have chosen.

Items 1–5:

A. **Nevertheless, Russia, like the United States, can get along with only a little importation of minerals from other countries.**

B. **Russia ranks next to the United States in the variety and extent of its mineral resources.**

C. **Iron ore, for instance, has to be transported long distances to reach deposits of coal, and many of the metals are in small deposits in remote parts of Siberia.**

D. **They are far inferior to those of this country, however.**

E. **Moreover, they are not well located.**

1. If the five sentences above were arranged in the best order, Sentence **A** would be placed
   1–1 first.
   1–2 directly after **B.**
   1–3 directly after **C.**
   1–4 directly after **D.**
   1–5 directly after **E.** ....1( )

2. Sentence **B** would be placed
   2–1 first.
   2–2 directly after **A.**
   2–3 directly after **C.**
   2–4 directly after **D.**
   2–5 directly after **E.** ....2( )

Published by permission of the copyright holder, Cooperative Test Division, Educational Testing Service, 20 Nassau Street, Princeton, New Jersey.

AN EXCERPT FROM COOPERATIVE ENGLISH TEST

should therefore be used cautiously in the placing of students in ability groups or in the sectioning and exemption of college freshmen.[17]

---

[17] Reprinted by permission of Oscar K. Buros, Editor, *The Third Mental Measurements Yearbook* (New Brunswick: Rutgers University Press; 1949). Page 223.

The main objection to the test is, then, that it does not measure the ability to compose or create. However, it was not intended for that use. According to the manual on the English Expression Tests, they would be valuable as supplementary to "the teacher's subjective judgment about his student's writing ability, gained from the cumulative experience with their actual work."

The test gives both speed of reading comprehension and level of comprehension scores. The correlation between the two for the higher level is .87, indicating that both elements are closely related on this test. The speed is dependent upon comprehension, not just on words read. Also the vocabulary in the reading sections was controlled so as to reduce the effect of word knowledge on the comprehension test.

Scores are transmuted into scaled units; consequently all parts of the test can be compared with each other. This comparability is extremely useful for understanding an individual's achievement levels in various areas and advising him educationally. Vocationally the test is useful only as vocational success is related to educational background and achievement.

This test, like the mathematics test, has standard errors of measure for the scores made, a good means of obtaining reliability. Norms are available for the parts of the English test, as well as the subtests and totals. They are based on large numbers of students in many different colleges. The scaled scores are also given in percentile units.

Summary

The major concern of this chapter was to describe and evaluate representative tests of intelligence, aptitude, and achievement. The tests were selected on the bases of the frequency of their usage in vocational counseling together with reasonable validity within the classification and variety.

Three tests of intelligence, 12 aptitude tests, and two achievement tests were described and evaluated.

The American Council on Education Psychological Examination is a time-limit group test of intelligence yielding a total score, a linguistic score, and a quantitative score. It is a good measure of academic ability.

The Ohio State University Psychological Test, a group test of intelligence, is a power test with no time limit. The test consists of three subtests: same-opposites, analogies, and reading comprehension. It has a high correlation with college success.

The Otis Self-Administering Test of Mental Ability is a short group test with 75 test items ranged in order of difficulty. The tests are economical to administer and score but one sacrifices validity.

The Bennett Mechanical Comprehension Test is a group test designed to measure a high level of mechanical ability. The test takes about 30 minutes and consists of 60 items involving the understanding of mechanical principles. It has reasonable validity for such jobs as machining precision parts and testing aircraft engines.

The Revised Minnesota Paper Form Board Test is a group test with a time limit of 20 minutes; it consists of 64 geometric figures. It measures spatial ability and is useful to predict success in such occupations and school subjects as drafting, blueprint reading, technical drawing and machine design.

The Minnesota Spatial Relations Test is a form board test administered individually. Since it measures simple spatial ability, it is more suitable to predict success in lower than in more highly skilled jobs.

The MacQuarrie Test for Mechanical Ability is a group paper and pencil test consisting of seven subtests. The separate subtests in various combinations show some validity for mechanical occupations.

The O'Connor Finger and Tweezer Dexterity Tests use two sides of the same apparatus. The tests are not highly correlated with each other. The Finger Dexterity Test has some validity where fine finger movements are required. The Tweezer Dexterity Test also has some validity for fine work.

The Minnesota Rate of Manipulation test is known as the placing and turning test. It is a performance test and measures gross movements of the hands and arms. It has been used most successfully in the selection of packers and wrappers.

The Purdue Pegboard yields five scores depending upon the task performed. This test measures gross as well as finer dexterities.

The Minnesota Clerical is a name and number checking task. It requires attention to detail and has been widely used in guidance and selection for a variety of jobs.

The Meier Art Judgment test was included as a sample of a test for special aptitude. Use of the test has been limited and its findings are not too clear cut. However, in combination with other tests it can be helpful to a cautious counselor.

The Seashore Measures of Musical Talents is most controversial. Interpretations of results on this test must be made with extreme care. It was primarily included to illustrate aptitude testing for music.

The two achievement tests included were selected from a very large number. The Cooperative General Achievement Tests in Mathematics and English are typical illustrations of measures of proficiency but are somewhat better standardized than many others in this area.

Bibliography

1. Adkins, D. C., *Construction and Analysis of Achievement Tests.* Washington, D.C.: U.S. Government Printing Office, 1947.
2. Anderson, E. E., *et al.*, "Wilson College Studies in Psychology: I. A Comparison of the Wechsler-Bellevue, Revised Stanford-Binet, and American Council on Education Tests at the College Level," *Journal of Psychology,* 14:317–326 (1942).
3. Andrew, D. M., "An Analysis of the Minnesota Vocational Test for Clerical Workers," I. *Journal of Applied Psychology,* 21:18–47 (1937).
4. ——— and D. G. Paterson, *Measured Characteristics of Clerical Workers* (Bulletin of the Employment Stabilization Research Institute, 3, #1), University of Minnesota, 1934.
5. ———, *Manual (Revised) for the Minnesota Vocational Test for Clerical Workers.* New York: The Psychological Corporation, 1946.
6. Baker, G., and J. G. Peatman, "Tests Used in Veterans Administration Advisement Units," *The American Psychologist,* 2:99–102 (1947).
7. Balinsky, B., and I. R. Stone, "A New Method of Finding the In-

telligence Quotient on Otis Self-Administering Tests, Higher Examination," *Journal of Social Psychology,* 10:459–465 (1939).

8. Barrett, D. M., "Aptitude and Interest Patterns of Art Majors in a Liberal Arts College," *Journal of Applied Psychology,* 29:483–492 (1945).
9. Barrett, P. W., "Prediction of Achievement in Typewriting and Stenography in a Liberal Arts College," *Journal of Applied Psychology,* 30:624–630 (1946).
10. Bennett, G. K., *Manual for Test of Mechanical Comprehension, Form AA.* New York: The Psychological Corporation.
11. ——— and R. M. Cruikshank, *A Summary of Clerical Tests.* New York: The Psychological Corporation, 1949.
12. ———, *A Summary of Manual and Mechanical Ability Tests.* New York: The Psychological Corporation, 1942.
13. Berdie, R. F., "The Prediction of College Achievement and Satisfaction," *Journal of Applied Psychology,* 28:239–245 (1944).
14. Blum, M. L., "A Contribution of Manual Aptitude Measurement in Industry: The Value of Certain Dexterity Measures for the Selection of Workers in a Watch Factory," *Journal of Applied Psychology,* 24:381–416 (1940).
15. ———, "Selection of Sewing Machine Operators," *Journal of Applied Psychology,* 27:35–40 (1943).
16. ———, in O. K. Buros (ed.), *The Third Mental Measurements Yearbook.* New Brunswick, N.J.: Rutgers University Press, 1949.
17. ——— and B. Candee, "The Selection of Department Store Packers and Wrappers with the Aid of Certain Psychological Tests: Study II," *Journal of Applied Psychology,* 25:291–299 (1941).
18. Brush, E. N., "Mechanical Ability as a Factor in Engineering Aptitude," *Journal of Applied Psychology,* 25:300–312 (1941).
19. Candee, B., and M. L. Blum, "A New Scoring System for the Minnesota Clerical Test," *Psychological Bulletin,* 34:545 (1937).
20. ———, "Report of a Study Done in a Watch Factory," *Journal of Applied Psychology,* 21:572–582 (1937).
21. Carroll, H. A., "What do The Meier-Seashore and The McAdory Art Tests Measure?", *Journal of Educational Research,* 26:661–665 (1933).
22. Cook, D. W., and M. F. Barre, "The Effect of Specialized Industrial Norms on the Use of the Minnesota Rate of Manipulation

Test as a Selective Instrument in Employment Procedure," *Journal of Applied Psychology,* 26:785–792 (1942).

23. Copeland, H. A., "Some Characteristics of Three Tests Used To Predict Clerical Success," *Journal of Applied Psychology,* 20:461–470 (1936).
24. Darley, J. G., and D. G. Marquis, "Veterans' Guidance Centers: A Survey of Their Problems and Activities," *Journal of Clinical Psychology,* 2:109–116 (1946).
25. Davidson, C. M., "Evaluation of Clerical Tests," *Personnel Journal,* 16:57–64, 95–98 (1937).
26. *Examiner's Manual, Minnesota Rate of Manipulation Test.* Minneapolis: Educational Test Bureau, 1946.
27. Failor, C. W., and C. A. Mahler, "Examining Counselors' Selection of Tests," *Occupations,* 28:164–167 (1949).
28. Farnsworth, P. R., in O. K. Buros (ed.), *The Third Mental Measurements Yearbook.* New Brunswick, N.J.: Rutgers University Press, 1949.
29. Ghiselli, E. E., "Tests for the Selection of Inspector-Packers," *Journal of Applied Psychology,* 26:468–476 (1942).
30. Green, H. J., I. R. Berman, D. G. Paterson, and M. R. Trabue, *A Manual of Selected Occupational Tests for Use in Public Employment Offices* (Employment Stabilization Research Bulletin 2, #3), University of Minnesota, 1933.
31. Greene, E. B., "Practice and Performance," *Occupations,* 15:51–56 (1936).
32. Guilford, J. P., in O. K. Buros (ed.), *The Third Mental Measurements Yearbook.* New Brunswick, N.J.: Rutgers University Press, 1949.
33. Harris, A. J., "The Relative Significance of Measures of Mechanical Aptitude, Intelligence, and Previous Scholarship for Predicting Achievement in Dental School," *Journal of Applied Psychology,* 21:513–521 (1937).
34. Hay, E. N., "Predicting Success in Machine Bookkeeping," *Journal of Applied Psychology,* 27:483–493 (1943).
35. ———, "Postscript to Predicting Success in Machine Bookkeeping," *Journal of Applied Psychology,* 31:235 (1947).
36. Humphreys, L. G., in O. K. Buros (ed.), *The Third Mental Measurements Yearbook.* New Brunswick, N.J.: Rutgers University Press, 1949.

37. Jacobsen, E. E., "An Evaluation of Certain Tests in Predicting Mechanic-Learner Achievement," *Educational and Psychological Measurement*, 3:259–267 (1943).
38. Jurgensen, C. E., "Extension of the Minnesota Rate of Manipulation Test," *Journal of Applied Psychology*, 27:164–169 (1943).
39. Kinzer, J. R., in O. K. Buros (ed.), *The Third Mental Measurements Yearbook*. New Brunswick, N.J.: Rutgers University Press, 1949.
40. Kuder, F., in O. K. Buros (ed.), *The Third Mental Measurements Yearbook*. New Brunswick, N.J.: Rutgers University Press, 1949.
41. Larson, W. S., in O. K. Buros (ed.), *The Third Mental Measurements Yearbook*. New Brunswick, N.J.: Rutgers University Press, 1949.
42. Levine, A. S., "Correcting Special Ability Test Scores for General Ability," *Journal of Applied Psychology*, 33:566–568 (1949).
43. Long, L., and J. Hill, "Additional Norms for the Purdue Pegboard," *Occupations*, 26:160–161 (1947).
44. *Manual, The Revised Minnesota Paper Form Board*. New York: The Psychological Corporation, 1948.
45. *Manual of Directions, MacQuarrie Tests for Mechanical Ability*. Los Angeles: California Test Bureau.
46. McDaniel, J. W., and W. A. Reynolds, "A Study of the Use of the Mechanical Aptitude Tests in the Selection of Trainees for Mechanical Occupations," *Educational and Psychological Measurement*, 4:191–197 (1944).
47. McQuitty, J. V., in O. K. Buros (ed.), *The Third Mental Measurements Yearbook*. New Brunswick, N.J.: Rutgers University Press, 1949.
48. Meier, N. C., *Examiner's Manual, The Meier Art Tests: I. Art Judgment*. Iowa City: Bureau of Educational Research and Service, State University of Iowa, 1942.
49. Morrow, R. S., "An Analysis of the Relations among Tests of Musical, Artistic, and Mechanical Abilities," *Journal of Psychology*, 5: 253–263 (1938).
50. Mursell, J. L., in O. K. Buros (ed.), *The Third Mental Measurements Yearbook*. New Brunswick, N.J.: Rutgers University Press, 1949.
51. Noyes, E. S., in O. K. Buros (ed.), *The Third Mental Measurements Yearbook*. New Brunswick, N.J.: Rutgers University Press, 1949.

52. Ohio College Association Bulletin No. 134, *Directions for Administering and Scoring the Ohio State University Psychological Test, Form 23*, 1947.
53. Ohio College Association Bulletin No. 139, *1948–49 (24th) Annual Report of the Committee on Technical Research.*
54. O'Connor, J., *Born That Way*. Baltimore: Williams and Wilkins, 1928.
55. Otis, A. S., *Manual of Directions and Key (Revised), for Intermediate and Higher Examinations*. New York: World, 1928.
56. Pallister, H., "American Psychologists Judge Fifty-three Psychological Tests," *Journal of Applied Psychology*, 20:761–768 (1936).
57. Paterson, D. G. (ed.), *Research Studies in Individual Diagnosis*, Bull. Empl. Stab. Res. Inst., Univ. Minn. 3, #4 (1934).
58. Pooley, R. C., in O. K. Buros (ed.), *The Third Mental Measurements Yearbook*. New Brunswick, N.J.: Rutgers University Press, 1949.
59. Purdue Research Foundation, *Preliminary Manual for the Purdue Pegboard*. Chicago: Science Research Associates.
60. Sartain, A. Q., "The Use of Certain Standardized Tests in the Selection of Inspectors in an Aircraft Factory," *Journal of Consulting Psychology*, 9:234–235 (1945).
61. Schneidler, G. G., and D. G. Paterson, "Sex Differences in Clerical Aptitude," *Journal of Educational Psychology*, 33:303–309 (1942).
62. Seashore, C. E., *Manual of Instructions and Interpretations for Measures of Musical Talent*. Chicago: C. H. Stoelting Co.
63. ———, "The Psychology of Music," *Music Educators' Journal*, 24: 25–26 (1937).
64. Seashore, H. G., "The Superiority of College Students on the Minnesota Rate of Manipulation Test," *Journal of Applied Psychology*, 31:249–253 (1947).
65. Shuman, J. T., "The Value of Aptitude Tests for Factory Workers in the Aircraft Engine and Propeller Industries," *Journal of Applied Psychology*, 29:156–160 (1945).
66. Staff, Division of Occupational Analysis, War Manpower Commission, "Factor Analysis of Occupational Aptitude Tests," *Educational and Psychological Measurement*, 5:147–155 (1945).
67. Stanton, H. M., *Measurement of Musical Talent*. University of Iowa Studies in Music (1935).
68. Stuit, D. B., in O. K. Buros (ed.), *The Third Mental Measurements Yearbook*. New Brunswick, N.J.: Rutgers University Press, 1949.

69. Super, D. E., *Appraising Vocational Fitness by Means of Psychological Tests.* New York: Harper, 1949.
70. Surgent, L. L., "The Use of Aptitude Tests in the Selection of Radio Tube Mounters," *Psychological Monographs,* 61:1–40 (1947).
71. Taylor, E. M., "A Study in the Prognosis of Musical Talent," *Journal of Experimental Education,* 10:1–28 (1941).
72. Teegarden, L., "Manipulative Performance of Young Adult Applicants at a Public Employment Office, I, II," *Journal of Applied Psychology,* 26:633–652, 754–769 (1942).
73. ———, "Occupational Differences in Manipulative Performance of Applicants at a Public Employment Office," *Journal of Applied Psychology,* 27:416–437 (1943).
74. Terman, L. M., and M. Merrill, *Measuring Intelligence.* New York: Houghton Mifflin, 1936.
75. The American Council on Education, *Manual of Instructions.* Washington, D.C.: The Council, 1946.
76. *The Cooperative English Expression Tests.* New York: The Cooperative Test Service, 1940.
77. *The Cooperative Reading Comprehension Tests.* New York: The Cooperative Test Service, 1940.
78. Traxler, A. E., "Correlations Between 'Mechanical Aptitude' Scores and 'Mechanical Comprehension' Scores," *Occupations,* 22:42–44 (1943).
79. Tuckman, J., "A Comparison of Norms for the Minnesota Rate of Manipulation Test," *Journal of Applied Psychology,* 28:121–128 (1944).
80. Wechsler, D., *Measurement of Adult Intelligence.* Baltimore: Williams and Wilkins, 1944.
81. Ziegfeld, E., in O. K. Buros (ed.), *The Third Mental Measurements Yearbook.* New Brunswick, N.J.: Rutgers University Press, 1949.

9

THE GUIDANCE USE OF INTEREST AND PERSONALITY TESTS

JUST AS THE preceding chapter attempted to familiarize the reader with specific tests of intelligence, aptitude, and achievement, this chapter is concerned with specific interest and personality tests. According to the four studies presented in Chapter 8, the tests chosen for discussion are widely used. There are other tests of interest and personality that might have been included; but those to be discussed illustrate the available interest and personality tests.

Two measures of interest and three of personality were selected for description and evaluation.

Interest tests

Kuder Preference Record. This interest test has seen wide usage since its original publication in the latter part of the 1930's. It has undergone revision with the accumulation of new data, and further revisions can be expected. It is a group test with no time limit. (College students ordinarily need 40 minutes and high school students a little longer.) No pencil is required. A special pin is supplied to pierce a hole in circles next to two statements of each grouping of three statements; the one liked most and the one liked least. Illustrated here are the directions and examples.

Form BB
Edition for self-scoring

KUDER PREFERENCE RECORD

VOCATIONAL

by

G. FREDERIC KUDER
Professor of Psychology, Duke University
Editor, *Educational and Psychological Measurement*

This blank is used for obtaining a systematic record of your preferences with respect to a variety of activities. The resulting scores can be used to help you select occupations to investigate and consider for your life work. The blank is not a test of ability. There are no right or wrong answers. An answer is right only if it is a true expression of your preference. Follow the instructions carefully in order that the results may be accurate and therefore of most value to you.

A number of activities are listed in groups of three on the following pages. Read over the three activities in each group. Decide which of the three activities you like most. Note the letter in front of it and punch a hole through the 1 beside this letter in the column at the right, using the pin with which you are provided. Then decide which activity you like least and punch a hole through the 3 beside the corresponding letter in the column at the right.

In the following example, two groups of activities are listed. The activities are lettered P, Q, and R in the first group, and S, T, and U in the second group. By punching a hole (indicated by the black dot) through the 1 in front of the letter R, the person answering has indicated that of the three activities listed in the first group he would most like to visit a museum. By punching a hole through the 3 beside the letter Q he has indicated that he would least like to browse in a library. In a similar manner he has indicated in the second group that he would like to collect autographs most and would like to collect butterflies least.

EXAMPLE

Put your answers to these questions in column O.

			O	
P.	Visit an art gallery		P	
Q.	Browse in a library		Q	←LEAST
R.	Visit a museum	MOST→	R	
S.	Collect autographs	MOST→	S	
T.	Collect coins		T	
U.	Collect butterflies		U	←LEAST

Some of the activities named in the following pages involve a certain amount of preparation and training. In such cases, make your choice on the assumption that you could first have the training and experience necessary for all the activities. Do not choose an activity merely because it is new or unusual. Make your choices on the basis of what you would like to do as a regular thing if you were equally familiar with all the activities.

In some cases you may find that you like all three activities in a group; in other cases you may find all three unpleasant. Please make your choices for every group even though the decisions may be hard to make.

Remember, a hole through the 1 before a letter indicates the activity you like most in the group. A hole through a 3 indicates the activity you like least of the three listed. Be sure there is a hole through a 1 and a hole through a 3 for each group in the booklet. Answer all questions so that your scores can be compared with those of others.

If you want to change an answer, punch two more holes close to the answer you wish to change; then punch the new answer in the usual way. Hold the pin straight up and down when you punch your answers.

Now go ahead with the activities listed on the next page.

Published By Science Research Associates, 228 S. Wabash Avenue, Chicago 4, Illinois

Copyright, 1942, by G. Frederic Kuder PRINTED IN U. S. A. *Patent No. 1,500,777*

By permission of G. Frederic Kuder and Science Research Associates

DIRECTIONS AND EXAMPLE FOR KUDER PREFERENCE RECORD, FORM BB, 1942

Nine general vocational areas are tested in Vocational Form BB: (1) mechanical, (2) computational, (3) scientific, (4) persuasive, (5) artistic, (6) literary, (7) musical, (8) social service, and (9) clerical. The actual test items are not put under the vocational headings. One hundred sixty-eight triads (three statements of different activities) are listed. The examinee, by indicating his preferences and dislikes, demonstrates his degree of interest in the various general areas. The activities have been carefully assembled by Kuder over a period of years to form consistent patterns among the areas, and only those statements that proved to be measures of an area have been retained. Each vocational area is therefore measured by certain of the statements.[1]

The triad form of presentation was developed to include more items in approximately the same time as the previous edition. Two choices in each triad must be correlated with a particular vocational area. The scoring system counts two of the three choices. The Manual (23) for the test gives the following illustration:

> Build bird houses
> Write articles about birds
> Draw sketches of birds
>
> Analysis of this item revealed that a preference for the first activity to the second is positively correlated with the mechanical scale. It was also found that preferring building bird houses to drawing sketches of birds is positively correlated with the mechanical scale. Including both of these choices in the mechanical scale means that the entire item should be scored to obtain the following results:
>
> A score of 2 should be obtained if the first activity is preferred to *both* of the other activities.
>
> A score of 1 should be obtained if the first activity is preferred to *one* but not both of the other activities.
>
> A score of 0 should be obtained if the first activity is preferred to neither of the other two activities.[2]

The scoring is simple and direct. Each time a pin-hole is made, it goes through a circle in the answer booklet. The circles are arranged

[1] A revised form, published in 1948, added a tenth vocational area known as "outdoor."

[2] By permission of G. Frederic Kuder and Science Research Associates.

for each general area so that the scorer can count the number of circles with holes inside them to obtain the score for each of the areas. The scores are then converted into percentiles, a percentile of 75 or better being considered significantly high. When more than one area exceeds the 75th percentile score, these areas are to be combined. Kuder in the Manual offers many occupations that fit the various areas and combinations. For instance, if the examinee rates significantly high in the mechanical and scientific areas, the list of occupations for each area should be considered as well as the list for the combined areas.

Where the examinee does not score above the 75th percentile, Kuder suggests, in the Manual, inspecting scores above the 65th percentile. He does not believe, however, that such scores can be regarded with as much confidence. He comments that no percentile can be regarded as a completely satisfactory cutting point; and he considers that the 75th is not only convenient, but has a valid statistical basis. Diamond (12) has criticized the employment of the 75th percentile for each area. He argues that more jobs are available in the mechanical area than in the scientific, and "that a low rank in one field may represent greater interest than a higher rank in another, less popular field." This is a cogent point and has general application to test interpretation. A number, score, or percentile should never be considered as a separate entity but should always be related to other information. Interest test scores should of course be checked with ability measures and the factors of motivation and knowledge as discussed in the interview.

The Kuder Preference Record has norms for high school students and for adults. These general norms allow for a comparison of the relative strength of different interests in an individual. This in itself is of importance to the individual, but it is also important to know how one's interest patterns compare in intensity to people in and preparing for various kinds of occupations. Kuder provides profile scores in the test manual for men in 44 various occupational groups and for women in 29. He also gives profile scores for female students preparing for various occupations. Berdie (5) is critical of the occupational norms because they are based on small samplings. However, he writes that the average scores on one or more of the nine areas obtained by the different occupational groups are "statistically different" from average scores earned by the base groups. Kuder himself requests that users of the test send him data on adults in different occupations so that he can add to the sampling upon which the norms are based. These additional data will check and possibly improve upon the present norms.

The average profile scores that Kuder supplies for different occupations are really indications of validity. For instance, he writes, "Chemists are found to be particularly high on the scientific scale, accountants on the computational scale, and so on."[3] Bolanovich and Goodman (8) report on the results of a study in which they employed the Kuder Preference Record. Kuder scores were available on 66 subjects selected for training in a 10-month course in the theory and practice of electronic engineering. The most successful were differentiated in the computational and scientific areas from those who dropped out of the course for reasons other than illness. Only the computational area differentiated the most successful in the course from the least. (The low correlation [.18] with final grade averages in the course is to be expected, since the test is not intended as a measure of ability.)

Shaffer (29) administered the Preference Record to 975 men and 205 women students in the graduating classes of 1947 and 1948 in the Indiana University School of Business. The test showed different patterns among the various business groups. For instance, the male advertising group was significantly different from the other business groups, with higher scores in the persuasive, artistic, literary, and musical areas, and lower in the mechanical, computational, scientific, social science, and clerical. However, only the persuasive and literary were above the 75th percentile in relation to the general base sampling. The male accounting group had relatively high scores in comparison with other business groups in the computational, scientific, clerical, and mechanical fields, and relatively low scores in the persuasive, artistic, literary, musical, and social science areas. However, in comparison with the general group norms, the accounting majors had

[3] By permission of G. Frederic Kuder and Science Research Associates.

scores above the 75th percentile in the computational, persuasive, and clerical areas. All the business groups, male and female, with the exception of the female commercial teacher group, had percentiles above 75 in the persuasive field when compared with general norms. Shaffer writes that, "The findings indicate that the Kuder is a useful tool in assisting students to choose a major within a school of business."

In counseling, the test is useful as a starting point for interviewing. It provides information about preferences that can be related to actual work. However, tests of ability must be taken into consideration too as well as other factors like need for more schooling and the sources of motivation for the preferences.

A caution must be interjected about the use of the test in selection. In selection, the individual is usually motivated to get the job more than to learn about his vocational possibilities. He may therefore answer as he thinks he should to obtain the position. Paterson (28) found the Kuder Preference Record to be more vulnerable to this tendency than the Strong Vocational Interest Blank. But Longstaff (24) found that both the Strong and the Kuder are decidedly fakable. He concludes from his data that, "The Strong test in general is easier to fake upward than the Kuder, while the Kuder is easier to fake downward than the Strong." He remarks that while the potential danger is present, it does not necessarily follow that much faking goes on in actual use of these tests. Apparently these tests are less valid for selection than they are for guidance purposes.

The reliability of the test is adequate, ranging from .81 to .98 for the different areas and on various groups. For individual prediction, however, it must be used together with other tests and the interview.

The Vocational Interest Blank. Strong's Vocational Interest Blanks have a relatively long history. The Blank for men was published in 1927 and revised in 1938. The test for women was standardized in the early 1930's and revised in 1947. The Vocational Interest Blank for men has been the subject of much research.

The Vocational Interest Blank for men (revised) may be scored for 39 occupations (30): accountant, advertising man, architect, artist, author-journalist, aviator, banker, carpenter, certified public accountant, chemist, city school superintendent, coast guard, dentist, engineer, farmer, forest service, lawyer, life insurance salesman, mathematician, mathematics-science high school teacher, minister, musician, office worker, osteopath, personnel manager, physician, physicist, policeman, president of a manufacturing concern, printer, production manager, psychologist, public utility salesman, purchasing agent, real estate salesman, sales manager, social science high school teacher, Y.M.C.A. physical director, Y.M.C.A. secretary.

Also it arranges the occupations into six groups and provides group scales. The six occupational groups are:

Artist, psychologist, architect, physician, and dentist.

Engineer and chemist, and (indirectly) mathematician and physicist.

Y.M.C.A. physical director, personnel manager, Y.M.C.A. secretary, social science high school teacher, city school superintendent, and minister.

Accountant, office worker, purchasing agent, and banker.

Sales manager, realtor, and life insurance salesman.

Advertising man, lawyer, and author-journalist.[4]

The occupational groups bring together several occupations that correlate quite high. The use of occupational groups allows for measurement of interest in an area rather than in a specific occupation. Strong (30) intends the group scales for use with younger people where a specific occupational interest is not yet warranted. He writes, "It seemed likely that a single group scale could replace a number of occupational scales when blanks of high school students were to be scored, and possibly about a dozen group scales could be developed which would replace thirty to fifty and possibly more specific occupational scales."[5] The specific occupational group is to guide the older student in specialization. However, the full program of devising occupational group scales was not carried out because Strong believes that "guidance should be based on high and low scores on all the

[4] Reprinted from *Vocational Interests of Men and Women* by Edward K. Strong, Jr., with the permission of the author and of the publishers, Stanford University Press.

[5] *Ibid.*

scales and not merely upon the single highest score."[6] He prefers the inclusion of secondary interests as well as low scores in the total appraisal. All these scores when considered together add to the accuracy of the decision.

The four non-occupational interests are: (1) interest-maturity (2) masculinity-femininity (3) occupational level, and (4) studiousness. Interest-maturity (I-M) is a measure of the degree to which one has the interests of 25-year-old men as contrasted with 15-year-old boys. In essence, the I-M scale attempts to measure changes of interest with age. Boys with low I-M scores will tend to show greater changes in interest at a later date than those with high scores. Also it must be noted that different occupations have higher or lower I-M scores. Strong reports (30), "... in interpreting I-M scores of young men one must take into account their occupational-interest scores. A future artist, for example, should have a much lower I-M score than a future minister."[7] Apparently the artist has interests more characteristic of adolescents than does the minister.

The masculinity-femininity (M-F) scale measures the interests of males and females. Some occupations are more feminine or more masculine than others. That is, they have more or less the characteristics that interest groups of males or females. (The Kuder Preference Record also can be scored for M-F.) Some distinctly masculine interests, according to Strong, are mechanical, scientific activities; physically strenuous, adventuresome activities; selling activities; legal, political, and army activities. Some distinctly feminine interests are musical and artistic, literary, and clerical. In interpreting the M-F score, caution must be taken to relate it to other personality factors. Not enough research has been done to enable us to conclude that a low M-F score (low masculinity) for a male indicates homosexuality. Scores of journalists, clergymen, artists, and musicians are relatively low in M-F. The interest in people and aesthetics may be somewhat

[6] Reprinted from *Vocational Interests of Men and Women* by Edward K. Strong, Jr., with the permission of the author and of the publishers, Stanford University Press.

[7] Reprinted from *Vocational Interests of Men and Women* by Edward K. Strong, Jr., with the permission of the author and of the publishers, Stanford University Press.

feminine if our standards of masculinity are toughness and interest in mechanical and scientific things, but this does not necessarily imply abnormality.

Occupational level (OL) contrasts the interests of men in the unskilled trades with those of business and professional men earning a certain minimum. This scale is useful in extending the significance of the specific occupational interest scales. In a general way, those men with high OL scores are similar in their interests to business and professional men, while the men with low OL scores have interests similar to workmen. However, no one is to be assigned to a specific occupation according to the OL score alone, since there is much overlap among various occupations.

The measurement of studiousness includes those interest factors other than intelligence that contribute to grades. This characteristic differentiates between superior and inferior students as well as men in occupations. The measure of studiousness has not as yet been sufficiently developed. Much more research is necessary to determine what vocational interests make for differentiation between the superior and inferior in any occupation and among students.

The Vocational Interest Blank for Men (revised), Form M, consists of 400 items. It is a group paper and pencil test without time limit. Most people can finish it in from 30 minutes to one hour. The first 100 items are occupations alphabetically arranged. The examinee is to indicate whether he likes, dislikes, or is indifferent to each. The second part has 36 school subjects to be evaluated similarly. The third consists of 49 different amusements; the fourth of 48 activities; the fifth of 47 statements of peculiarities of people all to be answered by like, dislike, or indifferent. The sixth part lists four sets of 10 activities. The examinee is to indicate the three in each set of 10 enjoyed most, by checking them in column 1. The three enjoyed least are to be checked in column 3; the remaining four are to be checked in column 2. In the seventh part, the examinee is to compare each of 40 pairs of activities. The eighth part consists of 40 statements on rating of present abilities and characteristics. This part is very much like the usual paper and pencil personality questionnaire. Excerpts of the test are illustrated on pages 272 and 273.

Part I. Occupations. Indicate after each occupation listed below whether you would like that kind of work or not. Disregard considerations of salary, social standing, future advancement, etc. Consider only whether or not you would like to do what is involved in the occupation. You are not asked if you would take up the occupation permanently, but merely whether or not you would enjoy that kind of work, regardless of any necessary skills, abilities, or training which you may or may not possess.

Draw a circle around L if you like that kind of work

Draw a circle around I if you are indifferent to that kind of work

Draw a circle around D if you dislike that kind of work

Work rapidly. Your first impressions are desired here. Answer all the items. Many of the seemingly trivial and irrelevant items are very useful in diagnosing your real attitude.

1 Actor (not movie) .. L I D
2 Advertiser .... L I D
3 Architect .... L I D
4 Army Officer ..... L I D
5 Artist .... L I D

46 Jeweler .... L I D
47 Judge .... L I D
48 Labor Arbitrator .. L I D
49 Laboratory Technician ..... L I D
50 Landscape Gardener L I D

Part II. School Subjects. Indicate as in Part I your interest when in school.

101 Algebra .... L I D
102 Agriculture .... L I D
103 Arithmetic .... L I D
104 Art .... L I D
105 Bookkeeping ...... L I D

Part III. Amusements. Indicate in the same manner as in Part I whether you like the following or not. If in doubt, consider your most frequent attitude. *Work rapidly.* Do not think over various possibilities. Record your first impression.

137 Golf .... L I D
138 Fishing .... L I D
139 Hunting .... L I D
140 Tennis .... L I D

Part IV. Activities. Indicate your interest as in Part I.

196 Interviewing men for a job .... L I D
197 Interviewing prospects in selling .. L I D
198 Interviewing clients L I D
199 Making a speech .. L I D
200 Organizing a play . L I D

Part V. Peculiarities of People. Record your first impression. Do not think of various possibilities or of exceptional cases. "Let yourself go" and record the feeling that comes to mind as you read the item.

234 Progressive people L I D
235 Conservative people L I D

Material on these two pages reprinted from Vocational Interest Blank for Men *by Edward K. Strong, Jr., with the permission of the author and of the publishers, Stanford University Press*

EXCERPTS FROM STRONG VOCATIONAL INTEREST BLANK

Part VI. Order of Preference of Activities. Indicate which three of the following ten activities you would enjoy most by checking (√) opposite them in column 1; also indicate which three you would enjoy least by checking opposite them in column 3. Check the remaining four activities in column 2.

	1	2	3	
281	( )	( )	( )	Develop the theory of operation of a new machine, e.g., auto
282	( )	( )	( )	Operate (manipulate) the new machine
283	( )	( )	( )	Discover an improvement in the design of the machine
284	( )	( )	( )	Determine the cost of operation of the machine
285	( )	( )	( )	Supervise the manufacture of the machine
286	( )	( )	( )	Create a new artistic effect, i.e., improve the beauty of the auto
287	( )	( )	( )	Sell the machine
288	( )	( )	( )	Prepare the advertising for the machine
289	( )	( )	( )	Teach others the use of the machine
290	( )	( )	( )	Interest the public in the machine through public addresses

Part VII. Comparison of Interest between Two Items. Indicate your choice of the following pairs by checking (√) in the first space if you prefer the item to the left, in the second space if you like both equally well, and in the third space if you prefer the item to the right. Assume other things are equal except the two items to be compared.

Work rapidly.

321	Street-car motorman	( )	( )	( )	Street-car conductor
322	Policeman	( )	( )	( )	Fireman (fights fire)
323	Chauffeur	( )	( )	( )	Chef
324	Head waiter	( )	( )	( )	Lighthouse tender
325	House to house canvassing	( )	( )	( )	Retail selling

Part VIII. Rating of Present Abilities and Characteristics. Indicate below what kind of a person you are right now and what you have done. Check in the *first* column ("Yes") if the item really describes you, in the *third* column ("No") if the item does not describe you, and in the *second* column (?) if you are not sure. (Be frank in pointing out your weak points, for selection of a vocation must be made in terms of them as well as your strong points.)

		YES	?	NO
361	Usually start activities of my group	( )	( )	( )
362	Usually drive myself steadily (do not work by fits and starts)	( )	( )	( )
363	Win friends easily	( )	( )	( )
364	Usually get other people to do what I want done	( )	( )	( )
365	Usually liven up the group on a dull day	( )	( )	( )

EXCERPTS FROM STRONG VOCATIONAL INTEREST BLANK

The validity of the test is inherent in its standardization. A "men-in-general group" is the base group to which all the various specific occupations are contrasted. For each occupation the 400 items receive weights that correspond statistically to the differences in responses from the "men-in-general group." By means of this process the items are scored differently, depending upon the specific occupation. According to Strong (30), "If a person says he would like to be an actor, he obtains 2 points toward having the interests of an artist and a minister, 1 point toward a musician, zero points toward a chemist, and –1 point toward a carpenter."[8] The scoring for each occupation should be differentiating from that of others. This in itself is a measure of validity.

Barrett (2) found high scores for the Artist occupation on the Strong's Vocational Interest Blank for Women to be associated more often than not "with successful specialization in art." Strong (30) reports a 10-year follow-up study based on the records of 197 men who were tested in 1927 when seniors in college and were tested again in 1937. Continuance in occupation was the criterion for measuring the predictability of the test. One hundred and sixteen made no change in occupation. Data were available on 95 of the 116, and showed their scores in their occupation to be almost the same later as earlier. The remainder changed their occupational choice. There were probably ample reasons for these changes, although Strong does not make that clear. However, such matters as second and third choices and the economic situation can probably explain a large number of the changes. The nine-year follow-up of college freshmen shows results similar to the 10-year college senior follow-up but there is slightly less agreement of interest scores with their early occupational choice. This is to be expected, since occupational choices of freshmen should be less stable. Both these studies show good validity for the test. But they also show the need for using results besides the highest score in interpreting the test, and the fact that the interest test is only one of the measures necessary for guidance. Strong emphasizes these facts many times.

---

[8] Reprinted from *Vocational Interests of Men and Women* by Edward K. Strong, Jr., with the permission of the author and of the publishers, Stanford University Press.

Strong has not included efficiency or happiness on the job as criteria of test validity. His assumption is that continuance implies fair adjustment in terms of ability and degree of satisfaction. Berdie (5) found that scores in the occupation of engineer on the Strong Blank and curriculum satisfaction of engineering students were not related significantly. The extreme scores may be differentiated, however.

Super (33) points out a very important aspect of validity of the Strong test: that of possible changes in interest patterns within occupations with time. He writes on the possibility of the change in the occupation of psychology as well as that of Y.M.C.A. secretary. The interests of the former are changing from emphasis on experimental, laboratory problems to clinical, industrial, and educational, whereas the latter seems now to emphasize the social rather than the religious-personal. A study by Kriedt (22) verifies the change in interests of the psychologists. A sampling of 1048 psychologists used by Kriedt shows them to be "more socialized than Strong's group, more interested in, more tolerant of, and more willing to help people, and less interested in mechanical and methodical work and in solitary activity." He suggests the use of a scoring developed on the later sampling of psychologists since the earlier scoring key is not as valid. Kriedt also found sub-group keys in clinical, experimental, guidance, and industrial fields to be useful for helping advanced psychology students determine their specialization. It would seem that new samplings of people in different occupations should be taken from time to time to check any changes in the interest patterns, especially among any occupations suspected of change.

The scoring of the Strong Vocational Interest Blank is by separate keys for each of the occupations and non-occupational interests. Scoring is laborious since there are many occupations. There are quicker methods available at a slight cost, like the Hollerith machine and I.B.M. method as well as the Hankes test scoring machine (31). The Kuder Preference Record has an advantage in its simplified scoring. The scores on the Strong test are transmutable into letter grades, A, B+, B, B−, C+, and C. The grade-letter A means that the individual has the interests of people successful in the occupation; ratings B+, B and B− are intermediate and indicate that the examinee probably has the interests but less certain than for grade-letter A; C+ and C indicate too little interest in the occupation. The ratings in as many occupations as possible, not merely the highest rating, should be the source of inferences about interests.

Darley (10) has classified the ratings as primary, secondary, and tertiary. The primary interest patterns are in those occupational fields largely A's and B+'s; the secondary, those largely B+ and B; and tertiary, largely B's and B–'s. By arranging the occupations in these classifications one can throw more light upon the stronger patterns.

The reliabilities of the different scales vary from about .73 to about .94. This means that extreme care should be exercised in interpreting the scores made by any one individual, since the scores themselves will vary from administration to administration.

Personality tests

The Adjustment Inventory. The Adjustment Inventory is a group paper and pencil questionnaire standardized by Bell in 1934. It is untimed and can be self-administered. It has two forms, adult and student. Only the student form will be described. It consists of 140 questions to be answered "Yes," "No," or "?." Four areas of adjustment are measured, each by 35 questions: home, health, social, and emotional. Bell (3) describes the areas in the Manual for the Student Form as follows:

> a. Home Adjustment. Individuals scoring high tend to be unsatisfactorily adjusted to their home surroundings. Fair scores indicate satisfactory home adjustment.
>
> b. Health Adjustment. High scores indicate unsatisfactory health adjustment; low scores, satisfactory adjustment.
>
> c. Social Adjustment. Individuals scoring high tend to be submissive and retiring in their social contacts. Individuals with low scores are aggressive in social contacts.
>
> d. Emotional Adjustment. Individuals with high scores tend to be unstable emotionally. Persons with low scores tend to be emotionally stable.[9]

[9] Reprinted from *Manual for the Adjustment Inventory, Student Form* by Hugh M. Bell, with the permission of the author and of the publishers, Stanford University Press.

The questions have letters a, b, c, or d next to them to designate the area being measured. Typical questions for each area are presented:

Home Adjustment
Do you sometimes feel that your parents are disappointed in you?
Do you feel that your parents have been unduly strict with you?
Has either of your parents dominated you too much?
Health Adjustment
Are you subject to hay fever or asthma?
Are you subject to eye strain?
Do you find it necessary to watch your health carefully?
Social Adjustment
Did you ever take the lead to enliven a dull party?
Do you enjoy social dancing a great deal?
Do you find it difficult to start a conversation with a stranger?
Emotional Adjustment
Do you frequently have spells of the "blues"?
Do you consider yourself rather a nervous person?
Do you get upset easily?[10]

In the Manual, Bell offers validity data that primarily indicate the test to be useful as a discriminant between well-adjusted and poorly adjusted students in the different areas. He offers no refinement to include the in-between group. For health, the criterion for adjustment is number of times absent from school because of ill health; for social adjustment, amount of participation (including leadership) in school activities during their freshman and sophomore years; for emotional adjustment, rating by counselors. The specific items in the questionnaire were so selected as to differentiate between the uppermost 15 per cent and the lowest 15 per cent of the group. This procedure in itself makes for differences between extreme cases in the original sampling. However, they may not show the same differences in a new sampling.

Clark and Smith (9) found correlations of —.319 to .165 between scores on the Inventory and faculty members' ratings of 138 students

---

[10] Reprinted from *The Adjustment Inventory, Student Form* by Hugh M. Bell, with the permission of the author and of the publishers, Stanford University Press.

on traits similar to those the Inventory measures. The low correlations are not unexpected, because the faculty ratings usually are based on different criteria than the test items and also because the test was not standardized to give fine gradings between people. Ellis (13) in his thorough review of the validity of personality questionnaires summarizes studies on several tests, including the Bell. Of the 12 times the Bell was employed in studies only once did it show positive validity. These data would indicate the danger in using the Bell for individual prediction. At best, scores showing poor adjustment should be investigated by other methods, like the interview and projective techniques.

Vocationally, the Bell Adjustment Inventory is used together with other personal information obtained from the interview as well as with other test data to help the individual find an occupation that will be more suitable and bring out his better traits. However, this procedure must be carried out on an individual basis, with elaboration of the personality findings in relation to work conditions. Generalizations as to degree of over-all adjustment or adjustment in any area cannot be made for an individual merely from the Bell scores.

The reliability of the total test is .93; for the separate areas, it varies from .80 for health adjustment to .89 for home and social adjustment. These reliability coefficients are not high enough for individual prediction. The test is easily scored. Each item that is answered in the direction of maladjustment is given a single point. The points are then added for each area to give the degree of maladjustment.

Bernreuter Personality Inventory. This group paper and pencil questionnaire is probably the most widely used test of its kind although its validity surely does not warrant such wide usage. It is not the only test that has become popular out of proportion to its worth; it is not to be singled out as the only "villain." It is cited as an example of the lack of relation between test validity and usage.

The test was published in 1931, at which time it represented "a new departure in the measurement of personality in that it measured several different aspects at one time" (7). It is untimed but takes about 25 minutes to complete. Originally the test measured four personality traits.

B1-N. This is a measure of neurotic tendency. Those who obtain a high score are considered to be emotionally unstable. If the score is above the 98th percentile, psychiatric help is recommended. Those who score low tend to be stable emotionally.

B2-S. This measures self-sufficiency. Those who score high prefer to be by themselves, and not take advice of others. Those who score low do not like to be alone, and often look for advice.

B3-I. This measures introversion-extroversion. The high scorers tend to be introverted; to live more within themselves. If the score is above the 98th percentile, psychiatric help may be indicated. Low scores mean extroversion. These people prefer action, do not worry as much and are not so sensitive as to be easily upset emotionally.

B4-D. This measures dominance-submissiveness. Those who score high will tend to dominate others. Those scoring low will tend to be submissive toward others.

Flanagan (14) factor-analyzed the test and found two traits that could be used in place of the original four. However, two traits, confidence in oneself (F1-C) and sociability (F2-S), were added to the four to give a total of six. This addition was made mainly because it was not considered practical to use only two traits in describing the complex matter of personality. Even six traits certainly are not enough for a full description. The correlations between B1-N, B3-I, and F1-C are so high, however, that little is gained by scoring for all three traits. One of the three can be used for all.

The Bernreuter Personality Inventory contains 125 questions to be answered "Yes," "No," or "?". The questions are similar to the Bell Adjustment Inventory. In fact, all personality questionnaires make use of similar questions. The first 10 questions, which illustrate the test, appear on page 280.

The validity of the Bernreuter test was determined by correlation of each of its four parts with a previously validated test designed to measure one of the traits. Thus the B1-N trait was correlated with the Thurstone Neurotic Inventory; the B2-S with the Bernreuter Self-Sufficiency Test; the B3-I with the Laird C2 Introversion Test; and the B4-D with the Allport Ascendance-Submission Reaction Study. Basically, the assumption is made that the four tests are valid and the

The questions on this blank are intended to indicate your interests and attitudes. It is not an intelligence test, nor are there any right or wrong answers.

In front of each question you will find: "Yes No ?"

If your answer is "Yes," draw a circle around the "Yes." If your answer is "No," draw a circle around the "No." If you are entirely unable to answer either "Yes" or "No" to the question, then draw a circle around the question mark.

---

1. Yes No ? Does it make you uncomfortable to be "different" or unconventional?
2. Yes No ? Do you day-dream frequently?
3. Yes No ? Do you usually work things out for yourself rather than get someone to show you?
4. Yes No ? Have you ever crossed the street to avoid meeting some person?
5. Yes No ? Can you stand criticism without feeling hurt?
6. Yes No ? Do you ever give money to beggars?
7. Yes No ? Do you prefer to associate with people who are younger than yourself?
8. Yes No ? Do you often feel just miserable?
9. Yes No ? Do you dislike finding your way about in strange places?
10. Yes No ? Are you easily discouraged when the opinions of others differ from your own?

Reprinted from The Personality Inventory *by Robert G. Bernreuter, with the permission of the author and of the publishers, Stanford University Press.*

SAMPLE QUESTIONS FROM BERNREUTER PERSONALITY INVENTORY

Bernreuter measures of its four traits will be as valid since the relationship between a Bernreuter trait and the corresponding test is high. However, the coefficients of correlation between each Bernreuter trait and the corresponding test are based on rather small samplings. The coefficients obtained, while high, were not perfect; this fact indicates that the Bernreuter and the original tests were not measuring precisely the same things.

The Bernreuter Personality Inventory has been used sufficiently and been the subject of enough research to enable us to estimate its validity by other means. Super (32), after a thorough review of the research on the test, writes, "The Bernreuter Personality Inventory has been shown to measure group trends with a reasonable degree of reliability; it can be used with individuals, but with some caution."[11] The test scores for an individual are not by themselves very valid; and the Bernreuter cannot distinguish among the abnormal although it may pick out maladjusted individuals. The degree and kind of maladjustment should be investigated by other means, like clinical interviews and other tests. Ellis (13) summarized 29 studies on the Bernreuter. Nine studies reported positive validation, six were questionably positive, and 14 were negative validations. He does not think much of the questionnaire as a means of distinguishing "between groups of adjusted and maladjusted individuals" and less as a means of diagnosing "individual adjustment or personality traits."

Vocationally, one should expect to obtain descriptions of traits of personality that could be matched with abilities and interests to help the individual choose the kind of work that would be most suitable. Not enough research has been done with the Bernreuter for this purpose. Super (32) in his review writes that the test was not helpful in the selection of efficient clerical workers and shed little light on work attitudes. He also pertinently reports that differences among occupational groupings were disappointing and that this might have been expected because of the considerable overlap among jobs. Varieties of personalities may be suitable for jobs in a given occupation. Flemming and Flemming (16) gave the Bernreuter in a battery of tests to help select salesmen. They found differences in traits among different kinds of salesmen. For instance, the sales engineers are less stable than 75 per cent of all salesmen. In another study the Flemmings (15) stress qualitative analysis of the tests. This is really clinical interpretation. It does not merely consider the test scores but involves interrelating the scores on all parts, analyses even of particular questions, and patterning with other tests. This more dynamic interpretation can

[11] D. E. Super, "The Bernreuter Personality Inventory: A Review of Research," *Psychological Bulletin*, 39:94–125 (1947).

then be related to different sales jobs. The Flemmings report rather good results on the qualitative analysis when judged against ratings by the salesmen's superiors.

For selection purposes, a caution must be mentioned. Although in most counseling situations, the individual will answer the personality questionnaire frankly and honestly because fundamentally he wants help, in hiring he may well try to show the traits he thinks desirable to obtain the position. This matter needs careful consideration and more research concerning its effect on the test.

The Bernreuter scoring is more complicated than the Bell. The test must be scored six times, once for each of the six traits when all are to be used. Each item or question on the test has a different weighting in each of the traits. Each item was weighted for its diagnostic value in each trait; the weights for the items range from plus seven to minus seven. The algebraic sum is the score for each trait. Norms in percentiles are available on college men and women, high school boys and girls, and adult men and women.

The reliability of the test as summarized by Super (32) ranges from about .70 to above .80. Bernreuter in the Manual reports coefficients of reliability ranging from .78 on the F2-S scale to .92 on the B2-S scale. These figures are not high enough even for great assurance with groups. With individuals, they magnify the need for using caution in making any interpretations whatever.

The Minnesota Multiphasic Personality Inventory. The M.M.P.I. test was devised by Hathaway and McKinley (18) "ultimately to provide, in a single test, scores on all the more important phases of personality."[12] It is different from the Bell and the Bernreuter tests in that it is designed for individual administration (a new group form has since been published) and tries to measure psychiatric characteristics rather than personality traits. Rather than measure traits like self-confidence, dominance-submissiveness and inferiority—traits that Hathaway and McKinley consider as "not having clear-cut abnormal implication"—the test measures such psychiatric classificatory terms

[12] The quotations from the Manual for the test are reprinted with the permission of The Psychological Corporation.

as hypochondriasis, depression, hysteria, psychopathic deviate, masculinity-femininity, paranoia, psychasthenia, schizophrenia, and hypomania.

The Hypochondriasis Scale (H_s) measures the amount of abnormal concern about functions of the body. Those with high scores are unduly worried over their health. As described by Hathaway and McKinley in the Manual for the test, "They frequently complain of pains and disorders which are difficult to identify and for which no clear organic basis can be found. It is a characteristic of the hypochondriac that he is immature in his approach to adult problems, tending to fail to respond with adequate insight."

The Depression Scale (D) measures the depth of depression. According to the Manual, "The depression may be the chief disability of the subject or it may accompany, or be a result of, other personality problems. A high D score indicates poor morale of the emotional type with a feeling of uselessness and inability to assume a normal optimism with regard to the future." Together with the hypochondriasis and hysteria scales this scale is supposed to identify a large number of people not under medical care and commonly called neurotic.

The Hysteria Scale (H_y) measures such symptoms as general pains and more specific complaints such as paralysis and heart and gastric disorders. Those with high H_y scores are also "especially liable to episodic attacks of weakness, fainting or even epileptiform convulsions." The hysterical people are the most immature.

The Psychopathic Deviate Scale (P_d) measures the degree of similarity with those persons who cannot profit from experience, who go counter to social custom and code, and who have little or no guilt feelings or anxiety about their behavior.

The Interest Scale (M_f) measures tendency to masculine and feminine patterns of interest. In cases of a high score for either sex, the indication is of a deviation away from the usual interest patterns toward the interests of the opposite sex. About this scale the Manual reports, "Males with very high M_f scores have frequently been found to be either overt or repressed sexual inverts. However, homosexual abnormality *must not be assumed* on the basis of a high score without confirmatory evidence. Among females high scores cannot yet be safely assumed to have similar clinical significance, and the interpretation must be limited to measurement of the general trait." This type of scale is used in the Kuder Preference Inventory and the Strong Vocational Interest Blank. It has some vocational meaning as was noted in discussion of the interest tests but implications about homosexuality must be guarded.

The Paranoia Scale (P_a) "was derived by contrasting normal persons with a group of clinic patients who were characterized by suspiciousness, over-sensitivity, and delusions of persecution, with or without expansive egotism." The diagnoses of the patients varied but all had the aforementioned paranoid characteristics. Hathaway and McKinley state that they have found very few paranoid persons who did not get high scores on the scale.

The Psychasthenic Scale (P_t) measures the degree of similarity with patients who have compulsions or phobias. Compulsive behavior may be overt like stepping on every crack in the street, washing hands every little while, or in terms of obsessional ideas that occur over and over again. Phobias are irrational fears that are symbolic of deeper disturbances. Thus a phobia for enclosed places may be symbolic of repressed guilt ideas concerning aggressive or sexual impulses.

The Schizophrenia Scale (S_c) is a measure of degree of similarity with those patients who are generally not in good contact with reality and whose ideas as well as behavior may be peculiar to the point of bizarreness. According to the Manual, "The S_c Scale distinguishes about 60 per cent of observed cases diagnosed as schizophrenia. It does not identify some paranoid types of schizophrenia, which, however, usually score high on P_a, and certain other cases which are characterized by relatively pure schizoid behavior." Hathaway and McKinley comment further on the need for more verification on the scale by reporting, "It is probable that one or two additional scales will be necessary to identify the latter cases, but this is not surprising in the light of the frequently expressed psychiatric opinion that schizophrenia is not a clinical entity but a group of rather heterogeneous conditions."

The Hypomania Scale (M_a) measures the characteristics of over-productivity in both ideational and behavioral content. Hypomania is a lesser state of over-productivity than mania. Hathaway and McKinley write that, "A principal difficulty in the development of the scale was the differentiation of clinically hypomanic patients from normal persons who are merely ambitious, vigorous, and full of plans."

They also report, "The hypomanic patient has usually gotten into trouble because of undertaking too many things. He is active and enthusiastic. Contrary to common expectations he may also be somewhat depressed at times. His activities may interfere with other people through his attempts to reform social practice; his enthusiastic stirring up of projects in which he then may lose interest, or his disregard of social connections. In the latter connection he may get into trouble with the law. A fair percentage of patients diagnosed psychopathic personality (see P_d) are better called hypomanic."

Four additional scores are available that are interesting attempts to increase the validity of the clinical scales; the question score (?), the lie score (L), the validity score (F), and a new score, the K factor. The question score is the total number of items answered as "Cannot say." A high question score invalidates the other scales. The lie score attempts to measure the attempt to choose the most acceptable response. A high lie score does not invalidate other scores but indicates that the true scores are probably higher than those obtained. The validity score acts as a check on the validity of the whole test. A high validity score means the subject was probably careless or did not understand the items, or errors were made in recording the scores. A low validity score is a reliable indication that the subject's scores were rational. The K scale is a correction factor that heightens the discriminatory power of the clinical scales. Those who try for "good" scores will tend to make higher K scores and those who try for "poor" scores will obtain lower K scores. Hovey (20) reports of the case of detection of circumvention by means of the K and L scores. Hunt (21) has used an F-K index for detecting malingerers. The value of these scores seems to be good, but requires more research.

The nine scales, together with the four additional scores, offer a wealth of personality descriptive material. However, just because they do, solid clinical training and experience are required for their interpretation. Hathaway and McKinley are aware of this fact and "strongly recommend that an accredited neuropsychiatrist, psychologist, or other person trained in the field of abnormal mental conditions should act either as consultant or as the person with direct responsibility in interpretation."

The test consists of 550 items (not all of which are yet used), which can be grouped into the various scales. There is room for additional scales. In the individual test each statement is printed on a single card. The subject is to sort the cards into three categories—True, False, and Cannot Say. The items resemble those in the Bell and Bernreuter as well as those in the Strong and Kuder, but they cover many more areas of the personality. The following are illustrative:

I like mechanics magazines.
I have a good appetite.
I would like to be a singer.
My judgment is better than it ever was.
I wish I could be as happy as others seem to be.
I do not worry about catching diseases.
Most nights I go to sleep without thoughts or ideas bothering me.
I liked school.
Someone has been trying to rob me.
Several times a week I feel as if something dreadful is about to happen.[13]

The time for administration varies from about 30 minutes to over 90 minutes. For older or dull persons, the examiner should illustrate by helping sort three or four items in the front of the box in which the cards are stacked. For others the test is self-administering. The test can be given to cooperative subjects about 16 years and older. The group form of the test (19) has 566 items; sixteen have been duplicated for a more economical method of scoring by machine. No time limits are required.

The scoring of the individually administered test is rather complex. Great care must be taken to sort the cards properly, and each atypical response must be recorded on the score sheet before results can

[13] Reprinted by permission of The Psychological Corporation.

be tabulated. However, Davis (11) has devised a new method of scoring that he asserts cuts the time about in half; Mullen (27) has extended the use of this method to the K scale. Norms are based upon normal groups of fairly good size; the scales are developed by contrasting scores of clinic cases with the scores of the normal groups.

In the Manual, the authors of the test report reliabilities of from .71 to .83 between the test and retest scores of a group of 40 normal subjects at intervals varying from a week or less to several years. These coefficients of reliability are of course not high. Great reliance must be put on the judgment of the examiner, in order to increase both the reliability and the validity of the test.

Wiener (36) used both group and individual forms and found little loss in using the group form. However, the test authors urge most strongly that the individual form be used for testing individuals and small groups, especially older people, hospital patients, and persons with little education and of low intellectual ability. Their preference for the individually administered form seems warranted; experience with group and individually administered tests indicates that the latter most often allow for a more valid description.

The Minnesota Multiphasic has been used mostly in psychiatric situations. Ellis (13) summarized 15 studies in which it had been employed and found positive validity in 10 instances, questionably positive in three, and negative in two. He regards the test as more valid than the personality questionnaire of Bell and Bernreuter. He attributes the better validity partly to individual administration. Gough (17) administered the test to 136 people consecutively admitted to a mental hospital. Their scores and patterns were compared to 27 normals as well as among themselves in terms of different psychiatric diagnoses. He found differentiation of the abnormals from the normals but not always clear differentiation among the abnormals; other studies (26, 4) support this view. He cautions against what might be called mechanical interpretation of the test, stating that the findings must be integrated into a meaningful picture in order to be useful in therapy. He also recommends that the test be finally interpreted by the psychiatrist or psychologist who has been working with the patient. These are recommendations that fit any test results. Altus (1) found that the schizophrenia scale of the Minnesota test in group form had a rather high correlation with certain signs of the group Rorschach. However, these signs were selected as having the greatest degree of association with the schizophrenia scale. Further research along these lines seems worth while.

Vocationally there have been few studies. Those by Lough (25) on college students and by Verniaud (35) on women workers employed in offices, department stores, and factories are generally direct interpretation of profile scores. No significant descriptive data were found that would differentiate one occupation from another. It is doubtful that this mechanical approach to test data will ever lead to anything significant. What is required is descriptive, dynamic interpretations of the scales to make as nearly complete a picture of the personality as possible. This picture can then be integrated in the interview and related to various characteristics and conditions of work.

The Minnesota seems to have possibilities for more complete personality descriptions that will be useful for the individual in relating himself to different working conditions. It certainly seems adequate as a screening device for those who may require personal counseling. The Bell or the Bernreuter can do a fairly adequate job of screening but do not lend themselves as well to a more comprehensive personality description.

Summary

The major concern of this chapter was to describe and evaluate representative tests of interest and personality. The tests were selected on the basis of the frequency of their usage in vocational counseling and as typical examples of pencil and paper tests in the areas. Five tests were described and evaluated; the Kuder and Strong interest tests and the Bell, Bernreuter, and Minnesota Multiphasic tests.

The Kuder Preference Record is an inventory of interests resulting in a profile. The nine general vocational areas are: mechanical, computational, scientific, persuasive, artistic, literary, musical, social-service and clerical. Each of these areas as well as their combinations are related to the variety of occupations available.

The Strong Vocational Interest Blank results in letter ratings of a variety of occupations for men and women.

The Bell Adjustment Inventory measures four specific areas of adjustment: home, health, social, and emotional. It also presents a total adjustment score.

The Bernreuter Personality Inventory can be scored for six personality traits: neurotic tendency, self-sufficiency, introversion-extroversion, dominance-submissiveness, self-confidence, and sociability.

The Minnesota Multiphasic Personality Inventory is a questionnaire designed to measure such psychiatric characteristics as: hypochondriasis, depression, hysteria, psychopathic deviate, masculinity-femininity, paranoia, psychasthenia, schizophrenia, and hypomania.

Bibliography

1. Altus, W. D., "Some Correlates of the Group Rorschach and the Schizophrenia Scale of the group M.M.P.I. Among Two Groups of 'Normal' College Students," *Journal of Consulting Psychology*, 12:375–378 (1948).
2. Barrett, D. M., "Aptitude and Interest Patterns of Art Majors," *Journal of Applied Psychology*, 29:483–492 (1945).
3. Bell, H. M., *Manual for the Adjustment Inventory, Student Form*. Stanford: Stanford University Press.
4. Benton, A. L., in O. K. Buros (ed.), *The Third Mental Measurements Yearbook*. New Brunswick, N.J.: Rutgers University Press, 1949.
5. Berdie, R. F., in O. K. Buros (ed.), *The Third Mental Measurements Yearbook*. New Brunswick, N.J.: Rutgers University Press, 1949.
6. ———, "The Prediction of College Achievement and Satisfaction," *Journal of Applied Psychology*, 28:239–245 (1944).
7. Bernreuter, R. G., *Manual for the Personality Inventory*. Stanford: Stanford University Press, 1935.
8. Bolanovich, D. J., and C. H. Goodman, "A Study of the Kuder Preference Record," *Educational and Psychological Measurement*, 4:315–325 (1944).
9. Clark, W., and L. F. Smith, "Further Evidence on the Validity of Personality Inventories," *Journal of Educational Psychology*, 33: 81–91 (1942).

10. Darley, J. G., *Clinical Aspects and Interpretation of the Strong Vocational Interest Blank.* New York: The Psychological Corporation, 1941.

11. Davis, C. E., "The Minnesota Multiphasic Personality Inventory: A New Method of Scoring and Analysis," *Journal of Clinical Psychology,* 3:298–301 (1947).

12. Diamond, S., "The Interpretation of Interest Profiles," *Journal of Applied Psychology,* 32:512–520 (1948).

13. Ellis, A., "The Validity of Personality Questionnaires," *Psychological Bulletin,* 43:385–440 (1946).

14. Flanagan, J. C., *Factor Analyses in the Study of Personality.* Stanford: Stanford University Press, 1935.

15. Flemming, E. G., and C. W. Flemming, "A Qualitative Approach to the Problem of Improving Selection of Salesmen by Psychological Tests," *Journal of Psychology,* 21:127–150 (1946).

16. ———, "Test-selected Salesmen," *Journal of Marketing,* 10:1–8 (1946).

17. Gough, H. G., "Diagnostic Patterns on the Minnesota Multiphasic Personality Inventory," *Journal of Clinical Psychology,* 2:23–27 (1946).

18. Hathaway, S. R., and J. C. McKinley, *The Minnesota Multiphasic Personality Inventory.* New York: The Psychological Corporation, 1943.

19. ———, *Supplementary Manual for the Minnesota Multiphasic Personality Inventory.* New York: The Psychological Corporation, 1946.

20. Hovey, H. B., "Detection of Circumvention in the Minnesota Multiphasic Personality Inventory," *Journal of Clinical Psychology,* 4:97 (1948).

21. Hunt, H. F., "The Effect of Deliberate Deception on Minnesota Multiphasic Personality Performance," *Journal of Consulting Psychology,* 12:396–402 (1948).

22. Kriedt, P. H., "Vocational Interests of Psychologists," *Journal of Applied Psychology,* 33:482–488 (1949).

23. Kuder, G. F., *Revised Manual for the Kuder Preference Record.* Chicago: Science Research Associates, 1946.

24. Longstaff, H. P., "Fakability of the Strong Interest Blank and the Kuder Preference Record," *Journal of Applied Psychology,* 32: 360–369 (1948).

25. Lough, O. M., "Teachers College Students and the Minnesota Multiphasic Personality Inventory," *Journal of Applied Psychology,* 30:241–247 (1946).
26. Morris, W. W., "A Preliminary Evaluation of the Minnesota Multiphasic Personality Inventory," *Journal of Clinical Psychology,* 3: 370–374 (1947).
27. Mullen, F. A., "The Minnesota Multiphasic Personality Inventory: An Extension of the Davis Scoring Method," *Journal of Clinical Psychology,* 4:86–88 (1948).
28. Paterson, D. G., "Vocational Interest Inventories in Selection," *Occupations,* 25:152–153 (1946).
29. Shaffer, R. H., "Kuder Interest Patterns of University Business School Seniors," *Journal of Applied Psychology,* 33:489–493 (1949).
30. Strong, E. K., Jr., *Vocational Interests of Men and Women.* Stanford: Stanford University Press, 1943.
31. ——— and E. J. Hankes, "A Note on the Hankes Test Scoring Machine," *Journal of Applied Psychology,* 31:212–214 (1947).
32. Super, D. E., "The Bernreuter Personality Inventory: A Review of Research," *Psychological Bulletin,* 39:94–125 (1942).
33. ———, *Appraising Vocational Fitness by Means of Psychological Tests.* New York: Harper, 1949.
34. Traxler, A. E., "Correlations between 'Mechanical Aptitude' Scores and 'Mechanical Comprehension' Scores," *Occupations,* 22:42–44 (1943).
35. Verniaud, W. M., "Occupational Differences in the Minnesota Multiphasic Personality Inventory," *Journal of Applied Psychology,* 30:604–613 (1946).
36. Wiener, D. N., "Individual and Group Forms of the Minnesota Multiphasic Personality Inventory," *Journal of Consulting Psychology,* 11:104–106 (1947).

10

CLINICAL PSYCHOLOGY IN RELATION TO VOCATIONAL COUNSELING

THE TERM "clinical" will be used in this chapter to refer both to a point of view toward counseling and to a certain type of test interpretation.

The clinical point of view toward counseling is the view that the individual is a unified whole. This attitude requires that any methods of counseling or use of tests take the entire individual into account. It requires, in other words, that the counselor (and the client) arrive at a true understanding of how the individual's patterns of behavior interact to make him behave as he does.

The "clinical" approach is the antithesis of the "analysis into elements" approach. It is not interested in a refined statistical treatment of small segments of an individual's behavior.

Tests that can be described as clinical are those that have been constructed with a firm belief in the clinical approach described in the preceding paragraphs; they have, as well, been more widely used in clinical psychology as adjuncts to psychiatric diagnosis. It is also possible to interpret vocational tests in clinical fashion.

For too long the fields of vocational psychology and clinical psychology have proceeded as separates which in fact they are not. This chapter will attempt to show briefly the close interrelation between these two fields and to encourage a closer integration. The clinical approach to vocational psychology will enrich it; it will allow for meaningful interpretations of individual cases and greater success in solving the vocational problems of individuals. It is really impossible to separate the individual's personality, interests, and motives from his aptitudes, abilities, and vocational aspirations. The clinical approach is an attempt to integrate the subject matter and problems of vocational psychology into a meaningful whole.

The tests described in the preceding chapter have in common the analytic approach, that is they attempt to measure certain basic aptitudes, personality traits, or the parts that contribute to general intelligence or achievement. They are relatively simple to administer and score. As vocational psychology had to struggle for its very existence rather simple instruments were often the most wise to use. As a result of this statistical-analytic emphasis these tests became more and more respectable and accordingly more and more acceptable. Few school teachers or counselors in this day will be brazen or foolish enough to say, "I don't believe in tests." In this respect these tests have served a dual purpose. They have not only been rather valid measures but they have encouraged the adoption of tests.

There have been two developments in recent years. The first has been the growth of the view that the clinical approach toward the traditional vocational tests is valuable. The second has been the adoption of clinical tests in vocational counseling.

Certain complex tests have been used for years in mental clinics and hospitals as aids in diagnosing personality problems of the more serious variety. The expansion of vocational counseling, especially promoted by the problems of the returning G.I., has forced the use of clinical techniques. On the adult level, people with vocational problems are likely to have accompanying personality problems. The problem of a counselor is sometimes to decide whether vocational guidance can take place or whether psychiatric referral is necessary. In the mild personality maladjustments the counselor may be required simultaneously to do some therapy as well as administer vocational guidance. Vocational counselors must therefore have training in and appreciation for clinical methods, techniques and instruments.

The two instruments most widely used in mental hospitals and mental hygiene clinics are the Wechsler-Bellevue Intelligence Scale and the Rorschach Inkblot Test. According to Baker and Peatman, (2), 52 per cent of 175 advisement units of the Veterans Administration used the Wechsler-Bellevue and 19 per cent used the Rorschach as a projective technique either once every 10 to 20 veterans or more rarely. The point is that these tests are being used in vocational counseling situations and it is to be expected that more frequent use of these tests will be made in the future.

The clinical approach in vocational psychology, then, demands that as far as possible all aspects of the total individual be studied in relation to vocational adjustment. Measures of ability, achievement, and interest are still important. But they must be recognized as parts of the larger whole, the organism or person. The counselor is to help the client understand the interactions of the various factors and help him to choose his vocational goal in the light of them.

Tests employed more traditionally in vocational counseling can be interpreted in an organismic and dynamic way. They can be enriched by cross-reference to other test scores, by including the background of the individual and his motivational and emotional states. They can be augmented by observations of the client's behavior while taking the tests. The clinical tests are more complex and measure at once various parts of the total person. Because of the complexities involved, the examiner needs greater skill and more training; but he is rewarded by a more dynamic picture of the client.

The clinical approach is not widely accepted in vocational psychology. The clinical tests are more vague than the traditional tests; they are difficult to score and interpret. They have not had wide vocational usage and their relationship to vocations is in many instances obscure.

As authors we respect the possibilities that the clinical approach offers to vocational psychology. We believe that the results of research indicate that integration has begun. Further research seems advisable concerning the possibilities of additional integration.

Clinical approach in vocational tests

To interpret vocational tests in an organismic and dynamic way all possible kinds of data must be obtained about the individual. These can be obtained by observing the client during the tests and the interview, as well as by obtaining test scores. The psychologist has the opportunity to observe the client taking various tests, especially the performance and individually administered ones. In some agencies he is permitted to interview the client. Where he cannot, he should have available the counselor's records of the interview or interviews. Successful weaving of test performance and interview behavior yields rich dividends in understanding the client.

As for the tests themselves, the psychologist should have knowledge of background information and psychological principles, as well as the specific validity, reliability, and norms as presented in the chapters on tests. The results can then be the more readily integrated toward possible vocational goals.

It is the authors' experience that reports based on dynamic interpretations carry more weight with counselors than simple direct interpretations of test results. They carry more weight because the counselor can use them more effectively in his effort to understand the client. We stress this fact because in many vocational counseling agencies the function is split between psychologists who administer tests and counselors who receive them as an aid in their interviews with the clients. If the counselors do not accept the report of the tests, testing will have served no real purpose. Di Michael (8) in describing a desirable psychological test report includes the following: observational material, technical results, interpretation of test results, recommendations, and summary.

To demonstrate the clinical approach, we offer here illustrations of observational data and vocational test reports.

Observations of the client. The examiner must be alert to the client's behavior before, during, and after taking tests. The behavior very often gives clues to work attitudes, approaches to different kinds of tasks, likes and dislikes, reactions to difficulties, social tendencies with others, and the like. These clues are valuable in interpreting test scores. They are also useful to the counselor, who can relate them to whatever he knows about the individual. The experienced examiners and counselors can sift the important from the unimportant; and, do not overemphasize the importance of any one segment of behavior.

There are guides to the beginner to help in the observation of behavior. They may also serve the experienced person as reminders. However, an experienced examiner should not have to rely on them. In some respects a check list is the antithesis of the clinical approach, but as a training device such check lists can have value. Bingham's (5) adaptation of Baumgarten's points on observing behavior is complete and well organized. He lists the details to which the examiner should pay attention.

I. During the Preliminary Instructions
  a. Looks steadily at the examiner, listening attentively
  b. Gazes around the room
  a′. Asks questions
  b′. Asks no questions
  c. Approaches the test
    a. quickly
    b. slowly
    c. hesitatingly
  d. Shows toward the task an attitude which is
    a. serious
    b. playful
    c. zealous
  e. Anticipatory expressions with reference to his own capacity for accomplishment
    a. Talks as if the task were easy
    b. Expresses enthusiasm
    c. Says he cannot do it
  f. Judgment upon or criticism of the task
    a. Aloud
    b. Through gestures

II. During Execution of the Task
  1. *At the start*
    a. Deliberates
    b. Does not deliberate
    c. Makes repeated starts

a. always in the same way
b. always in a new way

2. *While at work*

A. Direction of attention
a. Is attentive to the task
b. Attention wanders

A′. Degree of concentration
a. Attention highly concentrated (during the whole time does not avert his gaze from the task)
b. Distracted

B. Expression of Feelings and Emotions (Pleasure, Displeasure. Surprise)
a. Gives expression to feelings
a. during the entire test
b. during single phases
b. expresses no feelings

C. Bodily Movements
a. are well coordinated with the task
b. are not coordinated

D. Work Tempo
a. Quick
b. Slow

E. Movements of the Hands
a. Skillful, appropriate
b. Sure, steady
c. Quick, nervous

F. Manner of Work.

A′. As to Order
a. Works systematically
b. Works unsystematically, darting from one thing to another
c. Works regularly
d. Works irregularly
a. at first slowly, then more and more quickly
b. at first quickly, then more slowly
c. alternating, now slowly, now quickly, at intervals

B′. As to Kind of Performance
a. Careful, neat
b. Careless, sloppy

G. Handling of his Tools
During the working period, does he put the necessary tools in the same place?
a. Yes

b. No

3. *As difficulties emerge*
   A. Asks no help
      a. Maintains indifferent attitude
      b. Immediately throws up the sponge
      c. Overcomes incidental difficulties
         a. through correct methods
         b. through a trick
   B. Asks help
      a. Several times
      b. Once
   C. Conduct while being helped
      Receives help
      a. Indifferently
      b. Happily
      c. With a thankful glance
      d. Skeptically and gracefully
      e. Trustfully and credulously
      f. Showing offense
4. *Carries out the instructions*
   A. Exactly
   B. With deviations
      a. Of a positive kind
      b. Of a negative kind

III. Attitude Toward His Performance
   A. Notices his mistakes
      a. Occasionally
      b. At the end, when he checks his work for the first time
      c. During the work, always proving his results before he proceeds
   B. Does not perceive his mistakes or check his results
   C. Shows mild feeling

IV. Conduct at the End of the Test
   A. Remains silent and watches quietly
   B. Announces the result himself
   C. Asks questions, such as: "Isn't that good?"
   D. Expresses emotions of
      a. Satisfaction
      b. Vexation

V. After the Testing
   A. Leaves his tools
      a. In order
      b. In disorder

B. Disposes of the materials in ways which indicate that he is 1) economical; 2) wasteful

C. Leaves his place of work
   a. Quickly
   b. Slowly[1]

In specific instances the observations will enrich and explain the test scores. An individual may make a very fast time score on the Finger Dexterity Test but be slovenly or careless in procedure—the pins may fall out of his fingers and onto the floor and he may show no concern. His time score may be faster than someone else whose work is much neater. The score alone tells only part of the story. The same person may sigh with relief when he is finished with this test and when starting the Otis test remark, "This is much better!" Accordingly he settles down to work and concentrates fully. Obviously he prefers verbal material to a minute assembly task.

Di Michael (8) offers some rich examples of observation.

> The client seems most cheerful and at ease when the tasks were well within his level. When the tests challenged him the performance began to disintegrate and he did not hesitate to vent his anger on the materials and twice upon the tester.[2]

Another example is,

> . . . the client appeared long before the appointed time, dressed in fresh and neat clothes. He seems to be constantly trying to make a fine impression. This desire permeated his entire behavior during the testing. It may be the outcome of a well-concealed anxiety, a conclusion which is also indicated by his frequent attempts to convince the examiner that his inadequacies on difficult problems were caused by temporary nervousness.[3]

Still another example is,

> In conversations before the tests were administered, the (blind) client said that he had not yet learned to use his cane and might need assistance in finding his way around. This remark was made quite casually and indicated a realistic attitude toward the problem of dealing with his newly acquired handicap.[4]

---

[1] Reprinted by permission from *Aptitudes and Aptitude Testing*, by W. V. Bingham, Harper & Brothers, New York, 1937.

[2] Reprinted from *Journal of Consulting Psychology*, 12:433 (1948), by permission of the American Psychological Association, publishers.

[3] *Loc. Cit.*

[4] *Loc. Cit.*

These examples indicate how the observational data can make the tests more meaningful.

Interpretation of battery of tests. An effort should be made to combine a battery of test results so that they can be interpreted in an organismic and dynamic manner. The individual test results should not only be related to their norms and the results listed. This kind of listing is but a starting point. Separate test norms should be integrated with observational data, and the personal background information of the individual. Finally all the test scores, observations, and background must be woven into a whole. For vocational tests the total picture should emphasize work possibilities. Two batteries of tests are interpreted as illustrations of this point.

Joseph C. is 17 years old. He was placed in the ungraded classes in elementary school when he was nine years of age and remained there until leaving school. He comes from an economically poor home where both parents speak a foreign language. Joseph reports that his mother and father treated him well, and there is no evidence that he feels any hostility toward them. He feels rather close to them. He states, "There were many other mouths to feed in the family." Joseph spoke of his parents' lot as a hard one. He repeats over and over that they are good people. He wants to help himself and his family but he has had no training or skill; he does not know whether he was smart enough to ever acquire any. He has spoken with a State Employment Service worker, who referred him for counseling. His vocational test results follow:

Test	*Percentile*	*Norm Population*
Otis Intelligence Test, Intermediate Form	20	16-25 yr. old population—N.Y.C. general sampling
Minnesota Spatial Relations Test	72	"
Finger Dexterity	82	"
Tweezer Dexterity	78	"
Placing	81	"
Turning	90	"
Minnesota Paper Form Board	55	Male vocational school students, 11 and 12 grades

He also had a reading achievement test (Monroe Silent Reading) on which he rated fourth grade.

Joseph came early for his tests and waited patiently. He politely inquired when he was to start and, when told, sat down to wait. When another examinee arrived, Joseph smiled at him.

Joseph was not given the Otis test first, since a reading of his record revealed his poor schooling. The Otis might have been disturbing to him, as it has been to others with similar backgrounds. The manipulative tests were given first. On the Finger Dexterity Test, the young man listened intently to the directions and seemed most eager to do a good job. Yet he was not overly tense. He scored in the 82nd percentile when compared to a general norm group of 16–25 year olds. His work was rhythmic and neat. He picked up three pins at a time without difficulty and placed them together into the respective holes. He also improved on the latter half of the test. On the Tweezer Dexterity he rated almost as high, the 78th percentile, when compared to the same group. Again his work was rhythmic and neat. He seemed pleased at the end of these tests. He smiled and waited for his next assignment.

He was eager to start the Placing Test. He really tried to go as fast as he could and to make each trial better than the previous one. His rating was the 81st percentile when compared with the 16–25 year old group; this is a very good rating. On the Turning Test, he had no difficulty understanding the directions. His work was very smooth. At this time there was a clatter in the halls, but Joseph paid no attention to it. He scored in the 90th percentile when compared to the 16–25 year old group.

The Minnesota Spatial Relations Test seemed to be enjoyable to Joseph. He smiled all through it. He saw that the parts were grouped according to shape almost immediately and made good use of the grouping. He tended to pick up a piece and to deliberate before inserting it. He made very few errors. The second board was done faster than the first. The rating was in the 72nd percentile when compared to the 16–25 year old population.

He was then given the Otis. He tried very hard on this test. Occasionally he would call the examiner to inquire into the meaning of a word. Apparently his vocabulary was limited. Then he would brighten and try to do the problem. He was all bent over on this test and worked slowly. When the time was called, he remarked that the test was hard for him. His rating showed it; it was only at the 20th percentile when compared with the 16–25 year old group.

On the Minnesota Paper Form Board he did quite well, rating at the 55th percentile when compared to male vocational school students in the 11th and 12th grades. He made movements in the air with his pencil as well as attempts to measure sides of the parts with it. He remarked that the test was hard but he liked it. In order to check on his reading achievement, the Monroe Silent Reading Test was administered. His rating was the equivalent of the fourth grade in elementary school.

It appears as if the low score on the Otis test is due more to poor reading skill than to lack of intelligence. A check by means of the Wechsler-Bellevue Intelligence would probably bear this out, and if he can be re-scheduled this should be arranged. He will probably be able to profit from reading courses. Referral to a reading clinic might be desirable. He is capable of learning to do mechanical work on a semiskilled level immediately. If he could obtain some further training, he might be able to learn to do even a skilled job. If he were properly motivated, his reading skill might improve considerably.

Joseph was cooperative, showed good work habits, and evidence of ability to get along well with people. These characteristics will help him in his future vocational adjustment.

George K. is 19 years old. He is a sophomore in a business college and is not sure of his intended major. His grades have averaged B-, but he does not think he can compete readily with the better students. College means much to him. He believes that his parents are making a sacrifice by sending him there. He wants to be sure he is not just wasting his time, and is concerned about having the proper major. He discussed the matter with a friend, who recommended that he go for vocational counseling. The vocational test results follow:

Test	*Percentile*	*Norm Population*
American Council on Education	76	College Freshmen
Otis, Higher Examination	62	College
Minnesota Clerical		Accountants
Numbers	95	and
Names	90	Bookkeepers

Finger Dexterity	33	16–25 yr. old population
Tweezer Dexterity	50	"
Minnesota Spatial Relations	85	"
Bennett Mechanical Comprehension	55	Engineering Freshmen

George came on time for his test appointment. He chatted with other examinees who were waiting. Before he started on the tests he asked the examiner if the tests would tell him what he was suited for. The examiner answered that the test results would be discussed during the counseling interview together with any other matter he wanted to talk over with the counselor. George seemed satisfied to postpone any discussion until then. He cooperated fully.

He was given the Otis test first. When the time limit was called, he seemed reluctant to stop. He said the time went too fast and that he could do more if he had a few more minutes. His rating was at the 62nd percentile when compared with a college population. This is a substantial rating, which indicates that he should do better than average in academic work that emphasizes linguistic concepts. On the American Council on Education the total score was equivalent to the 76th percentile compared to college freshmen. He did a little better on the Quantitative part than the Linguistic. The fact that he rated higher on this test may be related to his protest against the time limit on the Otis. This test is supposed to be less influenced by speed. The slight advantage in the Quantitative part over the Linguistic is not in itself significant but may have some importance in a broader context. This possibility might be checked during the interview.

On the Minnesota Clerical Test, George was very intent in spite of regarding it as less challenging than the academic tests. He rated very high, 95th percentile on numbers and 90th on names when compared to accountants and bookkeepers. An analysis of the tests showed no errors on numbers and only one error on names. This demonstrates a very high level of accuracy on minute detail. His higher score on the number part may be related to the higher score on the quantitative part of the A.C.E.

George obviously did not feel comfortable with either the Finger or Tweezer Dexterity Tests. He smiled sheepishly and said they were silly. However, he kept to his work and could be readily motivated to do his best. He had difficulty picking up the three pins with his fingers and placing them in the holes together but did not become angry or too disturbed. Instead he disregarded neatness somewhat, so that by the time he was finished the test board was quite a mess. The rating of 33rd percentile when compared to a 16–25 year old population does not fully indicate the messiness of his work. He was neater on the Tweezer Dexterity Test, although his grasp of the pins with the tweezer was not always correct enough to prevent pins from shooting off once in a while. His rhythm was not sustained throughout. He remarked that he was not so good with "little things." However, he managed to achieve a score equal to the 50 percentile when compared to a 16–25 year old population on this test.

On the Bennett Mechanical Comprehension, George rated at the 55th percentile when compared to engineering freshmen. He enjoyed the test as a challenge but said he was "not quite up on his physics" and was not too much interested in it. Although this test is not supposed to be influenced much by knowledge of physics, it does make use of common principles found in physics. He did better on the Minnesota Spatial Relations Test, rating at the 85th percentile when compared to a 16–25 year old population. This test measures simple spatial ability.

George certainly has the ability for college, not engineering perhaps, but liberal arts or business. He may tend to be slow and deliberate in his studies, but still will probably manage quite well. Since he must decide on a major, a consideration of the non-engineering fields utilizing numbers, like accountancy, seems a possibility. Of course, this does not rule out other verbal areas for consideration. He should be given the Strong Interest Inventory or the Kuder Preference Record to serve as a basis for discussion of his interests. There was no time for these tests today but he can drop in for this the morning of his interview.

George seemed very cooperative and expressive and may well be able to clarify his interests during the interview. It appears that he would profit from a discussion of his ability to hold his own with other college students.

Vocational application of clinical tests

The Wechsler-Bellevue Intelligence Scale, the Rorschach Inkblot Test, and other clinical tests can become very valuable as vocational test instruments. About the Wechsler-Bellevue there is very little controversy. The Rorschach, however, still is disputed as a useful vocational instrument. Other tests like the Thematic Apperception Test and sentence completion tests have had little use so far. The Wechsler-Bellevue Scale is essentially an intelligence test. The others are personality tests much more complex than personality questionnaires like the Bernreuter and the Bell Adjustment Inventory.

The Wechsler-Bellevue Intelligence Scale. Although designed as a test of intelligence, the scale allows for descriptions of personality. There are 10 subtests (plus vocabulary, which may or may not be included). The background of the individual and his motivational and emotional states make for differences in scores on the various subtests. It is through the variations on the subtests that personality evaluations may be made. Reports are available of many researches on the variation of the test scores as indicators of personality problems. Rabin (18) has summarized the studies on the differences in Wechsler-Bellevue patterns among the mentally ill. Rapaport (19) has collated a large number of studies of his own and colleagues' research on test patterns in different forms of abnormal behavior. Wechsler (29) has devoted a complete chapter of the Third Edition of his book to the test's diagnostic and clinical features. It is not the present concern to go into the details of diagnosis by means of the Wechsler-Bellevue. Rather it is intended to discuss how the test may be used for its vocational implications.

Vocationally the test results in measures of abilities related to aptitudes. It permits a good deal of dynamic interrelating among the 10 subtests. It also allows for the observation of many behavioral aspects, because of the oral and individual administration as well as the variety of the subtests. However, it requires more training to learn to administer, and much more training to interpret results, than do the typical aptitude tests. A brief description of each of the subtests is necessary for better understanding its suitability for vocational testing.

1. *Information Test.* This subtest is not necessarily the first to be given. There is no standard order for administering the subtests; the order is left to the examiner's judgment. The information test consists of 25 items of information, most of which are commonly learned in school or elsewhere. These information items refer to important places, events, and things. The average person with average opportunity should have had contact with most of them. This subtest is administered orally with the examinee replying orally. It is verbal in nature and shows the alertness of the individual to things happening about him. It will, however, be subject to influences of limited schooling and restricted environment. The items in the subtest advance from easy to difficult, as do those in all the subtests. Some of the items are "Where is London?", "How many pints make a quart?", and "Where does rubber come from?"

2. *Comprehension Test.* This subtest consists of ten questions given orally and replied to orally. They involve social judgment. Wechsler (30) writes that,

> Success on the test seemingly depends on the possession of a certain amount of practical information and a general ability to evaluate past experience.

Some of the questions are "What is the thing to do if you find an envelope in the street, that is sealed, and addressed and has a new stamp?", "What should you do if while sitting in the movies (theatre) you were the first person to discover a fire (or see smoke and fire)?" and "Why should we keep away from bad company?"

3. *Arithmetical Reasoning Test.* This subtest consists of 10 problems. The first eight are read by the examiner, the last two are read by the examinee who continues to hold the cards with the problems on them until he solves the problems. If he cannot read well enough, they are read for him. They are all done mentally. The last two are given extra credits if done correctly within certain times. The computations do not involve arithmetical processes beyond addition, subtraction, multiplication, and division. The subtest is somewhat influenced by degree of education. Some of the problems are, "How much is four dollars and five dollars?", "If a man buys six cents worth of

stamps and gives the clerk ten cents, how much change should he get back?", "If a man buys eight cents worth of stamps and gives the clerk twenty-five cents, how much change should he get back?"

4. *Memory Span for Digits.* This subtest consists of two parts, digits forward and digits backward. Digits forward has series of digits ranging in length from three to nine. The examinee listens to each series as it is read aloud and repeats the series in the same order. Each series has two sets. When the individual fails the two sets in a series, the test is stopped. The digits backward has two sets each of series of three digits to eight digits. The digits are read and the examinee is to repeat them in reverse order. The stopping point is the same as for the digits forward. The subtest measures auditory rote memory, especially attention. It has little correlation with ability to reason.

5. *Similarities Test.* This subtest has 12 items; each is a pair of words that are alike in some way. The pairs are given orally and responded to orally. The words are quite common, and familiarity with them does not require a high level of education. The subtest essentially measures abstract verbal reasoning ability. It has a high correlation with the total score of the rest of the scale. Some pairs of words are orange and banana, coat and dress, and dog and lion.

The above five tests with the vocabulary subtest as an alternate to one of them, or in addition, consists of the Verbal Scale. The five subtests to follow make up the Performance Scale.

6. *Picture Arrangement Test.* This subtest consists of a sample and six sets of pictures to be rearranged. The score is derived from the six sets. Each set has pictures ranging from three in the easiest to six in the most difficult. The pictures are put down before the subject in a standard order with instructions that he rearrange them to make a sensible story. Extra credits are given for the more rapid performances in the last two sets. This test is subject to differences in cultural and social level; but because it is influenced by them, it gives clues about the cultural and social background of the examinee. It measures social judgment and ability to understand and organize parts of a total situation. The individual does not have to speak; he just rearranges the pictures.

7. *Picture Completion Test.* This subtest consists of 15 pictures

with parts missing. The pictures are of common things like a watch, a face, or a pig. The examinee must discover the missing part and name it or point to it. The subtest requires differentiation between essential and nonessential details, and perceptual ability. The score is the number obtained correctly. The test is not timed.

8. *Block Design Test.* This subtest is the best of the performance tests. It correlates quite high with the total scale and with the verbal tests. It is a good test of general intelligence. This is probably because it involves reasoning; it is necessary to analyze the designs and then build them into patterns.

The examinee is required to make designs out of blocks. Two demonstration patterns precede the actual test; seven designs make up the test. The first four are made up of four blocks; the next two of nine blocks; and the last one of 16 blocks. The designs are credited only if fully correct within quite ample time limits. Extra bonuses are given for speed on correct solutions.

9. *Object Assembly Test.* This subtest consists of three small form boards; a manikin, a profile, and a hand. The form boards have been cut into several pieces; the parts are laid out in a standard manner The examinee must put them together to form the whole object. The score is the number of parts correctly put together for each form board. Additional bonuses for faster time are given for the profile and hand. The subtest measures spatial ability.

10. *Digit Symbol Test (Also known as Substitution Test.)* This subtest consists of 67 boxes to be filled in as quickly as possible with certain symbols. The symbols correspond to numbers; both symbols and numbers are in full view of the examinee. The numbers are above the boxes; the examinee is to write in the box the symbol that corresponds to it. There is a time limit of 90 seconds. This subtest measures speed of making associations.

The results of the various subtests can be taken as indications of abilities that have vocational meaning. Balinsky (3) factor analyzed the Wechsler-Bellevue for different age groups. For the 25-29 age group a verbal factor was found in the Comprehension, Information, and Digit Symbol tests; a factor involving restriction in the solution in the Comprehension, Information, Arithmetical Reasoning, Picture

Arrangement, and Picture Completion tests; and a performance or spatial factor in the Picture Completion, Object Assembly, and Block Design tests. The verbal and spatial factors have most meaning vocationally, since they are related to verbal and mechanical occupations. It is interesting to note that the Digit Symbol test measures verbal ability, indicating that this particular test "is quite clerical in nature and has developed along with verbal ability." The Object Assembly and Block Design tests have the highest loadings in the spatial factor.

Diamond (7) reports a factor analysis of groups of subtests of the Wechsler-Bellevue and three aptitude tests. He combined the weighted scores of the Information, Comprehension, and Similarities subtests into a linguistic score; the Digit Span, Arithmetical Reasoning, and Digit Symbol subtests into a clerical score; and the Picture Completion, Object Assembly, and Block Design subtests into a spatial score. The O'Rourke Vocabulary, the Minnesota Clerical, and the Minnesota Spatial Relations were included to determine what relation each had with the groupings of the Wechsler-Bellevue subtests. He found that there was fairly high correspondence between the Wechsler-Bellevue linguistic subtests and the Vocabulary, between the clerical subtests and the Minnesota Clerical, and between the spatial subtests and the Minnesota Spatial Relations test. In addition to using the total score to measure intelligence, one can, according to Diamond, use these subtest groupings to indicate linguistic, clerical, and spatial aptitudes.

The measurement of vocational abilities alone, however, does not justify the use of the Wechsler-Bellevue in counseling. It also is the best measure of intelligence for adolescents and adults. The results on this test are least disturbed by differences in socio-economic and educational status, with their accompanying opportunities for development. People with limited education or poor environment are not as validly tested by the A.C.E., the Ohio State, or the Otis as by the Wechsler-Bellevue. But most important, the test allows for close observation of the examinee, since the tests are individually administered, and study of his performance on different subtests that have been standardized on the same population. A report on a girl of 18 who was given the Wechsler-Bellevue demonstrates its application in vocational counseling. It also shows the possibilities of the clinical approach. The report follows:

> The most striking result on this test is the significantly better handling of the spatial material than the verbal material. On the performance part of the test, the examinee rated bright normal while reaching only average on the verbal part.
>
> Analysis of the subtests shows the examinee to be superior on the Object Assembly test, which measures concrete spatial ability. She made a good score, but not as high, on the Block Design test. This test is more complex than the Object Assembly. However, she worked along steadily even when she was in apparent difficulty.
>
> When dealing with subtests that involve memory, the examinee was better with the Digit Symbol subtest than the Digit Span. Apparently having to hold the numbers in mind was more difficult than where she had the symbols before her. She tried hard on the Digit Span and commented that she could not easily retain the numbers. She was embarrassed because of this. She also did rather poorly on the Arithmetical Reasoning test where she had to retain the figures in order to solve the problems. Her schooling was irregular and this may account, in part, for her poor score on the Arithmetical Reasoning. The Information score was average. Here the score may have been better if she had had better opportunities for development. This was indicated by missing some easier items and answering correctly several difficult ones. The same was true for the Similarities on which she rated average. The score on the Comprehension test was above average, her best score on the verbal part. Apparently she has adequate understanding of social situations.
>
> She was fully cooperative but tense at times on the verbal material. She would often grope for words and correct herself even when no correction was necessary. Although she rates only average on the verbal part of the test, there are indications that she could do better. Her rating was impaired by irregular schooling. She most likely can profit from schooling, if this fits into her vocational planning.

The Rorschach Inkblot Test. The Rorschach was designed as an aid in personality diagnosis. It consists of 10 inkblots, selected from an originally larger number. The inkblots are unstructured or as Rorschach (25) called them "accidental forms." The forms of the blots do not have any specific meaning. The examinee perceives things in them in reference to his own intellectual, emotional, and motivational state. He projects into them his own interpretations. That is why the test is referred to as a projective technique. Five of the inkblots have color in them and five do not. There is no right or wrong answer in anything the subject reports. The directions simply request the examinee to tell what he sees in each inkblot.

This test demands more training and skill in scoring and interpretation on the part of the examiner than does the Wechsler-Bellevue, and considerably more than for the vocational tests. It is a complex test that reaches many aspects of the personality structure. Synthesizing the aspects into a dynamic whole is the goal in interpretation of the test. Interpretation requires knowledge of how the test measures personality and of the psychodynamics of personality. The test may take several hours to interpret. It is not our purpose to demonstrate how to interpret the test but to discuss its use vocationally. A brief description of its major terms will be given first to familiarize the reader with the test.

The examinee gives as many responses as he wishes to each of the 10 inkblots. The examiner takes down the responses verbatim, as far as possible. Each response is scorable in terms of location, determinant, and content. The location is the part to which the person made the responses; in the whole blot (W); a large part of it (D); or smaller and unusual places (d and dd). The determinant is what characteristics in the blot made for the response: the form (F); human movement (M); animal movement (FM); inanimate movement (m); shading alone or in combination with form (c, cF, Fc); color alone or in combination with form (C, CF, FC). The content represents the attributes of humans (H), human details (Hd), animals or animal details (A or Ad), objects (obj.), nature (nat.) and the like.

The location, determinant, and content responses are each summed separately. Percentages of the total number of responses (R) are taken for each. Certain relations or ratios are made. The particular kinds of response have meanings, but they must be buttressed by other responses and the relationships among them. Each response or sign may have more than one meaning. Therefore all signs must be weighed and patterned in such a way that all parts fit together to make a personality picture in accord with the principles of psychodynamics. The M responses indicate attitude toward self as well as intellectual level. The quality of the M is also important, in that it gives clues about the attitude toward the self. However, one can go further. The ratio of W:M indicates the relationship between drive, represented by W, and ability, represented by M. There may be too little drive in relation to ability or too much or balance. Again this may be modified or embellished by the locations of the M's. If in small and unusual locations, it may indicate unreality, attention to less practical details. The ratio of M : Sum C responses gives an indication of extroversion-introversion. Overbalanced M implies introversion; overbalanced C, extroversion. The forms may be too many in relation to the rest of the responses and this may indicate constriction; if few C's and more M's it may mean much thinking expended in unrealistic matters. The small c's have to do with control; they also may indicate anxiety. If there are color responses, which indicate impulsivity, the c's are important as checks upon it. However, many more signs and relationships must be considered than have too briefly been reported here. Klopfer and Kelley (11) have written an excellent text on the Rorschach; but book reading is not sufficient. Instruction and experience must be obtained, as well as a general clinical background.

Rorschach (25) recognized the possible vocational uses of his test; he included vocationally oriented descriptions in his analyses of some of his cases. He also described the personalities of artists as obtained from the test results. Since then, there seem to be three directions taken in the use of the Rorschach test vocationally: (1) attempts to find signs and give ratings that indicate success or lack of it in an occupation; (2) attempts to describe personalities belonging to different occupations; and (3) personality analyses of individuals to be used in selection and counseling.

The use of signs for prediction purposes yields inconsistent results. Piotrowski *et al.* (15) found four signs in the Rorschach that discriminated the relative success of young male mechanical workers: at least one m; responses to cards 4 and 6 as competent as those to 1, 2, 3 and 5; high evidence (reasons substantiating responses); and no whole form interpretation of cards 8, 9, and 10. Kurtz (13) reports on the use of ratings developed from signs on the Rorschach to distinguish between very satisfactory and unsatisfactory managers of life insurance agencies. The ratings were made by a Rorschach expert. They were found to discriminate managerial ability within the original group but not to discriminate when applied to another group. Munroe (14) successfully used an inspection technique of signs on the Rorschach to give ratings that distinguished among college students in terms of their over-all academic performance.

Harrower-Erickson (9) modified the procedure of the Rorschach to a multiple-choice group technique to give ratings for screening purposes. The modification lists responses for each blot from which the examinee selects those which he deems appropriate. The responses are not given spontaneously. Balinsky (4) used this procedure of the test on 100 individuals, varying in adjustment, who were referred for vocational counseling, and found that it did not prove adequate for screening the more poorly adjusted. Steiner (27), however, used this technique at the General Electric Company and found it useful in discovering disturbed cases. Much more research needs to be done with Rorschach sign interpretation as a predictor of vocational success.

The Rorschach has been employed in the attempt to determine personality characteristics of the people in various occupations. Kaback (10) attempted to discover differences in the responses of pharmacists and accountants by means of the group-administered Rorschach. She also analyzed the responses of male students who were planning to enter pharmacy and accountancy. Although differences were found between the pharmacists and accountants, they were not so distinct as to be used for making individual predictions. The same was true for the student group. Apparently there were no vocational personalities differentiating accountants and pharmacists. Steiner (27) reports descriptions of groups of student engineers, sales engineers, supervisors, copywriters, and artists or visualizers (commercial artists). The descriptions are rather meager and not clear cut.

Roe (23) administered the Rorschach to 20 outstanding painters. Neither she nor Dr. Bruno Klopfer, an outstanding Rorschach expert, could discover creativity by means of the test. Yet these were painters with works in the Metropolitan Museum of Art, in the Whitney Museum, or purchased by the Encyclopedia Britannica for their collection. Prados (17) studied another group of artists, not as famous, and found the more successful ones to deviate more from the average; but he found no real group artistic personality discernible. Andersen and Munroe (1) set out to determine if there is a difference in the responses on the Rorschach between students of creative painting and students of composition and design; and if the creative painting students had similar responses to Roe's and Prados' groups. They found some differences between the two groups of students but little similarity with the adult artist.

Roe's (24) study with scientists and technicians found them much more homogeneous than the artists. The scientists also gave certain responses differentiating them from the technicians. Rieger (21) reports on applicants interviewed and tested for different jobs, such as technical sales engineer, supervisor, administrator, and personnel worker. The Rorschach was also given. She found no clear-cut occupational personalities, but did find some statistically significant differences between the groups; the administrators as well as the supervisors and foremen differed from the others. It would appear that the personalities of individuals in different vocations are not distinctly different and that different personalities can be equally successful within the same vocation.

The most successful use of the Rorschach has been to describe an individual's total personality. Such descriptions can be aids in corroborating impressions obtained in either vocational or selection interviews. Rieger (22) describes the use of the test in conjunction with interview and other test data. She reports that if the Rorschach is given before the interview it can be of more value, because the interviewer can then follow up leads in the Rorschach. However, ratings on the basis of the Rorschach were occasionally assigned independently of the interview. When this was done for 30 applicants for different jobs and compared to the interview ratings, the coefficient of correlation was $+.75 \pm .05$. This is a good indication of validity, since the interview had already been demonstrated to have high predictive value.

Rieger comments, however, that the high correlation was achieved because she was closely associated with the interviewer over a fairly long period of time. They both knew the factors and relative weighting of the factors from which they made the recommendations. She suggests the use of the Rorschach together with other employment techniques.

In vocational counseling, the Rorschach can be an aid in planning with the client. Piotrowski (16) reports on a group of eight psychiatric student nurses sent because of many difficulties. The Rorschach was administered and the students classified according to the records they gave. Vocational recommendations were made, such as "Discontinue training"; "The girl could become a good child nurse without professional training" . . . "Continue training. Students probably will make satisfactory psychiatric nurses but not in responsible positions." All recommendations were followed. Only one girl dropped out of training which had been recommended. The others were doing what was expected of them after six to 30 months.

The Rorschach is not always used as a descriptive device in vocational counseling. Rather there is a tendency to use it as a diagnostic tool for possible referral to psychiatric help, or only with the maladjusted. This is a narrow function. Taylor (28) presents the issue admirably. He recommends the use of the Rorschach to enrich the descriptions of personality for the counselor. This is what Rieger does in vocational selection. Taylor presents a Rorschach description for illustration which we quote:

> The applicant had excellent ability to deal with small, practical matters in an impersonal, intellectual way. In these areas he displayed very superior discrimination, awareness, and intellectual sensitivity, but emotionally he was extremely cool, aloof and reticent. There was a basic constraint, lack of imagination and daring. He had little genuine interest in people and much anxiety in relating to people. In addition, there was considerable evidence of an immature, cautious personality. The Rorschach, then, suggested that the applicant would make inadequate relationships with his clients, that he was too immature to identify adequately with the real life problems of anxious, worried people, and that he had too little drive and vision to augur for success in certain community aspects of the job. In terms of cri-

> teria established for the position, this applicant was found lacking. However, the very qualities which suggested that he would do poorly in personnel work involving direct relationships with people suggested that he would make an excellent research worker. His very superior, discriminating type of intelligence in concrete, impersonal matters, his greater comfort in non-personal relationships and his ability to function more effectively in the latter area pointed to a more promising career in research work.

This kind of description gives many clues to the vocational counselor and can help him interview the client more effectively.

Other clinical tests. Other clinical projective techniques have had too little use vocationally to be properly evaluated. The Thematic Apperception Test (T.A.T.) has had rather wide clinical usage but its vocational use has been sporadic and limited. Possibly better scoring systems and further evidence of validity will enhance this test's vocational usage.

The T.A.T. consists of a series of somewhat unstructured pictures; the examinee is required to tell a story about each. Tomkins (29) recommends the use of the test as a supplemental aid in vocational guidance. He writes that the test can tell about such things as the meaning of work to the individual, his level of aspiration, and the conditions of work which may determine his vocational adjustment.

Sentence completion tests have been used in clinical procedures for a long time. The tests furnish the beginnings of sentences and the subject is required to complete the sentence. Each subject finishes the sentence in accordance with the way he thinks, feels or behaves. For example the sentence, "I feel . . .", can be completed in many, many, different ways. Research studies examining the reliability and validity of this technique are not numerous; most of those that have appeared are not clear-cut in their findings with reference to scoring and interpretation. However, in the hands of a good clinician these tests have been useful in diagnosis and better understanding of the subject.

A sentence completion test has been proposed by Rohde (20). It contains 64 items. Illustrative sentence beginnings include: "My school work . . ."; "I want to know . . ."; "At night . . ."; and "I become embarrassed. . . ."

This questionnaire is intended for use with individuals approximately 12 years of age and above, including adults. A validation study was conducted upon 670 students in the ninth grade of several schools. The results are interpreted according to a conceptual scheme proposed by Murray in his book, *Explorations in Personality.*

Spache (26) has developed a completion test recommended for industrial use. The items are varied and many are related to work situations. The test contains such items as "His wife . . ."; "My best boss . . ."; "When he was fired, he . . ."

The Szondi consists of six series of eight photographs, each of a mental patient. The diagnosis of the patients is known in each case. The examinee is to choose the two faces he likes most and the two he dislikes most from each set of eight. According to Klopfer (12), the basic assumption of the Szondi test is that an individual's affective reactions to the photographs of certain selected mental patients will reflect some basic characteristics of his personality. Deri (6) believes that this test has vocational implications, but no studies to determine whether it has, have been reported.

Summary

The term "clinical" has two aspects. One is the view of the individual as a unified whole; this view demands an organismic and dynamic approach in which all aspects of the individual are interrelated. The other is a certain category of tests, to be used as aids in diagnosis and description; and the view that vocational tests can be interpreted clinically.

The clinical approach is a useful technique in the interpretation of vocational tests. Observing the client while he takes a test is an important element. Another is the integration and more meaningful interpretation of a battery of psychological tests.

Certain clinical tests have been used in vocational batteries. The Wechsler-Bellevue and the Rorschach are two examples.

Bibliography

1. Andersen, I., and R. Munroe, "Personality Factors Involved in Student Concentration on Creative Painting and Commercial Art," *Rorschach Research Exchange and Journal of Projective Techniques,* 12:1–14 (1948).
2. Baker, G., and J. G. Peatman, "Tests Used in Veterans Administration Advisement Units," *The American Psychologist,* 2:99–102 (1947).
3. Balinsky, B., "An Analysis of the Mental Factors of Various Age Groups from Nine to Sixty," *Genetic Psychology Monographs,* 23: 191–234 (1941).
4. ———, "The Multiple Choice Group Rorschach Test as a Means of Screening Applicants for Jobs," *Journal of Psychology,* 19:203–208 (1945).
5. Bingham, W. V., *Aptitudes and Aptitude Testing.* New York: Harper, 1937.
6. Deri, S., "Editorial Comments," *Rorschach Research Exchange and Journal of Projective Techniques,* 11:6 (1947).
7. Diamond, S., "The Wechsler-Bellevue Intelligence Scales and Certain Vocational Aptitude Tests, *Journal of Psychology,* 24: 279–282 (1947).
8. Di Michael, S. G., "Characteristics of a Desirable Psychological Report to the Vocational Counselor," *Journal of Consulting Psychology,* 12:432–437 (1948).
9. Harrower-Erickson, M. R., "A Multiple Choice Test for Screening Purposes," *Psychosomatic Medicine,* 5:331–341 (1943).
10. Kaback, G. R., *Vocational Personalities,* Contributions to Education No. 294, Teachers College, Columbia University, New York (1946).
11. Klopfer, B., and D. M. Kelley, *The Rorschach Technique.* New York: World, 1942.
12. Klopfer, W. G., "An Investigation of the Szondi Test by the Association Method," paper delivered to 57th annual meeting of the American Psychological Association, abstract reported in *The American Psychologist,* 4:269 (1949).
13. Kurtz, A. K., "A Research Test of the Rorschach Test," *Personnel Psychology,* 1:41–51 (1948).
14. Munroe, R. L., "Prediction of the Adjustment and Academic Performance of College Students by a Modification of the Rorschach Method," *Applied Psychology Monographs,* No. 7 (1945).

15. Piotrowski, Z., B. Candee, B. Balinsky, S. Holtzberg, and B. Von Arnold, "Rorschach Signs in the Selection of Outstanding Young Male Mechanical Workers," *Journal of Psychology,* 18:131–150 (1944).
16. Piotrowski, Z. A., "Use of the Rorschach in vocational selection," *Journal of Consulting Psychology,* 7:97–102 (1943).
17. Prados, M., "Rorschach Studies on Artists and Painters," *Rorschach Research Exchange and Journal of Projective Techniques,* 8:178–183 (1944).
18. Rabin, A. I., "The Use of the Wechsler-Bellevue Scales with Normal and Abnormal Persons," *Psychological Bulletin,* 42:410–422 (1945).
19. Rapaport, D., *Diagnostic Psychological Testing.* Chicago: Year Book Publishers, 1945.
20. Rohde, A. R., "Explorations in Personality by the Sentence Completion Method," *Journal of Applied Psychology,* 30:169–181 (1946).
21. Rieger, A. F., "The Rorschach Test and Occupational Personalities," *Journal of Applied Psychology,* 33:572–577 (1949).
22. ———, "The Rorschach Test in Industrial Selection," *Journal of Applied Psychology,* 33:569–571 (1949).
23. Roe, A., "A Rorschach Study of a Group of Scientists and Technicians," *Journal of Consulting Psychology,* 10:317–327 (1946).
24. ———, "Painting and Personality," *Rorschach Research Exchange and Journal of Projective Techniques,* 10:86–100 (1946).
25. Rorschach, H., *Psychodiagnostics.* New York: Grune and Stratton, 1942.
26. Spache, G., *Manual for "An Incomplete Sentence Test for Industrial Use,"* 1949.
27. Steiner, M. E., "The Use of the Rorschach Method in Industry," *Rorschach Research Exchange and Journal of Projective Techniques,* 11:46–52 (1947).
28. Taylor, J. L., "Application of the Rorschach in a J. V. S.," Paper delivered at Mid-West Conference of J. V. S. Agencies, Chicago, Illinois (1948).
29. Tomkins, S. S., *The Thematic Apperception Test.* New York: Grune and Stratton, 1947.
30. Wechsler, D., *The Measurement of Adult Intelligence,* Third Edition. Baltimore: Williams and Wilkins, 1944.

11

INTEGRATING TESTS AND COUNSELING INTERVIEWS

VOCATIONAL COUNSELING is a dynamic process; all its parts must be interrelated to help the client achieve the insights necessary for stable vocational choice. Although six of the preceding chapters discussed the interview and tests separately, this procedure was followed for academic purposes. In practical guidance situations, tests cannot be considered apart from the interviews, nor interviews as separate from tests. It would not be amiss to say that the success of the counseling process depends to a large extent on how well the counselor integrates these two important tools of guidance.

Integration is achieved during the interview. It is only through the interview that the test results are appropriately relayed to the client. The manner in which this information is given is most important. The way the integration is effected can often be traced to the relative emphasis placed by counselors on tests and interviews. When tests are given the predominant role, the interview is often limited to direct interpretation of test results and thereby does not achieve its most effective purpose. When the interview has the predominantly major role, the tests, when given, may be completely disregarded. When both tests and interviews are considered they can be interwoven to make counseling an effective process. In this integration the manner in which the tests and their results are utilized is of primary importance.

The roles of tests and interviews will be presented first, but the manner of coordinating them will be given major consideration.

Role of tests

It is generally agreed that tests are a valuable part of the vocational counseling process, but tests alone cannot be considered as synonymous with counseling. Their function is to provide objective measures of intelligence, aptitude, achievement, interest, and personality that cannot be as readily obtained by interviews. They are essentially diagnostic instruments. As such they are to be used selectively to determine those characteristics of the client that the counselor needs to know to understand him.

Candee (5) reports that the function of a psychological department in a vocational counseling agency is "to contribute to the counselors' understanding of the clients with whom they deal." For this purpose, the psychological department employs tests wherever they may be useful to help the counselors "diagnose abilities and personality."

The counselor may feel the need for different kinds of tests for different clients. For the client who is definite in his desire to study engineering, mathematical and spatial tests should be emphasized. For the client who is vague, a more inclusive battery, with even more than one test of a kind is usually necessary. Where the personality factors do not emerge clearly in the interview, projective tests might well be added. The tests are to be chosen with the problem in mind.

Tests are sometimes given in stereotyped fashion, not particularly related to the needs of the client. In such instances, they may not delve into the major problem thoroughly, but touch several areas superficially. In such circumstances their results may have little value. And not too infrequently, tests administered in a haphazard fashion are summarized in a profile and given to the client rather than the counselor. Too often, in such a case, the client cannot interpret it himself. Moreover, it is often the case that when tests are given in this way that they are not worked into later interviews properly; they are used as the final authority in arriving at vocational objectives. This is often faulty counseling.

Although mainly diagnostic, tests can have the effect of making the person begin to think about himself more clearly. After taking tests, an individual may say that he thought he did better on a certain aptitude test than he expected. He may also become more aware of how he approaches tasks and reacts to difficult and challenging situations.

The fact that a client is treated with courtesy and understanding during test administration may help him react more cooperatively to further counseling. One of the authors in testing delinquents sent to Bellevue Hospital for mental examination found that the administration of aptitude tests helped establish the rapport necessary for future success in counseling. Such tests were considered by the delinquents as evidence of faith in their potentialities. They realized that these aptitude tests were a possible prelude to assistance in finding work, not further explorations which they could not understand and often resented. Small (10) also did some work along these lines and reports that aptitude test results served to reassure the clients. When these results were followed with interviews leading to jobs or job training, considerable progress was made with these delinquents.

Role of the counseling interview

The interview is the medium through which the individual gains insight about himself. Since the purpose of counseling is to have the individual gain a correct understanding of himself, it is obvious that the interview must be a part of counseling. Counseling can be conducted by interviewing alone but never by tests alone. It is best to include both.

There are instances of clients who have had sufficient work experience to evaluate their abilities rather correctly but still seek vocational counseling. They are not satisfied with their present jobs and want help in finding other possibilities. They may lack occupational information or insight into the relationship of their abilities and interests. The interview frequently helps them understand how their abilities and experiences can be utilized in other directions. In such circumstances the need for tests may never arise.

Harold is illustrative of such clients. He was 25 years of age and had worked since he graduated from high school. In seven years he had as many as 10 jobs; several were as shipping clerk, one as a laborer, and two as a helper in construction. Many of the jobs were seasonal; others he left of his own accord.

In discussing the various jobs, he admitted a liking for mechanics. But in none of his jobs did he think he had had the opportunity to learn something mechanical. He thought that he would make a good mechanic and spoke about how well he could fix all sorts of things around the house. On one job he occasionally had to assist in carpentry and thought he was very good at it. He had no doubt about his mechanical aptitude and said that he was really interested in a skilled trade.

However, he did not know much about such trades and had never properly evaluated them for himself. He had not yet decided on any particular trade. Since he wanted work, he generally followed the path of least resistance and took jobs that were immediately available or that paid comparatively high wages. The laborer and construction jobs, he thought, paid him quite well.

As the interview progressed, he talked of various possible trades. He was later given information about requirements and job possibilities of various trades and enthusiastically considered them. He made up his mind on the trade of carpentry and said he would try various leads he had to get him started.

Because he had no doubt about his abilities, he did not ask for tests; and they did not seem necessary. The interview was sufficient for him to come to a decision which he carried out successfully.

In those instances where emotional problems are in the forefront and impede vocational adjustment, tests may not always be needed. This is true especially when there is little question about aptitudes. Friend and Haggard (8) write, "There would, for instance, be little value in using extensive aptitude tests with the individual whose strengths are apparent but whose work history suggests that the difficulty lies in his capacity to mobilize them." Personality testing would be more suitable but the interview must play the major role. Balinsky (1) found the interview to be "the most significant part of the counseling process" in working both with clients whose problems were mainly vocational and with those whose problems were mainly neuropsychiatric. With the latter, vocational tests were hardly ever used, because such clients might not be able to accept the challenge that such tests sometimes present, and because they believed they possessed sufficient work experience to make a vocational decision. In such instances therapy would have to precede vocational testing.

Besides serving the major function of helping the individual gain insight, the interview may also offer diagnostic evidence about interests and personality. Culbert (6) states that interpretation of psychological tests is only one source of information about interests and personality, and that the interview can also provide such information. Super and Brophy (12) studied the role of the interview in vocational diagnosis. They found that the interview contributed largely to understanding the personality of the client and bringing out facts "which are occasionally missed by the more objective techniques." Although their study was on the interview as a diagnostic tool, they report that the function of the interview is "primarily an interpretive or treatment technique, the counseling method par excellence."

Integrating tests and interviews

It is apparent from the preceding discussion that although there are cases in which tests are not necessary, tests when given depend upon the interview for proper interpretation; and tests and interview are related parts of a dynamic whole. When the need for tests becomes apparent during an interview, the way in which they are to be introduced must be governed by the way the interview has proceeded. In interpretation, the personality of the client must be taken into account, and the results must be so presented that the client can think through whatever problems he may have. As well, test results may help determine the interviewing techniques to be used subsequently.

The remainder of this chapter will be a discussion of introducing and interpreting tests; the major emphasis will be placed on interpretation.

Introduction of tests. As previously indicated, tests are aids to the counselor. He may want them to obtain certain objective information. However, it is important to bear in mind that tests must be chosen in the light of what the counselor knows about the client. It is equally necessary to remember that tests should not be decided upon if this knowledge is inadequate, since under such circumstances the subject cannot be properly introduced and the wrong tests may be chosen.

However, many clients ask for tests without really understanding their full significance or implication. They expect the tests to give them the answer without further thought. Williamson (13) writes about the tendency for some students to think of aptitude tests in this way. He reports that, "One of the tasks of the guidance worker is to change the student's expectancy of magic into an appreciation of the complexity and clinical nature of guidance procedures."[1] The student must become aware of the motives behind his request for tests before they are introduced into the counseling process. He must also learn what they can do in general and for him in particular.

Consider the case of Howard K., who requested clerical aptitude tests almost immediately after the first interview started. When asked what he would like to get out of the tests he replied that they would tell him if he should go into white-collar work. Upon invitation to elaborate, he went on to say that he hoped the tests would tell him he was unsuited for the work because he did not like it. His mother did.

The interview then took another direction. He spoke about why his mother preferred clerical work even though he preferred mechanical work, and then said that he would like to take both kinds of tests.

He saw the reasons for wanting clerical tests. However, he seemed to prefer to rely on tests for the answer. It was necessary to explain the purpose of tests and what they could and could not do. After this was discussed with Howard, he readily understood the functions of the tests. He stated that he could answer incorrectly or not try as hard on the clerical tests and realized that this would not be a valid measure of his potential. He also understood that his feelings about clerical work were important and that he would have to discuss them as well

---

[1] From *How To Counsel Students* by E. G. Williamson. Copyright, 1939. Courtesy of McGraw-Hill Book Co.

as take tests. He said he wanted the tests anyway just to find out how good he was; he would discuss the results together with his feelings about different kinds of work in later interviews.

This case illustrates what tests may mean to an individual and how important it is that the person recognize the meaning of tests before he takes them. It also shows the need for explaining the purpose of tests as well as how they must be fitted into the total picture.

Very often the explanation of the purpose of tests helps define the counseling process for the client. Their purpose can be explained in several ways so as to give the client the proper perspective. At the time of registration for counseling, statements can be given to the client to read, or the intake counselor can offer them. The counseling process will be described, with tests mentioned as part of it but to be preceded and followed by interviews. However, such description may be insufficient, especially to the client who feels the need to rely upon tests. For such clients, the counseling process will need further redefinition during the interview. This can come at the beginning and may have to be repeated from time to time as the interviews continue. The tests will then be seen as measures required for more complete diagnosis. The client will be able to see tests in relationship to such other factors as background experiences, attitudes, and job possibilities.

Kilby (9) reports an illustration of defining the counseling process:

> Let me give you some idea of how we may use our time here. I can't solve this problem for you, nor will a test do it for you. No one can solve another's problems. But what we can do is this: A person is usually able to work out his own problems if he is able to talk them over with someone and get some new ideas, discover new ways out. And sometimes taking a test and talking over the results helps. So if you would like, we can think along on this together. Would you care to tell me a little more about this difficulty?[2]

He also gives another illustration in an interview context:

> Client: I came in to take those vocational tests. I can't decide between teaching and library work and have changed my major several times. Maybe the tests will tell me what to do.

[2] *Educational and Psychological Measurement,* 9:173 (1949).

Counselor: Well, now, taking tests will not tell you whether to go into library work or teaching, because tests can only give you information about yourself and cannot give you a decision. Nor can I tell you which to choose. But we can explore the two possibilities together if you wish, and maybe you will be able to reach a decision. And if there is something you find you need to know that a test will tell you, I'll mention a test and you can decide whether you want to take it. (These defining remarks need not be made in one continuous speech; plenty of opportunity is usually found to state the main ideas in a variety of ways.)[3]

Even the selection of certain tests may be involved when tests are suggested or introduced to a client. In attempting to apply non-directive principles in the introduction of tests, Bordin and Bixler (4) advocate giving the client the opportunity to share in the decision on the specific tests to be used. They do this by describing specific tests available in terms of what they measure and where the functions measured are important. An excerpt from a longer description follows:

> One type of test we have is one that gets at your general learning ability. You can get a comparison of your common-sense learning ability and your book-learning ability with that of the general run of people (Wechsler Adult and Adolescent Scales). If you wish, you can get a comparison of your book-learning ability with that of college students (American Council or Ohio State Psychological Examinations). We find that this last kind of measure when taken along with rank in high-school graduating class is the most accurate basis for predicting what a student will do in most types of college curricula.[4]

They present clinical evidence to the effect that this type of description brings about self-understanding on the part of the client. It helps the person see himself more clearly by giving him the opportunity to make a selection appropriate to himself. He will discuss why he selects certain tests. The counselor, however, still has "the responsibility for selecting in each area the test which is the most accurate for obtaining the judgment desired"[5] after the client decides that he would like tests in a certain area.

[3] *Loc. cit.*
[4] *Educational and Psychological Measurement,* 6:361 (1946).
[5] *Ibid.*

This presentation of tests deserves further study. Borden and Bixler propose among other things that the method be studied in terms of whether or not it helps the client accept the test results better. This is a very important matter for study, since it involves the other aspect of integration, that of interpreting the test results.

Interpreting test results. The basic premise in interpreting test results is that it be done with understanding of the client's possible reactions to them. The counselor must be prepared to give the test results in accordance with flexible interviewing standards.

The test results may or may not provide the main substance of the interview following their administration. In our experience many clients are prepared to continue the discussion of their vocational possibilities without receiving a description of their test results all at once. The results can be utilized at appropriate times during the interview as supporting evidence.

Bob is typical of these cases. He had already begun to discuss his problems. He was 16 years old and failing in some academic subjects in high school. Foreign languages, the sciences, and mathematics were his nemeses. He had arrived at the point where he no longer wanted to study. His father was concerned and it was he who referred him for vocational counseling.

Bob did not want to go on to college. He would try to stick out high school for his parents' sake but did not care for high grades. He had obtained a part-time job after school against his father's wishes and thought that he could eventually become a businessman or salesman. He was also good with tools but not sure whether he wanted to be a mechanic.

In discussing his aspirations, he said he believed that he was not bright enough for college and that he had no particular abilities, except perhaps with his hands. However, he had many friends and said he was able to get along very well with people his own age as well as those older than himself. After a discussion of tests, he thought he would like to have an interest test, personality test, intelligence test, and mechanical aptitude tests. He said that he would like to check on the ideas he had of himself.

When he came for his interview after the tests he was asked what he had been thinking about since he spoke to the counselor last. He said that he thought he had some good ideas. The main one was to take a mechanical course which would eventually lead to his starting his own business. He went on to say he thought he breezed through the mechanical aptitude tests and asked how he made out on them. He was told that he compared very favorably with students in training and that his chances for success were very good—that on one test he did better than 95 out of 100 of such students. On others he rated better than 90 out of 100 and 92 out of 100 when compared with people already at work.

After listening to this, he said that he really had thought of mechanical work before, but surreptitiously, because of his parents' attitude toward it. The results fortified him in his decision. He then turned to courses of study and said that he wanted to finish high school. The intelligence test result was brought in at this time. He was told that he had rated slightly above average, indicating he could manage to get through without much difficulty but that college might be more difficult. He asked about a possible change of course and was told about the non-college preparatory general course of study, in which he did not have to take many academic subjects. This course was for him, he said.

He then remarked that he could tell beforehand how he came out on the interest test. He really liked the mechanical and social activities and when he saw statements about them, marked them. The results of the interest test conformed to his own belief. He thought the personality test somewhat silly but the reason for this attitude was a defensiveness concerning his relations at home and with his parents. He began to talk about this matter, saying he felt guilty about not living up to his parents' expectations for him. He was able to resolve the feelings, however, and figured that by graduating from high school he would be satisfying his parents somewhat. He also thought that if he got into business eventually this would also ameliorate his relations with his parents.

He decided upon automechanics as his future work. The possibilities for owning his own business in this line also appealed to him.

Bob did not ask for his test results immediately. Asking him, "Did you do any thinking about your plans," led him to discuss vocational possibilities in a broader framework. The test results were brought in only as he asked for them and when the counselor thought they would be helpful in developing understanding.

A similar integration of test results is illustrated by the case of Miss J. K. This record was supplied by Allen V. Williams,[6] Director of the Lenox Hill Consulting Service. Because it clearly shows effective integration the case is presented in its entirety. The case is also presented to show how vocational problems on the adult level are also personal problems.

> Miss J. K. is thirty years old and has a position as an executive secretary. However she would like to go to college. Her vocational problem is complicated by emotional maladjustment. She was given the Rorschach Inkblot test, and other projective tests as well as tests of spatial relations, general intelligence, and interest tests.
>
> The record of interviews is reported. The words in italics represent Williams' interpretation of test results during the course of the several interviews. At times these tests are referred to but most often the interpretation of test results is made in context with the interview without even mentioning that the interpretation stems from the tests.
>
> 1/17/49 Miss K in on time. She is smiling but seems somewhat tense as she sits forward in her chair. I begin by saying that I guess she is pretty anxious to know how the tests came out. She replies she does want to know and goes on to say that the tests had really upset her. It seems that she felt all right during the testing but later at home she began to worry about some of her answers and what some of the tests meant. She thought about it so much that it was difficult for her to go to sleep for several nights. I say I have to share some of the responsibility for her getting so upset because in a way I had made it seem in our last talk that it was very important for her to do well on the tests. She denies that it was my fault and states that in fact I had given her the impression that the counseling was just as important as the tests. She feels that it is something in her which made her react that way. She knew that it wasn't a life or death matter. It reminded her of similar periods of anxiety she had when she was in high school. Although she did not obtain the highest grades in the class she was re-

[6] We are indebted to Allen V. Williams for allowing us to present his records of this case. Although some of his interpretation may be debated, we believe this case has value because it demonstrates how integration is necessary in the solving of a vocational and personal problem.

garded as the brightest, at least so the teachers told her. In fact she lived in a small town and everyone thought she had ability and because of this one teacher took a special interest in her and suggested she go to the city of M . . . where she would have much more scope in developing her abilities. But even though she made excellent grades and was very much involved in extra-curricular activities, particularly dramatics, she always became very upset when she was faced with an examination, or faced with some crucial situation where success was important. She just cannot understand why she became so upset when she knows that she almost always does well once she makes an attempt.

I nod that I know how this does feel to her and wondered whether somehow she is not telling me too that the tests had brought up a problem which she thought she had put behind her long ago. She is thoughtful for a few seconds, then states that perhaps this does bother her; that she had not realized it quite that way but it does tie up with so many other things. She might just as well tell me that she has had two years of psychoanalysis which she completed a few years back and she thought that she had gotten rid of some of these problems and suddenly here they are again. But she is not really worried about it, she knows that she can handle this—her problems—much better now, at any rate the reactions she has are not so strong as they used to be.

Miss K's mood changes at this point; she is calmer as she goes on to say that she has been relatively happy in her work and social life too. She talks at some length about the job. It seems that she is not really a good secretary; she does not work with steady persistence and sometimes two or three days will go by without getting much of the routine work done at all, but she gives the office a certain vitality, at least others there tell her that she has a quick mind which makes it possible for her to solve problems which are executive problems. She thinks this true in a way. She doesn't mean that she is running the business but various men who hold responsible positions do ask her what she thinks about particular problems and she often makes suggestions which they think are good and which they apply. She feels that her greatest value to them is in her ability to quickly size things up and come up with an idea. Also she likes to get along on this basis rather than as a straight secretary. In fact, she doubts that she would be able to stand a job which did not give her responsibility and a chance to say what she thinks. The more they use her ideas the better she likes it. Anyway, all in all, her work is satisfactory but still there is something missing. She doesn't know what it is but it's a feeling of wanting to do something and not knowing what it is or how to do it.

Then she adds tentatively that maybe the tests will throw some light on this—but then again the tests probably cannot . . .

I do not meet her request directly, but say lightly that I had begun to wonder whether we were going to get to the tests today; *I say that I think I should tell her—even though it is mean in one way after all her worry—that she really did quite well on the tests.* She acknowledges this with a smile and waits. I say that it is a little hard to know just how to begin with the test results but we might begin by talking about a few of the things that seemed important to her as a person. She agrees without comment, however, there is a slight trace of fearfulness in her facial expression. *I begin by saying that one of the things which seems to be quite central is her strong desire for independence. She certainly does not like being tied down. I can see how she would find straight secretarial work a pretty monotonous business unless she had a chance somehow to turn the job into something quite different than straight typing or filing or taking dictation.*

Miss K laughs in a puzzled way. She comments again at some length about how she just could not stand a routine job, but—well, though what I had said about "independence" is true, she is not sure that her desire to avoid being tied down is really a very good thing. After all everyone has to be tied down in some way.

I acknowledge that this is probably so and add that perhaps what I have raised did seem to be something of a problem in her and I am not sure exactly what to say about it.

She is quite thoughtful for a few minutes then in a tone of serious frankness asks if this means that she is immature. I say that I guess she is asking me if she is ever going to be completely happy and satisfied. Also, twice now her feelings have been upset and I guess she must be wondering more than ever what did result from her psychoanalysis. I know that just words aren't helpful to her, but I am quite sure that whatever comes up here about herself and her work can never really take away her gains in the analysis. As far as the desire not to be tied down is concerned, I do not think any one thing that we talk about will be the whole reason that she can or cannot make some change toward a happier experience in work. Miss K replies that she knows really that this is true. She talks for a little while of how the analysis was helpful to her but she puts in some doubt that she has solved all her problems and adds, "Of course, that is probably one reason for my coming here." Then she adds further that maybe instead of letting things that we talk about upset her, she ought to do some thinking about them first and will probably find out it's really not so bad. I nod agreement and accept this without further comment. I mention that we have gone a little overtime and probably we should stop for today. She agrees without comment. We make an appointment for next Friday at 6:00.

1/21/49: Miss K in on time. She is very friendly as we chat for a moment about the cold weather. Her mood shifts slightly now. She begins to talk more seriously. She says that she did some thinking about our last talk and she feels pretty good about what I had said to her, particularly in relation to her desire for independence. The more she had thought about this, the more she realized just how strong it is in her. She then tells me of how this really began when she was a very small child. Her mother and father had died during early childhood and she was raised by foster parents who were "wonderful" people, but even so she always felt that she had to stand on her own feet and not be a burden to them. Miss K goes on at some length to describe the early relationship at home. She projects only positive feelings about this part of her life and I do not raise any doubts about this. By telling me this, I think she is attempting to bring her need for independence into perspective, articulate it and focus it in regard to her present struggle with work. She goes on to say that it was not really hard for her to leave home and come to M . . . Her foster-father is dead now but her foster-mother is living and she helps to support her, though they live in separate towns. She describes these relationships as well as the various personal changes in her life in some detail and in a matter-of-fact way. I say that I guess her need for independence is pretty natural with her after being this way all these years and I could see too that she had used it in positive ways. She asks me how I meant this exactly. I say simply in the way in which it seemed to carry her forward—being able to leave home when she once decided to, being able to change jobs when they became unsatisfactory, and even in being able to take the initiative to come to a service like this one—all of these things showed she could take actions when she needed to. She seemed pleased at this. I think that it is important for Miss K to be aware of the fact that she can use herself (her independence) in positive ways. However, I know that there is another side of the same coin and at this point I raise a certain danger. I say to her that in mentioning her taking the initiative to come to a service like this one could be a positive action, but too, *I wonder whether it somehow is not hard to share her problems with others and in fact that this kind of sharing might really threaten the independence she does want.* She nodded yes that she knew what I meant but did not think that sharing her problems with me was really hard.

She said with a tone of discovery that so far it had been quite easy. I nodded acknowledgment of this and added lightly that at times I had made it a little painful for her. She knocked this aside by saying in effect that it could not all be pleasant and she was pretty sure she would not get anywhere if it always went smoothly.

Miss K changed the subject at this point. Since our last talk she has begun to wonder just what she could do about finding a different field of work. She brings in here the fact that once several years ago she was on the verge of registering in college but for one reason or another did not do it. She blamed this mostly on friends who discouraged her because they could see no point in her going to college unless it was directly related to her work. For example, her roommate said that she might take a course in personnel work or advertising—something which would help her to advance. She didn't exactly want this at the time and the result was that she did not enroll in school at all. I meet this by saying that I saw two parts in what she is saying: *First there is the part that says it is important for her to do the right thing: that is, that it matters to her to some extent what other people think. The other part is that she was not able to accept such fields as advertising or personnel. This is of interest particularly because from the test results she does seem to be a person who would just not feel comfortable in commercial work. I put in here that maybe the first question we have to try to look at together is the one of what relation exactly she does want with the world. All of us have our own way of structuring ourselves into the world and of structuring our surroundings. All of us have pretty definite lines of communication with life.* She replies that she thinks she sees what I mean. Yes she would like to talk about this. *I say that we might go back to her desire for independence. She seems to strive pretty hard to arrange her present work so that she is not tied down to the typewriter.* This is what I mean by "structuring" the situation. She needs to bring things around so that she can achieve her goal of independence. *She also seems to be strongly oriented to "ideas" rather than to "things." She is not the mechanic or engineer. One way she finds independence is through orienting herself to the world of ideas.* Miss K states that she is beginning to understand a lot of things now, things which had never become tied together before. She understands what I mean by her inclination to ideas. She talks slowly now. She seems to be pulling her thoughts together. She tells me about a girl friend who wanted to be a research worker in biology and gave up a great many material conveniences to complete her graduate studies. Other friends sometimes criticized this girl while she (Miss K) was always defending her, even though at times it was difficult for her to meet the arguments of her friends. She (Miss K) did not exactly envy this girl but she sometimes wished that it was she who was doing it. It was not a matter of just being ambitious either but of thinking she would like to be doing something like her friend was going to do—even if not in biology. The main argument of her friends is that the student friend was being impractical.

I say that I guessed in their eyes she was being impractical while in her friend's eyes she was being very practical. Somehow it depends upon the way in which each person has to express his own uniqueness as to whether they are being practical or impractical. Miss K says that she has always thought this too, but guessed she has always been too much influenced by the opinions of others to just follow completely her own thinking. *I put in here that in some way she is not as independent of the influence of others as perhaps her strong need for independence would indicate.*

Miss K is deeply thoughtful about this. She seems somewhat disturbed. *I know from the test results that a central dynamic lies at the core of Miss K's way of structuring. She has a very special way of relating to people and using people.* In challenging her thinking in regard to "independence vs. being dependent upon the opinions of others" I am attempting to open up this question.

I say that I sense that she is disturbed by what I have said. She answers that she is quite puzzled. Sometimes she doesn't care what people think and also she can be very persuasive with other people. At other times she cares a great deal. She referred back to what she had told me about her office work, particularly how she frequently comes up with ideas and is able to convince people above her that her suggestions are good ones, yet at times the opinions of others do get in her way. She went on to give several examples of how this is with her. She added with an exasperated laugh: that the more she thought about this the more mixed up she felt. Then as though to get rid of the confusion in some way she states definitely that whatever else is in the picture she knows that in any work she does she can't be completely isolated from people, in fact she wants to be in close contact with people.

I acknowledge this by saying that I thought this to be true too, both from what she had said and also from the test results. I wasn't clear either as to just exactly what being with people meant to her, but from what she had just told me I could see two parts: *one part which said it was important for her to be an influence with others and another part that said what she was in life was more related to what others thought she was and perhaps not enough dependent upon what she actually accomplished as a person. At times it is more important for her to do and say things to give others a certain picture of herself than to go ahead and do things simply for her own satisfaction.*

This seemed to be very meaningful to Miss K. She is quite enthusiastic for a moment then her expression again becomes thoughtful. She says, "You know, it is amazing to me how much of my analysis is being tied together by all of this." She told me of how she had followed "threads" for days upon end during the analysis and now she is beginning to tie up "the loose ends." I accept this but say too that I wasn't sure what she meant. She said one of the things which she had learned from the analysis was that she was a perfectionist and afraid of failure and this is why it is hard to just go ahead and do things. She then relates this to what we had just talked about. She says that when it comes to doing things which would test her in some way she would develop all kinds of doubts and use what others said against her ideas as a rationalization for not following through. This fits together with the attitude that she is only what others think she is. It is a different side of her need to be perfect. Also the fact that she has good ideas and can persuade others to use them was one way she had of not taking any risk herself. She said all of this rapidly as she formulated it in her mind. The extent to which she was able to organize all these thoughts did reflect the progress she was making here and also that she had gotten a good deal out of her analysis. I say to her that she certainly did seem to be tying a lot of loose ends together. I put in the doubt that just knowing all of this would make things different for her. She said that it did help her to see certain things about herself. As things become clearer in her own mind it seems to be easier to take action. She then states, "There is one thing I would like to ask you. Do you think I should go into sales work?" I say, "I guess this would be one way out, at least a way in which you could have 'good ideas and be persuasive' (her words) without too much risk and entanglement." There is a mixture of amusement and resignation in her tone as she replies, "It's the same old thing. I know I don't want a sales job. It is a way out and I've always taken some way like that, not necessarily sales but one thing or another. I'll have to think about this." The hour is up and we make an appointment for next Tuesday at 6:00.

1/25/49: Miss K in on time. She begins with the statement that yesterday she told her boss she would be leaving for a new job soon. There is obvious pride in the way she says this and she responds to the surprise in my own expression with a laugh and the comment that she does not blame me for being surprised but—, well she knows that she is going to do something else and it is only fair to let the company know. She has known this, the part about going into something else, for a long time and since talking with me is quite ready to make the change. I say lightly, yes, I am surprised. I know too that she wants to go ahead in some way. I guess she had gotten a little ahead of me. She laughed at this then told me how good it felt when she actually told Mr. V.... that she would be leaving. I acknowledge this by saying I can see how good it makes her feel. Then I say I feel good about it too, but in another way it frightens me because somehow it puts quite a bit on me. Miss K is thoughtful about this for a moment and acknowledges that she sees what I mean. She states that this is not really true because it will be herself who will be stuck unless she follows through. Then she says with much seriousness that actually she was not being impulsive or even "fixing" things so that she would have to do something. It came after a good deal of thought and when she went through with it, it felt very natural to her. Also it was something tangible which she could feel in a real way. It felt good. I accept this with the statement that I could not help but wonder just how the whole thing had really felt to her and as she says, it seems good.

It is important to maintain a control in the way Miss K uses herself and also uses me, particularly at this point in our relationship. In taking the step that she has in her work, there is enough natural fear on her part to blind and confuse her as she tries to go ahead. This can result in a negative relationship with me or rashness in her own actions. *The possibility of the development of a negative relationship with me must be understood against the background of a community view of "guidance" and "taking tests," a part of which implies that a person will be told the work for which he is most suitable as a result of the test findings.* I do not want Miss K to fall into this trap.

She takes a different direction now. She states that there is something inside her which makes her want to do work that is important. That's not it exactly, she does not know how to express it. It is not prestige. Neither does she want power or fame. In fact these things would not really interest her. She then expresses much negative feeling about industry. People are just cogs in a wheel and are driven both by the machine and by competition between themselves. She goes on at some length about this. I meet her feeling here by saying that I can see she is somehow through with the commercial world. She agrees and says that it is all right for some people but as far as she is concerned it would not satisfy her. She relates this back to the feeling of doing something important and ends by saying that she does not really know exactly what this is but she does know that it bothers her.

I state that what she is saying is interesting. *There is a part of her that needs the kind of work situation where she can feel that the work being done is of a "pioneering" kind. She needs to be free of the mundane and routine requirements of the everyday world and instead have the experience of exploring new territory, carrying out projects that push the frontiers of society outward.*

Miss K reacts as though what I have said is quite close to her. She confirms my statement with vigorous enthusiasm. "Yes, that's what I feel. It's not that I do something important but do something significant." *I add that this would bring together her interest in ideas and also in a way she would be doing work of importance in regard to people as a whole.* She understands this and comments, "It is amazing how all of these parts as you call them, fit together." I put in here that from many of the things we had talked about I wonder how she feels about herself in regard to not liking to be tied down. She replied that she knows she dislikes being tied down but she thinks she sees why now. More important, if some of her other goals were satisfied she would not mind doing the routine work which would be required. "Then routine and detail would be sort of secondary." I acknowledge this without comment.

There is a long pause, but without any tenseness between us. Finally she states that she had just been thinking about different fields of work. A lot of ideas pass through her head. It is hard to know. She asks tentatively, "What do you think I should do?" I say, "I know that it is hard for her to decide but I know too, that whatever I could suggest would be just words. In fact, I just don't know what would be best for her." She does not agree with me. She states that if she could be shown several "tracks to follow" she could select the one she wants. She adds that she could feel the direction pretty clearly now, but choosing a specific goal was hard for her. I say that I know how risky the jump is for her at this point. Then I put in that this could be something of a problem in itself. *Somehow she has a tendency to refuse to think through things and yet she is not a person who has to have specific rules as basis to go on.* She denied this with a good deal of defensiveness and told me again how easy it is for her to have ideas. Then she states that she is mentally lazy at times. She does not like to concentrate. She would hate to be a bookkeeper or an accountant. After several minutes of discussion she sums it up this way: she has ideas easily and they arise most easily when she is talking with others; on the other hand, she does refuse to think when faced squarely with a problem, whether it be a decision in regard to herself or a problem as for example in algebra. But she is intellectually curious. The whole matter confused her. She goes on to connect some of the problem with her fear of failure and her fear of risking herself in close quarters with a problem.

I say that I thought she did understand a good deal about her thinking. Apparently "how she thinks" depends upon the particular situation. She nods in agreement but she is not satisfied. I say, then that *perhaps the key to this is not in the way she thinks as such but somehow connected with the way she uses herself as a whole person, particularly in regard to the way she uses herself with people.* I recall that we had talked early about her relation to people, but probably did not really finish this—. She remembers but states that she does not see the connection, except in a vague way. That is, that people might blame her if she tries and fails at things. But she rejects this as not being very meaningful.

I say, that in sharing some of her problem, many of the central ways in which she structures herself in the world had come out. I mention some of these factors briefly, then say that at the core of all this is something else which we had not discussed. *It is as though there is a principle or a belief which says, "I am incapable of significant achievement myself, but I can realize my goals by being an inspiration to another person." "In other words," you say, "you get to your goals through someone else, by being the sensitive, intuitive influencer of others."* Miss K recognizes this instantly and then more slowly begins to articulate how it actually was in her everyday behavior. I could see that in grasping this principle she felt genuine insight. She says, "Yes, that is what I am doing. Except underneath I think I have it in me to achieve something significant even if I never try. You know, this is so true. It makes so many things that have puzzled me clear now. This is what I do with superiors at work. I try to . . . create the, I try to . . . it's almost like Pygmalion." She is greatly amused at this thought and then states that she "never went that far." She says that one of the things that always got her down at work was that she seldom met a man who could be the way she wanted. I put in here, "achieve your goals." She said, "Yes," and described in detail many of these people over the past years, contrasting herself as she now understands herself with their characteristics. She also talks at some length about various boy friends and states that in being this way she not only has not gotten into the right work but also this is probably the reason why she has not married. She has known men whom she thought she could "make into something" but they have been frightened by this quality in her. One told her that she made him insecure because she made him feel he had to accomplish more than he thought himself capable of. Another told her "you have the ideas and I have the drive; we would make a good pair." Either the particular man was afraid of her influence or else she did not like him enough to marry him. She told all of this with much eagerness. She appeared to feel quite clearly how she plays the role of the sensitive, artistic creator of others, a kind of "power behind the throne" using intuition as her intellectual approach rather than an objective, rational mental approach. I was able to relate this to her refusal to think. Thinking requires reaching into the problems themselves with one's intellect and when intuition is the primary mode, thinking becomes more of a reaching back into oneself. Refusal to think in the instance of Miss K is equivalent to refusal to act on the world in a direct way. Miss K. began to see how she had to change if she was going to go ahead and said so. We have gone overtime in this interview and we stop after making an appointment for next Monday at 6:00.

1/31/49: Miss K arrives 15 minutes early. I am free to see her. She begins by saying that she has made a decision since our last talk. She has decided to go back to school and major in science. I acknowledge this without comment. She states that she has written to her high school and asked them to forward her transcript to the University of C . . . . She had a talk with the registrar yesterday and it appears that she is eligible to enter.

I say that she had been doing a lot of thinking; it seems as though she has taken some action too. She laughs and states that in a way it seems crazy for her to go back to school. She is thirty years old. Her friends don't understand what she is trying to do; it's funny but that doesn't bother her anymore. Everyone has to live his own life. Miss K then expresses some of her own doubt. She states that she knows that if she goes to school she will have to continue to work. She will have to earn her own living just as she always has. It means that she probably will not be able to earn more than forty or forty-five dollars a week whereas if she simply went on working she could earn seventy to eighty dollars a week. I ask why she cannot earn the latter amount anyway since she does plan to work. She answers that while she is in school she wants a "nice, quiet job," perhaps as a receptionist or something at any rate where she will not "wear herself out." Her main effort will be devoted to school work. I say that it does sound to me like a pretty ambitious program and from what she has just said I can see too that her life will have to be pretty well organized for a while. She nodded in agreement and added that maybe it was too much to do. But she doesn't see any way around. There are no short cuts. She insists that she has thought the whole thing through very carefully and though she can see logically how to work the whole thing out, this is not the main thing. The main thing is . . . she doesn't know how to express it . . . the main thing is that going to college and preparing herself for really useful work where she personally can accomplish something in life just feels right to her.

I say that from the way she says it, I can see that it does feel right to her. I ask about the college work itself—she had mentioned majoring in science.

She answers this by saying she really is not sure yet. She thinks the best approach now is to explore the whole matter by taking several basic science courses. She smiles and states that maybe she will major in physics. She denies any knowledge of the subject but it seems like the type of material which she can get her teeth into. But she will not make up her mind about it finally until she has taken some courses. She will have to decide that when she comes to it. I can see that her mind is quite made up. There is a long pause. She seems to have little else to talk about. I say that it seems like things are pretty well worked out and remind her that when she first came in I had said we would probably see each other four or five times after the testing. Today is the fourth time and I'm beginning to think that coming in again would just be a burden to her though I did not really know. She replies that she is not sure what else there is to talk about at this point. She concludes that the remainder of the job is up to herself. She then asks me if we can leave any future appointment "open." She mentions that there may be difficulties in being admitted to school and if serious ones arise she would want to see me once again. I agree to this by saying that I thought if she had a specific question along those lines we could probably get together on it.

Miss K relaxes in her chair and her tone is conversational. She tells me that aside from helping her to get her vocational problem settled, our talks had meant much more than just that. She said that she was really quite confused about herself when she first came to the Service and so much that was hazy is not any longer. Furthermore what we had done wasn't at all like what she had expected. She expected to be told her IQ and interests and instead, "real problems that have been bothering me for years came up and I think I've already begun to make changes. At least, I feel differently about many things now." She appeared to have some difficulty in expressing just how this was with her but goes on to give several examples of it from everyday experience. She refers to our first talk when she spoke about the "rhythmical" desire to do something and not know just what it is she wants to do. She has not felt this at all during the past week. She is not sure whether she can trust its permanent disappearance for she adds that she should "knock on wood." She then states that she is beginning to find herself "thinking" rather than pushing serious thoughts away as she always has. She states an example of this in the office during the week when she was asked to set up a traffic schedule: "I got right in the middle of this before I knew it. Always before I procrastinated that type of a task or shoved it off onto someone else. But this time I even enjoyed doing it. It was fun." I say that I can see too that things are different for her now, not only from what she says but from the way she has taken real steps toward getting started in school. I add that she seems to be doing things on her own to make the changes something real in her everyday life. The hour is terminated at this point. Miss K thanks me as she gets up to go and I tell her that I will be interested to hear how things go with her after a little while of school. She promises to write and we say goodbye.[7]

In the above case the test interpretations weave in neatly with the development of insight. They are given in context to help the person think through his problems and occasionally as reassurance.

There are also times when it is necessary to use tests as evidence against an inadvisable vocational plan. But first other evidence from the individual's experience must be discussed and interpreted to him.

Charles represents such a case. He had rated an intelligence quotient of 75 on the Wechsler-Bellevue and lower on the performance part than on the verbal. He also tested low on spatial and manipulative tests. Yet he aspired to become a diamond-cutter. His older brother was one and he thought he could be too. He was asked about his schooling and began to speak of his grades—he was poor in mathematics but felt he was good in other subjects. He stated the teachers gave him low marks because they did not like him.

When asked about his work he also gave excuses for being fired. He was asked to explain further and in doing so told of finding it difficult to learn many operations and to follow directions. It was suggested that perhaps the work was too difficult and he accepted the

[7] From the files of the Lenox Hill Consulting Service, Inc., N.Y., N.Y., with changes in identifying data.

suggestion. It was then possible to go back to his school work and he admitted he was always very slow to catch on and that he was not too smart. He was told the tests indicated the same thing but that he might be able to learn to do some simple work. He accepted the test results and the suggestion about simple jobs.

In other instances where the suggestions are not accepted as readily, more direct advice and persuasion may have to be used to make the person recognize his abilities. Williamson (13) summarizes methods of using diagnostic evidence under the headings of direct advising, persuasiveness, and explanation. These methods are used after "adequate analysis and diagnosis have been made" and after "the student has been prepared for advice" by interviewing. According to Williamson, the counselor must also be alert to the client's reactions and modify his methods in accordance with them.

He recommends direct advising for "tough-minded" students who insist upon frank opinions of choice of action as well as for those "who persist with an activity or a choice which the counselor has reason to believe will lead to serious failure and loss of morale." However, in the latter case the counselor acts as an adviser, not as a dictator.

The persuasive method is recommended when the "case data indicate quite definitely that one choice is to be preferred over all alternatives." The counselor does not dominate but gives "the evidence in such a reasonable and logical manner that the student is able to anticipate clearly the probable outcomes of alternative actions."

The explanatory method is considered by Williamson to be "the most complete and satisfactory." It may need many interviews. In this method, the counselor explains the diagnostic data and points out where the student may use his potentialities. An example is given by Williamson:

> As far as I can tell from this evidence of aptitude, your chances of getting into the medical school are poor; but your possibilities in business seem to be much more promising. These are the reasons for my conclusions: You have done consistently failing work in zoology and chemistry. You do not have the pattern of interests characteristic of successful doctors which probably indicates you would not find the practice of medicine congenial. On the other hand you do have an

excellent grasp of mathematics, good general ability, and the interests of an accountant. These facts seem to me to argue for your selection of accountancy as an occupation. Suppose you think about these facts and my suggestion, talk to your father about my suggestion, see Professor Blank who teaches accounting, and return next Tuesday at 10 o'clock to tell me what conclusion you have reached. I shall not attempt to influence you because I want you to choose an occupation congenial to you. But I do urge that you weigh the evidence pro and con for your choice and for the one I suggest. Remember that we must both look for evidence of aptitude to succeed and that a mere desire to succeed is not sufficient evidence of the required aptitude.[8]

Interviews will necessarily follow this explanation of the diagnostic evidence. The evidence can be considered as "grist for the mill." In conducting subsequent interviews the counselor will be aware of the attitudes and personality needs of the client and gear his interview techniques accordingly.

Non-directive counselors who use tests in vocational counseling also emphasize alertness to the client's reactions to the tests, but use only the non-directive technique of interviewing. Bixler and Bixler (2) point out how the interpretation of tests can help the client express feelings and attitudes. "The primary factor is to divulge information, but not to encourage or discourage the client in other ways."[9]

They give an illustration from an interview with a crippled boy in engineering school. He was below average in two college aptitude tests and in mathematics and English. The illustration from the interview follows:

I briefly outlined his standing in relation to other students, pointing out that he rated above average in some things but below average in quite a number of things, especially some which seemed rather important. He then asked if that meant he had a 50-50 chance, and I asked him how he thought it stood and he said he felt it was less than a 50-50 chance. I explained that that was the way it seemed and mentioned that he was pretty disappointed, which was quite obvious. He said, "It's funny." I said, "It's funny in some ways, but it makes

[8] From *How To Counsel Students* by E. G. Williamson. Copyright, 1939. Courtesy of McGraw-Hill Book Co.

[9] *Journal of Clinical Psychology,* 1:186 (1945).

> you feel pretty unhappy, too." He said then that really a better word would be "strange" and that he had always had an uphill fight. Momentarily, he jumped into his personal anxieties and explained that they told him at one time that he would never walk, he would never be able to drive a car, and that he had to try to find those things out. I mentioned that he felt he had to give this a try, too. He said, "Yes. I'm certainly not going to quit."[10]

He was eventually dismissed from the university for poor grades. The Bixlers report that they did not try to dissuade him or to suggest alternatives. They state that it is "unlikely that a fixed and determined goal, no matter how inappropriate, can be altered by this means." Apparently they felt that the client was so determined that nothing could move him. This appears to be a moot point in need of verification. The integration might have been followed through more successfully by other interviewing techniques.

In a later report Bixler and Bixler (3) offer some good points on test interpretation. They recommend among other things giving simple statistical predictions based upon the test data and allowing the client to evaluate the predictions as they are applicable to himself. The following is an example:

> C. There are studies which demonstrate that students' ranks in high school along with the way in which they compare with other entering students in mathematics, are the best indication of how well they will succeed in engineering. Sixty out of one hundred students with scores like yours succeed in engineering. About eighty out of one hundred succeed in the social sciences (names several). The difference is due to the fact that study shows the college aptitude test to be important in social sciences, along with high school work, instead of mathematics.
>
> S. But I want to go into engineering. I think I'd be happier there. Isn't that important too?
>
> C. You are disappointed with the way the test came out, but you wonder if your liking engineering better isn't pretty important?
>
> S. Yes, but the tests say I would do better in sociology or something like that. (Disgusted.)
>
> C. That disappoints you, because it's the sort of thing you don't like.

[10] *Loc. Cit.*

S. Yes, I took an interest test, didn't I? (C nods.) What about it?

C. You wonder if it doesn't agree with the way you feel. The test shows that most people with your interests enjoy engineering and are not likely to enjoy social sciences.—

S. (Interrupts.) But the chances are against me in engineering, aren't they?

C. It seems pretty hopeless to be interested in engineering under these conditions, and yet you're not quite sure.

S. No, that's right. I wonder if I might not do better in the thing I like—maybe my chances are best in engineering anyway. I've been told how tough college is, and I've been afraid of it. The tests are encouraging. There isn't much difference after all—Being scared makes me overdo the difference.[11]

The subject decided to go into engineering.

The statistical prediction method of interpreting tests is impersonal and objective and would seem to be an effective way of presenting test evidence. Whether to follow it only by the non-directive interviewing method is another question. We would prefer to be more flexible; we advocate the non-authoritarian method of interviewing.

It is important to recognize that the integration of tests and interviews must be achieved if the client is to benefit from counseling. Often, both tests and the counseling interview present a very difficult learning situation for the client, since he is learning about himself in relation to the world of work. Clients sometimes find it difficult to terminate the relationship with the counselor and prefer to have some written report about the experience. Stone and Simos (11) describe a technique known as "Counseling Letters" which attempts to supplement the interview and leave the client with a permanent record. Such a record may help him subsequently in reviewing the mutually agreed upon possibilities, and may also be of some use in subsequent guidance, training, and work situations.

It should be emphasized that these letters are not variations of test profiles but rather are integrative interpretations of test interview results.

The figure given on the following page is a sample of such a counseling letter.

---

[11] *Educational and Psychological Measurement*, 6:143 (1946).

Mr. J. F. T.
St. Paul, Minnesota

Dear Mr. T.:

The following is a report of the results of the interviews and tests which you took at the Employment Research Center. We hope that this information will be helpful to you in seeking work or in preparing yourself for future employment by pointing out a number of job possibilities for which you seem to be fitted.

Work for Which You Appear Qualified by Experience and Training

On the basis of your work experience alone, your best immediate job opportunities would appear to be in work such as wrapper and packer or in the operation of some factory machines. You could also qualify as a painter's helper, plumber's helper, or possibly as a truck driver.

Job Opportunities Open to You on the Basis of Your Measured Capacities

An analysis of the results of your tests indicate that you have excellent mechanical ability and superior ability to work at jobs requiring the rapid and accurate use of your fingers and small tools. Your clerical ability is only fair, and it is not advised that you seek training for, nor employment in office work. It is also recommended that you do not attempt work as a salesman. Your interests are similar to those of men who are successful skilled tradesmen, as for example, men who work as painters, carpenters, printers, and machinists. These results indicate that you should be successful as a semi-skilled worker in a factory or working at machines which would not involve a long training period. The suggestions made in the preceding paragraph are further indicated by the test results.

Work for Which You Can Qualify if You Secure Additional Training

It is strongly recommended that you secure additional training in some trade. You should investigate the possibility of taking courses at the St. Paul Vocational School. Since there is considerable demand for these courses, however, you may find that you can obtain training more quickly in a reliable private trade school such as Dunwoody Institute in Minneapolis. Your excellent mechanical ability indicates very strongly that you should secure training in some trade, such as machinist, mechanic, plumber, or in some other mechanical trade in which you may have a special interest.

Use of This Letter

You may use this letter when applying for a job if you wish your prospective employer to know of your recommendations. If a prospective employer is intersted in obtaining additional interpretations of the interviews and tests, we shall be glad to supply further information at his request.

Very truly yours,

(signed)

Member of Research Staff

Reprinted from Journal of Applied Psychology *by permission of the American Psychological Association*

A COUNSELING LETTER

Summary

The counseling process is dynamic. It has two major tools, tests and interviews, and these must be integrated. The tests have primarily a diagnostic function, while the interview helps an individual gain insight about himself and his problems.

Tests should be introduced only after the interview has proceeded sufficiently. Their introduction will then be more meaningful to the client. They can be introduced by explaining their function in the total counseling process; and it should be mentioned during the introduction that they are only one means of obtaining evidence. Interviews must precede and follow them. They can also be introduced by explaining the function of specific tests selected with the participation of the client.

The manner of interpretation of test results is extremely important. It must be governed by understanding of the client's reactions to them. The reactions differ, and the counselor must stand ready to use interviewing techniques in a flexible manner.

In some instances, the interpretation of test results may take place throughout more than one interview—whenever the client asks for them, or when the counselor thinks they may be helpful in further developing the client's self-understanding. The test results may be used for reassurance and to facilitate interpretation of present attitudes and behavior.

Test results may also be integrated in such a way as to allow giving advice in a non-authoritarian manner or to persuade a client to accept one alternative over others, or to explain the data in such a way as to point out with evidence where the client may use his potentialities.

The non-directive counselors also use tests in vocational counseling. They also emphasize alertness to the individual's feelings and attitudes. They recommend the interpretation of tests in statistical predictive terms. This is done in an impersonal and objective manner with the counselor ready to continue the interview non-directively as the client evaluates the predictions in relation to himself. The statistical predictions seem valuable as a way of interpreting tests. However, the interview method need not be only non-directive but should rather be non-authoritarian.

To supplement the interview and allow for the client to have an integrated permanent record of the counseling experience of testing and interview, "Counseling Letters" appears to have some value.

Bibliography

1. Balinsky, B., "Vocational Counseling in Rehabilitation," *Bulletin of the Menninger Clinic,* 9:98–106 (1945).
2. Bixler, R. H. and V. H. Bixler, "Clinical Counseling in Vocational Guidance," *Journal of Clinical Psychology,* 1:186–192 (1945).
3. ———, "Test Interpretation in Vocational Counseling," *Educational and Psychological Measurement,* 6:145–155 (1946).
4. Bordin, E. S., and R. H. Bixler, "Test Selection: A Process of Counseling," *Educational and Psychological Measurement,* 6:361–373 (1946).
5. Candee, B., in J. F. Culbert and H. R. Smith, *Counseling Young Workers.* New York: Vocational Service for Juniors, 1939.
6. Culbert, J. F., "Counseling Young Workers," *The Child,* 10:116 (1946).
7. ———, and H. R. Smith, *Counseling Young Workers.* New York: Vocational Service for Juniors, 1939.
8. Friend, J. G., and E. A. Haggard, "Work Adjustment in Relation to Family Background," *Applied Psychology Monographs,* 16:1–150 (1948).
9. Kilby, R. W., "Some Vocational Counseling Methods," *Educational and Psychological Measurement,* 9:173–191 (1949).
10. Small, L., "Jobs and Self-esteem," Reprinted from Careers in Sight, *Better Times,* June 4, 1948.
11. Stone, C. H., and I. Simos, "Follow-up Study of Personal Counseling versus Counseling by Letter," *Journal of Applied Psychology,* 32:408–414 (1948).
12. Super, D. E., and D. A. Brophy, "The Role of the Interview in Vocational Diagnosis." *Occupations,* 19:323–328 (1941).
13. Williamson, E. G., *How to Counsel Students.* New York: McGraw-Hill, 1939.

12

STATISTICS IN TEST INTERPRETATION

STATISTICS is a useful tool. It brings order into data and allows one to compare test scores and see more clearly the relationships among them. Correct test interpretation demands basic understanding of statistical terms and concepts. This chapter will be concerned with discussing certain basic statistical concepts, not with calculation. For extensive treatment of statistics, Edwards (4), Garrett (6), Lindquist (8), or Peatman (11), as well as others, can be studied.

When an array of scores is obtained for a client, certain pertinent questions can be asked. Where does he stand in comparison with others? How much better or worse is he? What do the scores mean for the prediction of work or school success? How certain is the prediction? Do combinations of tests increase the certainty of prediction? What do the tests measure? These answers lie partly in statistics. The scores are also due to motivational and emotional factors; these important matters must be taken into consideration. In any event, to answer the questions at least in part, it is necessary to know something about measures of central tendency and of variability, about percentiles and standard scores, about the significance of differences between the averages of groups, about correlation, multiple correlation, and factor analysis.

Let us take the case of a client whom we shall call John and assume that he has taken a battery of eight tests. The tests included were the Wechsler-Bellevue, the A.C.E., the Bennett Mechanical Comprehension, the Minnesota Placing and Turning, the Revised Minnesota Paper Form Board, the Multiphasic, and the Kuder. The scores obtained are reported as follows:

Wechsler-Bellevue	*Raw-Score*	*Weighted Score*
Comprehension	15	13
Arithmetic	9	12
Information	17	12
Digit Span	13	11
Similarities	13	13
Verbal Total		61
Picture Arrangement	14	12
Picture Completion	12	12
Block Design	33	15
Object Assembly	25	16
Digit Symbol	56	13
Performance Total		68
Total		129

American Council on Education (A.C.E.)	
Total Score	130 points
Q-score (Quantitative)	60 points
L-score (Linguistic)	70 points
Placing Test	201 seconds
Turning Test	141 seconds
Bennett Mechanical Comprehension Test	57 points
Revised Minnesota Paper Formboard Test	57 points
Minnesota Multiphasic Personality Inventory	
Hypochondriasis (H_s)	3 points
Depression (D)	15 points
Hysteria (H_y)	9 points
Psychopathic Deviate (P_d)	0 points
Interest (M_f)	8 points
Paranoia (P_a)	5 points
Psychasthenia (P_t)	2 points
Schizophrenia (S_c)	4 points
Hypomania (M_a)	6 points
Kuder Preference Record	
Mechanical	97 points
Computational	45 points
Scientific	85 points
Persuasive	68 points
Artistic	52 points

Literary	50 points
Musical	16 points
Social Service	51 points
Clerical	32 points

From the test results as given very little can be said unless more is known about certain statistical concepts. It is impossible to interpret these results in terms of high or low. Nor can one know from the scores as given on which tests John did better than others. However, knowledge of statistical concepts will help to clear up the confusion.

Measures of central tendency

The arithmetic mean or average, the median, and the mode are measures of central tendency. They locate the most typical score in a group; and they identify a specific score as good or bad, depending upon whether such a score is above or below the average. A look at all the scores made by John conveys nothing without reference to certain statistical landmarks. The measures of central tendency are among the most frequently used.

The mean. The arithmetic mean, also called the average, is the most widely known of the measures. It is the sum of the scores made by a sampling of people divided by the number of people. Each score is given equal weight, each score contributing to the sum and accounting for one in the total number of people. A simple illustration is John's set of scores on the Wechsler-Bellevue. The weighted scores on the verbal part are 13, 12, 12, 11, and 13. The average or mean verbal score is the sum of the 5 scores divided by 5, or 12.2. The mean is the most reliable of the measures of central tendency, and useful if other statistics like the coefficient of correlation are to be computed.

The median. The median is the score made by the middle person or item in a series when the scores are arrayed in order of amount. It is the point above which and below which half the measures fall. The median is to be employed where there are extreme scores that would throw off the mean. For instance, if the scores were 4 on digit span but 13, 12, 12, and 13 on the other subtests, then the median should be calculated since it would more nearly typify the performance of the group. John might not have been paying close attention at the time the digit span was given. That score would not be representative and could therefore be disregarded in the calculation of the average. If it were to be included, the median should be taken and it would be 12, the middle score (4, 12, 12, 13, 13) of the five, one lower, one tied and two higher.

The mode. The mode is the score that is made by most people or that score which occurs most frequently. If the 10 subtest weighted scores on the Wechsler-Bellevue are examined in terms of frequency of occurrence, it will be seen that John obtained 11 once, 12 four times, 13 three times, and 15 and 16 once each. Twelve is therefore the mode since it occurred most often. This is a crude measure, used if only an approximation is needed.

Measures of variability

The range, the interquartile range, and the standard deviation are measures of variability, of dispersion about the measure of central tendency. They help one to judge more meaningfully how much a score varies from the central tendency. Their boundaries are additional landmarks. Like mileposts on a road, they help tell how distant the score is from the central location.

The range. The range is a crude measure of variability. Where there is a scarcity of data and where the size of the deviation need not be known too accurately, the range can be used. It reports merely the distance between the lowest and highest scores made by a group on a test. The range of one group of four-year male college students on the A.C.E. may be from 5 to 189 (9). If the mean is 105, it is clear that John's score of 130 is quite a bit better than the average; but it is not really clear how much better it is. Scores between 130 and 189 may have been obtained by very few people.

The interquartile range. The interquartile range includes the scores made by the middle 50 per cent of the people. It is the difference in scores between two specific points in the distribution. At one extreme is the score made by the person below whom there are 25 per cent of the scores; at the other end is the score made by the person below whom there are 75 per cent of the scores (and above whom are 25 per cent of the scores). In other words the interquartile range corresponds to the middle 50 per cent of the scores: 25 per cent of the scores are below and 25 per cent above. On the A.C.E. for four-year male college students the interquartile range is 52–123. This range gives an additional reference for interpreting John's point score. His A.C.E. score of 130 is better than at least 75 per cent of the scores or in the highest 25 per cent. The interquartile range is to be used for data with extreme scores. It can justifiably be used as the measure of variability when the median is reported as the measure of central tendency. Since the median is the score made by the person at the mid-point when the scores are arrayed in order from low to high, the interquartile range has 25 per cent of scores below and 25 per cent of the scores above the median.

The standard deviation. The standard deviation or sigma (σ) is the most reliable and most often used of the measures of variability. It measures the amount of deviation above and below the mean. A sampling of four-year male college students reported by Thurstone and Thurstone (9) yields a standard deviation of 25.14 points on the A.C.E. This means that one standard deviation equals 25.14 points, two standard deviations equals 50.28 points and three equals 75.42 points. These may be in either direction from the mean. The mean is 105; therefore, one standard deviation above the mean $(+1) = 105 + 25.14$, or 130.14; one standard deviation below the mean $(-1) = 105 - 25.14$, or 79.86; two standard deviations above equals $105 + 50.28$ or 155.28, and so on. John's score is 130 points. He is therefore approximately 1.0 standard deviation units above the average ($130 - 105$, divided by 25.14).

His Placing Test score is 201 seconds. What is the size of his deviation from the mean? In order to determine this it is necessary to know the mean and the standard deviation. On a set of industrial norms (3) the average for men on the Placing Test is 214 seconds, and the standard deviation as calculated by us from the data given is 14.82. Since a low score is desirable, he is therefore .88 standard deviation above the average of the male industrial group; 201 minus 214, divided by 14.82.

Comparability of scores

The scores reported for John are called "raw" scores except for the Wechsler-Bellevue weighted scores, which are standard scores. The raw scores are expressed in different kinds of units, either points, units of time, or errors. The points made on different tests do not have the same meaning. The raw scores must therefore be transmuted into units that have comparable or similar meaning from test to test. One can say the score on one test is better than that on another only if there is a basis for comparison. The measures of central tendency locate a score near the center that can be used as a point for making comparisons, but this single point is crude for such purposes. The boundaries of the variability measures add more reference points above and below the measure of central tendency. These allow for closer reading of position and more refined means of comparison among scores. The percentile and standard scores add still more reference points. In fact, a percentile and a standard score can be computed for every raw score in a distribution.

The percentile. A percentile is a point below which a certain percentage of the population scores. If the scores made by a sampling of people are distributed from lowest to highest and 20 per cent of the people make up to a certain score, the person who makes that score is better than the 20 per cent of the people who failed to reach the score. Such a person has a score equivalent to the 20th percentile. The percentiles range from 0 to 100 per cent of the number of people in the population. On the Placing Test (3) 248 seconds is at the 0 percentile. In the original standardization group nobody fails to reach the score. In practice a rare person may fail to reach it. Then any score slower than 248 seconds is assigned 0 percentile. Percentiles are easy to compute and relatively easy to understand. However, one major difficulty is involved in their use; it can be better understoood after the concept of the standard score has been discussed.

John's Placing Test score is 201 seconds. His percentile score based on the male industrial group referred to above is 84. This means that 84 per cent of the males in the group failed to reach 201 seconds; and, conversely, 16 per cent did better. The 84th percentile ranking means that he is as good as or better than 84 per cent of the male industrial group who have taken that test. He scored 141 seconds on the Turning Test. His percentile ranking when he is compared with both men and women in the industrial group (there are no sex differences) is 95; he is, therefore, as good as or better than 95 per cent of that group. Notice that he was at the 95th percentile on the Turning Test and at the 84th percentile on the Placing Test. It can be concluded that he did better on the former test.

When percentile norms are derived from different sorts of groups, however, then this must be considered in interpreting scores. By way of illustration, John's score on the Bennett Mechanical Comprehension Test is 57 points. According to the percentile norms supplied by Bennett (1), 57 is at the 95th percentile for Engineering School Freshmen, at the 99th percentile for technical high school seniors, and at the 85th percentile for candidates for engineering positions. In this case all the percentiles are high, but they are different for the same score when derived from different groups. The psychologist and counselor are required to use their judgment in referring to the most appropriate percentile table.

Percentiles are actually extensions of the median and the quartiles. The median is the 50th percentile. The lower end of the interquartile range, quartile 1, is the 25th percentile; the upper end, quartile 3, the 75th percentile. Percentiles include all the scores. Where the number of people in a sampling is small, quintiles (units of five percentiles) or deciles (units of 10 percentiles) are used. This procedure is followed because a single percentile does not make for a real difference in consecutive raw scores. If 50 people are in a sampling, 1 per cent accounts for only .5 of a person, 2 per cent for 1, 3 per cent for 1.5, and so forth. The scores corresponding to the percentages of people may be the same in such cases of small total population. A larger percentile unit, 5 or 10, is needed before differences in test score may occur.

The standard score. The standard score is a better norm or standard of reference than the percentile. It is derived from the mean and the standard deviation, which are, respectively, the most reliable measures of central tendency and variability. The standard score actually tells the position of any raw score in a distribution if the shape of the distribution is known. The raw score is expressed in units of the standard deviation in relation to the mean. When the standard deviation was previously presented, John's raw scores on the A.C.E. and the Placing Test were converted into standard deviation units. His A.C.E. score was 1.0 standard deviation unit above the average; his Placing Test score, .88 standard deviation unit above the average. He therefore did better on the A.C.E. If his friend got raw scores below the means of both tests his converted scores would be negative and lower than John's. The 1.0 and .88 are actually standard scores. However, to avoid negative numbers and decimals, various procedures for transforming standard scores to positive whole numbers have been devised. Transformed standard scores used to circumvent decimals and negative numbers are the T-scores (9), and the scores devised by Hull (7). Various standard scores are shown in the accompanying figure.

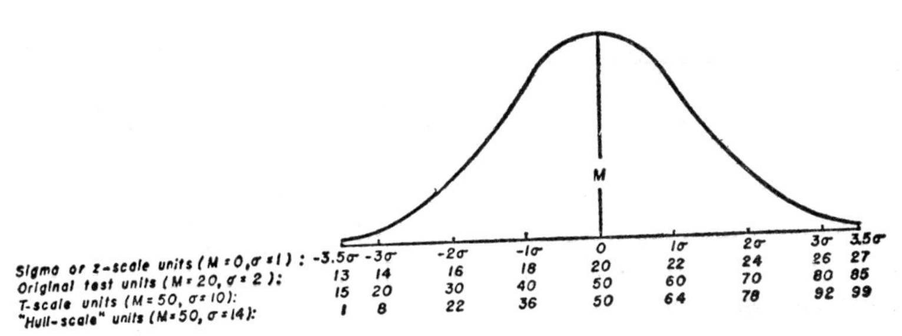

From A Simplified Guide to Statistics, *Rev. Copyright, 1938, 1946, by G. Milton Smith, published by Rinehart & Co., Inc.*

TEST SCORES EXPRESSED IN THREE STANDARD SCORE EQUIVALENTS: Z-SCORES, T-SCORES, AND HULL-SCORES

When the standard scores shown in this illustration of the normal distribution curve are interpreted, the 40 and 36 are one standard deviation below the mean and therefore signify the same distance. T-scores of 70 and Hull-scores of 78 are two standard deviations above the mean and therefore equally distant. This is true in spite of the difference in numerical value. Since the standard scores derived directly from the mean and the standard deviation give plus and minus values expressed in fractions or decimals, the T-scores and Hull-scores are to be preferred. In the T-scale the average is set at 50 with the standard deviation at 10. This means a score of 60 is 1 standard deviation above the mean, 65 is 1.5 standard deviations above, 40 is one standard deviation below the mean, and 35 is 1.5 below the mean. Since plus and minus three standard deviation units takes in most of the people in the distribution (997 out of 1000) and 3.5 takes in almost all (999 out of 1000) the range of most scores will go from 15 to 85 or 3.5 σ above and below the mean. The transformed standard scores used by Hull broaden the range of scores by setting the standard deviation equal to 14, leaving the mean conveniently at 50. The range for 3.5 σ above and below the mean is then from 1 to 99. This is more in agreement with the common usage of numbers.

It is to be noted that there are other systems of transforming standard scores. For example, Wechsler in his test uses a system of weighted scores whereby the average on any of his subtests is assigned the score of 10, and one standard deviation is assigned the score of 3. This client's performance of 13 on the comprehension subtest means that he has a weighted score 1 σ above average. On the object assembly, his weighted score of 16 means that he is 2 σ above average. If he had a score of 7, it would have meant that he was 1 σ below average on that test.

Another example is provided by the Army General Classification Test. In this test a system of weighted scores is used whereby the average score is assigned the score of 100 and one standard deviation is assigned the score of 20. If the client has been given this test and he received a weighted score of 130, he would be 1.5 standard deviation units above the average. If he had obtained a score of 80, which in his case is highly unlikely, he would be 1 σ below the average.

The standard score is statistically more accurate than the percentile score. For instance, near the average a difference of five percentile points usually signifies a lesser difference between two raw scores than the same difference does at some distance from the average.

John's raw score on the Revised Minnesota Paper Form Board is 57 points. When compared with first-year male engineering students it is equivalent to a percentile ranking of 94. A raw score of 64, seven points higher, rates a percentile score of 99. If John's friend received a raw score of 42, his percentile equivalent would be 45. A raw score of 43, the median, is equivalent to a percentile score of 50. Thus a difference of five percentile points around the average accounts for a difference of one point in raw score, whereas the same difference in percentile points much above the mean accounts for a difference of seven points in raw score. The differences in percentile scores, in other words, do not correspond to uniform differences in test scores. Because of this fact, it is incorrect mathematically to average percentile scores, even though this averaging is sometimes done.

Standard scores and transformed standard scores can be averaged without bringing in the same type of error, because differences in standard score are numerically proportional to differences in raw score. The Minnesota Multiphasic uses the T-score, a form of standard score. John received a raw score of three points on the Hypochondriasis Scale. This is equivalent to a 47 T-score. The T-scores are uniform throughout the scale, each raw score point accounting for two T-score points with only infrequent exceptions due to rounding off decimals. His friend, with a score of 4, would then receive a 49 T-score; another friend with 5, a T-score of 51, and so on. The same holds true for all the scales on this test.

Within a normal distribution, standard scores and percentiles bear a known relationship to each other and so can be converted into one another. Standard scores can be converted into percentiles by means of percentile equivalents for various standard scores. Table 14 gives some of the percentile equivalents.

The Hull-score of 36 is one standard deviation unit below the average. The area of the curve included between minus one standard deviation and the average is equal to 34.13 per cent of the total population. This means the Hull-score of 36 is better than 16 per cent of the people. Similarly, minus one standard deviation is equivalent to the 16th percentile. The Hull-score of 64 is one standard deviation above the mean. One standard deviation above or below the mean

TABLE 14

CONVERSION OF STANDARD SCORES INTO PERCENTILES

Standard Score Below Average	Percentile Equivalent (approx.)
−3.5	0.
−3.0	0.1
−2.5	1.0
−2.0	2.3
−1.5	6.7
−1.0	16.0
−0.5	30.8
0.0	50.
Above Average	
+0.5	69.2
+1.0	84.0
+1.5	93.3
+2.0	97.7
+2.5	99.0
+3.0	99.9
+3.5	100.0

includes 34.13 per cent of the total population. However, this score is better than that made by 84 per cent of the people (50 per cent up to the average and 34 per cent above the average). Each standard deviation unit includes a specific percentage of the area of the total curve, and the conversion from standard score to percentile can be made directly.

Statistical significance of difference between means. It is frequently valuable to know whether the difference between means in two groups is dependable or is to be attributed to chance or peculiarity of sampling. A test may be given to two groups differing in some way, such as degree of education, age, sex, subject matter studied, or experience. If, in these two groups, a difference between the averages is obtained, the question is whether such a difference can be attributed to the variable being investigated or whether the difference is due to chance.

For example, a group previously having a course in physics obtains a higher average score on the Bennett Mechanical Comprehension Test than a group that did not have such a course. The problem is whether this difference can be attributed to the effect that a previous course in physics has on the test performance, or whether the difference may be due to chance and therefore not be statistically significant. This question can be answered by testing for the significance of the difference between the averages of the two groups.

Bennett (1) cites a study in which this was done. The point at issue was whether or not previous training in physics had a real effect on the scores made on the Mechanical Comprehension Test. The difference between the averages was not found to be statistically significant, even though the physics group did have a higher average score. This finding means that a previous course in physics has not been proved to have an appreciable effect upon the score obtained in this test. However, other samplings may show a significant difference between means. As Mintz (10) demonstrates, a non-significant difference between means proves only that the variable, in this instance the physics training, may or may not have had an effect. It does not disprove the hypothesis that physics training may make an appreciable difference.

The test for significance or reliability of the difference between means uses the critical ratio or "t." In the ratio, the numerator is the difference between means, and the denominator is the standard error of the difference.

When a difference occurs between two means it is necessary to investigate the possibility that this difference may have arisen by chance and that in a population of infinite size no difference would be found. Were it possible to test an infinite population the difference might be zero (no difference at all). The critical ratio or "t" enables one to know the probability of reaching or exceeding a difference as large as the one obtained in the particular sampling if the true difference is really zero. In other words, is the obtained difference really significant? This can be answered only in terms of probability, and not absolutely.

The higher the critical ratio or "t," the less likely it is that the difference could occur by random sampling; conversely, the more confident one can be that the difference is dependable. The level of confidence is expressed in decimals or percentages; for example, a .05 or 5 per cent level of confidence. The level of confidence means the probability or chances in 100 that a value of "t" as large as the one obtained could occur on the basis of chance variation in the sampling. Thus a critical ratio of 1.96 has a level of confidence of .05 or 5 per cent and would occur only 5 times in 100 on the basis of chance variation in a large sampling from the same population. In other words, 95 times in a theoretical 100 chances this difference would not be due to chance. This ratio is therefore considered significant. Higher critical ratios offer even more certainty that the difference between the means is dependable. Table 15 gives the criteria of significance of the critical ratio or "t" in a normal distribution.

TABLE 15

CRITERIA OF SIGNIFICANCE OR CONFIDENCE LEVELS OF "t" IN A NORMAL DISTRIBUTION*

Level of "t"	*Level of Confidence*	*Rough Conclusion*
Below 1.65	Below .10 or 10% level	Insignificant
1.65	At the .10 or 10% level	Insignificant
1.96	At the .05 or 5% level	Significant
2.33	At the .02 or 2% level	Significant
2.58	At the .01 or 1% level	Very significant
2.81	At the .005 or 0.5% level	Very significant
Above 2.81	Beyond the .005 or 0.5% level	Very significant

* From *Fundamental Statistics in Psychology and Education* by J. P. Guilford. Courtesy of McGraw-Hill Book Co.

There are other matters to be considered in testing for the significance of the difference between means. These arc the size of the samplings and the question whether or not a correlation exists between the two sets of scores. If a sampling is below 30 in number, different probability tables applicable for small numbers must be used (5).

The coefficient of correlation

The coefficient of correlation is a measure of the degree of relationship existing between two variables. The variables may be related in similar or dissimilar directions. The coefficient tells how closely one test is related to another or to a criterion; for example, test performance to job success. It tells the degree of relationship between any two variables, whether tests, judgments of success or of personality characteristics, years of work experience, or others. If one correlates two tests, the correlation tells how often people with relatively high scores on one test tend to have correspondingly high scores on the other. If the correlation is high and positive, high scores on one test usually go with high ones on the other; if the correlation is negative, high scores usually combine with low ones on the other test; when the correlation is zero there is no recognizable rule.

The coefficient of correlation ranges from +1.00 through 0.00 to —1.00. Between 0.00 and ±1.00 the coefficient may be any size; for example, +.62, +.89, +.22, —.14, —.44, —.02. These are not to be misconstrued as percentages. They demonstrate the amount of overlap and can serve to indicate the improvement over chance relationship. A correlation of 0.00 represents no relationship at all, in other words a pure chance relationship. A correlation in either plus or minus direction indicates a relationship that is considered to be better than chance. Plus 1.00 is a perfect correlation with both variables always becoming larger or smaller in the same direction. Minus 1.00 is also a perfect correlation; but as one variable becomes larger, the other becomes smaller.

A group of individuals may be given the Placing Test and the Turning Test. All individuals have two scores, one on each test. One person may have the second highest score on the Placing Test and the eighth highest on the Turning; another may be 16th on the Placing and 24th on the Turning, and so on. The relationship of one test with the other is obtained from the plottings of the scores made by all the people in the group. A correlation does not imply a cause and effect relationship, for the scores made on each test may be due to a third factor common to both tests or to selective factors. The point is that the two tests have something in common.

In measuring validity, the coefficient of correlation is frequently used. Here each member of the group has test scores as well as a rating on work or school, depending upon what the test is thought to be valid for. The degree of the relationship between the test scores and the ratings is the measure of validity. If the two variables have enough in common, the test may be used as a predictor of success in work or school.

The coefficient of correlation is also used in measuring reliability. If the same test is repeated after a period of time, or a duplicate form given, then in either case two scores are obtained for each person in the group. Since the tests were the same or duplicate forms, the correlation must be high for the tests to be considered reliable.

Interpreting the coefficient of correlation. How high is high? How low is low? What can be said about the relationships expressed by the coefficients of correlation? Are the same criteria of interpretation used for groups as well as for individuals? How well can success on a job be predicted if a test score and the correlation with the criterion of success on the job is known?

A rough method of interpretation is the following:

Correlation coefficients from 0.00 to $\pm.20$ signify a negligible relation; from $\pm.20$ to $\pm.40$ a slight relation; from $\pm.40$ to $\pm.70$ a marked relation; from $\pm.70$ to ±1.00 a high relation.

In counseling, individual predictions must be made. These demand high correlation coefficients, because correlations express relationships between two groups and when the correlation is not perfect individual exceptions to the relationship occur. The lower the correlation the greater the number of individual exceptions, and accordingly the higher the error in individual prediction. A correlation of .70 may be substantial in making predictions about the relationships between tests or groups. For an individual it leaves much to be desired, since any one individual in the group may be the exception to the relationship.

The efficiency of prediction for individuals improves over chance as the correlation increases. A correlation of .866 between two variables is a 50 per cent improvement over chance, not an 86.6 per cent improvement. If the correlation were zero it would be a pure chance relationship. If .99, it would be 86 per cent better than chance. Reliability of tests should be at least .90, which would be a 56 per cent improvement over chance. Validity ought, theoretically, to be high to reduce guesswork. However, the difficulties with the criterion and the complexity of psychological measurement make high validities quite rare. This rarity means, of course, that too great faith cannot be put in any single test for predicting the fate of an individual. More tests and the interview may improve upon the validity of the counseling.

Bingham (2) refers to another statistical concept useful in interpreting test scores. This is concerned with the prediction of criterion performance when the standard score on a test and the correlation between the test and criterion are known. If the correlation between a test and an activity used as the criterion is calculated, it is possible to predict the performance in that activity when the standard score on the test is known.

If the correlation was calculated to be +1.00, the person's most probable performance rating would be perfectly predicted. The most probable performance rating estimated from the standard score on the test regresses toward the average performance as the correlation diminishes to zero. Thus, if John made a test score that was two standard deviation units above the mean (and therefore the standard score was known), and the correlation between the test and criterion was .75, the most probable performance on the criterion would be 1.5 σ above its mean. If the correlation was .50, the most probable performance would be 1 σ above the mean of the criterion. If .25 it would be 0.5 σ above the mean. Finally, if the correlation was 0.0 the most probable performance would be the average performance on the criterion.

A high correlation between two variables is necessary to accurately predict the performance on one variable given the standard score on the other variable. Super (12) very adequately elaborated on this problem.

Critical scores. A variation of the correlation technique that has had use in vocational psychology leads to the concept of the critical score. Often the critical score is obtained from an analysis of the plottings in a scattergram. It is a more crude measure of relationship than the correlation coefficient; but interestingly enough it has practical value, since it expresses directly the percentages of people who obtain scores defined as good, bad, and so on. As a step in computing the correlation coefficient, the two variables are plotted in a scatter-

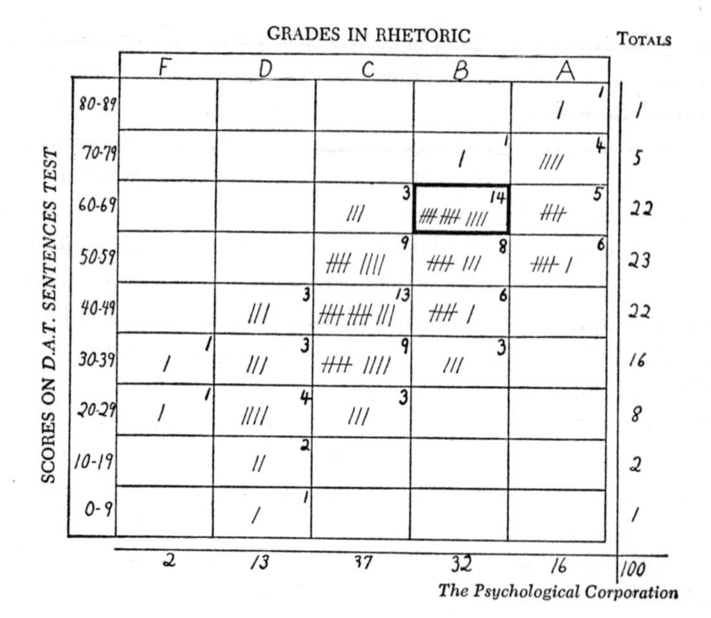

The Psychological Corporation

SCATTERGRAM TO ESTABLISH CRITICAL SCORE

Expectancy grid showing how students' grades in Rhetoric and previously-earned scores on the *DAT Sentences Test* are tallied in appropriate cells. (Data from Kansas State Teachers College; grade of F = failure, no grade of E given; N = freshman girls; mean test score = 48.58, S.D. = 15.2, r = .71).

Total No.	*Number receiving each grade* F	D	C	B	A	*Test Scores*	*Per cent receiving each grade* F	D	C	B	A	*Total Per cent*
1					1	80-89					100	100
5				1	4	70-79				20	80	100
22			3	14	5	60-69			14	63	23	100
23			9	8	6	50-59			39	35	26	100
22		3	13	6		40-49		14	59	27		100
16	1	3	9	3		30-39	6	19	56	19		100
8	1	4	3			20-29	13	50	37			100
2		2				10-19		100				100
1		1				0-9		100				100
100	2	13	37	32	16							

The Psychological Corporation

EXPECTANCY TABLE BASED UPON SCATTERGRAM

Expectancy table prepared from expectancy grid. The left-hand table summarizes the frequencies as they appear in the original grid. The right-hand table shows these frequencies converted into per cents.

gram. This scattergram itself is useful for analysis of the relationships between the sets of data. Wesman (14) demonstrates this in the two figures on page 366.

The first is a plotting of scores made on the Differential Aptitude Tests (D.A.T.) Sentences Test and grades in rhetoric. For instance, one person received a score of between 80–89 on the Sentences test and a grade of A in rhetoric. A tally is placed in the upper right-hand corner. Fourteen people received scores of 60–69 on the test and a grade of B in rhetoric. There are fourteen tallies in the cell which is blocked out. The second figure shows the number and per cent receiving each grade. Five people made scores between 70–79. Of these, four, or 80 per cent, made a grade of A; one, or 20 per cent, B. Sixteen made scores between 30–39. Of these, three, or 19 per cent, made a grade of B; nine, or 56 per cent, C; three, or 19 per cent, D; and one, or 6 per cent, F.

It is now easy, when the test score is known, to tell the probability of making a certain grade. For example, those who score between 60–69 on the Sentences test will in the future tend to score better than C in rhetoric. Those who score between 20–29 will tend to score less than C. The best and the poorest can be picked. This technique has application in vocational selection. One can set a certain score, known as the *critical score,* above which most people will be successful and below which most people will be unsuccessful. If the critical score were set at 40, only three people with B grades and 12 people with C grades would have been eliminated; three people with D grades would have been accepted, whereas 70 with grades of C or better would have been accepted and 12 with D and F grades eliminated.

Of course, the reliability may not be too great for each score, because of the small number of cases involved. But with larger sampling reliability becomes greater. The critical score should be re-evaluated from time to time, not only in the light of the additional data gathered but also in view of changes in the employment market.

Multiple correlation. A multiple correlation coefficient is an expression of the relationship between a combination of tests and a criterion. The tests are so combined as to have the maximal correlation with the criterion. A single test, as previously noted, may not yield too high a correlation with the criterion. When other tests are added to make a battery of tests and each one shows some relation with the criterion, then together they may show a higher degree of relationship. This technique has had more use in selection than in counseling, but is useful in both areas. The criterion of success at work can be more readily defined for selection because it involves a specific job. In counseling the criterion is more vague.

Factor analysis

Factor analysis is a statistical tool that allows for the summarization of correlations among many tests. Faced with a large number of correlations, the psychologist would have difficulty in analyzing the various relationships. Factor analysis permits an explanation of relations among numerous tests by the assumption that the tests have in common a few fundamental factors (or measures of ability) that can account for most of the relations. The factors are named on the basis of actual clinical experience. The statistical analysis does not name them; it merely suggests that certain tests measure the same ability—in other words, have a common factor. Identification of the factor is made by clinical analysis of these tests.

In order to make a factor analysis, one must correlate all of the tests with each other. The intercorrelations are arranged in a matrix for convenience, as in Table 16. Looking at the matrix, one cannot easily discern which tests are more closely related than others. One cannot tell how many factors can account for all the tests.

All of these intercorrelations are, so to speak, mathematically whirled about until no more factors can be extracted from them. The number of factors extracted is always smaller than the original number of tests. This is a saving in itself. After the factors are named, the examiner can deal with fewer concepts than before. Not only is the number of factors smaller; the factors are thought to be fundamental to many tests. When the factors are named, they can be used to tell what the tests measure and can make for finer discriminations in terms of what they measure. Table 17 demonstrates the end result of the mathematical whirling and rotation. The tests each have four

TABLE 16

SUMMARY OF INTERTEST CORRELATIONS FOR AGE 25–29 ON 9 TESTS OF WECHSLER-BELLEVUE SCALE

(N=135)

Test	*Compre-hension*	*Informa-tion*	*Arith-metical Reasoning*	*Digit Span*	*Picture Arrange-ment*	*Picture Com-pletion*	*Object Assembly*	*Block Design*	*Substi-tution*
Comprehension		.421	.206	.030	.186	.103	.075	.239	.188
Information	.421		.255	.033	.284	.236	.135	.229	.191
Arithmetical Reasoning	.206	.255		.226	.190	.188	–.104	.070	–.011
Digit Span	.030	.033	.226		.003	.062	–.112	–.017	.227
Picture Arrangement	.186	.284	.190	.003		.180	.059	.363	.134
Picture Completion	.103	.236	.188	.062	.180		.324	.305	.025
Object Assembly	.075	.135	–.104	–.112	.059	.324		.514	.168
Block Design	.239	.229	.070	–.017	.363	.305	.514		.205
Substitution	.188	.191	–.011	.227	.134	.025	.168	.205	

From B. Balinsky, "An Analysis of the Mental Factors of Various Age Groups from Nine to Sixty," ***Genetic Psychology Monographs,*** **23:191–234 (1941), p. 210.**

factors of appreciable size; they are "loaded" differently for each factor. Those tests which have significant loadings in a factor are said to have that factor in common.

TABLE 17

PSYCHOLOGICALLY MEANINGFUL FACTOR LOADINGS OBTAINED FOR AGE 25–29

Test	*A*	*B*	*C*	*D*
Comprehension	.540	.059	.270	.071
Information	.504	.018	.415	.125
Arithmetical Reasoning	.034	.182	.551	–.127
Digit Span	.051	.496	.126	–.106
Picture Arrangement	.244	–.087	.381	.246
Picture Completion	–.085	.115	.403	.379
Object Assembly	.025	.001	–.033	.729
Block Design	.174	–.048	.231	.743
Substitution	.395	.364	–.101	.208

Adapted from B. Balinsky, *op. cit.*, p. 216. The factor analysis was conducted according to L. L. Thurstone's method.

By looking down Column A, it can be seen that three tests, comprehension, information, and substitution, have high factor loadings in A. What makes these tests have high loadings and the others low? There must be something common to them that is not found to a significant extent in the others. To discover what the common factor is, the three tests must be analyzed clinically. Since the two highest are verbal and the other tests are not, the common factor must be verbal. A similar procedure is followed for all factors.

There can be further breakdowns. The common factor is verbal, but do the three tests measure the same aspects of verbal ability? Clinical analysis indicates that they do not. To determine the various aspects of verbal ability it would be necessary to use many other verbal tests, to obtain their intercorrelations, and to factor analyze them. Then certain verbal tests would cling together and have higher loadings in certain factors than others. Clinical analysis of the tests would determine the kinds of verbal ability.

The method of factor analysis can be employed to obtain fewer, possibly fundamental, variables in personality, interest, and other tests. Essentially it is an aid to the understanding of what we are really measuring.

Application of statistical concepts to John's test results

Understanding these various statistical concepts makes it possible to know how well John did on the various tests and to interpret the results: We can now interpret the degree of relationship between the tests he has taken as well as between a test and its criterion. We can also better understand what the tests measure and which tests measure similar functions.

His test battery consists of two intelligence tests, four aptitude tests, a personality test, and an interest test. The scores are not directly comparable because they are in different units. However, the Wechsler-Bellevue has weighted scores for its subtests. These are transformed standard scores. For these subtests the mean is 10 and the standard deviation 3. The A.C.E., the aptitude tests, and the interest test have percentiles available. The Minnesota Multiphasic has T-scores. These are transformed standard scores too. All the tests have norms or standards of reference. However, they are derived from different populations, and this fact must be taken into account in any interpretation.

Since the subtests of the Wechsler-Bellevue are given as transformed standard scores, they can be directly compared. Object Assembly is highest with a weighted score of 16. Then comes Block Design with 15; Comprehension, Similarities, and Digit Symbol with 13 each; Arithmetic, Information, Picture Arrangement, and Picture Completion with 12 each; and finally Digit Span with 11. The weighted scores can be totaled. In this case, the Performance total is higher than the Verbal. The total of all ten subtests is 129. How can we relate the data on this test to the A.C.E. and the tests of aptitude? It is necessary to relate the weighted scores to the percentile scores.

The average for John's age group on the total Wechsler-Bellevue is 98.8; the standard deviation is 19.0. His own score is 129. Therefore he is 1.59 standard deviation units above the average (or, in the 94th percentile). The A.C.E. percentile for the total score of 130 is 84. It must be remembered that the Wechsler-Bellevue is standardized on general population norms and the A.C.E. on a college population. One might expect that a person compared to such a select group would have a lower rating than when compared to a general population. John's percentile score on the verbal part of the Wechsler, where the mean and the standard deviation for his age group are 48.6 and 10.3 respectively, is 88. His percentile score on the performance part, where the mean and the standard deviation for his age group are 50.88 and 10.23, is 95. On the L-part (Linguistic) of the A.C.E., he received a raw score of 70, which is equivalent to a percentile of 72; on the Q-part (Quantitative), a score of 60, which is equivalent to a percentile of 97. Apparently he did less well on the verbal and linguistic parts than on the performance and quantitative parts in both tests. Notice that a higher score on the L-part of the A.C.E. receives a lower percentile than does a lower score on the Q-part. This is probably so because the average of the college population group is higher on the L-part than on the Q-part. Therefore a higher score is needed on the L-part to receive the same percentile as on the Q-part.

The raw score of 201 seconds on the Placing Test is equivalent to a percentile ranking of 84 in a group of industrial workers. The Turning Test score of 141 seconds is equal to the 95th percentile in that group. Both scores are high. The correlation between the two tests is usually not higher than .50. Therefore it is not to be expected that results on both tests will be uniformly high for every individual. In John's case they happen to be. Both tests have been found by factor analysis to measure gross manipulative ability. They also have correlations of the order of .40 with such jobs as those of operators and packers. These correlations are obviously not so substantial as to permit dependable prediction of success on the basis of these tests alone. In fact the high score on the intelligence tests would ordinarily point against success in such jobs.

John's Bennett Mechanical Comprehension Test raw score is 57 points. This would place him in the 95th percentile of male engineering school freshmen. The raw score on the Revised Minnesota Paper Form Board is also 57 points; this score places him in the 94th percentile of male engineering students. These scores are, then, both high. The correlation between the two tests varies with different populations, but occasionally is as high as .50. The two tests then have something in common but do not measure the same things. Both measure spatial ability but each measures it in addition to something else.

The Wechsler-Bellevue Scale has been factor analyzed. Block Design and Object Assembly measure spatial ability. John received the highest scores on these two subtests of the Scale. These scores are in agreement with the high scores on the Bennett and the Revised Minnesota.

The Minnesota Multiphasic makes use of T-scores, to which all the raw scores on the different scales are converted to make them comparable. The Hypochondriasis raw score is three points. This is equivalent to a T-score of 47. The 15 points on the Depression Scale is equivalent to a T-score of 46; the nine points on the Hysteria Scale to 36; the zero points on the Psychopathic Deviate to 14; the eight points on the Interest to 26; the five points on the Paranoia to 41; the two points on the Psychasthenia to 39; the four points on the Schizophrenia to 43; and the six points on the Hypomania to 32. It can be readily seen that the highest raw scores do not correspond to the highest T-scores. The T-scores on the different scales are related to different abnormal personality patterns. It so happens that John's T-scores are all within the normal range so that, according to this test, he is a well-adjusted person.

The Kuder Preference Record employs percentiles to make its various interest areas comparable. For John the 97 points in the Mechanical area is equivalent to a percentile score of 82; the 45 points in the Computational to 84; the 85 points in the Scientific to 85; the 68 in Persuasive to 56; the 52 in Art to 65; the 50 in Literary to 61; the 16 in Musical to 46; the 51 in Social Service to 24; and the 32 in Clerical to 3. The Mechanical, Computational, and Scientific have the highest percentile ranks. They are all over 75, and so are significant. John's interests are apparently in those areas where he has good ability.

Summary

The purpose of this chapter was to provide explanatory verbal descriptions of certain basic statistical concepts as an aid in the interpretation of tests. The concepts were measures of central tendency, measures of variability, comparability of scores, the significances of the difference between means, the coefficient of correlation, and factor analysis.

The measures of central tendency discussed were the mean, the median, and the mode.

The measures of variability presented were the range, the interquartile range, and the standard deviation. The standard deviation is the most reliable of the measures of variability.

Percentile and standard scores allow for the comparison and interpretation of raw scores. They are the most commonly used norms.

The test for the statistical significance or reliability of the difference between means uses the critical ratio, or "t." A difference between the means of two groups is significant if the critical ratio obtained could occur in less than five out of 100 times on the basis of chance variation. As the ratio decreases, the degree of certainty becomes less and the probability of chance factors increases.

The coefficient of correlation is the measure of the degree of relationship between two variables. It may be plus or minus. It is a useful expression for measuring validity and reliability.

The critical score provides a rather crude means of determining the possibilities of success of percentages of people in a population. It is frequently obtained by inspection of the scattergram and is most often used in personnel selection.

The multiple correlation is an expression of the maximal relationship between the best combination of tests and a criterion of success.

Factor analysis is a statistical tool that allows for the summarization of intercorrelations of many tests. By means of factor analysis tests that measure similar functions can be detected and the factors then named.

Bibliography

1. Bennett, G. K., *Manual, Test of Mechanical Comprehension, Form AA*. New York: The Psychological Corporation.
2. Bingham, W. V., *Aptitudes and Aptitude Testing*. New York: Harper, 1937.

3. Cook, D. W., and M. F. Barre, "The Effect of Specialized Industrial Norms on the Use of the Minnesota Rate of Manipulation Test as a Selective Instrument in Employment Procedure," *Journal of Applied Psychology,* 26:785–792 (1942).
4. Edwards, A. L., *Statistical Analysis for Students in Psychology and Education.* New York: Rinehart, 1946.
5. Fisher, R. A., *Statistical Methods for Research Workers,* Eleventh Edition. Edinburgh: Oliver and Boyd, 1950.
6. Garrett, H. E., *Statistics in Psychology and Education.* New York: Longmans, Green, 1947.
7. Hull, C., "The Conversion of Test Scores into Series Which Shall Have Any Assigned Mean and Degree of Dispersion," *Journal of Applied Pyschology,* 6:299 (1922).
8. Lindquist, E. F., *A First Course in Statistics.* Boston: Houghton Mifflin, 1942.
9. McCall, W. M., *How to Experiment in Education.* New York: Macmillan, 1942, Ch. X.
10. Mintz, A., "The Meaning and Research Implications of the Concept 'Unreliable Statistics,'" *Journal of the Intercollegiate Psychology Association,* 1:93–97 (1949).
11. Peatman, J. G., *Descriptive and Sampling Statistics.* New York: Harper, 1947.
12. Super, D. E., *Appraising Vocational Fitness.* New York: Harper, 1949.
13. Thurstone, L. L., and T. G. Thurstone, "Psychological Examination for College Freshman, 1946 Norms," *American Council on Education Studies,* 11:1–23 (1947).
14. Wesman, A. G., *Test Service Bulletin,* No. 38, The Psychological Corporation (1949).

13

THE CONCEPT OF INTEREST IN RELATION TO COUNSELING

THE KNOWLEDGE of a client's interests is most useful in the successful administration of vocational guidance. It is reasonably clear that interests can be distinguished from such concepts as personality, intelligence, aptitude, and achievement. However, the relationships between interests and these other concepts vary in different individuals. In some individuals, the interests and abilities are so intimately related that it is difficult to separate one from the other, for example, in the case of the interior decorator who has merged his hobby and his job. In other individuals there seems to be a clear separation of interests and abilities, as with the lawyer who prefers to paint. This varying relationship from individual to individual also applies to interests and personality, interests and aptitude, and even interests and intelligence.

Since the relationship between interests and the other four measurable dimensions of an individual is never perfect or even high, for individual prediction the problem is difficult. It may be that the person with no vocational problem is one whose balanced personality and direction of interests blends with the degree of intelligence, aptitude, and achievement he possesses. However, the counselor or psychologist rarely sees these people. He is more likely to work with individuals whose dimensions do not easily fit together.

Lack of clear understanding that interests are a basic dimension in guidance has led to much confusion. Even those who are aware that it is and have done much work in the field have not been too helpful in adding information that would clear up the many aspects of the problem. It must be admitted that despite the large amount of research conducted, the concept of interests has remained more elusive than lucid.

The earlier chapters on psychological tests include a discussion of some of the problems involved in interest measurement as well as illustrations of the more widely used interest tests. This chapter will not be primarily concerned with interest tests (although it is exceedingly difficult to separate interests from interest tests); rather, in it we shall attempt a clarification of the nature and characteristics of interests.

Definitions

Books that include chapters beginning with definitions may justifiably be accused of being too pedantic; yet in a chapter on interests it appears necessary. The various authorities who have done considerable research in this area usually offer definitions that differ somewhat from each other. In the authors' opinion the inability to agree is a manifestation of the complexity and elusive nature of interests.

Douglas Fryer in 1931 published *The Measurement of Interest* (12). This book was the first sustained effort to review comprehensively the many studies on the topic of interest conducted up to that time. It also attempted to organize the information systematically. Fryer considers interests the "vital key to many important situations."[1] He states:

> In social life, in personal adjustments, in education and in the occupational world interest is the vital key to many important situations. We all want to be *interested*, and we want to be *interesting*, that is, we want to be moved to act upon the world in a satisfying manner, and we want the world to react toward us in an equally satisfying

[1] From *The Measurement of Interests* by Douglas Fryer. Copyright 1931 by Henry Holt and Company, Inc.

> fashion. We are only now beginning to realize that the quality of being *interesting* may be cultivated; it has its development in each of us along with the growth of the capacity of being *interested.*[2]

Fryer differentiates between subjective interests and objective interests. He believes that (12) subjective interests are feelings that certain estimated experiences would be pleasant, and that subjective dislikes are feelings that certain estimated experiences would be unpleasant. Objective interests are acceptance reactions—positive reactions to stimulating objects and activities in the environment. Objective aversions are negative reactions to these stimulating objects. In other words, Fryer differentiates between subjective interests, which are estimated experiences, and objective interests, which are reactions or behavior. Fryer considered subjective interests as complex configurations, the criterion of which is feeling. These interests are estimated through either expressions of a person or his answers on standardized inventory blanks.

Tests of objective interests measure superficial and extensive information in a clearly defined field. Most of these measures are tests of extensive rather than intensive information. Another indicator of objective interests, according to Fryer, is the free association test.

Strong (21), in his book *Vocational Interests of Men and Women,* although primarily concerned with the analysis of the huge amount of data gathered in connection with his Vocational Interest Blank, also attempts a systematic treatment based upon a comprehensive analysis of available information. Strong's book appeared in 1943, 12 years after Fryer's work. Whereas Fryer considered almost all the work done up to the time of his publication, to a large extent Strong's volume is essentially an exposition of his test and secondarily a critique of the concept of interest.

Strong points out three conceptions of interest expression: (1) a single expression such as, "I like dogs"; (2) a general tendency towards a constellation of items as, "I have scientific interests"; and (3) a total score on an interest inventory, as for example a rating of "A" for interest in Psychology. He describes the relationship existing

[2] *Ibid.*

among abilities, interest, and achievements, by the analogy of a motor boat with a motor and a rudder. The motor (abilities) determines the speed of the boat, the rudder (interests) determines the direction in which the boat travels, and the distance travelled by the boat (achievment) is a result of the operation of both the motor and the rudder. Strong believes that "an interest is not a separate psychological entity but merely one of several aspects of behavior."[3] Consequently measurement of one interest is not a complete measurement of a unit of behavior. He recognizes that interest is an expression of satisfaction but not necessarily of efficiency. Fundamentally, Strong considers interest to be that which is measured by the Vocational Interest Blank. The information obtained from this test, according to Strong, indicates what the person wants to do and the general direction in which he should go in order to obtain enjoyment and satisfaction in life.

Bingham (5) defines an interest as "A tendency to become absorbed in an experience and to continue it."[4] He states:

> We therefore define interest not only in terms of the objects and activities which get attention and yield satisfaction, but also in terms of the strength of the tendencies to give attention to and seek satisfaction in these competing objects of interest.[5]

According to Bingham, to ascertain a person's interests beyond the kinds of activities in which he says he most likes to engage, one may obtain evidence by a study of the record of his previous activities, school subjects, recreations, and employment. Evidence may also be obtained by determining the person's relative achievement in these different fields. Bingham regards this sort of evidence as an indirect but objective indication of interest. Additional evidences of interest, according to Bingham, can be obtained by securing statements or ratings of supervisors, teachers, or associates, or by using a well-designed questionnaire.

Super (22) concludes that there have been four major interpreta-

---

[3] Reprinted from *Vocational Interests of Men and Women* by Edward K. Strong, Jr., with the permission of the author and of the publishers, Stanford University Press.

[4] Reprinted by permission from *Aptitudes and Aptitude Testing*, by W. V. Bingham, Harper & Brothers, New York, 1937.

[5] *Ibid.*

tions of the term interest: expressions, manifestations, tests, and inventories. Expressed interest is "the verbal profession of interest in an object, task, activity or occupation."[6] Manifest interest is "synonymous with participation in an activity or an occupation. Tested interest is measured by objective tests as differentiated from inventories which are based on subjective estimates. Inventoried interest is assessed by means of responses to lists of activities with experimentally determined numerical weight. It yields a score which represents, not a single subjective estimate as in the case of expressed interest, but a pattern which research has shown to be rather stable."[7]

The definition that seems most meaningful is offered by Berdie (3) who states:

> Vocational interests both as measured by tests and as indicated by occupational choices are expressions of liking and disliking as directed toward activities, objects and characteristics of the environment.[8]

Murphy (15) in describing interests offers a statement which is also etiological in character. He states, "Interests are conditioned stimuli pursued because of their relations to goal objects which are valued. Interests in turn are extinguished, as all other conditioned responses are extinguished, when the relations to the drives involved are destroyed."

A combination of the statements by Berdie and Murphy offers the best understanding of the term, "interests." Such a statement would describe interests as conditioned stimuli related to goal objects and expressed as likes or dislikes of activities, objects, characteristics or people in the environment.

Theories of interest

Since there is disagreement as to the exact nature of interest, even the best explanations must at the moment be regarded as only theoretical. At present there are a variety of theories proposed.

---

[6] Reprinted by permission from *Appraising Vocational Fitness,* by D. E. Super, Harper & Brothers, New York, 1949.

[7] *Ibid.*

[8] Reprinted from *Psychological Bulletin,* 41:137 (1944), by permission of the American Psychological Association, publishers.

Fryer proposes an acceptance-rejection theory of interest measurment. In the inventorying of likes and dislikes, the acceptance and rejection of objects of stimulation are measured. In the information test, applied to measurement of interest, there is an acceptance or rejection in a definite field of information. This acceptance or rejection takes place also in the free association test. Fryer believes that although motivation would seem to influence interest measures, its influence is the same as that upon a measure of ability. According to Fryer, motivation is extraneous to the measurement; it is distinguished from interest as a separate aspect of mental life. He believes that both objective interests and subjective interests may be regarded as acceptance-rejection experiences. He states, "It may be that the acceptance, or turning towards stimulation, and the rejection, or turning away from stimulation, is correlated with pleasant and unpleasant experience."[9] The major contribution of his theory, from his point of view, lies in its definition of interests and motivation as separate in mental life.

Strong proposes a two-fold hypothesis:

> First, if a student has sufficient interest to elect a college course, his grade in it will depend far more on his intelligence, industry, and previous preparation than on his interest . . .
>
> Second, interest affects the situation in causing the student to elect what he is interested in and to avoid courses in which he is not interested.[10]

The present writers must admit having difficulty in understanding exactly what this hypothesis means, if it is a hypothesis at all. It appears that Strong is referring to the relationship between interest and ability. This idea can be got from a quote that he apparently subscribes to, namely, "Interests and abilities seem to be independent variables, each one contributing its own quota to the ultimate success."[11]

---

[9] From *The Measurement of Interests* by Douglas Fryer. Copyright 1931 by Henry Holt and Company, Inc.

[10] Reprinted from *Vocational Interests of Men and Women* by Edward K. Strong, Jr., with the permission of the author and of the publishers, Stanford University Press.

[11] *Ibid.*

Darley (10) offers the hypothesis that occupational interest types are by-products of the development of personality types. Using as a basis an analysis of 1000 men who were given the Strong Vocational Interest Blank, he proposes that individual interpretation be guided by patterns of interest rather than specific occupational scores. Darley considers interest maturity, occupational level, masculinity-femininity, and "social intelligence" as four of the personality characteristics out of which interest types grow. Darley's hypothesis is interesting insofar as it proposes the relationship between interest and personality. However, it is based upon data from only the Strong test; this fact is unfortunate, since it may well be that the Strong Blank is not the best measure of interest nor the most meaningful approach to understanding the concept.

Super proposes an objective theory that recognizes multiple causation, the principle of interaction, and the joint contributions of nature and nurture. In many respects it is as much a summary of what is known of interests at the present time as it is a theory.

> Interests are the product of interaction between inherited aptitudes and endocrine factors, on the one hand, and opportunity and social evaluation on the other. Some of the things a person does well bring him the satisfaction of mastery or the approval of his companions, and result in interests. Some of the things his associates do, appeal to him and, through identification, he patterns his actions and his interests about them; if he fits the pattern reasonably well hc remains in it, but if not, he must seek another identification and develop another self-concept and interest pattern. His mode of adjustment may cause him to seek certain satisfactions, but the means of achieving these satisfactions vary so much from one person, with one set of aptitudes and in one set of circumstances, to another person with other abilities and in another situation, that the prediction of interest patterns from modes of adjustment is hardly possible. Because of the stability of the hereditary endowment and the relative stability of the social environment in which any given person is reared, interest patterns are generally rather stable; their stability is further increased by the multiplicity of opportunities for try-outs, identification, and social approval in the years before adolescence. By adolescence most young people have had opportunities to explore social, linguistic, mathematical, technical and business activities to some extent; they have sought to identify with parents, other adults, and schoolmates, and have rejected some and accepted others of these identifications;

> self-concepts have begun to take definite form. For these reasons interest patterns begin to crystallize by early adolescence, and the exploratory experiences of the adolescent years in most cases merely clarify and elaborate upon what has already begun to take shape. Some persons experience significant changes during adolescence and early adulthood, but these are most often related to endocrine changes, and less often to changes in self-concept resulting from having attempted to live up to a misidentification and to fit into an inappropriate pattern. Vocational interest patterns generally have a substantial degree of permanence at this stage: for most persons, adolescent exploration is an awakening to something that is already there.[12]

Berdie's (3) hypothesis concerning interest is most tenable. He regards interest as "a process of generalization, which may or may not be verbalized, or of which the person may or may not be aware, might play an important part in the development of these constellations or interest patterns. These interest patterns are not as likely to be influenced by fleeting experiences, as they are by conditions and situations enduring over long periods of time."[13]

Classification of interests

The one fact that appears indisputable in connection with our knowledge of interests is that they form patterns or constellations around either experiences or situations in the environment of an individual; and the concept of interests has become useful in successful vocational guidance insofar as interests have been accurately classified into types or groupings.

The major problem is to determine how many of these patterns need be recognized in order to make possible a complete description of a person's interests; and to allow a comparison of his interest patterns with those of other individuals.

Among the very earliest attempts to inventory interests was the approach by Moore (14), which was based upon a dichotomy of mechanical and social occupations—in other words a description of interests as centering on either people or things. Although people can be

---

[12] Reprinted by permission from *Appraising Vocational Fitness,* by D. E. Super, Harper & Brothers, New York, 1949.

[13] Reprinted from *Psychological Bulletin,* 41:154 (1944), by permission of the American Psychological Association, publishers.

described as being interested in either people or things, these two preoccupations are not mutually exclusive; and where they overlap, other patterns emerge. Consequently a twofold system is a slight over-simplification.

On the other hand, a classification system of interests, to be most meaningful, cannot be highly detailed. This is the major argument against a classification system having a large number of categories. It does appear that six is not too many for this purpose. One finds this number in Spranger's (20) six basic value types. These served as the basis for Allport and Vernon's construction of the test, Study of Values, which measures a person's values in the following categories: theoretical, aesthetic, religious, social, economic, and political. When interests are grouped into these categories, they tend to form patterns centered around either the first three listed or the second three; of course, there are exceptions. Sarbin and Berdie (17) found that by using the Allport-Vernon Study of Values, they could approximate certain occupational interest types as measured by the Strong test.

Strong's approach has been to relate interests to occupations; in fact, he defines an interest in an occupation as the pattern found among people who have been in the occupation for a minimum period of five years.

Men engaged in occupations have characteristic patterns of likes and dislikes that differentiate them from men in other occupations. However, the extent to which occupations may be differentiated varies greatly. Chemists and life insurance salesmen have interests patterns that are readily differentiated; chemists and engineers have interest patterns that are much more similar. The fact that occupational interest patterns can be compared as to degree of similarity has led Strong to propose six group scales each representative of certain occupations:

Artist, psychologist, architect, physician, and dentist.
Engineer and chemist, and indirectly mathematician and physicist.
Y.M.C.A. physical director, personnel manager, Y.M.C.A. secretary, social science high-school teacher, city school superintendent, and minister.
Accountant, office worker, purchasing agent, and banker.
Sales manager, realtor, and life insurance salesman.

Advertising man, lawyer, and author-journalist.[14]

Kuder has made a very scholarly analysis and treatment of data gathered by using his Preference Record; and from his findings he recommends that nine general areas of interest should be considered: mechanical, computational, scientific, persuasive, artistic, literary, musical, social service, and clerical. Depending upon the profile or pattern that is obtained by an individual, reference is made to a table in his manual in which suggested occupations are listed. There are lists for single patterns and for combinations. A few examples of occupations suggested in Kuder's manual are presented in Table 18.

TABLE 18

CLASSIFICATIONS OF OCCUPATIONS ACCORDING TO MAJOR INTERESTS

Major Interest	*Suggested Occupation*
mechanical	boilermaker, electrician, gunsmith, riveter, upholsterer
computational	accountant, surveyor, statistician, math teacher, actuary
scientific	biologist, oculist, physician, psychologist, veterinarian
persuasive	bill collector, buyer, politician, salesman, radio announcer
artistic	architect, barber, designer, sculptor, artist
literary	actor, author, teacher of languages, historian, journalist
musical	accompanist, musical composer, radio singer, musician, tap dancer
social service	case worker, teacher, dean, psychiatrist, farm adviser
clerical	file clerk, mail clerk, proofreader, stenographer, typist
mechanical-computational	cartographer, mechanical engineer, meteorologist, surveyor, accounting machine repairman
mechanical-scientific	beekeeper, chiropractor, dental hygienist, embalmer, truck farmer
mechanical-persuasive	construction foreman, hardware salesman, industrial engineer, radio dealer, supervisor—auto repair shop
mechanical-artistic	bookbinder, die maker, jeweler, taxidermist, window trimmer
mechanical-literary	writer of articles in machine trade journals, in fields of engineering trades such as electrical, popular mechanics
mechanical-musical	organ tuner, violin maker, sound-effects man, musical instrument repairman
mechanical-social service	safety engineer, shop work teacher, professor of engineering, handcraft instructor
mechanical-clerical	radio operator, shipping clerk, weighmaster, inspector of manufactured articles, compositor
computational-scientific	economist, mathematician, weather observer, claim appraiser, psychometrician

[14] Reprinted from *Vocational Interests of Men and Women* by Edward K. Strong, Jr., with the permission of the author and of the publishers, Stanford University Press.

computational-persuasive	brokerage salesman, claim adjuster, credit analyst, finance salesman, auditor
computational-artistic	art appraiser, draftsman, bookkeeper for art dealer
computational-literary	financial editor of newspaper, writer of articles on accounting, taxation, statistics, mathematics
computational-musical	business manager for orchestra or singer, accountant for musical firm
computational-social service	economic geographer, mathematics teacher, statistician in psychology, education or government
computational-clerical	bank cashier, express agent, timekeeper, purser, brokerage clerk
scientific-persuasive	druggist, salesman of dental and medical equipment, dealer in scientific apparatus, detective
scientific-artistic	botanical artist, photographer, structural designer, surgeon
scientific-literary	editor of scientific journal, literary critic, meteorologist, marine editor
scientific-musical	acoustician, radio engineer, music arranger, research worker in development of new musical instruments
scientific-social service	child psychologist, criminologist, occupational therapist, trained nurse
scientific-clerical	patent clerk, prescription clerk, time and motion study man fingerprint classifier
persuasive-artistic	advertising illustrator, art dealer, beautician, antique dealer
persuasive-literay	author, publicist, reporter, theatrical director, lawyer
persuasive-musical	band leader, music agent, choirmaster, music producer
persuasive-social service	clergyman, athletic coach, labor arbitrator, personnel director, juvenile court judge
persuasive-clerical	appointment clerk, census taker, floor manager, ticket agent, telephone operator
artistic-literary	actor, art teacher, fashion editor, primary-school teacher, writer on art subjects
artistic-musical	ballet dancer, chorus girl, dancing teacher, arranger of music for motion pictures
artistic-social service	home economics teacher, portrait painter, political cartoonist
artistic-clerical	clerk in art store, show card painter, vari-typist, draftsman
literary-social service	court reporter, greeting card writer, social worker
literary-clerical	bibliographer, court stenographer, legal secretary, manuscript reader, proofreader
musical-social service	music teacher, choir director, community music organizer
social service-clerical	switchboard operator, personnel clerk, secretary to a clergyman, stenography teacher[15]

Super was also concerned with an attempt to arrive at the basic interest factors and offers a neat summary in a table as follows:

[15] By permission of Science Research Associates and G. Frederic Kuder.

Table 19

INTEREST FACTORS REVEALED BY SIX STUDIES AND LOGICAL SYNTHESIS

Thurstone	*Allport-Vernon*	*Lurie*	*Strong* *Unrotated*	*Strong* *Rotated*	*Kuder*	*Synthesis*
Science	Theoretical	Theoretical	Science	Science	Scientific	Scientific
People	Social	Social	People	People	Social-Service	Social-Welfare
Language			Language	Language	Literary	Literary
			Things vs. People	Things vs. People	(Mechanical)	Material
				System	(Clerical) / Computational	System
Business	Economic / Political	Materialistic	Business			
				Contact	Persuasive	Contact
	Aesthetic				Artistic	Artistic
	Religious	Religious				
					Musical	Musical

Reprinted by permission from *Appraising Vocational Fitness,* by D. E. Super, Harper & Brothers, New York, 1949.

Examination of Table 19 reveals the close similarity between Super's synthesis and Kuder's nine major interest areas. With the present accepted method of measurement of interests it appears that a vocational counselor who is attempting to learn a client's interests from such things as his self-expressions, his work, school history, and hobbies would do well to consider a classification system based upon these nine major areas. On the one hand, the list is not so lengthy that it becomes unwieldy; on the other, it is not too specific for successful vocational application. It is sufficiently comprehensive to allow both the client and his counselor to work in areas sufficiently large as to scope, meaning, and vocational planning.

For example, a client's major interest in social service would allow for a considerable variety of occupations, any one of which might be equally interesting to the client. This of course applies to the other major areas included in the last two columns of Table 19.

Interest and the other dimensions of an individual

A person's interests may or may not be a clue to his personality. The very early work of Moore in classifying interests into the two major types, those centered on things and those centered on people; and Bingham's proposal that interests might be considered as essentially introvert or extrovert can be thought of as simple attempts to relate types of interest and personality. Since the best that can be said for the introversion-extroversion concept is that people have such tendencies but may also possess components of each, it is obvious that such an oversimplified system cannot be accurate.

Just as a person may have a hobby that is similar to his gainful occupation, so may a person have a hobby that is dissimilar. In the first instance we find reinforcement of the basic interest in two areas; in the second we may have a person making an adjustment to the basic interest or manifesting two interests that are equally strong. The same situation can exist in the case of personality. The basic interest and personality patterns can reinforce one another, or be different. When they are different, either the person adjusts or a problem arises. Along similar lines, Super (23) states:

> Men who find in their vocations an outlet for their major interests are likely to have hobbies which resemble their vocations, whereas men who do not have adequate vocational outlets tend to develop outside activities which rival their vocation in claiming time and thought. Those whose vocational activities supplement and extend their vocations not only tend to be better adjusted, but to be more stable vocationally. This shows how interests may operate to speed up or slow down the development of skills, the assimilation of knowledge, and vocational progress.[16]

One does not find studies reporting clear-cut relationships between interest and aspects of personality to a degree that would warrant positive generalization. For example, Tyler (25) investigated the relationship between scores on the Strong Test and other attitude and personality factors. The subjects were 55 men and 120 women in a college psychology course. One of the conclusions was that there was no appreciable relationship between neurotic tendency and any kind of interest score. The other major finding was that the more a male tends to avoid large numbers of acquaintances and indiscriminate social affairs, the more likely he is to show the interests of scientific men; and the more satisfaction he takes in social affairs, involving large numbers of people, the more likely he is to resemble salesmen in his interests. None of the other Strong groupings showed any consistent relationship to the personality factors investigated. Women show the same general sort of difference between persons with scientific and sales interests, but the nature of the social factor is less clearcut.

Seder (18) analyzed the responses of female physicians and life insurance saleswomen on both the Strong Vocational Interest Blank for Men and the Strong Vocational Interest Blank for Women. She concludes that the interests of men and women tend to be similar and that the differences between the sexes in an occupation are usually less frequent and less important than the similarities. Of course, it may well be that the interests of career women deviate from those of typical women; that they resemble the interests of the career, which are independent of sex.

---

[16] Reprinted by permission from *The Dynamics of Vocational Adjustment,* by D. E. Super, Harper & Brothers, New York, 1942.

There have been other similar studies, but most can be criticized for their extremely limited scope. That is, two tests are given to groups of perhaps 50 students and correlations are reported which may or may not be accurate. However, present knowledge indicates that the relationship between types of vocational interests and personality adjustment has not been established. Adjusted or maladjusted personalities can occur independent of interests.

The terms "like" and "dislike" are relatively simple and primary concepts in the hedonic aspect of life. Berdie (4) investigated the relationship between likes, dislikes, and vocational interests. The Strong Vocational Interest Blank was administered to 411 college freshmen. When the number of likes and dislikes was tallied, it was found that the person who likes more items tends to be a better student in both high school and college. He tends to be more sociable and to have more social skills. Conversely, the person who dislikes many items tends to be a poor student and has a less satisfactory social adjustment. People who check a preponderance of items as liked tend to have feminine interests, according to the Strong Masculinity-Femininity Scale. People who dislike many items also tend to have feminine interests. People who are indifferent to the items of the test tend to have masculine interests. Apparently marking extremes on this test is a feminine characteristic.

Berdie concludes:

> Emotional acceptance of their surroundings is typical of people in socially directed occupations. Rejection of these surroundings, perhaps an expression of cynical disillusionment, is characteristic of people in those occupations usually considered as revealing the realities of life with great emphasis. General indifference to these surroundings is characteristic of those people in the more mundane occupations which perhaps do not inspire too much enthusiasm on the part of the people in them.[17]

Differences in intelligence may be related to interests in specific occupations, but not to the wider occupational interest areas. A person with mechanical interests and with limited intelligence may be

[17] Reprinted from *Journal of Applied Psychology*, 27:188 (1943), by permission of the American Psychological Association, publishers.

a successful boilermaker; with more intelligence, a successful engineer. However, since interests are likely to be found in multiple areas, the problem becomes more complicated. It is for this reason that Table 19 is presented. It shows how wide the range of occupations can be when the interest factor is held constant.

A study by Skodak and Crissy (19) indicates that I.Q. categories do not differentiate interest scores of senior high school girls. Table 20 presents the percentage distribution of A scores on the Strong Blank in three I.Q. categories.

TABLE 20

NUMBER AND PERCENTAGE DISTRIBUTION OF STRONG A'S BY I.Q. CLASSIFICATION, SENIOR GIRLS

	Per cent			
	110+	*109–90*	*89–*	*Total*
Housewife	28.5	28.5	31.8	28.8
Stenographer	27.7	25.5	29.5	26.5
Office worker	28.1	24.7	26.1	25.8
Nurse	12.9	17.3	11.4	15.3
Math. Teach.	2.3	1.0	....	1.3
Soc. Stud. Teach.	....	0.6	....	0.4
H.S. Eng. Teach.	0.8	0.2	....	0.4
Y.W.C.A. Sec'y	....	1.0	....	0.6
Dentist	0.4	0.6	....	0.5
Lawyer	....	0.4	1.1	0.4
Social Worker	....	0.2	....	0.1
Life Ins. Sales	0.4	....	....	0.1
Physician	....	....	....	....
Librarian	....	....	....	....
Total A's	101.1	100.0	99.9	100.2

Reprinted from *Journal of Applied Psychology,* 26:71 (1942), by permission of the American Psychological Association, publishers.

This study also reported that approximately one fourth of all the stated interests of these girls on all levels of ability are in the field of office work. Interest in nursing, medical sciences, teaching, and social work is primarily found among superior or average girls. Interest in personal service, sales, and skilled trades is more frequently found among the average and below average girls. An analysis of the relationship between stated choices and A ratings on the Strong Blank showed nothing, since the predominant pattern of stenographer, office workers, housewife, and nurse overwhelmed all other differences.

According to Skodak and Crissy, this lack of discrimination as determined by Strong Interest scores offers little or no assistance in the choice of an occupation. They believe that this blank has less guidance value at the high school level than the stated occupational choices of the students themselves.

Intelligence requirements for different occupations have been suggested by the work that has compared scores on the Army intelligence tests in both world wars with success in civilian occupations. It therefore is possible to match in a crude way a person's intelligence with his major interest or combination of interests and find a group of suitable occupations.

According to Strong, interest is an indeterminant indicator of success. The reasons why interest is not directly related to achievement are: (1) Interest in an activity is an indicator of satisfaction but not necessarily of success; (2) an activity may be liked or disliked long after it has ceased to be carried on; (3) interest is often attached to an activity not because of its essential characteristic but because of some trivial aspect.

Strong believes that there are several reasons why a person enters an occupation other than the one in which there is a professed choice. These are knowledge, ability, personality, and physique.

It is impossible, according to Strong, to draw conclusions from the results of interest tests about abilities or other traits; he states that the correlation of occupational interest scores with intelligence is about zero. He believes that if a student has sufficient interest to elect a college course, his grade in it will depend far more on his intelligence, industry, and previous preparation than on his interest.

Williamson (26) points out that there are a number of factors that can interfere with a person's choosing an occupation realistically. Some of these are parental influence, too early choice, overestimate of earnings, and desire for social prestige. It is also possible for a person to have an occupational interest and not be aware of it.

According to Fryer (11), the correlations between vocational interests and abilities range between +.10 to +.60 in most of the studies investigating this area. Such results would warrant a conclusion that it is impossible to make individual predictions of ability based upon interest measurement.

There have been many specific studies that have reported a relationship between an interest test and an aptitude or achievement test. Most of these reports, however, conform to the generalization that knowing one dimension does not allow safely for the prediction of the other. An example of such a study is the one by Long (12), in which both the Strong Vocational Interest Blank and the Zyve Scientific Aptitude Test were administered to 200 college students. The findings indicate that students scoring high on the Zyve Scientific Aptitude Test rate higher on the Strong Technical-Nonmathematics and Technical-Mathematics groups, but lower on the Business Contact group than do those scoring low on the Zyve test. These results indicate that the Zyve test measures some phase of ability that separates students having interests like those found among the Technical-Mathematics and the Technical-Nonmathematics groups of the Strong from students without such interests.

Long concludes that the use of both of these instruments in counseling is better procedure than the use of either one, if the capacity of a student to do work in engineering or science is under consideration.

Development of interests

Superficial inspection of the developmental factors contributing to interest allows for the generalization that family, school, and general opportunity contribute. This generalization strongly implies that interests are basically determined by the environment. However, some who have worked in the field believe that interests are due to hereditary factors as well as the environment. For example, Berdie (3) believes that sex differences in interests are related to physiological or physical variables. He states further that "interest like personality is determined to some extent by inherited factors, if only insofar as these factors determine sensory and attentive limens. Although a concept of the inheritance of the specific interests appears somewhat ridiculous, when interests are conceived as specific personality patterns, this concept is more acceptable."[18]

---

[18] Reprinted from *Psychological Bulletin*, 24:154 (1944), by permission of the American Psychological Association, publishers.

Data based upon the administration of the Strong Blank to 120 pairs of twins yielded a correlation of +.50 for identical twins and +.28 for fraternal twins. This result enabled Carter (8) to conclude, "It seems probable that hereditary factors are more important in determining interests than are environmental factors." However, other studies do not support Carter's conclusion.

Berdie (3) reported that measured vocational interests apparently reach a point of relative stability soon after physical and intellectual maturity. He believes that the similarity of attitudes of parents and children may be due to exposure to mutual influences or due to a conditioning effect exerted by parents' attitudes upon the attitudes of the children. Family resemblances of vocational interests may be similarly explained.

Finch and Odoroff (11) administered the Strong Blank to junior high school students. They found that the number of occupational keys for which clear-cut sex differences appear is no fewer than the number of such differences occurring among the group from senior high school. They conclude that interests are well developed before 14 years of age.

Carter and Strong (9) conclude that vocational interests of the two sexes as measured by the Strong Blank show certain marked differences among the high school population.

From the preceding discussion it is clear that interests in boys and girls are different by the time they are about 14 years of age and that they resemble, respectively, the interests of men and women. It appears clear, too, that some familial resemblance occurs. What is not clear is the relative role of heredity and environment. Most of the preceding studies, and others, have pointed to the importance of the environment; but there is nevertheless the remote possibility that interests have an innate basis whose maturing is long and devious and therefore obscure. Since the evidence for such a statement is lacking, it should be accepted only as sheer speculation. It will be much safer to consider the development of interests as part of the conditioning process until evidence appears to the contrary.

Strong (21) states that interests are apparently little influenced by vocational training and actual experience in an occupation. His data indicate that occupational interest scores do not increase with occupational experience. According to Strong, "Apparently interests typical of occupations do not result from experience in the occupation, but rather the interests come first and the occupation is chosen because it provides a working environment in which the interests may be satisfied."[19]

According to Fryer (12), interests are primarily of environmental origin. They appear to have a chance relationship with abilities. Training and environmental factors, many of them chance stimulations, are the main cause of vocational interests.

Attempting to unravel the variety of environmental influences on interest is not particularly rewarding. Here, as in most other aspects, the conclusions are equivocal. According to Peters (16) the family is the greatest single agency in determining vocational choice.

Anderson (1) reports in a study that 12 per cent of a group of college males choose the occupation of the father. Forty per cent reported that the father had made vocational suggestions, and 27 per cent accepted the suggestion.

Berdie (2) found, in a study of 136 college students, that the sons of skilled tradesmen tended to have interests of skilled tradesmen and engineers. They did not have interests in social welfare or business but in engineering. Sons of businessmen were found to have interests in business. He found that people with technical interests tended to come from lower income families, while people with business interests tended to come from higher income families. Students with measured interests in engineering had greater ability than others. However, interests in the other vocations do not appear to be related to ability at all. High social adjustment scores accompanied interests in social welfare whereas students interested in engineering obtained low social adjustment scores. Students choosing business participate more in social activities. Berdie also found that hobbies were related to both expressed and measured interests.

School has an influence on vocational interest. In one group that

---

[19] Reprinted from *Vocational Interests of Men and Women* by Edward K. Strong, Jr., with the permission of the author and of the publishers, Stanford University Press.

Berdie (2) studied, 32 per cent reported as the reason for choosing a vocation the influence of a favored school subject. Another 10 per cent were influenced by their teachers. Berdie believes that hobbies and boyhood occupations are vital instruments in vocational selection. He concludes, "No one factor, ability, school or work experience, plays a large part in determining vocational interests yet all of these factors are related to interests to some extent. Vocational interest is a complex phenomenon resulting from a multiplicity of conditions. Family influences are among the more effective factors determining interests, and abilities are among the least effective factors."

It would be best in the analysis of a vocational problem to look to such major influences as family and school in trying to understand a person's interest.

Permanence of interests

In some respects the problem of the permanence of interests is crucial. If either interest estimates or measurements are subject to wide change, the measurement at any one time might in no way be related to the interest in the future. In other words, for prediction purposes interests would have to be relatively stable in an individual. This is the same requirement that holds for the I.Q. If it varies, the only value in measuring it would be to learn what it was at the moment. If it is rather constant, specific knowledge of an individual, and prediction, are possible.

The permanence of interests has been established. If evidence of interest is not a minute specific but rather a pattern then it is reasonably clear that interests have a relatively high degree of permanence.

Interests as measured by the Strong test are regarded by him as being highly permanent. The correlation between occupational interest scores when there is an interval of ten years between test and retest is +.75. Strong points out that such a correlation is representative of the average individual. For some, it is much greater and for others, much less. This fact would mean that in any individual case, the interest may not be as permanent as the figure suggests.

Part of the lack of permanence in interests is caused by changes in interest with age. But according to Strong, the correlation between the likes of 15-year-old and 55-year-old men is +.73; that between 15- and 25-year-old men, +.82; and that between 25- and 55-year-old men, +.88.

Taylor and Carter (24) administered the Strong Vocational Interest Blank to a group of 58 girls in the 11th grade. A second testing occurred one year later. During this period the girls had no vocational courses or systematic vocational guidance. They conclude that profiles of interest test scores from two administrations of the test reveal test result reliability and constancy of individual interest patterns. They further state, "The data are consistent with the hypothesis that the Strong Vocational Interest Blank for Women provides significant and valuable information about the interests of high school girls." Since this conclusion is practically opposite from the one drawn by Skodak and Crissy (19), the only remark that seems relevant is, "What paper do you read?"

Canning, Taylor, and Carter (7) believe that the Strong Blank indicates a rather high degree of score similarity between the sophomore and senior year. They found that if a high school sophomore received a C rating on the first test there would be an 83 per cent chance that he would receive the same rating, and only a 1 per cent chance that he would receive an A rating, two years later. If the boy received an A rating on the first test there would be an 88 per cent chance that he would receive a rating of B or higher, two years later.

Van Dusen (26) administered the Strong test to a group of college students first as freshmen and later as seniors. Among the individuals evidencing no change in anticipated life's work there is a significant increase in score over the college period on the vocation of their choice. Chosen vocations show a higher degree of consistency than other vocations. The results, according to Van Dusen, indicate that experiences affecting interests acquired during the college interval are largely determined by experiences acquired previous to college entrance.

Fryer (12), summarizing the various findings, estimates that there is an increasing permanence throughout elementary school, high school, and college. He concludes that there is considerable stability in the individual's interests, even though the degree of permanence is insufficient for the prediction of future interests.

Since the environment for most people is likely to remain relatively constant, and since a person's socio-economic status is relatively stable, it can be expected that they will be a stabilizing influence on his interests, thereby affording a degree of permanence of interests.

Most of the reported studies of interest are not very satisfactory. They are based upon a rather limited number of subjects in confined geographic areas, and the period of time is too short. It may well be that these findings apply only to the groups studied. Really worthwhile longitudinal studies and systematic clinical diagnoses are lacking. The work of Strong as reported in his *Vocational Interests of Men and Women,* although not subject to the criticism that its numbers are limited or its geographic regions too narrow, is primarily a report of the research in connection with a single measuring instrument, the Strong Vocational Interest Blank. If one grants that the Strong Blank measures interests, then the assumptions Strong makes and the conclusions he draws from his data are acceptable. However, if one is not prepared to accept the Strong Blank as the most valid measure of interest, much of this work can be regarded as confusing the issue rather than permitting the crystallization of basic facts. The writers consider that the Kuder test is in many respects a better instrument. The fact that its scoring system leads to an analysis of nine areas rather than of specific occupations is also to be approved. However, it is entirely possible that an instrument measuring interest is needed which in either administration or interpretation allows for a more clinically oriented view. It is highly probable that such a complex phenomenon as interest, with its lack of palpability, cannot be approached by asking a person to indicate a like or dislike preference for one item, or for that matter, for each of four hundred items. Perhaps an entirely fresh start is needed before we lose interest in interest because we cannot clearly understand what it is and how it is related to other concepts.

The authors would like to mention here, as speculation rather than discussion of definite findings, some of their unpublished research.

In their desire to obtain a more meaningful measure of interest, they constructed a series of pictures, four of which appear on pages 400 and 401.

Each picture is somewhat more structured than those in most tests that use pictures as a projective technique; yet they are deliberately not entirely structured. An attempt was made to cover most of the major occupational areas. It is believed that each picture is complex enough to allow a person to choose a role for which he might be suited. Although data have been gathered, and the authors have found the test helpful in estimating the person's interests and level of occupational aspiration, they are not prepared to offer it as a valid measuring device. Rather they suggest it as a different approach to interest measurement and understanding that may bear fruit.

Summary

There is no real agreement on a definition of interests or on a most acceptable theory. The preferred definition defines interests as conditioned stimuli related to goal objects and expressed as likes or dislikes of activities, objects, and characteristics of people in the environment. Interests can be considered as processes of generalization that form constellations or patterns influenced by conditions and situations over long periods of time.

A classification system is necessary if one is to make the greatest use of the concept of interests in vocational guidance. Kuder's nine-fold classification seems most appropriate. It includes mechanical, computational, scientific, persuasive, artistic, literary, musical, social service, and clerical interests.

Interests must be regarded as a separate part of the individual's makeup but as related to such other dimensions as personality, intelligence, aptitude, and achievement. The relationship between interest and these other aspects varies from one individual to another.

The influence of environment in the development of interests is readily recognizable; it may be that future research will reveal that heredity has some role.

When a sufficiently comprehensive measure of interests is ob-

SAMPLE PICTURES FROM BLUM AND BALINSKY INTEREST TEST

SAMPLE PICTURES FROM BLUM AND BALINSKY INTEREST TEST

tained, it is clear that interests are rather permanent. Although specific interests may change, interest patterns are stable. The Kuder leads to more meaningful interpretation of interest patterns than the Strong; but perhaps both the Kuder and the Strong tests are limited by their method, which is a summing of many specifics. Possibly a more clinical orientation toward interest measurement is needed.

Bibliography

1. Anderson, W. A., "Some Social Factors Associated with Vocational Choices of College Men," *Journal of Educational Sociology,* 6:100–113 (1932).
2. Berdie, R. F., "Factors Associated with Vocational Interests," *Journal of Educational Sociology,* 34:257–277 (1943).
3. ———, "Factors Related to Vocational Interests," *Psychological Bulletin,* 41:137–157 (1944).
4. ———, "Likes, Dislikes and Vocational Interests," *Journal of Applied Psychology,* 27:180–189 (1943).
5. Bingham, W. V., *Aptitudes and Aptitude Testing.* New York: Harper, 1937.
6. Burtt, H. E., *Principles of Employment Psychology.* New York: Harper, 1942.
7. Canning, L., K. Van F. Taylor, and H. D. Carter, "Permanence of Vocational Interests of High School Boys," *Journal of Educational Psychology,* 32:481–494 (1941).
8. Carter, H. D., "Twin Similarities in Occupational Interests," *Journal of Educational Psychology,* 23:641–655 (1932).
9. ——— and E. K. Strong, Jr., "Sex Differences in Occupational Interests of High School Students," *Personnel Journal,* 12:166–175 (1933).
10. Darley, J. G., *Clinical Aspects and Interpretations of the Strong Vocational Interest Blank.* New York: The Psychological Corporation, 1941.
11. Finch, F. H., and M. E. Odoroff, "Sex Differences in Vocational Interests," *Journal of Educational Psychology,* 30:151–156 (1939).
12. Fryer, D., *The Measurement of Interests.* New York: Holt, 1931.
13. Long, L., "Relationship Between Interests and Abilities: A Study of the Strong Vocational Interest Blank and the Zyve Scientific Aptitude Test," *Journal of Applied Psychology,* 29:191–197 (1945).

14. Moore, B. V., *Personnel Selection of Graduate Engineers,* Psychological Monographs, No. 138 (1921).
15. Murphy, G., *Personality: A Biosocial Approach to Origins and Structure.* New York: Harper, 1947.
16. Peters, E. F., "Factors Which Contribute to Youth's Vocational Choice," *Journal of Applied Psychology,* 25:428–430 (1941).
17. Sarbin, T. R., and R. F. Berdie, "Relations of Measured Interests to the Allport-Vernon Study of Values," *Journal of Applied Psychology,* 24:287–296 (1940).
18. Seder, M., "The Vocational Interests of Professional Women," *Journal of Applied Psychology,* 24:265–272 (1940).
19. Skodak, M., and O. L. Crissy, "Stated Vocational Aims and Strong Interest Test Scores of High School Senior Girls," *Journal of Applied Psychology,* 26:64–74 (1942).
20. Spranger, E., *Types of Man.* New York: Stechert, 1928.
21. Strong, E. K., Jr., *Vocational Interests of Men and Women.* Stanford: Stanford University Press, 1943.
22. Super, D. E., *Appraising Vocational Fitness.* New York: Harper, 1949.
23. ———, *The Dynamics of Vocational Adjustment.* New York: Harper, 1942.
24. Taylor, K., and H. D. Carter, "Retest Consistency of Vocational Interest Patterns," *Journal of Consulting Psychology,* 6:95–101 (1942).
25. Tyler, L. E., "Relationships between Strong Vocational Interest Scores and Other Attitude and Personality Factors," *Journal of Applied Psychology,* 29:58–67 (1945).
26. Van Dusen, A. C., "Permanence of Vocational Interests," *Journal of Educational Psychology,* 31:401–424 (1940).
27. Williamson, E., *How to Counsel Students.* New York: McGraw-Hill, 1939.

14

OCCUPATIONAL INFORMATION

It is only part of the counselor's task to know the aptitudes, abilities, interests, and personality of the client; he must match these to the jobs available in our culture. He must give the client accurate and usable information about jobs. Different jobs require more or less ability, different personalities, and varied interests. Consequently, a counselor must have considerable information about occupations if he is to achieve successful guidance of his clients.

One of the greatest sources of difficulty for people who are about to enter occupations is their lack of knowledge and even imagination concerning occupations. Too often a person has such extremely little knowledge about jobs that he decides his liking or disliking for them on superficial and even incorrect judgments. Furthermore, there are the vast number of occupations that he is not even aware exist. Stimulation is needed to persuade people to seek the less well-known occupations. Because of inertia and lack of originality, young people are sometimes herded into the common and often overcrowded occupations. From the point of view of vocational counseling, to encourage a person to seek a career in promising but less well-known fields is often rewarding, since it may make the difference between a calloused approach and a spark of enthusiasm on the part of a client.

According to Fredenburgh (8), occupational research has shown relatively little advance during the nearly three decades of its active utilization as a tool in occupational counseling. He states:

> It has failed to provide sufficiently reliable informational materials, and to a lesser extent, adequate methods of dissemination, to make of the *job analysis* aspect of vocational guidance an effective technique. Yet individual analysis and diagnosis (the *man analysis* aspect) has advanced with considerable rapidity under the persistent attacks of psychologists and psychometrists. Although it is quite true that individual analysis and diagnosis has not reached a point of proficiency approaching satisfaction even to the most skillful clinician, it has, nevertheless, won a place in the sun which it is not likely to lose. Yet the concomitant phase, the job analysis aspect of vocational guidance, has appeared to stagnate.[1]

The importance of the need for occupational information as well as the limitations of its present development are very clearly indicated by a further quote from Fredenburgh's article:

> Occupation information has grown into a virtual octopus harassing the adequacy of other techniques of vocational guidance. Despite its present vulnerability, and the tendency of some persons high in the fore-front of leadership to depreciate or ignore the fundamental character of this tool, occupational information has held and still holds the key to the mastery of one of the two or three weightiest personal problems confronting mankind.
>
> Uncounted thousands of men and women live lives of drudgery, unhappiness, frustration, and disillusionment due to faulty, inadequate or no occupational information and counseling. This is not the only problem confronting these unhappy folk, but it is a weighty one. Free choice of vocation is a mockery when we neither know what we may choose nor what we choose when we may.[2]

A major step in the direction of solving the problems expressed by Fredenburgh has been taken by Shartle. He has performed a great service in the field of occupational information. His book, *Occupational Information,* published in 1946, provides a most extensive and reliable coverage of the material (26). Shartle defines occupational information as the "accurate and usable information about jobs and occupations." He states:

> It also includes information about industries and processes insofar as such information is directly related to jobs. Occupational information

[1] Reprinted from *Journal of Applied Psychology,* 28:53–54 (1944), by permission of the American Psychological Association, publishers.

[2] *Ibid.,* page 66.

also includes pertinent and usable facts about occupational trends and the supply and demand of labor. These must be considered in planning personnel programs in industry, in carrying out vocational counseling and advisement, and in considering the planning of training courses and educational programs. Occupational information does not include the study of the abilities, aptitudes, and other characteristics of individual workers, job seekers or students. It is used as a tool, however, in evaluating an individual's capabilities in terms of the work he has performed. Occupational information is, of course, the principal tool in exploring with an individual, the jobs, occupations, families of occupations, industries, and relative opportunities that may be ahead for him if he makes certain vocational choices.

Job analysis

A job analysis is an accurate study of the various components of the job. It is concerned not only with the analysis of duties and conditions of work, but also with the individual qualifications of the worker. Although a counselor and others connected with vocational guidance need not know how to conduct a job analysis, they can make better use of the by-products if they understand the "hows" and "whys" of the procedure. Just as the family is the basic unit in our society, so the job analysis is the element out of which the huge field of occupational information emerges. Interestingly enough, industrial as well as vocational psychologists recognize the importance of job analysis, although the former does so for different reasons. The industrial psychologist finds four major uses for job analysis: (1) the derivation of training courses, (2) the setting up of personnel specifications, (3) the improvement of job efficiency, and (4) the establishment of wage structures (10).

A better understanding of the minute nature of job analysis can be gained by a reference to the headings in the job analysis form used by the United States Employment Service, as illustrated here.

After many job analyses have been performed and collated, the jobs may be classified. It is at this point that occupational information takes on direct meaning to the counselor and his clients.

1. Job title. 2. Date. 3. Alternate job titles. 4. Establishment No. 5. Industry. 6. Branch. 7. Department.

A. MINIMUM QUALIFICATIONS FOR EMPLOYMENT.

1. Sex. 2. Age. 3. Height. 4. Weight. 5. Education: S R W English; Other. 6. Special knowledge required: (*a*) None; (*b*) Specify. 7. Experience: (*a*) None; (*b*) Same job; (*c*) Recentness; (*d*) RNP; and (*e*) Similar job; (*f*) Title; (*g*) Recentness; (*h*) RNP; or (*i*) Similar job; (*j*) Title; (*k*) Recentness; (*l*) RNP; (*m*) Other job; (*n*) Title; (*o*) Recentness; (*p*) RNP. 8. Comments.

B. RELATION OF THIS JOB TO OTHER JOBS.

1. From what jobs are workers promoted to this job? 2. To what jobs (not involving promotion or demotion) may workers on this job be transferred? 3. To what jobs are workers on this job promoted? 4. Into what jobs is this job broken down in other establishments? 5. With what jobs is this job combined in other establishments? 6. Comments.

C. DETAILS OF JOB.

1. Seasonality of job: (*a*) Not seasonal; (*b*) Seasonal periods. 2. Machine set-up: (*a*) Done by worker; (*b*) Done by others. 3. Personal tools and equipment required: (*a*) None; (*b*) Specify. 4. Accuracy required: (*a*) Coarse; (*b*) Fine; (*c*) Exact. 5. Knowledge of special measuring devices: (*a*) No; (*b*) Name and use. 6. Knowledge of graphic instructions: (*a*) No; (*b*) Name and use. 7. Average production. 8. Comments. 9. In the opinion of management, what elements of this job require most skill from the worker? 10. Name of machine. 11. Maker. 12. Size or capacity. 13. Type. 14. Special attachments: (*a*) None; (*b*) Name and use. 15. Positions and activities: (*a*) Stand; (*b*) Sit; (*c*) Stoop; (*d*) Reach; (*e*) Walk; (*f*) Climb; (*g*) Lift; (*h*) Pull; (*i*) Push; (*j*) Other. 16. Transportation of materials: (*a*) None; (*b*) Hand; (*c*) Truck. 17. Strength needed most: (*a*) Back; (*b*) Legs; (*c*) Arms; (*d*) Fingers. 18. Surroundings: (*a*) Inside; (*b*) Outside; (*c*) Hot; (*d*) Cold; (*e*) Humid; (*f*) Dry; (*g*) Wet; (*h*) Noisy; (*i*) Dirty; (*j*) Dusty; (*k*) Oils; (*l*) Acids; (*m*) Fumes. 19. Hazards: (*a*) None; (*b*) Electrical; (*c*) Explosions; (*d*) Acids; (*e*) Poisons; (*f*) Falls; (*g*) Heat or burns; (*h*) Mechanical; (*i*) Specify. 20. Team Work: (*a*) No; (*b*) With whom. 21. Pacing: (*a*) Sets own pace; (*b*) Paced by machine; (*c*) Paced by management. 22. Supervision given: (*a*) General; (*b*) Close; (*c*) Inspection. 23. Supervision given: (*a*) None; (*b*) Number supervised; (*c*) Titles. 24. Contacts with public: (*a*) None; (*b*) Describe. 25. Comments.

D. JOB ELEMENTS.

United States Employment Service

HEADINGS IN THE JOB ANALYSIS FORM USED IN THE UNITED STATES EMPLOYMENT SERVICE

Job classification

According to Shartle (26), occupations can be classified according to variables of three types.

1. Variables concerning the characteristics of individuals who are or have been employed in the occupations.
2. Variables concerning the characteristics considered important for individuals to possess who enter the occupations.
3. Variables which are primarily the characteristics of the jobs in the occupations rather than of individuals who have been employed in the occupations, are now employed, or who may be selected later to fill such jobs.

The most comprehensive and widely used occupational classification system stems from the work of the Bureau of the Census. The 1940 Census classified all occupations according to 11 major occupational groups. The major groups are as follows:

Professional and Semi-professional Workers
Farmers and Farm Managers
Proprietors, Managers, and Officials, Except Farm
Clerical, Sales and Kindred Workers
Craftsmen, Foremen, and Kindred Workers
Operatives and Kindred Workers
Domestic Service Workers
Protective Service Workers
Service Workers, Except Domestic and Protective
Farm Laborers and Foremen
Laborers, Except Farm

This occupational classification system is the most comprehensive of all, since it includes the entire labor force of the United States. However, as might be expected, other systems have been proposed and used. One example is the proposal by Beckman (1). Essentially, he combined the Census titles into five major categories according to the degrees of intelligence, education, and training required. The scale is:

1. Unskilled manual occupations
   farm laborers, deliverymen, attendants, porters

2. Semi-skilled occupations
   fishermen, waiters, truck drivers, policemen
3. a. Skilled manual occupations
      bakers, mechanics, electricians, watchmakers
   b. Skilled white collar occupations
      bookkeepers, office clerks, canvassers
4. a. Sub-professional occupations
      opticians, undertakers, laboratory assistants, nurses
   b. Business occupations
      insurance agents, floorwalkers, owners of businesses (small)
   c. Minor supervisory
      foremen, captains, inspectors
5. a. Professional (linguistic)
      authors, editors, teachers, librarians
   b. Professional (scientific)
      architects, chemists
   c. Executive
      large company officials, government officials[3]

Fredenburgh (8) proposes a functional occupational structure which, although complete, is nevertheless simple enough to be utilized in the working limits of the practical counseling situation. It is illustrated in the figure on page 411.

As Shartle points out, most occupational classification systems are complex, and are determined on the basis of the several variables, usually of those in types two and three. It appears that the most promising classification methods for the future will come from the field of psychology, in which there will be more emphasis on the traits of workers than upon duties performed in the occupation. During and after World War II, considerable work in classification was performed. Lists of critical occupations and lists relating military jobs to civilian jobs are typical examples. However, it should be noted that the chief progress was made in expansion rather than in the development of new methods and techniques of classification.

The psychologist concerned with more rigorous methodology than the mere gathering of data can be expected to develop more precise measuring devices. In addition, he emphasizes the individual just as an engineer emphasizes the machine. These precise measuring

[3] Reprinted by permission from *Personnel Journal,* 13 (1934).

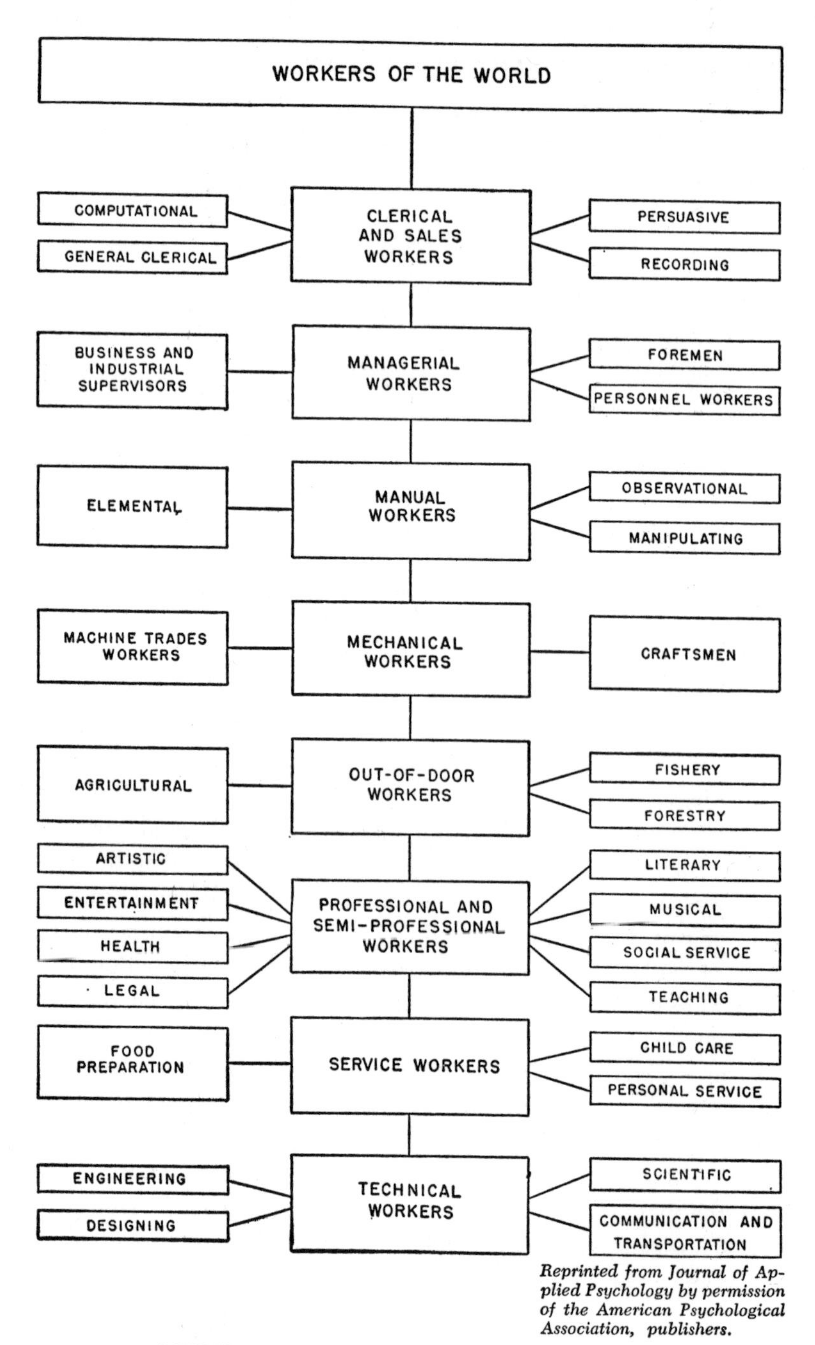

Reprinted from Journal of Applied Psychology by permission of the American Psychological Association, publishers.

A FUNCTIONAL OCCUPATIONAL STRUCTURE OF WORKERS OF THE WORLD

instruments and the emphasis on individuals, when related to occupational information, will result in much more effective vocational counseling.

The Dictionary of Occupational Titles

The *Dictionary of Occupational Titles* (4, 5, 6) is a most useful tool in the hands of a counselor. In many respects it is the most important contribution to the field of occupational information. The *Dictionary* can be considered as the central reference in any library of occupational information.

Its more important features are its definitions of occupations and an attempt at standardization of classifications of occupations in the United States. If a counselor needs to know what a pattern maker or a jigger does, or whether certain jobs are becoming obsolete, or what occupations are so interrelated that the skills from one job can be applied to others, then the *Dictionary* is most useful.

Part I of the *Dictionary* contains the definitions of 17,452 separate jobs. It also includes 12,292 alternate titles, so that 29,744 titles are defined. These definitions are based upon 54,189 job analyses (14). All job analyses resulted from the observation of actual operations of specific jobs. Each definition is composed of four parts: first, the main job title followed by alternate job titles; second, the industrial designation identifying the industry or type of work; third, the occupational code number used to symbolize the job in the classification structure; and fourth, the definition of the duties performed on the job (27).

In addition to these job titles and their definitions, the book contains a standardized occupational code structure, and an alphabetical list of common commodities sold in retail and wholesale trade together with the titles under which their vendors are classified.

Part II, "Titles and Codes," presents the structure of the U.S. Employment Service Occupational classification. It lists the titles defined in the *Dictionary* and the assigned codes in such a manner as to form related groups of occupations. These are arranged into major groups, divisions, and subdivisions. The major occupational groupings are:

Professional and Managerial Occupations
Clerical and Sales Occupations
Service Occupations
Agricultural, fishery, forestry and kindred Occupations
Skilled Occupations
Semi-skilled Occupations
Unskilled Occupations

Part III consists of information that supplements Parts I and II. Part IV, revised in 1944, is entitled "Entry Occupational Classification." (An entry occupation is one that does not require experience. It is simple; or it has on-the-job training facilities; or previous education and vocational training replace any experience requirement.) This section of the *Dictionary* gives six major occupational groupings for such occupations:

1. Professional, Technical and Managerial
   artistic work, musical work, literary work, entertainment, public service, technical and managerial
2. Clerical and Sales Work
   computing, recording, general clerical, public contact
3. Service Work
   cooking, child care, personal service
4. Agricultural, Marine and Forestry Work
   farming, fishery, hunting and trapping
5. Mechanical Work
   machine trades and crafts
6. Manual Work
   manipulative, machine tending, physical work

According to Zeran (29) the uses of the *Dictionary* in vocational guidance are (1) to aid in making a local occupational survey, (2) to learn in which industrial field a job belongs, (3) to learn the variety of jobs to which the same job title is applied in various industries, (4) to learn what work is performed in any given job, (5) to acquaint students with the vast number of ways to earn a living, (6) to prepare pupils for field trips to industrial establishments.

Work on the *Dictionary* has continued; and by 1945, six supplements had been issued. By the middle of 1945 nearly 38,000 job titles containing approximately 24,000 job definitions were included in the *Dictionary* and its supplements.

The rapid growth of the supplements, as well as the new jobs and new industries appearing, made it necessary to make many changes in the original volume. A revised *Dictionary of Occupational Titles* appeared in 1949. In the new *Dictionary,* Volume I is concerned with the alphabetical presentation of job definitions. Each definition describes the work performed and the essential elements of the job. Volume II contains the occupational classification and listing of jobs by classification code numbers (11). The new *Dictionary* contains slightly more than 40,000 job titles and 22,000 job definitions. It is an improvement over its predecessor, since it is easier to use and yields more up-to-date information.

Entry occupations

Counselors are likely to work, to a considerable extent, with people who have very limited job experience or none at all. They are likely, as well, to work with people experienced in one field who wish to (or must) change to another for which they are not fully qualified. It is therefore important for a counselor to be familiar with entry occupations. The most valuable work in this field is the compendium mentioned previously, Part IV of the *Dictionary of Occupational Titles.* In its listing of entry occupations, it will be highly useful to the counselor after he has acquired information about the client through interviews and tests. The counselor will know what jobs the client can get without previous experience and what will be open to him after he has acquired preliminary experience (18). The importance of matching even the inexperienced individual's characteristics to job characteristics cannot be too strongly emphasized.

For example, if the client is restricted because of size, weight, age, or immaturity to simple routine tasks not requiring much physical effort, he may be considered as eligible for the following entry occupations: box stackers (cigar box), counter (hat and cap), delivery boy, garment turner, handbill passer, route man helper, junior sales person, newspaper carrier, shoecleaner, or telegraph messsenger.

Occupational families

Occupational families are related occupations. It has been discovered through analyses of many jobs in many industries that there are groups of occupations which are fundamentally alike. Even though job titles and descriptions may differ, there are nevertheless resemblances from job to job in such items as basic skills required, ability, education, and tools used. Information about these can be useful as a guide in transferring workers, selecting workers for retraining, and curriculum planning in schools, as well as in placement and guidance procedures (34).

Occupational families may be constructed in different ways, according to Shartle (28). A single occupation family consists of occupations related to a certain occupation regardless of industry. For example, the occupations most closely related to that of machinist would be listed so that the placement of people with related skills could proceed smoothly when machinists were not available. Another type of occupational family is the industrial—comprised of related occupations for specific occupations in a particular industry. Such a listing is most useful in the up-grading or transfer of workers. In fact, occupational families may be constructed about any number of certain designated characteristics. For example, such a series might include, as Shartle points out, unusual strength, 8th grade education, and ability to run a machine. Job seekers who possess these three characteristics could then consider a number of occupations found in this family.

In developing occupational families it is obvious that the degrees of relationship must vary. For example, in the accompanying figure, Chart 1 presents the requirements of a wooden aircraft parts worker; Chart 2 presents the job metal and stone worker; and a comparison of these two charts shows that there is a resemblance between the two jobs.

According to Shartle (24), organizing jobs into families reveals information that is useful for two principal problems in vocational guidance:

1. It suggests a group of related occupations for which a person may be partially qualified because of his past experience, or for which he may receive basic training.

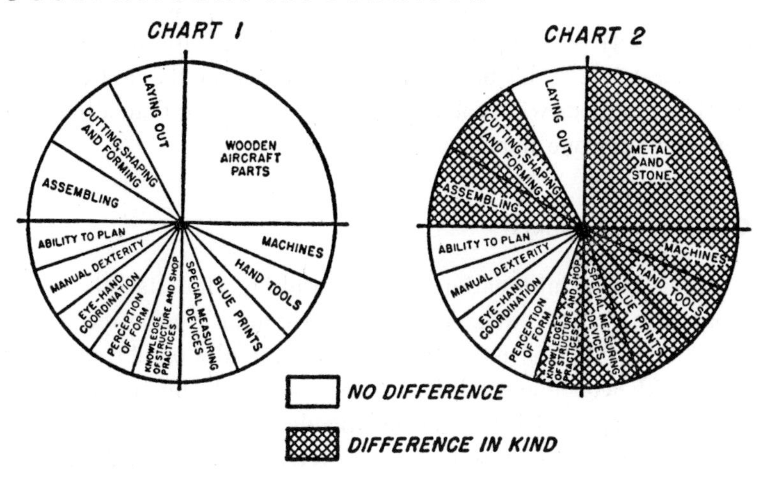

JOB REQUIREMENTS FOR A WOODEN AIRCRAFT PARTS WORKER AND FOR A METAL AND STONE WORKER

2. It suggests the type of training which may be taken by an individual in order for him to learn the basic duties of a large group of occupations.

Underlying the concept of job families, according to Toops (30), is the search for "traits" of occupations which can be measured in the same units as the traits of man to the end that reasonable judgments can be made as to whether a given man can do a particular job. Toops believes that measuring man and then allowing for the matching of jobs on the purely subjective basis without measuring jobs in comparable units is subject to considerable error. Toops states:

> just as in the taxonomy of botany one may arrive at various conceptions of what is a "family" (a sub-division of classifications) so one may arrive, by different routes, at different classification principles, at different aggregations of occupations which in the several classification systems logically may be called families.[4]

Accordingly there are several different methods of deriving job families, and it appears that although each method has certain advantages over the others no one is distinctly superior. Toops believes the common purpose of job families, if the multitude of purposes can be subsumed under one general statement, is to ascertain the paths of

[4] *Educational and Psychological Measurement*, 5:204 (1945).

transferability of occupations in accordance with the need to minimize retraining. If this be considered the criterion, the best elements of all the methods will probably yield a better result than a blind adherence to any one alone.

Occupational trends

Occupational information and its resulting vital statistics unfortunately are never static. At least two variables can be recognized. The first is the total number of people gainfully employed, which varies with economic conditions. The second is the fluctuation within an occupation, which may be independent of the total trend. This fluctuation could be caused by new developments within an industry.

Of course, in periods of prosperity jobs are more easily obtained; in recessions jobs are more scarce. However, in both prosperity and recession, there are more jobs in some fields than in others. Trends must be spotted and highlighted. Here the counselor is needed. The average person does not know how to obtain this information, or how to interpret it even when he has it.

An illustration of a study concerned with trends is the report by Palmer and Ratner titled, "Industrial and Occupational Trends in National Employment" (19). After a very careful and capable study of available statistics, they found a declining employment during the years from 1910 to 1948 in the extractive industries and increasing employment in manufacturing, trade, and services. However, they did not find any underlying trend for increased employment in the service industries *per se*. The decline in the extractive industries and personal services from the 1910 levels of employment was found to be major and those in construction and transportation, relatively minor. Within most of the broad industry groups studied, they found mixed trends in employment as technological changes modified labor requirements. Other factors contributing to these mixed trends were the substitutions of new materials for older ones and shifts in the consumption levels. By 1948 the number of women in jobs was double that of 1910. Palmer and Ratner's data reveal that, contrary to popular opinion, the number of craftsmen in relation to population actually increased. Although the trend for operatives was upward between 1910 and 1948, the decline in service occupations was greater over a longer span of time. The accompanying figure very clearly presents the changing occupational structure of industries in the United States. Careful study of it will reveal not only what is happening to employment figures within certain industries but also what changes have taken place in the jobs within each of these industries. These charts present a compelling argument for the education and guidance of individuals.

It is very important to see these changes in relation to the growth of the country, its standard of living, its style of living, and its ability to actively absorb its people in growth rather than decline. The counselor must have this broad view if he is to be truly effective.

Further, this bar chart is useful since it reveals the growth in the category of professional and semi-professional workers in all seven divisions represented. It shows the growth of clerical and sales workers. It shows the decline of laborers. It shows that skills and preparation for these skills have been becoming more important.

The survey by Palmer and Ratner is quite content to report the facts as they are; and it is obvious that counselors in familiarizing themselves with the data would make their own interpretations. As illustrative of a different use of trend figures the article by Professor Seymour E. Harris is relevant (10). Professor Harris begins by referring to the report of the President's Commission on Higher Education in which it has proposed for 1960 an enrollment of 4.6 million students in American institutions of higher learning. He points out that as late as 1900 the total enrollment in all institutions was only 238,000. As of 1947 this figure had increased to about 2.5 millions. As of 1940 the number of college graduates in the United States was approximately 3 per cent of the population.

If the recommendations of the Commission on Higher Education are carried out, the college graduate population would be as high as 25 to 35 per cent of the nation's labor force. As of the 1940 Census, nearly all of the college graduates belonged to the proprietorship, executive, managerial, and professional classes. If it is assumed that in the 1960's college men and women would seek the same kind of

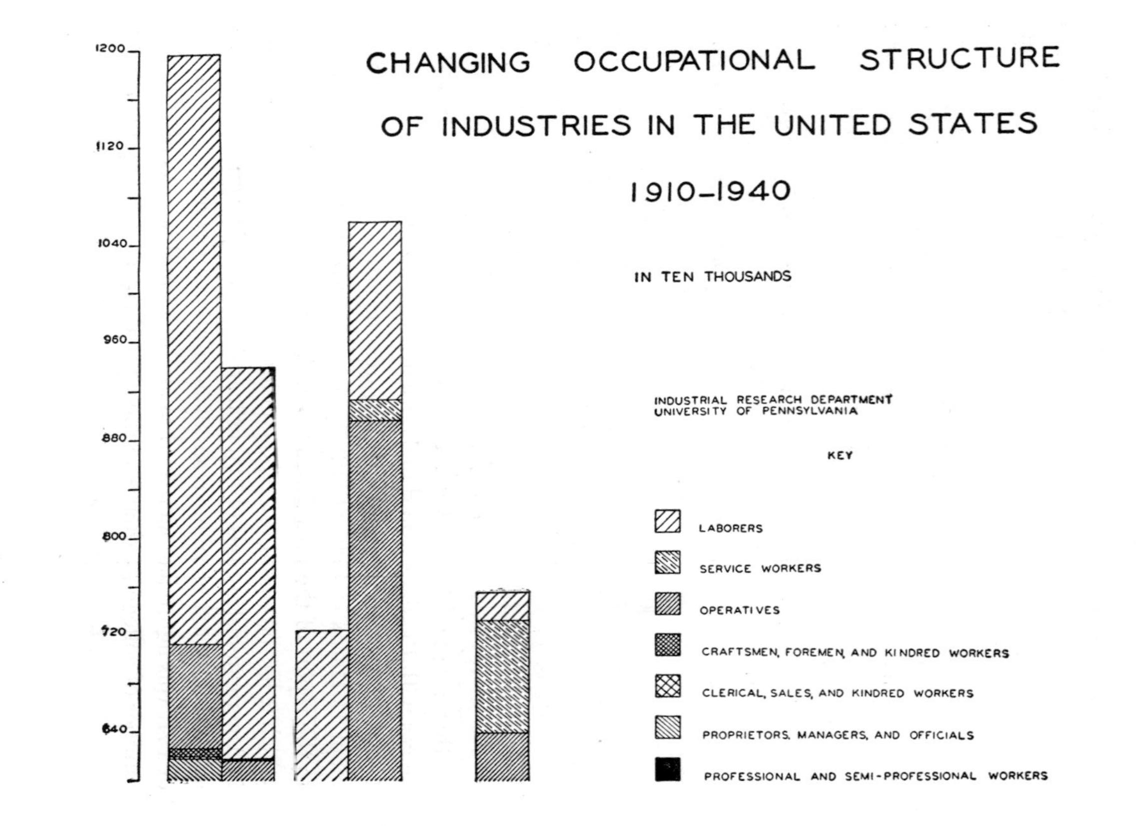
CHANGING OCCUPATIONAL STRUCTURE
OF INDUSTRIES IN THE UNITED STATES
1910-1940
IN TEN THOUSANDS
INDUSTRIAL RESEARCH DEPARTMENT
UNIVERSITY OF PENNSYLVANIA
KEY
LABORERS
SERVICE WORKERS
OPERATIVES
CRAFTSMEN, FOREMEN, AND KINDRED WORKERS
CLERICAL, SALES, AND KINDRED WORKERS
PROPRIETORS, MANAGERS, AND OFFICIALS
PROFESSIONAL AND SEMI-PROFESSIONAL WORKERS
1200
1120
1040
960
880
800
720
640

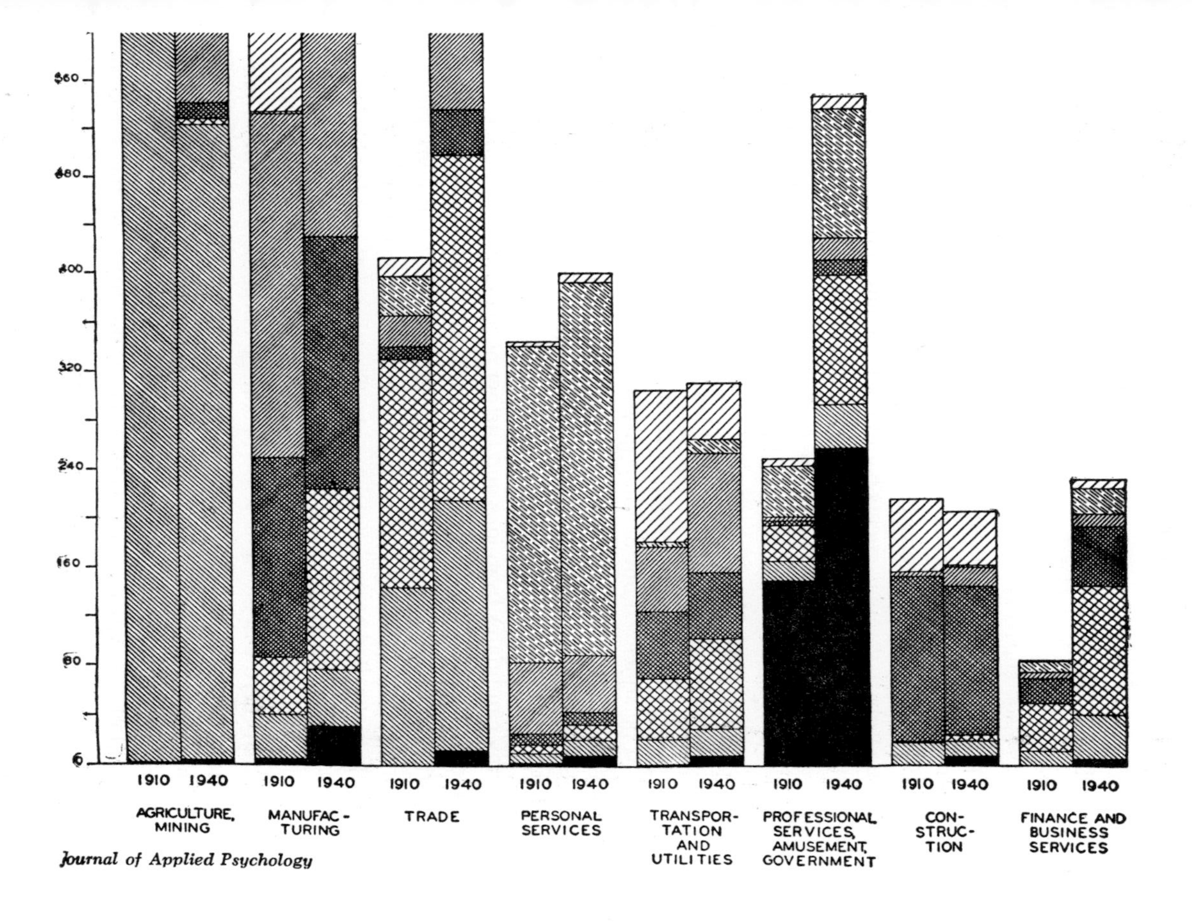

Journal of Applied Psychology

employment and in the same proportions as in the 1940's, then, according to Harris, there would simply be far more graduates than jobs.

Professor Harris is rather pessimistic. He points out that whereas the population in the period 1910 to 1940 increased by 36 per cent, the number of openings for executives was increased only 8 per cent. In 1940 the country supported one million teachers and these so inadequately that replacements could not be assured. It would require, according to Harris, a revolution in finance to increase teaching staffs by a mere 50 per cent within the next 20 years, and even then only a mere three sevenths of the anticipated number of teachers would be able to find jobs. Harris draws similar conclusions with reference to medicine, science, engineering, and law. He points out of course, with a greater surplus of college grads, many non-college men and women would be squeezed out of some professions, retailing and other employment. He believes however that a diploma should not serve as a passport when education does not contribute to the productivity of a profession. Too much insistence upon a college degree excludes other worthy candidates from jobs and further accelerates the stampede to college. According to Harris, if this trend is continued, the next generation of college graduates will have to find more and more justification for their college education on other than economic grounds. He believes that there must be a clarification of the objectives of a college education.

The authors do not share Harris' pessimism. They venture the opinion that there will be an increase in college enrollment but in no proportion to the increase which Harris accepts. In the 30-year period referred to, colleges have continually been offering broader educational opportunities. Whereas the liberal arts college with its study of Latin and Greek was a major emphasis in the 1910 era, the development of the science degrees, the business degrees, and more recently the junior colleges on a vocational level seem to be adequately coping with the need for more education that is appropriate to the times. The chances are that a compromise between the pessimism of Harris and the optimism of the authors will more nearly portray the reality of the situation in the 1960's. A reason for referring to the Harris report is to illustrate that every counselor must not only have the facts and interpretations, but must handle the problem as it pertains to each individual client.

Varied uses of occupational information

As already indicated the vocational counselor must have considerable occupational information if he is to be in a position to do an efficient job. Of course many clients of counseling agencies have previously sought some occupational information prior to their request for guidance or are very likely to have been stimulated in this direction by the counselor. However, many people do not seek or obtain formal guidance and yet their quest for occupational information goes on. Librarians are well aware of this need; many of them have shelves in the most conspicuous places of the library, in an attempt to meet it.

There are many other sources that need and make use of occupational information. To be sure, they may not be primarily concerned with the problems of vocational counseling but in many respects their problems closely interact.

For example, the state and federal employment services have a dire need for all varieties of occupational information. The *Dictionary of Occupational Titles* mentioned earlier was evolved to help meet this need. People seeking employment cannot be considerd as cases to be filed in folders and numbered. If their applications are to result in placement, then their previous experience must be properly classified according to title. If this classification is subjective, unsuitable placements, or none, result. If employment interviewers have occupational information as well as a clear understanding of job titles and duties, this kind of misdirection can be more easily avoided. (For example, it is desirable that secretaries be classified correctly. At present, confusion exists in the minds of many as to the differences in the respective duties of secretaries and stenographers. Since secretarial salaries are higher, many stenographers believe they are secretaries.) The *Dictionary of Occupational Titles* mentioned earlier was evolved to provide this sort of information.

Industry is concerned with improving its selection techniques. Industrial placement should be primarily concerned with matching the man and the job. Before an attempt is made to measure human aptitudes and abilities, accurate information about jobs must be on hand. There is no point to refined selection procedures unless the duties and requirements of the job are known.

Industry is also confronted with the task of training workers. Obviously, efficient training courses can be conducted only if one knows exactly for what job the worker is being trained. Other special problems occur in industry from time to time which demand a knowledge of occupational information. For example, placing handicapped workers is often rewarding to both the handicapped person and the employer. If the physical requirements of the job are known, it may become quite clear that the handicapped person is not really handicapped at all in relation to the job to be performed.

Educational institutions must have occupational information. Students as well as industry are often critical because the educational program has not been geared to the requirements of the job or the industry. At some point in any educator's career the question "education for what?" must arise. Admitting that all education should not have a completely vocational orientation, since at that point it would be training, it nevertheless may be true that an attempt to relate the curriculum of both high schools and colleges to a series of job analyses imposed by industries may make for more meaningful and highly motivated education.

Our educational institutions may make a further use of occupational information. They should make this material available so that their students may obtain a better understanding of the jobs they hope to seek.

The economic and social welfare of any community depends to a large extent upon its ability to employ its people. The hit-and-miss systems of the past have led to severe problems. Consequently, leading citizens have recognized that an inventory of their industries and business establishments is essential. Such inventory reveals the probable future need for workers, as well as the continued ability to absorb those in the area. One cannot be impersonal when an advertisement is seen in the business section of a newspaper, indicating that a large factory is available in a certain community. It often means that the community has failed to employ its available labor supply. When such a thing happens, the people are likely to seek other employment in more promising areas and accordingly leave. The industrial problem in the New England area as well as the ghost towns in various places point up this problem. Chambers of Commerce as well as local government officials are aware of these difficulties and attempt to offer concessions to potential employers so that existing facilities both physical and human may be utilized.

To portray forcefully the plight of a community unable to provide for its workers, a column by a newspaperman, Murray Kempton, is quoted directly.

> Cumberland, Md., Dec. 16, '49
>
> The winds of economic disaster are scuttling down the streets of this once prosperous coal and textile center with a chill force they never had in the bleakest days of 1932.
>
> The U. S. Dept. of Labor rates Cumberland as an "E" area; this is the letter technicians use to describe the few remaining concentration points of economic distress left over from last summer's little depression.
>
> Here in the coldest terms is what it means to live in an "E" area in the otherwise gilded Christmas season of 1949.
>
> Cumberland has 50,000 people. More than 7,500 of those who could work here and in surrounding Alleghany County are unemployed. And 4,148 of those jobless have exhausted the $650 annual unemployment checks to which the State of Maryland limits them.
>
> • • •
>
> **If a man is physically able** to work Maryland will not pay him direct relief. As a result, most of those 4,100 uninsured unemployed have no income beyond what straitened local governments and private charities can provide them.
>
> Whatever hope they have for Christmas rests with the Elks, the Salvation Army, the American Legion and a dozen other organizations which are pitching in manfully with the handout methods that proved so inadequate to meet the consequences of the 1929 crash.
>
> The weight of private charity is already proving too heavy for the shrunken incomes of those who still work around here. The city merchants who used to fill the Christmas baskets of Cumberland's few needy families with food can't come through this year.

They say they're already carrying hundreds of people on their books with no hope of getting it back any time soon, says Samuel Graham, the AFL printer who is chairman of the American Legion's child welfare department. As a result Graham's committee has asked the County Farm Bureau to set up food collection stations in rural areas.

• • •

It would take a war or a miracle to get back the jobs of the coal miners and textile workers who are the bulk of the area's unemployed. That grim fact is driving the young and the unattached out of Cumberland into places of greater economic promise.

Maybe a thousand have left this year. The letters come in to Celanese Local 1874 of the CIO Textile Union every day with the postmarks from Flint, San Diego, Erie and Toledo. Most of them ask for honorary withdrawal cards from the union, because the writers don't expect to come back.

Federal officials talk of channeling procurement orders in to Cumberland but so far none of the city's worried business men and union officers has noticed any. What's worse, nothing the government now plans could really solve the situation.

• • •

Cumberland was knocked off its feet by a one-two punch that strangely mixed decay with progress. Coal is dying because the fields that have sustained the area's economy for 100 years are thinning out and their methods are obsolescing. And textile jobs are falling because modern techniques enable the mammoth local celanese plant to produce just as much as it did two years ago with sixty per cent of the work force.

There are 5,000 coal miners in District 16 of the United Mine Workers Union here. A thousand of them were unemployed when John Lewis began his series of part-time strikes last summer. And most of the rest were on no better than a three-day week.

The ranking permanent Lewis lieutenant in Cumberland is William A. Morgan, a slow-spoken gentleman. He sits in an office surrounded with pictures of the master in various attitudes of challenge and response and says:

"The three-day week didn't mean anything around this area. This year a miner would have been lucky to make $1,500. Two hundred days' work would have been terrible high."

• • •

> **At its post war peak,** Celanese employed 8,000 people. It spent $23 million retooling. Now 5,100 workers are producing as much as the old force ever did.
>
> Those jobs are gone, and the people who held them, some as long as 20 years, have no skill and have never worked anywhere else.
>
> The unions and the business men are working as best they can together to find new industries. But there isn't much they can do yet. It's an ironic commentary on the situation that one of the best and smartest of them, Byron Kight, is at once president of the Cumberland Optimists Club and a funeral director.[5]

An outstanding example of the realization of this problem and its attempted solution is offered by the Upjohn Institute at Kalamazoo. This organization completed its fourth year of existence in July 1949. By way of focusing attention on the value of local effort in maintaining full employment, the Institute has chosen Kalamazoo County as the laboratory. Audits of local business firms designed to stimulate thinking along business stabilization lines are conducted. Census tracts have also been studied, with a view to advancing knowledge of local economic and social problems. Wage rate studies, on-the-job training programs for veterans, and surveys of industrial relations practices are among the many types of studies conducted by this group. Its main efforts are directed toward obtaining information on the local level which would better enable it to prevent unemployment. In other words, it is examining conditions before drastic needs arise. Although specific occupational information is not at present emphasized, this group deserves credit for at least being aware that a relation exists between the people in a community and the occupational opportunities present in it.

Steps in a Community Occupational Survey (33), a pamphlet published by the Federal Security Agency, briefly outlines the steps involved in planning and executing such a survey. The major divisions include: preliminary planning; determining scope, content, and method; preparing work plan and budget; introducing survey; directing survey personnel; collecting the data; preparing forms; editing and tabulating the data; interpreting the data and preparing the report; and using the report. In all, 71 specific steps are listed.

[5] Reprinted with the permission of the author.

Whether the approach is through a broad overall survey of the community as sponsored by the Upjohn Institute or a very specific and more confined survey as here suggested, communities have not only an obligation but a need for occupational information.

Occupational information sources

The major concern of the counselor is the application and extension of the findings in both job analysis and job classification. However, the final by-product known as occupational information can be no more valuable than the care exercised in obtaining it. It is for this reason that there are no short cuts to valid and usable information. Although there is much available information, it is important that one be able to differentiate hack writing from sound research.

Clark and Murtland (3) present one of the soundest reviews of the status of available occupational information. They are concerned with attempts to increase the scientific value of occupational information and have included in their article "Content of a Good Occupational Monograph" and "Distinguishing Marks of a Good Occupational Monograph" as working tools for the counselor.

A report by the Publications Committee, Occupational Research Division, N.V.G.A. (22), recommends standards for use in preparing and evaluating occupational literature. We reproduce them here.

Standards for Use in Preparing and Evaluating Occupational Literature

I. History of the occupation
II. Importance of the occupation and its relation to society
III. Duties
  A. Definition of occupation
    1. As determined by an official organization such as a union, trade, or professional association
    2. As given in the law; for example, licensing legislation for barbers, undertakers, and architects
    3. Carefully formulated definition acceptable to those in the occupation
    4. As defined in the *Dictionary of Occupational Titles*, Revised Edition, United States Employment Service,

Superintendent of Documents, Washington 25, D. C., 1949

(a) Specific job definitions may be found in Volume I of the *Dictionary of Occupational Titles.* These job definitions may not necessarily reflect the scope of the subject occupation. Volume II or Part IV of the *Dictionary,* however, will aid in determining the specific jobs embraced by the occupation. In such cases, job definitions from Volume I will serve as source data for the preparation of a composite definition for such occupation

B. Nature of the work
 1. Divisions of the work
 2. Specific tasks performed by workers
 3. Other occupations with which this work may be combined
 4. Tools, machines, and materials used in the performance of the work

IV. Number of workers engaged in occupation (Give source, date, and area covered by figures used)
 A. Present number
  1. Total number engaged in occupation
  2. Total males under 18; over 18
  3. Total females under 18; over 18
 B. Distribution
  1. Geographical distribution; numbers in specific areas, states, and regions
  2. Number of workers from special population segments, as broken down in the United States Census
 C. Trends and outlook
  1. Increase or decrease in number of workers
  2. Increase or decrease in number of workers in relation to population and other occupations
  3. Oversupply or undersupply of workers
   (a) Reasons
   (b) Centers of this maldistribution
  4. Trends affecting large numbers of workers
   (a) Short-term fluctuations
   (b) Long-term trends
   (c) Annual number needed to replace those dropping out

V. Qualifications
 A. Age
  1. Age range, if any, required for entrance

2. Age range, if any, required for retirement
3. Age qualifications preferred by employers

B. Sex

C. Special physical, mental, social, and personal qualifications, excluding those obviously necessary for success in all types of work

D. Special skills essential to performance on the job

E. Special tools or equipment essential for the performance of the job, which must be supplied by the worker

F. Scores on tests for employment or selection

G. Legislation affecting occupation
1. Laws regulating occupation
2. Requirements for license or certificate

VI. Preparation

A. General education
1. Necessary for successful performance of duties
2. Desirable for successful performance of duties
(a) Amount
(b) Special courses of value

B. Special training, including probable cost of training
1. Necessary. The minimum special training for successful performance of duties
2. Desirable
3. Special courses of value
4. Additional training recommended for advancement
5. Training centers
(a) Schools offering special training for this occupation. List of accredited, approved, or recommended schools with names of accrediting agencies, if any
(b) Training on the job, such as apprenticeship system, classes in the plant, in-service training for veterans, etc.
(c) Other types of training

C. Experience
1. Minimum necessary to enter occupation
2. Related experience in other occupations
3. Experience desirable for entrance
(a) Type
(b) Amount

VII. Methods of entering

A. Public employment service

B. Special employment agencies

- C. Civil service examination
- D. Apprenticeship
- E. License, certificate, etc.
- F. Other methods and channels

VIII. Time required to attain skill
- A. Special apprenticeship or union regulations
- B. Length of period of instruction on the job
- C. Length of time before median and maximum rates of pay are reached

IX. Advancement
- A. Lines of promotion; jobs from which and to which workers may be promoted
- B. Opportunity for advancement
  1. Difficulties or certainties of promotion
  2. Factors determining promotion
  3. Evidence, if any, of ratio between those in higher jobs and jobs described

X. Related occupations
- A. Occupations to which jobs may lead
- B. Occupations from which one may transfer

XI. Earnings
- A. Beginning wage range
- B. Wage range in which largest number of workers is found
- C. Maximum wage received by most highly skilled
- D. Median and average salary, if available, and differences for sex and age groups
  1. Deductions
     - (a) Uniforms
     - (b) Equipment
     - (c) Other
  2. Supplements
     - (a) Housing
     - (b) Lunches or other meals
     - (c) Commissions
     - (d) Tips
     - (e) Bonus
     - (f) Overtime
     - (g) Other
- E. Annual versus life earnings
- F. Regulations
  1. National legislation
  2. Minimum wage laws

        3 Labor Board rulings
        4. Union regulations
    G. Benefits
        1. Pensions
        2. Federal Old Age Security
        3. State Unemployment Insurance
        4. Other
    H. Rewards and satisfactions other than monetary
XII. Conditions of Work
    A. Hours
        1. Daily
        2. Weekly
        3. Overtime; frequency
        4. Irregular hours of shifts
        5. Vacation, with or without pay
        6. Regulations
            (a) State and Federal legislation
            (b) Labor Board rulings
            (c) Union regulations
    B. Regularity of employment
        1. Reason for regularity or irregularity
        2. If irregular
            (a) Normal periods
            (b) Busy periods
            (c) Dull periods
            (d) Frequency of shutdowns of plant
            (e) Cyclical unemployment
        3. Amount of irregularity
            (a) Number of workers employed during various seasons
            (b) Per cent of the force retained during dull periods
            (c) Per cent of the force added as extra workers during busy periods
        4. Attempts to regularize employment
        5. Effect of seasonal employment on the worker
        6. Effect of cyclical employment
    C. Health and accident hazards
        1. Special risks connected with the occupation and means of prevention
        2. State legislation, such as compensation for occupational diseases
        3. Mental health hazards
XIII. Organizations

A. Employees
   1. Function, purpose, activities, and strength. When there are two or more unions, technical or professional organizations for workers, the size of membership of each and other evidence of relative strength should be given, if possible
   2. Benefit funds, employment bureaus, or other services
B. Employers
   1. Function, purpose, activities, and size

XIV. Typical places of employment. An electrician, for example, may find employment in an electrical repair shop, power house, maintenance department of factories using electrical machinery, with construction companies, or with a gas and electric company

XV. Advantages and disadvantages not otherwise enumerated

XVI. Supplementary information
   A. Suggested readings; books, pamphlets, and articles
   B. Trade and professional journals
   C. Motion pictures, filmslides, and other visual aids
   D. Other sources of information, such as State and Federal government departments, reports of United States Census, State Employment Service, United States Employment Service, Bureau of Labor Statistics, etc.
   E. List of associations, firms, or individuals who may provide further information[6]

It should be clear that occupational information must not only be accurate but must be continually kept up-to-date; otherwise more harm than good could result. There are organizations devoting their time to the publication and dissemination of sound occupational information. Among such organizations, Science Research Associates of Chicago does a rather comprehensive job. They publish a series known as "Occupational Briefs on America's Major Job Fields." Each brief is four pages in length and includes job descriptions, present demand for workers, training needed, working conditions, probable future trends, and a bibliography of selected references. This series includes 250 job fields and as might be expected covers almost everything from citrus fruit and nut farmers to psychologists. A brief listing

[6] *Occupations, the Vocational Guidance Journal,* published by National Vocational Guidance Association, Incorporated, 28:320–321 (1950).

includes such fields as: frozen food workers, plastic workers, welders, jobs in government, funeral directors and embalmers, dancers, boxers and wrestlers, butchers, ophthalmologists and oculists, cooks and chefs, and tree surgeons.

A very desirable feature of this series is the continual revising of the briefs. Each year 50 briefs are revised so that no one can really become obsolete.

Science Research Associates also publishes a series of occupational monographs and life adjustment booklets. Among the occupational monographs are included twenty titles such as *Careers in Labor Relations, Highway Jobs, Occupations in Rubber, Your Future in Chemistry, Jobs in Horticulture,* and *Careers in Public Health.* The Life Adjustment Booklets number 18 and include such titles as *Getting Job Experience, Choosing Your Career, How To Live with Parents,* and *Growing Up Socially.*

Whereas the occupational briefs and monographs are useful primarily to the student, the Guidance Index and the Guidance Newsletter also published by this organization serve to keep the teacher or counselor informed. The former, issued each month of the school year, reviews pamphlets, leaflets, and books on occupational material. The latter, in typical newsletter style, serves to keep the counselor familiar with current occupational trends.

The Institute for Research publishes a series known as *Careers.* These are monographs discussing national surveys made with the cooperation of leading authorities in each field. By 1949, 207 monographs had been released and approximately 70 of these had been either printed or revised since 1948.

The procedure in producing these monographs is to review available literature after a field has been decided. Questionnaires are sent to leaders in various phases of the career. A draft is then sent to any national organizations existing in the field and ultimately a final draft is prepared. Over 13,000 school systems, libraries, and colleges use the Career Research monographs.

Among the various titles included in this series are: *Career as a Food Chemist, Botany as a Career, Career as a Tax Attorney, Service Station Operation as a Career, Careers in Geography, Mineral Eco-*

nomics as a Career, Careers for Women with the Air Lines, Osteopathy as a Career, Recreation Leadership as a Career, and *Cartooning as a Career.*

There are additional organizations doing similar work. For example, Personnel Services Incorporated publishes a series called *Occupational Abstracts.* Each abstract, approximately 2000 words in length, attempts to summarize the available literature regarding a specific occupational area. More than 125 abstracts have been published covering such diversified occupations as accountancy, cabinet making, office machine operating, guidance and personnel, airplane mechanics' work, barbering, industrial chemistry, and modeling. They also publish quarterly an occupational index that abstracts articles, books, and pamphlets on occupations. This service is most valuable to a counselor in need of contemporary references.

Vocational Guidance Monographs vary in length but are more lengthy than the previously described series. Very roughly they are about 6000 words, and have been issued in more than 75 occupational areas. The Commonwealth Book Company of Chicago, publishers of these Monographs, has released occupational information in such diversified fields as restaurant management, watchmaking and repairing, welding, forestry, tailoring, bee-keeping, and air conditioning.

This listing of private publishers has been presented with two purposes in mind: first, to make it known that such sources exist, and second, by deliberately and yet randomly picking titles, to indicate the wide range of information available in diversified occupational fields.

Not to be overlooked is the efficient job that the United States Government performs in disseminating occupational information through its Office of Education of the Federal Security Agency. The publications for sale from the Superintendent of Documents, U.S. Printing Office, Washington, D.C., are very valuable. They have the additional advantage of selling at very low prices. For example, they have a series of guidance leaflets, which usually sell for 5 and 10 cents, in such fields as nursing, librarianship, veterinary medicine, optometry, and osteopathy. These pamphlets cover such material as income, opportunities, and the colleges specializing in preparation, together with a list of the approximate cost of achieving the goal. In addition, selected references are furnished for each of the fields.

The government has also published a series of job descriptions in non-technical language. These are organized according to industry and include such items as duties, equipment used, job relationships, and qualifications for employment. Material has been published on the Laundry Industry, the Lumber and Lumber Products Industry, the Cotton Textile Industry, Industrial Service and Maintenance Occupations, Automobile Manufacturing Industry, and Office Occupations, among others.

From time to time, the government prints special pamphlets on current needs. For example, the pamphlet, *Teachers Are Needed* (29), printed in 1944, is written for the vocational counselor so that he may have the information indicating the shortage of qualified teachers as well as offering information to clients for more effective recruitment. Another pamphlet, *Why Industrial Training Needs Books* (32), forcefully calls attention to the need for printed materials in industrial training. A moment's thought will reveal that verbal people, and this often includes authors of books, are not likely to have the technical information required about machine tools and shops. On the other hand, the technical people are not likely to have the skills to write effective books in this field. The result is a dearth of much-needed material. One other example can be found in the publication *Professional Library Education* (2). Most people will superficially regard the librarian as only the person who stands behind the desk in the community library. Overlooked are the following aspects of a librarian's work: ordering, cataloging, reference department, periodical department, readers' advisory service, and school department, among others. The average grade school or high school student, seeing the very limited library facilities in his school, has no comprehension of the very comprehensive facilities of college and university libraries, which in many respects are the very centers of research. Also unknown to the average person are the rather adequate libraries of large business corporations and insurance companies. Other useful government sources of publication related to occupational information are the Occupational Outlook Division of the United States Bureau of Labor Statistics and the Women's Bureau of the United States Department of Labor.

Each year finds many books written on a wide variety of occupations. The following titles are just a few examples of the volumes upon volumes: *How To Run a Gift Shop* (20), a readable book on efficient gift shop management; *Photographic Occupation* (15), a discussion of the outstanding fields in photography; *Traffic Management* (31), an outline of the nature and scope of the work of the traffic manager; *How To Be a Successful Advertising Woman* (16), edited by Mary Margaret McBride and consisting of well-written descriptions of such careers as public relations, merchandising, and advertising art; *The Book of Opportunities* (21), which gives sidelights on 4000 American occupations; and *Twenty Careers of Tomorrow* (12), a book about the future in various fields of endeavor; *Job Guide* (13) which supplies authoritative information about employment opportunities, problems and conditions in such leading industries as air, chemicals, and rubber; and *Career Opportunities* (17), which gives such information as what they do, how to qualify, where one works, and how much one earns for such positions as accountant, statistician, hotel manager, reporter, editor, farmer, and teacher.

An additional source of occupational information is the large circulation magazine. From time to time, such magazines as *Life, Look, Pic* and *Glamour* publish accurate and readable information directly concerned with occupations. A very professional and authoritative article appeared in the August 1946 issue of *Glamour*, entitled, "Every College Major Leads to a Career" (7). Although in this article the point is well taken that the four years of college are not in any narrow sense the years for learning a trade, they are nevertheless important for professional preparation. A chart was compiled consisting of the 38 majors most often chosen, and for each of these fields important occupational information was given. The fields begin with accountancy, anthropology, and archaeology and run the entire alphabetical gamut ending with psychology, sociology, and zoology. The figure on pages 436 and 437 is a condensation of the chart published in the article.

MAJOR SUBJECT	ACCOUNTING	ANTHROPOLOGY	ARCHAEOLOGY	ARCHITECTURE
BEGINNING JOBS AND POSSIBLE SALARY RANGE *See Footnotes 1 and 3*	Statistical work; bookkeeping-machine operator; bookkeeper; junior accountant. $1800 or $2500 if applicant is well qualified. A minimum salary—$25 per week.	Odd jobs in museums classifying specimens; minor job with an expedition. Salary: depends on budget.	Junior assistant in a museum; minor job with an expedition (if you had a good major in a good institution). Volunteer basis, or a small salary.	Junior draftsman (must start in a routine job to get apprentice training). Model making. $24 to $40 per week perhaps.
PLACE TO APPLY GEOGRAPHICAL LOCATION	Employment agencies; college placement bureaus. Private business: banks, retail stores, insurance companies, utilities, public accounting firms. Not confined to one section of the country.	Museums and universities; educational and research institutions; Federal Government (Civil Service). Geographical location: Museums everywhere.	Museums (private and university). Try to join an expedition as a specialist. Teaching college. Widespread—girls usually have indoor museum jobs in cities. Experts go abroad.	Architectural firms; construction firms; Federal and State Government (Civil Service). Own business. Wherever people live or have places of business.
SPECIAL APTITUDES AND PERSONAL QUALIFICATIONS *See Footnote 4*	Analytical ability, liking for figures, ability to interpret facts and to make quick and accurate decisions, self-reliant and confident.	Keen interest in research. Specialize.	Should have a great interest in some particular region, field work, museums, deciphering inscriptions; specialize.	Artistic and scientific aptitudes; leadership; should be artist, engineer and business woman. Must have imagination, common sense and esthetic sense—ability to visualize good designs.
ADDITIONAL COLLEGE TRAINING DESIRED FELLOWSHIPS	College degree sufficient (B.S.). For C.P.A.—degree from accredited school with right professional standing; must also pass state C.P.A. examination. Inquire at your school about fellowships.	Graduate Degree M.A. or Ph.D.—essential for advancement. Inquire at your school about fellowships, scholarships, and assistantships.	Graduate work provides best opportunities and is essential for any real advancement. Consult your own school about fellowships, scholarships, and assistantships.	Additional year or two of specialization desired beyond B.A. Most schools take 6 or 7 years to complete course. Specialize. Inquire at your school about fellowships.

ADVANCED POSITIONS AND POSSIBLE SALARY RANGE *See Footnotes 2 and 3*	Chief accountant; general auditor; comptroller; credit manager; budget officer; treasurer; C.P.A.; teaching; actuary; tax specialist. Salary: $4000 and up.	Research (on level with university teaching). Field work; teaching; writing; administration; consultant. Salary—usually low, except for college teaching (see EDUCATION).	Excavating expert. With reputation may become a director. University lecturer; teaching—college; Federal Government (Civil Service). Salary—up to $4000.	Bide your time for a better job—skilled draftsman. Salary: $50 to $100 per week. Own business; teaching; writing; assistant editor; assistant curator. Total compensation—$5000.
GENERAL PROSPECTS	The opportunities are good for exceptionally well-qualified women but not for the person with mediocre ability.	 Limited opportunities. Little demand without thorough training.	Opportunities are poor, but depends on the job market, and what jobs are available. Many girls have become successful. Risky career.	This depends on your ability and aptitude. If you are serious about succeeding you should find good opportunities.
INCIDENTAL ADVANTAGES	You work in a professional atmosphere with a professional status. The work offers great variety and interesting and varied contacts. Business knowledge gained is invaluable.	Travel is unlimited. Advantages are personal.	Great deal of travel involved to remote parts of the world in advanced work. May become famous through field work.	Some jobs require a great deal of travel. It is a man's field primarily and most girls marry before getting very far.
DISADVANTAGES	Not a soft job—may have long hours during busy periods. A certain amount of overtime is inevitable. Considerable experience necessary for top jobs.	Exposure to all kinds of weather on field trips. Field reseatch rugged.	Definite physical hazards. Field work—primitive conditions.	Definite health and physical hazards. Confining work and tendency to overwork long hours. There is a prejudice against women.

Reprinted from the August, 1946, issue of Glamour *magazine, The Condé Nast Publications, Inc.*

ILLUSTRATION OF INFORMATION IN GLAMOUR'S CHART

A relatively new source of occupational information is visual aids. The Coronet Instructional Film Company of Chicago has produced some 16mm sound films in color; *Finding the Right Job* and *Choosing Your Occupation* are two examples. They require approximately 10 minutes and are useful as aids in group guidance techniques. A serious attempt is made to present the material accurately and yet interestingly enough so that high school students would be stimulated. A teacher's guide is provided. *Aptitudes and Occupation* and *I Want to Be a Secretary* have been prepared with the collaboration of Dean E. G. Williamson of the University of Minnesota and Dean M. E. Hahn of the University of California. A teacher's guide to enable better integration between film showing and class discussion is available for these films as well.

The use of films as a source of occupational information, although it attempts to be educationally valuable, is in its infancy. There is no doubt that people would rather see pictures than read, and therefore such attempts should be encouraged.

Future of occupational information

Although huge volumes could be filled with all the material there is on occupational information, this would only add to the quantity. The future value will depend on the refinement of techniques approximating scientific method. Emphasis must be given to ways and means of making material on occupational information available not only to counselors and teachers but also to young people. The knowledge that most people have on occupations is extremely limited. Possibly attention to occupational information orientation courses on all educational levels will result in improvement of the type of course offered; this improvement could result in educational administrators' being willing to introduce such courses on a wider level. However, other problems intimately related to occupational information must be considered. For example, the relationship existing between job level and job satisfaction must be accurately known. When jobs and men are matched accurately, then job satisfaction is possible. The range of jobs is as varied as the range of abilities in individuals.

The mismatching causes difficulty in the individual and ultimately in his family and in society. The tools of the psychologist for measuring the individual appear to be more highly developed at the moment than the instruments that measure occupational information. Future work, to be valuable, will require conscientious attention to the development of better instruments for recording occupational information. Considerable attention should also be given to relating occupational families and individual interests. When more is known in this area, better guidance can be administered.

Summary

Occupational information is necessary in the matching of jobs and men. A vocational psychology that emphasizes only the knowledge of individuals' characteristics and abilities is incomplete. Research in occupational information has lagged behind, and new and refined methods and instruments are needed.

Acquiring knowledge of facts about jobs begins with the technique known as job analysis, the accurate study of the various components of the job. This procedure leads to job classification; it is here that the information takes on significance for vocational psychology.

The *Dictionary of Occupational Titles* is in many respects the most important contribution to the field of occupational information.

Relating similar occupations regardless of industry or job title results in a grouping known as occupational families; knowledge of these is useful in job transfers and training.

In addition to specific knowledge about occupations, knowledge is important about trends in total number of people employed, as well as about changes within an occupation or industry which may be independent of the total trend.

Others besides vocational counselors need occupational information; two such groups are industry and educational institutions.

Sources of occupational information should be carefully checked for accuracy and recency. The evaluation of such material is aided by reference to such an outline as the "Content of a Good Occupational Monograph." Science Research Associates, the Institute for Research, and Personnel Services Incorporated are three private publishing firms that do a rather accurate job of publishing occupational information. The government publishes, at a slight cost, much useful material in this field.

Bibliography

1. Beckman, R. O., "A New Scale for Gauging Occupational Rank," *Personnel Journal*, 13:225–233 (1934).
2. Beust, N. E., *Professional Library Education*, Washington, D.C.: Library Service Division, Office of Education (1937).
3. Clark, F. E., and C. Murtland, "Occupational Information in Counseling: Present Practices and Historical Development," *Occupations*, 24:451–475 (1946).
4. *Dictionary of Occupational Titles.* Part I, "Definitions of Titles." Washington, D.C.: U.S. Government Printing Office, 1939.
5. *Dictionary of Occupational Titles.* Part II, "Titles and Codes." Washington, D.C.: U.S. Government Printing Office, 1939.
6. *Dictionary of Occupational Titles.* Part IV, "Entry Occupational Classification." Washington, D.C.: U.S. Printing Office, 1944.
7. "Every College Major Leads to a Career," *Glamour,* August, 1946.
8. Fredenburgh, F. A., "The Gordian Knot of Vocational Guidance," *Journal of Applied Psychology*, 28:53–66 (1944).
9. Greenleaf, W. J., *Dictionary of Occupational Titles,* Federal Security Agency, Washington, D.C., 1949.
10. Harris, S. E., "Millions of B.A.'s but No Jobs," *New York Times Sunday Magazine*, January 2, 1949, p. 9.
11. Heinz, C. A., "The Revised Dictionary of Occupational Titles," *Occupations,* 27:538–540 (1949).
12. Huff, D., and F. Huff, *Twenty Careers of Tomorrow.* New York: Whittlesey House, 1945.
13. Kasper, S. H. (ed.), *Job Guide.* Washington, D.C.: Public Affairs Press, 1945.
14. Lawshe, C., Jr., and G. A. Satter, "Studies in Job Evaluation, Factor Analysis of Point Ratings for Hourly Paid Jobs in Three Industrial Plants," *Journal of Applied Psychology,* 23:189–198 (1944).
15. Leyson, B., *Photographic Occupations; Choosing Your Career in Photography.* New York: Dutton, 1940.

16. McBride, M. M. (ed.), *How To Be a Successful Advertising Woman.* New York: McGraw-Hill, 1948.

17. Morris, M., *Career Opportunities.* Washington, D.C.: Progress Press, 1946.

18. Nichols, W. O., "A New Tool for Counseling: Dictionary of Occupational Titles, Part IV, Revised," *Occupations,* 23:447–451 (1945).

19. Palmer, G. L., and A. Ratner, *Industrial and Occupational Trends in National Employment* (University of Pennsylvania Research Report No. 11), Industrial Research Department, Wharton School of Finance and Commerce, 1949.

20. Peel, A. J., *How To Run a Gift Shop.* Boston: Cushman and Flint, 1941.

21. Platt, R., *The Book of Opportunities.* New York: Putnam, 1942.

22. Publications Committee, Occupational Research Division, N.V.G.A., "Standards for Use in Preparing and Evaluating Occupational Literature," *Occupations,* 28:319–324 (1950).

23. Schulz, C. L., *Your Career in Nursing.* New York: McGraw-Hill, 1941.

24. Shartle, C. L., "Vocational Guidance and Job Families," *Occupations,* 20:506–509 (1942).

25. ———, "Developments in Occupational Classification," *Journal of Consulting Psychology,* 10:81–84 (1946).

26. ———, *Occupational Information: Its Development and Application.* New York: Prentice-Hall, 1946.

27. Stead, W. H., "The Dictionary of Occupational Titles," *Occupations,* 19:16–20 (1940).

28. *Teachers Are Needed* (Vocational Division Leaflet No. 14), U.S. Office of Education, Federal Security Agency, Washington, D.C.

29. *The Occupational Dictionary as a Tool in Vocational Guidance Work,* Federal Security Agency, Washington, D.C., 1940.

30. Toops, H. A., "Some Concepts of Job Families and Their Importance in Placement," *Educational and Psychological Measurement,* 5:195–216 (1945).

31. Wilson, G. L., *Traffic Management.* New York: Appleton-Century, 1941.

32. *Why Industrial Training Needs Books,* American Library Association, Chicago, in cooperation with the U.S. Office of Education, Federal Security Agency, Washington, D.C., 1941.

33. Zapoleon, M. W., *An Outline of Steps in a Community Occupational Survey.* Washington, D.C.: Federal Security Agency, U.S. Office of Education, Vocational Division, 1941.
34. Zerga, J. E., "Job Analysis: a Resume and Bibliography," *Journal of Applied Psychology,* 27:299–367 (1943).

15

THE RELATION OF OCCUPATIONAL INFORMATION TO VOCATIONAL PSYCHOLOGY

OCCUPATIONAL information is a necessary part of vocational psychology. However, all the aspects of occupational information were not reported in the previous chapter. In order to emphasize the importance of knowledge concerning occupations such topics as job analysis, job classification, the *Dictionary of Occupational Titles*, entry occupations, occupational families, occupational trends, and varied uses of occupational information were presented.

For a more complete understanding of the matching of jobs and men one should have not only the two separate aspects of knowledge—occupational information and information about the individual—but an understanding of the relations between the characteristics of the job and of the man. This chapter has two objectives, first to relate these two fields, and second to demonstrate why occupational information, although not primarily psychological information, is nevertheless an important part of vocational psychology.

Possibly a good way to begin this interweaving is to review briefly some of the information concerning job satisfaction. Hoppock (6) in the epilogue to his study on job satisfaction proposes the following six major components of job satisfaction:

1. The way the individual reacts to unpleasant situations.

2. The facility with which he adjusts himself to other persons.
3. His relative status in the social and economic group with which he identifies himself.
4. The nature of the work in relation to the abilities, interests, and preparation of the worker.
5. Security.
6. Loyalty.

A tenable hypothesis is that a person is predisposed to job satisfaction or dissatisfaction prior to being employed. A review of such items as Hoppock proposes makes it clear that guiding people into jobs compatible with their intelligence, aptitudes, abilities, interests, and personality is more likely to result in job satisfaction than concentrating on specific and minor aspects of the job. Such aspects of personality as desire for recognition, desire for prestige, level of aspiration, and ability to accept challenges must be considered, along with many, many others. In other words, vocational psychology through both guidance and selection is a basic key to job satisfaction. What good will music during work or air conditioning or colored walls do for efficiency if the persons employed are on the wrong jobs? An individual with a long list of "gripes" will readily find opportunities to vent his wrath regardless of the job.

Occupational information is important in vocational guidance not only for uncovering facts about occupations but also for helping to solve the psychological problem of matching jobs and men so that maximum job satisfaction may be obtained. The problem of the relationship between occupational level and job satisfaction is a very real one; such information should be possessed by a counselor in addition to the facts about occupations. Super conducted a study in precisely this area (13). Although there were only 273 subjects, his findings are not only interesting but worth serious consideration. Super points out that since most workers are on the two lowest rungs of the occupational ladder, and since dissatisfaction is prevalent on at least one of these levels, the social implications of the findings concerning occupational level and job satisfaction are important. He suggests that remedial and preventive work should probably be done to change the aspiration levels of some individuals to bring them more in line with their abilities and with social possibilities. The specific major findings of Super's study were:

1. Slightly over 60 per cent of the group were satisfied with their jobs.
2. There is a significant, but not linear, relationship between occupational level and job satisfaction.
3. Two occupational scales were found to exist: one of white collar workers; the other of manual. Professional occupations are most productive of job satisfaction, Managerial next, Commercial least, in the white collar scale; skilled occupations rank highest in the manual scale.
4. These scales overlap when compared in terms of productivity of job satisfaction, the Skilled and the Semi-Skilled groups (two highest manual) ranking above the Commercial group (lowest white collar) in job satisfaction.
5. Amount of change of occupational level had little, direction of change considerable effect on job satisfaction.
6. Maintenance of the highest attained occupational status is the important factor in the relationship of change of occupational level to job satisfaction.
7. Roughly 70 per cent of the group had never changed occupational level; comparisons with an earlier study suggest that this may indicate a decrease in occupational mobility in recent years.
8. "Aspirational discrepancy", or the size of the gap between present occupational level and the level aspired to, is negatively related to job satisfaction.
9. The nature of the work itself appeared as the most frequent reason, in the minds of the men themselves, for disliking a job, economic reasons ranking second, and managerial policies an infrequent third.
10. Job satisfaction was found to develop cyclically, older adolescents (20–24) tending to be satisfied with their jobs, young men (25–34) dissatisfied, and older men satisfied, with a possible temporary decrease at the ages 45–54; this was taken as partial confirmation of Buhler's theory of life stages.
11. There is a tendency for men to rise in the occupational world as they get older; this is interpreted as explaining away the correlation of age with job satisfaction, reported by other investigators.[1]

Since these 11 conclusions by Super are clearly stated, there is no need to elaborate upon them here. It is justifiable merely to emphasize the fact that occupational information must be related to the psychological problem of job satisfaction. Guidance can be more effective

[1] Reprinted from *Journal of Applied Psychology,* 23:561 (1939), by permission of the American Psychological Association, publishers.

when such information and its relationships are more precisely known.

Paterson and Stone (12) sampled approximately 100 persons in each of seven occupational groups on two occasions. Their findings each time were rather consistent and indicated an occupational hierarchy of job satisfaction from the most dissatisfied (street-car men) to the most satisfied (employers). Paterson and Stone report a tendency for the dissatisfied to desire to change their life's work to professional, executive, or skilled trades even though their present jobs are on much lower levels. They interpret this to be rather unrealistic in adults.

Most researchers agree that the job satisfaction index rises with occupational level. Kornhauser (8) asked four economic groups seven questions dealing with personal satisfaction and in each instance found that higher income groups indicated greater personal satisfaction. The questions and answers are presented in Table 21.

It is to be noted that in only two questions the majority of the low-

TABLE 21

COMPARISON OF GROUPS ON PERSONAL SATISFACTION QUESTIONS
(Numbers refer to percentages.)

	Over $5000	$2000 to $5000	$1000 to $2000	Under $1000
1. Do you feel that your children have as much opportunity as they should have?	83	60	46	39
2. Do you like the kind of work you do?	95	91	81	67
3. Do you feel that your pay is fair?..	90	69	53	34
4. Would you say that you are treated well by the people you work for?..	96	90	86	77
5. Do you feel that there is any danger of losing your job?	89	80	72	49
6. Do you feel that you have as much opportunity to enjoy life as you should have?	82	69	55	36
7. Do you feel that you have a good chance to get ahead in life and become fairly well off?	96	78	69	43

* Reprinted from G. W. Hartmann and T. Newcomb (eds.), *Industrial Conflict*. New York: Cordon Press, 1939, page 242, by permission of the publishers and The Society for the Psychological Study of Social Issues.

est income groups give favorable answers; yet these two questions can be considered as the core of job satisfaction.

Shedding additional light on the problem of job satisfaction in relation to income is the report of Super (14). He found that men who believe that they had chosen their jobs for economic reasons tended to derive more satisfaction from their avocations than their vocations, whereas those men who believed they had chosen their jobs because of their interest in them derived more satisfaction from their vocation.

When the psychological characteristics of a person do not match the job, dissatisfaction is almost inevitable. Furthermore it is not correct to assume that an employer's attitude about employee job preferences is identical with employees' attitudes. Since this is a fact, then it becomes necessary to know the factors which influence job preferences of employees. Jurgensen (7), in a study of 1189 men applicants, found a rank order of job preferences as follows: security, achievement, type of work, company, co-workers, pay, supervisor, hours, working conditions, and benefits. His report, which resembles most of those in this area, does not find that pay is as important as it is ordinarily assumed. Surely, it does not rank first. Watson (15) and Blum and Russ (2) have obtained similar findings.

A job or future occupational life work must meet the needs of an individual as to interest, intelligence, and so forth. To be sure, it must be related to economic needs as well; but this correlation alone cannot be considered enough for job satisfaction.

Vocational counseling is not an academic or social welfare idealistic plan. It is at the core of job satisfaction. It can salvage many lives for future job satisfaction and happiness, since it proceeds by matching the individual and a job in accordance with both the person's and the job's requirements.

Psychological contributions to job analysis

The preceding chapter was concerned with a description of the technique of job analysis. However, this is primarily the job rather than the man aspect of work. Two distinct contributions relating the job and man aspect have emerged which show clearly how a job can be described in human characteristics. Viteles has proposed the job psychograph (17); the occupational ability pattern was devised by the Employment Research Institute of the University of Minnesota (4).

The job psychograph requires that each trait be rated on a five-point scale in accordance with its degree of importance for a specific job. Illustrated here is a job psychograph for a power machine operator (10).

JOB PSYCHOGRAPH FOR A POWER MACHINE OPERATOR*

	1	2	3	4	5	Remarks
1. Energy		X				
2. Rate of discharge			X			
3. Endurance		X				
4. Control	X					
5. Coordination A				X		
6. Coordination B					X	
7. Initiative		X				
8. Concentration			X			
9. Distribution (of attention)			X			
10. Persistence			X			
11. Alertness		X				
12. Associability		X				
13. Visual discrimination				X		
14. Auditory discrimination	X					
15. Tactual discrimination	X					
16. Kinesthetic discrimination			X			
17. Space perception				X		
18. Form perception		X				
19. Accuracy			X			
20. Visual memory		X				
21. Auditory memory	X					
22. Kinesthetic memory		X				
23. Understanding		X				
24. Understanding (Quickness)	X					
25. Observation			X			
26. Planfulness		X				
27. Intelligence	X					
28. Intellect	X					
29. Judgment	X					
30. Logical analysis	X					
31. Language ability	X					
32. Executive ability	X					

Key:
1. Negligible.
2. Barely significant.
3. Significant.
4. Of great importance.
5. Of utmost importance.

* *Occupations, the Vocational Guidance Journal,* published by National Vocational Guidance Association, Incorporated, 12:53 (1934).

It can readily be seen that the job psychograph rates a job in terms of specific human qualities; when persons have similar qualities, it is assumed that job and man can be matched. The implication for guidance is that a person without actual job experience can be assumed to be able to perform the job when his traits match those required on the job.

Paterson, Dvorak, and others on the staff of the Employment Research Institute of the University of Minnesota were also interested in carrying the job analysis technique to the point where job and man could be matched. The occupational ability pattern is a profile of test scores given to people in similar occupations. It is assumed that abilities on a job can be measured by a sampling of test results of people in that job. Typical sample patterns are illustrated on page 450.

It is obvious that this technique is useful in vocational guidance. By using it the counselor can recommend to the individual the job whose profile most nearly resembles his own.

Paterson (16) correctly evaluates the work of the Minnesota group in this area when he states that they promoted the integration of vocational tests and occupations. The test results of job applicants were utilized, chiefly through public employment agencies, in recommending jobs; this utilization resulted in transferring these people to more satisfactory work from fields in which they were experienced but with which they were not satisfied.

The use of occupational ability patterns led not only to suitable recommendations for inexperienced people but also, according to Paterson, to the concept of job families described in the previous chapter.

Paterson, Schneidler, and Carlson (11) have proposed a classification of occupations with respect to their requirements of abstract intelligence, mechanical ability, social intelligence, artistic ability, and musical talent. For each occupation, each characteristic is to be given a rating according to the degree to which it is required. Paterson *et al.* have made these ratings for about 400 occupations. Table 22 illustrates the rating scales for a few sample occupations.

Along similar lines but much more involved is the listing of occupational requirements by Oakley and Macrae (9). Each occupation

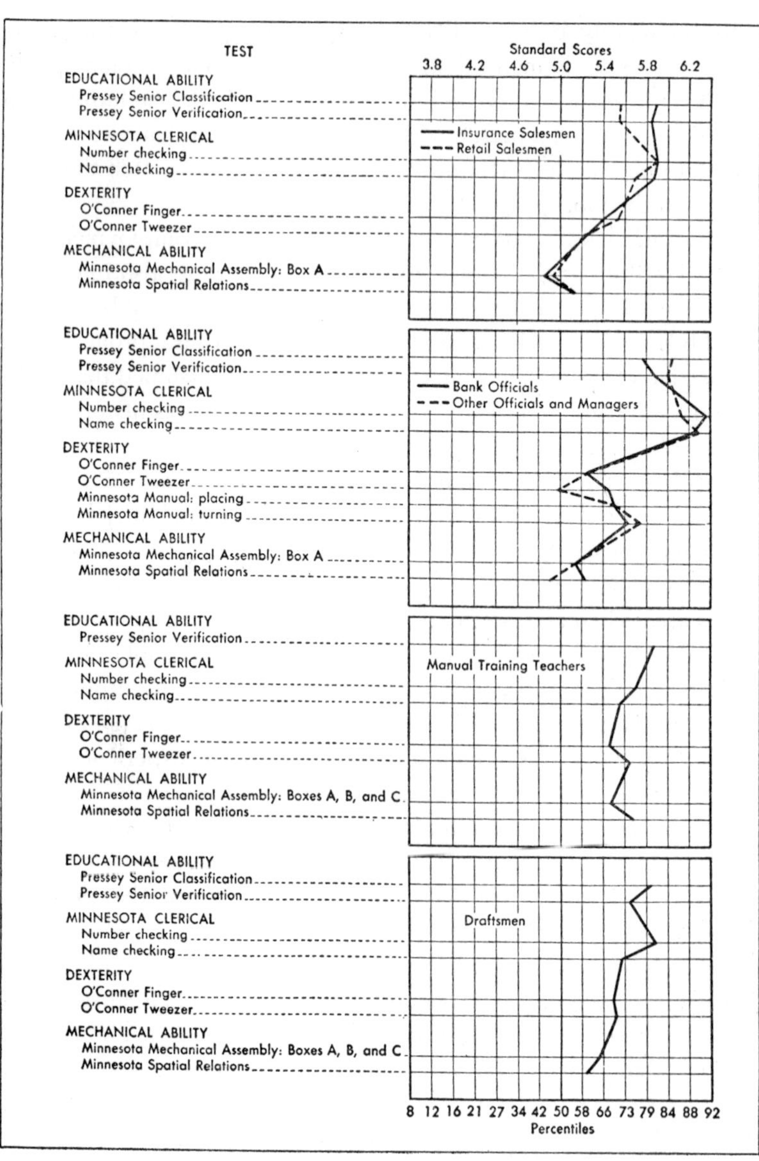

SAMPLE OCCUPATIONAL ABILITY PATTERNS

TABLE 22

MINNESOTA OCCUPATIONAL RATING SCALES

Occupation	*Abstract Intelligence*	*Mechanical Ability*	*Social Intelligence*	*Musical Talent*	*Artistic Ability*
Apiarist	4	5	6	6	6
Chemist, Industrial	1	2	6	6	6
Dentist, in city	2	2	2	6	6
Superintendent or principal of school	2	5	2	6	5
Portrait Painter	2	3	3	6	1
President, College	1	6	2	6	6

is rated for 23 abilities and qualities. Such items as scientific ability, manual dexterity, emotional restlessness, sense of beauty, and form perception are included and rated. A rather comprehensive listing of occupations, starting with accountancy and ending with wholesale selling, is included in the classification system.

The relation of job classification to vocational psychology

Psychological test data can be given increased meaning when related to occupational classifications. For example, the interrelation between scores on intelligence tests and men gainfully employed in specific occupational classifications has implication for vocational guidance. It can allow the assumption that certain levels of intelligence are required in certain occupations; recommendations can then be made accordingly. An example of how psychological test data and dictionary occupational title classifications can be related is afforded by a reference to a report by Christensen (3). Harrell and Harrell (5) reported the relationship existing between the scores on the Army General Classification Test and the civilian occupations of 18,782 enlisted men of the Army Air Forces. Christensen in his article presents a table of the average score obtained by people in various occupations together with the measure of variability known as the "1% confidence interval." In other words, variability from the obtained average beyond the range presented is likely to occur only once in every hundred cases. Related to these scores and occupational titles are the codes used in Parts II and IV of the *Dictionary*. Table 23 presents Christensen's data.

TABLE 23

OCCUPATIONS OF THE HARRELL-HARRELL SCALE OF OCCUPATIONAL INTELLIGENCE STANDARDS: BY PARTS II AND IV OF THE DICTIONARY OF OCCUPATIONAL TITLES CLASSIFICATIONS*

Mean AGCT Score	*One Per cent Confidence Interval*	*Occupation*	*Part II*	*Part IV*
128.1	125.8–130.4	Accountant	0-01.20	0-X7.11
127.6	124.7–130.5	Lawyer	0-22.10	0-X7.12
126.0	121.5–130.5	Public Relations Man	0-06.97	0-X3.5
125.9	122.3–129.5	Auditor	0-01.60	0-X7.11
124.8	116.8–132.8	Chemist	0-07.02†	0-X7.03
124.5	120.0–129.0	Reporter	0-06.71	0-X3.5
124.2	121.9–126.5	Chief Clerk	0-97.13	0-X8.10
122.8	120.7–124.9	Teacher	0-31.01†	0-X6.00
122.0	119.4–124.6	Draftsman	0-48.18†	0-X7.74
121.0	118.4–123.6	Stenographer	1-37.12	1-X2.3
120.5	115.3–125.7	Pharmacist	0-25.10	0-X7.03
120.1	117.2–123.0	Tabulating Machine Operator	1-25.64	1-X2.9
120.0	117.9–122.1	Bookkeeper	1-01.02	1-X2.0
119.0	114.4–123.6	Manager, Sales	0-97.61	0-X8.10
118.7	115.3–122.1	Purchasing Agent	0-91.60	0-X7.15
118.1	111.1–125.0	Production Manager	0-97.51	0-X8.41
117.6	114.0–121.2	Photographer	0-56.11†	0-X1.5
117.5	116.0–119.0	Clerk, General	1-05.01	1-X2.0
116.8	115.3–118.3	Clerk, Typist	1-37.34	1-X2.2
115.8	112.5–119.1	Installer, Telephone and Telegraph	5-53.030	4-X6.181
115.8	113.0–118.6	Cashier	1-01.52	1-X2.0
115.5	110.0–120.0	Instrument Repairman	5-83.971	4-X6.310
115.3	113.0–117.6	Radio Repairman	5-83.411	4-X6.185
114.9	110.8–119.0	Artist	0-04.01†	0-X1
114.0	112.2–115.8	Manager, Retail Store	0-72.91	0-X8.10
113.4	110.0–116.8	Laboratory Assistant	0-50.22†	0-X7.04
112.5	108.4–116.6	Tool Maker	4-76.210	4-X2.010
111.8	110.0–113.6	Stock Clerk	1-38.01	1-X2.8
110.9	106.5–114.3	Musician	0-24.12	0-X2
110.1	108.3–111.9	Machinist	4-75.010	4-X2.010
109.8	104.9–114.7	Watchmaker	4-71.510	4-X6.310
109.3	107.0–111.6	Airplane Mechanic	5-80.100	4-X2.103
109.2	107.4–111.0	Sales Clerk	1-70.10	1-X5.7
109.0	106.7–111.3	Electrician	4-97.010	4-X6.181
108.5	105.4–111.6	Lathe Operator	6-78.64†	6-X2.411
107.6	105.3–109.9	Receiving and Shipping Checker	1-34.15	1-X2.8
107.5	105.7–109.3	Sheet Metal Worker	4-80.010	4-X6.313

107.1	102.5–111.7	Lineman, Power and Tel. & Tel. . . .	5-53.410	4-X6.181
104.2	102.4–106.0	Auto Service Man	5-81.910	4-X2.103
104.1	101.5–106.7	Riveter	6-95.071†	6-X4.419
103.5	97.6–109.4	Cabinetmaker	4-32.100	4-X6.320
103.3	98.4–108.2	Upholsterer	4-35.710	4-X6.353
102.9	100.1–105.7	Butcher	4-09.205	4-X6.376
102.7	99.1–106.3	Plumber	5-30.210	4-X6.217
102.2	97.8–106.6	Bartender	2-21.10	2-X5.2
102.1	99.8–104.4	Carpenter, Construction	5-25.110	4-X6.220
101.9	96.5–107.3	Pipe Fitter	5-30.010†	4-X6.217
101.8	100.0–103.6	Welder	4-85.040	4-X6.280
101.3	99.2–103.4	Auto Mechanic	5-81.010	4-X2.103
101.1	95.2–107.0	Molder	4-81.010†	4-X6.343
100.8	97.4–104.2	Chauffeur	7-36.010	6-X2.492
99.5	96.9–102.1	Tractor Driver	7-36.510	6-X2.492
98.3	96.0–100.6	Painter, General	5-27.010	4-X6.246
97.9	93.5–102.3	Crane Hoist Operator	5-73.510	4-X2.493
97.0	91.8–103.2	Weaver	4-15.020	4-X2.452
95.3	90.1–100.5	Barber	2-32.01	2-X5.6
92.7	90.6– 94.8	Farmer	3-06.10	3-X1.00
91.4	89.6– 93.2	Farmhand	3-19.20	3-X1.00
90.6	86.5– 94.7	Miner	5-21.010†	4-X6.295
87.7	82.7– 93.4	Teamster	7-37.100	3-X1.11

* *Occupations, the Vocational Guidance Journal,* published by National Vocational Guidance Association, Incorporated, 25:99 (1946).
† These classifications are dependent upon this study's interpretation of the data supplied by Harrell and Harrell.

Christensen also presents the average scores on the A.G.C.T. for the major occupational groups. These are presented in Table 24.

TABLE 24

AVERAGE SCORE ON THE A.G.C.T. OBTAINED IN VARIOUS MAJOR OCCUPATIONAL GROUPS*

Classification	*Average Score on A.G.C.T.*
Professional	122.9
Managerial	118.8
Semi-Professional	117.6
Sales	112.1
Clerical	104.4
Skilled	101.7
Semi-skilled	99.6
Personal Service	98.7
Agricultural	92.0

* *Occupations, the Vocational Guidance Journal,* published by National Vocational Guidance Association, 25:97–102 (1946).

As Christensen points out, such data as reported have limited value at best; they are more suggestive than determinative. A counselor must recognize that factors other than intelligence are required in occupations. Interests, aptitudes, labor supply, and education must be considered. These tables may have their most appropriate use as indicators of intelligence requirements for certain jobs; even then exceptions must be considered possible.

Summary

Vocational psychology through its integration of occupational information and information about the individual matches jobs and men. An objective of vocational psychology is to increase the satisfaction of man in his work world; this can be done by knowing the factors in man that contribute to job satisfaction.

The job psychograph and the occupational ability pattern are two outgrowths of the job analysis technique that attempt to describe jobs in human qualities. The former depends upon ratings, while the latter is a profile resulting from a battery of psychological tests. Two other systems that stress the human qualities are the Minnesota Occupational Rating Scales and the listing of occupational requirements proposed by Oakley and Macrae.

Determining the intelligence scores of people in occupations results in a scale of occupational intelligence standards.

Bibliography

1. Bingham, W. V., *Aptitudes and Aptitude Testing.* New York: Harper (1937).
2. Blum, M. L., and J. Russ, "A Study of Employee Attitudes Towards Various Incentives," *Personnel,* 19:438–444 (1942).
3. Christensen, T. E., "Dictionary Classification of the A.G.C.T. Scores for Selected Civilian Occupations," *Occupations,* 25:97–102 (1946).
4. Dvorak, B. J., *Differential Occupational Ability Patterns.* Minneapolis: University of Minnesota Press (1935).
5. Harrell, T. W., and M. S. Harrell, "Army General Classification Test Scores for Civilian Occupations," *Educational and Psychological Measurement,* 5:229–239 (1945).

6. Hoppock, R., *Job Satisfaction.* New York: Harper, 1935.
7. Jurgensen, C. E., "Selected Factors which Influence Job Preferences," *Journal of Applied Psychology,* 31:553–654 (1947).
8. Kornhauser, A., "Analysis of Class Structure of Contemporary American Society," in G. W. Hartmann and T. Newcomb (eds.), *Industrial Conflict.* New York: Cordon Press, 1939.
9. Oakley, C. A., and A. Macrae, *Handbook of Vocational Guidance.* London: University of London Press, 1937.
10. Otis, J. L., and K. R. Smith, "Job Psychograph in Job Analysis," *Occupations,* 12:47–56 (1934).
11. Paterson, D. G., G. Schneidler, and J. S. Carlson, "Minnesota Occupational Rating Scales," from Bingham's *Aptitudes and Aptitude Testing.* New York: Harper, 1937, pages 130–137.
12. Paterson, D. G., and C. H. Stone, "Dissatisfaction with Life Work among Adult Workers," *Occupations,* 21:219–221 (1942).
13. Super, D. E., "Occupational Level and Job Satisfaction," *Journal of Applied Psychology,* 23:547–564 (1939).
14. ——— "Avocations and Vocational Adjustment," *Character and Personality,* 10:55–61 (1941).
15. Watson, G., "Work Satisfaction," in G. W. Hartmann and T. Newcomb (eds.), *Industrial Conflict.* New York: Cordon Press, 1939.
16. Williamson, E. G. (ed.), *Student Personnel Work.* Minneapolis: University of Minnesota Press, 1949.
17. Viteles, M. S., *Industrial Psychology.* New York: Norton, 1932.

16

THE COUNSELOR

THERE ARE many different kinds of counselors, serving in schools, private and public agencies, prisons, hospitals, industry, and private practice. The backgrounds of training and experience vary considerably; probably the only characteristic common to all is the title of counselor.

The reason for the variation among counselors is probably that there is no real agreement as to what a counselor does, and no common core of training. Counselors are known to have different duties; some may even unjustifiably function as disciplinarians. Cochrane (1) reports that he found counselors in schools still using the "scare technique." For example he reports the following: "If Johnny didn't get busy and do his lessons, he was told he was doomed to be a 'mere' manual worker, and to be bossed around by pupils who learned their conjunctions."

The training objectives are obscure. Jager (6) writes that much of counselor training "has been directed at an obscure target" and that much of it "has been too specific, concentrated on high skill in certain techniques without enough orientation to the whole task of the counselor or even to the functional effect on the counselee.'

The day is passing when anyone with inadequate preparation can be known as a counselor. The field is in process of professionalization. Standards are being developed. In line with this trend is the amendment to the By-Laws voted by the National Vocational Guidance

Association (7) in 1948 in regard to Professional Membership. Professional Members are defined as "persons who are technically competent in the fields of guidance and personnel and who possess the following minimum qualifications":[1]

A. A Bachelor's Degree from a recognized college or university, plus the completion of 30 semester hours of appropriate professional graduate courses (the list of such courses to be determined by the Board of Trustees).

B. Four years' work experience in education, business, industry, social service, and/or government, at least two years of which were in guidance and personnel fields, including any of the following activities, singly or in combination:

1. Actual performance in, or immediate supervision of
   (a) Educational and vocational counseling.
   (b) Teaching classes in guidance and personnel topics in secondary schools and colleges.
   (c) Research in developing information techniques or procedures in guidance.
   (d) Job placement or adjustment of workers, involving counseling.
2. Engagement in the preparation of professionally competent people in the above fields.

C. The endorsement of two professional members signifying that the candidate is technically competent and ethical in practice.[2]

Recognizing that there are professionally competent counselors without the prerequisite college training, the National Vocational Guidance Association added section "D" to allow such people to be considered for professional membership. This is often referred to as the "Grandfather Clause."

D. Prior to July 1, 1950, guidance experience satisfactory to the Professional Membership Committee may be substituted for college training as follows:

Two years of guidance experience for the 30 semester hours of appropriate professional graduate courses. One year of guidance experience for each year of undergraduate college training. (This means that a person with a bachelor's degree and no

---

[1] *Occupations, the Vocational Guidance Journal,* published by National Vocational Guidance Association, Incorporated, 26:511 (1948).

[2] *Loc. cit.*

graduate training will need at least six years of experience, and one with no college training will need at least 10 years of relevant experience.)[3]

The Professional Membership Committee does not choose indiscriminately. Although there were about 4600 members in the Association as of 1950, only about 800 were Professional Members (8).

The problem is not only to increase the requirements and standards for those who are at present known as counselors but also to devise more adequate means for the training of future counselors.

Jager (6) suggests the job analysis approach to study what various counselors do and to find a common core of training for all. In addition to this common core would be added training in the various special skills required for specific counseling positions. Among the desirable trends in training counselors Jager reports changes in the curriculum, the addition of in-service training, and new methods of teaching by seminar and workshop, where the students obtain practice as well as book-learning.

The job analysis approach can yield significant information about counseling occupations; conferences among leaders in the field can lead to agreement on qualifications, training, and experience. Both of these methods have already yielded results that will not only help stabilize the training in counseling but also eventually give it definitive professional status.

Sample job descriptions of counseling occupations

A counselor is often known by other names. Shartle (9) describes the duties, qualifications, and prospects for such related occupations as: College Counselor; Psychologist for Physically Handicapped; Consulting Psychologist; Employment Interviewer; Employment Counselor; and Vocational Counselor.

Six occupations, as reported by Shartle, follow:

Counselor, College

(Social Adviser, Director of Vocational Guidance, Junior Dean)

---

[3] *Loc. cit.*

DUTIES:

The combinations of duties vary considerably with specialization in one or two phases frequently occurring.

Assists college students to understand their backgrounds, potentialities, and interests and to make intelligent educational and vocational plans. Uses personal interview, test results, school and college grades, reports from instructors, course requirements, and other data.

Performs various types of guidance such as personal and social, in addition to educational and vocational guidance with students by personal interview.

Assists students in finding full or part time work; may conduct an employment agency for campus work for students during school year and attempt to place graduates in suitable vocations.

May have charge of a testing program and administer group tests as well as individual psychological tests for guidance purposes. In larger institutions testing may be largely individual in nature with the general program under separate direction. Interprets test results in student counseling.

Frequently contacts college instructors regarding students' programs and progress. Positions which are combined with Freshman Adviser involve reports to parents, principals, and students in assisting the orientation of the students.

May serve as veterans' counselor in colleges selected by local Veterans Administration agencies to test and counsel veterans regarding choice and suitability of vocational objectives and certification for vocational rehabilitation.

May teach several classes in psychology and personnel depending on size of institution and extent of duties.

QUALIFICATIONS:

At least an M.A. degree is necessary and a Ph.D. is desirable. Courses in adolescence, personnel administration, education, guidance, sociology, tests and measurements, abnormal psychology, counseling, clinical psychology, and occupational information are important. A well rounded college training is helpful as is some teaching experience. While courses in psychology are important, a degree in guidance, education, or personnel work may be preferred.

Several months of supervised practice is sometimes provided, especially in larger institutions.

Previous experience in interviewing, counseling, or industrial personnel work is often necessary.

Both men and women, preferably 25 years of age or older, are employed in these positions. They should be able to make good first impressions, establish rapport with students, and be sincerely interested in students' problems. They may be required to supervise other counselors and to sell the program to administrators.

PROSPECTS:

There is a chance to advance from perhaps an Adviser on a part time basis to Counselor to Assistant Director to Director of the Personnel Bureau. Further promotions may be either toward administrative or teaching positions in other branches of the college.

Most colleges have expanded their counseling staffs with recently increased enrollments, and the advent of veterans to the campus and use of college counseling and psychometric staffs by the Veterans Administration. The employment level should remain permanently higher than before World War II because of increased enrollments and the greater emphasis on this type of work in the regular college program. Some positions in large schools are part time in nature making it possible for the individual to pursue graduate studies.

Beginning full time salaries range from $2400 to $3600 with those of Director of Personnel or Dean ranging from $3500 to $6000 and a few at higher levels.[4]

Psychologist for Physically Handicapped

(Rehabilitation Training Officer, Vocational Psychologist for Handicapped)

DUTIES:

Administers and may devise special intelligence and aptitude tests for deaf, blind, and other handicapped who are entitled to state aid. Uses test results as aid in recommending state vocational or educational aid or placement.

Recommends hearing aids, orthopedic aids, lip or Braille lessons, and other techniques to aid handicapped persons to rehabilitate themselves. May supervise training.

Gives vocational, educational, and other types of counsel on basis of interviews and tests. In most cases counsel is given to those persons who qualify for state aid in order to make them employable. Any

[4] Reprinted from *The American Psychologist,* 1:563–564 (1946), by permission of the American Psychological Association, publishers.

schooling, correction of handicaps, or training is aimed at vocational rehabilitation of the individual. In this counseling, a knowledge of sign language and lip reading is valuable if not essential.

QUALIFICATIONS:

The B.A. or M.A. degree is preferred with a major in psychology, speech, or rehabilitation. Desired courses are in psychometrics, vocational rehabilitation, counseling, personality maladjustments, neurology, anatomy, and others depending on field of specialization.

Some experience in testing, counseling, or work with handicapped persons in speech clinics, schools for deaf or blind, or other is valuable. At least a year is preferred.

One must be patient and understanding and able to gain confidence of client. Since this work often involves working and living in an institution, personal adaptation to institutional living may be essential. Loss of hearing or sight may not be a disqualifying factor in many cases.

PROSPECTS:

There seems to be an increase in state services for the handicapped and a demand for more skilled workers. Eventually much of the work of the Veterans Administration in regard to disabled veterans will be delegated to state agencies. Federal subsidies for vocational rehabilitation have given impetus to better services in this area and will apparently continue to do so.

In the state bureaus for vocational rehabilitation there are beginnings as a Vocational Counselor working up to District Supervisor or State Supervisor. Or opening positions might be in various schools for deaf or blind in teaching, counseling, and testing. States vary as to the amount of centralization of these agencies.

The salary varies from $1500 to $4500 because of the variety in types of positions ranging from a Speech Psychologist with a B.A. degree to a Vocational Psychologist with a Ph.D. who is directly responsible to the Director of the Vocational Rehabilitation Bureau.[5]

Consulting Psychologist

(Personnel Psychologist, Clinical Psychologist, Educational Psychologist, Industrial Psychologist, Personnel Consultant)

[5] *Ibid.*, page 573.

DUTIES:

The duties under this title vary considerably according to the field of specialization. The psychologist works as a member of a consulting firm or service or as an individual consultant. The psychologist usually specializes in one of the following areas:

Consultation with industry regarding personnel procedures, particularly selection methods including testing. May perform research for the client in order to determine facts necessary for developing improvements and for evaluating new procedures.

Consultation with school systems regarding the establishment and maintenance of psychological services. May personally test, interview, and treat problem cases.

Consultation with individual clients in private practice. Tests, interviews, and treats individual cases who seek assistance or are referred by schools, industry, and other organizations. May specialize in vocational guidance, remedial work, or psychotherapy.

Consultation with social agencies. Examines clients, holds staff conferences, may perform research.

QUALIFICATIONS:

A Ph.D. degree is necessary with specialization in the area in which consultation is given.

Several years' experience in the area of specialization is necessary, unless the consultant is a member of an organization and works under supervision of another consulting psychologist.

Must be able to make good first impressions and to deal with clients tactfully and cooperatively. Skill in written and oral expression is important. Must have high ethical standards.

PROSPECTS:

There has been an increase in consulting work during the war. It may reduce somewhat but will not go back to prewar levels. Competition may be intense and many persons not qualified in psychology oversell their services and discredit consulting work generally.

In most instances the psychologist is pretty much "on his own" and his achievements are determined by his ability to render a competent, satisfactory service.[6]

Employment Interviewer

DUTIES:

Interviews applicants to determine if applicants possess proper qualifications, and, in public employment offices, classifies them

[6] *Ibid.*, pages 575–576.

occupationally according to qualifications. May administer and interpret trade tests and may interpret aptitude test scores.

In public employment offices, matches worker qualifications to job requirements, and refers applicants to employers. In a business establishment sends applicant to appropriate foreman for final approval.

May visit employers (in positions in public employment offices) and by interview with personnel officer or by observing job, notes requirements and assists company in finding suitable workers from those registered for work. Maintains contacts with employers as to their current needs and their job specifications.

By interview and by having applicant fill in forms, obtains information regarding experience, schooling, and other factors. May classify applicant according to *Dictionary of Occupational Titles* occupational code. In private industry may obtain badge photos, fingerprints, and may interpret pay deductions and regulations, and explain union membership, retirement, and hospitalization. May maintain file of application cards.

QUALIFICATIONS:

This position may require a B.A. degree which includes work in testing, interviewing, personnel administration, occupational information, and perhaps some courses in clinical psychology and statistics. Often persons with no formal psychological training are employed.

In government service, year for year training and experience may be substituted for college education. Experience should include personnel work and a knowledge of oral trade questions and aptitude tests. In industry hiring requirements may vary considerably.

One must be able to keep forms and records correctly, be able to analyze qualifications well, and be able to meet people and gain their confidence.

PROSPECTS:

This is an entry occupation for work in either industrial personnel or public employment service and may lead to a position in general personnel administration, occupational analysis, counseling, or psychological testing.

At present there are several thousand workers employed in public employment offices and turnover is quite large. Industry will probably create little increased demand for this type of position as turnover decreases and the labor demand and supply become more settled. In case of large unemployment, needs for these workers in public employment offices will increase.

Salary ranges are from $1500 to $2400.[7]

Employment Counselor

DUTIES:

By interview obtains pertinent facts regarding education, experience, and interests. Utilizes work history information and test results and discusses with the client possible occupational alternatives. Gives occupational information and other information and assists the client in reaching a vocational decision.

Has client fill out forms, and records facts obtained through interviews. Indicates test batteries to be administered to the client and may personally administer tests. Interprets and records test results.

Advises clients regarding job duties and opportunities and where and how to secure training.

Secures pertinent occupational information from published sources and from visits to plants in order to advise clients about the qualifications required of jobs, sources of training, and vocational trends.

QUALIFICATIONS:

For work in public employment offices in most states, education up to five years of college may be substituted for experience in vocational counseling or related work—but at least one year of experience is necessary. Valuable college courses include tests and measurements, interview techniques, occupational information, and industrial psychology. In private agencies there is greater emphasis on educational standards. A B.A. or M.A. degree is usually required with major work in psychology, guidance, and related subjects.

Ability to gain rapport with clients is essential. A counselor must be able to evaluate and analyze problems and qualifications of clients and transform them into vocational possibilities. In higher levels of counseling it involves ability to plan, instruct, and supervise.

PROSPECTS:

The public employment services employ several hundred such counselors. Future numbers will increase or decrease according to appropriations. The salary, promotional possibilities, and the number of counselors employed vary considerably according to the states. Salary grades are related to the general level of salaries paid by the

[7] *Ibid.*, pages 577–578.

particular state government. Veterans' preference regulations also vary among the states.

There has been considerable increase in the demands of private agencies.

Entrance salaries vary from $1500 to $2400. More responsible positions range from $2800 to $3200. Supervisory positions range up to $4500.[8]

Vocational Counselor, Community Agency
(Psychologist, Community Center)

DUTIES:

Provides free educational and vocational counsel to applicants at a social center or community supported agency; refers cases to appropriate community agencies; plans future program.

Selects and administers appropriate tests to applicants, scores them, attends case conferences with other counselors and interprets findings. Gives counsel on basis of interviews, test results, and case conference.

Places applicants desiring jobs within limits of agency or advises clients of other agencies for placement.

Sends cases to other social or welfare or employment agencies to aid counselees in other ways than that particular agency can serve. May recommend agencies for financial, medical, legal, and other assistance.

Organizes programs in conjunction with fellow workers as to improvement or enlargement of services, research projects, and organizational changes.

Conducts group guidance for young people regarding problems of vocational adjustment.

QUALIFICATIONS:

An M.A. degree is usually required with courses in clinical, abnormal, social, and vocational psychology. It is desirable to have some college work in sociology, economics, case work, guidance, and statistics.

Clinical, educational, or vocational work is valuable experience but may not be required for employment.

One must be able to gain rapport of counselees, work congenially with others, and be able to meet the public.

[8] *Ibid.*, page 578.

PROSPECTS:

This may be an entry position for various types of counseling. One may start as a Junior Psychologist and work to Chief Psychologist or Guidance Director of the social agency.

Communities seem to be expanding their work in this area. One should get in touch with the various community and social agencies regarding opportunities. Salaries range from $1770 to $3000.[9]

From these six job descriptions, one can see that counselors may hold varied positions. They require different degrees of responsibility and different amounts of training and experience. However, each counselor deals with human beings in an interview situation and should be familiar with psychological tests. Each, regardless of his specialization, is required to be familiar with educational, vocational, and personal counseling. The preparation of the counselor should therefore not only have a common core of basic techniques and be intensive in a specific area but should also be general enough to allow for successful awareness of related area problems.

Counselor preparation

The kind of training and experience that counselors should have is not yet standardized.

The counselor in a school will have not only curricular and vocational problems to deal with but also social and emotional ones. School counselors are frequently teachers who are given an extra assignment as counselors. They may not be prepared academically, by experience, nor by personality to do counseling. This situation must be recognized as faulty and in need of correction. An attempt to remedy it is indicated by a committee report (3) to the eighth National Conference of State Supervisors of Guidance Services and Counselor Trainers. The report is concerned with proposing the duties, standards, and qualifications for counselors employed in schools. It may also serve as a basis for a training program.

The qualifications and training of the counselors is described in terms of education, experience, and personal fitness:

---

[9] *Ibid.*, pages 579–580.

A. Education
   1. General
      A counselor must have a bachelor's degree from an accredited institution and must meet fully the regular State educational requirements for a teacher's certificate valid for the grade level in which the counselor is employed.
   2. Professional
      A counselor must have at least the equivalent of a master's degree with emphasis in the essential areas of the guidance program. A basic course in "Principles and Practices of the Guidance Program" should be a prerequisite to this training. The essential areas in each of which some training is required are:
      a. Core areas of training
         (1) The counseling process
         (2) Understanding the individual
         (3) Educational and occupational information
         (4) Administrative relationships of the guidance program
         (5) Research and evaluation procedures for counselors
      b. Training supplementary to the core areas. In addition to the above required core areas of training, counselors shall have had or shall secure training in psychology, economics, and sociology.

B. Experience
   A practicing counselor must have had at least 2 years of successful teaching or counseling experience, at least 1 year of cumulative work experience in a field or fields other than school work, 3 to 6 months of supervised counseling experience or internship, and sufficient experience in activities of social significance, such as volunteer work in the community, to reveal interest in working with others and to indicate leadership ability.

C. Personal fitness
   The personal qualifications of a prospective and practicing counselor can be placed in four groups: Scholastic aptitude, interests, activities, and personality factors. Any one of these sources may not provide sufficient evidence, but the four combined should indicate a pattern of interest in and an ability to work with people.[10]

The description of personal fitness is incomplete. This is evidently so because of the difficulty in determining what is personal fitness

[10] *Proceedings of 8th National Conference of State Supervisors of Guidance Services and Counselor Trainers,* Federal Security Agency, Office of Education (1949).

for a counselor. To indulge in glittering generalities and list positive favorable traits is useless. The combined judgment of instructors in courses and supervisors of training might be an effective rating method until a more adequate determination is made available. In any case, the judgment about personal fitness should be made before the person actually undertakes counseling as a profession; or he may materially damage the people he counsels.

The descriptions of education and experience requirements is a step forward in the training of school counselors. The counselor with such training will be better prepared for dealing with his clients.

Vocational counseling will also profit from an improved training program. The vocational counselor as well as other counselors must understand the individual as a whole. This understanding is necessary for clients whose problems are essentially educational or vocational as well as for those whose problems are personal. In the cases where the problem is primarily educational or vocational, little attention need be given to the personal aspect. Where the educational and vocational problems are interlocked with personal ones, then the latter must be resolved. If they are neglected, the educational and vocational problems cannot really be solved.

When the personality maladjustment is primary, this should be recognized by the counselor. If the maladjustment is determined by the temporary situation rather than by deeper conflicts, a well-trained counselor will be able to cope with it. If major, such as a deep neurotic condition or a psychotic illness, it becomes the function of the counselor to help the client obtain therapy. As the very sick individual recovers, the counselor will be able to help him make a vocational adjustment. In cases of major personal maladjustment the counselor would probably best function as part of a mental hygiene team consisting of psychiatrists, clinical psychologists, and social workers as well as counselors.

In order to function effectively counselors must have knowledge of psychological theory and technique, be skilled in interviewing techniques, learned in psychological tests and clinical methods. This essentially psychological training must also be supplemented for those counselors who are to do vocational or school counseling with such special skills as occupational information, group guidance techniques, and administration.

These requirements seem very exacting. However, if counseling is to reach the level of a profession, they would seem to be unavoidable. It may well develop in practice that there be generalists who will be able to deal with all sorts of problems and specialists who will handle the complicated specialized problems. This is often what actually happens in the other professions. The generalist counselors might be able to handle educational and vocational problems but not know enough about certain occupational areas. The clients would then be sent to a specialist in that area who would also be a skilled counselor. The generalist should also be able to spot clients whose personal problems are such that they cannot deal with them. A specialist in that area may then be called upon to take over the counseling. However, each counselor no matter what his duties are must be trained in vocational as well as psychological techniques.

Evidence from various sources points to a trend to both broaden and deepen the training of counselors. The emphasis is at least on a core of training common to all.

Froehlich (4) has been active in meetings with representatives of various professional counselor organizations. In a report for the Counselor Training Committee to The Division of Counseling and Guidance of the American Psychological Association, he describes the content of psychological courses needed by counselors. The report states:

> The training a counselor needs should be determined by those duties he will be called upon to perform. The planning of all counselor training programs should be predicated upon this principle. Many of the counselor's duties are determined by his area of specialization or place of employment. But not all duties are unique to the particular situation in which he works. To perform those duties common in all counseling, counselors need a basic core of training. One element in this core is training in psychology.
>
> That a working knowledge of psychology is requisite for all counselors is universally accepted. But at the same time, there exists a wide range of opinion regarding the content of this training. The Counselor Training Committee of the Division of Counseling and Guidance Psychologists of the American Psychological Association

has considered what psychological training might reasonably be expected of all counselors. This committee recommends that all counselors receive training in each of the following areas of psychology:

1. The foundations of psychology, including an overview of the various fields of psychological study.
2. The psychology of growth and development with special emphasis on the age group to be served by the counselor.
3. Nature of individual differences, and the implications of these differences for counseling.
4. Principles of learning and their application in education and other pertinent situations.
5. Personality development and mental hygiene.
6. Psychological tools and techniques for the study of individuals and diagnosis of their problems including tests and other procedures.
7. Principles and procedures of counseling.
8. Supervised practice in diagnosis and counseling.
9. Statistics and research methods used in those psychological investigations ordinarily used or undertaken by all counselors.[11]

This report is concerned only with psychological courses. However, other kinds of training more directly related to educational and vocational problems are also necessary.

In 1947 the National Vocational Guidance Association, through the Division of Professional Training and Certification, appointed a "planning committee" to write a manual on counselor preparation. A general plan for the manual was prepared in tentative form. Eight other professional organizations joined the N.V.G.A. in its proceedings and a joint committee was formed. The eight participating organizations were:

1. American College Personnel Association.
2. American Psychological Association, Division of Counseling and Guidance.
3. National Rehabilitation Association.
4. National Vocational Guidance Association.
5. Office of Education, Federal Security Agency.
6. National Association of Guidance Supervisors.
7. U.S. Employment Service, Federal Security Agency.
8. Veterans Administration.

---

[11] *Counseling News and Views*, 2:11–12(1949).

Each organization appointed an official delegate to represent it on the joint committee; every delegate was aided by no more than two consultants. The report drawn up is entitled *Counselor Preparation* (2). Leonard M. Miller, chairman of the Joint Committee and Planning Committee, writes in the preface to the manual that,

> It was made clear to each organization that participation in the preparation of the statement did not mean endorsement. The materials presented in this report are intended to be used as a guide for all agencies and organizations who wish to improve standards for counselors. There are some who would prefer to set minimum standards much higher than those presented in this manual but it was the feeling of the committee members that if these standards become effective within the next five years, marked progress will have been made.[12]

He further reports,

> Immediate steps should be taken by agencies so inclined to work out standards which go beyond those set forth here. As these are put into practice, new standards will be accepted. It is hoped, therefore, that within five years a revised manual can be prepared with an even greater number of agencies and organizations participating.[13]

The committee is aware of many more problems to be faced and solved. The manual prepared is not by any means the final one, although it is a great step forward. Froehlich (5) in summarizing and commenting upon it has correctly stated, "The Committee does not present its report as a dogmatic statement. *Counselor Preparation* should rather be regarded as a preliminary statement which can be used as a starting point for a discussion of counselor preparation." However, it can serve immediately as a guide for the training of counselors.

The manual does not delineate specific courses. It describes the aims and objectives as well as the areas of training. The character and extent of preparation is very extensive, more so than any previously

---

[12] From *Counselor Preparation.* New York: The National Vocational Guidance Association, 1949, pages v–vi. By permission of *Occupations, the Vocational Guidance Journal,* published by National Vocational Guidance Association, Incorporated.

[13] *Loc. cit.*

agreed upon. Not only is it on a graduate rather than an undergraduate level but it includes practice in counseling.

An outline of the areas of training will allow for an understanding of the kind of preparation suggested. The areas included are:

I. Philosophy and principles
    A. Every individual has intrinsic worth as a person.
    B. Society has an obligation to help each individual to live a life that is individually satisfying and socially effective.
    C. Knowledge of self is basic for intelligent choice and for the attainment of maximum efficiency.
    D. Understanding of choices available to the individual is essential to wise selections.
    E. Every individual has a right to receive assistance in making satisfactory choices and adjustments.
    F. The individual has a right to that kind of assistance which will continually increase his ability for self-direction.
    G. The guidance worker has a responsibility to society as well as to the individual.

II. Growth and development of the individual
    A. Growth and maturation
    B. Learning
    C. Emotional development
    D. Motivation
    E. Individual differences
    F. Personality adjustment
    G. Social and cultural factors affecting behavior

III. The study of the individual
    A. Observation
    B. Autobiographies
    C. Interview
    D. Tests and inventories
    E. Records
    F. Physical capacities appraisal
    G. Reports from professional sources
    H. Questionnaire methods
    I. Rating scales
    J. Anecdotal records
    K. Projective techniques
    L. Sociometric techniques
    M. Home visits
    N. Synthesis of data

IV. Collecting, evaluating, and using occupational, educational and related information
  A. Classification of jobs and industries
  B. Description of jobs and industries
  C. Occupational trends in relation to socio-economic changes
  D. Sources of information
  E. Evaluation of occupational information literature
  F. Maintaining occupational information materials for reference use
  G. Information for local use
  H. Training facilities
  I. Placement facilities
  J. Use of occupational information with groups and with individuals

V. Administrative and community relationships
  A. Administrative problems and relationships
  B. Organization of guidance services
  C. Community relationships

VI. Techniques used in counseling
  A. The counseling interview
  B. Information about the counselee
  C. Utilization of experience
  D. Referral sources
  E. Records of counseling data
  F. Initiation of counseling relationship
  G. Termination of counseling relationship
  H. Evaluation of counseling effectiveness

VII. Supervised experience in counseling
  A. Field visits
  B. Participation in activities in the guidance service
  C. Actual counseling under supervision[14]

The training program is designed as a common core for all counselors. Counselors so trained will have a sound basis upon which they could handle educational and vocational as well as personal problems. However, the preparation outlined is not considered maximal. Indeed the National Vocational Guidance Association prepared a supplement to it for educational and vocational counselors that adds still more areas of training: group methods in guidance; placement as a function of the process of vocational adjustment; follow-up tech-

[14] *Ibid.*

niques and uses; and methods of research and evaluation including statistics.

Other organizations may add still more. The agreement on such a common core of preparation with further agreement on supplementary training, will certainly lead to advances in the field of counseling. The varieties of counselors will resemble each other more closely and function on a recognized professional level.

Summary

Counselors differ greatly in their training and experience. They are by no means all sufficiently qualified. However, there is active concern about stabilizing the field of counseling and bringing it up to professional status.

Two steps are being taken in the process of raising the level of counseling: the job analyses of counseling occupations and agreement on training programs. These will probably make for progress.

The descriptions of counseling occupations as reported by Shartle are a significant contribution. They clarify the duties and qualifications of present counseling positions. The next step taken is the series of conferences among the professional organizations. These conferences have contributed reports on standards, training, and qualifications.

The manual *Counselor Preparation* is a major contribution along these lines. The description of the training program is very thorough and comprehensive and could be applied in the training of all counselors. It is expected that this program will be revised and improved with further experience.

Bibliography

1. Cochrane, R., "The Competent Vocational Counselor," *Occupations,* 28:118–120 (1949).
2. *Counselor Preparation.* New York: The National Vocational Guidance Association, 1949.
3. "Duties, Standards, and Qualifications for Counselors Employed

by Schools, Report of Committee," *Proceedings of 8th National Conference of State Supervisors of Guidance Services and Counselor Trainers,* Federal Security Agency, Office of Education (1949).

4. Froehlich, C. P., "Report of the Counselor Training Committee," *Counseling News and Views,* 2:11–12 (1949).
5. Froehlich, C. P., "Content of the Manual on Counselor Preparation," *Occupations,* 27:541–545 (1949).
6. Jager, H. A., "Trends in Counselor Training," *Occupations,* 26:477–482 (1948).
7. "Report of N.V.G.A. Delegate Assembly," *Occupations,* 26:511 (1948).
8. "Reports by Divisions and Committees to the 1950 Delegate Assembly," *Occupations,* 28:542 (1950).
9. Shartle, C. L., "Occupations in Psychology," *The American Psychologist,* 1:559–582 (1946).

17

EVALUATION OF GUIDANCE

Whether guidance is to remain an art or reach the status of a science will depend ultimately upon systematic evaluation. Although some of the instruments and methods used in guidance meet objective standards, the process cannot be evaluated in terms of its parts alone. It is necessary to evaluate the end product as an integrated total before the assessment can be considered complete.

Throughout the entire presentation of the subject matter in this book critical evaluations were offered. This approach has been applied to types of guidance centers, the interview technique, psychological tests, occupational information, the concept of interests, and even to the standards necessary for counseling. The major objective was to encourage a strengthening of the parts of the counseling process. The clinical approach has been recommended in order to achieve the most meaningful and positive results.

From the academic point of view the attempt at critical evaluation is very desirable. One should continually strive to improve and perfect instruments and in addition strengthen the theoretical base upon which sound guidance can be offered. Moreover, the skeptic has the right to ask whether anything is known about the values or validity of counseling as a total process.

Despite the fact that there are multiple goals in guidance and the criteria are rarely as objective as they might be, it does appear that guidance is worth while. The worth-whileness does not result from "do-gooders" just wishing, or from others becoming round-shouldered from back-slapping. There is evidence, and research will be presented not only to demonstrate the present status of counseling but also to point to the next steps in the evaluative process.

Evaluation of the guidance process has proceeded by essentially five different methods. The first is reviews of the literature. These are usually critical of the methods and approaches used and attempt to point the way toward improved research. The second is primarily "expert" evaluation. Judges who are considered competent in the field make independent evaluations of the outcomes, the quality of the counseling, or the directions that research should take. The third is the "follow-up" method. In these investigations the counselees are contacted by various means to learn of their current status; this is related to the previous counseling.

The fourth introduces an aspect of the experimental method known as the "control group." In these investigations two groups are to be compared according to certain criteria. One group, called the experimental group, has been counseled; the other group, the control group, has not been counseled.

The fifth method is an attempt to evaluate changes in behavior by measures of "before and after." Measures of certain characteristics of the counselees are obtained before and after counseling to note changes.

The major difficulty in evaluating the "evaluative studies" is that they employ different techniques as well as different criteria. Typical studies in each of the five lines of investigation will be reviewed. The criteria used and conclusions drawn will be noted and discussed. In this way, comparisons can be made among the investigations that not only will allow for understanding the methods employed, but also will help form a critical frame of reference that can possibly point to ways to improve upon the evaluative studies.

Reviews of the literature

Froehlich (12) has attempted a comprehensive review of the literature concerning the evaluation of guidance. His survey covers literature reported during the period from 1921 to 1947 and includes 177 sources. He classifies the studies according to method employed and briefly summarizes the findings. In concluding the review, he reports the need for research on the methods themselves as well as on criteria against which success may be better measured.

Froehlich classified the investigations on the basis of the methodology employed, listing seven categories:

1. External criteria, the do-you-do-this? method.
2. Follow-up, the what-happened-then? method.
3. Client-opinion, the what-do-you-think? method.
4. Expert opinion, the "Information Please" method.
5. Specific techniques, the little-by-little method.
6. Within-group changes, the before-and-after method.
7. Between-group changes, the what's-the-difference method.[1]

These seven categories correspond rather closely to the five employed in this book. The "external criteria" classification makes use of experts who recommend approaches and procedures. This category is included in our "expert evaluation." The "expert opinion" classification is also part of the same group. The "follow-up," "within-group changes," and "between-group changes" correspond to our "follow-up," "before and after," and "control groups" respectively. The "client-opinion" category is part of the "follow-up" since most of the studies using client opinion use follow-up to obtain the opinions. The "specific techniques" category evaluates particular tools and techniques rather than the counseling process. Froehlich reports that this technique has many weaknesses. He writes, "In the case of tests, validity depends upon the use that is made of the test by the counselee and the counselor in a particular instance rather than on any validity inherent in the test itself." The specific technique must then be evaluated as part of a whole; this evaluation can be carried out by other methods. The "review of the literature" category was added to include such over-all evaluations as Froehlich's.

Travers (22) critically reviewed evaluative techniques in guidance. He believes that guidance is essentially a learning situation and that it could be evaluated by techniques used in education. He writes,

[1] *Federal Security Agency, Office of Education, Misc. No. 3310* (1949).

"Usually, in these learning situations the guidance worker is attempting to help the student to learn new behaviors which may solve immediate social difficulties or establish new long-term goals."[2] He also reports that the approach taken by the guidance worker is clinical in order to understand the person as a whole. The educator uses the organismic approach, which is essentially the same as the clinical. Since both are similar, the evaluative techniques employed in education might be used in guidance. "In organized learning situations in education, goals are established, procedures are developed for attaining those goals, and methods are devised for determining the extent to which the goals are achieved."[3] This is an orderly and scientific approach to evaluation.

Travers criticizes the criteria employed in determining the outcomes of guidance. He classifies them as subjective and objective. The former include the client's estimates of such matters as job satisfaction, adequacy of social life, and personal happiness. The latter are academic grades, income after a period of time, frequency of job change, and the like. Travers finds that the criteria employed are not really satisfactory. Further, he reports that most of the evidence on the effectiveness of guidance comes from subjective sources, which may "be influenced by wishful thinking and other irrelevant factors."[4] There is a paucity of objective evidence because of the difficulty in obtaining it.

Williamson and Bordin (25) have also critically reviewed evaluative methods. They believe that progress in evaluation has been hindered by two types of counselors; those who evaluate by arm-chair methods and those who do not evaluate because they maintain that research will impair their efficiency as counselors. They write,

> On the other hand, those who believe that counseling can and should be evaluated have taken one of three approaches. First, there is the approach which clings to traditional statistical methodology in utilizing only those criteria that are objectively quantifiable. This approach is based upon the premise that a straightforward statistical

[2] *Educational and Psychological Measurement,* 9:211 (1949).
[3] *Ibid.,* page 212.
[4] *Ibid.,* page 223.

> analysis of such data as grades, years in college, number of jobs held or wages earned, are sufficient criteria for evaluation experiments. Second is the approach which utilizes non-statistical case study methods of evaluation. The third approach attempts to avoid the objections to the other two methods by using various objective and systematically derived criteria which are combined by means of impartial judgmental treatment in contrast with statistical summations.[5]

The criteria must be spelled out carefully. They must be applicable to the situation being studied as well as to each individual used in the study.

Williamson and Bordin advocate the formulation of clear hypotheses and the establishment of experimental designs suited to the testing of various hypotheses. They conclude:

> 1. All available methods of evaluation have weaknesses.
> 2. Composite criteria which avoid arithmetic computation of the part-criteria are at present least open to question, although still being crude measures.
> 3. The problem of securing sufficient data without doing violence to the concept and practice of counseling is a real one. Involved also are the inadequacy and incompleteness of most available case records.
> 4. The proper time interval to use for evaluation is extremely important because of the possible relationship between the intervention of confusing factors and the length of time between counseling and evaluation.
> 5. The methods used for validation of diagnostic and prognostic tools (e.g., tests) may not be applicable because of the uniqueness of each counseling situation. Stated another way, the methods of studying students in general may not be applied to the study of individual students with particular problems.
> 6. An impediment to more exact evaluation is the inability to control conditions for an adequate test of counseling recommendations.[6]

The reviews of the literature by Froehlich, Travers, and Williamson and Bordin show clearly the assets and liabilities of this method of evaluation. Since these authors have not been content to merely abstract studies but rather have been critical of the reported studies,

---

[5] *Educational and Psychological Measurement,* 1:6 (1941).
[6] *Ibid.,* page 22.

they obviously point the way to improvements. The authors have also logically collated the data with the attempt to systematize the available knowledge. For these two reasons reviews of the literature have value. However, the main liability is that they are always subjective evaluations of someone else's research.

"Expert" evaluation

Kefauver and Davis (15) constructed an inquiry form which they gave to 51 professors of courses in guidance and to 10 directors of guidance. They listed 10 kinds of investigations and asked the respondents to indicate the importance or need of the different kinds on a five-point scale. The directions continue: "If you consider a line of investigation to have no importance, place an '0' on the line in front of the statement; if you attach little importance, place a '1'; if you attach considerable importance, place a '2'; if you attach large importance, place a '3'; and if you attach very large importance, place a '4.' Importance should be interpreted to include need and promise of value to guidance workers."

The ten kinds of investigations were:

1. Secure objective evidence of need for guidance service.
2. Analyze and describe guidance practices.
3. Investigate occupational conditions and opportunities.
4. Summarize judgments of specialists in guidance concerning desirable objectives and practices in guidance.
5. Describe training and experience of guidance workers.
6. Construct and validate improved measures of characteristics of students.
7. Investigate the nature and extent of the variation of the capacities of the individual.
8. Make follow-up studies of students who go out from school into higher institutions and into vocations.
9. Measure results obtained by existing programs of guidance.
10. Set up a well-planned program of guidance, follow a group of students through this program, make complete records at each step or grade level, and make a careful measure of the results obtained by this well-planned guidance service.[7]

---

[7] *Occupations, the Vocational Guidance Journal,* published by National Vocational Guidance Association, Incorporated, 12:18–19 (1933).

Item 10 is in many respects the most idealistic and challenging. It allows a "fresh start" basis for research. It was rated as most desirable by the professors, but second to highest by the directors. It is evident that they were somewhat more concerned with the effectiveness of their own program than with building a new setup to allow for possibly better-controlled research. This is quite typical of the research in guidance as conceived by many administrators.

The professors rated number 3 second highest, number 9 third highest and number 8 as fourth highest. The directors rated number 10 second highest, and numbers 3, 6, 7, and 8 were tied for third place.

Evidence of need for guidance service obtained an average rating of ninth by the professors and tenth by the directors. Descriptions of training and experience of guidance workers was rated tenth by the professors and ninth by the directors. Both these lines of investigation are probably considered least important because it is taken for granted that investigations along the broader lines of items 9 and 10 will include them.

However, a survey of the training and experience of guidance workers may be rewarding, especially in the light of the wide varieties of training and experience among counselors. Darley and Marquis (9) made a survey among contract clinics listed by the Veterans Administration, and included data on the personnel. Of 210 full-time and part-time personnel who could be traced from the identifications given, 132 were counselors and 78 psychometrists. Thirty-five of the counselors were members of the American Psychological Association and only nine of the psychometrists were. Three counselors and no psychometrists were members of the American College Personnel Association. No data are given on membership in the National Vocational Guidance Association. For the psychometrists, this is a rather poor showing. Moreover, the bachelor's degree is "typically the highest degree reached" at the psychometric level. However, Darley and Marquis state that having advanced students in the larger universities serve as counselors as part of their training affects the educational level. Among 86 counselors, 16 had the Ph.D. or Ed.D, 42 the M.A., 27 the B.A., and one had no degree.

As part of the counseling process, counselors frequently make judgments about clients' vocational choices. Berdie (5) checked their judgments by employing the "expert opinions" of five counselors. Twenty folders on pre-college male students were selected from the files of the Testing Bureau of the University of Minnesota. Each of these students had made a vocational choice which had been judged as appropriate or inappropriate by his counselor in the first counseling interview. A case reader reviewed the notes on the client to verify the judgment of the counselor. Then duplicate folders were prepared for each of the 20 students with no identifying data present. The folder contained test scores, preliminary interview report, and other material on the students.

These folders were given to the five counselors with instructions to make judgments on the vocational choices and to give reasons for their judgments. Each counselor rated every case. The combined judgments were compared with the originals. The judgments of the majority of the counselors (three or more) agreed with the original judgments in 18 of the 20 cases. There was greater agreement when the student's choice was appropriate than when inappropriate.

The results indicate that the original counselor's judgment is quite accurate even though he made it in the first interview. However, there is one point in the method that may have had some positive effect on the results. In 14 of the 20 cases the original counselor was also one of the judges and not one disagreed with his original decision. Berdie believes that because all identifying data were removed and several months had elapsed, the counselors would not remember the cases. This belief needs verification. On the other hand, as Berdie reports, it is of interest to note that the counselors tend to arrive at the same judgments from a review of case data that they did from the interview.

Follow-up investigations

Many researches make use of the follow-up method. The purpose is usually to determine the general effectiveness of the total counseling process. One of the earlier studies using follow-up was conducted by Viteles (23) on 75 young people two years after they were counseled. He reports that 58 per cent followed the recommendations completely and 21 per cent partly. None of those who followed the advice failed to find employment, and only seven held more than two jobs. Although those who failed to follow the recommendations were earning more money, they were mostly in blind-alley jobs. Of those still in school, there were more failures among the pupils who did not follow the recommendations.

A similar pattern seems to have been followed in later researches employing the follow-up method. The concern is generally with whether or not the clients followed the decisions reached and how they were faring. There are variations among the methods employed in the follow-up, the criteria used in determining the degree of effectiveness, and the length of time since counseling was completed.

Coe and Habbe (6) studied 50 clients selected at random from a large number of cases and deemed by them to be representative, even though they acknowledge that the group was younger and had more initiative. They used the interview as a means of obtaining information about the clients' status. Follow-up occurred after only a six-month period. The purpose of the follow-up was to determine how nearly the clients achieved the goals set in counseling. Of the 16 who had sought educational advice primarily, 10 had acted upon it, four planned to act upon it, and two did not plan to act upon it. Of the 32 who sought vocational guidance primarily, 17 had acted upon the advice, three planned to act upon it, three had acted upon it in part, and nine did not plan to act upon it. This study would have been more significant if the follow-up period had been longer. Six months is too short a time to determine the effects of the counseling.

Coe and Habbe obtained other information on the counseling process. They report on the counseling being "total" and the clients' dwelling on the meaningfulness of the whole experience. The clients felt the counseling to be warm and vivid and make such statements as: "They didn't talk down to me"; "They encouraged me when I was blue"; "They helped me to keep faith in myself." The guidance workers had stressed the "total situation" in their work with the clients.

Webster (24), in a follow-up study two to five years after counseling, mailed letters and received 66 replies from former clients. He was able to contact 15 other clients in person or by telephone. The letters and other sources supplied data about the educational and vocational status of the clients and Webster made subjective estimates on the basis of the data of the degree of educational and vocational "success." This was then compared to the recommendations reached in counseling. Webster reports on 116 instances where vocational or educational recommendations were available as well as the work or academic record. For these cases, he combined the educational and vocational predictions to determine their accuracy; he found the predictions to be correct in 87 cases, incorrect in 13, and doubtful in 16.

A further analysis of the data yields some interesting information. Webster reports that the counselor or psychologist is given credit not only for help with educational and vocational matters but also for the more important help in correcting personality deficiencies. The counselor or psychologist also receives credit for vocational recommendations if new careers were suggested, rather than those contemplated by the client.

Barber (3) conducted a follow-up by interview of 87 clients and by mail of six who lived at too great a distance to be interviewed personally. The group was the first class of high school graduates to have had opportunities for guidance throughout their four years in high school. The follow-up was made five years after graduation, a more respectable period, to allow for at least one year after college for those who attended. The criteria used in the evaluation include completion of college, kind of work, and salaries. Barber reports that the students generally followed the occupations they selected in school and that they were apparently well adjusted, since they expressed happiness with their homes and surroundings. This study would have profited by the inclusion of a control group against which the results found with the counseled group could be compared. Also the findings are given in too general terms.

Studies by Long and Hill (18), Barnette (4), Failor and Isaacson (10), and Anderson (2) are in the same pattern as the ones previously cited. Long and Hill conducted a follow-up study on 300 veterans.

These data were collected from the information files on each client, for some after a period of 12 months and for others after approximately 15 months. Criteria for judging success included whether the client started a training program, and whether he stayed in it. Of 206 cases for whom a training program was recommended, 166 began the training and 40 did not. The progress made by 148 veterans who began training in the originally planned program was as follows: six completed it; six discontinued and were considered rehabilitated; 53 discontinued and were not considered rehabilitated; and 83 were being completed. Long and Hill collected data on reasons for not beginning the training program and for discontinuing it. The most frequently given reasons were: physical condition, lack of interest in training, mental condition, and acceptance of a job. The authors of the study note that the reasons given may not be the actual ones. They are also concerned with the reasons why so many veterans did not begin their training or dropped out. The study indicates the need for such research.

Long and Hill report an additional finding which may be significant. It is that there is a relationship between the type of program and percentage of drop-outs. There is less drop-out from college than from special courses and from on-the-job training programs. This fact might be worth investigating further.

Barnette used a questionnaire to obtain follow-up information on two groups of veterans counseled at least one year earlier. The criterion was whether training was begun and continued. In one group of 104 veterans, 2 per cent completed the training and were satisfied, 45 per cent were still in training and satisfied, 9 per cent began the training but dropped, and 38 per cent never began the training. In the second group, 3 per cent completed the training and were satisfied, 64 per cent were still in training and satisfied, 6 per cent began the training but dropped, and 18 per cent never began. Fifty-three per cent in the first group and 79 per cent in the second were considered "successes" by Barnette; that is, their occupational pursuits were in agreement with the projected aims. However, the reasons for the difference in per cent between the two groups and for those who were not "successes" are not analyzed.

The study by Failor and Isaacson employed a rather detailed questionnaire consisting of 20 items on the counseling process to measure the reactions of veterans to completed advisement. The questionnaire includes such items as:

How do you feel about the amount of time that was allowed for your counseling and testing? It was: (*Check one*)

——very ample time, without hurry
——probably enough time given
——seemed somewhat pressed for time, but most of my problems were considered
——time so short that I felt adequate consideration was not given to my problems
——I was just pushed through, and felt that little thought was given to my problems.

During the interviews: (*Check one*)

——I did practically all of the talking
——I talked all I wanted to
——I had opportunity to talk on most subjects
——I had very little opportunity to talk
——I "couldn't get a word in edgewise"

Do you feel that the counselor: (*Check one*)

——made the decision of a training program for you
——high-pressured you into a decision
——counseled with you, but let you make your own decision
——let you make most of the suggestions as well as the final choice

——gave you little help of any kind

How many veterans entering training should receive counseling? (*Check one*)

——all
——most
——about half
——some
——none

At the present time: (*Check one*)

——I am making good progress in the job objective selected
——I am making poor progress in the job objective selected

——I did not make satisfactory progress and have changed objectives
——I started the training program, but quit
——I never entered into a training program[8]

Out of 1604 questionnaires mailed, 658 usable returns were received. The length of time since counseling varied up to about three years and the counseling was done at five guidance centers. The returns indicate "a very favorable attitude toward the counseling process, as well as an attitude indicating that the process was ably administered, professionally handled, and of considerable personal value to the veterans responding."[9] However, there was "considerable variation in percentage of returns when the centers were compared."[10] Failor and Isaacson anticipated this variation because of the differences among the completed cases in the various centers. Apparently the centers with college student clients had the largest percentage of returns. This is a fact that might have influenced the results. Another point is that those who did not complete advisement were not included in the sampling

Anderson used a questionnaire too. She studied two groups. One group consisted of industrial employees who were counseled at company expense. This group answered the questionnaire to evaluate their counseling experiences. The other group consisted of ex-service men for whom the practical outcomes of counseling were studied.

Out of 1086 questionnaires distributed to the industrial employees, 658 were returned.

> The results indicate that: 71 per cent got a better idea of their strongest abilities; 38 percent found they had underestimated their aptitudes for particular jobs, 32 percent in general; 71 percent got a better understanding of themselves; 65 percent and 59 percent respectively got a better understanding of their personalities in relation to fields of work or of ways of promoting their personality development. Although 33 per cent reported ambitions not supported by test results for particular jobs, and 20 per cent reported general

[8] C. W. Failor and L. E. Isaacson, "The Veteran Evaluates Counseling," *Occupations, the Vocational Guidance Journal*, published by National Vocational Guidance Association, Incorporated, 28:21–23 (1949).
[9] *Ibid.*, page 20.
[10] *Ibid.*, page 19.

> ambitions not supported by test results, 58 per cent reported increased self-confidence; only 6 percent, decreased self-confidence.[11]

Also, 53 per cent got a better idea of possibilities of transfer to other work; 50 per cent expect that the counseling will influence their future work or training decisions. The counseling was in line with the decisions of 29 per cent who had already made choices. Those who had the occasion to apply their counseling or who were to change their employment replied more favorably to the questionnaire.

Other findings showed that the older men—41 years and over—derived less personal benefit from the counseling than the younger men. However, they reported an increase in self-confidence to the same degree as the younger men. The group with grammar school education reported less favorably than the groups with more education. The more favorable responses are from the group with highest ability.

In the second part of the study, Anderson checked placement outcomes against counseling recommendations. This was done with 444 ex-service men available for follow-up.

> Of these, 82.4 percent were satisfactorily placed in recommended jobs according to their own and their employers' statements; 10.9 percent had been placed in other jobs. At the time of the last follow-up, 7 percent were not yet employed. The last group included a number of men in upper economic brackets who had not sought employment.[12]

The employment stability record was also noted. Of those employed, 11 men, or less than 3 per cent, had changed jobs during a period of 19 months.

The studies cited in this category all seem to have as their major purpose the measure of the general success of the counseling process. They apparently were not planned before counseling with well-designed experiments to test various hypotheses, but rather as a check on the counseling already completed. This in itself is insuffi-

---

[11] Reprinted from *Journal of Applied Psychology,* 33:464–465 (1949), by permission of the American Psychological Association, publishers.

[12] *Ibid.,* page 472.

cient. From the studies it can be concluded that counseling is a good thing. But there remains much to be studied about the dynamics of counseling.

The investigations employed different methods, such as study of the case records, questionnaires, letters, and the interview. The period of follow-up varied from six months up to five years. Although the conclusions were generally positive, they differed in detail.

Investigations using control groups

The use of control groups in following the progress of clients is an important addition to the research in this field. The control groups serve as a basis for comparison against differences in the experimental groups. However, when control groups are employed, great care must be taken to have them originally comparable to the experimental groups. This is often a most difficult matter to accomplish because of the complexities of human beings.

Cole (7) evaluated the vocational guidance program of a boys' club by using two groups of 100 each, one that had vocational guidance and one that did not. The groups are described as "nearly alike" in such factors as age, intelligence quotient, class grades, and marks. The follow-up was conducted after a six-year period had elapsed. This is a substantial length of time. Criteria used were objective and in such terms as still in school, school retardation, leaving school during semester, employment, kind of employment, change of jobs, and earnings

According to the criteria, the counseled group after six years was getting along better than the non-counseled group. The more subjective criterion of job satisfaction, obtained from expression of views by the individuals in the group, showed that the counseled group had nearly five times as many boys happy in their jobs as the non-counseled group. There was only one delinquent in the counseled group (and he reformed), while six of the 11 delinquents in the non-counseled group were recidivists. This study demonstrates the value of counseling.

The investigation by Toven (21) is an intensive four-year study of

188 counseled college students whose progress is compared with a non-counseled group of 188 students. They were matched on the basis of an intelligence test score, and by sex, age, college class, race, religion, and curriculum chosen. The criteria for assaying success of the counseling were graduation from college, persistence in college, scholastic action by the faculty, cumulative college grade averages, college grades, and number of points completed.

The experimental group was counseled systematically over four years by faculty advisers appointed by the dean. The control group had no counseling. The students in the experimental group had counseling on "problems touching education, finance, health, personal matters, spiritual and vocational aspects of student life, separately, or in combination." The findings indicate that the counseled group made better records according to all the criteria except grades received by those who graduated. Here they were identical with the control group.

This is a well-planned study. It demonstrated the value of a systematically planned counseling program. The number of students in the study was quite large, the control group well matched, and the criteria objective and several in number. It does not, however, go into an analysis of the counseling techniques and the ways in which they achieved or failed to achieve their purposes.

Kirchheimer, Axelrod, and Hickerson (16) studied the case records of counseled and non-counseled veterans, utilizing the objective criterion of grade point averages. The veterans were presumed to be a random sampling of students in the same college, which the writers considered had a homogeneous population. They therefore did no matching. The number in the sampling groups studied is small for each group and could not dogmatically be considered as matched. The results indicate that the counseled groups improved in grade point average significantly more than the non-counseled groups. This study sustains the merit of counseling but adds little to understanding of the counseling process. The authors of the study are aware of this when they write, "From the standpoint of evaluating counseling, we cannot, of course, generalize beyond the particular type of counseling under study."

The investigation by Aldrich (1) includes more evaluative criteria and the follow-up is for the substantial period of eight years. She had small samplings—31 in the experimental group and 28 in the control. However, they were carefully matched by means of tests and on group and individual high school activities. This research is different from the others in that it is on the effectiveness of social rather than vocational guidance. Both groups had gone through the usual testing and counseling procedures, but the experimental group also received guidance in social adjustment and was directed toward extracurricular activities.

The follow-up consisted of a check of the records of all individuals in the study through the campus agencies of the Student Counseling Bureau, Student Activities Bureau, Bureau of Admissions and Records, Disciplinary Committee, Mental Hygiene Clinic of the Students' Health Service, and the Alumni Association. The results show the general effectiveness of the social guidance given; the experimental group exceeded the control group in such things as the average number of college activities, committees, and offices and a less severe diagnosis for those who contacted the Mental Hygiene Clinic. Aldrich writes, "The problem was, however, essentially an investigation of a method and as such the results should be emphasized only as a justification for the further use of the method."

Measures of "before and after"

Other investigations use different techniques and experimental designs which may also include follow-up or control groups. These researches employ objective tests to measure changes attributable to the counseling. They may also have a more refined experimental design to obtain data on the relationship of various aspects of the counseling process.

An investigation by Williamson and Bordin (26), designed to evaluate clinical counseling done at the Testing Bureau of the University of Minnesota, was concerned not only with how many students profited by the counseling but also with the conditions and characteristics of students that may be related to successful counseling. The latter concern leads to a better understanding of the counseling process; one that may lead to improvement in counseling techniques.

The investigators employed several checks on evaluating the effectiveness of the counseling: two trained workers read the case data, each client was interviewed, and finally trained evaluators reviewed both the case data and the report on the interview to arrive at a judgment on the effectiveness of the counseling. The adjustment of the counselee was scaled in the five categories of satisfactory adjustment, some progress, no change, slightly worse, and much worse, rather than in just two categories.

Study was directed to the relationship between degree of cooperation and adjustment, as well as such matters as the expectancy of adjustment according to type of problem, the expectancy of adjustment according to status of vocational choice, aptitude and achievement in relation to adjustment and cooperation, number of interviews versus adjustment and cooperation, and time interval versus evaluation. Among the results are such findings as the fact that cooperation by the client with the counselor was positively related to adjustment; and that cooperation led to adjustment in a shorter period of time. Also, the educational and vocational problems were more successfully handled than the personal. These findings are in addition to the discovery that the counseling was effective for over 80 per cent of the students.

Worbois (27), using the Luria technique, studied an experimental group and a control group to determine how two different kinds of guidance affected emotional development.

The Luria technique is objective and makes use of word association combined with motor responses in the hands. A word association test is given. The individual is to respond to each word by saying the first word that comes to mind and simultaneously pulling down a plunger with the right hand. The left hand is to remain motionless. If there is anxiety, motor and associative behavior will show disorganization. The words spoken by the subject may be infrequently used or the association may be blocked. The right hand will show irregularities by holding on to the plunger too long or letting up slowly with muscular tremors. The left hand may also show tremors and downward pressures. These actions will indicate emotional disturbance.

Two groups of 233 each were studied. The ninth grade in a public intermediate high school was divided into two groups, and matched in age, sex, and intelligence and achievement test scores. The experimental group was given intensive guidance by two well-trained counselors who maintained close contact with each of the students. The control groups received the "regular" school guidance program. The results on the Luria technique showed the experimental group to have less "emotional conflict" than the control students.

Another investigation in the area of personal counseling utilized psychological tests before and after counseling. Muench (20) evaluated non-directive counseling by this means. The Rorschach test, the Kent-Rosanoff Word Association test, and the Bell Adjustment Inventory were given to 12 clients before and after the completion of counseling. The changes in the tests were studied for evidence of personality change in the clients. The counselors also made judgments on the outcome of the cases; these estimates were compared to the test results. The relationship between judgments and results on tests was quite high. The use of tests before and after is an objective and acceptable technique for evaluation. This study was designed only to investigate the effectiveness of the non-directive technique. It did not analyze the degree of adjustment or relate it to the characteristics of the clients and aspects of the counseling process.

Cowen and Combs (8) report a follow-up study of 32 clients who were counseled non-directively. This study has a much more elaborate experimental design and goes into the dynamics of the counseling process. Its purposes were to obtain an idea about the effectiveness of non-directive methods as applied at a particular counseling center; to examine the accuracy of prediction of the counseling; and to evaluate some of the principles of non-directive counseling in order to improve its practice and to establish hypotheses that might be suitable for future investigations of the dynamics of non-directive counseling.

The cases used in the study were concluded at least five months before the time of investigation; in each case there was more than one interview. Twenty clients were interviewed in the follow-up; twenty-seven (of whom 15 were among those interviewed) had a Bernreuter Personality Inventory before and after counseling. Before the follow-up interview each case was studied and categorized as successful, making progress, or failure. The follow-up interviews were recorded and transcribed for three judges who were to evaluate the outcome. This procedure was followed because a pooled judgment is usually better than a judgment by a single individual.

The evaluation is not in over-all terms but rather includes evidence on such matters as the warmth in counseling, the reactions to non-directive structuring, the effect of student counselors, interpersonal factors, transferring of cases, and termination of counseling. Warmth in counseling was found to be extremely important as setting a healthy atmosphere. Not all clients could accept the passivity of the non-directive interview; some wanted more counselor participation. Student counselors were not as effective as professional counselors. The sex of the counselor was important in some instances. Sometimes cases had to be transferred because of poor interpersonal relationships between client and counselor. The termination of therapy seemed, from this study, to be important in non-directive counseling because some clients did not experience the feeling of completion. These findings are important to the development of counseling and guidance. They go beyond merely determining how many people improved or did not improve when counseled.

Although it is not a direct evaluation of counseling, the study by Friend and Haggard (11) is very significant because it analyzes the characteristics of clients, their reactions to counseling, and the possibilities of adjustment to vocational opportunities. The vocational counseling was done in a case work setting and was clinical. Much was learned about the feelings and attitudes of the clients. In order to have a tool for statistical evaluation, a check list of characteristics was prepared for the use of the counselors. They rated each client on the items in the check list. The information was obtained from the case records of the district case worker and the vocational counselor and occasionally from records of other agencies. The rating schedule consisted of the following seven general sections:

1. Early life
2. Mature or current family life
3. Early or beginning jobs
4. Response to counseling
5. Personality patterns and general work reactions
6. Reactions to specific working conditions
7. General work capacities, adjustment, and improvement.[13]

The rating schedule consisted of 173 items spread over the seven general sections. Comments were encouraged on the interaction of forces that were felt to be important in the attitudes of the clients toward work. Although the rating schedule consisted of items, they were dynamically patterned.

The study was limited to 80 cases "because the scrutinizing of the vast body of data on each, and the rating according to the 173 items of the schedule required the expenditure of a sizable block of time."[14] The clients had come to the Vocational Counseling Service during the years from 1934 through 1943, referred by the case workers for vocational help. All of them had a least six and some as many as 15 interviews with the counselor, ranging over periods of from four to nine years.

Those who adjusted well and poorly were identified and the items analyzed for each group. The items were dynamically interrelated to throw light on the course of counseling and the possibilities of adjustment. Some of the findings are:

> One of the tightest links in our findings draws together the person's work and his personal adjustment. With the Lows (the poorly adjusted), their parents' attitudes were clearly perpetuated in their immediate families as well as in their job reactions. But the healthier Highs (the well adjusted) wrenched free from the early pressures

---

[13] Reprinted from *Work Adjustment in Relation to Family Background, Applied Psychology Monograph #16,* by Jeannette G. Friend and Ernest A. Haggard, with the permission of the authors and of the publishers, Stanford University Press.

[14] *Ibid.*

which were generally less acute, and tended to reverse the patterns of their families. Through the satisfactions which the Highs derived perhaps from school, from their starting jobs, from fellow-workers, or from their current families, they were helped to counteract the very real difficulties they encountered.

Similarly, the special values or demands which the worker makes of the job are often a later chapter of his experiences as a child. How much he prizes and accentuates special appreciation as a reward varies inversely with the degree of unity in his early family group, and seems to be a means through which the individual strives to secure for himself a place with, and status in, the current work group. The worker appears to compromise with life by going after the identical and specific satisfaction in work denied him years before. The over-dominated boy often strives to be completely free from supervision on his job. This clarification is one of the most useful results of our investigation. There is clearly a consistency permeating the worker's reactions; each element is an integral part of a whole and bears a relation to his present-day job attitudes. As such, these emotional constants have real significance for those who work with people in relation to jobs.[15]

Additional implications for the counselor concern finding a positive source of satisfaction at work and following through on linking the needs for satisfaction with the kind of work that could supply it. The timing of referrals and the interpretation of the purpose are also important to the results of the counseling. If a client is under severe economic pressure, passive counseling will make him impatient.

Summary of findings and critique of investigations

The investigations described yielded some important information about guidance and the counseling process. They used different samplings, different interviewing methods and tests, and various research methods. All these must themselves be investigated further. Some of the findings may be modified by later research and, of course, new findings will eventuate. However, the findings in the investigations indicate the present state of knowledge of counseling. They are

[15] *Ibid.*

listed both to summarize this knowledge and to provide possible hypotheses for future research.

Summary of findings. There is need for research on methods used in evaluating guidance as well as on criteria against which success is to be measured.

Guidance is essentially a learning situation and can be evaluated by techniques used in education.

In evaluating guidance, clear hypotheses should be formulated and experimental designs made to suit the testing of the various hypotheses.

Professors in the field of guidance rate highest the line of investigation that sets up a well-planned program of guidance, follows a group of students through this program, makes complete records at each step or grade level, and makes a careful measure of the results obtained by this well-planned program.

Directors of guidance agencies rate highest the line of investigation that measures results obtained by existing programs of guidance.

Judgments on the appropriateness of vocational choice made by three or more of five counselors agreed in 18 out of 20 cases with the original counselor's judgment made during the first interview.

Older men, 41 and over, derive less personal benefit from counseling than younger men. However, they report an increase in self-confidence to the same degree as younger men.

A group with grammar school education reported less favorably on the effects of guidance than those with more education.

Those with the highest ability reported more favorable responses toward guidance than those with less ability.

Vocational counseling is worth while because it is effective in aiding the vocational adjustment of many individuals.

The percentage of successful adjustments varies from study to study but few analyses were made of the reasons for the variations in success.

Those who are counseled are more successful in their work adjustment than those who are not.

The counselor is likely to be given more credit by the client if he helps correct personality deficiencies and also if he suggests careers different from those the clients have been contemplating.

Those students who have been counseled generally follow the occupations they selected while in school.

There is a relationship between dropping out of school and type of training program; the least drop-outs are from college, the next from other institutional programs, and the most from on-the-job training programs.

College students who are given intensive counseling are more likely to graduate than those who are not given it.

Those who obtained social guidance plus vocational guidance adjusted better in social matters than those who had only vocational guidance.

The cooperation of the client is positively related to adjustment and leads to adjustment in a shorter period.

Educational and vocational problems are more successfully handled than the personal.

Emotional conflicts are reduced by intensive guidance.

Non-directive counseling is generally successful in aiding the adjustment of clients.

The accuracy of prediction by non-directive counselors of the outcome of client adjustment is quite high.

Warmth in counseling is extremely important to the success of counseling.

Not all clients can accept the passivity of non-directive counseling.

Student counselors in non-directive counseling are not as effective as professional counselors.

The sex of the counselor is important as an aspect of interpersonal relationships in non-directive counseling; and it may hinder progress for some clients.

The termination of non-directive counseling presents problems to some clients in regard to the feeling that they may not have made definite decisions.

Parents' attitudes are perpetuated in the immediate families as well as in job reactions.

The poorly adjusted vocationally are not free from earlier pressures. The better adjusted are much freer.

People require from jobs, satisfactions that are related to earlier needs.

The need for certain satisfactions should be linked to jobs that can supply them.

If a client is under severe economic pressure, passive counseling will make him impatient.

Critique of investigations. It is apparent that investigating a complex process like guidance is a difficult matter. There are many factors that require control—the interviewer, the kind of interview, the tests, the number of interviews, the influences outside of the interviews, the length of the follow-up period, the kinds of problems, and the age and sex of the clients. However, these difficulties will not forever remain insurmountable. Some progress has already been made by well-planned researches.

The over-all surveys of guidance that determine whether or not the guidance is successful have not added substantially to the understanding of guidance as a process. Those reported in the literature are always positive and indicate little beyond the fact that guidance is worth while. This fact needs no further support. However, no one can yet say that guidance is as effective as it might be. Further research must determine the degree of effectiveness and point to ways for increasing its effectiveness. That should be the purpose of evaluations in guidance.

Froehlich (12) correctly states that "Evaluation is a prerequisite to progress. Guidance programs have had the benefit of relatively few evaluative studies to point out strengths and weaknesses." Travers (22) reports that most of the studies have failed to provide much in the way of "objective evidence concerning either specific aspects of guidance and counseling or the process as a whole."[16] In writing of the evaluation of outcomes by non-directive counseling, Grummon and Gordon (13) report that the method of evaluation is "very puzzling." They indicate that their evaluative methods are complicated

[16] *Educational and Psychological Measurement,* 9:223 (1949).

and involve objective measurements as well as other criteria, but they do not describe them.

The criteria employed in researches are extremely varied. They may be grades in school, earnings on job, changes in job, kind of employment, number and kind of social activities, opinions of the clients, and so on. Kitson and Crane (17) in an earlier survey of the evaluative studies did not find that they were adequate. Lurie and Weiss (19) report on the variability of criteria and write that "occupational adjustment" can mean many things. If wealth is a criterion of success, what about the wealthy but dishonest gambler and, on the other hand, what about the poor but cultured professor? They believe that the occupational adjustment of any individual can best be understood clinically in relation to achievement in various areas. The criteria cannot be summed but must be dynamically integrated. This requirement may mean that more extended as well as more intensive follow-up is necessary.

The periods of time for follow-up in the investigations are certainly varied. Some relate to school success and do not go beyond it; few follow long enough in the life situation. Hoppock (14) believes that classroom criteria are intermediate and that the ultimate criterion lies beyond them. Kitson and Crane report that the follow-up should cover 10 years after high school. However, the length of time cannot be absolutely defined. It would seem to have to be related to what is to be discovered about the guidance process. The same holds for the use of criteria.

The objectives of the research need to be more clearly defined before an investigation is undertaken. Since counseling deals with individuals and their adjustment, the objectives must necessarily be related to the identification of the problems of the individuals and the methods for resolving the problems. As Travers (22) has written, this means that the objectives to be achieved are to be carefully defined, the group in which they are to be achieved specified, instruments developed for measuring the extent to which the objectives are accomplished, and finally the program carried out and its outcomes measured by suitable criteria. Williamson and Bordin (25), in writing on the evaluation of counseling, have reported that the problem was

"What counseling techniques (and conditions) will produce what types of results with what types of students?"[17]

Further refinements in terms of sex, age, education, economic status, intelligence quotient, aptitudes, and the like can be made through limiting the research to defined groups. The problems will be identified, the goals or objectives defined, the methods to be employed described, and the criteria for measuring the outcomes established. A hypothesis can be formulated such as: Given a certain problem found in individuals with certain characteristics, will this method of counseling bring about changes in terms of certain adjustment criteria? This kind of investigation would be more scientific and without doubt would yield valuable contributions.

Summary

The evaluation of guidance as a total process is difficult but necessary. Progress depends upon it. Typical investigations of guidance make use of reviews of the literature, the expert opinion, the follow-up, control groups, and measures of "before and after."

Many investigations are concerned with the over-all effectiveness of the guidance. They do not go into a study of the process itself. Those that do have thrown light on the dynamics of counseling and indicated additional areas for further research.

The findings from the investigations of guidance were summarized and the investigations criticized. It was pointed out that although the over-all effectiveness of guidance is established, the dynamics needed further investigation by more scientific methods in order to ascertain and improve the degree of effectiveness.

Bibliography

1. Aldrich, M. G., "A Follow-up Study of Social Guidance at the College Level," *Journal of Applied Psychology*, 33:258–264 (1949).
2. Anderson, R. G., "Reported and Demonstrated Values of Voca-

[17] *Ibid.*, 1:8 (1941).

tional Counseling," *Journal of Applied Psychology*, 33:460–473 (1949).

3. Barber, J. E., *Evaluating School Guidance*. Buffalo, N.Y.: Foster and Stewart, 1946.
4. Barnette, W. L., "Preliminary Report on a Follow-up of Veterans Counseled at the Vocational Service Center, Y.M.C.A. of the City of New York," *Counseling*, 6:1–2 (1948).
5. Berdie, R. F., "Judgments in Counseling," *Educational and Psychological Measurement*, 4:35–55 (1944).
6. Coe, B. H., and S. Habbe, "The Adult Guidance Service of New Haven: An Evaluation Study," *Occupations*, 18:338–343 (1940).
7. Cole, R. C., "Evaluating a Boys' Club Guidance Program," *Occupations*, 17:705–708 (1939).
8. Cowen, E. L., and A. W. Combs, "Follow-Up Study of 32 Cases Treated by Nondirective Psychotherapy," *Journal of Abnormal and Social Psychology*, 45:232–258 (1950).
9. Darley, J. G., and D. G. Marquis, "Veterans' Guidance Centers: A Survey of Their Problems and Activities," *Journal of Clinical Psychology*, 2:109–116 (1946).
10. Failor, C. W., and L. E. Isaacson, "The Veteran Evaluates Counseling," *Occupations*, 28:18–24 (1949).
11. Friend, J. G., and E. A. Haggard, *Work Adjustment in Relation to Family Background*, Applied Psychology Monographs, No. 16 (1948).
12. Froehlich, C. P., "Evaluating Guidance Procedures: A Review of the Literature," *Federal Security Agency, Office of Education*, Misc. No. 3310, 1–26 (1949).
13. Grummon, D. L., and T. Gordon, "The Counseling Center at the University of Chicago," *The American Psychologist*, 3:166–171 (1948).
14. Hoppock, R., *Group Guidance*. New York: McGraw-Hill, 1949.
15. Kefauver, G. N., and A. M. Davis, "Investigations in Guidance," *Occupations*, 12:17–26 (1933).
16. Kirchheimer, B. A., D. W. Axelrod, and G. X. Hickerson, "An Objective Evaluation of Counseling," *Journal of Applied Psychology*, 33:249–257 (1949).
17. Kitson, H. D., and M. Crane, "Measuring Results of Vocational Guidance," *Occupations*, 16:837–843 (1938).
18. Long, L., and J. Hill, "A Follow-up Study of Veterans Receiving

Vocational Advisement," *Journal of Consulting Psychology,* 11: 88–92 (1947).

19. Lurie, W. A., and A. Weiss, "Analyzing Vocational Adjustment," *Occupations,* 21:138–143 (1942).
20. Muench, G. J., "An Evaluation of Non-Directive Psychotherapy," *Applied Psychology Monographs,* No. 13 (1947).
21. Toven, J. F., "Appraising a Counseling Program at the College Level," *Occupations,* 23:459–466 (1945).
22. Travers, R. M. W., "A Critical Review of Techniques Evaluating Guidance," *Educational and Psychological Measurement,* 9:211–225 (1949).
23. Viteles, M., "Validating the Clinical Method in Vocational Guidance," *Psychological Clinic,* 18:69–77 (1929).
24. Webster, E. C., "A Follow-up on Vocational Guidance," *Journal of Applied Psychology,* 26:285–295 (1942).
25. Williamson, E. G., and E. S. Bordin, "The Evaluation of Vocational and Educational Counseling: A Critique of the Methodology of Experiments," *Educational and Psychological Measurement,* 1:5–24 (1941).
26. ——— "A Statistical Evaluation of Clinical Counseling," *Educational and Psychological Measurement,* 1:117–132 (1941).
27. Worbois, G. M., "Effect of a Guidance Program on Emotional Development," *Journal of Applied Psychology,* 31:169–181 (1947).

18

EMPLOYEE COUNSELING

VOCATIONAL COUNSELING is not only for the individual who does not know what job to seek, but also for the individual who has already had one or more jobs. The term vocational counseling implies that the client seeks help outside and away from the job. However, even if vocational guidance were scientifically perfect, it would not be the ultimate or final need of an individual seeking help. It is necessary to recognize that a complementary form of guidance must be available. This is known as employee counseling in industry.

Industrial counseling includes all the methods and techniques previously discussed, except that the counseling takes place within the industrial establishment in which the worker is employed.

If all individuals received vocational counseling prior to entering industry, the number of industrial misfits would be greatly reduced. However, it would be unrealistic to believe that they would be eliminated. They would not be eliminated because on the adult level, vocational maladjustment and emotional maladjustment are likely to be found together. These two forms of maladjustment can be present in individuals in different proportions; and interestingly enough, the original presence of one may react upon the other and increase its intensity. Another way of understanding this relationship is to consider that vocational and emotional maladjustment can have a continuous reversible cause and effect relationship.

Allowing for the possibility that an individual is ideally placed in a job, as a result of the most sound counseling, there is no reason to assume that future situations will not result in emotional problems. These, in turn, may result in vocational maladjustment. When it is recognized that most people have not obtained any vocational counseling, then it is reasonable to expect that, for many, their job histories begin and continue with vocational maladjustment. The view that vocational counseling should be a continual process was expressed earlier. In fact, the present setup of administering guidance on a piece-meal basis was criticized. Schools on all levels have more than they can do to take care of their own student bodies because of budget problems. Private and public agencies must specialize because none are large enough to handle all the ramifications of vocational problems. Both these types of agencies function outside the framework of industrial establishments. Since it is true that people have problems when they start work, and since these problems can become more intense while people are gainfully employed, it therefore appears obvious that counseling should be continued in industry. To date very few industrial organizations, unfortunately, have recognized this principle. If they did, they would be not only contributing to a more well balanced and adjusted society but also quite definitely increasing employee morale, production figures, and ultimately profits. Probably the chief exception to the prevailing neglect of industrial counseling can be found at the Western Electric Company. Other companies have introduced such programs from time to time, but either they did not become a part of the basic philosophy of the company or else the sporadic attempt indicated that it was considered a whim or luxury.

The meaning of the terms "psychology" and "psychiatry" are not clearly understood among most people. Both terms, however, are in almost everyone's vocabulary and their misuse spreads confusion. When a responsible business executive accepts the term "psychology" he usually limits its industrial application to the job of testing. The terms "clinical psychology" and/or "psychiatry" are regarded by most executives as having no place in industry.

The following is an example of the confusion. Some years ago one of the authors had occasion to call upon the first vice-president of a very large corporation. He was surprised to be admitted into the inner sanctums so rapidly. His elation did not last long because the vice-president started the interview with the following remarks: "The reason why I admitted you to my office was because I wanted to see what a psychologist looks like. Furthermore," he continued, "I can assure you we have no 'nuts' in our employ and if we did we would fire them." Here we find an executive who believes industrial psychology is synonymous with clinical psychology and psychiatry.

Industrial psychologists have a body of knowledge and of course many are actively engaged working directly in companies or performing consulting roles to the companies. Among all the tasks they are likely to perform in industry, counseling is not among the more widely accepted. Industry has been concerned with its production problems more than the adjustment of its human problems. Industry can continue as it has pretty much in the past to shut its eyes and assume that maladjusted people are not its responsibility. Industry may argue that the cost of treating maladjusted people is not its burden. It seems clear that if industry does not pay the bill directly it does pay a great deal more indirectly, through either limiting its production, limiting consumption, or contributing heavily to philanthropic and benevolent agencies that correct maladjustments. It may, as well, pay more taxes to municipal, state, and federal government treasuries to support the maladjusted people while they are out of work; or, in extreme cases, while they are being rehabilitated in varieties of hospitals.

Candor forces a recognition that all has not been well with leadership in industry, and this applies on all levels whether it be the president, or a line foreman. The same applies to union president or shop steward. Serious personality maladjustments in these people result in frustration of large groups and the attendant industrial problems confronting us. Labor disputes, for example, can be better understood in terms of the tragedy of poor human relations rather than economic problems. Poor human relations may often be understood in terms of maladjusted people in key positions projecting their own unconscious shortcomings on to many. The resulting flare-ups are the tragedy of our industrial scene.

Industrial counseling should not be regarded as a decent program to be introduced at some time in the distant future. Industrial counseling does not have as its basis for existence a desire to live in a utopia. It is just as pragmatic, realistic, and related to profits as the manufacturing process itself. It is the continuation of the counseling process on the adult level while a person is gainfully employed. It attempts to reduce vocational and emotional maladjustment in industry. It recognizes that the individual business organization has a responsibility to perform this task for its employees. Industry and business must recognize that in the final analysis they do not escape the social obligations of the community.

Anderson (1) believes that about 20 per cent of all employees are what may be called "problem" individuals. From the point of view of the employer they are production problems, chronic health problems, chronic attendance problems, discipline problems, and so forth. Studying the case histories of these "problems" often reveals emotional maladjustments within the individual, or else the mis-matching of the job and the man. When management is confronted with such problems, it prefers to attach incorrect labels rather than understand the causes and solve the problems. According to Anderson,

> Faulty ways of meeting situations, unhealthy preoccupations, inferiority feelings, anxiety states, fears and hatreds, irrational attitudes, pessimistic moods, prejudices, obsessive reveries, in the average normal person, go undetected and therefore receive no special care or consideration. But to these conditions in supposedly normal people, may be attributed a large proportion of work failures, domestic difficulties, and serious social complications.[1]

As a result of Anderson's work in industry, he concludes that

> Work failure in the majority of instances does not seem to be due to the lack of ability, . . . (i.e., as far as measurable aptitudes for the performance of the task are concerned) as to the presence of factors of a more dynamic nature that influence the total personality and the general health of the worker, that handicap or interfere with the use of such abilities as he actually possesses.[2]

---

[1] Reprinted by permission from *Psychiatry in Industry*, by V. V. Anderson, Harper & Brothers, New York, 1929.
[2] *Ibid.*

McMurry (10) believes that nearly one third of those gainfully employed are victims in some degree of vocational or emotional maladjustment. Since it is acknowledged that most people obtain their life's work as a result of chance or fortuitous circumstances rather than guidance it is no wonder that there are so many problem cases. McMurry, like Anderson, is of the opinion that labeling a person a "problem" achieves nothing. He has found through experience that upon investigation, such problem employees usually are people who have either a vocational or an emotional maladjustment. The antisocial, the eccentric, the insubordinate, the supicious, the daydreamer, the chronic absentee can better be understood in terms of the real issues involved. Counseling affords the opportunity to clear up the basis for the difficulty and as the worker is more adequately adjusted his label "problem employee" disappears.

Review of counseling programs in industry

Counseling in industry has its roots in two very different types of studies. One was conducted at R. H. Macy's and the other at the Hawthorne plant of the Western Electric Company. Because each of these programs was so vastly different in origin and procedure it is necessary to describe each so that the reader may not only gain a better perspective toward the different kinds of programs that can be called "counseling in industry" but also see more clearly the results of such studies and their applications to a wide variety of industrial organizations regardless of their size. In addition two other programs will be described as illustrating work of more recent origin. These are the programs at Oak Ridge and at the Caterpillar Tractor Company.

R. H. Macy. Dr. V. V. Anderson described the results of a four-year study which he directed in this large department store in the book *Psychiatry in Industry* (1). From his experience, Anderson concluded that the minimum basis for undertaking a sound and constructive research program into the personnel problems of industry is a working team consisting of a psychologist, a psychiatrist, and a psychiatric social worker. Dr. Anderson's primary concern was with the "problem" employee. Accordingly, he discovered that problem cases may be divided into four main groups.

> Group A includes those problem employees whose main difficulties lie in their own make up and the disorder of their own personality, rather than that they are in the wrong job. A careful psychiatric inquiry discloses the nature of these difficulties and the important causative factors underlying the problems presented. Treatment of these cases involves adjustment of the employee right within his department. This is accomplished through frequent contacts with the psychiatric social worker or the psychiatrist, and a well-planned therapeutic regime is followed over a sufficiently long period to bring about changes in the behavior of the employee.[3]

Group B includes those employees in which

> the job maladjustment or misplacement, rather than the personality disorder of the employee, stands out as the most important factor in the situation. To be sure, there are often other issues to face, but the transfer to more suitable work, with proper training and adjustment on the job, is what is needed.[4]

Group C includes those people who present outstanding personnel problems and who "following upon a careful psychiatric examination, show physical and mental conditions of such a nature as to justify us in believing that an adjustment of their difficulties cannot be brought about satisfactorily, under store conditions."[5]

Group D included those employees who were kept on the job during treatment but did not respond and so had to be dismissed.

Anderson analyzed the results obtained by reviewing 500 successive referrals. In all cases the referrals were made because the employees were "problems." The varied reasons for their being problems were briefly put as: "bad attitude, nervousness, constant disciplinary problem, indifferent, resents authority, day-dreamer, etc."[6] Of this group of 500 employees, 67 per cent were still in the Company's employ at the time of the review; 23 per cent had been dismissed; 8 per cent had resigned; and the remaining 2 per cent had been pensioned.

---

[3] *Ibid.*
[4] *Ibid.*
[5] *Ibid.*
[6] *Ibid.*

There is no doubt that a good percentage of the 67 per cent would not have been in the employ of the store if the "problem" employees had not been investigated. From the point of view of the store itself, savings resulted in the employment, training, and placement of new people who would have had to be hired in their place; and, probably, at least one fifth of these new employees would also have turned into "problems." Beyond this, however, one cannot overlook the satisfaction of the individual that resulted from his newly-found adjustment. This satisfaction must pay dividends not only to the store but to the community at large.

Anderson points out that many medical cases reaching an industrial medical department must be thought of as patients for the psychiatrist rather than the general M.D. The authors would agree with this, except that they would use the clinical psychologist as well. Among such cases are included the chronic hospital users, the situation reaction cases, the fatigue problems, and those in whom nervous and mental diseases are suspected.

Among the chronic hospital users are those in which there is a fixation of interest and attention on themselves and their bodily organs. For them illness is a compensation for defeat because of difficulties; it serves as a comforting and attention-getting device. Very often medical treatment alone serves only to intensify the condition.

The situation reaction cases include those employees who find the hospital a retreat from a difficult job or an irritating home situation. The medical symptoms of these employees are never quite as clear as in the former group. Whereas the former group includes the headache and pain-in-the-back variety, the latter suffers from eyestrain or "nervousness."

Among the fatigue cases, the major causes may be physical conditions, personality maladjustment, home problems, or the job situation itself. For this group the "tonic treatment" is not likely to be very effective.

According to Anderson, it is generally agreed that approximately 25 per cent of the patients in general hospitals suffer from psychoneuroses. He is convinced that in an industrial medical clinic the percentage is higher. Psychotics or severely disoriented persons are not to be found only in hospitals or in the ranks of the chronically unemployed. They were discovered at R. H. Macy's and are equally as likely to be found in all other business establishments. Sometimes, oddly enough, they are in key positions. The disabilities of these people are often not recognized and as a result they cause havoc with the lives of others who work with them.

Although a careful study of Anderson's book reveals obvious shortcomings and a point of view that is surely not shared by most competent psychiatrists and clinical psychologists, as to the roles each is capable of playing, Anderson's work has nevertheless more than historical interest. Since its publication in 1929 he has continued his interest in industrial psychiatry, or as the present authors would prefer to state, counseling in industry. Anderson should be given credit for his awareness that detecting "problem" employees merely by the symptom of their problem behavior accomplishes little, but that approaching the underlying causes and administering psychotherapy while the person is on the job may result in his adjustment. The benefits accrue not only to the individual but to the industrial establishment of which he is a part.

Western Electric. The most significant industrial counseling program is to be found at the Western Electric Company. It has its roots in the now famous Hawthorne Studies, which were conducted at the Hawthorne plant of the Western Electric Company. This series of studies is all the more remarkable in relation to their implications for interviewing because originally they had nothing to do with interviewing. The first phase concerned experiments on illumination. The objective was to determine the relationship existing between changes in illumination and production. A series of experiments was performed in which controls were introduced and the conclusion was reached that a one-to-one relationship between changes in illumination and production could not be established. As a result of these findings, the second phase of the study known as the Relay Assembly Test Room was started.

In an attempt to control conditions more carefully, a group of girls performed their job of assembling relays in a separate room, apart from the factory, so that exact production records and observations of the employees at work could be made. They were subjected to a wide variation in conditions, such as change in financial incentive, variations in rest periods, and decreases in the work day. Despite the changes taking place, production tended to rise. The chief result was to demonstrate the importance of employee attitudes. The relay assembly test room showed very clearly that as the girls' attitudes improved toward each other, their work, and the supervisor, their production increased. It was during this phase that the experimenters realized that they were not studying the relationship between output and fatigue but were performing a sociological and psychological experiment.

Whereas management had believed that its supervision was good, the employees' remarks were exceedingly disparaging. This contrast could mean either that management knew little about what constitutes good supervision or that they did not know the attitudes of the employees on this subject. It was decided to include instructions for improving employee morale in a supervisory training course. At this point, it was learned that there was a dearth of facts on how to improve supervision. Because of this discovery, the management decided to interview employees.

In other words, the interviewing program at Western Electric started essentially as a plan for improving supervision. It is important to recognize that interviewing in this company got started, as it were, "through the back door." The reason, then, was not that the company recognized the importance of providing therapy to its employees. Its original objective was simple and straightforward—to gain information about employee attitudes. The program started with the selection of three men and two women who were to do the interviewing. The only qualification considered essential was the knowledge of shop conditions, so that the person being interviewed would feel that his statements were understood. The fact that neither psychiatrists, psychologists, or psychiatric social workers were selected to conduct the interviews shows very clearly that the intent was simply to gain information concerning shop conditions and the attitudes resulting therefrom. Each interviewer was given the following list of instructions:

1. Each interviewer was assigned a certain territory to cover. From the foreman of each department in his territory he was to obtain a list of the employees' names.

2. When the interviewer was ready to start interviewing in any department, it was recommended that he first go to the foreman in charge and make his presence known.

3. It was recommended that the interviewer select the man he wanted to interview because otherwise the supervisor might be tempted to give him all his "problem cases" first. However, the interviewer was to cooperate with the supervisor so that the operation of the department would be interfered with as little as possible.

4. The interviewer was to ask the supervisor's advice about where the employee should be interviewed—whether away from the job or on the job. (Subsequent experience showed that it was usually advisable to interview an employee away from his work. Thereafter it was recommended that the interviewer ask the department chief for a bench or desk where he could conduct the interviews without interruption.)

5. The interviewer was to make sure that the necessary arrangements were made for paying the employee his average earnings for the time consumed in the interview.

6. In his contacts with supervisors the interviewer was to be careful not to betray the confidence of any employee and to refrain absolutely from discussing the content of the interviews with the supervisors.

7. Only a few employees from any one location were to be interviewed on the same day, so that the work of the department might go on normally and without undue confusion or curiosity.[7]

Careful instructions with regard to approaching the employee and conducting the interview were also given the interviewers:

1. Whenever possible, the employee was to be formally introduced to the interviewer by the supervisor. Interviewers were not to interview employees whom they knew, because the acquaintance might influence the employees' comments.

2. When the interviewer and employee were seated and ready to proceed with the interview, the employee was to be told the interviewer's name again.

[7] Reprinted by permission of the publishers from Fritz Jules Roethlisberger and William John Dickson, *Management and the Worker*, Cambridge, Mass.: Harvard University Press, 1939.

3. The interviewer was to explain to the employee the purpose of the interview, i.e., why any comments, either favorable or unfavorable, that the employee cared to make about his supervisors, working conditions, and job were being solicited.

4. The employee was to be told how the interviews would be used; for example, any complaints he had about working conditions would be investigated together with those of the other employees and, as far as practicable, remedial action would be taken. The manner in which the material gathered from the interviews was to be used in supervisory training conferences was also to be explained.

5. The interviewer was to make clear to each employee that the interviews would be kept strictly confidential; i.e., the employee could tell the interviewer anything, no matter how bad it was, without getting in trouble himself or getting his supervisors or his coworkers in trouble. The interviewer was to explain that no names or company numbers would appear on any records and that the people who read the interviews or heard them read would not be told who the employee was or where he worked. Anything the employee said which might identify him with his supervisor would be deleted from his interview.

6. The employee was to be told that the company was as much interested in the things he liked as in those with which he was dissatisfied and which he thought needed to be corrected.

7. The interviewer was to take almost verbatim notes as the employee talked. He was to explain to the employee that he was writing down what was said word for word so that there would be no possible chance of misrepresenting or forgetting anything. (At first it was thought that taking notes might make the employee reluctant to talk, but this was found not to be true.)

8. The interviewer was to be sympathetic and a good listener, and to let the employee know that he was really interested in his problems and complaints.

9. Strict care was to be taken to express no agreement or disagreement with the complaints the employee made. The interviewer was to let the employee know that he himself was in no position to judge the correctness or incorrectness of what the employee was saying.

10. The interviewer was not to inform the employee of the nature of the complaints made by other employees.

11. The interviewer was not to give the employee advice as to what he should do. In rare cases he might advise an employee to see his supervisor, or tell him about the various benefit plans, the Hawthorne evening school, or similar things. However, the interviewer

was not to hesitate to offer encouragement to any employee if he thought it would do him good.

12. The interviewer was to write up the interview under six headings. The opinions of the employee were to be divided first into three categories: working conditions, supervision, and job. Each of these headings was to have two subclassifications, likes and dislikes.[8]

This interviewing program received rather widespread acceptance from not only the employees but also the supervisors. Many employees commented upon the recognition by management of the workers' point of view, which they believed was implied in the program. Typical quotes revealing this were: "It's a good idea to interview the operators as they may have something on their minds that they want to talk over with someone and this gives them a chance to do it," or "I think interviewing is a good idea. It helps some people get a lot of things off their minds."

Although the original interviews were never conducted as if a questionnaire were being administered, the interviewer had certain questions in mind for the purpose of eliciting material. Such questions were, "How does your boss treat you?" or "What do you think of the Company as a place to work?" In other words, the interviewer led the conversation and the employee followed. In this type of interview it was often reported that the subject would wander from the topic. Feeling that this material was irrelevant the interviewer would try to lead him back. Too often, there was one subject uppermost in the mind of the person being interviewed and it was about this that he wished to talk. At this point, certain defects in the direct question method of interviewing were realized. It tended to put the person in a yes or no frame of mind, and prevented spontaneity of response. This led to the adoption of a different interviewing technique, which they called "the indirect approach." Most briefly, this method allowed the employee to choose his own topic, and talk spontaneously. The interviewer was not to interrupt or change the topic. He was to listen attentively to anything the worker said and to take part in the conversation only to keep the employee talking. This change in technique resulted in a drastic change in the length of the interview.

[8] *Ibid.*

Whereas in the direct method the interview lasted approximately 30 minutes, it now increased to one and one half hours.

At this point it is necessary to note that the indirect method of interviewing as developed by the Hawthorne group is rather similar to the non-directive technique developed by Rogers. Careful check by the authors reveals that both of these techniques developed quite independently of each other. It is an interesting observation in scientific methodology as well as fact, that very often two people working quite independently will, at approximately the same time, evolve similar contributions. For example, in psychology, James and Lange contributed similar theories explaining emotions and of course, the development of atomic physics similarly illustrates this point.

As the importance of the interview method was realized, it was extended so that finally 21,126 employees were interviewed. It is desirable to remember that this interviewing program was not started, modified, nor continued simply because a psychologist wanted to do research, or because a social reformer wished to demonstrate that industry had a responsibility to its workers. It was a practical program that had very practical results for the company. For example, it resulted in drastic changes in the training of supervisors. This resulted in better supervision, because there was a tendency for supervisors to become less dogmatic and because it encouraged a growing appreciation of the effects which methods of supervision might have on the attitudes, morale, and working effectiveness of employees.

Another use to which the interviews were put was a content analysis of complaints, as well as an investigation of those complaints which were specific. For example, during 1929, some 40,000 comments, including 28,000 complaints and 12,000 approvals, were sent to the organization responsible for the regulation and maintenance of physical plant conditions. Such things as aisles, furniture, lockers, fumes, smoke, and stairwells were investigated.

However, in many respects, the most important results from the interviewing program were those that were unexpected. Among these were: (1) The existence of the interviewing program created a change in supervision. Apparently it stimulated the supervisor to greater effort. (2) The interviewers began to understand the importance of taking into consideration the thoughts and the reflections of workers, and they were very instrumental in developing techniques of understanding employees. (3) Employees appreciated being recognized as individuals who had valuable comments to make. They seemed to benefit as individuals because of the opportunity to express freely their feelings and emotions.

Benefits resulting from the interviewing program were the correction of unfavorable working conditions, better training courses for supervisors, and psychological benefits accruing to the person interviewed. Possibly one of the most important things in connection with the interviewing program was the realization that employee comments had a dual character: They not only served to communicate facts, but also to express sentiments; and too often, it was extremely difficult to differentiate clearly between fact and sentiment. A classification of comments resulted in a trifold analysis. One group of complaints involved primarily the sensory experiences of seeing and touching. For example, "The tool is dull." The second group included those in which sensory experiences played a large role, but also involved sensations arising within the organism. For example, "The room is hot" or "The job is dangerous." In class C sensory experiences played a small role and sentiment a very large one. The comments can be understood only in relation to the social settings that inspired them. Such comments would include, "The rates are too low," or "Ability does not count." The complaint of one person with less education than others is, "The company attaches too much importance to education." Another individual with more than average education says, "Brains do not count." It is especially in this class of comments that we see the confusion between fact and sentiment. However, even in the first group mentioned, "The tool is dull" may not be a fact, but a complaint of a poor worker and therefore a sentiment.

To understand the confusion between fact and sentiment, one must differentiate between the manifest content, that which is said, from the latent content, the real meaning of the comment. For example, a worker complains that the rates are too low. This is the manifest content. The latent content as revealed by the interview is that the man's wife is sick and he has large doctor bills. To understand many employee complaints one must find the individual meaning behind the verbalization. The Hawthorne group discovered that certain complaints could not be treated as facts but as symptoms of personal situations which needed exploration.

The Hawthorne group evolved a series of rules of orientation and of conduct in connection with their interviewing procedure. Rather close agreement can be discovered between these rules and those we suggested in the chapter on the interview. However, the rules of the Hawthorne group are equally important and deserve separate and complete consideration. The rules of orientation are as follows:

1. The interviewer should treat what is said in an interview as an item in a context.

1A. The interviewer should not pay exclusive attention to the manifest content of the conversation.

1B. The interviewer should not treat everything that is said as either fact or error.

1C. The interviewer should not treat everything that is said as being at the same psychological level.

2. The interviewer should listen not only to what a person wants to say but also for what he does not want to say or cannot say without help.

3. The interviewer should treat the mental contexts described in the preceding rule as indices and seek through them the personal reference that is being revealed.

4. The interviewer should keep the personal reference in its social context.

4A. The interviewer should remember that the interview is itself a social situation and that therefore the social relation existing between the interviewer and the interviewee is in part determining what is said.

4A1. The interviewer should see to it that the speaker's sentiments do not act on his own.[9]

The rules of conduct are:

1. The interviewer should listen to the speaker in a patient and friendly, but intelligently critical manner.

[9] Reprinted by permission of the publishers from Fritz Jules Roethlisberger and William John Dickson, *Management and the Worker,* Cambridge, Mass.: Harvard University Press, 1939.

2. The interviewer should not display any kind of authority.
3. The interviewer should not give advice or moral admonition.
4. The interviewer should not argue with the speaker.
5. The interviewer should talk or ask questions only under certain conditions.
   a. to help the person talk.
   b. to relieve any fears on the part of the speaker which may be affecting his relation to the interviewer.
   c. to praise the interviewee for reporting his thoughts and feelings accurately.
   d. to veer the discussion to some topic which has been omitted or neglected.
   e. to discuss implicit assumption, if this is advisable.[10]

At this point one can readily see that the development of interviewing at Western Electric had gone a long way, from attempting to understand employee attitudes to the realization that complaints were related to personal adjustment. Difficulties in the personal situation of workers could be relieved or exaggerated depending upon the immediate work situation. Indifferent methods of supervision often left the employee without social support; this deficiency would be interpreted by such an individual as a threat to his security. Personal situations in which there was a serious disorientation of general attitude frequently were accompanied by a reduced capacity for work. The interviewing program showed that the source of most employee complaints is not some single cause, but rather a complex situation which can be understood only in terms of the worker's adjustment to the interferences. By now, the reader can see that we are no longer talking about interviewing but rather counseling or psychotherapy. This point is stated very well by Roethlisberger and Dickson (12) as follows:

> Inasmuch as in most cases the worker could not adequately specify the locus of this dissatisfaction, it was important that the supervisor be alert to interferences of many types and kinds, those arising from within as well as from without the immediate working environment. By encouraging the worker to talk freely and by refraining from hasty disapprobation, the supervisor was in a better position to "spot" the locus of the interference and consequently to handle his employees

[10] *Ibid.*

more intelligently. This was the lesson which had been learned from the interviewing program.[11]

The personnel counseling program as developed at the Hawthorne plant serves the employees and management equally well. There is absolutely no doubt that the method of interviewing developed is one of the acceptable methods of psychotherapy. The vast number of cases compiled by this group as well as those from the rather related non-directive technique of Rogers demonstrates this clearly. Psychological disturbances do interfere with an individual's efficiency and are sometimes manifested in the classification, "dissatisfied worker." This interviewing program has led to the adjustment of otherwise maladjusted people. However, it is also important to point out that management benefits equally. Not only has the production of the recently adjusted workers increased; management now has a very effective tool to improve its system of communication. Too often management is preoccupied with the organization of effective communications down the chain of command and assumes erroneously that all is well. It has no way of knowing to what extent its orders and policies are actually carried out. The close personal and intimate contact that these interviewers, in a distinctly non-supervisory capacity, can have with employees is not often matched by other employer-employee relationships. These interviewers also afford the most meaningful way of safely channeling communications from employee to management.

Because Western Electric learned all this the hard way, they not only are aware of the significance of their industrial counseling but regard it as very important in their scheme of management. The fact that they discovered so many important things which in some respects were in no way related to their original objective possibly makes them all the more appreciative. In any event, personal counseling continues at Western Electric. For example, Dickson (6) has recently reported that in the Chicago Division there are 40 counselors equally divided among men and women. Each counselor is assigned a territory comprising some 300 employees to whom his entire time is de-

[11] *Ibid.*

voted. The contacts are of two kinds: off-the-job interviews and on-the-job contacts. The former are held in a private room; employees are interviewed as often as seems necessary. These interviews average about an hour and 20 minutes, and average earnings are paid for the time spent with the counselor. The counselors are also expected to keep in touch with the employees and integrate themselves in the work group. They maintain such contacts by visiting the worker at his work place, in the aisles, restrooms, and so forth. As for the potential power of the interviewing method, Dickson reports a rather dramatic case in which a person in a relatively short time was made an effective member of society at little cost.

> The man was about 45 years of age with twenty years of service with the company. As a younger man he had progressed rapidly and had risen to the rank of supervisor. Then something happened and his course trended downward. When he came to the counselor's attention he had been assigned to the lowest grade of work in the department and was not doing well at it. His supervisor said that they had been concerned with his output and quality of work for a long time and had tried every method they knew for improving him but without results. He had become so nervous they hardly dared approach him for fear he might incur an accident on his machine.
>
> In the interviews, the man seemed very willing to talk although at first he had great difficulty in expressing himself and there were long pauses in the interviews. Briefly, the picture was one of extreme social isolation. He had no friends or relatives except a brother whom he saw only infrequently. After work he ate his dinner and then locked himself in his room. His medicine cabinet was stocked with all sorts of nostrums and after dosing himself with these he usually went to bed and read detective stories or occasionally drank himself into a stupor.
>
> His locker at work also resembled a small drug store which he drew upon frequently during the day. He said that one of the things which bothered him most was the way his supervisors continually spied on him. Every time he turned around he could see his supervisor staring at him and even when his back was turned he could feel his supervisor's eyes boring a hole in his back. This was the general pattern revealed.
>
> The counselor began interviewing this person daily for about three weeks and then less and less frequently as the need diminished. Within a relatively short period his fears began to diminish, his performance

to improve, and he seemed to take a new interest in the people around him. Shortly afterward he improved sufficiently to justify his supervisors in recommending him for a higher grade of work and increase in pay.

Today, six years later, he has married, established a home, risen to a responsible position, and seems to have overcome his former difficulties completely.[12]

As for the variety of problems that are covered by such interviewers, Dickson offers the following selection from the interviews of two counselors which are regarded as typical:

1. An employee who feels that his progress is too slow and who cannot see any chance for further progress in his department.
2. An employee in a group which expects to be transferred soon is disturbed by the insecurity of the situation.
3. A young man who is worried about being drafted.
4. An employee who has been offered a higher paid job elsewhere but cannot decide whether to accept it.
5. A young woman having difficulties with parents over getting married.
6. A man with a neurotic wife.
7. A young woman whose husband has deserted her.
8. Friction with other workers on the job.
9. A woman disturbed by her supervisor's criticism of her work.[13]

Needless to say, the rules of interviewing evolved some years earlier are still followed. The interviewer merely encourages continued conversation. Any restatements by the interviewer are always addressed to the feeling of the employee rather than to the logical content of what is said. The counselor is a skilled listener who shows a real interest in the person. He never interrupts, argues, or gives advice. He does not indulge in any evaluation. He relates himself to everyone in the counseling territory in exactly the same way—to supervisor, shop steward, and worker.

This system of interviewing, according to Dickson, provides an emotional release and a release from tensions. It also stimulates the employee to re-examine his beliefs and phantasies. Frequently, as a result, he modifies his interpretations of his experiences.

[12] *American Journal of Orthopsychiatry,* 15:344 (1945).
[13] *Ibid.,* page 345.

A counseling program is also conducted at the Kearny Plant of Western Electric. This program is conducted according to the recognition that counseling helps to solve personal employee problems, especially related to "work situation," and improves supervision. Counseling helps supervisors understand that supervision must cover more than production, quality, and cost. This program has been effective in improving the communication skills of supervisors.

A tender spot in the counseling situation is the relation of the counselor and the supervisor. To gain the cooperation of the supervisor, the counselor does not take responsibility or assume authority for straightening out the problem on hand. This is the supervisor's duty; the counselor through interviewing technique attempts to help the supervisor develop insight.

Oak Ridge. Oak Ridge grew in a very short time from hilly farm land to a city of 75,000 with all the conveniences of a well organized community (5). It was assumed because everyone would be employed at good wages and would be supplied with adequate housing that there would be no social or personal problems for the workers. Here the realists would be able to demonstrate that if you give a man and his family adequate salaries and living conveniences, personal problems would not arise. How wrong this assumption proved to be! The problem of transplanting people did not work out so easily. Very soon it was realized that the family breadwinners, their wives, and their children had problems—and so did the single workers. Life for the 12,000 housed in dormitories was not as smooth as expected. Either the newly-found freedom or the impersonal living resulted in frightened, insecure, and homesick behavior. Pilfering, gambling, and other problems were present. Because of these problems dormitory counselors were introduced.

Young children coming from widely different school systems presented educational-emotional problems as well as the typical varieties of juvenile delinquency. Because the workers could not indulge in "shop talk," there were difficulties in husband and wife relations, especially among the scientific group. General ignorance of the purpose of the project further contributed to the difficulties. The large quantities of materials that poured into Oak Ridge as well as the conspicuous absence of any visible project being shipped out, when coupled with the high degree of specialization of task, and the inability to determine the relationship between it and other jobs, contributed greatly to a wide variety of emotional and psychosomatic disorders. The most common mental illness was the type known as anxiety neurosis—in many respects similar to the diagnosis known as battle fatigue, found in overseas units. Fatigue reactions with associated tensions were common. Another pattern that evolved in Oak Ridge was the widespread unfounded rumor of undue health hazards (which resulted in anxieties).

In Oak Ridge, a vast and complex system of security safeguards was emphasized. For many men and women, the importance of their war work was stressed and although they did not really understand the importance, this factor served as a stabilizing influence. However, this emphasis did not help people with paranoid tendencies, (those who are likely to suffer from delusions, especially of personal reference). To these, the frequent inspections and continual need for identification were regarded with personal suspicion. An individual having such a basic pattern was likely to become even more excited and more susceptible to a breakdown.

In other words, jobs at good salary, with more or less adequate housing facilities, apparently are not enough to prevent personality disorders. One simply cannot overlook the personality pattern of the worker and the members of his family. Apparently these are even more important. To be sure, substandard jobs and substandard housing, can bring on a crisis, but their correction, in and of itself, is not a preventative. And so, it was necessary to set up a program that those who know nothing at all about psychology might call social welfare, but that those with greater knowledge would call counseling.

The program at Oak Ridge had three main divisions. The first was hospital service for in-patients and out-patients, who already showed evidence of mental sickness. The second was a community service which included child guidance and family counseling. The third aspect of the program was geared to prevent mental breakdown within the plant by detection and early treatment. This threefold service served a very useful purpose. For example, if in the third or industrial aspect, a worker was encountered who revealed anxiety on the job and there was a strong surmise that the root of the difficulty was in the home, it was possible, through the other services, to observe the children of this man in the school. If tensions in the child existed, then a visit to the home, ostensibly to go into the child's problem, could be made. Such a situation does not make obvious the connection between the father's tension at work and the home picture. However, at this point, the three-pronged attack on the problem can be found to clear the entire picture. To be sure, most industrial plants attempting such a program would not only meet with strong resistance but would be accused of paternalism. However, in the Oak Ridge situation, because of the peculiar circumstance of the job and community being rather integrated, such a plan was feasible. In a typical industrial picture, modifications of this plan might still be possible—that is, the industrial counselor might be able to contact the various school or community agencies and so obtain a more comprehensive understanding of the worker's disorder. Leggo, Law and Clarke (9) have drawn the following conclusions concerning industrial psychiatry as a result of their Oak Ridge experiences.

1. Causes of emotional disturbances in industry lie primarily within the individual, and the exciting mechanisms lie in the home or in his social surroundings. Our experience is that in not more than approximately 10% of the on-the-job emotional disturbances can exciting factors be recognized as lying in the industrial environment.
2. An adequate minimum amount of treatment results in conspicuous on-the-job improvement. This minimum will average two hours individual time and will rarely exceed three hours.
3. Therapeutics directed to on-the-job patients is economically profitable by preventing non-disabling maladjustments from developing into major disabling breakdowns.
4. Seriously disturbed cases or those in which deep or prolonged therapy is required should not be handled on the job but referred to outside therapists.
5. The community gains from a sound industrial psychiatric program by the increased number of home adjustments accomplished by on-the-job therapy.
6. Institutional or private practice psychiatric techniques may require

considerable modification before they are applicable in industry.

7. A program which we believe will justify the employment of a psychiatrist by an industry for a given period of time consists of:
   (a) Treatment of individual cases with particular reference to their value as educational material for the regular medical staff.
   (b) In-service training for the medical staff.
   (c) Improvement of emotional attitudes through conference methods with medical, nursing, counselor, or supervisory staffs.
   (d) Training for employment interviewers for methods of screening for emotional instability.
8. Criteria justifying the permanent employment of a psychiatrist are beyond the scope of this paper.[14]

The Caterpillar Tractor Company. Whereas a psychiatrist introduced the program of counseling at Macy's, a psychologist performed such a task at Caterpillar. This program was rather comprehensive and included testing, training, and counseling, all within the framework of mental hygiene.

Prior to being hired, an applicant was interviewed to ascertain his "status of emotional fitness"; findings from this interview were integrated with results of the employment test battery, which included intelligence, mechanical, and emotional adjustment tests. The integration of testing and interviewing allowed for the decision of hiring and specific placement.

Employees were either referred to or voluntarily visited the psychologist, who was known as the Personnel Consultant. The type of counseling offered was directive. According to Weider (13), who was in charge of the program: "It is practicable and feasible to offer counsel, advice and make referrals, in an effort to remedy, alleviate and 'cure' various conditions contributing to an employee's emotional and/or vocational maladjustment." At Caterpillar the task of counseling was to make the employee aware of the "true" conflicts that underlay his complaint. When this awareness was reached, the symptom either was alleviated or disappeared.

The psychologist at Caterpillar, in addition to counseling, also included in the program mental hygiene training. He worked with

[14] *Industrial Medicine,* 15:254 (1946). Reprinted by permission of the Industrial Medicine Publishing Company.

employment interviewers by conducting a continuing series of lectures on personality and applied psychology, and by supervising interviews.

All employees were reached, in an attempt to put across mental hygiene education, through articles in the employees' magazine and by the organization of a program called bibliotherapy. Bibliotherapy consisted of a careful selection of 200 books which were made available to employees. These books, on various psychological topics, were chosen because of appropriateness of subject matter and simplicity of language. The experiences at the company showed that bibliotherapy was useful as a supplement to employee counseling.

At Caterpillar recourse was made to outside community agencies, in order to effect a more complete vocational and emotional adjustment.

Integration

Four rather comprehensive industrial counseling programs have been described. Each is different from the other, not only in name and in original objective, but also as to the background of the personnel involved. At Macy's a psychiatrist who relegates the psychologist to the specific role of testing has demonstrated the efficacy of a counseling program. Many workers on the job with emotional or vocational maladjustments have been salvaged and made more productive.

At Western Electric, the counseling system evolved was far removed from the confines of the psychiatrist. The counselors were trained in a specific manner of interviewing which rather closely resembled the non-directive technique of Carl Rogers, a psychologist, and there is not a doubt that it amounts to psychotherapy. However, it must be stressed that the system developed at Western Electric, although in many respects valid, was developed the hard way over a long period of time and with many detours.

At Oak Ridge, the problem was forced. Here were war workers doing a secret and very important war job which, by its very nature, required the workers to live and work in a fashion much more confined than is usual in industry. Again we find the psychiatrist in charge, but we see the recognition that counseling can take place not only as a curative but also as a preventative, while the worker is on the job and before he is completely broken.

At Caterpillar the clinical psychologist comes to the forefront. Demonstrated here is the fact that psychology in industry is not confined to testing solely for selection purposes; but rather that testing can become integrated in an ultimately more meaningful program of counseling the worker on the job, thereby leading to a decrease in vocational and emotional maladjustments. Dorcus and Case (7) have abstracted 116 of the 456 titles appearing in a three-year period ending July 1943 on the subject "Mental Hygiene Problems in Industry." Such industrial programs are a part of either the plant medical service or the personnel department. Correcting individual maladjustments, reducing accidents, and relating off-the-job adjustment to on-the-job adjustment are among the more commonly reported results of such programs. Dorcus and Case conclude their survey by stating, "While one is impressed with the volume, we are disappointed that there are relatively few factual and experimental studies. It is quite apparent that the field is one in which a vast amount of work needs to be done."

Despite the fact that some large-scale and many sporadic attempts to either promote or demonstrate the various uses of counseling in industry have been going on for 20 years or so, it must be acknowledged that this is a largely unexplored field. The psychologist has not been satisfied with the experimental evidence, the industrialist still cannot see that a maladjusted worker is his problem, and the number of psychiatrists who have even worked in industry is small.

A program must emerge. This field is not one which intrinsically belongs to psychiatry, clinical psychology, or even to people who have been trained in an interviewing technique. It may be that a new profession should emerge. For lack of a better name it could be called industrial counseling, and in its formative stages should draw people from many different professional backgrounds. Different techniques of therapy should be used but more than self-evaluated data must ultimately be gathered. It will be then that the best techniques will emerge. Until that time, bold recognition must be given to the fact that the absentee, the quarrelsome worker, the chronic hospital user, the high accident rate employee are very likely vocationally and/or emotionally maladjusted individuals. The particular problems they present in industry are only a symptom. Cures cannot be effected in either physical or mental illnesses only by treating symptoms. One must reach the cause. A worker on the job does not leave his home problems at home. The reverse is true. Problems on the job also affect the worker in his home and community relations. An individual, even the first day he works on his first job, presents degrees of adjustment or maladjustment. The job history from then on will serve either to increase or decrease the personal adjustments the worker has made. Incidentally, although the term worker has been used throughout this chapter, by no means has there been an attempt to preclude the employer. Employers are workers, too. In fact, one way of possibly demonstrating the efficacy of a counseling program in industry is to introduce the program by counseling the employers first. It may be that then, recognizing the value of such a program, they will be more able to see that counseling should spread to the lower echelons in our industrial society.

Counseling in industry should therefore be regarded as another stage in the continuum of guidance. The first phase might be known as educational guidance, the second phase as vocational counseling, and the third phase as industrial counseling. A very strong case can be made for industrial establishments, rather than a wide variety of community agencies, handling this problem. The meaningfulness of counseling in the industrial situation is greater than in the typical community setting, which sometimes serves only to separate the segments of a personality that is striving for integration.

Summary

Industrial counseling takes place within the industrial establishment. Since vocational and emotional problems can have a continuously reversible cause and effect relationship, and since some job histories begin and continue with vocational and emotional maladjustment, it is advisable to recognize that counseling must be continued in industry.

The argument that it is not the responsibility of industry to bear the costs of adjusting these problems of people is not valid. If industry does not pay directly, then the indirect costs of taxation and philanthropic bequests are likely to be even greater.

Not very much work in this area has been performed in industry. Anderson, a psychiatrist, as a result of some work at R. H. Macy, reports that 20 per cent of all employees are what may be called "problem" employees.

The most intensive type of counseling program in industry has been developed and carried on at Western Electric. The interview procedure resembles rather closely the non-directive technique. It is interesting to note that counseling developed as a by-product of a research study rather than as a direct objective or plan. Western Electric has discovered that such a counseling program benefits both management and employee.

Oak Ridge demonstrates that giving people jobs at good salaries and also providing workers with satisfactory housing will not solve all problems. A counseling program had to be introduced to help solve the personal and emotional difficulties of the people living and working in Oak Ridge. The fourth illustration of a counseling program described was the work at the Caterpillar Tractor Company. In this company a psychologist was in charge.

Counseling in industry should be regarded as a stage in the continuum of guidance. The meaningfulness of counseling in the industrial situation can be greater than in the typical community setting.

Bibliography

1. Anderson, V. V., *Psychiatry in Industry*. New York: Harper, 1929.
2. ——— "Psychiatry in Industry," *American Journal of Psychiatry*, 100:134–137 (1944).
3. Blum, M. L., *Industrial Psychology and Its Social Foundations*. New York: Harper, 1949.
4. Cantor, N., *Employee Counseling*. New York: McGraw-Hill, 1945

5. Clarke, E. K., "Psychiatric Problems at Oak Ridge," *American Journal of Psychiatry*, 102:437–444 (1946).
6. Dickson, W. J., "The Hawthorne Plan of Personnel Counseling," *American Journal of Orthopsychiatry*, 15:344–347 (1945).
7. Dorcus, R. M., and H. W. Case, "Mental Hygiene Problems in Industry," *Review of Educational Research*, 13:485–489 (1943).
8. Friend, J. G., and E. A. Haggard, *Work Adjustment in Relation to Family Background*, Applied Psychology Monographs, No. 16 (1948).
9. Leggo, C., S. G. Law, and E. K. Clarke, "Industrial Psychiatry in the Community of Oak Ridge," *Industrial Medicine*, 15:4, 243–254 (1946).
10. McMurray, R. N., *Handling Personality Adjustment in Industry*. New York: Harper, 1944.
11. National Research Council, *Fatigue of Workers*. New York: Reinhold, 1941.
12. Roethlisberger, F. J., and W. J. Dickson, *Management and the Worker*. Cambridge, Mass.: Harvard University Press, 1946.
13. Weider, A., "Mental Hygiene in Industry—A Clinical Psychologist's Contribution," *Journal of Clinical Psychology*, 3:309–320 (1947).

19

RELATION OF VOCATIONAL GUIDANCE TO VOCATIONAL SELECTION

VOCATIONAL SELECTION is the process whereby applicants for positions become employees. In such a situation, there is a job available and there are many people seeking it. Of course, the number of people who want the job varies with economic conditions and the resulting labor supply.

The ideal in vocational selection is to choose the one person who best qualifies for the job. In actual practice this ideal is never reached, since it is undoubtedly true that many people are equally fit for any one job. It is therefore more accurate to state that in vocational selection the primary problem is to select among the many applicants the one person who is likely to perform the job as well as can be expected.

The frame of reference in vocational selection is the opposite of that in vocational guidance. In selection there is one job and many people. In guidance there is one individual and many potential jobs. This reversal requires a rather different orientation even though the tools, instruments, and techniques used in guidance are similar to those used in selection. The major difference is in orientation. In guidance it can be assumed that the client is seeking help. As a result he is likely to be more honest in his statements to a counselor. In selection the applicant wants and often needs the job and will try to "beat" the personnel department by elaboration, and sometimes even prevarication. In selection the person doing the hiring is under pressure to make a choice that would be best for the company and very often seemingly tangential explorations concerning the individual are not possible. In guidance the counselor, even though he might be under pressure, must always remember that he is dealing with an individual; consequently the process is likely to be more lengthy. Possibly the biggest difference between guidance and selection is in the social significance of the two for the community. In selection it is assumed that when the decision is made not to hire an applicant the company has no further obligations to the individual. In guidance it is not an exaggeration at all to state that the client's social welfare and economic well-being are in the hands of the counselor. An incorrect decision not to hire a person is not nearly so critical because if the person is employable, he will seek and obtain another job. An incorrect decision in guidance may be serious insofar as the person may wind up in a job that is not capable of satisfying his needs. Ultimately, this mismatching results in either vocational or emotional maladjustment; and not only the individual but even the style of life of the individual's present or future family is affected.

Although it is true that guidance and selection are very different, it can be noted that theoretically this difference need not exist. In Utopia, guidance and selection would be merged into a continuing process. Every individual would be employed in a job that is most suited to his abilities, and so on. Under present conditions, the problems of attempting to integrate guidance and selection become so great as to be insurmountable. For example, many more people aspire to be M.D.'s than can be admitted to medical schools. The number of applicants is so large that it is really difficult to understand the validity of the process by which medical schools accept candidates. For a physically healthy United States many more doctors should be trained. However, medical schools show little inclination to expand to meet this need. The result is a shortage of doctors as well as a chaotic and overcompetitive system of selecting qualified applicants. Another example might be the field of accountancy. For any of many reasons, college students will study accountancy. The facilities to do so on the college level are not restricted. This allows all who are qualified to study accountancy and eventually enter the profession. Such a practice must lead to overcrowding and force some not to practice accountancy who are qualified. The point being made is that at present we have either unrestricted educational opportunities with resulting overcrowding or restricted educational opportunities with resulting shortages.

Despite the laments of G.I.'s, the closest this country has ever come to an acknowledgment of the importance of integrating guidance and selection has been in the practices of the Armed Forces during World War II. There is not a single case on record of an individual once having received his "greetings" being told by the interviewer, "Sorry we have no job for you today. Suggest you try us again in the near future." The personnel job done by the Armed Forces can be considered as miraculous, at least when compared with the practices of our educational institutions as well as the personnel departments of most companies. Despite the huge growth of manpower in the Armed Forces which of course was unparalleled, guidance and selection were at once an identical process. This is not to say that individual mistakes were not made. However, it must also be recognized that certain civilian occupations were severely restricted with reference to the military. Lawyers were at a disadvantage, since we were fighting rather than arguing with the enemy. On the other hand the need for pilots and navigators existed out of proportion to the previous civilian needs and so training was required. Since the need for personnel was great and training was necessary in unprecedented numbers, it became important to select people for various assignments with a more thorough understanding of the principles of vocational guidance than otherwise usually exists in personnel departments.

Much if not all of the subject matter of vocational guidance, as discussed in the previous chapters, applies to vocational selection, even though in practice there are obvious differences between them. In other words, the members of a personnel department, to be most effective, should know more than how to use certain selection tools. They should understand the theory and applications underlying the counseling interview, psychological tests, occupational information, and so on. They should evaluate the specific techniques used in relation to other available techniques.

Rather little sound and systematic research has been carried on to refine selection techniques to the point where they can be said to possess proven scientific validity. Personnel departments seem quite content to exist on self-evaluation systems. They have generally remained insecure because most companies do not consider them really important; consequently, financial retrenchment in companies often hits them first.

Since almost everyone considers himself a good judge of "human nature,"—whatever that is—the backgrounds of people in personnel have been varied, and too often unrelated to psychology and its related disciplines. Stagner (36) obtained replies to a questionnaire from 36 companies employing approximately 815,000 people. These replies are therefore to be considered as representative only of large companies. One of the questions was whether professionally trained psychologists were employed in the personnel department. Only 30 per cent indicated "yes"; but further, only 53 per cent considered them desirable. In the same study, 42 per cent of the companies had an employee counseling system and 53 per cent considered such a system desirable. It is interesting to note that the attitudes of these corporate executives were in part negativistic. That is, 19 per cent did not consider the employment of a trained psychologist as desirable, and 11 per cent did not consider employee counseling systems desirable. At this point it might be mentioned that there is less resistance to psychological tests than there is to psychologists, since 56 per cent of the companies administered intelligence tests and 58 per cent administered performance tests. Only 3 per cent did not consider intelligence tests desirable and 11 per cent did not consider performance tests desirable.

Scientific aids in selection

In practice there are six aids in the selection of employees. They are: recruitment, interviewing, the application blank, letters of recommendation, checking claims of the applicant, and psychological tests. The amount of scientific work done in connection with each of these varies.

Refinement of recruitment policies. Industrial establishments obtain employees in any of a wide variety of ways, but if a generalization is possible it is that the usual recruitment policy is haphazard. Employees are just hired. Sources of securing employees include personal contact of executives; personal contact of fellow employees; employment agencies, either government or private; want ads or situation wanted ads in newspapers or trade magazines; and direct solicitation on the part of the applicant. In the instance of some companies, in relation to college graduates, there is active recruiting by having company representatives interview college seniors on the campus.

To the best of the authors' knowledge, very little worth-while research has been done in this area. It appears obvious that depending upon the type of job, the industry, or the geographic location, some of these recruitment systems might be better than others. Very worthwhile research can be conducted in the future by companies conducting follow-up studies to determine which type of recruitment has led to the most successful employee. In the meantime there does not seem to be any definite information. Directors of personnel will enthusiastically swear by the system they use, but really have no data to prove that it is the best system. Even such a statement as this is likely to result in attacks of a defensive nature. If it does, then it will be all to the good, since it may lead to evaluating recruitment programs.

The interview. The selection interview attempts to discover whether the candidate has sufficient qualifications for the job. In industry there are two types of employment interviews. The first might be called the preliminary or rail interview. This is a very brief interview, likely to last as little as three minutes. The interviewer with a specific job analysis in mind will run through a batch of applicants at one time to hire a packer, at another time a sales clerk, and so forth. Very obvious qualifications such as age, education, and experience are kept in mind and only those people are selected who meet the definition of the job, in terms of the certain specific qualifications.

The second type of the interview is more lengthy, and for lack of a better name, might be called the final interview. It is during this interview that a more serious attempt is made to know the applicant's potentialities. Gardiner (12) reports that 57 out of 60 employment managers replied "Yes" to the question, "Do first impressions count?" Not nearly so many psychologists would be that optimistic concerning first impressions.

The greatest single means of improving the selection interview would be to require that interviewers be trained. Almost everyone believes that he can interview, and as long as "self-evaluation" is the criterion, this belief is never shaken. For example, in the review of interviewing policies in a certain company in which approximately 40 interviewers stationed throughout the country reported their "system," it was found that each one, without training, had varied ideas and widely different behavior in interviewing. Some interviewers were content with a five-minute interview, whereas others interviewed an applicant for three hours. One interviewer never saw an applicant unless he kept him waiting one and a half hours, whereas another in the same company never interviewed an applicant until he took him to lunch. In each of these cases, the interviewer was very definite about the reasons why his system was best.

As has been pointed out in an earlier chapter on the interview, there are basically three types: authoritarian, non-directive and non-authoritarian. It is inconceivable that a person should attempt to conduct an employment interview without at least a knowledge of the fact that there are different types of interviews and that each has a different theoretical structure. The early studies that reported the lack of agreement among interviewers will not be referred to except to point out that different methods of interviewing on the part of interviewers with varied training must, of course, lead to differences. The contributions of psychologists cannot be overlooked. To be an employment interviewer, one need not be trained in either psychoanalysis or non-directive counseling. But it might be added that such training would be helpful. Admitting that the interview in industrial selection is conducted under time pressure and must be brief, one must ask a basic question, why an interview? If it cannot accompish something besides what the other aids in selection accomplish, there is no point to it. Nevertheless, the interview is in many respects the most important part of the selection process. Some executives who insist on conducting a final interview believe that an interview is a pep talk. For example, one of the authors was told by the head of a psychology department "that all appointments to our staff are made upon our recommendation to the president, but he insists on the final interview." This interview turned out to be a 15-minute one-way conversation, with the president doing all of the talking. There is absolutely no evidence that college presidents are less capable than their corporate brothers in conducting interviews. Much nonsense in industry goes on under the guise of employment interview.

A useful pamphlet to improve the employment interview is *Employee Evaluation Manual for Interviewers,* by Fear and Jordan (11). They suggest that interviewers use an employee evaluation form as an aid in conducting the interview. They recommend that the interview have three major headings: work experience, training, and personal history. It is their belief that having the applicant talk first about his work experience is the best way to begin an interview, since it is a subject that the applicant knows and can talk most easily about. It is easy to lead the person from previous experience into training and then finally touch upon the more subtle areas of the interview. The manual is also valuable insofar as it provides illustrations of worth-while lead questions. For example, "I see by your application that you worked for the —— Company. Suppose you begin by telling me just what you did there." To determine relations with former supervisors such questions are suggested as, "How good a job did your foreman do in supervising his men?" or, "Was he fair in his dealings with the men?" A very difficult part of the employment interview is determining the reasons for leaving previous jobs. Such questions as, "How did you happen to take the job at the Company?" when followed with, "and leave the job" can allow the trained interviewer to explore tactfully these difficult matters. For example, the interviewer might probe further by stating, "This job doesn't seem to represent very much improvement in either wages or opportunity,—Why do you want to make the change?" The employment interviewer should be able to determine the reasons for job termination. Lack of flexibility, temper, job wandering, dissatisfaction with job conditions should be considered as possible predictors of adjustment on the new job. The interviewer can ferret out this information.

Although there is no statistical evaluation in connection with the manual by Fear and Jordan, it at least, to a certain extent, presents specific information in conformance with sound psychological practice. It is for this reason that it is recommended as an aid to improving the interview.

Included in the manual is an illustration of a form that Fear and Jordan designed for use in interviewing. The form provides a check list of questions under such general headings as previous experience and training; space for rating the applicant as below average, average, or above average in each general characteristic; and space for a brief comment about each. It provides as well for a record of test results, an over-all rating for the specific job, and for a summary of the interview. We give here the general instructions to the interviewer, the check list, and the over-all rating.

EMPLOYEE EVALUATION FORM FOR INTERVIEWERS

NAME .... JOB CONSIDERED FOR ....

INTERVIEWER .... DATE ....

INSTRUCTIONS: Rate the adequacy of the applicant's work experience, training, and manner and appearance only as they apply to the job for which he is being considered. For your aid in writing interview summary, mark a check (√) in box before question items to which answers are favorable and a cross (X) where responses are unfavorable. Mark only those items which have a bearing on the requirements of the particular job in question. Place a check (√) on each line to indicate your estimate of how well the applicant satisfies the requirements of the factor considered. Note brief facts which substantiate your decision in space below each line.

I PREVIOUS EXPERIENCE

A [X] Similar job duties?
B [X] Required hand and machine tools?
C [X] Same type materials?
D [X] Similar working conditions?
E [X] Same degree of supervision?
F [√] Shown development on the job?

II TRAINING

- A [√] Sufficient formal school education?
- B [X] Best liked or least liked subjects related to job requirements?
- C [√] Required mechanical, mathematical or other specialized training?
- D Required "on the job" training?
- E [√] Any special training since leaving regular school?

III MANNER AND APPEARANCE

- A [X] Favorable, unfavorable mannerisms? (gestures, facial expressions, speech)
- B [X] General appearance satisfactory? (features, poise, dress, personal hygiene)
- C [X] Evidences of cultural background? (speech, courtesy, interests)
- D [X] Voice and speech acceptable?
- E [√] Physical qualifications adequate? (height, weight, stamina)
- F Any physical disabilities?
- G [√] Appear nervous, high-strung?
- H [√] Appear aggressive, self-confident?

IV SOCIABILITY (TEAMWORK)

- A [√] Any job experience requiring special teamwork?
- B [√] Participate in school social activities?
- C [√] Take part in community affairs?
- D [√] Engage in any group recreation?
- E [√] Interests reflect liking for people?
- F [√] Appear friendly, the kind of person who can get along with others?

V EMOTIONAL STABILITY

- A [√] Friction with former supervisor? ("chip on shoulder" or "sour grape" attitude)
- B [√] Unsound reasons for leaving jobs? (incompetence, quick temper, inflexibility)
- C [√] Unsatisfactory job stability? (easily dissatisfied or discouraged)
- D [√] Reasons for leaving school? (reaction to failure: frank or defensive)
- E [√] Difficult adolescent period? (parents divorced, all work–no play, etc.)
- F [√] Lonely, poorly balanced life now? (inadequate social contacts, etc.)

VI MATURITY

- A [√] Work after school or summers? (earliest contribution to family income)

B [√] Decisions dominated by family? (lean on family for moral support)

C [√] Ever lived away from home? (had to make own way)

D Ever handle more than one job at a time? (economic drive)

E [√] Good sense of responsibility? (considered transportation, wages, hours, family in making change of jobs; how much life insurance)

F [√] Why did he apply for work here? (any logical occupational goal)

VII LEADERSHIP CAPACITY

A [√] Ever had leadership experience? (in school, former job, community)

B [√] Does he want to be a leader? (why)

C [√] Seem like natural leader type? (dominate or inspire confidence, respect)

D [√] Reasonably aggressive, self-confident and self-sufficient?

OVER-ALL RATING FOR SPECIFIC JOB

Considering all the facts you have learned about the application, how well is he fitted for this job in comparison with other men already doing this work in the plant?

___ Above Average
___ Average
_√_ Below Average[1]

Hovland and Wonderlic (21, 39) have developed an instrument called the Diagnostic Interviewers' Guide. This form includes questions designed to cover four areas: work history, family history, social history, and personal history. The information elicited enables the interviewer to ask himself certain questions about the applicant and the resulting judgments are reduced to quantitative ratings. Two different interviewers using this Guide obtained judgments of applicants that had a correlation of + .71. A follow-up in an industrial establishment showed that the successful group of employees, that is, those who had longer periods of employment, received original higher ratings on the Guide than the dismissed group of employees.

Otis (31) has reviewed methods of improving the employment interview and concludes that there is a marked trend toward the use of some type of guide in the employment office. Although no one guide has been found to be distinctly superior, most make it possible for several interviewers to agree more consistently. It has been learned that rating scales offer further aid. Otis concludes that

[1] Reprinted by permission of The Psychological Corporation.

> research studies in the validity and reliability of the interview show that the employment interview does not have to have low reliability and validity and that in some cases it meets acceptable statistical standards. The study of the interview procedure under controlled conditions indicates possibilities of even greater improvement in the future.[2]

The major difference between employment and vocational interviews is that the former tend to be more standardized. When people whose background and training are inadequate conduct interviews, they must be supplied with aids or crutches. If employment interviewers had more sound information in vocational psychology, guides would not be necessary. A standardized interview has the advantage of leaving little to the judgment of the interviewer. Where the judgment of the interviewer cannot be trusted, this limitation is necessary. It would be better to hire more competent interviewers and allow them the spontaneity that interviews often afford.

Application blank. The application blank is one of the most commonly used tools in the employment screen. It is usually a standardized form, and requests personal history items from the applicant. Its two most common uses are: (1) to form a live file of applicants to be used when needed; and (2) to prepare the interviewer and give him sufficient orientation to ask more meaningful questions during the interview. There are two additional uses of the application blank. Under proper conditions it can become a predictor of success; and it can validly aid in the selection of candidates. Innumerable studies have been conducted, in which it has been found that personal history items differentiate the successful from the unsuccessful applicants. For example, Tiffin (37) reports how a laundry relieved its problem of high labor turnover among female pressers, as a result of the analysis of certain personnel data. Table 25 shows that women pressers who remain on the job tend to be older, shorter, and heavier, and to have less formal education than those who leave the job within a short period of time.

Since Tiffin does not record any further data, it is impossible to

---

[2] Reprinted from *Journal of Consulting Psychology*, 8:68 (1944), by permission of the American Psychological Association, publishers.

TABLE 25

PERSONNEL DATA ON WOMEN EMPLOYED AS PRESSERS IN A LAUNDRY

(after Tiffin)

	Those Employed More Than 8 Months	*Those Who Worked Less Than 6 Weeks*
Average age when hired	27.2 yrs.	22.2 yrs.
Average height	5′2.3 in.	5′3.7 in.
Average weight	145 lbs.	125 lbs.
Average yrs. of school	9.3 yrs.	9.9 yrs.

Adapted from J. Tiffin, *Industrial Psychology* New York: Prentice-Hall, 1947.

determine whether these differences in age, height, weight, and education approach statistical significance.

The important fact to be determined from any statistical analysis of differences between averages is whether the difference may be attributed to chance, due to the particular sampling, or whether the difference existing is a real one and would occur again in another sampling. To enter into a complete discussion of the derivation of statistically reliable differences at this point would not only be too involved but would be a digression from the objective of the chapter. (See the chapter on statistics.) However, it is necessary to call to the reader's attention the fact that it is sometimes not advisable to draw conclusions from differences in numbers, percentages, or averages unless the proper statistical checks have been made.

As early as 1922, the application blank was statistically refined as an aid in the selection of salesmen. Goldsmith (15) determined that by assigning weights to such items as marital status, previous occupation, membership in clubs, and others, the successful salesmen could be differentiated from the unsuccessful. Adopting a critical score, 54 per cent of the failures would have been eliminated and 84 per cent of the successes would have remained in the company.

Ohmann (30), in a careful study, determined that 13 items on the application blank were very meaningful in differentiating successful from unsuccessful salesmen in the company investigated. The items, together with the scoring weights assigned, are presented in Table 26.

It must be emphasized that the experiences in each company, the

Table 26

SCORING WEIGHTS FOR PERSONAL HISTORY ITEMS

(after Ohmann)

	Score
1. *Age*	
50	4
45–49	5
40–44	2
up–39	7
2. *Height*	
72″–up	7
70″–71.9	5
69″–69.9	4
up–68.9	3
3. *Marital status*	
Married	5
All others	3
4. *No. of dependents*	
4 or more	0
3	3
2	6
1	7
None	3
5. *Thousands of ins.*	
10 or more	5
5 to 10	6
1 to 5	3
None	6
6. *Amount of debts*	
None	4
Current	6
$500 or more	5
7. *Years of education*	
Grades 1–8	6
9, 10, 11	3
12, Col. 1	6
Col. 2, 3	0
Col. 4, more	5
8. *Number of clubs*	
None	6
One	4
Two	6
Three, more	3

	Score
9. *Years on last job*	
Less than 1	5
1 to 1 yr. 11 mo.	1
2 to 2 yrs. 11 mo.	3
3 to 3 yrs. 11 mo.	6
4–5 yrs. 11 mo.	8
6–9 yrs. 11 mo.	10
10. *Experience in maintenance*	
None	3
Any amount	6
11. *Average no. years on all previous jobs*	
1–2½	3
3–6	5
6½–10	8
12. *Average monthly earnings on last regular job*	
Up to 150	5
150–199	4
200–249	8
250–349	1
350–399	5
400-up	6
13. *Reason for leaving last regular job*	
Still employed	10
Job discontinued (depression) (Co. folded) (also illness and circumstances beyond man's control)	7
To better self (positive reasons)	5
Was let go–dismissed (but if because of conflict with management, score as negative reason)	4
Negative reasons (friction)	2

Critical Score ± 62

The experience of the company is that 70% of those scoring above 62 are still working, while only 30% of those scoring below 62 are still employed.

Adapted from O. A. Ohmann, "A Report of Research on Selection of Salesmen at Tremco Manufacturing Company," *Journal of Applied Psychology*, 25:18–29 (1941). Used by permission of the American Psychological Association, publishers.

type of personnel employed, and the type of product sold are so different that it is extremely unlikely that any success would be obtained by simply using these 13 items together with the specific weights. This material is included merely as an illustration. For this company, these 13 items were the ones that were useful. They might not be similarly useful in other companies. The original application blank included 31 items.

Most of the work in the refinement of the application blank has been done in the selection of insurance salesmen. Kornhauser and Schultz (24), Bills (4), and Kurtz (25) are among the many who have reported success in the selection of applicants by means of an application blank standardized through the statistical refinement of its various items. There is absolutely no reason to believe that selection through the application blank should be predominantly limited to life insurance salesmen. The authors believe that analysis of application blanks for most of the jobs available can result in improvement in the selection procedure.

There is still another use for the application blank, which the authors would be remiss not to report. This use is not to be condoned in any manner or form. The authors do not believe that by mentioning it, they will further its use, but rather hope that they will help reduce or even ultimately eliminate this crime in employment practices. Many employers and even their personnel departments promote prejudice by including, in the job specifications, characteristics of the individual which in no way can be found to be related to a job analysis. The prejudices of people are as many as they are illogical, but the most common concern religion and skin color. There are many direct and indirect items on the application blank which allow the promotion of prejudice in hiring procedures. Among the most direct questions are those about race or skin color, religion, and nationality. Many unknowing applicants who are Americans foolishly enter nationality as different from citizenship.

Among the indirect questions are: father's nationality, mother's nationality, or the counterpart, father's and mother's place of birth. No one has ever established a statistical relationship between parents' nationality and job requirements and so obviously, the only point in the inclusion of such an item on the application blank is to promote the prejudice of the employer. Some forms include a space for supplying information on grandparents' place of birth. Other items in the indirect question category include mother's maiden name, change of name if any, a request for listing church organization, requiring as a reference the listing of a clergyman, and the request to list languages spoken at home in addition to English.

Another item in this category is the request for a photograph to be submitted along with the application blank. In certain very large organizations, this may serve a future identification purpose, in which case it may be regarded as innocent. However, there are two additional reasons for the inclusion of the photograph. One is to promote prejudice and the other is to encourage amateur physiognomists. Neither have a place in a selection procedure designed to hire on the basis of merit.

Letters of recommendation. Many employers request that the applicant furnish a listing of references. However, very few follow up with a request for a letter of recommendation from the listed references. It must be recognized that when personal references are given, it is obvious that only those will be named who can be estimated in advance as furnishing good references. And thus, the value of a letter of recommendation might be related to the ability of the letter writer, but hardly related to the ability of the applicant. This is not to say that the practice of writing letters of recommendation should be discontinued. However, the limitations of this procedure in employment screening must be recognized. At best, one may find these useful only insofar as they determine gradations of positive qualities. Letters of recommendation from former employers may have more value, but then since the motive of the letter writer cannot be known, the value judgments obtained from such letters must be limited.

Many large firms have decided upon the policy of limiting the letter of recommendation to merely a statement of the former employee's job title and the dates of employment. Such letters can serve to check on the honesty of the applicant's statement of his previous employment history. It may well be that this is the only value of letters of recommendation. No scientifically conducted study has been performed to determine the value of letters of recommendation. This might be a worth-while field of investigation, and ultimately there may be a rating scale devised to better evaluate these subjective appraisals. For the time being, their use should be limited.

Checking claims of applicant. As surprising as it may sound, it is nevertheless true that many firms employing otherwise sound selection procedures do not check the claims made by the applicant. Most are quite content with allowing the interviewer to decide on the honesty of the applicant and his application blank. This of course is not the most objective manner of checking honesty. Depending upon the importance of the job, deliberate attempts should be made through either mail or personal interview to check educational and work history of applicants. It is not suggested that investigations equal to those conducted by the Federal Bureau of Investigation be conducted for most jobs, but it is equally ridiculous not to check such very obvious items as the two previous jobs held and the last educational institution attended.

Donald G. Paterson writes, in private correspondence, "It is strange that in forty years of personnel work little or no data are available on the validity or accuracy of work histories as given by different occupational, age, sex and educational groups." A study by Keating, Paterson, and Stone (22) attempts to shed some light on the accuracy of work histories given during an interview held with unemployed persons registering for employment. Each statement as to salary, duration of job, and duties was checked with the former employers' records. The conclusion drawn by Keating *et al.* is, "Validity remained high for histories secured for jobs held up to six years prior to the interview. In terms of correlation coefficients, the validities may be generalized as being from +.90 to +.98."

Since the atmosphere during an interview in an agency employment office may be different from that in a personnel department, it is unsafe to conclude from this study that applicants always state facts about previous jobs with complete accuracy. More research in this area is needed.

Tests. The greatest single contribution of psychologists to employment procedures has been the development and use of psychological tests for selection purposes. Chapters 6 through 9 have described characteristics, developments, and types of psychological tests in use; and of course, all of this information applies to the use of tests in selection. To avoid repetition, much of this will not be discussed here, except to mention that the frame of reference of testing in the employment department is different from that found in guidance. In vocational selection, tests must be related to those important characteristics predicting success on the job. Further, testing in industry is under much greater pressure as to both time and money. If one remembers that tests are used primarily for screening, he will realize that many more people must be given the test than are ultimately selected. For example, if a client in a guidance agency is given a battery of tests lasting three hours, it is very likely that all of the information obtained will be very useful. However, in industry, if experience shows that only one out of every four applicants possesses the ability to pass the test battery, then four times more time must be spent than is actually productively used by the company. It is primarily for this reason that industrial test batteries must be brief, especially for the typical job. For example, if a packer is to be hired, and his salary is nominal, unless one exercises extreme caution, the cost of testing applicants may exceed the cost of hiring packers without tests. As previously pointed out by Blum (6), an improvement in job performance of 10 to 20 per cent is often all that can be expected as a result of the use of a valid testing program.

The widest use of tests in industry has been the adoption of shorter forms of intelligence tests. Wonderlic (38) has devised a brief twelve-minute test of intelligence. This is an abridgement of the Otis Self-Administering Test which has either a 20- or 30-minute time limit. For industrial selection purposes, such brief testing of intelligence is justifiable provided that one wants merely a crude estimate of the intellectual level of the applicant. There are other brief tests of intelligence such as those constructed by Tiffin and Lawshe, Otis, and Pressey.

Whether aptitude or ability tests are to be used in industrial selection depends entirely upon the hiring policy of the firm. If inexperienced people are to be hired and trained, then aptitude testing is important. On the other hand, if experienced people are hired, then achievement testing, or as it is known in industry, "trade testing," is desirable. In the hiring of factory workers assembling small parts, the Finger Dexterity Test has been found to be helpful, especially when inexperienced applicants are considered. In the hiring of a typist a standardized typing test can more directly determine the speed and accuracy of a typist than any lengthy interview.

Applicants may successfully bluff their way through an application blank and an interview, but faking on a good test is more difficult. For example, one of the authors in hiring sewing machine operators was unable to judge the ability of applicants during an interview. The introduction of a sewing machine in the interview room improved the judgment of the interviewer. In fact, the mere presence of the machine tremendously cut down the many exaggerated claims on the part of applicants. If the decision is made to employ psychological tests as an aid in selection, two things must be immediately remembered. First, the tests will be able to predict only those aspects of the job that the test measures. For example, if it can be truly determined that finger dexterity is a component of job success, and if a perfect measure of finger dexterity is available, at best it could predict only that component. There is no reason to believe that a measure of finger dexterity can in any way measure the other components. Intelligence and other aptitudes and abilities, as well as varieties of personality patterns and motivation, must be directly measured in addition if accurate prediction is to be made.

Another important principle of industrial testing is that a testing program must be paralleled with research in the specific firm. Very briefly, a correlation must be established between success on the job and success on the test battery. A priori judgments can be used only as preliminaries to the testing. Unless a relationship is found to exist between test results and job success there is no justification for the use of tests. When employers become dissatisfied with tests as selection aids, it is more often because the tests are misused than because they are inadequate. Much work is entailed in determining whether tests can be useful for selection purposes. In the first place a measure of job success must be available. Sometimes this is defined as total production; at other times it may be a foreman's rating. In addition to actually knowing what the criteria for success is for a specific job, the psychologist must do the following before the test can be used.

First, a complete analysis of the job must be made. Before determining the abilities required for successful performance, the job must be analyzed to determine the abilities required on the job. Second, a preliminary selection of tests is made based upon the leads furnished in the job analysis. Familiarity with the wide variety of tests available is necessary, and of course, such factors as length of time necessary to perform the test must be taken into consideration.

Third, this preliminary battery of tests must be administered to a group of employees or applicants in order to determine the range of variability in scores, and to enable the psychologist to predict the chances of success of the battery. Assuming that all has run relatively smoothly up to this point, the next step is to obtain a correlation between the results on the test and a measure of job performance. If the tests are found to differentiate between groups of employees whose success on the job varies, the likelihood is that the tests will be useful. If however, statistical differentiation is not obtained, then of course, one must either discontinue the project or begin all over.

The next to the last step involves an extended statistical analysis of the test items to determine which of the items are more diagnostic. The final step in developing a test or a test battery for industrial use is to administer it to a new and preferably larger group. Sometimes, a preliminary battery shows considerable promise; but when administered to another group, does not give positive results. This failure means either that the findings for the original group were not statistically reliable, or that the original group was unique and not representative of the population.

Of all types of psychological testing in industry, personality testing has been least used. This neglect may be due to the fact that it has had the least success for selection purposes. In some respects, this may be considered the tragedy of testing for selection purposes. Most authorities agree that labor turnover is due primarily to personality problems rather than limitations of ability. For most jobs a person either has the necessary abilities, or can soon learn to perform the job. In any event, ability and aptitude tests have been moderately successful. The same can not be said of personality tests. As previously stated, personality tests may be classified into two types. The first are of the questionnaire or inventory variety; the second use projective techniques. In the first type, a series of questions is asked and the subject is encouraged to answer them candidly and truthfully. For example, such questions as: "Do you worry over possible misfortunes?" or, "Does discipline make you discontented?" are typical. The major limitation of such tests for selection purposes is obvious. The applicant's answer may indicate not what he really thinks but what he believes he should answer in order to get the job.

A more meaningful approach to the measurement and understanding of the personality requirements for a job may be the use of projective techniques. Answers to the relatively free type of situation afforded by projective techniques are neither right nor wrong, nor can the applicant know in advance which is best.

Piotrowski (32), one of the leading authorities in the use of the Rorschach test, is enthusiastic about the possibilities of the applicability of the Rorschach in selecting candidates for occupations, especially those that involve dealing with people. He has found this test useful in work with student nurses, and together with Candee, was able to select outstanding mechanical workers. Balinsky [2] has administered the Rorschach for the selection of a plant superintendent.

Batteries of tests have been useful in selecting a wide variety of workers. Blum (5) has found tests useful in selecting watch factory assemblers. Hay (18) was able to predict 91 per cent of the better bookkeeping machine operators on the basis of a battery of tests. Sartain (34) used tests successfully to select inspectors in an aircraft factory. Knauft (23) has had some success with psychological tests in the selection of bake shop managers. Abt (1) has demonstrated that a battery of tests can aid in the selection of technical magazine editors. Ghiselli (13) has carefully reviewed over 100 researches specifically related to the validity of psychological tests as selection devices. He states, ". . . with few exceptions no single type of test will give satisfactory predictions of success for any occupational group. Clearly the indication is that batteries of tests will almost be a requirement if a reasonable level of accuracy in selection is to be achieved."[3] Ghiselli did not find evidence to support the widespread notions that intelligence tests are more effective in the "higher" than in the "lower" occupations. At best the effectiveness is only slightly greater there.

According to Ghiselli, "the measures ordinarily used in the selection of clerical workers, namely intelligence, immediate memory, substitution, arithmetic, and name and number comparisons tests appear well justified."[4] For salespersons the best predictors are measures of personality, interest, and personal background. Intelligence tests have been found to have substantial validity for the selection of supervisory personnel. For selection of factory supervisors and skilled workers, spatial relations and mechanical principle tests are of demonstrated value.

A most useful reference for the person interested in the problem of deciding what test to use in varieties of personnel situations is the selected and annotated bibliography, *Employment Tests in Business and Industry,* compiled in 1942 and revised in 1945 by the Industrial Relations Section of the Department of Economics and Social Institutions at Princeton University (7). Approximately 350 references are included, and good judgment has been exercised in the selection of the material. Since it presents a brief survey of the various kinds of tests that have been used for selection purposes, it should prove useful to those contemplating using tests in industry as selection aids. Samples of the brief reviews follow:

> Harrell, Willard. "A factor analysis of mechanical ability tests." *Psychometrika,* March, 1940. pp. 17–33.
>
> An analysis of the Minnesota mechanical ability tests, Stenquist I, the O'Connor wiggly blocks, the MacQuarrie test, and several tests of spatial relations ability and dexterity for perceptual, verbal, manual agility, and spatial factors. A practical finding was that the factors measured by mechanical ability tests can be measured by paper-and-pencil tests.[5]

---

[3] Reprinted from "The Validity of Commonly Employed Occupational Tests" by Edwin E. Ghiselli, *University of California Publications in Psychology,* Vol. 5:9, University of California Press, 1949.

[4] *Ibid.*

[5] D. J. Brown, *Employment Tests in Business and Industry,* page 5. Reprinted by permission of the Industrial Relations Section, Princeton University.

Tiffin, Joseph and R. J. Greenly. "Employee selection tests for electrical fixture assemblers and radio assemblers." *Journal of Applied Psychology,* April, 1939. pp. 240–263.

Tests administered to three groups of operators included O'Connor Finger Dexterity Test, a precision of hand movement test, Keystone Visual Safety Tests, and the Otis Advanced Intelligence Test. Value of these tests varied in accordance with type of work performed by each group. Combinations effective in selecting efficient operators in each group were reported.[6]

Otis, Jay L. "Procedures for the selection of salesmen for a detergent company." *Journal of Applied Psychology,* February, 1941. pp. 30–40.

Outline of a program established for a small company hiring only 5 or 6 salesmen a year.[7]

Blum, Milton L. and Beatrice Candee. "The selection of department store packers and wrappers with the aid of certain psychological tests." *Journal of Applied Psychology*, February, 1941. pp. 76–85; June, 1941, pp. 291–299.

Reports of studies conducted by the New York State Employment Service in two New York City department stores. The results indicated that clerical speed and accuracy have a higher relation to production on both jobs than scores on manual dexterity tests.[8]

Another compilation of abstracts from the literature on employee testing was made by Dorcus and Jones (9). Four hundred and twenty-seven references comprise the body of this book. These were carefully selected after examining over 2000 sources. Only those references were included that gave such definite information as: specific type of employee investigated, number of subjects, description of tests used, explicit statement of criterion, validity (through statements of actual results and evidence of reliability). A sample of a typical abstract follows:

Sartain, A.Q.: The use of certain standardized tests in the selection of inspectors in an aircraft factory, *Journal of Consult. Psychol.*, 9:234–236 (1945).

1. Subjects: 46 inspectors, aircraft factory

---

[6] *Ibid.*, page 18.
[7] *Ibid.*, page 23.
[8] *Ibid.*, page 24.

2. Tests: (1) MacQuarrie Test for Mechanical Ability, (2) Otis Self-administering (3) Cardall Test of Practical Judgment (4) Revised Minnesota Paper Form Board (5) Purdue Industrial Classification Test (6) Bennett Test of Mechanical Comprehension (7) O'Rourke Test of Mechanical Aptitude.
3. Criterion: ratings by 2 instructors who also knew job performance
4. Validity: multiple correlation of tests and criterion:

Tests	R
All	.79
1,3,4	.78
1,3	.76

5. Reliability: correlation between the ratings of 2 raters: .77.[9]

A third source on testing for hiring is Lawshe's *Principles of Personnel Testing* (26). This book is a practical treatment of the problems and procedures in the use of tests in employment. It cites pertinent illustrations from the various reports of research to indicate specific situations in which tests have been useful. Since this book did not have as its aim merely the presentation of bibliographic material, it differs markedly from Dorcus and Jones even though both cover the area of employment tests.

Another sourcebook in the area of employment testing is Burtt's *Principles of Employment Psychology* (8). Although it covers subjects besides testing, more than half of the material is on the use of tests for personnel purposes. It is both more theoretical and more statistical than Lawshe's book, but is nevertheless a very useful reference for those who need to know more about psychological tests in employment offices.

Relation between vocational and industrial psychology

The relation between vocational and industrial psychology is close. Separation of the subject matters of these two applications of psychology is sometimes difficult and exceedingly arbitrary. Industrial psychology is concerned with enhancing the satisfactions of employers and employees and thereby increases efficiency. Vocational psychol-

[9] From *Handbook of Employee Selection* by Dorcus and Jones. Copyright, 1950. Courtesy of McGraw-Hill Book Co.

ogy, through either guidance or selection, is also concerned with enhancing the satisfactions of man by correct placement of present or future employees. Although guidance and selection have not been synonymous concepts, a broad social view demands that the personnel department consider more than the specific techniques it uses. It demands that each employee, in accordance with his intelligence, aptitudes, abilities, personality, and interests be given the chance to work on that job which will give him the greatest individual opportunities and the fewest frustrations.

It is obvious that a good start can be made toward this objective by insuring that hiring policies and procedures are designed to help achieve it. However, one must go further if the objective is to be ultimately and permanently attained. Industrial psychology is not only concerned with the personnel hiring policies but continues with the individual in his work-life situation.

Of course, industrial psychology and vocational psychology overlap in testing, interviewing, and other techniques. They overlap and feed each other in such areas as occupational information, training, job satisfaction, incentives, and morale.

For example, an incentive system can be only as effective as it is meaningful to the employees. If the employer offers an incentive such as a bonus for increased production and the employee has a need for security, then the incentive may not be very strong. Incentive systems are likely to be effective as the interests and other characteristics of the employee are known. Similarly, hiring employees who are not intelligent enough or who are too intelligent for the job can create problems in training and morale. The need for occupational information in both vocational and industrial psychology becomes apparent under such circumstances, since matching the job and individual characteristics is a necessity.

There are many professionally competent books in industrial psychology. Those by Bellows (3), Blum (6), Ghiselli and Brown (13), Harrell (17), Ryan (33), and Tiffin (37) are among the recent treatments of this topic.

Bellows' book has four parts. Part I is concerned with goals and historical development of personnel methods. Part II discusses the tools for effective use of personnel. Part III is concerned with personal relations through counseling, communication, and similar problems. Part IV describes the process of professionalization taking place and summarizes current trends.

Blum's work is concerned primarily with the social foundations of industrial psychology. It considers testing as a part of the entire system but not its major part. Attitude, job satisfaction, and industrial morale are emphasized, and the goal of industrial psychology is set as the encouraging and promoting of democracy in industry. Critical evaluations of time and motion study, work environment, and accident proneness are considered among other topics.

Ghiselli and Brown offer a sound and orthodox treatment of the subject and include job analyses, personnel selection techniques, work efficiency and methods, training, and safety problems among their major topics.

Harrell's book has three parts. The first is essentially on selection; the second is concerned with problems of human engineering or work improvement through training and eliminating fatigue. The third part covers the area of human relations.

Ryan's publication is a thorough review of the problems of work in relation to fatigue and emphasizes the laboratory and experimental approach. It is not concerned with problems of selection but rather with the psychological and physiological aspects of the cost of work.

In Tiffin's book approximately one half the content is devoted to psychological tests with heavy emphasis on visual skills, tests, and inspection problems. Briefer treatments of job evaluation, work and fatigue, accidents, and attitudes are also included.

As can be inferred from these thumb-nail sketches, different authors treat the subject of industrial psychology with different emphases. However, the knowledge of this subject goes hand in hand with a knowledge of vocational psychology and together greater individual satisfactions are achieved.

Advice to job seekers

Very little information of scientific value is available concerning the other aspect of vocational selection, namely, how we get a job. Few if any conclusions have been drawn from either experiment or data.

Much in the field is the kind of generalization which results from the experiences of a person sitting on the other side of the desk. As a result, much advice is available and as is typical of advice it is highly opinionated. Recognizing this, the authors nevertheless believe that they too should add to the confusion by giving advice.

Apply appropriately. Much time in job seeking is wasted because the individual does not estimate correctly the job for which he is qualified. In applying for a job it is important to be specific. One should not apply for any job that may be available in an organization but rather for a specific job such as sales clerk, shipping clerk, messenger boy, vocational counselor, or instructor in psychology. If a person has any orientation at all, he must surely know that an employer will not consider the applicant who is qualified for a teaching job as a shipping clerk. And yet, many job seekers make the big mistake of believing they can do anything. Not only is this belief unfounded, but the potential employer is not likely to share it. Of course it is true that an individual can do any one of many jobs equally well. In fact, the theme of this book is in accord with such a view. Guidance and selection operate differently, however. In selection there is always the specific job and the applicant must recognize this.

In seeking a specific job, the applicant must seek the most meaningful sources. Especially among young people, although this is true of all job applicants, personal contacts play a very important role. Too often this source is overlooked. A shipping clerk is likely to know about openings in his department and so is a psychology instructor. A good lead as to whether one is applying for an appropriate job is whether one has friends working on similar jobs. Assuming that education, age, interest, and economic status are factors in forming friendship, it follows that individuals who are friends are likely to have opportunities for jobs on approximately equal occupational levels. A girl whose friends are primarily factory workers is likely to work more successfully in a factory than an office. The college graduate who seeks a job as a buyer, and yet does not know intimately any buyers, is more likely to obtain employment as an assistant buyer or follow-up clerk—the sort of job that his friends are most probably holding. This is not to say that he has no friends doing other kinds of work. It merely means that you can determine to some extent whether a job is appropriate for you by learning whether other people with qualifications like yours hold the same kind of position.

During periods when there are more applicants than jobs, personal contact plays a very important role in obtaining a job. Of course there are other sources of jobs, but one should not overlook as an important source the personal contact of friends and relatives. Employment agencies are another source. These agencies, both public and private, should be visited, and the applicant should attempt to estimate the activity in the agency, as well as the likelihood that the agency would place him. If after a number of visits no promising leads are furnished, it might be better to try a different agency.

Ads appear in newspapers of both the Help Wanted and Situation Wanted variety. In an unpublished study by a student of one of the authors, very little relationship was found to exist between the specific items in each of the two types of ads. Whereas Help Wanted ads emphasized salary expected, experience, age and education, Situation Wanted ads were cluttered up with such glittering generalities as "intelligent, aggressive young man desires position requiring judgment and initiative." Direct solicitation, either in person or by letter of application, sometimes leads to employment, but it is not likely except in rare cases that such solicitation will lead to a job offer.

Be prepared for interview. Preparation for the interview takes two forms. In the first place, it is well for an applicant to prepare an application form in advance. This will make it easy to complete an application blank in the employment office. Omitting such items as addresses of references is likely to be prejudicial. Further, exact dates can be accurately given in connection with previous employment, education, and so on. The prior completion of an application form also allows the applicant to leave with the prospective employer a brief statement of the individual's personal history as well as educational background and work experience.

Although one cannot completely predict all the questions that will be asked in an interview, certain things can nevertheless be presumed. For example, the applicant should be prepared to state the reason for leaving the previous job, or the reason for seeking a change in employment. He should be prepared to start the conversation with a direct statement. The most direct of all is applying for a very definite job.

It might be mentioned that one should be appropriately dressed, since employment managers agree that first impressions count. The appropriateness of dress, of course, varies with the type of job. It is likely that a model would be dressed differently from a girl seeking a routine office job in a conservative bank.

The applicant should be prepared to state the starting salary he wants. If one is applying for an appropriate job, he knows the salary range for that job. The problem of salary is very often related to the number of dependents the applicant has. If dependents exist, they should be mentioned in a matter-of-fact manner and not used as a means of begging for a job. Employers or personnel people realize the advantages of an employee with dependents: they are likely to be a factor in reducing turnover. They recognize also that the appropriate salary is determined not only by the labor supply but also by the standard of living of people in the particular occupational level.

Watch application blank for traps. The safest way to accurately complete an application blank is to have prepared for it in advance. In addition, however, as has been previously mentioned, some employers use an application blank to obtain information that they would be too embarrassed to ask during an interview. Mother's maiden name and languages spoken at home are extremely unlikely to be related to job requirements. An applicant who does not fill out items such as these is likely to be at a disadvantage; but then if he does, and reveals information toward which the potential employer is prejudiced, he is not likely to obtain the job either. Not only are such unfair employment practices dubious but they are a blight on American democracy. Possibly such laws as the "Fair Employment Practices Act" will curtail these practices. Peculiarly enough, in New York State an applicant is legally protected when he furnishes incorrect information provided that the correct information would have prevented him from obtaining employment. It must be recognized that although two wrongs do not make a right, such a practice can truly be condoned, since no employer in New York State or anywhere else has the right to deny a person a livelihood because of characteristics in no way related to the job.

Use stunts sparingly. A stunt in employment seeking is an unusual means of obtaining employment. The types of stunt that have been used vary not only with the imagination but also the eccentricity of the applicant. Decorating the envelope to attract attention, advertising that the person is the laziest alive, or in many other ways using startling means to attract attention is typical. Although most employers frown upon the use of stunts, it must nevertheless be admitted that all an applicant needs at any one time is one job to be provided by one employer. If, by any chance, the eccentricity of the applicant matches the idiosyncrasy of the employer, a stunt may result in a job. The authors believe that stunts should be used very sparingly, if at all; but if they are used, they had better be unusual and of high calibre. Included in the category of stunts, but nevertheless on a more acceptable level, would be the preparation of a brochure. Such a printed folder is likely to command attention, and incidentally reveal creativeness. If such an ability is a component of the potential job then the brochure may give the applicant an advantage in obtaining the job.

Use care when taking tests. The chances are that the readers of this book are not only test-conscious but also test-wise, and so are not likely to be as frightened in a test situation as most other adults. Among the items not a credit to our educational institutions is the fear that teachers sometimes instill in students in connection with tests. As a result, many people become tense and highly emotional when confronted with a testing situation. This attitude will be generally transferred to all types of tests situations, especially those used for employment selection. The advice that can be given to applicants is brief. First, read directions fully and carefully. Too often the person taking the test is in such a rush that he cannot be bothered with wasting time reading directions. This can prove fatal. The second hint is to pay attention to the examiner and do as he instructs. Practice periods, often a part of many psychological tests, better prepare the individual for the actual test.

One should spend time on test items in proportion to their weight. If an item cannot be answered, one should, unless otherwise directed, skip it and go on to the next one. Since many tests have items arranged in order of difficulty, it is best to begin at the beginning and work as rapidly as one can toward the end. This allows one to answer more items and thereby receive more credit. Psychological tests are not puzzles, tricks, or games, especially when they are used for industrial selection.

Summary

The orientation in vocational selection is different from that in vocational guidance. With one job and many applicants available, both the applicant and the personnel representatives can be expected to conduct themselves differently from the way they would in a client-counselor situation. In practice, guidance and selection operate independently. The closest we have approached to unification was in the instance of personnel practices in the armed forces.

Six aids in the selection of employees are: recruitment, interviewing, the application blank, letters of application, checking applicant's claims, and psychological tests.

Evaluation of various recruitment systems in use is needed before the differences in effectiveness can be known. The employment interview has been improved in effectiveness through the use of manuals in conducting the interview.

From an analysis of those personal items that differentiate among the successful and unsuccessful employees, the application blank has been found to be a useful selection device.

Letters of recommendation are reported to have little value and at best may indicate gradations of the positive qualities of the applicant. More attention should be devoted to the applicant's claims.

Tests are widely used as aids in selecting employees. For inexperienced applicants, aptitude tests are appropriate, and trade tests are most appropriate for experienced applicants. Intelligence tests are commonly used, but personality tests for selection, while important, have not been used too successfully. Tests should be used in industry only when the relationship between test performance and job success is known.

The relation between vocational and industrial psychology was briefly presented and six of the professional books on industrial psychology were very briefly reviewed.

Advice to job seekers was offered with the caution that much, if not all, information, instead of being fact based upon data, is opinion, based upon experience on the other side of the desk. The suggestions to applicants were: to apply appropriately, to be prepared for the interview, and to watch the application blank for traps.

Stunts in job seeking were not generally recommended, although it was admitted that in rare instances they do achieve their purpose.

Bibliography

1. Abt, L. E., "A Test Battery for Selecting Technical Magazine Editors," *Personnel Psychology*, 2:75–91 (1949).
2. Balinsky, B., "A Note on the Use of the Rorschach in the Selection of Supervisory Personnel," *Rorschach Research Exchange and Journal of Projective Techniques*, 3:184–188 (1944).
3. Bellows, R. M., *Psychology of Personnel in Business and Industry*. New York: Prentice-Hall, 1949.
4. Bills, M. A., "Selection of Casualty and Life Insurance Agents," *Journal of Applied Psychology*, 25:6–10 (1941).
5. Blum, M. L., "A Contribution to Manual Aptitude Measurement in Industry," *Journal of Applied Psychology*, 4:381–416 (1940).
6. ———, *Industrial Psychology and Its Social Foundations*. New York: Harper, 1949.
7. Brown, D. J., *Employment Tests in Business and Industry*. Princeton, N.J.: Industrial Relations Section, Dept. of Economics and Social Institutions, Princeton University, 1945.
8. Burtt, H. E., *Principles of Employment Psychology*, Revised Edition. New York: Harper, 1942.
9. Dorcus, R. M., and M. H. Jones, *Handbook of Employee Selection*. New York: McGraw-Hill, 1950.
10. Child, H. A. T., "Industrial Planning and Vocational Guidance," *Occupational Psychology*, 18:69–76 (1944).

11. Fear, R. A., and B. Jordan, *Employee Evaluation Manual for Interviewers*. New York: The Psychological Corporation, 1943.
12. Gardiner, G. L., *How You Can Get A Job*. New York: Harper, 1945.
13. Ghiselli, E. E., "The Validity of Commonly Employed Occupational Tests," *University of California Publications in Psychology*, 5:253–288 (1949).
14. ——— and C. W. Brown, *Personnel and Industrial Psychology*. New York: McGraw-Hill, 1949.
15. Goldsmith, D., "The Use of the Personal History Blank as a Salesmanship Test," *Journal of Applied Psychology*, 6:149–155 (1922).
16. Hardtke, E. P., "Aptitude Testing for Metal Working Occupations," *Psychological Bulletin*, 42:679–694 (1945).
17. Harrell, T. W., *Industrial Psychology*. New York: Rinehart, 1949.
18. Hay, E. N., "Predicting Success in Machine Bookkeeping," *Journal of Applied Psychology*, 27:483–493 (1943).
19. Hearnshaw, L. S., "The Present Position of Selection Tests," *The Human Factor*, 9:395–404 (1935).
20. Holliday, F., "The Relation between Psychological Test Scores and Subsequent Proficiency of Apprentices in the Engineering Industry," *Occupational Psychology*, 17:168–186 (1943).
21. Hovland, C. I., and E. F. Wonderlic, "Prediction of Industrial Success from a Standardized Interview," *Journal of Applied Psychology*, 23:537–546 (1939).
22. Keating, E., D. G. Paterson, and H. Stone, "Validity of Work Histories Obtained by Interview," *Journal of Applied Psychology*, 34:6–11 (1950).
23. Knauft, E. B., "A Selection Battery for Bake Shop Managers," *Journal of Applied Psychology*, 33:304–315 (1949).
24. Kornhauser, A. W., and R. S. Schultz, "Research on Selection of Salesmen," *Journal of Applied Psychology*, 25:1–5 (1941).
25. Kurtz, A. K., "Recent Research in the Selection of Life Insurance Salesmen," *Journal of Applied Psychology*, 25:11–17 (1941).
26. Lawshe, C. H., Jr., *Principles of Personnel Testing*. New York: McGraw-Hill, 1948.
27. Long, W. F., and C. H. Lawshe, Jr., "The Effective Use of Manipulative Tests in Industry," *Psychological Bulletin*, 44:130–148 (1947).
28. Lowe, F. W., and W. Raphael, "Seven Years' Experience of Tests for Sales Assistants," *The Human Factor*, 11:137–146 (1937).

29. Misselbrook, B. D., "The Short Personnel Selection Interview," *Occupational Psychology*, 20:85–98 (1946).
30. Ohmann, O. A., "A Report of Research on the Selection of Salesmen at Tremco Manufacturing Company," *Journal of Applied Psychology*, 25:18–29 (1941).
31. Otis, J., "Improvement of Employment Interviewing," *Journal of Consulting Psychology*, 8:64–69 (1944).
32. Piotrowski, Z. A., "Use of Rorschach in Vocational Selection," *Journal of Consulting Psychology*, 7:97–102 (1943).
33. Ryan, T. A., *Work and Effort*. New York: Ronald, 1947.
34. Sartain, A. Q., "The Use of Certain Standardized Tests in the Selection of Inspectors in an Aircraft Factory," *Journal of Consulting Psychology*, 9:234–235 (1945).
35. Slater, P., "The Economics of Vocational Selection," *Occupational Psychology*, 20:12–24 (1946).
36. Stagner, R., "Attitudes of Corporate Executives Regarding Psychological Methods in Personnel Work," *The American Psychologist*, 11:540–541 (1947).
37. Tiffin, J., *Industrial Psychology*. New York: Prentice-Hall, 1947.
38. Wonderlic, E. F., "Personnel as a Control Function," *Personnel*, 14:31–39 (1937).
39. ——— and C. I. Hovland, "The Personnel Test: A Restandardized Abridgement of the Otis S-A Test for Business and Industrial Use," *Journal of Applied Psychology*, 23:685–702 (1939).

INDEX OF NAMES

INDEX OF SUBJECTS